Roman Catholicism in the United States

Catholic Practice in North America
Series co-editors:

Angela Alaimo O'Donnell, Associate Director of the Francis and Ann Curran Center for American Catholic Studies, Fordham University
John C. Seitz, Associate Professor, Theology Department, Fordham University

This series aims to contribute to the growing field of Catholic studies through the publication of books devoted to the historical and cultural study of Catholic practice in North America, from the colonial period to the present. As the term "practice" suggests, the series springs from a pressing need in the study of American Catholicism for empirical investigations and creative explorations and analyses of the contours of Catholic experience. In seeking to provide more comprehensive maps of Catholic practice, this series is committed to publishing works from diverse American locales, including urban, suburban, and rural settings; ethnic, postethnic, and transnational contexts; private and public sites; and seats of power as well as the margins.

Roman Catholicism in the United States

A Thematic History

Margaret M. McGuinness and James T. Fisher, Editors

FORDHAM UNIVERSITY PRESS

NEW YORK 2019

Fordham University Press also publishes its books in a variety of electronic formats. Some content that appears in print may not be available in electronic books.

Visit us online at www.fordhampress.com.

Library of Congress Cataloging-in-Publication Data available online at https://catalog.loc.gov.

Printed in the United States of America

21 20 19   5 4 3 2 1

First edition

CONTENTS

Part III.   Prophetic Catholicism

Roman Catholicism in the United States

Writing American Catholic History

Margaret M. McGuinness and James T. Fisher

Historians have—until recently—followed a rather standard chronology when recounting the story of Catholicism in the United States. The narrative began by retracing the trail of Franciscan missionaries in the sixteenth-century Southwest—which was blazed prior to the arrival of Anglo-Protestants along the Eastern Seaboard—and moved on to Jesuits in New France (Canada) early in the following century. These historical accounts drew on primary sources originally intended to record the Catholic encounter with Native American peoples and their environment, including the astounding reports filed by Jesuits in Canada to their religious superiors in France, which constitute some of the earliest works of American literature, anthropology, and theology and offer an alternative New World "creation narrative," with the Upper Midwest and Mississippi Valley playing the role the Atlantic Coast colonies later fulfilled for British Protestants.[1] The forcibly diminished French and Spanish presences within the future United States of America consigned their legacies to the shadow side of the new nation's history, but Catholicism itself became a visible presence in the new nation, often serving as a live object of ambivalence among nineteenth-century Protestants.

By 1850 Catholicism was the largest religious denomination in the United States; so it remains to this day. American Protestant Christianity has always boasted a substantial *aggregate* majority of religious adherents, but Protestantism was broken into so many movements by the mid-nineteenth century that no single Protestant group equaled in size the nation's Catholic populace. Roughly 12 percent of the U.S. total by 1850, Catholicism's "market share" of the nation's believers would double by 1900.

Many mid- to late nineteenth-century Protestants who cherished their deep spiritual roots in the nation's soil fretted that the growing Catholic presence in America was disproportionate to the church's status as an ancient religion in a new country. The U.S. church was organized into dioceses—territorial jurisdictions led by bishops—linked in turn to often-unwieldy structures of authority administered by the Holy See in Rome. Protestants worried about this "Roman connection," which would indeed strengthen throughout the nineteenth century, but American Catholics were generally much less interested in Rome than in Brooklyn, Philadelphia, Milwaukee, and dozens of other burgeoning communities where spiritual and material services provided by the church filled pressing needs and opened vast frontiers of opportunity. In the half-century that followed the Civil War, U.S. Catholics built the largest network of private elementary schools in world history; took possession of the Democratic Party's political machinery, which operated most of the nation's largest cities; raised hundreds of orphanages and hospitals staffed largely by members of booming Catholic women's religious communities; and opened scores of colleges and universities for women and men.

The rapid growth of American Catholicism, along with the schools, hospitals, and orphanages built to serve the needs of the Catholic population, often led to the development of an American anti-Catholic—or "nativist"—impulse that sometimes targeted not just the church as an institution, but those vestigial Catholic forces and institutions bedeviling Protestants. In August 1834, for example, the Ursuline convent at Charlestown, Massachusetts, was burned to the ground by a nativist mob, but the girls' school destroyed in the conflagration (staffed by Ursuline nuns from the convent) enrolled daughters of the locally unpopular Unitarian [Protestant] elite in greater numbers than it did Catholic schoolgirls.

Hostility to Catholicism was one thing; in practice this impulse was often refracted through struggles *between* Protestant Americans divided by social class, political outlook, or geography. The enduring complexity of American Protestants' "Catholic problem" was one good reason, as historian R. Laurence Moore astutely noted in *Religious Outsiders and the Making of Americans* (1986), that "after the Civil War virulent anti-Catholicism was a weaker force in American life than Catholicism." This relative degree of security enabled late nineteenth-century Catholic leaders to expansively debate the proper role for their church in the United States or, as Moore put it, "to imagine more than one way to press their collective fortunes in America."[2]

The literature of U.S. Catholic history has both recorded and reflected that debate; at times historical works have even shaped the dialogue. While it is true that U.S. Catholic historiography from the mid-nineteenth to the mid-twentieth century ritually extolled heroic explorers and church hierarchs while eschewing potentially divisive issues, at least one biographical study of a prominent Catholic triggered a late nineteenth century intrachurch controversy that resulted in a harsh, ill-informed, but momentous response from the Holy See. In 1891 Walter Elliott, an American priest of a religious community known as the Paulists, authored a hagiography of the congregation's founder, Isaac Hecker, a German American from a Protestant immigrant family and a one-time Transcendentalist who in 1844 communed for six months with fellow nature mystics and utopians at Brook Farm in Massachusetts. Hecker converted to Catholicism shortly after leaving the commune, and as subsequent leader of the Paulists his ardent cultivation of the Holy Spirit's stirrings fostered a uniquely openhearted, optimistic, and distinctly American Catholic spirituality.[3] A French translation of Hecker's biography led to Leo XIII issuing a condemnation of what came to be called "Americanism." The church was neither a democracy nor an instrument for cultural and political adaptation, the pontiff scolded James Gibbons—the highly influential cardinal archbishop of Baltimore—in the 1899 "apostolic letter" *Testem Benevolentiae*.[4]

During the first six decades of the twentieth century, American Catholic historians, whose work was shaped by the Americanist controversy, chose to move away from the nineteenth-century debate over the place of the church in the United States and focus on the more genteel elements of their community's past. As William M. Halsey explained in *The Survival of American Innocence* (1980), accounts of the putatively orderly lives of notable and less-notable bishops and priests affirmed "the American Catholic labor of mind to maintain a sense of control over experience" just at that moment when "the American scene drifted into the unpredictable." In Halsey's persuasive argument, early and mid-century American Catholic intellectuals of the twentieth century sought to uphold that serene quality of "innocence" long forsaken by others in the light of personal experience, scientific revelation, and the newfound existential *frisson* of religious doubt.[5]

Only in the decade following the Second World War did Catholic historians acknowledge their own complacency, most notably in a ringing jeremiad leveled by the church's leading professional historian, Msgr. John Tracy Ellis of the Catholic University of America. In "American Catholics and the Intellectual Life" (1955), Ellis blasted Catholic educators for aping the least attractive features of American life while spurning its more desirable traditions of intellectual and creative freedom. Surmounting these obstacles proved a tall order: Ellis was himself given to a somewhat mannered, courtly style of historical scholarship. The deeply engrained "labors of mind" identified by William M. Halsey proved difficult to break.[6]

Beginning in the late 1960s and across the long scholarly generation that followed, Catholic and secular historians alike systematically dismantled historic claims to American "exceptionalism." Although the militant legacy of Catholic anti-Communism often continued to contribute to the structure of the narrative—some Catholic and ex-Catholic historians helped expose the U.S. church's role in promoting holy-war interventions in Southeast Asia—other historians deftly sidestepped the dominant anti-Communist paradigm by reconstructing alternative histories of Catholic pacifism and "countercultural" or "prophetic" movements of resistance to militant nationalism.[7] The unsavory tone of U.S. Catholic anti-Communism chronicled by these scholars helped account for the rebirth of the Catholic Worker movement as a staple of historical inquiry during and after the Vietnam War era. The Catholic Worker is rooted primarily in the United States, but studies of less well-known movements such as the Grail, an enduring rural communitarian experiment for Catholic laywomen poised somewhere between a vocation to religious life and more worldly callings, the Young Christian Workers, and the Young Christian Students reminded readers that other groups were European born and adapted themselves to American soil.[8]

Historians of U.S. Catholicism trained far less attention on issues demanding a comparative perspective linking Catholic action to secular American social movements, especially labor activism and its encounter with Catholic forces strategically deployed far outside the church's traditional confines. In secular accounts focusing on the "age of the CIO"—in historian Michael Denning's phrase—Catholics were largely absent beyond an often-grudging admission that they dominated the rank and file in most major industries organized by the fledgling, industrial union–oriented Congress of Industrial Organizations. (One most revealing episode from that fugitive history, the fervid struggle waged during the interwar decades between Catholics and Communists for the allegiance of African Americans, is treated herein for the first time in all its revealing particulars.)[9]

The confluence of political, religious, and intellectual tumult in the 1960s and 1970s finally yielded a "post-Americanist" Catholic historiography signaling the most dramatic paradigm shift in the tradition's history. Several distinct strains gradually emerged in the spirit of the Second Vatican Council (1962–65), whose invitation to a renewed Catholic intellectual life engaged forms of secular thought customarily off-limits to Catholics. The first phase can be identified as a vigorously interdisciplinary mode of historical scholarship that began in the early 1980s and overlapped with a small but influential American Catholic Studies movement that emerged during that same decade. Popular devotions, Catholic material culture, and the meanings of sacred space were among topics explored in scholarly depth for the first time during these years by historians of U.S. Catholicism. These studies were often methodologically innovative and even daring; they drew on approaches fostered by secular fields of cultural and literary studies and engaged issues of gender, sexuality, and social class more forthrightly than earlier scholarship in the field. The cultural-studies turn within U.S. Catholic historiography yielded rich material for incorporation within broader narratives of U.S. social and cultural history, though its influence was more deeply witnessed in the field of religious studies than in U.S. history proper.[10]

A second wave of post-Americanist historical scholarship highlighted the "prophetic" dimension of Christian thought and practice championed by moral theologians and ethicists. These scholars were located most often in religious studies and theology programs, where growing numbers of U.S. Catholic historians experienced some of their intellectual and spiritual formation. From this perspective, devotees of the prophetic turn viewed Americanist historiography as not simply outdated but nearly idolatrous in its desire to reconfirm the enduring compatibility of American and Catholic traditions. At the same time, a newly minted "radical orthodoxy" movement found favor among substantial numbers of younger Catholics attracted to the uncompromising zeal of these prophetically inclined scholars, whose quest for a purified Catholicism pointed away from the comparative, boundary-crossing scholarship of the 1980s and early 1990s in favor of rediscovered classic Christian sources, most notably the tradition of natural law, that buttressed many works of contemporary apologetics.[11]

A third stream of post-Americanist historiography found some younger scholars exploring themes like natural law and the historic Catholic quest for moral order not as advocates of these traditions' prescriptive or normative value, but simply because such forces—generally downplayed by the Americanist school—may be discerned empirically, at work throughout much of U.S. Catholic history. These historians reexamined the relationships between Catholic authority and the conditions in which it operated, from colonial Maryland to nineteenth-century frontier missions to the twentieth-century national mission against Communism and moral disorder.[12]

Contemporary chroniclers of U.S. Catholicism—like most historians generally—are driven less by methodological or ideological concerns than by the desire to tell a good and meaningful story. Contributors to *Roman Catholicism in the United States: A Thematic History* vary in outlook and approach, but all share herein with readers compelling stories of women and men bearing witness to intimately held convictions in ecclesial, political, and social-historical settings. Many of these essays are linked by a common desire to enrich narratives of United States history via attentiveness to the engagement of American Catholics with the *public* and *communal* dimensions of American life. All of the essays blend materials from religious and historical studies in illuminating the U.S. Catholic experience.

The essays in this volume represent ways of looking at the history of U.S. Catholicism that move beyond hierarchical organization and parish structure. They are loosely grouped into three categories: "Beyond the Parish," "Engaging the World," and "Prophetic Catholicism." The essays in Part I, entitled, "Beyond the Parish," focus on aspects of Catholic history that are not connected to the "traditional" urban immigrant parish. Part II, "Engaging the World," offers readers some examples of how Catholics and Catholic culture interacted with the larger society from a variety of perspectives. In Part III, entitled "Prophetic Catholicism," readers will find examples of how prophetic and creative aspects of Catholicism have played important roles in both church and society.

The scholars represented in this volume explore ways the faithful practiced their beliefs while engaging Americans holding different faith convictions or none; applied their faith to political issues; created art and literature; and prayed and worked for social change. These studies all convey a vivid sense of Catholic *presence*, the recognition of which by readers and scholars can only enhance prospects for narrative wholeness in subsequent works of U.S. social and religious history.

Part I: Beyond the Parish

The "immigrant church" (roughly covering the period 1830s–1940s) motif is so integral to American Catholic historical identity that alternative models are rarely proffered. Yet long before the advent of that immigrant church there was a Southwest borderlands Hispanic church, an Upper Midwest French church, and a California mission church. There was also a European Catholic Church of history and myth that—despite its remoteness in time and space—inhabited a large region in the imaginations of American Protestants who likely never encountered an actual Catholic person. The essays in Part I identify and treat formative locations of American Catholicism found in places other than the urban-immigrant parish neighborhood. These works affirm a much broader foundation of Catholic presences than found in canonical versions of United States history.[13]

The opening essay, "Ambiguous Welcome," by Patrick Allitt, examines aspects of American Catholic history that lay outside the commonly told story of parishes and immigrants by surveying the efforts of American Protestants—from the colonial era to the present—to properly map that Catholic place in the life of their nation and their own religious sensibilities. Allitt shows how the ambivalent greeting initially extended to Catholic immigrants by U.S. Protestants was shelved for outright hostility during the nativist era prior to the Civil War, when the mass emigration of impoverished, famine-stricken Irish Catholics greatly aggravated preexisting fears of "popish superstition."

At the same time a number of Protestants—often from elite backgrounds—found themselves powerfully drawn to Catholic art and ritual, and more than a few took the plunge into religious conversion. If mass immigration largely shaped the social contours of American Catholicism, Catholic converts proved extraordinarily influential in the spiritual and intellectual life of the church, from Elizabeth Ann Bayley Seton—who founded a women's religious community in the early nineteenth century and was canonized in 1975 as the first native-born American saint—to Dorothy Day and Thomas Merton, surely the two most influential spiritual leaders in twentieth-century U.S. Catholic life. Allitt also shows that beyond the mixed feelings many Protestants harbored toward the Catholic Church lay a host of substantive and genuinely divisive issues, responses to which not only shaped Protestant-Catholic relations but eventually prompted American Catholics to assert their convictions when the church deliberated on matters of social justice, religious liberty, and theologies of pluralism.

In the 1970s public controversies linking religion and politics saw some Catholics forge extra-ecclesial alliances as oppositional blocs against Catholic-led groups holding divergent views. The clerical sex abuse scandal that broke out in 2002 (nearly a decade after this catastrophic phenomenon first received widespread attention) revived some ancient hostilities toward the church; much more importantly, it prompted Catholics to demand accountability from their appointed leaders and to assume greater responsibility for the church's direction.

Regionally focused essays by Timothy Matovina and Jeffrey Burns invite the repositioning of American Catholicism's early and expansive Western presence at the heart of U.S. historical narratives. The Catholic prehistory of America rarely garners detailed treatment in standard accounts of the nation's origins. Yet, as Timothy Matovina explains in "Latino Catholics in the Southwest," the Catholic presence in that borderlands region is nearly twice as old as the United States itself. Colonial-era Latinos were not immigrants; a new and ever-expanding American nation-state migrated during the nineteenth century into terrains called home by Latinos for centuries. Later many Latinos *did* migrate to the American Southwest: first from Mexico, and later from all precincts of Latin America. The multifaceted Latino Catholic communities they created gave birth to forms of Christian witness and worship integral to contemporary American Catholic life—especially in parishes where changing demographics meant a tradition from congregations traditionally composed of Catholics of European descent to those that primarily identify as Hispanic—notwithstanding the habit of scholars to equate the origins of devotional Catholicism largely with European immigrant peoples.

Timothy Matovina reaffirms that many Native Americans dreaded the notorious Spanish missions—-the original Catholic institutions founded in the future United States—as "alien and coercive," but in recovering the early nineteenth-century leadership role at southern California's San Gabriel Mission of Eulalia Perez, Matovina begins to highlight "an element of Latino Catholicism that has been significant throughout the history of the region: the faith and leadership of women." Latinas not only took the lead in community rituals and annual Guadalupe feast-day celebrations, he explains, but later pioneered in advocacy for social justice via such organizations as *Las Hermanas* ("the sisters") founded in 1971 by members of women's religious communities in Texas.

In "Left Coast Catholicism," Jeffrey Burns argues that independence, innovation, bold action, and openness to change—traditions uniquely nurtured in California from its beginnings—shaped Catholic experience in the Golden State. Burns's treatment of the formative California missions focuses on the "first dissenter," Fray José Maria Fernandez, a critic of the exploitation of Indians in the late 1790s who was persecuted by enemies (and later by many historians) as mad or brain-damaged yet endured in his advocacy work. Burns's essay is replete with vivid, often stubborn Californians alternately viewed in their time as visionaries, troublemakers, or dissidents, yet nearly all found spaces in which to operate as Catholics. In California, Burns explains, dissent was understood as an integral component of local Catholic tradition.

In the twentieth century, California Catholics engaged issues of great importance for the whole church; the local church engaged in vigorous dialogue that transcended parish boundaries. Archbishops, labor priests, and rank-and-file union members, for example, addressed questions of work and social justice with a directness and intensity rarely witnessed in eastern cities, where ethnic tribalism so often undermined concerted action, especially action that called the church to account for failures to practice its own social teachings. The independent spirit demonstrated by women's religious communities in the postwar Golden State similarly presaged national developments and set high standards for integrity and commitment.

The urbanization of California Catholicism was one development that lagged behind the national trend. By the time San Francisco—and much later Los Angeles—became major Catholic centers, the image of American Catholicism as an overwhelmingly urban-immigrant phenomenon was already well established. U.S. Catholicism's primal urban character is *so* familiar that the story told by Jeffrey Marlett in "Strangers in Our Midst" will jar even some practitioners of American religious history. Marlett recovers the distinctive spirituality and culture of agrarian Catholicism across an array of geographic locales. Church officials actively promoted rural colonization schemes for immigrants throughout the nineteenth century; once relocated, these pioneers shaped an agrarian spirituality blending Catholic tradition with communal folkways rooted in the Jeffersonian-American legacy.

By the time the church authorized an official "Catholic Rural Life Movement" in the early twentieth century, an eclectic Catholic rural culture was already well established and thriving. Though agrarian Catholicism varied by region, boundary-crossing innovation was a pervasive element, as was the adaptation of Catholic social thought to local

conditions. The very remoteness of rural Catholics from an ever-centralizing church authority structure demonstrates a kind of American church not tied to urban parishes with
well-defined geographic boundaries and allows agrarian Catholicism to be viewed as a site
of authentic, enduring creativity.

Roy Domenico's essay entitled, "An Embassy to a Golf Course?" treats the most con-
spicuously Catholic location on earth; here the Eternal City doubles as a political capitol
engaged in shifting patterns of diplomacy with an emerging North American nation. Conducted as an amiably low-key, informal relationship in the post-revolutionary period
("Unlike the French," as Domenico explains, "the Americans never invaded the Papal
States, nor did they kidnap and kill the pope"), the growth of American power—and an
even more rapidly growing Catholic population—intrigued the Vatican, which in turn in-
furiated many non-Catholic U.S. citizens whenever the prospect of formal diplomatic
recognition loomed. Protestants and other Americans questioned why the nation's lone
church beholden to a foreign potentate should be thus rewarded.

When the Lateran Treaty of 1929 guaranteed Italy's recognition of Vatican City's sovereignty, the U.S government was faced with the delicate task of reckoning with—and
sometimes abetting—the church's global diplomatic initiatives. The Holy See was impli-
cated in the enigmatically transatlantic political outlook of U.S. Catholics: while fully
one-quarter of the nation's populace was at least nominally allied with the universal church,
these numbers never yielded anything like a unified bloc in support of an increasingly
imperial papacy. Yet there remained an undeniably if elusively transnational component
to American Catholic identity: critics of diplomatic recognition observed not unfairly
that this Catholic "difference" factored into U.S. diplomatic calculations often favorable to the Holy See's interests. By relocating Rome in the American religious and political landscape, Domenico's comparative transnational perspective illuminates the complex
triangular relationship among the American faithful, their national government, and the
Holy See.[14]

Part II: Engaging the World

As *individuals*, Catholics helped to shape American culture from its origins. As the Catholic *Church* grew stronger by the mid-nineteenth century it generated a vast network of
agencies and apostolates (initiatives inspired by the devotion of Jesus Christ's apostles) serving the faithful. Increasingly self-confident displays of the church's organizational prow-
ess enshrined a robust version of "public Catholicism" difficult for fellow citizens to miss.
Yet Catholics operating *as Catholics* in the public arena often plied two fronts, engaging
the broader public while subtly dismantling the mutually imposed quarantine estranging
their church from non-Catholic America.[15]

In "American and Catholic and Literature," literary historian Una Cadegan notes that
sixteenth- and early seventeenth-century European Catholic explorers and missionaries
invented "American literature" (in the form of diaries, journals, and descriptive accounts

of their work intended for European sponsors). With the development of a print culture in the early national period, an American literature designed for a domestic audience began to emerge. The U.S. Catholic Church soon grew sufficiently well organized to generate its own separate literary apparatus meeting the varied needs of immigrants and acculturated readers alike. Catholics were melded into a parallel reading public by their common faith, largely insulated from a national literary industry supplying Protestant readers with tales of moral uplift and sentimental piety not so very different from the Catholic versions.

In the early twentieth century, when a canon of classic American literary artistry finally emerged—immortalizing the likes of Hawthorne, Melville, Emerson, and Margaret Fuller—Catholic authors were excluded; erased too was the persistent engagement of these Protestant writers with Catholic themes in their major works, including perhaps the most canonical work of all: Nathaniel Hawthorne's *The Scarlet Letter*. For decades, as Cadegan explains, American literary studies ignored the "complicated and ambivalent reactions" of these authors to Catholicism. A separate Catholic print culture continued to thrive, beyond whose parochial boundaries a small cohort of American Catholic authors crafted notable works "defined not just by their relationship to the church but individual encounters, with the transcendent reality the church embodies and mediates, with the time and place in which they live, and with their own personal history and circumstances."

A Catholic subculture steeped in the idea that one ought to be at least partially identified by parish membership was able to simultaneously orchestrate an astoundingly global network of missionary enterprises. Although the U.S. church inhabited "mission territory" in the Holy See's estimation until 1908—despite being the richest and most generous national branch of the universal church—American Catholic overseas missionary work commenced in earnest before the turn of the century. In "Gospel Zeal," Robert E. Carbonneau treats the dramatic multifront campaign pursued by American Catholic missionaries to China. These zealots negotiated relationships with the Chinese people, Protestant missionaries, U.S. government representatives, and with the Vatican, whose Asian interests rarely converged with American ambitions. Carbonneau also details the most vital missionary relationship of all: that between members of religious orders conducting expensive overseas apostolates and the "armchair missionaries" who supported them materially and followed the real missionaries' exploits in popular magazines like *The Sign*, a publication of a missionary religious community of priests and brothers, the Congregation of the Passion (or "Passionists").

Few non-Catholic Americans ever encountered a Roman Catholic missionary, but nearly all were familiar with "the sisters," members of women's religious communities ("nuns," strictly speaking, were members of cloistered communities; most U.S. sisters pursued active vocations outside monastic settings). These "women religious" were surely the most conspicuous signs of Catholic presence in the Unites States from the Civil War era (so many served as nurses in the war that for many servicemen of all faiths "sister" and "nurse" became virtual synonyms) through the 1960s. Members of women's religious communities taught millions of parochial school students; others provided social services to immigrants and the poor. As Margaret M. McGuinness demonstrates in "Northern Settlement Houses and Southern Welfare Centers," the Sisters of Our Lady of Christian Doctrine—among dozens of communities responding to the needs of immigrants—adapted the settlement house tradition founded by secular reformers with whom they shared many concerns with one fundamental difference: a sacramental worldview inspiriting apostolic work for personal rebirth and social renewal.

Religious communities like the Sisters of Our Lady of Christian Doctrine provided women with opportunities for lives in leadership and service, sometimes in daunting locales. Having established a successful neighborhood program on New York's Lower East Side, the sisters were invited in 1940—with Al Smith himself as broker—to open a community welfare center in an impoverished, overwhelmingly Protestant corner of South Carolina. The women fostered handicrafts and cultural programs, adapting again a borrowed form—in this case the New Deal's culture-based regional uplift strategy—with creativity and passion. Soon the local community "embraced the sisters as both neighbors and friends." But by the 1960s the sisters were compelled to close both their northern and southern centers amid a precipitous decline in sisterly vocations and a growing shift toward state-sponsored social services. The demise of such innovative ministries marked the end of an era that saw women religious forge enduring relationships with the immigrant and rural poor and with elite non-Catholic reformers.

Sisters enhanced the public image of U.S. Catholicism and the self-appraisal of their coreligionists. An analogous process was on display at the movies in the twentieth century. In "Pulp Catholicism," Anthony Burke Smith assays some of the roles Catholics played in the art form/industry that shared with jazz music a distinction as the most influential American cultural product of the twentieth century. Smith uncovers a rich, nearly lost history of apostolic film production—launched prior to 1920!—under the auspices of the Catholic Art Association. Catholic tastemakers' relatively sophisticated embrace of visual mass culture stood in marked contrast to the later heavy-handed censorship motive that was often ascribed to the church. As Smith shows in this nuanced account, the film industry's original production code was written in 1930 by the prominent film-friendly Jesuit and theatrical impresario Daniel Lord; in later incarnations a harsher code was enforced with gusto by a small group of highly influential laymen.

Smart-talking Irish Catholics were virtually synonymous with the archetypal urban American ubiquitous in popular films of the 1930s. The two decades that followed witnessed a spate of transethnic Catholic films in several genres: favorite themes ranged from the sentimental piety of beloved nuns and clerics to hard-boiled urban adventure. Catholic directors like John Ford made classic movies (Westerns, in Ford's case) expeditiously in service of a studio system faintly analogous at least to the hierarchical church (with Ford as on-set hierarch, especially in his dealings with actors). When that system finally cracked in the 1960s, gifted cinematic insurgents like Martin Scorsese—bearing a pedigree in classic cinema studies *and* mean city streets—potently blended ethnic Catholic experience and Hollywood convention into "sacraments of genre," in film scholar Leo Braudy's memorable phrase.[16]

Part III: Prophetic Catholicism

Dismay over the clergy sex abuse crisis helped revive a movement among younger Catholic intellectuals in the new century: an impulse that had first surfaced a decade earlier. The brand of prophetic Catholicism sought by these scholars and activists was itself a reinvention of a 1930s movement—at once radical and anti-modernist—blending liturgical innovation and social action. For prophetic Catholics of that earlier era, communal worship performed vital apostolic *work* in and for the mystical body of Christ. Six decades later historians found this tradition attractive both as research subject and source of an uncompromising scholarly vocation.

This prophetically Catholic impulse animates Christopher Shannon's "American Catholic Social Thought in the Twentieth Century." Shannon argues that the best early twentieth-century Catholic social thinkers engaged the broader culture but were never assimilated by it. Their sacramental imaginations and openness to supernatural intervention represented a sign of contradiction against the faith-free academic social science in rapid ascent at the time. This prophetic option was especially appealing to converts, anti-modernists, and ex-radicals, but in the 1930s and 1940s it slowly found favor among a cohort of young ethnic Catholics, particularly those exposed to the Catholic Worker movement.

Shannon advances the highly provocative argument that sporadic attempts by prophetic Catholics to influence secular culture undermined the movement's spiritual foundation. John A. Ryan is the pivotal figure here: Shannon privileges Ryan's uncompromising Catholic militancy—as he sees it—over against the pragmatic coalition-building "Right Rev. New Dealer" evident in Ryan's ardent minimum-wage advocacy. That Ryan could fill both roles indicates just why debates within the tradition of Catholic social thought/action confound recourse to the facile binaries of liberal vs. conservative, radical vs. traditionalist, or modernist vs. reactionary.

The creative and prophetic dimension of Catholic social thought often disclosed itself in times of moral and political crisis. As Cecilia Moore demonstrates in "Catholics, Communism, and African Americans," the integrity of "integral Catholics" was put to a stern test by the American church's willingness to countenance racism in the early and middle decades of the twentieth century. Although white ethnic communities had been provided with national parishes of their own since the late nineteenth century, expressions of African American ethnic/racial solidarity were widely viewed as an affront to the all-encompassing theology of the mystical body of Christ. Moore shows how this patronizing racial ideology was shaken only after the Communist Party won substantial numbers of black converts in the 1930s and beyond.

This unprecedented challenge from the Left mobilized a Catholic interracial apostolate led by patrician clerics in collaboration with such black leaders as Dr. Thomas Wyatt Turner, head of the Federated Colored Catholics, an advocacy group that worked with the prominent Jesuit John LaFarge and others to highlight the church's more progressive racial teachings. Goaded from within the church by Catholic radicals like the priest-sociologist Paul Hanly Furfey and from without by Communists, the interracial movement sought the "prudent" integration of Catholic institutions in the late 1930s and 1940s. Collegian-activists were mobilized (especially on Catholic women's campuses), and a racial justice ideology slowly developed.

"Catholics, Communism, and African Americans" shows how the issue of race was refracted through the church's balky political and ideological apparatus, even as racism itself posed an enduring challenge to U.S. Catholicism's moral standing. Rivalry with Communists on the ground—whether in black urban enclaves like Harlem or in the Jim Crow South—exerted a transformative effect on many Catholics, even if their initial motive was to shore up the church's left flank against ideologically motivated attack. Some Catholics succeeded in recasting racial segregation from an unfortunate vestige of "original sin" to a *social* and *personal* sin committed by confirmed Christians in the present moment. In 1944 the Jesuits' Saint Louis University became the first institution of higher learning in a former slave state to admit black students, but only after a Jesuit preacher implored students attending a Mass to stand up and acknowledge the sinfulness of racial exclusion (that Jesuit, Claude Heithaus, was quickly banished from his campus post).

When the young Milwaukee priest James Groppi was asked in 1965 why he marched alongside local African American children boycotting public schools to protest racial inequality, he replied, "I didn't think I had a choice." Groppi is profiled in James P. McCartin's "Praying in the Public Square." McCartin reaffirms that deep into the postwar era "integralism—the integration of Christian practice into all activities of one's everyday life—provided the spiritual foundation for Catholic activism." Integral Catholics heeded the call of American Jesuit Gerald Ellard to "live . . . with the life of Christ living within us." As McCartin demonstrates, this practice of piety changed politics, and then piety itself was changed via personal experiences of prophetic Catholicism in action. This prophetic mode became Dorothy Day's "radical" daily witness beginning in the 1930s; three decades later it approached normative status among a wide swath of Catholics from all walks of life.

Widespread Catholic discontent with U.S. foreign policy during the Vietnam War era swelled the prophetic ranks; that same war exposed deep and ominous fissures within the church itself. Growing political divisions among Catholics always overshadowed doctrinal dissent; as McCartin explains, the battle over legalized abortion in the post-Roe years did not polarize Catholic opinion as dramatically as it introduced a wholly new national political dynamic that wrecked the historic alliance of urban Catholics and the Democratic Party. Before the abortion issue was largely reduced to a culture war between the religious right and secular liberals, some Catholics activists applied the same kind of prophetic witness to the pro-life cause as they had to the peace movement of the 1960s. But the realignment of national political culture resulted in a pro-life movement dominated by conservative evangelicals and a segment of the Catholic community opposed to abortion as part of a wider neo-traditionalist reaction against modern culture.

The collapse of the putatively insular American Catholic subculture in the decade after the Second Vatican Council is a familiar trope pending exhaustive historical inquiry. The stirring opening of the church to the world proclaimed at the Council was surely welcome news to American Catholics transfixed by the epochal event, whose four successive autumnal sessions were held in Rome's St. Peter's Basilica between 1962 and 1965. The Council's inspiriting metaphor of *aggiornamento* ("bringing up to date") resonated globally but was celebrated in a special way by Americans, who saw their unique if undervalued traditions vindicated in several key documents from Vatican II.

In her essay "The Resurrection Project of Mexican Catholic Chicago," Karen Mary Davalos offers a historical ethnography of community building in Chicago's historic Pilsen neighborhood on that city's Near West Side. Davalos's narrative focuses on the Resurrection Project, a post–Vatican II interparish coalition of solidarity coordinated by Mexican Catholic women who create from their work "a Catholicism that unites the mundane and the sacred through a precondition that envisions salvation on Earth." Though Davalos intentionally locates her subjects outside "the historiography of American Catholicism in its description of clergy, ministry, and devotional practices *inside* the church," this essay bears a strikingly prophetic quality not only for where the U.S. church is heading but also for where it *has been*—a story that may stand outside canonical historiography but surely not the lived experience of Catholic people.

There is a tantalizingly unique dimension of Davalos's narrative, likely due to the special conditions of Mexican Catholic history in Chicago—a story that begins in 1916 with the arrival of railroad workers (and sometime strikebreakers) on the city's Near West Side. Chicago's first Mexican Catholics were immediately subject to Americanization schemes sponsored by the local archdiocese; just as quickly they found themselves agents of ethnic succession when a historically Italian parish (originally German) was converted to a Mexican church. St. Francis Assisi parish soon sponsored carnivals and *Guadalupana* devotions, the primal stuff of urban Catholic myth and memory.

In later years support from the church for reconstituted Mexican Chicago communities ebbed and flowed: sometimes the community was blessed by the presence of a remarkable worker-priest; at others Mexicans were viewed with indifference by church officials, leaving the community to draw deeply from its own resources. Women took the lead, but laity and their clergy alike, Davalos suggests, learned to "use their social experiences as the starting point for theological discourse." That social experience included racism in the form of a commonplace belief that Chicago's Mexicans are all illegal aliens and structural economic disadvantage rooted in the now-ancient post-industrial character of Pilsen and surrounding areas. The Resurrection Project "responds to the *materiality* of Mexican Chicago," as Davalos explains. The reversal of conventional Catholic expectation in this unabashed grounding of the spiritual in the material generated modes of theological reflection that in turn *changed* a community's social and religious experience.

In the concluding essay, "The People of God," Chester Gillis shows that the Second Vatican Council called the whole church to engage the world in a spirit of joy and hope. The U.S. Catholic bishops—following an unprecedented process of consultation with other citizens—gradually adopted a prophetic stance as world citizens rather than imperial monarchs. In the 1980s, the U.S. bishops attracted global notice via their pastoral letters on nuclear weaponry and economic justice. As Gillis explains, there were no more bars to the church's wholehearted participation in the public arena, but the bishops' intended audience—especially including many Catholics—now ascribed an advisory role at best to these shepherds' teachings. Church leaders operated within a competitive marketplace of ideas—ideas warily assessed by consumers regardless of their source. Chester Gillis's essay reflects historian James P. McCartin's contention earlier in this volume that the political realignment of abortion foes in the 1980s and 1990s cast many bishops as transparently partisan operatives whose dictates were widely viewed as strictly advisory. And all this came *before* the scandal of sex abuse and its cover-up was reignited in 2002, which Gillis rightly calls the "most painful, disturbing and publicly embarrassing chapter" in U.S. Catholic history.

In light of the challenges facing historians of U.S. Catholicism—including the sexual-abuse scandal that rocked the church during the first decade of the twenty-first century and the growing divide between traditionalist and progressive bishops and laypeople, the essays in this volume are exemplary for the good will and generosity that complement the originality of their scholarship. The communal spirit underlying these works is palpable, as though to reaffirm the vitality *and* the sense of solidarity that has marked U.S. Catholic historical scholarship for decades and now extends to the next generation of scholars as they embrace the joys and challenges of this enduring tradition.[17]

NOTES

1. For a plausible claimant as the original work of American literature, see Álvar Nuñez Cabeza de Vaca, *Adventures in the Unknown Interior of America*, trans. Cyclone Covey (Albuquerque: University of New Mexico Press, 1983). This narrative begins with an account of the Spanish expeditionary force that landed in 1528 near present-day Sarasota, Florida. Cabeza de Vaca was among only four members of the party of three hundred to survive the subsequent misadventure. For even richer accounts of European–Native American encounters and exchange, see the truly mind-boggling *Jesuit Relations and Allied Documents: Travels and Explorations of the Jesuit Missionaries in New France, 1610–1791*, published by Burrows Bros. in seventy-three volumes between 1896 and 1901, including the original French, Latin, and Italian texts, with English translations and notes.

2. R. Laurence Moore, *Religious Outsiders and the Making of Americans* (New York: Oxford University Press, 1986), 50–51.

3. The first prominent U.S. Catholic historian was John Gilmary Shea (1884–1947), who studied missionary explorers and later wrote the first American Catholic history textbook; his successor was Peter Guilday (1884–1947), best known for his studies of early national–era bishops John Carroll (Baltimore; the first American bishop) and John England (Charleston, South Carolina). For Hecker, see David J. O'Brien, *Isaac Hecker: An American Catholic* (Mahwah, N.J.: Paulist Press, 1992).

4. For classic studies of the Americanism controversy, see Robert D. Cross, *The Emergence of Liberal Catholicism in America* (Cambridge, Mass.: Harvard University Press, 1958), and Thomas T. McAvoy, C.S.C., *The Great Crisis in American Catholic History, 1865–1900* (Chicago: Regnery, 1957); for the subsequent related Modernist controversy, see R. Scott Appleby, *Church and Age Unite: The Modernist Impulse in American Catholicism* (Notre Dame, Ind.: University of Notre Dame Press, 1992).

5. William M. Halsey, *The Survival of American Innocence: Catholicism in an Era of Disillusionment, 1920–1940* (Notre Dame, Ind.: University of Notre Dame Press, 1980).

6. John Tracy Ellis, *American Catholics and the Intellectual Life* (New York: Fordham University Press, 1955); see also Walter J. Ong, *Frontiers in American Catholicism: Essays on Ideology and Culture* (New York: Macmillan, 1957). For a different way of looking at the much-ballyhooed Catholic intellectual dilemma of the 1950s, see James T. Fisher, "Alternative Sources of Catholic Intellectual Vitality," in *U.S. Catholic Historian* 13 (Winter 1995): 81–94. For an overview of U.S. religion in the postwar era, see Fisher, "American Religion Since 1945," in *A Companion to Post-1945 America*, ed. Jean-Christophe Agnew and Roy Rosenzweig (New York: Blackwell, 2002), 44–63.

7. For Catholic-American patriotism and anti-Communism, see Christopher J. Kauffman, *Faith and Fraternalism: The History of the Knights of Columbus, 1882–1982* (New York: Harper and Row, 1982); Donald J. Crosby, *God, Church and Flag: Senator Joseph R. McCarthy and the Catholic Church, 1950–1957* (Chapel Hill: University of North Carolina Press, 1978); Patrick Allitt, *Catholic Intellectuals and Conservative Politics in America, 1950–1985* (Ithaca, N.Y.: Cornell University Press, 1993). For a dramatic case study of Catholic anti-Communism yoked to the fortunes of political leaders, see Seth Jacobs, *America's Miracle Man in Vietnam: Ngo Dinh Diem, Religion, Race and U.S. Intervention in Southeast Asia, 1950–1957* (Raleigh, N.C.: Duke University Press, 2004). For the emergence of an American Catholic peace church, see William A. Au, *The Cross, the Flag and the Bomb: American Catholics Debate War and Peace, 1960–1983* (Westport, Conn.: Greenwood, 1985); David J. O'Brien, *The Renewal of American Catholicism* (New York: Oxford University Press, 1972); Charles Meconis, *With Clumsy Grace: The American Catholic Left, 1961–1975* (New York: Seabury, 1979); Murray Polner and Jim O'Grady, *Disarmed and Dangerous: The Radical Lives and Times of Daniel and Philip Berrigan* (New York: Basic, 1997). For tensions between segments of the church militant and the nascent peace church, see Fisher, *The Catholic Counterculture in America, 1933–1962* (Chapel Hill: University of North Carolina Press, 1989).

8. O'Brien, *American Catholics and Social Reform: The New Deal Years* (New York: Oxford University Press, 1968); Mel Piehl, *Breaking Bread: The Catholic Worker and the Origin of Catholic Radicalism in America* (Philadelphia: Temple University Press, 1981); Nancy Roberts, *Dorothy Day and the Catholic Worker* (Albany: SUNY Press, 1984). For the European Catholic revival, see Stephen Schloesser, *Jazz Age Catholicism: Mystic Modernism in Postwar Paris, 1919–1933* (Toronto: University of Toronto Press, 2005). For an evocative overview of the Catholic revival's mystique in the United States, see Dolores Elise Brien, "The Catholic Revival Revisited," *Commonweal* 106 (December 21, 1979): 714–16. For the lay apostolate movement, see Dennis Robb, "Specialized Catholic Action in the United States, 1936–1949" (Ph.D. dissertation, University of Minnesota, 1972). For the Grail, see Janet Kalven, *Women Breaking Boundaries: A Grail Journey, 1940–1995* (Albany: SUNY Press, 1999), and Alden V. Brown, *The Grail Movement and American Catholicism, 1940–1975* (Notre Dame, Ind.: University of Notre Dame Press, 1989).

9. For a notable exception to the rule that Catholic action and the labor movement were treated separately, see Steven Rosswurm, *The CIO's Left-Led Unions* (New Brunswick, N.J.: Rutgers University Press, 1992). Historians of labor—and race—who might once have eschewed the Catholic issue are becoming more attentive: see, for example, Bruce Nelson, *Divided We Stand: American Workers and the Struggle for Black Equality* (Princeton, N.J.: Princeton University Press, 2001). For a work that avowedly bridges the very different but coterminous worlds of Catholic/secular radical-reform politics, see Fisher, *On the Irish Waterfront: The Crusader, the Movie and the Soul of the Port of New York* (Ithaca, N.Y.: Cornell University Press, 2009); see also Michael Denning: *The Cultural Front: The Laboring of American Culture in the Twentieth Century* (New York: Verso, 1997); David W. Southern, *John LaFarge and the Limits of Catholic Interracialism* (Baton Rouge: Louisiana State University Press, 1996). For a heretofore unexplored case of Catholic/Leftist ideological/spiritual competition, see the essay herein by Cecilia Moore, "Catholics, Communism and African Americans."

10. For the American Catholic Studies phenomenon, see Fisher, "The (Longed For) Varieties of Catholic Studies," *Listening: Journal of Religion and Culture* 42 (Winter 2007): 54–67. A gathering of Catholic Studies voices is found in Thomas J. Ferraro, Special Issue editor, *Catholic Lives/Contemporary America*, *South Atlantic Quarterly* 93 (Summer 1994). The original essays and new material were published under the same title by Duke University Press in 1997. Among the most influential early (and ongoing) work in the field is that of Robert A. Orsi; see *The Madonna of 115th Street: Faith and Community in Italian Harlem, 1880–1950* (New Haven, Conn.: Yale University Press, 1985); see also Orsi, *Thank You St. Jude: Women's Devotion to the Patron Saint of Lost Causes* (New Haven, Conn.: Yale University Press, 1996); and Orsi, *Between Heaven and Earth: The Religious Worlds People Make and the Scholars Who Study Them* (Princeton, N.J.: Princeton University Press: 2005). For works treating literature and the visual arts, see Paul Giles, *American Catholic Arts and Fictions* (Cambridge: Cambridge University Press, 1992); Debra Campbell, *Graceful Exits: Catholic Women and the Art of Departure* (Bloomington, Ind.: University of Indiana Press, 2003); Colleen McDannell, *Picturing Faith: Photography and the Great Depression* (New Haven, Conn.: Yale University Press, 2004). For popular culture and popular devotions, see McDannell, *Material Christianity: Religion and Popular Culture in America* (New Haven, Conn.: Yale University Press, 1995); Julie Byrne, *O God of Players: The Story of the Immaculata Mighty Macs* (New York: Columbia University Press, 2003); Ann Taves, *The Household of Faith: Roman Catholic Devotions in Mid-Nineteenth Century America* (Notre Dame, Ind.: University of Notre Dame Press, 1986); and the four excellent essays in James M. O'Toole, ed., *Habits of Devotion: Catholic Religious Practice in Twentieth-Century America* (Ithaca, N.Y.: Cornell University Press: 2004), 187–236.

For innovative studies of women's religious communities treating issues of gender and sexuality, see Carol Coburn and Marsha Smith, *Spirited Lives: How Nuns Shaped Catholic Culture and American Life, 1836–1920* (Chapel Hill: University of North Carolina Press, 1999); Amy Koehlinger, *The New Nuns: Racial Justice and Religious Reform in the 1960s* (Cambridge, Mass.: Harvard University Press, 2006); Maureen Fitzgerald, *Habits of Compassion: Irish Catholic Nuns and the Origins of New York's Welfare System, 1830–1920* (Urbana: University of Illinois Press, 2006); Leslie Woodcock Tentler, *Catholics and Contraception: An American History* (Ithaca, N.Y.: Cornell University Press, 2004); Margaret M. McGuinness, *Called to Serve: A History of Nuns in America* (New York: NYU Press, 2013); Paula M. Kane, *Sister Thorn and Catholic Mysticism in Modern America* (Chapel Hill: University of North Carolina Press, 2013).

For works blending Catholic and ethnic studies, see Ferraro, *Feeling Italian: The Art of Ethnicity in America* (New York: New York University Press, 2005); Thomas Tweed, *Our Lady of the Exile: Diasporic Religion at a Cuban Catholic Shrine in Miami* (New York: Oxford University Press, 1997); Timothy Matovina and Gary Riebe-Estrella, eds., *Horizons of the Sacred: Mexican Traditions in U.S. Catholicism* (Ithaca, N.Y.: Cornell University Press, 2002); Matovina, *Guadalupe and Her Faithful: Latino Catholics in San Antonio, from Colonial Origins to the Present* (Baltimore: Johns Hopkins University Press, 2005).

For other notable historical studies that incorporated interdisciplinary approaches, see, among many others, Allitt, *Catholic Converts: British and American Intellectuals Turn to Rome* (Ithaca, N.Y.: Cornell University Press, 1997); Kane, *Separatism and Subculture: Boston Catholicism, 1900–1920* (Chapel Hill: University of North Carolina Press, 1994); Mark S. Massa, *Catholics and American Culture: Fulton Sheen, Dorothy Day and the Notre Dame Football Team* (New York: Crossroad, 1999); John Seitz, *No Closure: Catholic Practice and Boston's Parish Shutdowns* (Cambridge, Mass.: Harvard University Press, 2011); Thomas Rzeznik, *Church and Estate: Religion and Wealth in Industrial-Era Philadelphia* (University Park: Penn State University Press, 2013); Byrne, The Other Catholics (New York: Columbia University Press, 2014).

For a work that brilliantly reconstructs the conflicting intellectual worlds that virtually ensured U.S. Catholic history would be "received" as problematic by the secularizing academy, see John T. McGreevy, *Catholics and American Freedom: A History* (New York: W. W. Norton, 2003). For an interpretive survey of relatively recent U.S. Catholic historical scholarship, see Leslie Woodcock Tentler, "On the Margins: The State of American Catholic History," *American Quarterly* 45 (March 1993): 104–27. Tentler's essay is reprinted in *U.S. Catholic Historian* 21 (Spring 2003): 77–126; themes treated in the essay are discussed and updated in a symposium featuring commentaries by historians John Bodnar, Madeline Duntley, Patricia O'Connell Killen, Joseph A. McCartin, and John T. McGreevy.

For the influence of Catholic Studies in other fields, see—for only one example among dozens of volumes by the same author—Andrew M. Greeley, *The Catholic Myth: The Behavior and Beliefs of American Catholics* (New York: Charles Scribner's Sons: 1990). Greeley both appropriated—primarily from theologian David Tracy (the inaugural holder of the Greeley Chair at the University of Chicago)—and popularized the notion of a uniquely "Catholic imagination" that became a staple of Catholic Studies scholarship, despite the trope's failure to stand up very well at all under comparative-historical scrutiny. See also Paul Elie, *The Life You Save May Be Your Own: An American Pilgrimage* (New York: Farrar, Straus and Giroux, 2003), which treats a quartet of the most canonical American Catholic writers of the twentieth century: Dorothy Day, Thomas Merton, Flannery O'Connor, and Walker Percy.

11. For a representative introduction to themes characterizing U.S. Catholic scholarship in the prophetic mode, see Michael J. Baxter, "Notes on Catholic Americanism and Catholic Radicalism: Toward a Counter-Tradition of Catholic Social Ethics," in *American Catholic Traditions: Resources for Renewal*, ed. Sandra Yocum Mize and William Portier (Maryknoll, N.Y.: Orbis, 1997), 53–76. See also Baxter, "Writing History in a World Without Ends: An Evangelical Catholic Critique of United States Catholic History," *Pro Ecclesia* 5 (Fall 1996): 440–69; Christopher Shannon, *Conspicuous Criticism: Tradition, the Individual, and Culture in American Social Thought from Veblen to Mills* (Baltimore: Johns Hopkins University Press, 1996); Eugene McCarraher, *Christian Critics: Religion and the Impasse in Modern Social Thought* (Ithaca, N.Y.: Cornell University Press, 2000).

12. Maura Farrelly, *Papist Patriots: The Making of an American Catholic Identity* (New York: Oxford University Press, 2012); Michael Pasquier, *Fathers on the Frontier: French Missionaries and the Roman Catholic Priesthood in the United States, 1789–1870* (New York: Oxford University Press, 2010); Rosswurm, *The FBI and the Catholic Church, 1935–1962* (Amherst: University of Massachusetts Press, 2009).

13. The immigrant church model has obtained among historians of the United States since the publication of Oscar Handlin, *Boston's Immigrants, 1790–1865: A Study in Acculturation* (Cambridge, Mass.: Harvard University Press, 1941). Among other notable works, see Jay P. Dolan, *The Immigrant Church: New York's Irish and German Catholics, 1815–1865* (Notre Dame, Ind.: University of Notre Dame Press, 1975); Dolan, *Catholic Revivalism: The American Experience, 1830–1900* (Notre Dame, Ind.: University of Notre Dame Press, 1978); Tyler Anbinder, *Five Points: The 19th-Century New York City Neighborhood that Invented Tap Dance, Stole Elections, and Became the World's Most Notorious Slum* (New York: Free Press, 2001).

14. See also Peter D'Agostino, *Rome in America: Transnational Catholic Ideology from the Risorgimento to Fascism* (Chapel Hill: University of North Carolina Press, 2003); before Peter D'Agostino's life was tragically cut short, he was known and admired by many of the contributors to this volume.

15. See O'Brien, *Public Catholicism* (Maryknoll, N.Y.: Orbis, 1996); see also McGuinness, "Let Us Go to the Altar: American Catholics and the Eucharist, 1926–1976," in *Habits of Devotion: Catholic Religious Practice in Twentieth-Century America*, ed. James M. O'Toole (Ithaca, N.Y.: Cornell University Press: 2004), 187–236.

16. Leo Braudy, "The Sacraments of Genre," in *Native Informant: Essays on Film, Fiction and Popular Culture* (New York: Oxford University Press, 1991), 22. See also Christian Smith, *Soul*

Searching: The Religious and Spiritual Lives of American Teenagers (New York: Oxford University Press, 2005); Jerome P. Baggett, *Sense of the Faithful: How American Catholics Live Their Faith* (New York: Oxford University Press, 2009); for background on Catholic colleges, see Philip Gleason, *Contending with Modernity: Catholic Higher Education in the Twentieth Century* (New York: Oxford University Press, 1995).

    17. Jason Berry, *Lead Us Not into Temptation: Catholic Priests and the Sexual Abuse of Children* (New York: Doubleday, 1992), treated many of the issues that would only receive sustained attention with the relentless revelations of clergy sex abuse beginning in January 2002. For other works that treat the crisis, see also Peter Steinfels, *A People Adrift: The Crisis of the Roman Catholic Church in America* (New York: Simon & Schuster, 2003); David Gibson, *The Coming Catholic Church: How the Faithful Are Shaping a New American Catholicism* (San Francisco: HarperSanFrancisco, 2004); Berry, *Render unto Rome: The Secret Life of Money in the Catholic Church* (New York: Crown, 2011).

PART ONE

Beyond the Parish

ONE

Ambiguous Welcome: The Protestant Response to American Catholics

Patrick Allitt

Introduction

The United States has a long history of bigotry, intolerance, and violence against outsiders and minorities. The Catholic Church and Catholic immigrants, at times, were among the victims. The nation also has a long tradition of civility and tolerance, of which at other times Catholics were the beneficiaries. The story of America's attempts to persecute, exclude, or reject Catholics should be balanced against its welcome for and inclusion of them. Otherwise the development of an immense, thriving, fully acculturated U.S. Catholic population by the mid-twentieth century would be incomprehensible. This chapter surveys the history of Protestant reactions to Catholics and their church from the colonial era to the present. It demonstrates that verbal and physical attacks on Catholics were, in many eras, offset by some Protestants' attraction to Catholicism and that the phenomenon of public anti-Catholicism, potent in the nineteenth century, disappeared almost completely after the 1960s.

The three or four thousand Catholics in the pre-revolutionary American colonies came mainly from England. About four million Irish and German Catholic immigrants swelled their ranks between that era and the Civil War and transformed the character of U.S. Catholicism. In the late nineteenth and early twentieth centuries, eight or ten million more at least nominally Catholic immigrants arrived from Italy, Poland, and Southeastern Europe. In the twentieth century as many again arrived from Central and South America, the Philippines, and Vietnam. Most of these immigrants, in each generation, overcame initial difficulties, found work, intermarried, sent their children to American schools, enjoyed upward social mobility, and benefited from the First Amendment's guarantee of religious freedom.

Other Americans, the vast majority of whom were always Protestants, rarely welcomed them. Why? The historian Barbara Welter once imagined a typical American Protestant's objections to Catholicism as going something like this: "[W]e dislike [your] arrogance and elitism of claiming to be the 'one, holy, catholic and apostolic' church; we dislike [your] reliance on authority rather than on individual judgment; we dislike [your] substitution of a parochial for a public school system; we find celibacy unwholesome and perverse for the clergy . . . we oppose inflexible social rules masquerading as immutable natural laws; we oppose censorship in books; we prefer to read the Bible for ourselves and scorn official interpretation; we deplore the level of taste in architecture, statuary and hymns; [and] we shudder at the superstition surrounding the Virgin and the saints."[1] All the themes she noted in this hypothetical tirade have indeed played a role in U.S. Protestant-Catholic relations, and many of them persisted from the colonial era well into the twentieth century.

Nevertheless, the Catholic way of life, which revolted some Protestants, attracted others. Many admired the Catholic Church from outside, especially its artistic, architectural, and literary achievements. Others modified their own religious practices and ideas under the influence of Catholic examples. A few even became convinced by its theological claims and converted to Catholicism. Attitudes were rarely religious alone, however; questions of religion were nearly always intermixed with questions of politics, race, ethnicity, and social class.

The Colonial Era

The first English migrants to the New World in the 1600s, nearly all of them Protestants, brought with them a vivid set of convictions about Catholics. They understood the Reformation of the 1520s and 1530s as the moment when Christendom had emerged from the dark night of Catholic cruelty, superstition, and infamy and thought of it as part of the great cosmic drama being fought out between God and the Devil. They recalled that several leading English Protestants, notably, bishops Cranmer, Ridley, and Latimer ("the Oxford Martyrs"), had been burned at the stake by Catholic Queen Mary I during her attempt to undo the English Reformation in the 1550s. They read lurid accounts of these executions in John Foxe's *Book of Martyrs* (1559), one of the most popular Protestant books to make the crossing to the colonies, and one that would stay in print from the 1560s right into the twentieth century.

Catholics, according to Protestants nurtured on Foxe and his successors, were tyrannical, immoral, cruel, and idolatrous. They were also active or latent traitors to England. Protestant settlers recalled Queen Elizabeth I's defeat of the Spanish Armada in 1588 not merely as a naval victory over a rival power, but as a manifestation of divine providence. Their narratives emphasized that a "Protestant wind" had blown in the English Channel to aid Francis Drake's ships and confound those of Spain. Catholicism, under the leadership of a sinister pope in alliance with foreign tyrants like Philip II of Spain, seemed to Protestants a constant threat to England and its colonies.

The Puritan colonies founded in the 1600s—Plymouth (1620), Massachusetts Bay (1629), Rhode Island (1636), Connecticut (1636), and New Haven (1638)—were accordingly zealously anti-Catholic right from the beginning. Cotton Mather (1663–1728), the most prolific Puritan writer of the colonial era, echoed a common view when he argued that one of the principal reasons for the Protestant settlement of America was "to carry the Gospel into those parts of the world, and to raise a bulwark against the kingdom of Antichrist, which the Jesuits labor to rear up in all parts of the world." By "Antichrist" he meant the pope. "[I]n the Pope of Rome, all the characteristics of that Antichrist are so marvelously answered that if any who read the Scriptures do not see it, there is a marvelous blindness upon them."[2] Anti-Catholic woodcuts, playing cards, and cartoons featuring lecherous priests could be found throughout colonial New England. A popular children's schoolbook, the *New England Primer* (1683), blended lessons in the alphabet with a vigorous anti-Catholicism in passages like this: "Abhor the whore of Rome and all her blasphemies, and drink not of her cursed cup; obey not her decrees."[3]

Not all seventeenth-century settlers in the American colonies were as fanatically opposed to Catholics as the New England preachers, to be sure. King Charles I granted a colonial charter to a Catholic convert, Cecilius Calvert, the Second Baron Baltimore, in 1632. The settlers who crossed the Atlantic to this new colony, Maryland, celebrated Mass on American soil for the first time in the spring of 1634. Maryland's population was religiously mixed from the outset; its Toleration Act of 1649 imposed fines on anyone who tried to stir up intra-Christian conflict. Even in New England, moreover, the pattern was mixed. The chance arrival of individual Catholics (after a shipwreck, for example) was often taken calmly, so long as they carried no ecclesiastical authority. Gayle Brown, a historian of colonial-era anti-Catholicism, writes that "individual lay Catholics confronted on a face-to-face basis were less threatening to ordinary Protestants, and hence less likely to be the target of verbal or physical attack."[4]

The succession of colonial wars fought between Britain and France in the eighteenth century, culminating in the French and Indian War (1754–60), strengthened the idea that Catholicism meant, potentially, loyalty to the enemy. Indian tribes allied to the French had sometimes become at least nominally Catholic under Jesuit instruction; colonial commentators linked their ferocity in war to the idea of Catholic brutality. Narratives written by colonists taken captive in these wars often blended criticism of the Indians with criticism of their French Catholic allies. At the same time their Protestant authors expressed an uneasy awareness that the Jesuits had done a far better job at converting the Indians than they themselves. One captive wrote, "Oh, may not the zeal of Papists, in propagating Superstition and Idolatry, make Protestants ashamed of their lukewarmness, in promoting the religion of the Bible?"[5]

The Revolution

Among the acts of Parliament that galvanized American revolutionary opposition to Britain was the Quebec Act of 1774, which offered religious toleration to the Catholic majority in Canada, the land Britain had recently won from France in the French and Indian Wars, and permitted tithing for the support of Catholic clergy in French Canadian districts. Bostonians were almost as incensed by this last concession as by the closing of their port, viewing it as a foot in the door for religious tyranny. They had been agitated, since 1763, by the rising possibility that an Anglican bishop might be sent to their colony. Bishops, in their view, were a vestige of Catholicism, a symbol of England's incomplete Reformation, and an augury of tyrannical royal power. The Continental Congress replied to the Quebec Act by sending an address to the people of Britain listing a lengthy history of Catholic persecutions and atrocities.

When the fighting began in 1775, nevertheless, most American Catholics sided with those advocating revolution. In recognition of the need for Catholic support, General George Washington suppressed Boston's "Pope's Day," the annual anti-Catholic festival held every November 5 (to commemorate a failed Catholic attempt to blow up the Houses of Parliament in 1605). Over the years it had become a riotous apprentices' parade, in which drunken workmen paraded an effigy of the pope through the streets before burning it on the town common. Aware that the success of the revolutionary cause depended in part on forming an alliance with Catholic France, and recognizing that the allegiance of colonial Catholics would also be useful, Washington urged a new interreligious discretion. An American army marched to Quebec and Montreal in the hope of enlisting Canadian aid to the revolutionary cause. General Washington reminded its commanders that they and their soldiers must treat Catholics and their institutions with respect and restraint.

The army's failure to do so—and some soldiers' provocative insults and plundering of Canadian Catholics—contributed to the inability to win the Canadians' allegiance. Charles Carroll, the richest and most prominent Catholic in Maryland, joined Benjamin Franklin in a delegation to Canada but found the Canadians resolute against joining the patriot cause. Carroll was a popular figure among pro-independence Marylanders for his outspoken criticism of the colony's proprietors. In 1776 he became the one and only Catholic signatory of the Declaration of Independence. His dedication to the cause made a favorable impression on other revolutionary leaders. John Adams, for instance, wrote that Carroll "continues to hazard his all, his immense fortune . . . and his life," while Benjamin Rush described him as "an inflexible patriot, and an honest independent friend to his country."[6] His enthusiasm for the revolution outweighed old suspicions of his faith, as he was well aware, and contributed to the muting of anti-Catholic sentiment. His home state, like Virginia, introduced the principle of complete religious liberty in its new constitution.

Despite Carroll's example, popular anti-Catholicism persisted on both sides of the revolutionary divide. An alliance with Catholic France from 1778 made some of the revolutionary leaders, such as Samuel Adams, uneasy, but most of them held their noses and accepted it for reasons of political convenience. It offered a propaganda opportunity to loyalists, however, who were quick to point out the hypocrisy and the hazards of such an alliance. A New York Anglican rector, Charles Inglis, reproached the revolutionaries: "Is popery then changed? Is it purged from error and become less persecuting? No—it is now the very same as formerly. Its Inquisition still reeks with the blood of Protestants."[7]

Ironically, many of America's most zealous Protestants had now decided to ignore Inglis's warning and risk their future in an alliance with one of the great Catholic powers.

Antebellum Tensions

American Catholics' support for the Revolution won the enthusiastic gratitude of Washington, Adams, Franklin, and Jefferson, but these revolutionary leaders had a more pragmatic, this-worldly outlook than most of their contemporaries. Militant Protestants throughout the new republic continued to believe that Catholicism was not merely another branch of Christianity but was, in effect, its antithesis, the religion of Antichrist. As the Second Great Awakening, a vast Protestant revival, gathered power after 1800, its Methodist and Baptist champions worked to disseminate the King James Bible and to "missionize" settlers on the rapidly expanding frontier. They worked in sharp rivalry not merely against each other, but against the imagined threat of Catholic infiltrators. Nativist newspapers like *The Protestant* and the *American Protestant Vindicator* (both published in New York during the 1830s) warned that Jesuits, the pope's shock troops, were disguising themselves as "puppet show men, dancing masters, Music teachers, peddlers of images and ornaments [and] barrel organ players" in frontier territories, imperiling Protestant souls.[8]

Rumors spread in the old Northwest that Catholics might try to take over the Ohio Valley and close off a vast area from Protestant settlement. The Leopoldine Foundation, according to this theory, had been founded by Prince Klemens von Metternich, a diplomat of the Austro-Hungarian Empire, to achieve this goal. If the theory were true, the arrival of German Catholic migrants in the Ohio country became a sinister fulfillment of the plot rather than a poor immigrant group's simple search for economic opportunity. Lyman Beecher, one of the most famous Protestant preachers of his day (and father of Harriet Beecher Stowe), followed the Ohio migration and became president of Lane Theological Seminary in Cincinnati. He took seriously some of these nativist rumors, imagined that papal armies might actually seize Cincinnati, and told parishioners that the Catholic Church was "the most skillful, powerful, dreadful system of corruption to those who wield it, and of slavery and debasement to those who live under it."[9] His tract, *A Plea for the West* (1835), urged Protestants to rescue "the west" from the devious plans of Europe's Catholic reactionaries, men like Metternich. Samuel Morse, an art professor at New York University who is best remembered today for his invention of telegraphy and Morse code, was even more zealous in his attacks. "We are the dupes of our hospitality," he warned in *Foreign Conspiracy against the Liberties of the United States* (1834). "The evil of immigration brings to these shores illiterate Roman Catholics, the tools of reckless and unprincipled politicians, the obedient instruments of their more knowing priestly leaders."[10]

Morse here linked anti-Catholicism with opposition to immigration. The two issues would be closely connected from then on for at least a century, especially when the immigrants in question were Irish. Prior to 1800 the nearly half million Irish immigrants in the United States were Protestants (the Scotch-Irish), but after 1800 growing numbers of

Irish Catholics also crossed the Atlantic, about 250,000 of them between 1820 and 1840. Many of them settled in East Coast cities, notably New York, Philadelphia, Baltimore, and Boston. They originated in rural Ireland, but poverty forced most to become city dwellers in the United States. The Catholic stream became a flood during the mid- and late 1840s when famine in Ireland prompted emergency emigration on a huge scale—over a million in the five years after 1846, and three and a half million more between then and the end of the century. Malnourished immigrants were vulnerable to typhus, cholera, and other infectious diseases, with the result that many immigrant ships arrived off America bearing corpses and travelers on the brink of death. Horrified U.S. onlookers regarded them, not surprisingly, as a health menace. New York and Boston sent away many fever ships without letting them land; at least 30,000 immigrants who were permitted to come ashore in Montreal died within a year of their arrival. Charitable impulses led some Americans to help the suffering, but the famine created such an enduring impression among Protestants that the terms "Catholic," "Irish," "destitute," and "diseased" became virtually interchangeable.

A large-scale immigration of German Catholics further increased tensions. The establishment of Catholic churches, schools, and convents to help the new immigrants in East Coast and midwestern cities that had previously been predominantly Protestant provoked a strong negative reaction. Older American groups (who, confusingly, referred to themselves as "Native Americans") not only feared the Catholics' religion but resented them as competitors for jobs. Growing friction between Protestant and Catholic groups culminated in pitched street battles between teenage gangs and Protestant attacks on Catholic institutions. In August 1834, for example, a working-class Protestant mob burned to the ground a convent school in Boston run by Ursuline sisters, alleging that it held girls against their will and permitted priests to abuse them sexually. Although upper-class Protestants expressed disapproval at this act of vandalism, their eventual reaction suggests a less than wholehearted condemnation. Thirteen men, arrested red-handed at the scene of the crime and tried for setting the fire, were acquitted by sympathetic juries amid Protestant rejoicing.

Street fighting in Philadelphia between Irish Catholics and anti-immigrant nativists lasted for three days in 1844 and ended with the destruction of the Irish Kensington neighborhood and the burning of several churches. Conflicts flared up again later that year and featured nativists firing scrap metal out of cannons into Catholic churches. Thirteen men died in the fighting, with hundreds more injured. At least twenty more were killed in Louisville, Kentucky, on August 6, 1855, "Bloody Monday," when anti-Catholic politicians prevented naturalized Irish and German citizens from voting. Fights broke out at the polls, and a drunken Protestant mob rioted, vandalizing Catholic districts and beating residents. The mob set fire to an entire block of houses in one area and gunned down the residents as they fled from the flames.[11]

Contributing to the interreligious tension from the 1830s to the 1850s was a lurid body of anti-Catholic literature. Much of it purported to describe the horrible and perverted lives of nuns in convents. The most famous example was the *Awful Disclosures of Maria Monk, or The Hidden Secrets of a Nun's Life in a Convent Exposed* (1836). Ostensibly the autobiography of a young Protestant girl who had converted to Catholicism and entered a religious community as a novice, it was in fact a fake, probably written by a Protestant minister named J. J. Slocum. It described her life in a Montreal convent as a form of torture, in which every aspect of liberty was denied and every opportunity to think for herself was taken away. Monk alleged that, after taking her vows, she and the other women became the sex slaves of lecherous local priests. She added that to avoid scandal in the outside world, they gave birth to babies in secret, baptized them, but then had to strangle them for burial in a mass grave underneath the convent. Those who did not cooperate were tortured, sometimes to death. William Leete Stone (1792–1844), a skeptical New York newspaper editor, investigated the convent in question with the local bishop's permission and demonstrated the book's falsity. The real Maria Monk (1816–49), a mentally retarded prostitute and pickpocket, died in prison a few years later. Nevertheless, the book itself remained in print throughout the nineteenth century and far into the twentieth, widely believed, despite its fraudulence having been proved repeatedly by Catholic (and fair-minded Protestant) investigators.

Protestant activists thought of Catholics not only as poverty-stricken peasants or sexually predatory priests, but also as the tyrants of old Europe, natural opponents of enlightened political change. They drew on U.S. political idealism to condemn the Catholic Church's role in the European politics of the 1840s and 1850s. The papacy in those years opposed Hungarian independence from the Austro-Hungarian Empire as well as the movement for Italian unification, which threatened the Papal States in central Italy. This reaction to the era's great political changes confirmed old Protestant fears that the church loved tyranny and dreaded liberty. A defrocked Italian monk, Alessandro Gavazzi (1809–89), now an Italian nationalist, toured the United States in the early 1850s preaching against the Catholic Church. He asserted that the pope's representative, Archbishop Gaetano Bedini, who was visiting the country at the same time, had led papal troops in a massacre of Italian nationalists during the siege of Bologna in 1849. Worst of all, said Gavazzi, Bedini had killed the patriotic priest and nationalist hero Ugo Bassi that same year.[12] Vast Protestant crowds turned out to hear Gavazzi confirm their worst fears. Meanwhile, the United States' easy military victory over Mexico in the war of 1846–48 gave Protestants a sense of superiority over a decadent Catholic foe. The victors forced the vanquished to end the war by signing a humiliating treaty at Guadelupe-Hidalgo, scene of an apparition of the Virgin Mary, one of the holiest Catholic sites in Mexico, and a symbolic center of Mexican nationalism.

Anti-Catholic sentiments took political shape in the creation of the American or "Know-Nothing" Party, an ostensibly secret political organization founded in 1854, whose sworn Protestant members were supposed to disavow all knowledge of its activities. It grew out of the Order of the Star-Spangled Banner (founded 1850), whose members took an oath to work against all Catholic officeholders, never to hire Catholics, and never to vote for Catholic political candidates. The members were no good at keeping secrets, but they did influence the politics of the 1850s, as the Whig Party was breaking up. They even adopted as their own presidential candidate the ex-Whig president Millard Fillmore in 1856. Among the party's proposed policies was an attempt to minimize immigrants' growing political significance by changing the naturalization laws; immigrants would have to wait twenty-one years, instead of a mere five, before being allowed to vote. At street level, their heroes, like the New Yorker "Bill the Butcher" Poole (1821–55), led Protestant gangs against rival Catholic gangs affiliated with Democratic Tammany Hall.

The Know-Nothings thrived on pseudo-ancient rituals, special forms of communication, secret handshakes, and conspiracy theories. When, as a gesture of good will to the United States, the pope sent an ancient carved stone from the Roman Temple of Concord to be built into the Washington Monument (then under construction on the Washington Mall), the Know-Nothings suspected the worst. Alleging that the stone's incorporation into the completed monument would be the signal for a Catholic coup d'état, which would give the pope political power over the country, they stole it. It never reappeared. To make doubly sure of forestalling the coup, Know-Nothings seized control of the Monument Society, which oversaw construction of the monument, to prevent it from being finished. So it remained, a half-finished stump, until twenty years after the Civil War.

If prejudice against Irish and German Catholics dominated the pre–Civil War story, however, it is offset in part by an undeniable attraction that some Americans felt for Catholicism. Among the American elite, in particular, the opportunity to visit Rome and see Catholicism "at home" fascinated a generation of travelers. The invention of transatlantic steamships made the journey much safer and faster after about 1840 than it had been in sailing ships. For some of these visitors, admittedly, the sights of Rome confirmed their belief that Catholicism was a gaudy fabric of superstition and idolatry. Others, by contrast, admired the city's immense artistic heritage, its beautiful old churches, and the sense it gave of an ancient faith practiced the same way through the generations. Protestantism suddenly seemed to them, by contrast, to be rootless and callow. Struck by the romantic possibilities of Catholicism after a visit to Rome, the poet James Russell Lowell (1819–91) described the church as a "loving mother" and as "the only church that has been loyal to the heart and soul of man." In the same vein Ralph Waldo Emerson (1803–82) wrote in a letter to Margaret Fuller, in 1843, "It is a dear old church, the Roman I mean, and today I detest the Unitarians and Martin Luther." Shrewd Catholic observers became aware of the attraction Protestants felt to the Catholic way of life and their tendency to romanticize it. One wrote that "our everyday life is the romance of their dreams."[13]

Similarly, some American historians began to think about aspects of Catholic tradition in more positive ways. The nationalist historian George Bancroft, writing in the late 1830s, made heroes, not villains, out of the Jesuit priests who had pioneered the exploration of the American interior. "Their cloisters became the best schools in the world," he wrote. "Their missionaries, kindling with a heroism that defied every danger and endured every toil, made their way to the ends of the earth. . . . The history of their labors is connected with the origin of every celebrated town in the annals of French America; not a cape was turned, not a river discovered without a Jesuit's having shown the way."[14] This kind of celebratory rhetoric made a jarring contrast to that of preachers like Beecher and Morse, who depicted the Jesuits as sinister, devious, and corrupt.

While the majority of these observers drew a line between admiring the Catholic heritage on the one hand and despising the Irish immigrants on the other, a few, both men and women, took the next step and converted to Catholicism, often rising to leadership roles among their new brethren. Among the earliest was Elizabeth Ann Seton (1774–1821), who converted in 1805, founded a community of women religious known as the Sisters of Charity of St. Joseph, and was eventually named a saint. Another was Isaac Hecker (1819–88), a friend of the Transcendentalist philosophers, who had become fascinated by Catholicism and underwent a succession of mystical experiences. Converting in 1844, he entered the priesthood and founded the Missionary Society of St. Paul the Apostle (Paulists), whose special mission was to convert Protestants. Sophia Ripley (1803–61), wife of the founder of the Transcendentalist commune Brook Farm, was another convert. A fourth was Orestes Brownson (1803–76), a restless religious seeker and religious controversialist who had made his way through most of the Protestant denominations before coming to rest in the embrace of Catholicism. *Brownson's Quarterly Review*, nearly all of whose four thick annual issues he wrote himself, became the principal intellectual journal of U.S. Catholicism for the next quarter century. Even after his conversion, however, Brownson was not shy about writing critically about the Irish and lamenting that many Americans confused "Irish" with "Catholic."

The impact of conversion to Catholicism, usually the result of intense theological study, was far more profound than the impact of conversion to one of the rising Protestant denominations. It required converts to abandon many of the fundamental ideas they had grown up with and to endure the dismay—sometimes the hostility—of friends, neighbors, and family. As one historian observed, "For Catholic converts, the process entailed a series of radical ideological inversions, in which the Whore of Babylon became the Mother Church and the Antichrist became the venerated Pope."[15] Conversions sometimes occurred among groups of religious friends for whom theological exactitude was important, especially groups of Episcopalians. They were impressed not only by the venerable qualities of Catholicism, but also by news from England about the Oxford Movement then sweeping through the Anglican Church and the conversion to Catholicism of such Anglican leaders as John Henry Newman (1801–90).

Most Protestants, however, kept their distance. Conversion to Catholicism was exceptional, and anti-Catholicism was still far more common than admiration. During the Civil War a series of street riots even more violent than those of the foregoing decades broke out, led by Irish immigrant protestors against the military draft. Some Irish immigrants fought for the Union but others, avoiding military service, attacked free blacks, whose competition for jobs they feared. They also attacked prominent Republicans, who symbolized class bias in the draft (according to which wealthy young men could buy an exemption). The riots caused more than one hundred deaths and intensified anti-Catholic revulsion throughout the urban North.

The Era of Mass Immigration

Europeans' migration to America increased from year to year through the late nineteenth century, and more than a million immigrants were arriving each year by the early years of the twentieth. Most of them were Catholics and Jews from Southern and Eastern

Europe, and they provided a dramatic contrast to older immigrants and old-stock Americans. Among the Catholics, settlers from Germany and Ireland continued to arrive in large numbers. In addition almost four million Italians came between 1899 and 1924 (though around half of them later reemigrated), along with two million Poles, nearly one million French Canadians, half a million Slovaks, and hundreds of thousands more Ruthenians, Lithuanians, Slovenians, and Hungarians. Numerous American writers and politicians declared that Slavs, Russians, Italians, Poles, Greeks, and Bohemians could never be assimilated and claimed that they threatened the integrity of the nation. Tom Watson of Georgia, sometime governor, senator, and presidential candidate, wrote in 1912, "The scum of creation has been dumped on us. . . . The most dangerous and corrupting hordes of the Old World have invaded us. The vice and crime which they have planted in our midst is terrifying."[16]

Were they scum? Even Emma Lazarus, the Statue of Liberty's poetess, herself a Jewish immigrant, referred to the immigrants as the "wretched refuse" of Europe's "teeming shores." Part of the criticism directed against the New Immigrants was similar to what had been used earlier against the Irish; it took the form of ethnic or cultural slurs, alleging that Southern and Eastern Europeans were naturally "slavish" and lacked Northern Europeans' capacity for freedom and democracy. Madison Grant, a writer who favored banning immigration from Southern Europe, belonged to a generation of eugenicists, pseudo-scientists who believed that inferior peoples would contaminate America's exceptional population and cause a decline in the quality of its racial stock. Immigration commissioner Francis Amasa Walker, meanwhile, had noticed that native-born populations had much lower birth rates than immigrant Catholics, which he saw as further evidence that the good old American type would soon be swamped. By one of the great ironies of history, most of the states passed their first anti-abortion laws in the 1870–1900 period as anti-Catholic measures, in the hope that the Protestant birth rate might rise to keep pace. A century later, Catholics would become the most passionate supporters of these laws because of their church's teaching that life begins at the moment of conception.

Protestant observers disagreed about how to react to the new immigration. Some sought ways to prevent any more Catholics from emigrating, picking up elements of the Know-Nothing tradition. An Iowa lawyer, Henry Bowers, founded the American Protective Association in 1887 as an anti-immigrant and explicitly anti-Catholic society. It grew rapidly in the following years, recruited half a million members, blamed Catholics for "stealing" jobs that should have gone to "real Americans," and held the church responsible for deliberately causing the business crash of 1893. Its journal, the *Patriotic American*, printed forged papal documents, one of which alleged that the papacy planned a massacre of all American Protestants. Contributors even found a way to blend anti-Semitism with their anti-Catholicism, arguing that Jewish immigrants were working on behalf of the pope. One APA member wrote, "The Jews have been brought in to wage war with Rome against America and Americans."[17] Lobbying by such groups contributed to immigration restriction laws after World War I.

The government of rapidly growing, immigrant-packed cities like New York, Chicago, Philadelphia, and Cleveland was dominated by corrupt ethnic "machines," often Catholic, which the older WASP population detested but found difficult to displace. The young Theodore Roosevelt (1858–1919) built his political career in the 1880s as a Republican opponent of Tammany Hall, the Irish and Democratic machine that ran New York for most of the late nineteenth century and would continue to do so into the twentieth. Roosevelt, however, made a distinction between good "Americanized" Catholics, especially if they were among the small majority that had joined the Republican Party, and bad "ultramontanes" (loyalists to the pope and Roman traditions) who resisted assimilation. Nowhere was political hatred of the Irish and Catholics illustrated in his generation more vividly than in Thomas Nast's editorial cartoons. Nast (1840–1902), like Roosevelt a Republican and a "good government" reformer, depicted the Irish as brutal subhumans with simian features and Catholic priests as fat, scheming hypocrites. In one of his cartoons, a sinister pope and his bloated cardinals plotted their takeover of the United States from the dome of St. Peter's. In another, crocodiles appeared to be coming out of the "American River Ganges" to attack innocent American children and their public schools. On closer inspection viewers realized that these crocodiles were really Catholic bishops on all fours— their mitres like gaping jaws.

Anti-Catholicism in the late nineteenth and early twentieth centuries, then, was part ethnic and part political. A third element was intellectual. The church appeared to its critics to be turning away decisively from important trends in U.S. intellectual life and to be throwing its weight against the discovery of new truths. Pope Pius IX's "Syllabus of Errors" (1864) condemned many of the propositions on which modern society was based and that modern intellectual life presupposed. The encyclical criticized freedom of speech and religious freedom, condemned secular education and the separation of church and state, and ended by condemning the idea that "the Roman Pontiff can, and ought to, reconcile himself, and come to terms with progress, liberalism and modern civilization." First under Pius IX (1846–78) and then with renewed vigor under Pope Pius X (1903–14), the Catholic Church attacked evolutionary biology, the historical-critical method of biblical scholarship, and the application of comparative and anthropological approaches to the study of religion.

To non-Catholic observers the church seemed almost willfully obtuse in its resistance to all these rich and promising lines of development. A prominent New York scientist, John William Draper, countered with *The History of the Conflict between Religion and Science* (1874), while the president of Cornell University, Andrew Dickson White, wrote *The History of the Warfare of Science with Theology in Christendom* (1896). Both these authors argued that the intellectual history of the last few centuries had been a prolonged struggle by truth-loving scientists to throw off the yoke of Catholic obscurantism and dogma. Draper, concentrating his attack on Catholicism and treating papal persecution of Galileo as emblematic, claimed his book was "a narrative of the conflict of two contending powers, the expansive force of the human intellect on one side, and the compression arising from traditionary [sic] [Catholic] faith . . . on the other."[18] Between the late nineteenth and mid-twentieth centuries, writers from a wide array of academic disciplines had virtually nothing favorable to say about U.S. Catholic scholarship (most of which was indeed defensive, unimaginative, and weak). These were the years, moreover, in which U.S. intellectual life was losing its traditional religious moorings and becoming a more secular enterprise. Scholarship based not just on Christian, but on explicitly Catholic, principles seemed all the more irrelevant.

Anti-Catholicism is not the whole story in this era, however, just as it had not been earlier. Some Protestants, averse to Catholicism but influenced by theologians in the social gospel tradition, held out helping hands to poor, hungry, and unemployed immigrants. Dismayed by the harsh consequences of industrial capitalism but no less frightened by the rise of socialism (because it was usually presented as explicitly atheistic), they regarded the evolving nonsocialist Catholic critique of capitalism as a welcome third way. Washington Gladden (1836–1918), one of the best-known social gospel writers, said he admired Pope Leo XIII (1878–1903) for his social teachings, especially the encyclical *Rerum Novarum* (1891), which condemned the utilitarian rationalism of industrial capitalism and tried to create a humane alternative. Gladden explained that he admired the pope's "large intelligence and quick human sympathy."[19]

Social Gospellers hoped to persuade immigrants to adopt American standards of cleanliness, punctuality, and republican virtue and to convert them, when possible, to Protestant forms of Christianity. The settlement house movement was guided by these ideals; Jane Addams was its brightest star and her Hull House settlement in Chicago (founded 1889) its best-known center. It provided an array of social services, emergency relief, childcare, and education to the area's Irish and Italian immigrants. Addams discovered that Italian immigrant *men* were often bitterly anticlerical. To the exasperation of the local Catholic bishop, she offered a meeting place to the Giordano Bruno Club, an anti-Catholic men's society. On the other hand, Addams was careful to specify that her mission included practical care for people in need, whatever their faith, and she had a talent for local community building. "[F]ortunately," she wrote in her autobiography, "our friendly relations remained unbroken with the neighboring priests from whom we continued to receive uniform courtesy as we cooperated in cases of sorrow and need. Hundreds of devout [Catholic] communicants identified with the various Hull House clubs and classes."[20]

Addams's sensitivity to other cultures and her eagerness to protect and preserve Irish, Italian, and Slavic languages, customs, and folk crafts stood in healthy contrast to the era's often heavy-handed efforts to enforce "one hundred percent Americanism." Addams's friend and long-time coworker Ellen Gates Starr, who not only worked among Catholic immigrants but was increasingly attracted to Catholicism for theological reasons, ultimately converted after World War I. For decades, Starr claimed, she had been deterred because of the church's "reactionary attitude . . . in the matter of social and political progress, its organized and authoritative opposition of socialism, and its obstructive policy toward social reform movements."[21] Now that the National Catholic War Council's program for social reconstruction (1919) had realigned the church with the era's progressive political forces, however, she was glad to join and anticipated many more conversions.

Starr was not alone. Some Americans in the late nineteenth century began to wonder whether their country, as it became an industrial giant and left its traditional and rural ways behind, was becoming worse rather than better. Disenchanted with industrialization and looking nostalgically for an older, simpler world, a generation of educated antimodernists romanticized the Catholic Middle Ages and began to borrow, selectively, from its forms and ideals. A few, as in the antebellum era, went so far as to convert; thousands more stayed outside the Catholic Church but looked on it with newly sympathetic eyes.

Nowhere was this new attitude more striking than in patterns of church architecture. The revival of medieval Catholic "gothic" style had begun earlier in the century in England, achieving maturity with the new Houses of Parliament (completed in 1855), designed by Charles Barry and decorated by the Catholic convert Augustus Pugin. Neogothic became the favored building style of both the Church of England in the late nineteenth century and its American counterpart, the Protestant Episcopal Church. Even Protestant denominations in the Puritan tradition, such as Congregationalists and Presbyterians, began to construct churches with gothic arched windows and doorways, buildings whose symbolism would have been anathema a century before. Ralph Adams Cram, one of the American architectural leaders of the era, admitted to himself in 1886 that the great art of the past thousand years drew its inspiration not from "the life of rationalism and physical science and liberal Unitarianism but very specifically [from] the life of the Catholic Church."[22] After a conversion experience in a European Catholic church, he became an Anglican and began to build U.S. churches that paid homage to the Catholic cathedral style of the thirteenth and fourteenth centuries. His chapel for Princeton University, one of the greatest gothic-style buildings in the United States, is a magnificent example.

Few Americans were more impressed by Catholic architecture than Henry Adams (1838–1918). Grandson of one president and great-grandson of another, he was also among the first professional historians in the United States. His book *Mont St. Michel and Chartres* (1904) and a famous chapter, "The Virgin and the Dynamo," of his autobiography *The Education of Henry Adams* (1918), were sustained tributes to Catholicism and the Catholic sensibility. After surveying the French abbey at Mont St. Michel, for example, Adams rhapsodized over the Crusades that had inspired it. This was an episode from which earlier Protestant historians would have shrunk. "The outburst of the First Crusade was splendid even in a military sense, but it was great beyond comparison in its reflexion in architecture, ornament, poetry, color, religion, and philosophy. Its men were astonishing and its women were worth all the rest. Mont Saint Michel, better than any other spot in the world, keeps the architectural record of that ferment."[23] Such pro-Catholic effusions certainly did not mean that Adams smiled on the typical U.S. Catholic of his own day; nevertheless, views such as his contributed to softening anti-Catholicism among the educated American elite.

In Protestant literature, too, Catholicism was now sometimes depicted as alluring rather than repellent. Harold Frederic's *The Damnation of Theron Ware* (1896) is a case in point. Its central character, the Methodist preacher in a small upstate New York town, became fascinated by the rituals of a nearby Catholic church, its priest, and his learned friends. He recognized their superior learning and sensed that they represented an unbroken Christian tradition stretching back to the earliest days of the church. Beside them he felt shabby and threadbare, and before long he was indulging in a dangerous flirtation with the richest Catholic girl in town. Frederic depicted the Catholics as exotic rather than fully domesticated to the U.S. scene, but he also juxtaposed the weak-willed and undereducated

Methodist minister with the suave, worldly Catholic priest in a way that avoided all the old anti-Catholic cliches. Similarly Willa Cather, in *O, Pioneers!* (1913) and *My Antonia* (1918), drew a sympathetic portrait of Catholic immigrants on the Nebraska plains. Antonia's father, a likeable Catholic character, visits the Protestant narrator's family, kneels, and crosses himself when Christmas tree candles are lit. "I saw grandmother look apprehensively at grandfather. He was rather narrow in religious matters and sometimes spoke out and hurt people's feelings." But grandfather respected this Catholic neighbor and afterward told his own family that "the prayers of all good people are good."[24]

This period between the Civil War and 1920 witnessed a persistent anti-Catholicism on the one hand, but a rising philo-Catholicism on the other. It also bore witness to the first stages of secularization, especially among more highly educated and urban populations. As the historian John Higham has noted, the character of anti-Catholicism was changing in these circumstances. "During the nineteenth century the tradition [of anti-Catholicism] drew its main strength from the larger towns and cities where Catholics were actually settling. . . . But in the twentieth century it re-emerged most actively in rural America, where adherents of the hated faith were relatively few."[25] Mid-nineteenth-century Americans disliked the Catholics they knew, whereas mid-twentieth-century Americans would dislike the Catholics they had never met.

The Mid–Twentieth Century

Immigration restriction laws, passed by Congress in 1921 and 1924 in response to decades of nativist agitation, which were intensified by fears of foreign radicals, Jews, and "Bolsheviks," severely diminished Catholic immigration to the United States. As a result, new generations of Italian, Polish, South German, and Irish arrivals from Europe no longer swelled urban ghettos. Those who had come in the preceding half century moved through the various stages of acculturation, adopting U.S. work habits, learning the English language, getting better jobs, intermarrying (though usually with other Catholics), and serving in the U.S. armed forces during World War II. An Americanized Catholic population, eager to share the benefits of a wealthy U.S. society, became steadily less objectionable to nativists than their unassimilated parents and grandparents had been. Nevertheless, sources of tension remained for several reasons.

First, the Catholic Church was religiously uncompromising. It continued to insist that there was no salvation outside the church ("*extra ecclesiam nulla sallus*" was the Latin phrase) and that Protestants who knew about the Catholic Church but failed to join it were condemning themselves to eternal damnation. This teaching's effect on a young Catholic girl anxious about her beloved Presbyterian grandfather's immortal soul is humorously recounted in Mary McCarthy's *Memories of a Catholic Girlhood* (1957), but it could sometimes be destructive of good community relations. The church continued to deny that religious freedom in the United States was a positive good, regarding it, rather, as a necessary evil behind which Catholics could protect themselves while aspiring to eventual exclusivity.

Second, most dioceses were busy erecting schools and colleges, resulting in a Catholic educational system stretching from kindergarten to graduate school, whose purpose was to preserve young Catholics' faith and prevent them from assimilating too fully into the wider society. Nativist groups periodically attacked this separatist Catholic system, looking for legal or financial ways to undermine it. In 1922, for example, an Oregon referendum, promoted by Freemasons and the Ku Klux Klan, mandated that every child in the state between eight and sixteen years of age attend public schools run by the state. The Klan, refounded in 1915, was now as much anti-Catholic and anti-Jewish as anti-black, and it influenced political life in some northern and western states. National Catholic organizations responded by suing the state of Oregon, on behalf of the Society of Sisters of the Holy Names of Jesus and Mary, who administered Catholic schools and orphanages. They pursued their case all the way to the Supreme Court and eventually won a favorable unanimous verdict. *Pierce v. Society of Sisters* (1925) safeguarded Catholic schools' existence from then on but never silenced rumblings about either their separatism, their inculcating different values than the public schools, or their divided loyalties. In the late 1940s, critics noted that Cardinal Francis Spellman of New York and other Catholic leaders were trying to secure public funds for their nonpublic schools. One Methodist bishop, G. Bromley Oxnam, called Spellman "a prelate with a prehensile hand."[26]

Meanwhile, the Democratic Party's selection of New York governor Al Smith, a Catholic, as its 1928 presidential candidate marked a new epoch in U.S. political history. The choice itself suggests a diminution in the intensity of anti-Catholicism; such a selection would have been hard to imagine fifty years before. A combination of factors, however, kept Smith out of the White House. First, his Republican opponent, Herbert Hoover, was an overwhelmingly popular national hero who would probably have defeated any opponent. Second, Smith's electoral plans were opposed by the campaigns of explicitly anti-Catholic opposition groups. Among them, once again, was the Ku Klux Klan. Klansmen ostensibly supported Prohibition, whereas German, Irish, and Italian Catholics all favored alcohol as central to their traditions of conviviality and hospitality. For the Democrats to win national elections they had to garner southern whites' votes as well as those of northern urban workers. Klan lobbying and southern whites' suspicion of Catholics broke the "solid South" that year, so that Hoover's landslide included the states of Florida, Texas, North Carolina, and Virginia.

After the 1920s, the kind of flagrant anti-Catholicism practiced against Al Smith began to decline. In its place, Catholics, in districts where they were numerous, worked out a *modus vivendi* with their neighbors, with varying degrees of warmth. The people of Mechanics Grove, Illinois, for example, gratefully renamed their town Mundelein, in honor of the archbishop of Chicago, Cardinal George Mundelein, who built his seminary there and brought prosperity to the town's business community. Chicago's leaders recognized Mundelein as a tough-minded businessman and a skilled church politician whose projects benefited the city as a whole. Like many of the hard-headed bishops of his generation, he seemed to the non-Catholic community as much a businessman as a spiritual figure. One admirer wrote that "there was a great mistake in making you a bishop instead of a financier, for in the latter case Mr. Morgan [the era's most famous multimillionaire] would not be without a rival in Wall Street."[27]

Mundelein was one of a series of mid-century Catholic leaders who wielded great power locally, men whom the rest of the community felt it prudent to cultivate and conciliate. The Hollywood movie industry, likewise, recognized in the 1930s that it could not afford to provoke or alienate Catholic religious leaders, even when it resented their high-handedness. The Legion of Decency, founded in 1933 by the Catholic archbishop of Cincinnati, vetted films for their presentation of moral issues. If the legion condemned a new movie, priests would preach against it, parishioners would heed their priests and refuse to attend, and it would do no business in Catholic areas. Since moviegoing was a staple of Depression-era entertainment and since nearly one-third of all Americans were Catholic, this was an audience the studios could not afford to antagonize. Studio heads, afraid of losing their Catholic audience and equally afraid that Catholic lobbying might lead to government censorship, introduced their own strict Production Code (1934), which governed the content of films for the next thirty years. Drafted for the studios by the Jesuit Daniel Lord, in conformity with Catholic natural-law principles, it strictly limited depictions of sexuality, violence, and vengeance, and it prohibited movies that suggested crime might be profitable.

Millions of white Americans, Catholics and non-Catholics alike, fought shoulder to shoulder during World War II and shared its sacrifices (while African Americans served and suffered in segregated units). Wartime propaganda and the reality of life in military service both underlined the ethnic and religious diversity of America in its struggle against Germany and Japan and probably contributed to the decline of intergroup prejudices. Even so, the early postwar years bore witness to another round of anti-Catholic polemics, in which many of the old themes sounded out once more, but with a new emphasis to suit the rising Cold War. Even as U.S. Catholics tried to position themselves as natural leaders of the anti-Communist cause (McCarthyism drew some of its most fervent support from Catholics), a few Protestant and liberal writers persisted in regarding Catholicism as the same kind of authoritarian threat as Communism itself. The Presbyterian fundamentalist Carl McIntire, one of the best-known mid-century Protestant leaders, argued in the late 1940s that Catholics posed, if anything, a worse threat to the republic than the Russians. "As we enter the postwar world," he wrote, "without any doubt the greatest enemy of freedom and liberty that the world has to face today is the Roman Catholic system. . . . America has to face the Roman Catholic terror."[28]

McIntire's was by no means a lonely voice. Paul Blanshard, a liberal journalist who contributed to *The Nation* and other left-of-center U.S. magazines and had little else in common with fundamentalists, published *American Freedom and Catholic Power* in 1949. The book's first few sentences claimed:

> There is no doubt that the American Catholic hierarchy has entered the political arena, and that it is becoming more and more aggressive in extending the frontiers of Catholic authority into the fields of medicine, education, and foreign policy. . . . It tells Catholic doctors, nurses, judges, teachers and legislators what they can and cannot do in many of the controversial phases of their professional conduct. It segregates Catholic children from the rest of the community in a separate school system, and censors the cultural diet

of these children. It uses the political power of some twenty-six million official American Catholics to bring American foreign policy into line with Vatican temporal interests.[29]

Blanshard's three-hundred-page indictment scored the Catholic Church for its teachings on education, medicine, birth control, divorce, democracy, and labor, arguing that in every instance it represented the antithesis of American freedom. As a religion, he added, Catholicism was harmless, but as a political force it was as threatening as Communism. To Blanshard's own surprise, and to most Catholics' dismay, it became a bestseller. The historian John McGreevy has shown that even in the late 1940s and early 1950s Blanshard enjoyed respectful reviews in nearly all the mainstream media, rather than denunciation for what now looks like his thinly veiled bigotry.

The mid-twentieth century, during which the Catholic community attained an unprecedented degree of maturity and authority, ended just as it had begun: with a Catholic presidential candidacy. John F. Kennedy's presidential campaign of 1960, his victory, and then his premature death would do more than anything else to silence anti-Catholicism as a respectable option in American life. As late as March 1960 the editor of the *Catholic World* believed it was impossible for a Catholic to win a national election because most voters were "not psychologically and emotionally mature enough." Besides, added the editor, a Catholic president "would work under the intolerable strain of prying, lynx-eyed scrutiny from censors who would smell Vatican influence in every Presidential utterance."[30] When Kennedy was campaigning, two organizations raised alarms about a Catholic president. Protestants and Other Americans United for Separation of Church and State was one; the other was the National Council of Citizens for Religious Freedom. Respectable Protestant figures in public life, such as the evangelical leader Billy Graham, the Episcopal bishop of San Francisco, James Pike, and the Methodist minister and best-selling author Norman Vincent Peale, joined these groups, apparently sincere in their fear that a Catholic in the White House would mean Vatican influence over U.S. foreign and domestic policy.

Unlike Al Smith in 1928, however, Kennedy and his advisors believed they could appeal to non-Catholics' reluctance to appear bigoted. He addressed a gathering of Protestant ministers in Houston a few weeks before the election and scored a rhetorical victory by convincing them that his religion would never compromise his political actions. As president he made good on the promise. When the Supreme Court ruled against prayer and Bible-reading in schools he declined to support legislation or a constitutional amendment for their restoration. Neither would he support proposals for the use of public funds in parochial schools.

1965 and After

Two events, with profound implications for U.S. Catholics, make 1965 a pivotal year in this story. First, the Second Vatican Council, which began in 1962, ended. Its decrees removed many of the sources of friction between Catholics and other Americans. No longer were Catholics to regard Protestants as heretics journeying toward damnation. Now they were to be thought of as "the separated brethren," real Christians following their own path to salvation. Catholics had, until 1965, been prohibited from entering the churches of any Protestant denomination; now their leaders encouraged them to do so and to create interreligious friendships. The mid-1960s marked a flowering of ecumenical and interreligious cooperation, a novelty whose drama was captured by pictures of priests, men and women religious, ministers, and rabbis joining hands with southern Baptists like Martin Luther King Jr. in Selma, Alabama, in one of the civil rights movement's most dramatic moments. By 1977 Rev. Billy Graham, probably the preeminent U.S. Protestant of the era, could be found leading a revival in the University of Notre Dame's football stadium!

Not that anti-Catholicism disappeared overnight. Expressions of indignation and outrage were still found in the literature of "population-ists," intellectuals of the 1960s who feared that the world's rapid population growth was dangerous and that drastic policies were needed to slow it. When Pope Paul VI's encyclical letter *Humanae Vitae* (1968) affirmed an older Catholic ban on the use of artificial contraceptives, writers like Paul Ehrlich regarded him as hardly better than an environmental criminal. In the "What Can You Do?" section of his book *The Population Bomb*, Ehrlich followed a time-honored approach by rhetorically separating the good ordinary parishioners from their bad leaders, urging "responsible" Catholics to "let your church know that you strongly disapprove of its policies on birth control. You can withdraw your financial support from the diocese and channel it into liberal Catholic causes."[31]

The other great event of 1965 was passage by Congress of the Immigration and Nationality Act (the Hart-Cellar Act), which repealed all racial and national-origins preferences for immigrants. From then on, large-scale immigration from Asia resumed, having been almost impossible since the 1890s. It included a million Filipinos and more than 500,000 Vietnamese Catholics (especially after the Vietnam War ended in 1975). From Latin America, at the same time, and especially from Mexico, documented and undocumented Catholic immigrants (almost certainly more than ten million of them) also streamed into the United States, transforming the character of the church in California, Texas, Arizona, and Florida. Just as earlier generations of immigrants aroused Protestant opposition, so in the 1970s and 1980s neonativist political movements tried to limit this new immigration and to limit the use of the Spanish language in schools and in public life. Opposition was more likely to be linguistic than religious, however, and public expressions of outright anti-Catholicism became unusual by 1980.

By this time, interreligious alliances with political objectives, such as the Moral Majority, were taking the place of interreligious antagonisms. In fact, the entire religious landscape was modified as politically conservative Protestants, Jews, and Catholics found themselves united on several political issues against liberal Protestants, Jews, and Catholics. Robert Wuthnow's *The Restructuring of American Religion* (1988) schematized this shift, which was making rifts within churches (including the Catholic Church) more important than the gulf between them.[32]

The anti-abortion movement, for example, galvanized into action by the Supreme Court's permissive decision in *Roe v. Wade* (1973), began as a largely Catholic movement but gathered widespread conservative Protestant support after 1980. In Operation Rescue, the mass anti-abortion movement of the late 1980s, Catholic and Evangelical Protestant activists demonstrated side-by-side and were arrested together under the leadership of a born-again Protestant, Randall Terry. At one point they even agreed on liturgical rules for their "rescues"; Catholics agreed not to pray the rosary while Pentecostal Protestants agreed not to speak in tongues. On the opposite side of the political spectrum, the "sanctuary movement" of the 1980s that aimed to shelter illegal immigrants from El Salvador on the grounds that they were really political refugees brought together elements of the Catholic and Protestant Left. Here too differences of organization and style, especially between Catholics and Quakers, entailed tensions and the need to create internal ground rules. Participants agreed, however, that their common political objective was much more important than their religious differences.[33]

As Wuthnow and other scholars have shown, a citizen's political ideas were, by the 1980s, more likely to generate controversy than the fact that he or she was a Catholic. Catholics remained slightly unusual because their leaders failed to line up along the national left-right spectrum of issues. If the bishops' prolife posture looked conservative, their outspoken condemnation of nuclear weapons in the pastoral letter *The Challenge of Peace* (1983) looked extremely liberal. From the bishops' point of view, both policies grew out of the Consistent Life Ethic, which emphasized reverence for human life in all situations.

In other areas, ideas about Catholics experienced a sea change in the 1970s and 1980s. One such idea involved education and the changing reputation of Catholic schools. According to one stereotype, favored by ex-Catholic school children themselves (such as the novelist Mary Gordon) and echoed by progressive educational theorists, Catholic schools were repressive, intellectually inferior, and staffed by ignorant nuns who relied more on corporal punishment than love of learning. A vigorous internal critique of Catholic higher education, led by John Tracy Ellis, also lamented Catholic universities' lackluster intellectual achievements. By the 1970s, however, educational theorists were granting Catholic schools a new respect. As public schools gained a reputation for crime, faddishness, and philistinism, their Catholic counterparts won an offsetting new reputation for holding on to the old verities, for teaching manners, discipline, smartness, and the "basics" of reading, writing, and arithmetic. Advocates of educational reform even began to argue that Catholic schools provided a model, especially for poor and minority children looking for an educational road out of poverty and privation. One detailed study from 1993, for example, noted that "more academic coursework is required of all students in Catholic schools, and the emphasis is especially noticeable for students enrolled in general and vocational programs. Of particular importance, our analysis indicates that disadvantaged students benefit most from attending schools in which there is a strong normative pull toward a core of academic work for everyone."[34]

Catholics' reputation was, by the late twentieth century, mixed, partly because of the decline of overt interreligious prejudice and partly because the post–Vatican II, post-JFK church was no longer ethnically, economically, or ideologically unified. Just when it seemed possible that all interest in the "Catholic image" might disappear, however, the question revived in a huge and horrible way. Beginning in the late 1980s and reaching a climax in

2002, revelations of child sexual abuse by certain priests severely damaged the formerly good reputation of the clergy in general. Successive discoveries by reporters from the *Boston Globe* demonstrated that numerous priests had sexually abused children and teenaged boys, that their superiors had often known about it and had conspired to cover it up, and that church leaders around the nation had collaborated in moving offenders to new ministries where they had repeated their offenses.

The fallout from these revelations showed the persistence of some old attitudes and the expression of several new ones and underlined the power of the U.S. press to shape popular perceptions. The *Globe* stories led to Boston cardinal Bernard Law's resignation in December 2002. Some commentators on the scandal used the revelations as evidence of the unhealthiness of priestly celibacy. Pope John Paul II's continued refusal to open Catholic sexual teachings to debate, wrote one observer, had contributed to "the current crisis in the church," which was creating "a pressure cooker atmosphere that will eventually blow up."[35]

Other observers saw in the scandal a new confirmation of the old charge that the church was secretive, manipulative, and anti-democratic. Frank Keating, head of a lay investigative board of the U.S. Conference of Catholic Bishops, resigned in disgust after discovering that many of the bishops would not cooperate with his investigation; in a controversial press statement he compared them to "la Cosa Nostra" (the Mafia). In the face of earlier scandals, Catholics' instinct was usually to close ranks. Now, by contrast, few criticisms were made by non-Catholics that were not also being voiced by indignant members of the church itself. Keating himself was a Catholic. Catholic groups like Voice of the Faithful and Survivors' Network of Those Abused by Priests (SNAP) denounced the lack of democracy in the church, its lack of transparency in responding to allegations, and some bishops' instincts to seek legal loopholes rather than offer full disclosure and public penance.

Conclusion

Here was the ironic outcome of two centuries' struggles against prejudice and bigotry: Catholics were now echoing from inside the church allegations that had long been flung at it from the outside. Stereotypes are tricky; they often promote misunderstanding and intolerance but they sometimes embody real insights. The Catholic Church *had* historically been autocratic, sometimes Machiavellian and intolerant, had played a sordid role in nineteenth-century Italian politics, and had earlier sought to manipulate regimes throughout the Christian world. No wonder generations of American Protestants had feared and mistrusted its power; now Catholic critics were joining in from inside the church. On the other hand, such stereotypes as the persistent claim that Catholic convents were really priests' brothels had always been groundless, springing from Protestants' psychological projection. In the late twentieth century Catholics were speaking out as loudly as anyone else about the Catholic priesthood as a realm of sexual perversity and crime. But whatever the negative stereotypes, Catholicism was an established and permanent part of American life. As a religious entity it had created a liturgically rich and psychologically gratifying world for many of its members and a way of life deeply reassuring to uprooted immigrants. These attractions had proved powerful enough to a few sympathetic outsiders in every generation to win a steady stream of new converts. In the opening years of the twenty-first century it emerged chastened from perhaps its worst U.S. crisis, vulnerable to a new pattern of observers' ideas, prejudices, and associations.

NOTES

1. Barbara Welter, "From Maria Monk to Paul Blanshard," in *Uncivil Religion: Interreligious Hostility in America*, ed. Robert Bellah and Frederick Greenspahn (New York: Crossroad, 1987), 44.

2. Cotton Mather, quoted in Le Roy E. Froom, *The Prophetic Faith of Our Fathers* (Washington D.C.: Review and Herald, 1946), 3:113.

3. Quoted in Gayle K. Brown, *A Controversy Not Merely Religious: The Anti-Catholic Tradition in Colonial New England* (Ph.D. diss., University of Iowa, 1990), 9.

4. Ibid., 165.

5. Robert Eastburn, quoted in ibid., 160.

6. John Adams, quoted in James Hennessey, *American Catholics: A History of the Roman Catholic Community in the United States* (New York: Oxford University Press, 1981), 58–59.

7. Charles Inglis, quoted in Brown, *Controversy*, 286.

8. David H. Bennett, *The Party of Fear: From Nativist Movements to the New Right in American History* (Chapel Hill: University of North Carolina Press, 1988), 36–37.

9. Lyman Beecher, *Plea for the West* (Cincinnati: Truman and Smith, 1835), 142.

10. Samuel Morse, *Foreign Conspiracy against the Liberties of the United States* [1835] (New York: Arno, 1977), 59, 62.

11. See George H. Yater, *Two Hundred Years at the Falls of the Ohio: A History of Louisville and Jefferson County* (Louisville: Filson Club, 1979).

12. Ira Leonard and Robert Parmet, *American Nativism: 1830–1860* (New York: Van Nostrand Reinhold, 1971), 89.

13. Jenny Franchot, *Roads to Rome: The Antebellum Protestant Encounter with Catholicism* (Berkeley: University of California Press, 1994), 272, 202, 199.

14. George Bancroft, *History of the United States* [1840] (Boston: Charles C. Little, 1846), 3:120, 122.

15. Franchot, *Roads to Rome*, 280.

16. Tom Watson, quoted in Bennett, *Party of Fear*, 165.

17. Bennett, *Party of Fear*, 174.

18. Draper, quoted in Jon H. Roberts, *Darwinism and the Divine in America* (Madison: University of Wisconsin, 1988), 79.

19. Washington Gladden, quoted in John McGreevy, *Catholicism and American Freedom* (New York: Norton, 2003), 126.

20. Jane Addams, *Twenty Years at Hull House* [1910] (New York: Signet Classics, 1981), 292.

21. Ellen Gates Starr, quoted in Patrick Allitt, *Catholic Converts: British and American Intellectuals Turn to Rome* (Ithaca, N.Y.: Cornell University Press, 1997), 148.

22. Ralph Adams Cram, quoted in T. J. Jackson Lears, *No Place of Grace: Antimodernism and the Transformation of American Culture, 1880–1920* (New York: Pantheon, 1981), 204.

23. Henry Adams, *Mont St. Michel and Chartres*, in *Novels, Mont Saint Michel, The Education* (New York: Library of America, 1983), 371.

24. Willa Cather, *My Ántonia* [1918] (New York: Bantam, 1994), 73.

25. John Higham, *Strangers in the Land: Patterns of American Nativism, 1860–1925* [1955] (New York: Atheneum, 1965), 181.

26. John Cooney, *The American Pope: The Life and Times of Francis Cardinal Spellman* (New York: Times, 1984), 179.

27. George Duval letter to Mundelein, quoted in E. Kantowicz, "Cardinal Mundelein of Chicago and the Shaping of Twentieth-Century American Catholicism," *Journal of American History* 68 (June 1981): 55.

28. Carl McIntire, quoted in Mark Noll, "The Eclipse of Old Hostilities," in Bellah and Greenspahn, *Uncivil Religion*, 87.

29. Paul Blanshard, *American Freedom and Catholic Power* (Boston: Beacon Press, 1949), 4.

30. John Sheerin, quoted in Allitt, *Catholic Intellectuals and Conservative Politics in America: 1950–1985* (Ithaca, N.Y.: Cornell University Press, 1993), 84.

31. Paul Ehrlich, *The Population Bomb* (1968; repr. New York: Ballantine, 1970), 181.

32. Robert Wuthnow, *The Restructuring of American Religion* (Princeton, N.J.: Princeton University Press, 1988). For empirical elaboration of Wuthnow's sociological outline, see also Allitt, *Religion in America Since 1945: A History* (New York: Columbia University Press, 2004).

33. Allitt, *Religion in America*, 163–64 (Operation Rescue and Randall Terry), 174–80 (Sanctuary Movement).

34. Anthony Bryk, Valerie Lee, and Peter Holland, *Catholic Schools and the Common Good* (Cambridge, Mass.: Harvard University Press, 1993), 304.

35. A. W. R. Sipe, "The Crisis of Sexual Abuse and the Celibate/Sexual Agenda of the Church," in *Sin against the Innocents*, ed. Thomas G. Plante (Westport, Conn.: Praeger, 2004), 61.

Latino Catholics in the Southwest

Timothy Matovina

Spanish-speaking Catholics have been continuously present in what is now the southwest United States for almost twice as long as the nation has existed. In 1598, eight Franciscans and other members of the Juan de Oñate expedition crossed into present-day El Paso, Texas, and established the initial Catholic foundations in the region. Two and a half centuries later, the war between the United States and Mexico (1846–48) resulted in Mexico's loss of nearly half its territory: the present-day states of Texas, Nevada, California, Utah, and parts of New Mexico, Arizona, Colorado, and Wyoming. Subsequently Francis Baylies, who had accompanied the victorious U.S. forces on their march through Mexico, wrote a book that clearly reflected U.S. views on the history of the region and the U.S. takeover of the former Mexican territories. Baylies applauded the Spanish missionaries who worked in the Texas missions to convert Native Americans during the eighteenth century, but claimed that after Mexico won independence from Spain

> everything went to decay. Agriculture, learning, the mechanic arts, shared the common fate; and when the banners of the United States were unfurled in these distant and desolate places, the descendants of the noble and chivalric Castilians had sunk to the level, perhaps beneath it, of the aboriginal savages; but it is to be hoped that the advent of the Saxo-Norman race may brighten, in some degree, the faded splendor of the race which has fallen.[1]

While many Latinos and other observers assert that the U.S.-Mexican War resulted in an unjust conquest of Mexican lands,[2] Baylies's depiction of Mexican backwardness and corruption allowed him to claim that U.S. westward expansion redeemed culturally and spiritually desolate peoples and territories.

Like many historians of the Southwest, Baylies implicitly divided the history of the Southwest into three major eras: the "golden age" of the missions, Mexican corruption, and Anglo-American redemption.[3] Historians today criticize such interpretations of Southwest history in various ways. The focus on a golden age in which Spanish missionaries selflessly taught Christianity, Spanish culture, and European civilization to native peoples fails to account for indigenous perspectives on the mission system, including the cultural shock, harsh treatment, and death from European diseases that many Native Americans experienced in mission communities. It also leads to the false presumption that the only Catholic religious institutions in the Spanish colonies were the missions, when in fact parishes and military chapels have been the homes of Latino Catholic faith communities from colonial times until the present day. These enduring communities of faith reveal that, even after Mexico won its independence from Spain in 1821 and then lost the war with the United States, many Mexican Catholic communities in what is now the Southwest persevered despite the upheaval all around them. Indeed, for many the arrival of U.S. rule did not represent an Anglo-American redemption of Mexican corruption, but a tumultuous period of social, political, economic, and demographic change that forced established Mexican residents into a defensive posture that continued well into the twentieth century and in some ways even down to the present day.

This chapter summarizes new trends in scholarship on the U.S. Southwest by expanding and refining the three-era schema of Southwest history illustrated in Baylies. In what follows, Latino Catholicism in the Southwest is divided into a thematic schema: colonial foundations, enduring communities of faith in the wake of the war between Mexico and the United States, the rejuvenation and diversification of Latino Catholic communities with the arrival of numerous immigrants from Mexico and throughout Latin America, and the struggle for rights in church and society that accelerated during the second half of the twentieth century.

Colonial Foundations

The first Spanish subjects to visit present-day San Antonio, Texas, a locale that Native Americans called "Yanaguana," were soldiers and Franciscan friars in the 1691 expedition led by Domingo Terán de los Ríos. Arriving on the Feast of San Antonio de Padua (June 13), the newcomers named the site "San Antonio." Though San Antonio's climate and setting were highly favorable, the threat of French incursion in the borderlands well east of the site led the Spanish crown to wait nearly three decades before establishing settlements at San Antonio as part of its claim to Texas. But by 1731 Spanish subjects had founded a *presidio* (garrison) and civilian settlement, along with five missions dedicated to propagating Christianity among local indigenous groups. San Fernando parish, the church that soldiers and civilian settlers jointly founded in 1731, has remained a predominantly Hispanic congregation under the flags of Spain, Mexico, the Republic of Texas, the United States, the Confederate States of America, and then the United States again. Today portions of the original parish church still comprise the sanctuary of San Antonio's renowned San Fernando Cathedral, while south of the downtown area four of the original missions have been renovated and restored as the San Antonio Missions National Historical Park, landmarks managed by the U.S. National Park Service that also house active Catholic parishes.[4]

Historic preservation efforts and places of worship still used today, like San Fernando Cathedral and the San Antonio missions, are visible reminders that Latino Catholicism in the regions from Texas to California originated with communities planted during the late sixteenth through early nineteenth centuries. Of course, subsequent immigration from Latin America during the nineteenth and especially the twentieth and twenty-first centuries deepened and brought new vibrancy and expansion to these communities, but the story must begin with the original foundations. The planting and development of Hispanic Catholic communities in the region by Spanish, Indian, African, and *mestizo* (mixed-heritage) peoples was a highly conflictive and coercive but also cooperative and integrative imperial enterprise; it was a story of conquest, violence, cultural confrontations, accommodations, change, and the emergence of new traditions.

The "arrival" of Christianity in what is now the Southwest began with Spanish expeditions into the area, such as the fated Pánfilo de Narváez expedition, from which only Alvar Núñez Cabeza de Vaca and a handful of companions survived after an eight-year ordeal of hunger, captivity, and an overland trek from Florida to New Spain (present-day Mexico). Later Spanish subjects established settlements to stake territorial claims for the Spanish crown, pursue economic gain, and propagate Catholicism among native populations. Pueblos (towns) with formal civil and church institutions, military garrisons, and missions provided historically tested structures around which Hispanic frontier communities emerged.

Catholic missionaries, usually Franciscan friars, accompanied exploratory expeditions and then were an integral part of Spanish efforts to establish settlements. Sometimes the friars founded missions within or near settled indigenous communities. In other cases, they induced nomadic peoples to settle down at newly established missions, usually near Spanish pueblos and military garrisons. While initially the prospect of entering the missions to stave off enemies, starvation, and harsh winters seemed attractive to some Native Americans, many eventually found mission life too alien and coercive. Not only were they not accustomed to the Spanish work routines and religious lifestyles, they also found unacceptable the friars' demands that they shed their traditional ways. A number of them made the transition into these new lives and eventually embraced Christianity, but many others became resentful and left the missions at the earliest opportunity. In some cases outright rebellion ensued, such as in 1680 when New Mexico's Pueblo Indians exploded into open violence under the leadership of a shaman or spiritual leader named Popé, driving the Spaniards and their loyal indigenous subjects from the region and purging their communities of Catholic symbols and everything Spanish.[5] Though the Spanish reconquered them once again beginning in 1692 and Franciscan missionary efforts resumed, the revolt illuminated the clash of civilizations often evident in mission life.

Despite the drawbacks and difficulties of mission life, some Native Americans remained within the world of the missions, accepted Christianity, and took on Hispanic and Catholic identities. For the missionaries, Hispanicizing the natives entailed creating living spaces for their charges around impressive churches and chapels that became the center of everyday life. The missionaries worked diligently inculcating Catholicism, defining work regimes, establishing predictable daily life routines, teaching the Spanish language, overseeing social interactions, enforcing Christian-appropriate gender relations, and generally changing or modifying any and all cultural practices among the natives that they deemed contrary to Christianity.

The Spanish crown viewed the missions as temporary institutions whose role was to prepare Native Americans to become good Spanish subjects. Spanish officials envisioned the missions as temporary institutions destined for secularization—that is, transference from missionary to civil authority once the friars completed the work of Hispanicizing the natives. A number of missions were already being secularized in New Spain's northern regions by the end of the eighteenth century. At that same time, however, new mission establishments emerged in California that were not secularized until the 1830s. Secularization, then, varied from region to region, depending on government policies, interests of local officials, the socioeconomic realities of the communities and the missions, the level of cooperation among Native Americans, and the interests of the missionaries themselves.

In theory, the indigenous people at the mission were to receive individual land allotments and other assets in the secularization process; these material possessions would aid them in their transition to a new status as Hispanicized Catholics. In numerous cases, however, this did not occur. Rather, the Native Americans simply lost everything in their former missions to unscrupulous officials or other Hispanic residents, often moving into the Hispanic pueblos where they occupied the bottom of the social structure. However the mission residents fared, the secularization process transformed their communities from corporate entities under the authority and protection of specific missionary orders to independent communities that became another element of Hispanic civil society.

Extant mission records were almost entirely produced by men and tend to accentuate the perspectives, accomplishments, and struggles of the male friars. Nonetheless, the missions reveal an element of Latino Catholicism that has been significant throughout the history of the region: the faith and leadership of women like Eulalia Pérez, who became a prominent figure at Mission San Gabriel (near Los Angeles). A native of Loreto, Baja California, Pérez moved to the mission in the early nineteenth century with her husband, who was assigned there as a guard. After her husband's death, Pérez lived at the mission with her son and five daughters, where she became the head housekeeper (*llavera*), a leadership position in the mission community that grew increasingly significant as the number of friars decreased. Her duties included overseeing supplies and their distribution, as well as supervising Native American workers.[6]

Though the dozens of missions founded in New Mexico, Arizona, Texas, and California were clearly the predominant Catholic institution in the northern stretches of New Spain, parishes and military chaplaincies also played a crucial role in establishing and maintaining Catholicism. Unlike the missions in which the population consisted exclusively of Native Americans save for a few friars and Hispanic military personnel, parishes and military chaplaincies provided for the spiritual welfare of Hispanic civilian and military settlers and their descendants, as well as for some natives who eventually joined these communities. Parishes first appeared with the establishment of formal towns and grew in number as some missions were secularized and became ordinary parishes. Local residents built the churches and sought to obtain the services of priests, either religious-order priests or diocesan priests—that is, clergy primarily trained to serve existing Spanish-speaking Catholic communities rather than to work for the conversion of Native Americans. In Spanish colonial times, Hispanic Catholics established parishes in places like San Antonio, Laredo, Santa Fe, Albuquerque, Los Angeles, and San Jose, along with military chapels in other locales, such as Monterey, California, where the current Catholic cathedral has its origins in a colonial military chapel.

During the Spanish colonial era and the period that the Southwest was under Mexican rule (1821–36 in Texas; 1821–48 elsewhere), New Mexico was the most populous territory and thus the one with the largest number of Catholics. By the beginning of the nineteenth century, the diocesan clergy in New Mexico had begun the process of slowly displacing the Franciscan missionaries who had served in the region since the late sixteenth century. This was, of course, a natural and predictable course of events, since the missions had always been viewed as temporary institutions dedicated to preparing the indigenous communities for parish life as Hispanic citizens. In 1798 the diocese of Durango, which encompassed New Mexico, introduced the first diocesan pastors to the region, one for the parish at Santa Fe and the other at Santa Cruz. As the Franciscan numbers declined, particularly after Mexican independence, when many Spanish friars left the new republic out of loyalty to their native Spain, the diocesan priests increased, thanks to recruitment of local youth who went to seminary in Durango. Between 1823 and 1826, four New Mexicans completed their training and returned home to begin their ministries. By the end of the 1840s, the Franciscans had all left or died, and some seventeen or eighteen diocesan priests (most recruited locally) served the spiritual needs of New Mexico's parish communities. In the end, the church's viability in New Mexico depended on the communities themselves, especially their ability to recruit their youth into the priesthood.[7]

Enduring Communities of Faith

Padre Antonio José Martínez (1793–1867) was the leading figure among nineteenth-century New Mexican priests. His numerous accomplishments include a distinguished academic career as a seminarian in Durango, the establishment of a primary school and seminary preparatory school in his hometown of Taos (from which some thirty students went on to be ordained for the priesthood), the operation of the first printing press in what is now the western United States, authorship of numerous books and pamphlets, formal certification as an attorney, and extensive service as an elected New Mexican representative in legislative bodies under the Mexican and later the U.S. governments. In 1854, Frenchman

Jean Baptiste Lamy (1814–88), the newly arrived first bishop (and later first archbishop) of Santa Fe, instituted mandatory tithing and decreed that heads of families who failed to comply be denied the sacraments. Martínez publicly contested the prelate's action in a newspaper article and a series of letters, actions that eventually led to Lamy's excommunication of Martínez from the Catholic Church and to a schism between Martínez's supporters and the official leaders of the Santa Fe diocese.[8]

The struggles of Father Martínez and his backers illustrate the efforts of Mexican-descent Catholics to endure and defend themselves—both within the Catholic Church and within the wider society—during the turbulent half century following the U.S. take-over of northern Mexico. U.S. military victory led to the 1848 Treaty of Guadalupe Hidalgo, which brought an official end to this war, but military defeat merely initiated the process of U.S. conquest and expansion. After the territories changed hands, law enforcement personnel, judicial officials, and occupying troops imposed U.S. rule. Violence against Spanish-speaking residents at times reached epidemic proportions, but the judicial system afforded little if any protection for Spanish-speaking citizens.

Anglo-American newcomers also consolidated the conquest by asserting their dominion over political and economic life. When Texas became a state in 1845, for example, Mexican San Antonians lost control of the city council their ancestors had established and led for more than a century; over the following century they held less than 5 percent of city council posts. At the same time, after Texas statehood citizens of Mexican heritage increasingly became a working underclass and lost most of their land holdings. Demographic shifts facilitated the diminishment of Mexican political and economic influence. Nowhere was this shift more dramatic than in California, where the Gold Rush altered the demographic profile almost overnight. Even southern California settlements relatively distant from the gold mines experienced a rapid influx of newcomers.[9]

Hispanic hegemony in religious life and public celebrations also dissipated as population growth among Anglo-Americans and other groups facilitated the formation of new congregations and public festivities. By 1890 in the formerly "Catholic" town of Los Angeles, for example, there were seventy-eight religious organizations, including groups such as Congregationalists, Jews, Buddhists, Baptists, Unitarians, and an African Methodist Episcopal congregation.[10] Parishes and other elements of Catholic life were not immune to change during the tumultuous period of transition. Dioceses were established at places like Galveston (1847), Santa Fe (1850), San Francisco (1853), Denver (1887), and Tucson (1897). European clergy and women religious served in many areas of the Southwest, with the French predominating in Texas, New Mexico, and Arizona and the Irish in California.

Frequently differences in culture and religious practice led newly arrived Catholic leaders to misunderstand and criticize their Mexican coreligionists. One French priest claimed that, among the Mexican-descent Catholics he encountered in Texas during the 1840s and 1850s, "the religion of the great majority is very superficial, the great truths of the faith are overlooked, and the most essential duties of a Christian neglected." To be sure, in some instances foreign clergy acclaimed the religious practices of Spanish-speaking

Catholics. Bishop Jean Marie Odin, the first bishop of Texas, participated in Mexican religious feasts like local celebrations in honor of Our Lady of Guadalupe and spoke enthusiastically of the religious zeal demonstrated in these celebrations.[11] Nonetheless, criticism and conflict frequently marked the relations between established Mexican Catholic communities and the Catholic religious leaders who arrived in the wake of U.S. conquest.

Conquered Mexicans resisted the U.S. takeover in various ways. Some offered military resistance to the foreign invaders. California defenders during the war between the United States and Mexico won battles in the Los Angeles area and at the hamlet of San Pasqual, although subsequently they came to terms peaceably when the larger and well-armed invasion force overwhelmed them. Even after the war ended, armed resistance erupted in various locales. Contemporary Mexican Americans still acclaim Joaquín Murieta for his vigorous defense of his people and his family honor in California after the U.S. war with Mexico.[12]

In other instances, Spanish-speaking residents defended their rights in the political arena. Native Texan José Antonio Navarro made various legislative attempts to protect the ancestral lands of Mexican Texans. While his fellow lawmakers did not enact any of his land-claim proposals, at the 1845 Texas Constitutional Convention Navarro was able to prevent passage of an "odious" and "ridiculous" law that restricted suffrage to the "free white population." Like Navarro, native Californian Pablo de la Guerra futilely tried to protect the land claims of Mexican-descent residents in his state. In an often-quoted 1856 speech to fellow members of the state senate, he described Mexican Californians as "strangers in their own land" whose plight was caused in part by "a legislature hungry to take away from us our last penny simply because the [Anglo-American] squatters are more numerous than the native Californians."[13]

Lay Catholic leaders also took initiative to defend their religious traditions and faith communities. At Nacogdoches in east Texas (near the Louisiana border), where Spanish-speaking Catholics first established a settlement in 1716, Anglo-American ascendancy led to ethnic tensions and outbreaks of violence with Mexican Catholics. The local pastor, Father José Antonio Díaz de Léon, died mysteriously in 1834, probably at the hands of an Anglo-American assassin. Subsequently Anglo-Americans expelled or killed numerous Mexican-descent residents and burned the local Catholic house of worship to the ground. No resident priest replaced Father Díaz de Léon until 1847. But in the thirteen years the local community was without a priest they continued to conduct Sunday services on their own and organized rituals for feast days and funerals, gathering in private homes after their parish church was destroyed. The resilience of Nacogdoches residents illuminates that, far from eradicating their initiatives to persevere, fear and anger at their subjugation could perpetuate and even intensify religious fervor and the desire to maintain Mexican Catholic pride and identity.[14]

Many residents in conquered territories sought to endure as Mexican Catholic faith communities by celebrating and asserting their collective identity through their long-standing rituals and devotions. From Texas to California, various Mexican Catholic communities continued to enthusiastically enact established local traditions such as pilgrimages, devotion to Our Lady of Guadalupe, *los pastores* (a festive proclamation of the shepherds who worshiped the newborn infant Jesus), Holy Week, Corpus Christi, and established patronal feast days.[15] The persistence of established religious traditions was particularly striking in light of newly arrived Catholic and Anglo-American Protestant leaders' attempts to ban, replace, and condemn these traditions. In the face of such efforts, as well as military conquest and occupation, indiscriminate violence and lawlessness, political and economic displacement, rapid demographic change, the erosion of cultural hegemony, and the appointment of Catholic leaders from foreign lands, Spanish-speaking Catholic feasts and devotions had a heightened significance. These religious traditions provided an ongoing means of public communal expression, affirmation, and resistance to Anglo-American and other newcomers who criticized or attempted to suppress Mexican-descent residents' ethnic and religious heritage.

Women frequently played a key leadership role in public worship and devotion. At Santa Rita, Texas, and Conejos, Colorado, young women served in public processions as the immediate attendants for the image of Our Lady of Guadalupe, the principal ritual object in annual Guadalupe feast-day celebrations. Young women occupied similar places of prominence in processions at Los Angeles for the feasts of the Assumption and Corpus Christi; at Ysleta, Texas, for the Feast of Our Lady of Mount Carmel; and in Arroyo Hondo, New Mexico, for the Feast of St. John the Baptist. The contribution of women in preparing and enacting public religious traditions illuminates what Ana María Díaz-Stevens calls the "matriarchal core" of Latino Catholicism—that is, women's exercise of autonomous authority in communal devotions despite the patriarchy of institutional Catholicism and Latin American societies.[16]

The most renowned lay group that served as the protectors of treasured local traditions was the brotherhood of *Los Hermanos de Nuestro Padre Jesús Nazareno* (Brothers of Our Father Jesus the Nazarene), or *Penitentes. Penitente* brotherhoods evolved in towns and villages of northern New Mexico and southern Colorado well before the U.S. takeover of the area. Their most noticeable function was to commemorate Christ's passion and death during Lent and, in particular, during Holy Week, although they also provided community leadership and fostered social integration. Organized as separate local entities, *Penitente* brotherhoods had a leader named the *Hermano Mayor* (literally "older brother") and a *morada* (literally "habitation") or chapter house where they held meetings and religious devotions. Despite the sharp criticism they often received from outsiders and some Santa Fe archdiocesan officials' attempts to suppress the brotherhoods and their ritual and devotional practices, the *Penitentes* (and their female collaborators) continued to provide leadership for prayer and social life in numerous local communities.[17]

To be sure, some communities in the Southwest struggled for their very survival; in the process their observance of long-standing traditions often abated or even ceased. Nonetheless, as Bishop Henry Granjon of Tucson noted in 1902 during his first pastoral visit to Las Cruces, New Mexico, in the Southwest, Mexican-descent Catholic initiatives "to observe their own traditions and customs as they did before the annexation of their lands by the American Union" enabled them to "maintain the unity of the Mexican population and . . . resist, to a certain extent, the invasions of the Anglo-Saxon race."[18] The story of

Latino Catholicism in the Southwest after the U.S.-Mexican War is primarily a tale of ethnic Mexican Catholics' struggle to defend their dignity and endure as communities of faith.

Immigrants

Latino newcomers to the Southwest also took initiatives to foster communal solidarity and faith. In 1871, Spanish-speaking Catholics at San Francisco proposed a national or "ethnic" parish to serve the growing Latino population in their city. Although most Spanish-speaking residents were émigrés or long-standing California residents of Mexican descent, representatives from the consulates of Chile, Peru, Nicaragua, Colombia, Bolivia, Costa Rica, and Spain were among the leaders in this effort. These leaders printed a circular letter in which they contended that a national parish was necessary both for monolingual Spanish speakers and for bilingual Catholics who longed to pray in "the sublime language and in the same prayers their tender mother taught them." They also proclaimed that their proposal to construct a national parish for Latinos was "not only consistent with evangelical doctrine" but also, given the demographic ascendancy of Anglo-Americans in the city since the Gold Rush two decades earlier, "reestablishes, in this great city, the splendor, brilliance, and influence of our race." Four years later, their vision and funding efforts proved successful as Archbishop Joseph Alemany formally established the national parish of Our Lady of Guadalupe.[19]

The participation of Central and South American consul officials and Mexican émigrés in the establishment of Our Lady of Guadalupe parish reflects the expanding Latino presence in the Southwest through a history of immigration that continues to this day. Though the vast majority of these newcomers have arrived from Mexico, in more recent decades increasing numbers have also come from Central America, Puerto Rico, Cuba, and South America. As with most immigrants, numerous Latinos came to the United States to escape forces of instability and displacement they had little control over. They came for a number of reasons, including difficult conditions in their countries of origin and forces created by North American economic and political expansionism that intimately linked Latin America to the United States.

Following the end of the U.S. Civil War, railroad construction, mining, and agriculture in the regions from Texas to California, and then in Mexico itself, linked the regions economically, creating migration flows of Mexican labor north. The Porfirio Díaz regime in Mexico (1876–1911) promoted economic growth linked to foreign interests, leading to prosperity for some but displacement and migration for others who went to the United States looking for work. Mexican immigration accelerated substantially after the outbreak of the Mexican Revolution in 1910. Intermittent periods of relative calm followed the enactment of the 1917 Mexican Constitution, but spontaneous violence erupted once again in central and western Mexico when President Plutarco Elías Calles enforced and expanded anticlerical articles of that constitution. The resulting guerrilla war, known as the Cristero Rebellion (1926–29), drove even more émigrés north to the United States, many fleeing religious persecution. During the Depression era of the 1930s Mexican migration all but came to a halt, and in fact deportations created a significant return migration. But the northward flow of Mexicans resumed during World War II, a trend strongly influenced by the infamous guest worker or Bracero Program (1942–64). It brought some five million contracted workers north from Mexico, a number of whom stayed or eventually returned to establish homes in the United States. Many undocumented migrants also crossed the Mexican border into the United States. A number of them stayed permanently. After the Bracero Program ended, the number of undocumented workers increased dramatically, a trend that has continued to the present.[20]

Meanwhile, urbanization, increases in birth rates and life spans, growing expectations for better lives, improved transportation, ties with family members already in the United States, and the communications revolution brought people from all over Latin America to the Southwest. The Cuban revolution in 1959 initiated an exodus from the island that brought some Cubans to the region, while civil wars in El Salvador, Guatemala, and Nicaragua during the 1970s and 1980s brought thousands of Central Americans. Increasing migration to the region from Puerto Rico and South America has made Latino communities in the Southwest all the more complex and diverse.

A continuing flow of immigrants, along with the proximity of their native countries, has enabled numerous Mexicans and other Latinos in the Southwest to maintain ties with their homeland and its language, culture, and religious traditions far more readily than did European Catholic immigrants during the nineteenth and early twentieth centuries. For example, although he moved from his native Sonora to Tucson in 1882, Federico José María Ronstadt (1868–1954) revealed in his memoirs that he returned home regularly to visit family members and celebrate traditional religious feasts like Christmas and Holy Week. Similarly, Catholics who live in borderland cities have noted that Catholic life, ministry, and devotion transcend the political border that "divides" Mexico and the United States. Residents of the El Paso–Juárez area commended the service of local priests Ramón Ortiz and Carlos Pinto, whose terms of service collectively spanned the seven decades between the U.S. war with Mexico and the end of the Mexican Revolution. Like their parishioners, these priests blurred national boundaries through their activities and ministrations on both sides of the border.[21]

Of course, not all Latinos reside directly on the U.S.-Mexican border, nor can all immigrants return home at regular intervals. Today numerous immigrants who lack documentation refrain from visiting their homeland because they fear they won't be able to return, others go home rarely (if at all) because of limited financial resources or the political situation in their native country. Nonetheless, many immigrants remain in contact with their country of origin (and other countries where Spanish is spoken) through Spanish-language newspapers and television programs, improved communication technologies, commemorations of their national heroes and patriotic holidays, and a variety of local community networks and associations. Latino religion in the Southwest cannot be fully understood without taking into account the transnational character of borderlands life for Mexican-descent residents and other Latinos.

As in society at large, in the Catholic fold Latino initiatives are significantly influenced by their interactions with other U.S. residents, particularly Euro-Americans. At times these interactions have been cordial and cooperative, but in other instances they have resulted in disagreement and even painful prejudice and conflict. On the official ecclesial level, this diversity of interrelations is illustrated by Latino attempts to establish national parishes like Our Lady of Guadalupe in San Francisco as safe havens that reinforce their language, culture, and Catholic faith and provide a base for ethnic solidarity and pride.

Interactions with Protestants have also influenced Latino Catholics, a number of whom have worshipped in Protestant churches or even become active congregants. Latinos in the Southwest first embraced the Protestant faith during the first half of the nineteenth century. Initially Latino Protestant numbers were comparatively small and centered in denominations like the Methodists, Presbyterians, and Baptists. The famous Azusa Street Revival in Los Angeles lit the Pentecostal spark among Latinos and other racial and ethnic groups beginning in 1906. Subsequently the growth of Pentecostalism and evangelicalism became a major trend in Latino religion. Today Latinos lead and participate in a wide array of religious and spiritual groups, movements, and practices. This pluralism shapes the religious sensibilities of immigrant and native-born Latinos alike. Even Catholics who elect to make a more conscious commitment to their faith are often influenced by the "competition" with other denominations and faith traditions.[22]

The Mexican Revolution and the Cristero Rebellion fostered the expansion of Mexican Catholic parishes in the Southwest by accelerating the existing migration from Mexico to a massive movement of newcomers during the first three decades of the twentieth century, especially into California and Texas. Among those arriving in the United States were Catholic priests targeted by anticlerical revolutionaries. One estimate is that 25,000 political refugees had arrived in San Antonio by 1913; they were joined by thousands more during the next two decades. By August 1914, the archbishops of México, Michoacán, Oaxaca, Durango, and Linares and the bishops of Sinoloa, Saltillo, Aguacalientes, Zacatecas, Guadalupe, Tulacingo, Chiapas, and Campeche resided in exile at San Antonio. Even more Mexicans went to Los Angeles. Over 150,000 migrants arrived in that city by 1925; that number nearly doubled when the Cristero Rebellion erupted. By 1928 some 1,000 Mexican priests lived in Los Angeles. Exiled priests, along with lay leaders and women religious, played an important role in the creation of new Mexican parishes and missions and revitalizing local Mexican worship traditions. In Los Angeles, twelve Mexican parishes were founded between 1923 and 1928. By 1936 there were sixty-four Mexican parishes in the Archdiocese of Los Angeles alone, many started or staffed by exiled priests from Mexico.[23]

The Mexican laity and church hierarchy, along with some Catholic clergy from the United States, managed to keep the issue of the Mexican government's "socialistic" and anti-Catholic leanings highly visible. Their efforts were particularly conspicuous at a 1934 public procession for the feast of Our Lady of Guadalupe in Los Angeles held in the wake of renewed church-state tensions after Mexican president Lázaro Cárdenas's election. Organizers announced the event as "a memorial service for those who had suffered persecution in Mexico." The Mexican consulate urged all "real Mexicans" to boycott the procession, but 40,000 participants reportedly took part, some bearing placards that read "atheism reigns in Mexico City and Moscow." A week later the Mexican vice consul in nearby San Bernardino unsuccessfully petitioned local officials to cancel the parade permit for a similar event. He then published a letter in a Spanish-language newspaper calling for a boycott. Mexican Catholics bought or stole all the copies of the paper they could find and burned them. They then wrote President Franklin D. Roosevelt, accusing the Mexican consuls of attempting to deny their constitutional right to freedom of religion; subsequently Mexican officials reassigned the consuls stationed at Los Angeles and San Bernardino to posts outside the United States.[24]

The widespread policy of establishing national parishes for various Catholic immigrant groups began to change by the 1920s, when Cardinal George Mundelein of Chicago became the first major U.S. prelate to reverse this policy. Mundelein contended that these parishes increased nativist anti-Catholic sentiment and that the rise of the second generation among many immigrant groups warranted a greater use of English and a more integrationist approach. Soon other bishops followed Mundelein's lead in seeking both to prohibit new national parishes and "Americanize" existing parishes. For example, while the 1870s effort to create a Spanish-speaking national parish at San Francisco was successful, a 1950 attempt to establish another such parish at San Jose (at the time still part of the San Francisco archdiocese) was not. In this instance the attitude of archdiocesan authorities had clearly shifted from the approach of their predecessors some eight decades earlier; these authorities denied the 1950 petitioners' request because they perceived national parishes as segregationist.[25]

Despite the widespread disinclination among church leaders to establish national parishes since World War II, however, today a number of Latinos comprise territorial parishes that in effect are national parishes, since their congregations are overwhelmingly Latino. Many Latinos gravitate to such parishes because they feel more *en su casa* (at home) in them. Moreover, whether in mixed or predominantly Latino parishes, numerous Latinos have established, supported, and refashioned feast days, devotional practices, organizations, and renewal movements that enable them to formulate and express their Latino Catholic faith and identities on their own terms. Besides the Feast of Our Lady of Guadalupe (December 12) commemorated in numerous locales, in recent decades feast day celebrations in the Southwest have included the Cuban Virgen de la Caridad del Cobre (September 8) in Houston, the Nicaraguan La Purísima (Immaculate Conception, December 8) in San Francisco, the Guatemalan Cristo Negro de Esquipulas (January 15) in San Antonio, and the El Salvadoran Divino Salvador del Mundo (Feast of the Transfiguration, August 6) in Los Angeles. Like the national parishes of yesteryear, these celebrations serve both a religious and a social purpose: they foster faith and devotion but also provide a sacred ambiance in which Latinos can feel at home in a church and society that often appear unfamiliar and distant.

Parish associations like the Guadalupanas, Hijas de María (Daughters of Mary), Santo Nombre (Holy Name Society), and Adoración Noctura (Nocturnal Adoration Society) have provided both spiritual sustenance and organizations that affirm ethnic heritage and

a sense of belonging. Over the past half century the popularity of these devotional societies has shifted toward renewal movements like the *Cursillo de Cristiandad* (Brief Course
in Christianity), which has had a significance among Latino Catholics in the Southwest
(and elsewhere in the United States) that is impossible to exaggerate. Spanish-speaking
Catholics organized the first Cursillo retreat in the United States at Waco, Texas, in 1957.
As a lay-run movement that trained participants to actively live and spread their Catholic
faith, the Cursillo has offered numerous Latinas and Latinos the opportunity to exercise
ecclesial leadership. Moreover, the Cursillo gave numerous U.S. Latino Catholics a "turf"
of their own where they could express themselves in their own language, customs, and
devotional style. In large part, the Cursillo's popularity among Latinos stemmed from its
significance as a means of collective self-expression.[26]

Similarly, the Charismatic Renewal, a movement of Pentecostal-type prayer and formation for Christian living that emerged among English-speaking U.S. Catholics in 1967,
has provided a means for numerous Latinos to form Spanish-language prayer groups and
express their faith in their own way. The growth of U.S. Latino Catholic Charismatics to
more than five million is "one of the largest overlooked popular grass roots religious movements in the U.S."[27] But at least one conclusion about the continuing vitality of the Charismatic Renewal among Latinos is clear: the desire for ecclesial structures that provide
Latinos with a sense of ownership and belonging is far from quenched.

Struggles for Justice

In 1973 Sisters Carmelita Espinoza and María de Jesús Ybarra publicly denounced the use
of Mexican nuns as low-paid domestic workers in U.S. Catholic institutions, asking rhetorically, "Is it necessary to profess vows to be a waitress or a house maid?" Espinoza and
Ybarra spoke as the national coordinators of Las Hermanas (the Sisters). The organization
had been founded two years previously through the initiative of Sister Gregoria Ortega,
a Victory Noll sister and community activist from El Paso, Texas, and Sister Gloria Gra-
ciela Gallardo, a Holy Ghost sister from San Antonio who worked as a catechist and
community organizer. These two leaders convened fifty sisters at Houston, Texas, in
April 1971 and established Las Hermanas. The charter membership declared that the organization's purpose was "to meet the needs of the Spanish-speaking people of God, using our
unique resources as Spanish-speaking religious women." Subsequently a more focused
commitment to Latina women emerged. The organization concentrated its national conferences and projects on issues that Latinas face, such as sexuality, domestic violence,
leadership skills, and the empowerment of women. While initially comprised primarily of
Chicanas, other Latina religious, particularly those of Caribbean heritage, soon joined
their Chicana sisters in forming Las Hermanas; by 1975 lay Latinas were also accepted
into organizational membership. Las Hermanas thus became the only national Catholic
organization of Chicana/Latina women.[28]

Las Hermanas is one of numerous organizations and efforts that Latinas and Latinos
initiated to struggle for their rights in church and society. Whether entering the United

States as the result of U.S. territorial expansion or as émigrés, all Latinos face the common challenge of adapting to life in a new country. One of their most defining challenges has been confronting the persistent racism and rejection of the dominant society. At a very practical level, the dominant society's derisive stereotypes and prejudicial attitudes led to discriminatory practices that have been historically debilitating and isolating and have had severe implications for daily life. Latinos in the Southwest have often expressed outrage at Euro-American supremacist attitudes and struggled to defend themselves from a generally aggressive anti-Latino attitude in the United States. Both emigrés and native-born Latinos have actively combated racism, poverty, and other social maladies. Through their community organizations and activism, which included mutual aid societies, newspapers, labor unions, political organizations, and civil rights groups, Latinos have struggled to ensure dignity, self-determination, and the right to full participation in U.S. society.

A group of predominantly Mexican immigrant parents at Lemon Grove, California (near San Diego), won a landmark desegregation lawsuit in 1931 after local school board officials sought to impose an all-Mexican school on their children. In other instances, U.S.-born Hispanics led efforts to combat discrimination and prejudice, at times excluding their immigrant counterparts for political expediency. Organizations like the League of United Latin American Citizens (LULAC), founded in 1929, restricted their membership to U.S. citizens of Mexican or Spanish descent. Although LULAC promoted good citizenship, the use of the English language, and even "Americanization," it also focused considerable attention on issues like school reform, increased Mexican American representation for juries and other public duties, and an end to discrimination. Similarly, in the wake of World War II Mexican American veterans formed the American G.I. Forum. While primarily intended to lobby for the rights of veterans, forum members also promoted social and political reforms that benefited their fellow Mexican American citizens.[29]

Like the struggles of African Americans and other minority groups, Latino activism increased dramatically during the 1960s. While their activism was most visible to the general public in the efforts of Chicano leaders Cesar Chavez, Dolores Huerta, and the United Farm Workers (UFW), it was also evident in predominately Chicano groups like the Mexican American Youth Organization (MAYO), La Raza Unida Party, and the Crusade for Justice, all of which were founded in the Southwest.[30] This increased activism, along with the reforms of Vatican II, the 1968 Latin American episcopal conference at Medellín, and the inspiration of Latin American liberation theology, influenced many Latino church leaders in the Southwest and beyond who consequently initiated efforts for ecclesial and social reform. The expanding Latino population and the growing number of Latino leaders and professionals also facilitated Latino activist efforts that have shaped both church and society in the United States since the late 1960s.

Many Latino Catholic organizations founded in the Southwest strove primarily to promote Latino equality within the church itself. PADRES (Padres Asociados por los Derechos Religiosos, Educativos, y Sociales, or Priests Associated for Religious, Educational, and Social Rights) emerged out of a Chicano priests' support group in San Antonio, Texas, and played a major role as a catalyst for the advancement of Latino leadership and concerns within the church during the 1970s and 1980s. In 1972 PADRES member Virgilio Elizondo led the effort to establish the Mexican American Cultural Center (MACC, now the Mexican American Catholic College) in San Antonio as "a response to the struggles, frustration, and disappointments" many Latino Catholics felt within the church. Elizondo served as MACC's founding president from 1972 to 1987. Las Hermanas and lay leaders joined Elizondo and other PADRES in establishing the Center. Elizondo's successors as MACC president, Father Rosendo Urrabazo, C.M.F., Sister María Elena González, R.S.M., and Arturo Chavez, have continued to enact and develop the vision of MACC as a language and pastoral training institute, as well as an advocate for Latino ministry and justice in church and society. The staff at MACC has also engaged in an ongoing ecumenical, interethnic effort to train leaders for cross-cultural work in a variety of contexts and played a leading role in publishing groundbreaking research about Latino liturgy, faith expressions, history, and theology.[31]

The work of organizations founded in the Southwest like PADRES, Las Hermanas, and MACC reflects the multiplication of national Latino Catholic organizations over the past five decades, all of which encompass the significant involvement and leadership of Latino Catholics from the Southwest. Today there are national organizations for Latino deacons, priests, women, diocesan directors of Hispanic ministry, youth, theologians, liturgists, and catechists, among others. One such organization founded in the Southwest is the National Catholic Council for Hispanic Ministry (NCCHM), which Jesuit priest Allan Figueroa Deck, catechists, religious congregations of men and women, and lay leaders established in 1991. NCCHM leaders envision the council as a clearinghouse and source of unity for national and regional organizations involved in Hispanic ministry.

In 1945 San Antonio archbishop Robert E. Lucey (1891–1977) was instrumental in establishing the Bishops' Committee for the Spanish Speaking, the U.S. bishops' first collaborative effort in Hispanic ministry. This ongoing initiative led to the 1974 creation of the Secretariat for Hispanic Affairs of the United States Conference of Catholic Bishops, which subsequently provided national leadership under the directorship of Pablo Sedillo and his successor, Ron Cruz, until the secretariat was subsumed into a new Secretariat of Cultural Diversity in the Church in 2007. Four national *encuentros* of Hispanic Catholic leaders from across the United States gathered in 1972, 1977, 1985, and 2018, respectively, to develop pastoral strategies and advocate for Hispanic ministry. The Secretariat for Hispanic Affairs and other Latinos also played a prominent role in convoking an *encuentro* in 2000 that brought together leaders from the various racial and ethnic groups in U.S. Catholicism to engage in a broader process of pastoral planning and collaboration. Mexican American bishop Patricio Flores became the first Latino bishop in 1970; since then more than fifty Latinos have become Catholic bishops. Their efforts on the national scene are reflected in the U.S. Catholic bishops' 1983 pastoral letter on Hispanic ministry, the 1987 *National Pastoral Plan for Hispanic Ministry,* and the 2002 follow-up to the Pastoral Plan, *Encuentro and Mission: A Renewed Pastoral Framework for Hispanic Ministry.*[32]

While Latino Catholics have focused considerable time and energy promoting a more vibrant ministry to their people, in other instances they have sought to address broader social issues. Cesar Chavez (1927–93) is arguably the most renowned figure among Latino leaders in the Southwest, and indeed in Chicano history. Born near Yuma, Arizona, he moved with his family to California in 1939. There he followed in his parents' footsteps, laboring as a farm worker in the San Joaquin Valley. In 1952, Chavez began organizing with the Community Service Organization (CSO) at San Jose, California, where his family lived when they were not working the fields. Chavez was deeply influenced by his training in community organizing and Catholic social teaching, as well as the faith he nurtured and expressed in frequent Mass attendance, his experience of *Cursillo*, spiritual fasts, the discipline of nonviolent protest, and devotion to Our Lady of Guadalupe. During the 1960s, he collaborated with Dolores Huerta to establish the National Farm Workers Association (later known as the United Farm Workers), the first union to secure contracts and official recognition from California growers. The union's significance extended far beyond the fields as the efforts to gain farm workers' rights helped ignite the Chicano struggle in many other areas of church and society.[33]

In various towns and cities across the Southwest significant numbers of Latino Catholics have participated in local faith-based community organizations. Many of these efforts are staffed by organizers from national networks like the Pacific Institute for Community Organization (PICO), which is headquartered in Oakland and led by the Jesuits and their lay collaborators, and the Industrial Areas Foundation (IAF), which staffs various organizations in Texas, California, New Mexico, and Arizona. The Catholic Campaign for Human Development (CCHD), which the U.S. Catholic bishops launched in November 1969, has provided more funding for faith-based community organizations than all other religious givers combined. Though somewhat dated, the latest pertinent study showed that CCHD support totaled nearly one-fifth of all income for faith-based community organizations nationwide.[34]

The most renowned of the local faith-based community organizations is Communities Organized for Public Service (COPS), an IAF-affiliated organization in San Antonio. Lay leaders like founding president Andrés Sarabia, professional organizer Ernie Cortés, and priests such as Edmundo Rodríguez and Albert Benavides collaborated in the 1974 effort to establish COPS among six ethnic Mexican Catholic parishes on San Antonio's west side. Their first major issue was the horrendous drainage and frequent flooding in their neighborhoods, which had caused school closings, accidents, damaged homes, impassable roads, bridge collapses, a dearth of business establishments, even deaths. When COPS members discovered that many drainage projects had actually been authorized in bond issues passed as far back as 1945, they filled city hall during a council meeting to voice their outrage. Stunned by the crowd and the overwhelming evidence presented, Mayor Charles Becker ordered the city manager to devise a drainage project implementation plan. COPS then took the lead in passing a $46.8 million bond issue for fifteen west-side drainage projects. Led primarily by Latina leaders like Beatrice Gallego, Carmen Badillo, Beatice Cortés, Sonia Hernández, Patricia Ozuna, and Virginia Rámirez, subsequently the organization achieved more than $1 billion in infrastructure improvements for primarily low-income and working-class neighborhoods, as well as significant advances in community issues like educational reform, job training, economic development, and living wages. More importantly, members attest that "the most positive change [because of COPS] has been in the attitude of our people. Twenty-five years ago, we couldn't imagine that a city council member would attend our meetings, now we know that with the power of educated, organized people, anything is possible."[35]

Southwest Latinos and U.S. Catholic History

Recent general histories of U.S. Catholicism evidence a growing trend to address more adequately the Latino Catholic presence and contribution in this country. For instance, most historians now begin the U.S. Catholic story with a treatment of the Spanish colonial era that predates U.S. independence by two centuries. Woven into the narrative of noteworthy works like those of James Hennesey, Jay Dolan, and James Fisher are further references to topics such as Latino Catholic leaders, organizations, movements, religious traditions, social activism, immigration patterns, and demographic shifts.[36] Nonetheless, the contention that U.S. Catholics of European roots have become "Americanized" to a significant degree remains an important point of departure and interpretive lens through which a number of scholars and other observers examine Catholicism in the United States.

Clearly the notion that U.S. Catholics are immigrants on the road to rapid Americanization does not reflect fully the Latino experience in the Southwest (and elsewhere). In fact, Latino Catholics in the Southwest during the mid-nineteenth century were not immigrants but enduring communities of faith that survived the U.S. takeover of northern Mexico following the war between the two nations. While the saga of nineteenth-century European Catholic émigrés is one of seeking an immigrant haven in a new land, the story of the first Mexican American Catholics is in large part a tale of faith, struggle, and endurance within their ancestral homeland.

Moreover, though there was some previous immigration, massive Mexican immigration began only after the outbreak of the Mexican Revolution in 1910, just a decade before restrictive U.S. immigration laws vastly diminished the flow of European émigrés. Thus, precisely during the era when European immigration declined and descendants of European immigrants were purportedly on their way to becoming full-fledged Americans, Latino Catholic immigrants were repopulating and revitalizing enduring communities of faith in the Southwest and establishing scores of Mexican Catholic communities in the Southwest and beyond.

Today Latino immigration shows no sign of diminishment. An expanding Latino population is part of larger demographic shifts within U.S. Catholicism. The U.S. Catholic Church is no longer an overwhelmingly immigrant church, as it was a century ago, nor is it solely an "Americanized" church. Rather, it is a church largely run by middle-class,

European-descent Catholics with growing numbers of Latino, Asian, and some African immigrants, along with sizeable contingents of native-born Latino and African American Catholics and some Native Americans. Latino Catholics in the Southwest add not just another chapter to the general history of U.S. Catholicism, but a lens through which to examine colonial origins, westward expansion, ongoing immigration, and the struggles of non-European groups as significant components of that history.

NOTES

1. Francis Baylies, *A Narrative of Major General Wool's Campaign in Mexico* (Albany: Little, 1851), 11.

2. Mexicans, Puerto Ricans, Cubans, Salvadorans, Guatemalans, and others from countries where Spanish is a primary language have employed the umbrella designations "Hispanic," "Latino," and its feminine form "Latina" to reflect and promote perceptions of a common language and heritage and a common struggle adapting to life in the United States. No clear consensus on any one term is evident in common parlance, though "Latino" and the gender inclusive "Latino/a" and "Latinx" are gaining ascendancy among scholars. During the twentieth century the designation "Mexican American" emerged among those of Mexican heritage born or living in the United States, often as an expression of pride in their dual heritage. But since the 1960s some ethnic Mexicans have rejected the term as assimilationist and instead called themselves "Chicanas" and "Chicanos," usually as a means of expressing a strong ethnic consciousness and orientation toward social struggle and justice. In this essay I attempt to reflect the self-referential language in primary sources, including both the diverse expressions of individual informants and the general usages in specific historical eras.

3. Robert E. Wright, "Local Church Emergence and Mission Decline: The Historiography of the Catholic Church in the Southwest during the Spanish and Mexican Periods," *U.S. Catholic Historian* 9 (Winter/Spring 1990): 27–48.

4. Timothy Matovina, *Guadalupe and Her Faithful: Latino Catholics in San Antonio from Colonial Origins to the Present* (Baltimore: Johns Hopkins University Press, 2005); Thomas S. Bremer, *Blessed with Tourists: The Borderlands of Religion and Tourism in San Antonio* (Chapel Hill: University of North Carolina Press, 2004).

5. David J. Weber, ed., *What Caused the Pueblo Revolt of 1680?* (Boston: Bedford and St. Martin's, 1999).

6. Matovina and Gerald E. Poyo, eds., *¡Presente! U.S. Latino Catholics from Colonial Origins to the Present* (Maryknoll, N.Y.: Orbis, 2000), 38–41.

7. Wright, "How Many Are 'A Few'? Catholic Clergy in Central and Northern New Mexico, 1780–1851," in *Seeds of Struggle / Harvest of Faith: The Papers of the Archdiocese of Santa Fe Catholic Cuarto Centennial Conference on the History of the Catholic Church in New Mexico*, ed. Thomas J. Steele, Paul Rhetts, and Barbe Awalt (Albuquerque: LPD, 1998), 219–61.

8. Juan Romero, with Moises Sandoval, *Reluctant Dawn: Historia del Padre A. J. Martínez, Cura de Taos* (San Antonio: Mexican American Cultural Center Press, 1976); Angélico Chávez, *But Time and Chance: The Story of Padre Martínez of Taos, 1793–1867* (Santa Fe: Sunstone, 1981).

9. Matovina, *Tejano Religion and Ethnicity: San Antonio, 1821–1860* (Austin: University of Texas Press, 1995), 50–52, 68; Albert Camarillo, *Chicanos in a Changing Society: From Mexican Pueblos to American Barrios in Santa Barbara and Southern California, 1848–1930* (Cambridge, Mass.: Harvard University Press, 1979), 117.

10. Michael E. Engh, *Frontier Faiths: Church, Temple, and Synagogue in Los Angeles, 1846–1888* (Albuquerque: University of New Mexico Press, 1992), 189–90.

11. Matovina, *Tejano Religion and Ethnicity*, 43–44, 67.

12. Leonard Pitt, *The Decline of the Californios: A Social History of the Spanish-Speaking Californians, 1846–1890* (Berkeley: University of California Press, 1966), 33–35; Zaragosa Vargas, ed., *Major Problems in Mexican American History* (Boston: Houghton Mifflin, 1999), 143–46.

13. José Antonio Navarro, *Defending Mexican Valor in Texas: José Antonio Navarro's Historical Writings, 1853–1857*, ed. David R. McDonald and Timothy Matovina (Austin, Tex.: State House, 1995), 19–20; Pablo de la Guerra, Speech to the California legislature, in *El Grito: A Journal of Contemporary Mexican-American Thought* 5 (Fall 1971): 19–20.

14. Matovina, "Lay Initiatives in Worship on the Texas *Frontera*, 1830–1860," *U.S. Catholic Historian* 12 (Fall 1994): 108–11.

15. Matovina and Poyo, *¡Presente!*, 44–89.

16. Ibid., 65–85; Ana María Díaz-Stevens, "The Saving Grace: The Matriarchal Core of Latino Catholicism," *Latino Studies Journal* 4 (September 1993): 60–78.

17. J. Manuel Espinosa, "The Origins of the Penitentes of New Mexico: Separating Fact from Fiction," *Catholic Historical Review* 79 (July 1993): 454–77; Alberto López Pulido, *The Sacred World of the Penitentes* (Washington, D.C.: Smithsonian Institution Press, 2000).

18. Henry Granjon, *Along the Rio Grande: A Pastoral Visit to Southwest New Mexico in 1902*, ed. Michael Romero Taylor, trans. Mary W. de López (Albuquerque: University of New Mexico Press, 1986), 39.

19. Spaniards and Hispanic Americans of San Francisco, *Lo que puede y necesita la raza española en San Francisco* (circular letter printed in San Francisco), 1871; copy in Bancroft Library, University of California, Berkeley.

20. Lawrence A. Cardoso, *Mexican Emigration to the United States, 1897–1931* (Tucson: University of Arizona Press, 1980); David M. Reimers, *Still the Golden Door: The Third World Comes to America*, 2nd ed. (New York: Columbia University Press, 1992).

21. Federico José María Ronstadt, *Borderman: Memoirs of Federico José María Ronstadt*, ed. Edward F. Ronstadt (Albuquerque: University of New Mexico Press, 1993), esp. 108–9; Mary D. Taylor, "Cura de la Frontera, Ramón Ortiz," *U.S. Catholic Historian* 9 (Winter/Spring 1990): 67–85; Lilliana Owens, *Reverend Carlos M. Pinto, SJ, Apostle of El Paso, 1892–1919* (El Paso, Tex.: Revista Católica, 1951).

22. Paul Barton, *Hispanic Methodists, Presbyterians, and Baptists in Texas* (Austin: University of Texas Press, 2006); Juan Francisco Martínez, *Sea la Luz: The Making of Mexican Protestantism in the American Southwest, 1829–1900* (Denton: University of North Texas Press, 2006); Gastón Espinoza, *Latino Pentecostals in America: Faith and Politics in Action* (Cambridge, Mass.: Harvard University Press, 2014).

23. Jay P. Dolan and Gilberto M. Hinojosa, eds., *Mexican Americans and the Catholic Church, 1900–1965* (Notre Dame, Ind.: University of Notre Dame Press, 1994), esp. 33, 162–63, 184–87.

24. Francisco E. Balderrama, *In Defense of La Raza: The Los Angeles Mexican Consulate and the Mexican Community, 1929–1936* (Tucson: University of Arizona Press, 1982), 73–90.

25. Philip Gleason, *Keeping the Faith: American Catholicism Past and Present* (Notre Dame, Ind.: University of Notre Dame Press, 1987), 48–49; Jeffrey M. Burns, "The Mexican Catholic Community in California," in Dolan and Hinojosa, *Mexican Americans and the Catholic Church*, 167–68, 226.

26. Gina Marie Pitti, "The Sociedades Guadalupanas in the San Francisco Archdiocese, 1942–1962," *U.S. Catholic Historian* 21 (Winter 2003): 83–98; Kristy Nabhan-Warren, *The Cursillo Movement in America: Catholics, Protestants, and Fourth-Day Spirituality* (Chapel Hill: University of North Carolina Press, 2013).

27. Gastón Espinosa, "The Impact of Pluralism on Trends in Latin American and U.S. Latino Religions and Society," *Perspectivas* 7 (Fall 2003): 15–21; Matovina, *Latino Catholicism: Transformation in America's Largest Church* (Princeton, N.J.: Princeton University Press, 2012), esp. Chap. 4, "Parishes and Apostolic Movements."

28. Lara Medina, *Las Hermanas: Chicana/Latina Religious-Political Activism in the U.S. Catholic Church* (Philadelphia: Temple University Press, 2004).

29. *The Lemon Grove Incident* (New York: Cinema Guild, 1985), videocassette; Benjamin Márquez, *LULAC: The Evolution of a Mexican American Political Organization* (Austin: University of Texas Press, 1993); Henry A. J. Ramos, *The American GI Forum: In Pursuit of the Dream, 1948–1983* (Houston: Arte Público, 1998).

30. F. Arturo Rosales, *Chicano! The History of the Mexican American Civil Rights Movement* (Houston: University of Houston Press, 1996).

31. Richard Edward Martínez, *PADRES: The National Chicano Priest Movement* (Austin: University of Texas Press, 2005); Matovina and Poyo, *¡Presente!*, 224–26; Virgilio Elizondo, "The Mexican American Cultural Center Story," *Listening: Journal of Religion and Culture* 32 (Fall 1997): 152–60; Mario T. García, *Católicos: Resistance and Affirmation in Chicano Catholic History* (Austin: University of Texas Press, 2008).

32. Moisés Sandoval, "The Organization of a Hispanic Church," in *Hispanic Catholic Culture in the U.S.: Issues and Concerns*, ed. Jay P. Dolan and Allan Figueroa Deck (Notre Dame, Ind.: University of Notre Dame Press, 1994), 131–65.

33. Richard Griswold del Castillo and Richard A. García, *César Chávez: A Triumph of Spirit* (Norman: University of Oklahoma Press, 1995); Alan J. Watt, *Farm Workers and the Churches: The Movement in California and Texas* (College Station: Texas A&M University Press, 2010); Luis D. León, *The Political Spirituality of Cesar Chavez: Crossing Religious Borders* (Berkeley: University of California Press, 2015).

34. Richard Wood, *Faith in Action: Religion, Race, and Democratic Organizing in America* (Chicago: University of Chicago Press, 2002).

35. Mark R. Warren, *Dry Bones Rattling: Community Building to Revitalize American Democracy* (Princeton, N.J.: Princeton University Press, 2001).

36. James Hennesey, *American Catholics: A History of the Roman Catholic Community in the United States* (New York: Oxford University Press, 1981); Jay P. Dolan, *The American Catholic Experience: A History from Colonial Times to the Present* (1985; repr. Notre Dame, Ind.: University of Notre Dame Press, 1992); James T. Fisher, *Communion of Immigrants: A History of Catholics in America* (2000; new ed., New York: Oxford University Press, 2008).

THREE

Left Coast Catholicism: The Tradition of Dissent in the California Church

Jeffrey M. Burns

California has long occupied a special place in the American imagination. From the Gold Rush to the Summer of Love to Governor Jerry Brown, California has been regarded as a land of possibilities, innovation, and new beginnings. Berkeley, San Francisco, and other California communities are virtually synonymous with the spirit of cultural and political radicalism and creative innovation. Journalist/historian Carey McWilliams equated the California experience with "a spirit of independence and a tradition of bold action."[1] None of these attributes—change, innovation, independence, bold action—are values traditionally associated with Catholicism in popular thought. Rather, the church has represented stability and tradition, if not outright reaction. To many, the church is a monolithic institution insisting on uniformity in directing the lives of its faithful, who ostensibly march in lockstep. This stereotype does not fit the reality of the Catholic Church in California.

The church in California has been made up of a vast array of personalities seeking to respond to the prompting of the spirit and to live out the gospel call in their time and place. This effort has often brought California Catholics into conflict with their age and, at times, with their church. These individuals were "dissenters" for their disruption of the status quo in church and society. Most of these individuals did not consider themselves "dissidents" or radicals. Rather they saw themselves as loyal Catholics struggling to work out their vocation in fidelity to the church in a complex and, at times, hostile world. Often, it was the circumstance in which they found themselves that led to dissent. For the most part, these men and women were unaware of one another and did not define themselves as part of this tradition. Nonetheless, they share several basic principles. First, they identified with the poor, the outcast, and the dispossessed, recognizing the human dignity of each person. Second, they tended to be personalists, placing the value and well-being of the person over that of the institution. Finally, the breadth of their vision could not be limited to narrow institutional concerns. For their efforts, these Catholics were branded as troublemakers, agitators, or simply insane: they were in fact part of a tradition of dissent that has surfaced in almost every era within the history of the Catholic Church in California.

The Mission Era

Catholicism was first established in California by the Franciscan fathers under the leadership of Father Junipero Serra (1713–84) at Mission San Diego in 1769. (He was recently canonized in 2015). Between 1770 and 1823 twenty additional missions were built along the coast stretching from San Diego to Sonoma. The missions were designed to secure the northernmost province of the Spanish Empire in the so-called New World. The missionaries were to "pacify" the native peoples by effecting a dual conversion—to Christianity and to Spanish culture. Once natives were converted they were required to stay at the missions; if they ran away, soldiers were sent to return them to the missions, whose complexes were designed to be self-contained and self-supporting. Buildings were erected, fields planted and toiled, industrial products produced, all by California Indian labor.

The missions have been a source of controversy from their beginning. Critics of the missions existed within Spain and Mexico and among Spain's imperial rivals. In the 1880s, Californians rediscovered the missions (they had been secularized in the 1830s), rebuilt the decaying mission structures, and created the California Mission Myth. The missions were depicted as utopian communities where loving padres tended trusting natives, who joyfully returned the padres' love. An anti-myth later emerged, depicting the missions as agents of genocide and torture. In reality each mission and each padre functioned differently, as did each tribe and each Native American. A recent study of Franciscan missionaries from the 1790s by Rose Marie Beebe and Robert Senkewicz suggests that some, including our "first dissenter," Fray José Maria Fernandez, were critical of mission policies and practices.[2]

Fernandez was born in Madrid in 1770, joined the Franciscans at an early age, and left Spain in 1795 for mission work in Mexico; he was sent to San Francisco the following year. Fernandez found a mission site there where more than two hundred indigenous "neophytes" (converted Native Americans) out of approximately nine hundred had died recently from an epidemic; three hundred more had run away claiming they were hungry, overworked, punished too severely, and fearful of death from disease. Fernandez increased the food allotment for the neophytes and generally created a better atmosphere within the mission, quickly earning a reputation as a kind and loving padre: one soldier described him as one "in whom resides gentleness, affability, and good treatment." Fernandez was openly critical of the two other padres at the mission. He wrote a letter to the governor of California complaining of their abusive treatment of the native peoples and calling for their removal. He was further upset when his colleagues sent a band of neophytes to the East Bay to reclaim a group of runaways in June 1797. Two years earlier a similar expedition had ended in disaster, when seven neophytes were killed. The 1797 expedition led by a Baja California neophyte named Raymundo fared slightly better. Raymundo's band was repulsed by the "fugitives" and their non-Christian allies. In a scathing letter to the governor, Fernandez attributed the debacle to "the terrible suffering they experienced from punishment and work . . . they longed for the opportunity to take revenge against those two fathers."[3]

Fernandez was labeled a malcontent, whose only real complaint, it was said, was that he was not listened to by the other padres. Junipero Serra's successor as mission president, Father Fermin de Lasuen (1736–1803), accused him of conspiring with Indians against the other mission priests: Fernandez was then accused of insanity and returned to Mexico. Fernandez has been treated just as badly by mission historians who have derided him as "demented," incapacitated by "an accidental blow on the head," or a victim of "hallucinations." Whatever the cause, Fernandez was "not a well man." The historical record, however, supports Fernandez's position. Even Lasuen acknowledged that the Indians were overworked, though he denied physical abuse. Rather than the ranting of a lunatic, Fernandez's observations were those of a Franciscan deeply concerned about the welfare of the native people. On leaving for Mexico the padre offered a sharp rebuke to his critics: "If I had been listened to last year, all this danger would have been avoided. But no one believed me. I was taken for a fraud, a troublemaker. I was accused of conspiring with the secular authorities for sinister purposes. I am quitting because I am choked to the core with feelings."[4] The life of a dissenter was never easy.

Transitional California

In 1821, Mexico achieved its independence from Spain; by 1836 all twenty-one California missions had been shut down or "secularized." All temporal authority was removed from the missions, the neophytes released, and the missions reduced to simple parish status. The era of the great land grant ranchos began as a *Californio* elite established the vast estates that dominated California life. Former missionary Francisco Garcia Diego y Moreno (1785–1846) was appointed first bishop of California in 1840; he arrived two years later and established his episcopal see at Santa Barbara. In 1846 (the same year Garcia died), war broke out between the United States and Mexico; California quickly fell to U.S. forces. On February 2, 1848, California was formally transferred to the United States in the Treaty of Guadalupe Hidalgo. In 1850, Spaniard Joseph Sadoc Alemany, O.P. (1814–88) was appointed the first U.S. bishop; in 1853 he was made the first archbishop of the newly created Archdiocese of San Francisco. The southern portion of the state was split off with the creation of the Monterey (later Los Angeles) diocese, where Thaddeus Amat, C.M. (1810–78) was appointed the first bishop in 1854.

Bishop Amat disapproved of the spiritual practices of his Mexican Californians. According to historian Michael Engh, Amat "envisioned a local Catholic community, Roman in orientation, uniform in expression, and obedient to him in its actions."[5] He attempted to Romanize and Americanize his new diocese, Engh contends, by standardizing ritual and strengthening discipline by subscribing "to measures adopted in Baltimore [by the national hierarchy] and confirmed in Rome."[6] Symbolic of this new direction, he chose a Roman saint, Vibiana, to be patroness of the diocese, replacing the Mexican patroness, *Nuestra Senora de Refugio*. His efforts were met with little enthusiasm from the Mexican Californian community. Complicating matters, Amat resented the enduring popularity of the Franciscans among the disenfranchised Mexican Californian population, who faced loss of their land and constant verbal and physical assault from the Yankee newcomers. In 1855 the anti-Catholic, anti-immigrant American Party (known as the "Know-Nothings" for their secretive ways) saw one of its members elected governor of California. The following year Bishop Amat issued a pastoral letter criticizing what he considered the dismal quality of Catholicism he found in Santa Barbara, the seat of the Monterey diocese. He even forbade the much-loved traditional Midnight Mass at Christmas, scandalized by the celebrations that surrounded the Mass.

An exceptionally popular Mexican Franciscan, Father José Gonzalez Rubio (1804–75), emerged as a reluctant dissenter against what he called this "bishop endowed with a vivid imagination, resourceful cleverness, and an exaggerated notion of episcopal dignity."[7] Born in Mexico, Rubio had served as a missionary, as administrator of the California church following Bishop Garcia's death, and as vicar general since Alemany's arrival. Rubio was so beloved that, upon being summoned back to Mexico in 1855, the people of Santa Barbara prevented his departure by "kidnapping" him and locking him away until his ship had departed. Rubio remained to oversee the Franciscan seminary in Santa Barbara and to serve as pastor of the downtown parish, both named Our Lady of Sorrows. Amat asked the Franciscans to relocate to an Indian mission at San Luis Rey—an offer the friars rejected on grounds they would have to shut their seminary down if they accepted this ministry.

Amat then took his complaints to the Congregation of Propaganda Fide, the Roman congregation in charge of mission affairs, accusing the Franciscans of promoting superstition by allowing the practice of selling burial shrouds, which the bishop complained were regarded as the "key to heaven" by Catholics in the diocese. Amat's supporters later charged that the Franciscans encouraged "nominal and superstitious Christianity that scandalized American Protestants with its shameful version of Christianity."[8] Before traveling to Rome to plead his case personally against the Franciscans, Bishop Amat suspended the priestly faculties of Rubio and two other friars at Santa Barbara and forbade them from any public ministry. Rubio and the Franciscans were supported throughout their ordeal by San Francisco Archbishop Alemany, who sent many missives to Rome on their behalf. Of Rubio, Alemany wrote, he is "the most venerated man in all of California for his knowledge, prudence, and virtue."[9] Alemany argued that Amat's actions were unjust and ill-founded and counseled the Franciscans to pursue a policy of respectful dissent.

Father Rubio acceded to Amat's injunction, though he believed it to be illegal and urged Franciscans in Rome to press his case "to seek reparation for the grievous deed done to this community, with scandal and prejudice to the local community."[10] He continued to direct the seminary, and by 1860 three seminarians were ready for ordination; that same year the Propaganda Fide decided in favor of the Franciscans, and Rubio's faculties were restored, though the dispute dragged on for another four years. Rubio was respectful and restrained throughout the controversy: not a dissident by nature, he dissented to protect his fellow friars and the Santa Barbara Mexican Catholic community. He took little joy in his vindication, observing that a lasting solution depended "not on the clinching of arguments, nor on the concrete expression of juridical formulas, nor on the ingenious handling of investigations, but solely on that victorious grace that animates the human heart."[11] That victorious grace would be the source of much of the dissent in the California church as individuals tried follow what they perceived to be their vocation.

The Plight of the Native American

Following the secularization of the missions, the California Indian population was left to its own devices. Some drifted into towns and *ranchos* and became part of the workforce. Some remained at the missions, while others left for the interior. With the onset of the Gold Rush, the condition of the Native Californians significantly deteriorated as gold seekers abused the women, stole their children, and hunted and killed the "dangerous" Indian. California governor Peter Burnett (1807–95)—a Catholic convert—suggested that extermination might be the only answer to the Indian problem. Massacres became regular occurrences, and the California Indian population dropped dramatically to below 30,000 by 1870. "Uprooted from their homelands and neglected by the federal government," explained historian George Phillips, "the Indians of California experienced both material and psychological deprivation."[12] In 1862 Archbishop Alemany welcomed to San Francisco a number of seminarians from Mexico after they were expelled by the anticlerical government of President Benito Juarez (1806–72). Among this group was Luciano Osuna (c. 1830–94), who became the most prominent missionary of the post-secularization period. Osuna served communities of Spanish-speaking Indians in Mendocino, Lake, and Sonoma counties and later ministered to native peoples on the Round Valley Indian Reservation at Ukiah.

Osuna's unorthodox evangelical methods were grounded in his intense identification with his native parishioners. In 1872 he wrote to Archbishop Alemany:

> I have been with the Indians most of the time. They are sick and hungry and so I am hungry with them. We have no place where to live, nothing to do to work for our living. . . . The Indians are starving in both respects in the body and in the soul and with good desires and words we will not relieve them. We must do something otherwise our charity will not reach them.

Osuna proposed establishing a mission at the reservation that would provide the natives with gainful employment. He concluded his letter by challenging the bishop to "do all that is in your power to do, to raise all kinds of help in provisions, in money, in clothing, in blankets . . . and on the last day we will avoid that terrible sentence of our Lord, you saw me hungry and naked and did not recognize me."[13] Osuna's work exposed him to the violently anti-Indian feelings prevalent in 1873. From Sunol, he wrote Alemany that his attempts to purchase land for a mission were hindered by the white community who "know the church is to be for the good of the Indian, do not like it and don't want to help." He concluded his letter, "Every day I am more convinced of the necessity of caring for the Indians, much more because the Indians have become the prey of all and they have no one to offer them a friendly hand."[14] Later that year Osuna confided to Alemany, "Each day I am more convinced that I can do nothing with Indians unless I live with them."[15] Live with them he did, often teaching in their sweathouses. Osuna cared little for his physical appearance. Observers variously described him as "barefooted, unwashed, uncombed, torn robe, cow manure and mud between his toes and on his feet."[16] Another noted, "In appearance he was a very filthy, barefooted, miserable, looking fellow."[17]

Osuna was no ecumenist or proponent of religious diversity: when a Methodist Indian agent was appointed to oversee the reservation he had been tending, Osuna refused to ask the agent for permission to enter the reservation to evangelize. He believed his relationship to the Indians superseded any government official, especially a Protestant one. "These Methodists won't stop until they infiltrate with their errors," he complained in a letter to Alemany. "The principal weapon they have is the lie."[18] Osuna was arrested and jailed several times for visiting the Indians without permission. His outlandish dress and intransigence provoked the charge that he was insane. At his trial, Archbishop Alemany and Bishop Eugene O'Connell (1815–91) of the newly established Grass Valley diocese supported him. O'Connell wrote, "In order to gain over the Indians to Christianity Padre Osuna conforms to their mode of living. He goes without shoes and wears sandals, therefore he is insane! He eats, drinks, and sleeps after the fashion of the Indians therefore he is insane!"[19] O'Connell concluded that St. John the Baptist would no doubt be found insane by contemporary standards. Ultimately, Alemany and O'Connell went through proper government channels to get St. Turibius Indian Mission established in 1875, where Osuna continued to minister until he returned to Mexico in 1879.

Father Peter C. Yorke and Archbishop Riordan

By the turn of the twentieth century a steady stream of immigrants reestablished Catholicism as a major force in California, particularly in San Francisco. With its large foreign-born population, San Francisco's political life had a very Catholic "feel": in 1896, Irish American Catholic James D. Phelan (1861–1930) was elected mayor. But it was Father Peter C. Yorke (1864–1925) who came to dominate the era. A true original, the combative Yorke would find himself at odds with politicians, employers, fellow Catholics, and even the archbishop himself.

Born in 1864 in Galway, Ireland, Yorke came to the United States in 1886 and was ordained for the Archdiocese of San Francisco in 1887; he then enrolled as one of the first students at the new Catholic University of America in the nation's capital. Yorke returned to San Francisco in 1891 and was promoted rapidly: in 1894, he was appointed chancellor and secretary to Archbishop Patrick W. Riordan (1841–1914), as well as editor of the arch-diocesan newspaper, *The Monitor*. By 1896, Yorke had emerged as the champion of San Francisco's Catholics as he "vanquished" the newly formed anti-Catholic American Protective Association (APA) by publishing a series of exposes of its members and engaging its leaders in highly publicized debates in the local press. At this time, Yorke developed his acerbic and slashing rhetorical style in which he first dissected, then bludgeoned his opponents. Many complained that Yorke's rhetoric was not appropriate for a priest. Yorke ignored these complaints, observing, "The horsewhip is the only corrective for such abuses."[20]

As quickly as Yorke's ecclesial star had risen, it began to fall. In 1896 his nomination for a bishopric was derailed by a Jesuit theologian from Santa Clara College who questioned his orthodoxy, writing that Yorke had a "tendency to modernize and Americanize theology, as some of the clergy modernize and Americanize the Church."[21] Americanism and Modernism were separate issues that tended to be conflated by church traditionalists: the former represented an attempt to reconcile American social and political practices with Catholic teaching; the latter was primarily a movement among a small cohort of English and Western European Catholics looking to adapt modern scholarly methods to the study of theology. By 1907, both "movements" were condemned as heresies, though Peter Yorke escaped censure on either account. He remained active in California political life, even though Archbishop Riordan—in a rare move—informed the *Sacramento Bee* newspaper in 1898 that Yorke did not speak for the church, but "alone is responsible for his utterances."[22] During the mayoral campaign of that year Riordan expressed his support for the incumbent Mayor Phelan after Yorke staunchly promoted the candidacy of his opponent. Yorke resigned as editor of *The Monitor* and traveled to Europe, only to discover on his return in late 1899 that Riordan had failed to appoint him to a parish; he was reduced to accepting a position as assistant at St. Peter's in San Francisco. He became a harsh critic of his archbishop, claiming that Riordan failed at "grappling with the great questions that are now troubling the minds of men." He was "too much engaged in ledgers, or writing letters to priests and religious, about paltry matters that could be well arranged by vicars . . . the whole Pacific slope is waiting, opened mouthed, for every word that falls from our Archbishop."[23]

Despite his demotion, Yorke continued to command considerable respect in San Francisco. During the Teamsters' and Waterfront strike of 1901, Yorke reasserted his leadership. During that strike Yorke placed the church in San Francisco firmly on the side of labor. He became the spiritual adviser of Teamster leader Michael Casey, as well as the union's most popular publicist. Yorke argued that his defense of labor was based on papal teaching as articulated in the seminal social encyclical *Rerum Novarum*, issued by Pope Leo XIII in 1891, a claim supported by Archbishop Riordan. The strike turned into a bloody and brutal struggle: 5 workers were killed and another 336 injured. In response to declining morale, Yorke rallied the strikers with an electrifying speech at the Metropolitan Temple in San Francisco on August 8, 1901; he affirmed the justice of the workers' claims, asking, "Shall men for whom Christ died to teach them that they were free men, with free men's rights, be crushed beneath the foot of the least bright of all the angels that fell from heaven, Mammon, the spirit of Greed?"[24] Yorke gave a second speech on September 21, where 15,000 pressed in to hear him speak. To those who questioned a priest's involvement in the labor struggle, Yorke later answered, "As a priest my duty is with workingmen, who are struggling for their rights because that is the historical position of the priesthood and because that is the Lord's command."[25]

In the course of the strike, Yorke took direct aim at his fellow Irish Catholic, Mayor Phelan. Elected in large part by the Irish vote, Phelan now gave police protection to strikebreakers. Yorke dubbed Phelan "Jimmy the Rag" because he was "as useful to labor as a dishcloth on top of a pole." More damning, Yorke began referring to the mayor as "Clubber Phelan," because after a meeting with the mayor, Yorke claimed the mayor had told him, "If they [the workers] don't want to get clubbed, let them go back to work."[26] Ultimately, the union survived the strike, and organized labor emerged as a major power in the city. Yorke's prestige in the city soared, particularly among the Irish. "Yorke was undeniably one of their own," wrote historian James P. Walsh, "and they gloried in his attack on employers and religious bigots. They liked his style. He was a fighter and they could vicariously share in his victories over the respectables."[27]

Though Riordan defended Yorke's role in the strike, their relationship remained stormy. Riordan named Yorke pastor of St. Anthony's parish in Oakland in 1903 in an ostensible promotion, but many San Francisco priests viewed an appointment across the bay as a form of exile. The previous year Yorke had established his own newspaper, *The Leader*, which gave him a platform to cover his two favorite concerns—labor and the struggle for an Irish free state. The establishment of *The Leader* came in part as a reaction to *The Monitor*'s feeble coverage of the 1901 strike: its militant tone rankled Archbishop Riordan, who lamented in 1906, "I am powerless to stop him. If I did, we would have worse trouble on our hands than McGlynn caused in New York." (Edward McGlynn was a radical New York City priest of the late nineteenth century.) In 1909 a high-ranking Vatican official registered his concern about Yorke's publication. Riordan responded that he had done everything but issue an edict banning his priests from "editing or publishing newspapers and periodicals without the consent of the Ordinary [bishop]. I have been of the opinion that this latter method is the only one that will have any effect and I doubt then it will have the desired effect. . . . I almost despair of having him stopped should he wish to go on with his publication."[28] Riordan succeeded in getting Yorke to step down as editor of *The Leader* in 1909, though he continued to guide the publication.

For the remainder of his career, Yorke distinguished himself as a cofounder of the National Catholic Educational Association; as author of a series of *Textbooks of Religion* that adapted the *Baltimore Catechism* and inserted grade-appropriate biblical and liturgical materials; as an early advocate of liturgical renewal, encouraging congregational singing and developing a children's Mass that included recitation of responses in English (the vernacular); and finally as a major advocate for an Irish free state, raising funds and organizing support for that cause. When Peter Yorke died on Palm Sunday, 1925, the sorrow was deep and widespread in San Francisco. The anniversary of Yorke's death became a major annual celebration for the Irish and San Francisco labor. Labor and state and civic dignitaries gathered for Mass at St. Peter's followed by a procession to Yorke's grave at Holy Cross

Cemetery in Colma. Even Eamon de Valera, president of Ireland, attended on several occasions. An annual highlight was the recitation of the poem "Rest, Warrior Priest," in honor of Yorke: "The priest with the heart of the warrior bold/rest now for the battle is ended."

Modernism

Peter Yorke's nemesis, Archbishop Riordan, occasionally displayed what historian Kevin Starr called "a slightly rebellious streak" of his own.[29] In 1905 Riordan invited a suspected "modernist" theologian, the Irish-born Jesuit George Tyrell (1861–1909), to visit San Francisco. Even after Tyrell was condemned as a heretic by Pope Pius X in 1907 over his alleged willingness to adapt church teaching to the spirit of the age, Riordan sent Tyrell a message via his secretary, Monsignor Charles A. Ramm, that conveyed the breadth of Riordan's vision of church. Ramm wrote to Tyrell of Riordan, "He spoke in a most feeling way of you saying—'there is a place for him and plenty of work for him to do in this great Church of Christ.'"[30]

Archbishop Riordan faced his own modernist crisis at home. In 1907 he campaigned to promote the Reverend Edward J. Hanna (1860–1944), a professor at St. Bernard Seminary in Rochester, New York, as his successor. Accusations by a seminary colleague that Hanna harbored modernist tendencies derailed his campaign. Hanna had written a series of articles for a lively, controversial Catholic intellectual journal, the *New York Review*, on "The Human Knowledge of Christ," that were considered suspect, and so his candidacy was undermined. Riordan remained loyal to Hanna, and five years later succeeded in having Hanna appointed his auxiliary bishop. Riordan received him enthusiastically and without reservation. He wrote to a friend, "It was a great triumph . . . for until now he was under a cloud, and evil minded people were disposed to carp at him because he had been rejected a few years ago but I kept my counsel and remained loyal to him, and at last, for his sake, I brought him through triumphantly."[31] Edward J. Hanna went on to become the most beloved of all the archbishops of San Francisco. In his dealings with Tyrell, Hanna, and even with Peter Yorke, Patrick W. Riordan displayed a breadth of vision for the church that even Yorke might have been surprised to admit.

Los Angeles Ascendant and Mary Julia Workman

By 1900, while San Francisco remained the economic, cultural, and political center of California, Los Angeles was on the rise. Los Angeles had surpassed San Francisco in population and in relative importance by 1920, in part due to the devastating earthquake that destroyed San Francisco in 1906 and in part due to Los Angeles' emergence as the center of the burgeoning movie industry. Los Angeles was named an archdiocese in 1936, making California the only state with two archdioceses. And in 1953, the Archbishop of Los Angeles, James Francis McIntyre (1886–1979) was named cardinal, much to the dismay of Catholic San Franciscans.

In 1901, while Peter Yorke championed labor in San Francisco, Los Angeles found itself in the midst of an ardent Progressive reform movement from which emerged an exceptional Catholic woman, Mary Julia Workman (1871–1964). As historian Michael Engh has pointed out, Workman was a Progressive liberal Catholic woman in a church that was conservative, clerical, male-dominated, and suspicious of Progressive reformers.

Workman was born in 1871 in Los Angeles, the daughter of a Protestant father, who later served a term as mayor of Los Angeles, and an Irish Catholic mother. She was trained in convent schools before entering the State Normal School to become a teacher. Graduating in 1902, Workman served as a public school teacher in inner city Los Angeles from 1901 to 1921. While in college, Workman encountered the settlement house movement popularized and championed by Jane Addams. She began to work at the College Settlement House, where "college trained women used their intelligence and their educational opportunity to aid in the solution of community problems."[32] In 1901, she joined a group of women in founding the Brownson Settlement House in Los Angeles, the first Catholic settlement house established in the West and only the third in the country. Working at the house transformed Workman and brought her into conflict with her church and her age. Brownson House provided typical settlement services to the poor inner-city neighborhood, made up primarily of immigrants, as well as offering religious instruction and sacramental preparation. As the neighborhood changed, the settlement house increasingly served people of color, especially Japanese and Mexican immigrants, even as the national mood grew increasingly anti-immigrant and racist. Discriminatory immigrant restriction legislation was passed by the U.S. Congress in 1924. These currents were reflected locally in an intense animus that was directed against the Japanese and the Mexicans. In the midst of this, Workman and Brownson House welcomed these immigrants, working with them and, at times, defending them from their fellow Catholics.

Like many prominent figures in the settlement house movement, Mary Julia Workman was an advocate of Americanization, by which she meant immigrants should learn English and basic civics and participate in American democracy. She had no use for the crass 100 percent Americanism campaigns that prevailed during and after World War I. Workman placed the burden of Americanization on U.S. citizens. She wrote, "Americanization is pre-eminently dependent upon the exemplification of American ideals by the native born American, and upon the conditions which he creates."[33] Michael Engh summarized her philosophy: "The immigrant would learn to love America from personal contact with fair-minded citizens and 'from the measure of social justice he receives.'"[34] Work for social justice was also integral to evangelization. "When a man or woman is hungry, overworked and exploited, you cannot teach Catechism to him, you must first remedy his condition. When children live eight or nine people in one room, you cannot expect the grace of First Communion to perform a miracle."[35]

In 1917, Los Angeles welcomed a new bishop, John J. Cantwell (1874–1947). Cantwell was a progressive who set about modernizing and centralizing the church bureaucracy to make it more efficient and fiscally responsible, a trend reflected in the larger society as well. He appointed Reverend William Corr (1882–1940), a university-trained social worker, to centralize the diocese's charities into the Associated Catholic Charities (later the Catholic Welfare Bureau). Its formation reflected national trends of organization and efficiency. The founding of the National Conference of Catholic Charities in 1916 promoted just such objectives. Workman balked at the move to professionalize and centralize charities and to incorporate Brownson House into Catholic Charities; it violated her sense of the importance of local control. The settlement's success was based on the intimate contact and collaboration with the poor, a contact she believed was mutually beneficial, benefiting both the settlement worker and the poor. Local control promoted an intimate knowledge of the neighborhood that made for more effective responses. She intuited what in later times would be called "local control" to empower the poor; people should have some say in decisions that affected their life. To Workman, professionalization of social work seemed to make it cold and distant; the poor became "clients" instead of partners.

After repeated clashes with William Corr, she resigned from Brownson House, followed by the other members of her board. The conflict may have involved more than professionalization—beneath the surface lurked gender concerns and issues of authority. While Cantwell and Corr organized a more effective and centralized authority, Workman called for "democratic lay activity,"[36] a feature not highly prized in American Catholicism. Moreover, she suggested gender was an issue. "We pleaded for the development of Catholic women for public service through the bearing of responsibility. We pleaded for liberty under the law. . . . As a consequence of the 'autocratic regime,' our Catholic women are losing interest and going into non-sectarian organizations. In this day of democracy such direction as comes from the 'Bureau' here *kills* or *drives* away the energy needed for our Catholic activities."[37]

After leaving Brownson House, Workman remained active in many charitable and civic affairs and reforms, working with the League of Women Voters, the Municipal League, the League of Nations Association, the Democratic Party, and many other groups, including Catholic organizations; she chaired the newly formed diocesan branch of the National Conference of Catholic Women in 1924, and later worked for the Catholic Association for International Peace. As her biographer Michael Engh concluded, she remained in the "vanguard of social progress to the time of her death" in 1964.[38]

Preconciliar Times

The post–World War II era witnessed a tremendous expansion of parishes in the archdioceses of San Francisco and Los Angeles, particularly in suburban areas. The Archdiocese of San Francisco reaffirmed its traditional support of labor, a support that had been mobilized during the Depression with the creation of a Labor Management School at the University of San Francisco; the founding of a branch of the Association of Catholic Trade Unionists in 1938; and implementation of a seminary curriculum that included courses on the papal social encyclicals. The most innovative movement to emerge in the postwar era grew out of work among the migrant and *bracero* farm workers by a group of priests who came to be known as the "Spanish Mission Band."

The Spanish Mission Band was created in 1950 when four recently ordained priests—Donald McDonnell, Thomas McCullough, John Garcia, and Ralph Duggan (later they were joined by Ronald Burke)—were released from parish ministry to minister to the migrant and *bracero* workers in California's agricultural fields. They were sent to attend to the spiritual needs of the migrants, who, it was feared, were being lost to the Catholic Church. Their primary mission was to say Mass, preach, hear confessions, recite the rosary, and sponsor other devotions for the men and women in the fields. The Band was distinguished by their personal contact with the migrants. As Duggan recalled, their approach was "direct contact with the people: the poor and needy who had little or no association with the regular parish."[39] The close contact spawned exceptional responses. They identified the migrant and bracero as Christ. The often sung "Ballad of Christ the Bracero" affirmed, "I see you O Christ in the face of the *bracero*/ You come Christ Our King disguised as Ricardo."[40] Close contact also exposed the Band to the living conditions of the migrants, and they were shocked by what they discovered. It became clear to them that it was not enough to meet the spiritual needs of the workers, and they turned slowly in the direction of social action.[41]

In 1957, a resolution inspired by the Band following a *bracero* priests' conference in Sacramento captured the transition: "The priest is a man of Christ. . . . He is the agent of God, and his mission is to save men's souls. Yet his very care for souls will sometimes lead him among men whose physical, moral and economic conditions have become not only highly conducive to vice, but also offensive to Christian customs and religious practice."[42] This realization pushed the Band toward labor organizing, the only way they believed they could obtain just wages and better living conditions for the workers. This was a daunting task because, to date, there had never been a successful labor organization among the California farm workers. The Band opposed the *bracero* system, which they believed was destructive to both the migrant laborer and the *bracero*, and inhibited labor organizing. According to historian Gina Marie Pitti, the Band came to realize that "the entire system of agribusiness . . . must be reformed."[43] McDonnell wrote Archbishop John Mitty, "The main effort of the Church should be directed to insisting on the human dignity of the men who labor in the fields of America."[44] McDonnell and McCullough were given permission to "explain the teachings of the Church" on social issues.[45] By 1957, McDonnell and McCullough became actively involved in the labor struggle, going so far as to assist Dolores Huerta (1930–) in writing the constitution of the nascent Agricultural Workers Association (AWA) in 1958.

The Band found themselves in conflict with Catholic growers and conservative clergy who did not think its activities were appropriate for priests. A typical complaint to the Archbishop of San Francisco read, "Father McCullough has been antagonizing the good will of farmers in the county," and, "As a Catholic farmer, I am disturbed by the fact that the Catholic Church is developing a statewide reputation as being anti-farmer."[46] Until 1961, the Band operated freely despite complaints because they had the support of Archbishop John J. Mitty (1884–1961) of San Francisco. In 1961 Mitty died, and the Band was quickly dismantled. Shortly before Mitty's death, McCullough and McDonnell attended a rally in support of striking lettuce workers in El Centro. They had received permission from San Diego bishop Charles Buddy (1887–1966) to offer an invocation, but when a newspaper reported that the priests had led the workers in a rousing chorus of "Glory, Halleluia, the Union Makes Us Strong," Buddy protested that priests should limit their activities to the spiritual, affirming one farmer's complaint, "Keep Catholic priests out of the camps. They are agitators and troublemakers."[47] The division of the Archdiocese of San Francisco in 1962, which created the dioceses of Oakland, Santa Rosa, and Stockton, provided the circumstance of the Band's dismantling; without Mitty to protect them, their adversaries gained the upper hand.

Perhaps the Band's most enduring legacy was their support and encouragement of the early efforts of Cesar Chavez (1927–93) and Dolores Huerta, who in 1962 established the National Farm Workers Association (the forerunner of the United Farm Workers). Chavez recalled of Father McDonnell, "I began to spend more time with Father McDonnell. We had long talks about farm workers. . . . [In his office] he had a picture of a worker's shanty and a picture of a grower's mansion; a picture of a labor camp and a picture of a high priced building in San Francisco owned by the same grower. When things were pointed out to me I began to see."[48] And, "He sat with me past midnight telling me about social justice and the Church's stand on farm labor, and reading from the encyclicals of Pope Leo XIII in which he upheld labor unions."[49] McDonnell's influence on Chavez played an important role for a movement that blossomed in the 1960s, transformed the face of California agriculture, and entered national political consciousness when *la causa* was ardently embraced by Senator Robert F. Kennedy.

Brother Antoninus / William Everson

One of the most intriguing figures in the history of California Catholicism is convert poet William Everson (1912–94), who for a period of eighteen years served as a Dominican brother. Born in Sacramento in 1912, Everson grew up in Selma in the San Joaquin Valley. In 1934, he entered Fresno State College, where he discovered the nature poetry of Californian Robinson Jeffers, inspiring him to become a poet himself. At the onset of World War II he registered as a Conscientious Objector and served at the C.O. Camp in Waldport, Oregon, during the war. After the war, Everson moved to the San Francisco Bay Area, where he became associated with poet and critic Kenneth Rexroth's circle and with what came to be known as the "San Francisco Renaissance" and later as the "Beat" movement. He also became an expert fine arts printer, purchasing his own letterpress.

Everson's conversion to Catholicism began after two failed marriages. In 1948, while attending Midnight Mass on Christmas Eve at St. Mary's Cathedral in San Francisco, he had a mystical experience. As he later recalled the moment, he gazed on the Tabernacle and reflected, "What can you be that I should come here and wait for your word? If the hills and the sky and the stars have not spoken, what hope from you? O lifeless bread housed in the lifeless bronze! If the vast cosmic god hears not, nor cares, why should any man speak to you?" He then had an experience in which he understood the world as sacrament:

> When the fir-smell reached me across the closed interior air of the Cathedral, binding as it did the best of my past and the best of my future, shaping for the first time that synthesis of spirit and sense I had so needed and never found, I was drawn across, and in the smell of the fir saw it for the first time, not merely as an existent thing, but as a *created* thing, witness of the Word, the divine Logos, who made all earth, and me, a soul in His own image, out of very love. And I saw in the fact of Creation the end of Creation; and in the end of Creation saw indeed the unspeakable Lover who draws the loved one out of the web of affliction, remakes him as His own. . . . That was the night I entered into the family and fellowship of Christ—made my assent, such as it was—one more poor wretch, who had nothing to bring but his infirmities.[50]

The following year William Everson was baptized at St. Augustine's Church in Oakland.

Feeling called to deeper prayer, Everson considered monastic life, but did not want to give up his poetry. He worked for fourteen months at the Oakland Catholic Worker House, attracted by the Worker's radical anarchism and appreciation for the arts. While there he followed a rigorous regime of praying the rosary and had another intense mystical experience: "I was seized with a feeling so intense as to exceed anything I had previously experienced. . . . It was as if all the aspects of human love I had ever known, both spiritual and physical, were suddenly brought forward a thousandfold, and thrust against my heart. It was as if His very lips, as if his mouth wonderfully sweet, were pressed to my heart."[51] Again and again Everson returned to these themes in his poetry: the wonder of nature as an encounter with God, the overwhelming love of God for his creation, and the sensuous relationship of God and humanity.

In 1951, Everson entered the Dominican Order in Oakland as a lay brother, taking the name Antoninus. He began a routine of manual labor and prayer and ultimately began writing deeply personal religious poetry. He published three collections of poetry during his time with the Dominicans: *The Crooked Lines of God* (1959), *The Hazards of Holiness* (1962), and *The Rose of Solitude* (1967). Brother Antoninus's poetry was described by U.S. poet laureate Robert Hass as "God-haunted." It reflected the mystical struggles and passions within Antoninus and employed the naturalistic style of his hero, Jeffers. Most objectionable to some Catholics, however, was his poetry's erotic quality; sexual images abounded, causing some to protest its lack of decency. In *Hazards of Holiness* his description of Salome's dance and the story of Judith and Holofernes were seen as far too explicit. For instance, when describing Judith, he wrote, "The light of her loins, the numinous fire/fluxing out of her breasts' slow fall." Other lines were even more explicit.

By the late 1950s, Antoninus's public readings were as important as his writing. In typical Beat style, his readings were more than polite recitals of his poetry; they were cathartic encounters engaging poet and audience. His reading at Dominican College in San Rafael was reported: "The first word echoed from every corner of the room—a word which no one remembered because of the emotion and love from which it sprang. It was a cry in the wilderness . . . a communion with the people sitting before him."[52] Beyond just adapting the Beat style, Antoninus revived his connection with Rexroth and the Beat Movement and was dubbed by *Time* magazine as the "Beat Friar." Of the Beats Everson later reflected, "I was proud to be identified with them, however. I knew it was a revolt needed in American letters."[53] Everson's revolutionary temperament often proved a poor fit for 1950s Catholicism. He once observed, "I believe the Church does not mean for us to be slaves to formulas, not even meaningful formulas."[54] His poetry and stage performances exploded the formulas of acceptable Catholic art. In 1959, the archbishop of San Francisco banned Antoninus from performing public readings in his Dominican robes for fear that he might be mistaken for a priest, though by 1961 he was back performing in full habit.

As the 1960s began, Antoninus's fame grew, and he sought to deepen his commitment to the Dominicans. In 1964, he made first vows to become a First Order Dominican Brother. Ironically, he was simultaneously engaged in a passionate affair with Rose Moreno, a young woman who pushed his poetry forward. Out of this relationship came the highly erotic and mystical *The Rose of Solitude*. He broke off with Moreno in 1965, but shortly thereafter took up with another young woman, Susanna Rickson, for whom he left the order and married. On December 7, 1969, he performed his last reading as Brother Antoninus at the University of California at Davis. At the end of his reading, he took off his Dominican habit and left the stage. When he married, he also left the church, though he wrote Susanna, "I will leave the Order and even the Church to marry you. Not really leave the Church in my heart. Never that. But I would step aside her proscription to marry you."[55] William Everson once again, he lived out the rest of his life as poet-in-residence at the University of California Santa Cruz.

The 1960s

During the 1960s, the dissenting tradition that had existed somewhat on the periphery of Catholic life in California exploded into the religious mainstream. The forces unleashed by the Second Vatican Council (1962–65) coalesced with the extraordinary social turbulence of the 1960s to create a chaotic time where dissent became the norm. The civil rights movement, the antiwar movement, the counterculture, the riots, the assassinations, and much else shattered American society. The church in California was not immune to these forces. A brief listing of some of the major conflicts in the California church during the 1960s reflects the new trends. In 1964, Father William Dubay (1934–) of Los Angeles accused his cardinal, James Francis McIntyre, of forbidding him to preach on civil rights. He called for McIntyre's removal, charging him with "gross malfeasance of office" and "abuse of authority."[56] Shortly thereafter, Monsignor John Coffield (1914–2005) was exiled from the Archdiocese of Los Angeles due to his passionate advocacy of civil rights. In 1965, César Chávez and Dolores Huerta launched a major strike against grape growers that pitted Catholic farmworkers against Catholic growers. Ordinary Catholics across the country rallied to their support. In 1966, Catholics in San Francisco took to the streets to protest the construction of a magnificent new cathedral, arguing that the money would be better spent serving the poor. In 1967, Jesuit Robert Brophy defied his superiors and testified in the famous "Love Book" obscenity trial on behalf of the defendants. In 1969, Chicano Catholics in Los Angeles—acting in solidarity with the San Francisco

Cathedral protests—expressed their objections to the construction of a grand new church, St. Basil's, by disrupting Christmas Eve Midnight Mass. In 1971, the priests of the Archdiocese of San Francisco threatened to go on strike. Throughout this entire period the Catholic laity, clergy, and religious communities of men and women played significant roles in all of the cultural and political protests of the era.

Sister Corita Kent

In one of the most celebrated and publicized confrontations of the 1960s, the Immaculate Heart of Mary Sisters (IHM) clashed with the cardinal archbishop of Los Angeles, James Francis McIntyre, over the renewal of their congregation's constitutions. While the main issues centered on the proper education of teaching sisters and the modification of the habit, the core issue became the cardinal's authority. Lurking not too far beneath the surface was his dis-ease at working with a group of highly educated, articulate, creative women, who tended to be "liberal." Long before the conflict peaked in 1967, McIntyre expressed discomfort with the sisters' liberality, particularly as it was personified in Sister Corita Kent (1918–86).

Frances Elizabeth Kent was born November 20, 1918, in Fort Dodge, Iowa. In 1936, she entered the Sisters of the Immaculate Heart of Mary in Los Angeles, taking the name Sister Mary Corita. She was schooled at the sisters' Immaculate Heart College, where she received her B.A., and in 1951, she received her master's degree in art history from the University of Southern California. She taught art at Immaculate Heart College from 1951 until 1968. In 1951, Corita began making prints and serigraphs, which became her primary means of artistic expression. Her early art treated traditional religious themes in a nontraditional expressionistic manner. She noted, "In the early days, I was trying to make 'religious art' that would be not quite as repulsive as what was around."[57] In another early print, *Benedictio*, she used words in her print, an innovation that was well received and that became a standard part of her serigraphs.

During the 1950s Corita's popularity grew. By the end of the decade she traveled extensively throughout the United States producing shows and giving lectures. In 1958, she and her students produced a banner exhibit for the National Gallery of Art in Washington, D.C. In 1964, she produced a forty-foot mural entitled the "Beatitude Wall" for the Vatican Pavilion at the New York World's Fair, which gained her international fame. The following year she created IBM's Christmas exhibit in New York City entitled, "Peace on Earth, Good Will Towards Men," using large decorated boxes. By the early 1960s Corita was at the forefront of an emergent Catholic Pop Art, using bright colors, simple forms, and simple sayings and openly embracing modern popular culture. She made frequent use of advertising slogans and billboard motifs in her serigraphs, attempting to illustrate the often-hidden beauty of modern culture. As theologian Harvey Cox put it, for Corita, "Art meant transforming even the ugliest parts of the urban environment into testimonies of joy."[58]

Corita expressed her own philosophy of art in this way: "Our time is a time of erasing the lines that divided things neatly. Today we find all the superlatives and the infinite fulfillment man hungers for portrayed not only in fairy stories or poems but also in bill-boards and magazine ads and TV commercials. . . . This sign language is almost infinitely rich. . . . Up and down the highways (good symbols too) we see words like 'Cold, clear, well-water,' 'The best to you each morning,' 'Have a happy day,' 'Sunkist,' 'Del Monte's catsup makes meatballs sing,' that read almost like contemporary translations of the psalms for us to be singing on our way. The game is endless, which makes it a good symbol of eternity which will be a great endless game."[59]

Corita's innovations were not limited to art. In 1964, she transformed Immaculate Heart College's traditional Mary's Day celebration into a vibrant event, which *Newsweek* described as "black robed nuns parading in flowered necklaces, poets declaiming from platforms and painted students dancing in the grass, Mary's Day became a prototype for the hippies' 1967 be-in in San Francisco."[60] These innovations brought her (or at least Immaculate Heart College) into conflict with the archbishop of Los Angeles, as did some of her "religious art," most notably her print that referred to Mary as "the juiciest tomato of them all." As former IHM Superior Anita Caspary observed of Cardinal McIntyre, "Sister Corita's colorful new look of religious art was to him, as well as to some traditional Catholics, sacrilegious."[61]

By the mid-1960s, Corita had developed a friendship with noted activist Father Daniel Berrigan, S.J., who opened Corita up to the struggle for social justice, and her prints took on an increasingly political edge, with some protesting the Vietnam War (such as "Stop the Bombing"), and others in support of the civil rights movement, César Chávez and the UFW, and other causes. Though Corita never engaged in protest marches, Harvey Cox called her an "urban guerilla with a paint brush,"[62] as her art served as her form of protest. In 1968, Corita's intense schedule, combined with the struggles her community was experiencing with local church authorities, deeply affected her. She confided to a friend, "The suffering here is much but it is creative I think," and "This morning my stomach is sick—but that's all this damn mess—reaction at the 'office' to our Chapter." And "Battle needs to be fought if absolute monarchs are to be encouraged to just love instead of squashing—excuse my violence—but it's so hard not to be."[63] In the summer of 1968, Corita departed on a sabbatical to Boston, but it was more than that. She also left the sisterhood and the Catholic Church. Corita remained in Boston, retired from teaching, and devoted herself completely to her art. She retained her religious name, "Corita."

Father Eugene Boyle

Like Corita, Father Eugene Boyle found himself at the center of the tumult of the 1960s. That Boyle became one of the great symbols of protest came as a surprise even to him. Ordained to the priesthood for the Archdiocese of San Francisco in 1946, he served as an assistant pastor at various parishes until 1956, when his gift for preaching earned him an appointment to the Archdiocesan Mission Band. In 1960, Boyle was appointed director of Vallombrosa Retreat Center for Women, where he remained until 1968. In 1958, he began a radio program entitled "Underscore: Catholic Views in Review," advertised as "adult radio voicing the dialogue of religion and modern life." The show treated contemporary church issues and social justice concerns and gave Boyle the reputation for being San Francisco's "leading liberal Catholic intellectual."[64] In 1962, when the infant Catholic Interracial Council (CIC) of San Francisco went looking for a new chaplain, Boyle was the obvious choice.

The CIC became increasingly involved in the black struggle for equal rights. Initially, it focused on education, though it quickly moved to protest. Boyle was reluctant. He observed:

> Though I was becoming intellectually aware and sympathetic to the purposes of the heightening civil rights struggle, I was viscerally repulsed by many of the tactics employed, the street marches, the demonstrations, the sit-ins. . . . Somehow, I was convinced cool-headed reason would prevail; surely knowledge, understanding, rational discourse were sufficient to persuade the people of this freedom loving country to change its laws.[65]

Boyle engaged in his first public protest march in May 1963 to protest the bombing of a Birmingham, Alabama, motel where civil rights leader Dr. Martin Luther King Jr. had been staying. He joined with other black and white leaders for a march around San Francisco City Hall. Boyle later reflected, "I recall distinctly how embarrassed I was feeling doing this, because this was just not the thing we were brought up to do . . . even when you are standing up for people's rights, and for the poor, and for justice . . . there would be a sense that you were not doing the work that you were ordained to do as a priest."[66] By the end of the 1960s Boyle had grown accustomed to this new public style, but Archbishop Joseph T. McGucken had not. He repeatedly admonished Boyle not to neglect "the work of your principal concern."[67]

Boyle was far more at ease speaking and preaching, which he was often called on to do. In September 1963, in his sermon at the City Hall rally to memorialize the children who had died in the bombing of a Birmingham church four months after the motel bombing, Boyle asserted, "The world cannot be saved if the Christian withdraws into an antiseptic island and limits himself to hurling indiscriminate invectives at a world he considers wholly bad and clearly beyond redemption. The Christian must believe the world is capable of regeneration, open to love and grace though wounded. He must leave hate to others who are too weak to love."[68] These themes emerged again and again in Boyle's preaching.

Between 1964 and 1974, Eugene Boyle would vigorously oppose the anti-fair housing initiative (Proposition 14), begin the Archdiocesan Social Justice Committee, march with and assist César Chávez and the United Farmworkers, teach a social action class at the seminary college that produced an application of the national Kerner Report (on urban unrest) to San Francisco and generated a storm of criticism by predicting a race riot in San Francisco, and become pastor of inner city parish Sacred Heart in San Francisco, where he permitted the Black Panthers to open their Breakfast Program for Children in his church hall. In 1969 Archbishop Joseph T. McGucken removed Boyle from his teaching position at St. Patrick's College; his ouster resulted in one of the first due process cases in the history of the Catholic Church in the United States, which led to Boyle's reinstatement. Five years later Boyle ran unsuccessfully as a candidate for the California State Assembly over

McGucken's objections and censure. In 1975, he became chaplain at the Newman Center of Stanford University.

Boyle's vision of church embodied the spirit of Vatican II. "The law of love—here and now—demands that together with the people we work to lay bare the root causes of poverty and degradation . . . we must join with the community's constructive efforts to move established institutions toward a greater measure of justice for all people."[69] The church can no longer "think of its own survival, of its membership statistics, of the grandeur of its brick and mortar, and the prestige of its leaders." Rather, like Christ, the church had to locate itself "at the center of broken reality, in the messy mainstream of man's alienated history."[70]

Archbishop John R. Quinn

The last dissenter is, again, an unlikely one, John R. Quinn (1929–2017), the sixth archbishop of San Francisco. Quinn would bristle at being labeled a dissenter: nothing in his background indicated such a direction, but like others from this exceptional group of Californians, Quinn's fidelity to truth and to his vocation led him at times into conflicts. Born in Riverside in 1929, he studied at the North American College and Gregorian University in Rome and was ordained in 1953. In 1967 he was named auxiliary bishop of San Diego; in 1972 he was named bishop of Oklahoma City and Tulsa, becoming archbishop of Oklahoma City in 1973. In 1977 Quinn came to San Francisco. He served as president of the National Conference of Catholic Bishops from 1977 to 1980, and on two sensitive pontifical commissions in the 1980s—one examining religious life in the United States and one resolving the Archbishop Raymond Hunthausen controversy in Seattle. Such credentials place him in the mainstream of the U.S. church.

Even so, Quinn has stood outside the mainstream on a number of occasions. In 1980, he caused a major controversy at the Synod on the Family in Rome by suggesting the way the church's proscription on artificial contraception was taught needed to be reevaluated. To even suggest that the issue be discussed caused a furor. In 1981, he condemned the nuclear arms race and became one of the outspoken doves during the preparation of the U.S. bishops' pastoral on war and peace. The following year, he sanctioned an archdiocesan committee to examine violence against gays and lesbians. The result was a radical document calling for a change in the church's teaching on homosexuality; rather than condemn the document outright—it had been the result of consultation—he gently distanced himself from the document, then trumped it with a new policy, developed by the Council of Priests and approved by him, that was not only more consistent with traditional church teaching, but heralded new modes of ministry to the gay community.[71] Throughout the 1980s, Quinn was an outspoken critic of United States policy in Central America, calling for an end to military aid. In addition, he expressed support for Latin American refugees, going so far as to endorse the Sanctuary Movement.

After his retirement in 1995, he published the highly controversial book *The Reform of the Papacy: The Costly Call to Christian Unity*, which called for, among other things, an overhaul of the Roman Curia. Though the book's tone is calm and rational, its publication met with significant criticism from conservative Catholics, most of it unwarranted. Quinn's distinctive stances are not radical, but they do put him out of step with contemporary church attitudes. John Quinn has been the most thoughtful of U.S. bishops, never applying rote answers to complex problems, but rather basing his decisions and views on study, reflection, prayer, and consultation. During the 1987 Papal Visit to the United States, Quinn reflected, "We cannot fulfill our task simply by an uncritical application of solutions designed in past ages for problems which have qualitatively changed or which did not exist in the past." Quinn called for dialogue and mediation "to lay new foundations for a critical mediation in a transformed cultural and social context."[72] Quinn's method, if not something new in the U.S. church, is largely something untried.

Conclusion

From José Maria Fernandez to Archbishop John Quinn, the church in California has fashioned a tradition of exceptional men and women who have disrupted the status quo, confronting society and, at times, the church. They have been driven by a vision of a church that values the dignity of each person; of a church that sides with the lowly, the poor, and the outcast. At times they have had to recall the church to its own mission; to call the church to be faithful to the gospel values it proclaims. Though not seeking the role of dissenter or even liking the designation, these men and women have established an important tradition upon which all can draw as we journey through the complexities of the twenty-first century.

Note: I want to thank a variety of scholars who shared their scholarship with me and assisted in the completion of this essay. Special thanks to Michael Engh, S.J., William Issel, Robert Senkewicz, Rose Marie Beebe, Michael Neri, Gina Marie Pitti, and James Fisher.

NOTES

1. Carey McWilliams, *California: The Great Exception* (Berkeley: University of California Press, 1949), 49.

2. Rose Marie Beebe and Robert Senkewicz, "Uncertainty on the Mission Frontier: Missionary Recruitment and Institutional Stability in Alta California in the 1790s," in *Francis in the Americas: Essays on the Franciscan Family in North and South America*, ed. John F. Schwaller (Berkeley: Academy of American Franciscan History, 2005), 295–322.

3. Quoted in Ibid., 314, 316.

4. Lasuen quoted in Francis Guest, *Fermin Francisco de Lasuen: A Biography* (Washington, D.C.: Academy of American Franciscan History, 1973), 214; Zephyrin Engelhardt, *San Francisco or Mission Dolores* (Chicago: Franciscan Herald Press), 129, 216; Maynard Geiger, *Franciscan Missionaries in Hispanic California, 1769–1848* (San Marino, Calif.: Huntington Library, 1969), 84; quoted in Randall Milliken, *A Time of Little Choice: The Disintegration of Tribal Culture in the San Francisco Bay Area, 1769–1810* (Menlo Park, Calif.: Ballena, 1995), 145.

5. Michael Engh, *Frontier Faiths: Church, Temple, and Synagogue in Los Angeles, 1846–1888* (Albuquerque: University of New Mexico Press, 1992), 175.

6. Ibid., 185.

7. Michael Neri, *Hispanic Catholicism in Transitional California: The Life of Jose Gonzalez Rubio* (Berkeley: Academy of American Franciscan History, 1997), 110.

8. Ibid., 90.

9. Quoted in ibid., 85.

10. Quoted in ibid., 98.

11. Quoted in ibid., 111.

12. George H. Phillips, *The Enduring Struggle: Indians in California History* (San Francisco: Boyd and Fraser, 1981), 53. See also Benjamin Madley, *American Genocide: The United States and the California Indian Catastrophe, 1846–1873* (New Haven, Conn.: Yale University Press, 2016).

13. Osuna to Bishop, August 29, 1872. Original in the Archives of the Archdiocese of Los Angeles. Copy in the Archives of the Archdiocese of San Francisco (Hereafter referred to as AASF).

14. Osuna to Alemany, June 17, 1873, AASF.

15. Osuna to Alemany, November 2, 1873, AASF.

16. J. L. Burchard, U.S. Indian Agent, June 15, 1875, AASF.

17. E. B. Bateman, U.S. Commissioner, June 15, 1875, AASF.

18. Osuna to Alemany, April 6, 1874, AASF.

19. Eugene O'Connell, quoted in John T. Dwyer, *Condemned to the Mines: The Life of Eugene O'Connell, 1815–1891* (New York: Vantage, 1976), 151.

20. Peter C. Yorke, quoted in James Gaffey, *Citizen of No Mean City: Archbishop Patrick Riordan of San Francisco* (New York: Consortium, 1976), 155.

21. Ibid., 157.

22. Yorke, quoted in James P. Walsh and Timothy J. O'Keefe, *Legacy of a Native Son: James Duval Phelan and Villa Montalvo* (Villa Montalvo, Calif.: Forbes, 1993), 71.

23. Gaffey, *Citizen of No Mean City*, 174.

24. Quoted in Richard Gribble, *Catholicism and the San Francisco Labor Movement, 1896–1921* (San Francisco: Mellen Research University Press, 1993), 43.

25. Quoted in ibid., 44–45.

26. Walsh and O'Keefe, *Legacy of a Native Son*, 77.

27. Walsh, *Ethnic Militancy: An Irish Catholic Prototype* (San Francisco: R. and E. Research Associates, 1972), 6.

28. Riordan to Falconio, January 20, 1909, AASF.

29. Kevin Starr, "A Bold Experiment: The Creation of the Archdiocese of San Francisco," in *Catholic San Francisco: Sesquicentennial Essays*, ed. Jeffrey M. Burns (Menlo Park, Calif.: Archives of the Archdiocese of San Francisco, 2005), 15.

30. Ramm to Tyrell, July 20, 1909, AASF.

31. Quoted in Richard Gribble, "A Rough Road to San Francisco: The Case of Edward Hanna, 1907–1915" (Santa Barbara: Santa Barbara Mission Archive-Library, 1996), 236; reprint from *Southern California Quarterly*.

32. Quoted in Michael Engh, "Mary Julia Workman: The Catholic Conscience of Los Angeles," *California History* 72 (Spring 1993): 13.

33. Quoted in Engh, "Religion, Immigrants."

34. Quoted in ibid.

35. Quoted in ibid.

36. Quoted in Engh, "Mary Julia Workman," 13.

37. Quoted in ibid., 13–14.

38. Quoted in ibid., 18.

39. John Duggan, "My Mind to Me a Kingdom Is: An Autobiography" (unpublished manuscript, 1984), copy in AASF.

40. Henry Anderson, "Ballad of Christ the Bracero," copies in AASF.

41. See Josephine Kellogg, "Ministry, Hispanics, and Migrants: The San Francisco Mission Band, 1949–1961" (unpublished revision of 1985 master's thesis, Franciscan School of Theology), copy in AASF; Jeffrey M. Burns, "The Mexican Catholic Community in California," in *Mexican Americans and the Catholic Church, 1900–1965*, ed. Jay P. Dolan and Gilbert Hinojosa (Notre Dame: University of Notre Dame Press, 1994); and Gina Marie Pitti, "To 'Hear About God in Spanish': Ethnicity, Church, and Community Activism in the San Francisco Archdiocese's Mexican American Colonias, 1942–1965" (Ph.D. diss., Stanford University, 2003).

42. "Resolution of the First Bracero Priest Conference, February 12, 1957," AASF.

43. Pitti, "To 'Hear About God in Spanish,'" 320.

44. Quoted in ibid., 320; McDonnell to Mitty, August 21, 1956, AASF.

45. Bishop Hugh Donohoe to McDonnell, April 6, 1954, AASF.

46. Quotes from Bracero file, AASF.

47. Quoted in Kellogg, "Ministry," 110.

48. Jacques E. Levy, *Cesar Chavez: Autobiography of La Causa* (New York: W. W. Norton, 1975), 91.

49. Quoted in Joan London and Henry Anderson, *So Shall ye Reap* (New York: Crowell, 1970), 143–44.

50. Brother Antoninus, "Pages from an Unpublished Autobiography," *Ramparts* 1 (September 1962), 61, 64.

51. Quoted in Lee Bartlett, *William Everson: The Life of Brother Antoninus* (New York: New Directions, 1988), 120.

52. Quoted in ibid., 189.

53. Quoted in ibid., 172.

54. Quoted in ibid., 194.

55. Quoted in ibid., 208.

56. See William H. DuBay, *The Priest and the Cardinal: Race and Rebellion in 1960s Los Angeles* (Create Space Independent, 2016).

57. Quoted in transcript of oral history interview by Bernard Galm, *Los Angeles Art Community: Group Portrait: Corita Kent* (not published, UCLA Oral History Project, 1977).

58. Harvey Cox, "Corita Kent: Surviving with Style," *Commonweal*, October 24, 1986, 550.

59. Sister Mary Corita Kent, Harvey Cox, and Samuel Eisenstein, *Sister Corita* (Philadelphia: Pilgrim, 1967), 11–12.

60. Sister Corita, quoted in "The Nun: A Joyous Revolution," *Newsweek*, December 25, 1967, 46.

61. Anita Caspary, *Witness to Integrity: The Crisis of the Immaculate Heart Community of California* (Collegeville, Minn.: Liturgical Press, 2003), 136.

62. Cox, "Corita Kent," 550.

63. Letters from Corita to Father Robert Giguere, July 30, 1967, October 25, 1967, January 18, 1968, AASF.

64. John Delury, personal interview, October 4, 1967; tape of the interview housed in the AASF Oral History Collection.

65. Eugene Boyle, "Social Justice in the Archdiocese of San Francisco, 1962–1972: A Personal Reflection" (unpublished, copy in AASF), talk delivered at the Conference on the History of Bay Area Catholicism, 1991.

66. Boyle interview, July 14, 1987, AASF.

67. Quoted in Boyle, "Social Justice."

68. Boyle, quoted in "Birmingham Memorial," *San Francisco Monitor*, September 27, 1963, 8.

69. Boyle, "Sacred Heart Urban Team and the Western Addition Community: A Theological Reflection," *San Francisco Monitor*, June 5, 1968, 11.

70. Ibid.

71. Jeffrey M. Burns, "Sexuality After the Council: Gay Catholics, Married Clergy, Rights, and Change in San Francisco, 1962–1987," in *Catholics in the Vatican II Era: Local Histories of a Global Event*, ed. Kathleen Cummings, Timothy Matovina, and Robert Orsi (Cambridge: Cambridge University Press, 2017).

72. Archbishop John R. Quinn, quoted in "Dissenters Not Necessarily 'Bad Catholics,' Says Archbishop Quinn," *San Francisco Catholic*, October 1987, 4.

Strangers in Our Midst: Catholics in Rural America

Jeffrey Marlett

Do any American Catholics like country music? Have singers like Merle Haggard, Shania Twain, or Dierks Bentley attracted Catholic listeners? Do any Catholics appreciate environmental activists, Wendell Berry, or Pope Francis's *Laudato Si*? Why should it matter? Answering those questions goes a long way toward understanding America's polyvalent rural Catholic heritage. Urban life pervades most historical studies of U.S. Catholicism. The well-established, but mostly overlooked, traditions rural Catholics have created receive far less attention. Yet Roman Catholicism has enjoyed a long presence in America's rural environs: from Maine to California, northern Michigan to Louisiana's Acadiana parishes, Catholics helped populate rural America. While their numbers may never have been large, Catholics have lived and worked and worshipped in rural areas since colonial times.

Rural Catholicism posed challenges—pastoral, spiritual, environmental, and social— for a church self-identified with the cities where a largely immigrant, second and sometimes third-generation membership staked a most conspicuous claim. Rural America, once idealized as the foundation for a virtuous Protestant-American republic, saw that Jeffersonian inheritance threatened by economic and political setbacks. These deprivations restricted opportunity and gave rise to popular stereotypes of rural life as violent, crude, culturally impoverished, and spiritually deadening. While struggling with these misperceptions, rural Catholics also discovered in most times and places that their religious convictions set them apart from their neighbors.

An organized Catholic effort to address rural and agricultural issues did not unfold until the 1920s. During that decade the Catholic "rural life movement" emerged as church leaders discerned that urban centers were not the only American locales in need of context-specific ministries. The Catholic rural life movement enjoyed its greatest popularity during the 1930s and 1940s, when it promoted an agrarian worldview blending Catholic theology with an ecological consciousness. A fertile brand of conversation soon engaged some of the nation's most creative proponents of Catholic social action, including Dorothy Day and Peter Maurin of the *Catholic Worker* (which promoted its own romantic agrarian vision), Rev. Virgil Michel, O.S.B., of the Liturgical Movement, the women of the Grail in Loveland, Ohio, and Rev. John La Farge, S.J., founder of the Catholic Interracial Council. Significantly, Catholic rural life leaders also worked enthusiastically with Protestant and Jewish agrarian organizations.[1]

Decades before the 1960s-era discovery of environmentalism, Catholic agrarians bemoaned the ways in which "Nature's nation" misused and abused the natural world. They warned prophetically of the time when America's industrialized modern life would simply exhaust itself, leaving only the scarred environment and a populace ignorant of sustaining itself "on the land." Catholic agrarians believed a new society might emerge from the old: a new order both "green" and spiritually attuned to Roman Catholicism. Peter Maurin wrote in the *Catholic Worker* of the "Green Revolution" and of "building a new society within the shell of the old." Other Catholic agrarians decried urbanization and ecological degradation and extolled the nation's tradition of small-scale family farms. Rural America, it was believed, harbored the only sites where work, earth, and spirituality united in a truly organic American dream.

Beyond the visions of Catholic agrarian theorists, the history of Catholics in the rural United States engages three narrative strands. The role of the institutional church—its schools, churches, monasteries, and hospitals—and its clergy represent perhaps the most visible strand. Then there is the story of rural Catholic people themselves: where they came from, what they did (not all worked in agriculture!), and how their religious faith separated them from their non-Catholic rural neighbors. An often-tense relationship between the city and the country constitutes the third strand; stereotypes aside, rural America has never existed in isolation from American cities. This dynamic was especially evident in the history of rural Catholics. That history generated some of its own quintessentially "American" images: family farms, wholesome church life, the simplicity and honesty of small town life; but these images were inevitably read as anomalous when Catholics staked their proprietary claims.[2]

Building the Catholic Presence in Rural America

Spain, England, and France established three separate paths of Catholic colonization in the New World. The Spanish experience imparted the greatest influence on rural Catholic history: by 1680 a rural/urban division was already present in New Spain. Larger settlements had turned into cities, supplying smaller communities in outlying areas with protection, materials, and clergy. The Spanish crown dealt enterprising Spanish laymen large tracts of land to farm. In exchange, the owners agreed to provide religious instruction for the native populations relocated to provide labor. This New World recreation of the feudal system was called the *encomienda*. The system required comparatively few Catholics and enabled the Spanish to plant a Catholic presence throughout western North America. From the Pacific coast east to the Mississippi River and from the Rio Grande to Great Bend, Kansas (the northernmost bend in the Arkansas River), Spanish Catholicism demonstrated what could be achieved on a shoestring missionary budget.

The *encomienda* system also encountered resistance. In 1680 the Pueblo in New Mexico revolted, taking control of Santa Fe until 1692. The Pueblo rebellion foreshadowed the decline of Spanish American plantations. In the eighteenth century, the plantation owners regularly provided insufficient funds to the missions, despite their pledges to the Spanish crown. Vestiges of the *encomienda* survived long past the departure of their Spanish patrons. From Santa Monica and San Luis Obispo in California through Santa Fe, New Mexico, and over through east Texas, the Spanish footprint remains quite clear on a road atlas. Centuries later, Mexico's Cristero Revolt or *La Cristiada* (1926–29) demonstrated the resilience of the original Spanish presence. The *encomiendas* were long gone, but allegiance to the far-flung Catholic presence had endured. Mexican Catholics rose to defend parishes and church landholdings when threatened by troops led by revolutionary dictator Plutarco Calles.[3]

The French and English enjoyed their own successes, but on smaller scales. English Catholic settlement was confined to the Maryland colony. Even that small endeavor dwindled after the Glorious Revolution of 1688. Anglican authorities curtailed all Catholic missionary efforts, even among African slaves. French settlement was much more expansive. It began in Quebec in 1612, where Samuel de Champlain's exploration of the St. Lawrence River and the eastern Great Lakes created an enormous territory. Marquette and Joliet's travels further west and down the Mississippi established a French crescent territory around the English colonies. French-speaking Catholicism stood well established in New Orleans to the South and Montreal and Quebec in the Northeast. In between, several French colonial villages based on agriculture emerged. These included St. Genevieve, Missouri (1735), Vincennes, Indiana (1732), and Fort Duquesne (1754; later Pittsburgh, Pennsylvania). Prior to colonization, this vast territory had been traversed by French Jesuit missionaries seeking to convert Native Americans. Isaac Jogues, murdered by the Iroquois near Fonda, New York, in 1644, was one of several French Jesuits martyred during these endeavors. Jogues and his colleagues sought more converts like Kateri Tekakwitha ("the Lily of the Mohawk") but were not able to effect large-scale changes to native agriculture practices as the Spanish did further west. The English victory in the French and Indian War (1763) marked the end of French-Catholic rural settlements in the future United States. In Quebec, though, rural Catholicism survived and became a potent cultural and political force until the late 1960s.

In the United States, the rural Catholic population grew rapidly after mass migrations from Europe after 1820. European immigration increased significantly with each decade; Irish and German Catholics and then later impoverished immigrants from Eastern and Southern Europe all swelled the populations of northeastern and midwestern cities. This emergence of the immigrant Catholic underclass tells a familiar story. Less well known are the implications for rural America. On the surface, burgeoning urban Catholic centers fueled anti-Catholic nativism. Renowned Presbyterian minister and Lane Seminary president Lyman Beecher led popular resistance to Catholic expansion in both city and country. "American travelers at Rome and Vienna assure us," wrote Beecher in *Plea for the West* (1834), a series of sermons the Cincinnati-based preacher delivered on a return visit to Massachusetts, "that in the upper circles the enterprise of reducing our western states to spiritual subserviency to the see of Rome is a subject of avowed expectation, and high hope, and sanguine confidence." Anti-Catholic rhetoric soon led to violence. Beecher's sermons contributed to the 1834 burning of the Ursuline convent by a Boston mob in nearby Charlestown. When nativists marched to intimidate Catholics, in some cities, such as Philadelphia and St. Louis, the immigrants fought back.

Some Catholics were motivated by such outbursts to seek a better fate beyond the city limits. Rural America's agricultural bounty and open space literally promised greener pastures. Catholics thus joined the nation's great westward expansion. Amid mixed and peripatetic company Catholics helped establish towns and businesses and built parishes across the interior of the United States in the middle decades of the nineteenth century. In some locations Catholic settlers were pioneers, the first Americans to settle permanently in an area. In still others, they joined established rural communities. Frontier expansion complemented the West's resident population—some of whom were descended from Spanish colonizers or the colonized.

Catholics' role in expanding the nation's western frontier was fostered in part by colonization projects supervised by Catholic clergy. During the nineteenth century, according to one historian, it seemed as if "almost every bishop in the American hierarchy . . . had a pet colonization scheme." From 1827 to 1836, Boston bishop Benedict J. Fenwick counseled Irish immigrants in Maine to pursue agriculture as the best vehicle to prosperity. A product of rural Catholic Maryland, Fenwick purchased land in Maine for an Irish Catholic colony in 1834. Christened "Benedicta" by Fenwick, it came to play an important role in establishing potatoes as northern Maine's cash crop. In the mid-1830s, Bishop Mathias Loras established Dubuque, Iowa, as a new agricultural center for Catholic immigrants struggling in eastern cities. Father Ambrose Oschwald established St. Nazianz, Wisconsin, in 1854, as a quasi-monastic community. Father Jeremiah Trecy founded St. John's City, Nebraska, in 1857. Occupying a prominent location atop a Missouri River bluff, the community erected an enormous crucifix to signal home for later arrivals. Around the same time but further south, Father Joseph Hogan established a small rural Catholic community between the Eleven Point and Current rivers in the Missouri Ozarks. The town "Wilderness" provided refuge from the urban drudgery of St. Louis. Apparently, Hogan also envisioned the tiny community as a matchmaking enterprise. He specifically sought single Catholics as settlers in hopes that they would meet, marry, and remain in Wilderness to raise large Catholic families.[4]

Immigrant aid societies proliferated in the nineteenth century as important sources of direction and assistance rooted in the newcomers' native lands (and, later, northeastern

American cities). While many served primarily as benevolent societies, some directed funding streams toward efforts at rural colonization. In 1822 French Catholics established the Society for the Propagation of the Faith at the urging of Bishop William DuBourg of St. Louis and New Orleans, who viewed his dioceses as missionary territory in dire need of help from European philanthropic sources. *Propaganda Fide* became a leading source of personnel and funding for mission operations within the nation's interior. Other aid societies were largely based on ethnic identity. The Leopoldine Missionary Society (*Leopoldinen-Stiftung*), founded in Vienna in 1829, sought two missionary goals. First, the conversion of the Ojibway Indians of the Upper Great Lakes resembled the French *Propaganda Fide* endeavor. Second, honoring the legacy of Maria Leopoldina (1797–1826), the young Austrian archduchess and wife of Brazilian emperor Pedro I, the Leopoldine Society also assisted Slovenian and German Catholics to settle in the same areas. One priest in particular, Father Francis Pierz, worked tirelessly to create rural ethnic enclaves. His signature project made Stearns County, Minnesota, "probably the most rural Catholic county in the United States." The *Ludwig Missionverein* (Louis Mission Society) of Munich likewise served German Catholics. In 1857 the Swiss Colonization Society of Cincinnati purchased land in Indiana for a colony on the Ohio River named "Tell City" (after the Swiss hero William Tell). Numerous Irish and Irish American Catholics endorsed similar efforts, first as individuals, then after 1856 under the auspices of the Irish Immigrant Aid Society, convened in Buffalo, New York, by layman Thomas D'Arcy McGhee. The Polish Roman Catholic Union emerged in 1873 and included rural colonization along with its insurance and philanthropic concerns.[5]

Individual recruiters also drew Catholic immigrants to rural settlements. James La Ray and his son Vincent established eleven Catholic colonies in northern New York between 1800 and 1830. The timber industry augmented farming and drew immigrants from France, Ireland, and Germany. Further west, in 1844, Alexander Faribault, a second-generation fur trader, organized a French Canadian community in Rice County, Minnesota. In 1842 Catholics from Baltimore and Philadelphia founded the German Catholic Brotherhood to escape those cities' anti-Catholic nativism. Later that year they purchased thirty-five thousand acres in northwestern Pennsylvania to establish a colony; one hundred families hacked out of the woods the future St. Marys, Pennsylvania.[6]

Midwestern states also witnessed the emergence of immigrant communities created intentionally to preserve religious and ethnic identity through agriculture and relative isolation. In 1835, the German Catholic Colonization Association of Philadelphia established the town of Hermann along the Missouri River west of St. Louis. Frustrated with the same East Coast nativism that sparked St. Marys, colonizers defiantly arranged Hermann's main street ten feet wider than Philadelphia's. The town became so successful in preserving German cultural practices that enclaves of German Lutherans and Reformed immigrants also moved there. The area became known as "the Missouri Rhineland," with Hermann as its capital. One observer called the town "New Germania" for the small Missouri town's reproduction of the homeland's religious dynamic.[7] Prior to the Civil War, German immigrants populated both cities and farming regions in the mid-Atlantic and midwestern states.

After the war, the German Catholic population was centered in the nation's midsection, where the mythic "German triangle" emerged in the area between St. Louis, Cincinnati, and Milwaukee. The region took on a decidedly Teutonic flavor. Economics, politics, and religion combined to make emigration to the rural Midwest attractive for German Catholics. Above all, the area offered German Catholics an uncontested chance to practice their faith. Several events in German principalities prompted corresponding waves of German immigration, especially among Catholics, to the United States. The 1848 revolutions across Europe spurred the already-strong process. Later in the 1870s, Bismarck's *Kulturkampf* ("Culture War") against German Catholicism's alleged political power spurred additional immigration.

The rural Midwest became the most popular location for these immigrants because the region offered an unfettered chance to pursue Old World farming, despite some obvious climate and geological differences. Several areas within the Midwest took on a specifically German Catholic rural identity. The American interior offered land and room enough for these Germans to build communities centered on an agricultural vocation, ethnic identity, and religious practice. Teutopolis, Illinois, a pan-Germanic community established in 1839, offered Catholic immigrants to Cincinnati an opportunity to escape from the city. Oldenburg, Ferdinand, Fulda, and Jasper all were German Catholic colonies in southern Indiana. Father Joseph Kundek, who organized Ferdinand, grasped how rural America insured religious freedom: "Many a German Catholic is agreeably surprised to find he can travel four, five, or even ten miles in a wooded region settled by Catholic families and discuss matters pertaining to religion without fear and without contradiction. Here a German is really independent and respected."[8]

While priests were often the most successful recruiters for immigrant colonization schemes, their presence in the colony itself was far from guaranteed. Oldenburg in eastern Indiana did not enjoy a resident priest; Ferdinand further west did. Joseph Kundek served as the town's priest, community planner, exemplary farmer, and best recruiter among German Catholics living in eastern states or abroad. Other locations were not so blessed. Only a few miles away in Jasper, a German Catholic community began building a chapel while waiting for a German-speaking priest to serve them. Catholics in New Vienna, Iowa, waited for three years after completing their building before a priest arrived in 1851. Belgian priest Ferdinand Helias, S.J., moved to Westphalia, Missouri, as the town's first resident priest, and subsequently traveled throughout the Missouri River Valley serving other parishes as well. Looking much like the Methodist circuit rider, Helias rode from town to town, administering the sacraments as he went. Much further north, Father Edward Jacker traveled among the mining towns of Michigan's Upper Peninsula until a parish could be built in Calumet.[9]

By 1900 rural America featured many of the same denominational fault lines that divided the nation's cities. Historian David Bovee calculated that the Catholic population in some regions was in fact predominantly rural. One such area was the Upper Midwest: Iowa, Wisconsin, Minnesota, North Dakota, and South Dakota. The other was the Southwest: Arizona, New Mexico, Louisiana, and Texas. Louisiana contained perhaps the largest rural Catholic population in the country. If considered nationally, a "rural Catholic minority" certainly existed. In certain locations, though, a rural Catholic *majority* prevailed. Catholics maintained their influence in pockets of the rural United States despite sporadic eruptions of nativism. Rural Catholics were certainly no less "Catholic," if by that term one means religiously observant. From another perspective, they could have been perceived as more "American" since they engaged in the occupation that the nation's forefathers had ordained as the "natural" national livelihood. All rural Catholics, living on farms or small towns, could identify with this national character they shared with the rest of rural Americans. In some situations, ethnic Catholics were no different than ethnic Protestant immigrants or separatist Holiness churches. The farming life cycle and small-town ways formed a common core that Catholics shared with their neighbors.[10]

While Catholics were not the most populous faith community in the rural Midwest, the church's presence was far from insignificant. Some areas—such as southern and central Minnesota—were primarily ethnic Catholic in character. Outside St. Cloud, Minnesota, Stearns County's population was almost entirely rural Catholic. This included the towns of Collegeville and St. Joseph, where Saint John's College (for men) and the College of Saint Benedict (for women), the epicenter of Virgil Michel's liturgical work, were located. In other areas of the Midwest, Catholics were to some degree "separate" from people of the same ethnic group, such as German Catholics and Lutherans in the Missouri Ozarks. Rural Catholics, ethnic or not, were as much a part of the agrarian American landscape as its iconic Protestant church scenes. Rural Catholics endured and overcame blizzards, prairie fires, and the arduous labor involved with establishing farms and rural communities. The twentieth-century Catholic rural life movement originated with the premise that the rural church was "weak," a presumption of spiritual and social destitution that discounted the varieties of vital rural Catholic territories throughout the United States.

Shaping and Organizing the Rural Catholic Identity in the United States

Addressing the inaugural National Catholic Rural Life Conference (NCRLC) convention in 1923, Bishop Vincent Werhle of Bismarck, North Dakota, remarked that "there is something sacramental about rural life." An oft-repeated mantra of the Catholic rural life movement—"Christ to the Country, the Country to Christ"—expressed a similar view. The two phrases captured the conference's imaginative theological appreciation of American Catholic rural life. Agriculture was not merely an occupation, but an analogy for the soul's relationship with the divine life. Farmers worked with God's natural gifts to produce food, just as Christians cooperated with God's grace to hasten God's kingdom. Like the church's seven sacraments, farming conveyed grace in a form inaccessible elsewhere.[11]

The crowning achievement of the Catholic rural life movement was embodied in the National Catholic Rural Life Conference. This organization, which is headquartered in Des Moines, Iowa, and remains active in farming and environmental causes, emerged through the singular efforts of one priest, Edwin V. O'Hara.[12] Born in 1881, O'Hara grew up in Lanesboro, Minnesota, and graduated from St. Thomas College and Seminary in St. Paul. He quickly moved onto graduate studies in sociology at the Catholic University of America. There he studied under Monsignor John A. Ryan, who later became the best-known Catholic supporter of Franklin D. Roosevelt's New Deal. From Ryan, a fellow Catholic from rural Minnesota, O'Hara gained an appreciation for the programs of Catholic Action and the possibilities of applying Catholic social thought to rural issues. After graduation, O'Hara accepted an assignment in Oregon, a state still classified entirely as "mission territory." He soon encountered the Ku Klux Klan's concerted efforts to marginalize Catholic life in the state. Oregon's Klan was the most active in the West, achieving more than Klans in traditional southern states. The Klan had successfully elected one of its candidates as governor, and in 1916 Oregon voters supported a Klan referendum requiring public school attendance for all children younger than sixteen. The measure clearly aimed at limiting, and hopefully eradicating, Catholic parochial education. Serving as both parish priest and chaplain for the Newman Club at Oregon State University, O'Hara quickly organized the Catholic opposition. In 1925 the U.S. Supreme Court struck down the Oregon law. Oregon's Catholics also faced internal crises. O'Hara became dismayed at how poorly Oregon Catholics exhibited their own faith and realized that the situation required a new rural remedy.

O'Hara's assessment was not elitist. He knew very well that "rural" did not necessarily reflect negatively on "Catholic." His own life experience disproved the assumption, already becoming commonplace among Catholic leaders, that rural America and Catholic were mutually exclusive. Instead, following a hunch, O'Hara collected sociological data indicating that lack of resources, and specifically a shortage of rural ministries, largely created the rural Catholic spiritual vacuum. O'Hara created, distributed, and collected the survey data—evidence of his previous sociological training—with his own funds. He spent the next decade spreading news of the survey's results. He discovered that rural Protestants, and even a small group of rural Jews, faced similar financial and staffing crises. O'Hara was aware of the Catholic Church Extension Society, a rural missionary enterprise founded by Monsignor Francis Kelley in 1905. However, O'Hara also realized that Extension sought only to address rural shortcomings through fund-raising. His own sociological data indicated that only a holistic solution would solve rural America's, and thus rural Catholicism's, myriad problems.

O'Hara also uncovered some disconcerting demographic evidence. The 1910 census indicated that for the first time the nation's population lived primarily in urban, not rural areas. Further, Catholic birth rates lagged behind the national and Protestant averages. O'Hara calculated that the urban Catholic population would dwindle precipitously. Building up the rural Catholic population seemed to be the only answer. He feared, however, that rural Catholics did not possess nearly the same sort of Catholic identity as their urban coreligionists. O'Hara realized that a Catholic organization was needed that would address both problems: increasing the number of rural Catholics and improving the faith of those who lived there. Unnerved by the presumably declining urban birth rate and thus that of the church, O'Hara and his allies insisted that rural Catholics provided the church's future membership. As he bluntly asserted, "Cities are relatively sterile, and country relatively fertile."[13]

The Rural Life Bureau (RLB) was his first organizational endeavor. O'Hara himself ran the operation from his rectory in Corvallis, Oregon. The RLB was a branch of the National Catholic Welfare Conference's Social Action Committee. O'Hara appreciated the legitimacy lent by the bishops' offices in Washington, D.C., but he desired greater independence. In the Country Life Movement, a loose affiliation of rural sociologists, reformers, and Protestant clergy, O'Hara saw the blueprint for a new start. Organized by President Theodore Roosevelt in 1909, the Country Life Movement sought to improve and refine rural America to better serve the needs of the nation's burgeoning cities. A central focus highlighted the apparent uselessness of so many rural churches. Country Life clergy sought to consolidate rural Christians into well-ordered congregations under the aegis of mainstream Protestant denominations (Methodists, Baptists, Presbyterians, Lutherans, etc.). In 1919 the American Country Life Association (ACLA) emerged from the various Country Life activities to provide oversight and Protestant-influenced spiritual direction. O'Hara signed on in 1920, becoming the only Catholic member of the ACLA. For the 1923 ACLA convention in St. Louis, O'Hara organized a parallel convention signaling the inaugural meeting of the National Catholic Rural Life Conference (NCRLC). O'Hara and the ACLA leaders arranged the event so Catholic and Protestant members could attend their counterpart's meetings. Thenceforth the two religious agrarian groups scheduled their annual meetings to coincide. By 1941, the NCRLC drew larger numbers than the ACLA.[14]

A large part of the NCRLC's appeal—to members and supporters alike—lay in its midwestern location. That region was quickly supplanting the South as the quintessential site of "rural America" and afforded opportunities for outreach to contiguous regions. The 1935 convention was held in Rochester, New York; two years later the NCRLC convened its annual meeting in Richmond, Virginia. The conference completed its national expansion two years later when it convened in Spokane, Washington. Nevertheless, the Midwest remained central to the conference. It was headquartered first in Saint Paul, Minnesota, prior to moving its central office to Des Moines, Iowa, in 1940. During World War II, national conventions were confined to Missouri, Illinois, Ohio, Iowa, and Wisconsin, states that held a majority of the conference's clerical and lay members. The midwestern character was expressed quite clearly in 1946 when *Land and Home* announced the upcoming "Victory" convention. The headline read, "All Roads Lead to Green Bay." An accompanying map of the Upper Midwest, with Green Bay prominently located, listed such cities as Kansas City, St. Louis, Detroit, Omaha, and Toledo. Chicago shared Illinois with Cairo. Although the map included the New England and mid-Atlantic regions, where most of the nation's Catholics lived, the easternmost city marked was Buffalo, New York. The conventions with the largest attendance were held in St. Cloud, Minnesota, in 1940, and La Crosse, Wisconsin, in 1948.[15]

Populated with Catholic clergy and leading Catholic lay leaders like the Central Verein's Frederick Kenkel, the new organization stood apart from, but still worked with, the

Rural Life Bureau. O'Hara eventually transferred his RLB duties to the Benedictine monsignor Edgar Schmiedeler (later known for his work opposing artificial contraception). The NCRLC leadership originally consisted of an annually elected president, but by 1940 an executive secretary had taken over daily affairs and general direction. In 1930, O'Hara was appointed bishop of Great Falls, Montana, but remained the conference's inspirational leader. In 1939 O'Hara became bishop of Kansas City, Missouri. This relocation to his native Midwest only solidified O'Hara's identification with the Catholic rural life movement. In his place, several Catholic agrarian leaders took turns leading the NCRLC. William H. Bishop, later founder of the Glenmary Home Missioners, served as NCRLC president from 1928 to 1934. Bishop focused specifically on the "back to the land" movement and, not surprisingly, missionary work among non-Catholic rural Americans. After O'Hara, though, the most prominent Catholic rural life leader was Monsignor Luigi Ligutti. Born in Italy in 1895, Ligutti was ordained in the United States and immediately began work in rural Iowa. He established the nationally recognized Granger Homesteads in 1933. His infectious enthusiasm, communication skills, and homespun rural wit invigorated the conference. Ligutti served as executive secretary from 1941 to 1960, when he became the Vatican's observer to the World Health Organization. Following Ligutti's departure, the NCRLC continued to extol rural Catholic perspectives, especially regarding state and federal agricultural policies. The specifically Catholic agrarian perspective, however, diminished by the 1960s.[16]

Environmental and Spiritual Currents in the Catholic Rural Life Movement

Catholic agrarianism's theological worldview expressed a uniquely American and Catholic appreciation of the natural world. It thus represented the first incarnation of American Catholic environmentalism. Catholic rural-lifers blended aspects of U.S. culture with the Catholic Revival motifs associated with neo-Scholastic philosophy in the 1930s and 1940s, particularly the focus on "restoring all things in Christ." The U.S. farmer embodied everything "American," while simultaneously symbolizing the dawn of a new order built on Catholic principles. God's gift of the land to the farmer supplied the basis for both claims. While American agribusiness became increasingly oriented toward large-scale farming, Catholic agrarians posited "bio-dynamic farming" as the best means by which to realize the divine fertility of God's creation. They also envisioned rural Catholics as modeling fertility—both spiritual and biological—in their own family farm operations. Rural America had the space to accommodate large Catholic families, thus lending some ecological support for natural family planning. By tending the soil correctly and praying correctly, under the tutelage of NCRLC, rural Catholics would constitute a uniquely well-grounded and spiritually balanced subculture. By working for the redemption of both the land and the soul, the Catholic rural life movement brought the church further into the mainstream of American life. It countered the persistent image that American Catholicism was essentially an urban phenomenon. At times the Catholic agrarian worldview corresponded neatly with that of the laity in general. When it could not, the laity reverted to their own designs, generating an innovative body of American Catholic thought and practice.

The Catholic Revival turned American Catholics toward the social criticism of the English decentralists and their American followers. American decentralist intellectuals, such as Herbert Agar, Ralph Borsodi, and the "Vanderbilt Agrarians," followed Catholic intellectuals Hilaire Belloc and G. K. Chesterton in their condemnation of mass production and intrusive bureaucracies.[17] Published in 1930 by "Twelve Southerners," *I'll Take My Stand* lauded the Southern traditions of agriculture and religion as solutions to the crises of American life. One of the twelve, Allen Tate, helped start *Free America* as a journal of decentralist thought and homesteading activities. (Tate's fascination with religion and rural life later led him to convert to Catholicism.) Borsodi's *This Ugly Civilization* blamed urban pollution and human corruption on the mass production of the factory. Another Borsodi book, *Flight from the City*, recommended an escape from urban problems through "domestic production" on the land. Not surprisingly, Catholic agrarians were enthusiastic. In 1941, both the *Catholic Rural Life Bulletin* and the *Catholic Woman's World* hailed Borsodi for his "School of Living" in Suffern, New York. Instead of separating the church from the world, like the urban "Catholic ghetto" areas of the East did, the predominantly midwestern Catholic rural life movement engaged other agrarians in a creative yet critical embrace of American culture.[18]

The NCRLC's environmental message clearly reflected this midwestern orientation. Large-scale farming received univocal condemnation and was blamed for such environmental calamities as the 1930s Dust Bowl. When St. Louis' auxiliary bishop Christian Winkelmann was named bishop of Wichita, the *Catholic Rural Life Bulletin* commented:

> Anyone conversant with the agricultural tragedy of the last thirty years will realize all too
> well the tremendous task which will be his. The once rich, fruitful land of Kansas lies
> near to exhaustion. It has taken a merciless beating. In some places there isn't even a spark
> of life left. In others, synthetic, inorganic fertilization, get-rich-quick, one-cropping,
> large-scale, mechanized land-bleeding, not to mention absentee ownership, long ago
> ridiculed to oblivion any meager attempts to bring about a true ruralism.

"A true ruralism" meant one not invaded by "urban" forms of life and that included farming methods. Factory farming had stripped God's creation of all fertility, and now the United States faced a Dust Bowl in its midsection. The subsequent economic and spiritual rural poverty only further resembled the city's captivity. "With the general mechanization of life all chance of genuine freedom is suffering. Men lack economic freedom, and in that fix to speak of their being politically free is to use ideal if not ironic words."[19]

Catholic anti-urbanism encompassed both people and the land itself. Following O'Hara's proposal, if cities were sterile and corrupt, rural areas were inherently fertile, physically as well as spiritually. The land possessed salvific qualities for both the natural life and the supernatural. It offered a sacramental relationship with God. With the acknowledgment that the earth possessed its own spiritual, as well as physical, value came the criticisms of one-crop farming. The church thus came to play an important role in demanding protection for the environment. Urban Baer, a priest from Wisconsin, insisted that Aquinas established "the principle that all creatures and consequently all earthly goods, can, of their very nature belong to God alone." Only Catholic farmers with the correct spiritual vision could truly honor God's creation. The embrace of such wisdom, it was argued, might have prevented the Dust Bowl:

> Considering land as a sacred trust, [the farmer] would not have permitted speculators to make the farmer a chore boy for unhealthy individualism. It must emphasize and re-emphasize that the very ground the farmer breaks, the very earth he plows, ultimately belongs to God; that the farmer is only the trustee, the guardian thereof, and must one day render an account of his stewardship to the Divine Harvester.[20]

This success could be replicated anywhere, since both land and human beings possessed natural capabilities when it came to farming.[21] The unreflective productivity of nature, and thus farming, was simply assumed by Catholic agrarians. If one lived correctly on the land, it would provide. "LIVE IN THE COUNTRY—WORK IN THE CITY," proclaimed one NCRLC handout. "Holy Mother Church shows the way to a holier, richer life on the land for farm, small-town, and suburban families through the NCRLC."[22] In 1940, Ligutti and John C. Rawe, S.J., published *Rural Roads to Security: America's Third Struggle for Freedom*. The subtitle evoked two struggles, the Revolutionary War (for democracy) and the Civil War (for freedom for all Americans), to situate the third: the struggle against the dehumanizing and environmentally harmful aspects of urban living. A stinging decentralist indictment of modern industrial life, *Rural Roads to Security* offered an accurate expression of the Catholic agrarian theological appreciation of nature. The fertility and stability of "life on the land" stood as the nation's line of defense against the encroachment of a harmful, technocratic culture. Achieving the vision of *Rural Roads*, though, required work informed by Catholic agrarian theology, so that the land's fertility and stability, as well as that of believing Christians, might be preserved.[23]

Catholic agrarians argued that farm work uniquely augmented Christian faith and practice. "On the land, also, one is very near to our Lord in His earthly life—the toil in the heat of the day, the weariness, the sitting down to rest. Try carrying heavy oak fence posts on your shoulder for an hour, and then see, the next time you say your rosary, how much more the Carrying of the Cross means to you than it ever did before."[24] In other words, simple manual labor received renewed appreciation. All the work had a point, however, or in Scholastic language, a goal or "telos." Because they valued the land and the created order as a God-given gift, Catholic agrarians insisted that correct farming methods must be used. Consequently, the Catholic rural life movement contributed the first Catholic voice to the budding environmental movement, better known through secular works like Aldo Leopold's *Sand River Almanac* (1948) or even Rachel Carson's *Silent Spring* (1961). Only just use of natural resources would stave off environmental catastrophe. In fact, preventing ecological and social crises went hand in hand. Unlike those works, though, the Catholic rural lifers believed religious traditions still had essential contributions to make. Walter Lowdermilk, an assistant director of the Soil

Conservation Service, declared that proper use of the soil preceded a just and peaceful social order: "Only by conservation can we be led on to a higher spiritual and physical development which will express itself in stewardship of the earth for the well-being of humanity for all time."[25]

"Bio-dynamic farming" provided the primary means by which Catholic agrarians pursued their environmental concern for the social-religious order. The term originally appeared in the work of Rudolf Steiner, the Austrian philosopher who founded the quasi-eastern, esoteric religious movement known as Anthroposophy in 1912. The Catholic rural lifers rarely mentioned this connection. "What do we mean by bio-dynamic farming?" asked Catholic agrarian reformers John Thomas and James McShane in a 1941 essay. "The word means methods that conserve the health and fertility of the soil by several means. Among these means are the use of animal and vegetable fertilizer and the avoidance of certain harmful fertilizers." Materials like manure and compost revitalized the land naturally and were, of course, readily at hand. Artificial fertilizers were an additional expense farmers could do without and provided merely temporary help. Cognizant of the land's supernatural connection, bio-dynamic farming accentuated its powers of physical and spiritual regeneration.[26] "Animals and crops are living things, and they follow laws of nature that we must respect." John C. Rawe, S.J., argued:

> We too are living things—spiritual living things, but rather than adjust ourselves to the laws of life in a material and spiritual being, we have in recent years spent most of our time in an amazingly destructive effort to reduce ourselves to machinery.

Bio-dynamic farming helped achieve the integration of life and religion for agriculture that proponents of the Catholic Revival sought in literature and other professions.[27] Thus Bishop Wehrle's 1923 remarks about rural life's sacramentality included the very farmland itself. Catholic agrarians preached a rather stringent environmental ethic with transcendent implications. Care for the earth reflected one's care for earthly existence as well as the soul.

More practically, perhaps, Catholic agrarians created devotions specifically for rural Catholics. A foundation for this lay in those devotions available to all Catholics. "The Little Flower"—St. Therese de Lisieux—became quite popular even before her 1925 canonization. Catholic agrarians rarely missed an opportunity to emphasize the floral symbolism's union of natural life and supernatural piety. Both Father Charles Coughlin's suburban Detroit shrine and W. Howard Bishop's first rural life organization bore her name for this reason. The *Catholic Worker* published A. de Bethune's woodcut prints of biblical images. "The Sower" and "Christ the Tree of Life" provided visual counterparts to Peter Maurin's Green Revolution. The Liturgical Movement also created specifically rural images for all American Catholics. The natural simplicity of rural life embodied the purity liturgical reformers sought. Shorn of all human accoutrements, not cluttered and crowded like a city, the new Mass would offer a purified spiritual experience just as rural life offered a pure natural one.

Luigi Ligutti's dislike for prayer books that were "too urban" led him to create a more suitable rural version. Published in 1956 and edited by Alban Dachauer, S.J., *The Rural Life Prayerbook* contained translated sections of the Mass, prayers, and blessings whose character reflected Catholic agrarianism's blend of traditional devotional prayers with specifically rural ones. "A Prayer for the Wood-Lot" separates "A Prayer to Simon of Cyrene" from "To My Friend Jesus." Blessings included those for candles on the Feast of St. Blaise, diseased animals, bees, tractors, and a "reserved" blessing to "ward off destructive insects and other small animals" for which, Dachauer noted, the priest must receive his Ordinary's approval.[28]

One practice stood above all others in its embodiment of Catholic agrarianism and its popularity among rural Catholic laypeople: the devotion to St. Isidore the Farmer, a Spaniard of the late eleventh and early twelfth centuries. A devout peasant and dutiful husband, Isidore's patient faith was rewarded when, after being rebuked by his overseer, two angels helped him plow the fields. The patron saint of Madrid, Isidore was canonized the same day as Francis Xavier, Teresa of Avila, and Philip Neri. Despite his patent suitability, NCRLC only cultivated devotion to Isidore after his embrace by the Liturgical Movement. Pius XII named St. Isidore the NCRLC's patron saint in 1948. The following year the conference began conducting pilgrimages to Isidore's shrine in Madrid; an American version was located within the NCRLC headquarters in Des Moines.[29] The St. Isidore devotion was Catholic agrarians' clearest mark at high tide of the postwar devotional revival. Urban Catholics from Chicago and Brooklyn were as enamored of the devotion as their rural coreligionists; in 1956 one hundred thousand faithful participated in the St. Isidore novena, a devotional form conducted over nine days of prayer and meditation. By 1958 membership in NCRLC had soared past the ten-thousand mark.[30] Interest soon peaked, then gave way to a steady decline among rural Catholics who, according to historian David Bovee:

> seemed mainly attracted by the Conference's spiritual program, not its rather self-sacrificing economic message. Thus, when the Church entered the era of Vatican II, with its emphasis on modernization and social justice, not old-fashioned devotions, NCRLC membership declined rapidly.

Conference membership had not always focused so heavily on the laity. Yet once rural Catholics began to join the conference and the Company of St. Isidore, the church itself turned its attention from the very niche created for rural laypeople by the conference claiming to minister to their needs. Ironically, some of this transformation was led by the heirs of the Liturgical Movement, which originally had organized the devotion. One commentator has remarked that "while Vatican II made eating meat on Friday permissible for Roman Catholics it did not necessarily make them feel good about it." Something similar might be said about the dominant form of piety replaced by the Council. Devotional life was certainly reformed, but at least in the case of the NCRLC, the difference between the intended effects and that which occurred was greater than expected.[31]

The rupture between the NCRLC and the rural Catholic laity over St. Isidore reflected greater distances between the realities of American Catholic rural life and the images after which Catholic agrarians wished the laity would pattern their lives. Unaware perhaps of its intellectual origins, the Catholic agrarians replicated the ACLA's mistake of distancing itself from the farmers it thought needed its help. The structure of the Catholic agrarian worldview led its adherents to separate themselves from the rural Catholic laity on more than just a spiritual level. When the worldview failed, it did so completely. No longer connected with Catholic farmers politically, regionally, or spiritually, Catholic agrarians found themselves with a message but no audience.

Part of the Local Color: Rural Catholics

At certain times, such as in the early 1930s, the Catholic agrarian message reached a sympathetic and needful audience. Yet after World War II this enthusiasm could not be recaptured. The NCRLC's membership fluctuated dramatically before and after the Second World War. Groups such as the Central Verein and the Catholic Workers likewise could not sustain the members or the interest, despite constant calls to embellish U.S. Catholicism with Catholic agrarian principles. In fact, the frustration Catholic colonizers experienced stemmed in part from the frequent reluctance of rural Catholics to trade their rural lives for the purportedly "improved" one offered by Catholic agrarians. The transformations within rural life in the United States and the established means by which rural Catholics created their own identities established a certain insular mindset that Catholic agrarians only infrequently influenced. Examining the origins of the Catholic presence in rural America reveals the depth of rural Catholics' independence as well as the reasons for their readiness, frightening to many Catholic leaders, to simply blend into their surroundings.[32]

Catholic agrarians hoped to reform U.S. agriculture according to their theological image of farming. Religion aside, agriculture itself underwent a dizzying array of changes during the first half of the twentieth century. Both Catholics who farmed and those who lived in areas dependent upon agriculture were affected by these transformations as much as any other group. In some regions (Louisiana, central and northern Minnesota, southern Indiana, or along the Missouri River in Missouri), they had maintained their vibrant communities since settling there in the previous century. Elsewhere the relationship had become indistinct. In either situation, agriculture and its varying fortunes served as a unifying medium. Technological advances and the national image of rural life itself provided similar experiences. With the exception of religious affiliation, therefore, rural Catholics shared a great deal of their lives with their non-Catholic neighbors.[33]

Rural Americans, Catholic and non-Catholic alike, were quite familiar with what agricultural historian David Danbom calls "the universality of hard work." Quite simply, "life on the land" was based on long hours of manual labor, and it included every member of the family over the age of five or six. An observation in James Agee's 1941 account of impoverished southern sharecroppers, *Let Us Now Praise Famous Men*, might have been extended to all rural Americans: "The family exists to work . . . and children come into this world chiefly that they may help with this work."[34] Yet agriculture was at the same time becoming a highly rationalized industry like any other: the ability to acquire the most efficient equipment and learning to use both new tools and scientific methods generally spelled the difference between viability and oblivion.[35] The technological and economic changes that accompanied the New Deal and the years following the Second World War were of such magnitude that it is no exaggeration to treat the period in terms of a paradigm shift faced by all rural Americans, including its Catholics. Better machinery usually meant better returns (weather permitting), but it also added to unemployment figures as sharecroppers and small-scale farmers became extraneous or uncompetitive.[36] The most revolutionary change in rural America was the introduction of electricity; tasks that formerly took hours now consumed only minutes. Electricity brought connections with the world: first radio then television provided daily contact with experiences and peoples far removed from farm work.[37]

The onset of food shortages following World War II gave U.S. agriculture the opportunity to show its productive might. Agribusiness' distinguishing characteristic—massive and efficient production of food—was viewed as the outcome of modernizing rural America. Anything that caused *too much* work with inadequate reward was now vilified. Those who remained on the farm were encouraged to look disdainfully on the immediate, nonindustrial past. "We used to eat inside and shit outside. Now we eat outside and shit inside!," one southern Illinois woman commented enthusiastically. After homesteaders moved into the Granger, Iowa, properties directed by Ligutti of the NCRLC, a visitor from *Commonweal* noted that neighborhood boys had taken to tipping over the abandoned outhouses, even under the threat of gunfire. Such persistent tomfoolery indicated a deep cultural shift: the old days—symbolized by the outhouse—were definitely on the way out.[38]

Most rural Catholics had built lives without undue recourse to agrarian theology, making them indistinguishable in many respects from their non-Catholic neighbors. Just as a *Spoon River* epitaph claimed that when all of the town's church bells rang together one "could no longer distinguish . . . any one from the others," rural Catholics could at times comprise yet another U.S. subcommunity negotiating the religious marketplace.[39] At other times, they could find comfort in such exclusivist fraternal organizations as the Knights of Columbus and the German Catholic Central Verein, groups that partly bridged the gulf between rural and urban Catholic life, promoted social reform, and combated the influence of the Ku Klux Klan and other manifestations of organized anti-Catholicism.[40]

The same flexible network remained after Catholic agrarianism faded. The Knights of Columbus's promotion of Catholic identity, American fraternalism, and social awareness remained strong in the rural United States long after threats to the community diminished. As a Knight in Flush, Kansas, buoyantly put it in 1954, "The Knights of the present continue to manifest the same spirit of cooperation and aggressiveness. Their enthusiasm and good will are not limited to the four walls of the council chamber; they extend to every project that is for the good of the parish and the community." The evolution of rural Catholicism confirmed historian Catherine Albanese's observation that "whatever their ascribed religious identity, Americans were professing religions that bore the signs of contact with those who were other and different." Rural Catholics in fraternal organizations, whether they squared off against the Ku Klux Klan or preserved ethnic identity (or both), found themselves engaged in new relationships with cultural and religious forms familiar to their non-Catholic rural neighbors.[41]

Rural Catholic parishes could serve as sites of interreligious community building. In the midst of the early 1930s Dust Bowl, the Catholic women's club of St. Martin's parish in Caldwell, Kansas, met one November day in the basement of the Christian Church (Disciples of Christ) for a turkey dinner. Everyday rural life allowed for such interaction between Catholics and non-Catholics and occasionally necessitated it. Even seemingly significant differences in religious practice could be acknowledged without the bigotry others ascribed to rural life. Advertisers in a Kansas parish's jubilee history included a non-Catholic grocer who boasted "Fresh Fish for Fast Days." Another advertisement sent "Best Wishes to Our Catholic Friends."[42]

The technology that was revolutionizing agriculture provided another avenue by which rural Catholics fostered familiarity with their non-Catholic neighbors. If wired for electrical service, the rural household possessing a radio encountered literally a new world as entertainment, news, and politics poured into the home. The Grand Ol' Opry, for instance, became a southern, and then national, weekend institution. Its product—country-and-western music—expressed a very accessible form of agrarianism. The NCRLC sponsored radio programs in the cities hosting the annual convention. A Catholic Worker from central Illinois wrote Dorothy Day about hearing the radio broadcast of Pope Pius XII celebrating Mass.[43] In 1940 the Paulist Fathers based in Winchester, Tennessee, began a program that "goes out over the powerful station, WSM, an NBC outlet in Nashville. It is directed to the country people and follows immediately the National Farm and Home Hour." The same station every Friday and Saturday night broadcast the Grand Ol' Opry. (This happened before the Opry moved to the now-famous Ryman Auditorium, which quickly became labeled "the Mother Church of Country Music.") Few associations between religion and rural life could have been stronger.[44]

Faced with planting for the financial future or planting on the basis of theological principle, most Catholic farmers chose the former and went to Mass as usual. Their spiritual relationship with the land and the church expressed itself differently than the formulas of Catholic agrarianism. Facing the greatest agriculture boom in the nation's history, yet one fraught with peril for those unwilling to "modernize" both their outlooks and their practices, Catholic farmers largely eschewed the gospel of self-denial inherent in clerically promoted versions of agrarianism. Witnesses to the rush to cash exhibited by neighbors, they found little wisdom in Luigi Ligutti's message of simplicity and self-denial.[45] Before 1960 rural American Catholics acknowledged the discrepancy between rhetoric and reality by hesitating to join or support the organization church leaders had erected for their benefit.[46] "In the externals of life there is little to distinguish the Catholic suburbanite from his Protestant neighbor," wrote Andrew Greeley in 1959. Many rural Catholics had already experienced that very reality for decades. They did so, though, without undermining their legitimacy as Catholics.[47]

Conclusion

Just when it seemed to the Catholic agrarians that the nation might heed the Catholic agrarian message, the postwar world presented unavoidable material and spiritual distractions. The devotional, liturgical, and theological changes brought about by the Second

Vatican Council only accelerated the distance most rural Catholics cultivated from both recent and remote pasts. The significance of the rural life movement was almost wholly lost to history, furthering the habit of virtually equating the American Catholic experience with urban immigrant history. Insofar as we fail to consider just how Catholics in Springfield, Missouri, Havre, Montana, or Winchester, Tennessee, or any location considered "rural" have understood their Catholic faith, our understanding of the national Catholic experience suffers.[48] In standard historical accounts, Catholicism continues to represent that "new" element of U.S. life against which rural America defended the nation. Until that most elemental of biases in American Catholic and American history diminishes, the smaller but no-less-vital rural populations will remain consigned to obscurity.

That lack of awareness, though, does not mean rural Catholics starve for recognition. The old assumption that equated "rural" with greater environmental awareness has been broken. For some environmental activists, rural Americans pose as much a threat to nature as urban pollution. Catholics now can side either with radical agrarians like Passionist priest Wendell Berry or the more pragmatic approach of the Catholic bishops' agricultural lobby in Washington, D.C. The bishops themselves continue to produce statements praising rural life and theologically grounded environmental stewardship. Meanwhile, groups of "green sisters" maintain their own ecological witness, borrowing from Catholic agrarianism as well as ecofeminism. All Catholics find both challenges and comforts in Pope Francis's recent environmental encyclical *Laudato Si'* (2015). Besides that broad Catholic social tradition, rural Catholics still find guidance in the stubborn resilience embodied in country music. Inspired by the popes and sustained by the sacraments, they probably also find solace in Hank Williams Jr.'s "A Country Boy Can Survive" or Sugarland's "Something More."[49]

NOTES

1. On these participants, see Michael J. Woods, S.J., *Cultivating Soil and Soul: Twentieth-Century Catholic Agrarians Embrace the Liturgical Movement* (Collegeville, Minn.: Pueblo, 2010), 34–100.

2. Robert P. Swierenga, "Theoretical Perspectives on the New Rural History: From Environmentalism to Modernization," *Agricultural History* 56 (1982): 495–502.

3. See Matthew Butler, *Popular Piety and Political Identity in Mexico's Cristero Rebellion: Michoacan, 1927–1929* (New York: Oxford University Press, 2004).

4. David S. Bovee, *The Church and the Land: The National Catholic Rural Life Conference and American Society, 1923–2007* (Washington, D.C.: The Catholic University of America Press, 2010), 9–12; Jeffrey Marlett, *Saving the Heartland: Catholic Missionaries in Rural America, 1920–1960* (DeKalb: Northern Illinois University Press, 2002), chap. 2.

5. Maureen A. Harp, "The Leopoldine Foundation, Slovene Missionaries, and Catholic Rural Migration," *Mid-America* 75 (January 1993): 23–43; Mary Gilbert Kelly, O.P., *Catholic Immigration Colonization Projects in the United States, 1815–1860*, United States Catholic Historical Society Monography Series no. 17 (New York: United States Catholic Historical Society, 1939), 4, 230–37; Mary Evangela Henthorne, *The Irish Catholic Colonization Association* (Champaign, Ill.: Twin Towers, 1932), 34; Henry W. Casper, S.J., *Catholic Chapters in Nebraska Immigration, 1870–1900*, vol. 3, *The History of the Catholic Church in Nebraska* (Milwaukee, Wisc.: Bruce, 1966), 148.

6. Kelly, *Catholic Immigrant Colonization Projects*, 19–26, 37–47, 120–22; Edward McCaron, "A Brave New World: The Irish Agrarian Colony of Benedicta, Maine in the 1830s and 1840s," *Records of the American Catholic Historical Society of Philadelphia* 105 (1994): 1–15.

7. Jette Bruns to Heinrich [Geisburg, her brother], August 1839, in *Hold Dear, As Always: Jette, a German Immigrant Life in Letters*, trans. Adolf E. Schroeder, ed. Adolf E. Schroeder and Carla Schulz-Geisberg (Columbia, Mo.: University of Missouri Press, 1988), 98; Kelly, *Catholic Immigrant Colonization Projects*, 116–18.

8. See Russell Gerlach, *Immigrants in the Ozarks: A Study in Ethnic Geography* (Columbia: University of Missouri Press, 1975); Kelly, *Catholic Immigrant Colonization Projects*, 132–39; Joseph Kundek to the Leopoldine Society of Austria, December 23, 1844, quoted in Albert Kleber, O.S.B., *Ferdinand, Indiana, 1840–1940: A Bit of Cultural History* (St. Meinrad, Ind.: n.p., 1940), 64; Yda Schreuder, *Dutch Catholic Immigrant Settlement in Wisconsin, 1850–1905* (New York: Garland, 1989), 3–5.

9. Kelly, *Catholic Immigrant Colonization Projects*, 65, 152; *St. Joseph's Sesquicentennial: Westphalia, Missouri, 1836–1986* (Westphalia, Mo.: n.p., 1986), 4; *Sacred Heart Jubilee: Calumet, Michigan, 1868–1918*, Catholic Central Union of America archives (CCUA), St. Louis, Missouri, Drawer 28, Reel 7.

10. Bovee, *The Church and the Land*, 14–16. Bovee includes statistics for every state in 1900 on the basis of 1900 census reports. Louisiana had the largest rural Catholic population (approximately 300,000), and New Mexico's small-town and rural Catholics constituted approximately 66 percent of the state's population (143,009 of 216,328).

11. Vincent Yzermans, *The People I Love: A Biography of Luigi G. Ligutti* (Collegeville, Minn.: Liturgical Press, 1976), 58. After Ligutti became NCRLC executive secretary, this particular phrase became part of the conference's letterhead. For the use of analogy in theology, see David Tracy, *The Analogical Imagination: Christian Theology and the Culture of Pluralism* (New York: Crossroad, 1981), 404–38.

12. See Timothy Dolan, *Some Seed Fell on Good Ground: The Life of Edwin V. O'Hara* (Washington, D.C.: The Catholic University of America Press, 2012); and Woods, *Cultivating Soil and Soul*, 1–13.

13. Edwin O'Hara, "The Clergy and Rural Life," *St. Isidore's Plow* 2 (October 1923): 3.

14. For the ACLA, see Kevin M. Lowe, *Baptized with the Soil: Christian Agrarians and the Crusade for Rural America* (New York: Oxford University Press, 2016).

15. The map appears in *Land and Home*, June 1946, 31. An insert in *Catholic Rural Life*, November 1925, 5, ranked the states according to subscription to the publication. In descending order it listed Iowa ("with four hundred names"), Michigan, Missouri, Illinois, Minnesota, "and thirty-five states, Canada, and South America." For NCRLC attendance, see Bovee, *Church and the Land*, 141–43, 162–63.

16. The preceding two paragraphs are explained in much greater detail in Marlett, *Saving the Heartland*, chap. 1.

17. Jay P. Corrin, *G. K. Chesterton & Hilaire Belloc: The Battle against Modernity* (Athens: Ohio University Press, 1981), 1–28; Peter Huff, *Allen Tate and the Catholic Revival* (New York: Paulist, 1996), 13–14.

18. Huff, *Allen Tate and the Catholic Revival*, 38, 48, 67–69; Corrin, *G. K. Chesterton & Hilaire Belloc*, 162; William H. Issel, "Ralph Borsodi and the Agrarian Response to Modern America," *Agricultural History* 41 (April 1967): 157–59; "Notes and Comments: Mr. and Mrs. R. B," *Catholic Rural Life Bulletin*, May 1941, 45; Mildred Jensen, "Back to the Land," *Catholic Woman's World*, January 1941, 43, 48–49.

19. "Notes and Comments: Bishop Winkelman," *Catholic Rural Life Bulletin*, February 1940, 15; Leo Ward, C.S.C., "The Land and Human Values," *Catholic Rural Life Bulletin*, August 1938,

2–4, 18; cf. Per Binde, "Nature in Roman Catholic Tradition," *Anthropological Quarterly* 74, no. 1 (2001): 15–27.

20. Urban Baer, *Farmers of Tomorrows* (Sparta, Wisc.: Monroe, 1939), 37–38; Luigi M. Ligutti, "What's Wrong with Farmers?" *America*, April 24, 1943, 66; C. E. Wolf, "I Left College to Become a Farmer," *Catholic Rural Life Bulletin*, February 1941, 1.

21. Louise Owen, "Kill . . . and Cure," *Land and Home*, June 1943, 52; Jensen, "Back to the Land," 48; "Cracked Corn: Part-Time Farming Works," *Land and Home*, March 1945, 20.

22. "Cracked Corn: Part-Time Farming Works," 20. The flyer on "LIVE IN THE COUNTRY" is in Marquette University Archives (MUA), NCRLC Series 7/1, Box 13. The same image and phrase served as the front cover for Reverend Patrick Quinlan's *Standing on Both Feet: The Rural Homestead; A Necessity for an Era of Reconstruction* (Des Moines, Iowa: NCRLC, n. d.). Edward Skillin Jr., "Armchair Husbandry," *Commonweal*, March 27, 1942, 554.

23. Peter McDonough includes many of the points made here in an explication of *Rural Roads to Security*'s expression of the Jesuits' search for a new social order in mid-century American life; see McDonough, *Men Astutely Trained: A History of the Jesuits in the American Century* (New York: Free Press, 1992), 89–95.

24. Willis D. Nutting, "The Catholic College and the Land," *Catholic Rural Life Bulletin*, November 1938, 3.

25. Walter C. Lowdermilk, "'Lebensraum'—Agrarianism vs. War," *Catholic Rural Life Bulletin*, November 1940, 21; cf. Christopher Hamlin and John T. McGreevy, "The Greening of America, Catholic Style, 1930–1950," *Environmental History* 11, no. 3 (2006): 464–99.

26. John Thomas and James McShane, "Farmers Must Reform Methods of Farming," *Catholic Rural Life Bulletin*, November 1941, 101; Bovee, *The Church and the Land*, 121–22; cf. John C. Rawe, S.J., "Biological Technology on the Land," *Catholic Rural Life Bulletin*, August, 1939, 1–3, 20–22; Rawe, "What, Where and Why of Bio-Dynamics," *Land and Home*, September 1943, 67–68.

27. Thomas and McShane, "Farmers Must Reform," 102; John C. Rawe, S.J., "Home on the Land," *Catholic Rural Life Bulletin* 2, February 1939, 24–25.

28. Yzermans, *People I Love*, 61; Alban Dachauer, S.J., ed., *The Rural Life Prayerbook* (Des Moines, Iowa: National Catholic Rural Life Conference, 1956), 56–99, 130.

29. Raymond Witte, S.M., *Twenty-Five Years of Crusading: A History of the National Catholic Rural Life Conference* (Des Moines, Iowa: National Catholic Rural Life Conference, 1948), 212–15; St. Isidore prayer card, undated; MUA, NCRLC, Series 1, Boxes 10 and 11. Robert F. Jardes, undated memo on national shrine to St. Isidore, MUA, NCRLC, Series 1/1, Box 11. Jardes suggested that the work had already begun in those two dioceses.

30. Company of St. Isidore folders; Edna Barrett to Michael Dineen, December 4, 1957; "The Company of St. Isidore, List #3"; all in MUA, NCRLC, Series 1, Box 10. The outdoor shrine advertisement is held in Series 5/1, Box 8; *St. Isidore Patron of the Farmer* (Des Moines, Iowa: National Catholic Rural Life Conference, n.d.), 18. For Our Lady of the Fields, see Mary Jean Dorcy, *Our Lady of the Fields* (Des Moines, Iowa: Land and Home Booklets; National Catholic Rural Life Conference, 1957); Bovee, *The Church and the Land*, 167–69.

31. Bovee, *Church and the Land*, *331*; James Hudnut-Beumler, *Looking for God in the Suburbs: The Religion of the American Dream and Its Critics, 1945–1965* (New Brunswick, N.J.: Rutgers University Press, 1994), 177. Jay Dolan, *The American Catholic Experience: A History from Colonial Times to the Present* (1985; repr. Notre Dame, Ind.: University of Notre Dame Press, 1992), 429–33, discusses the postconciliar development of devotional "rearguard actions" and "liturgically advanced" parishes (these terms appear on 429 and 430).

32. The 1940 convention in St. Cloud had 18,000 attendees, and the 1948 convention in La Crosse, Wisconsin, brought in 30,000. No other convention before or since drew nearly as many.

33. Pamela Riney-Kehrberg, *Rooted in Dust: Surviving Drought and Depression in Southwestern Kansas* (Lawrence: University Press of Kansas, 1994).

34. David Danbom, *The Resisted Revolution: Urban America and the Industrialization of Agriculture, 1900–1930* (Ames: Iowa State University Press, 1979), 4–6; Carmen Delores Welch, "From an Illinois Farm," MUA, DD/CW, W-4, Box 1, "Nazareth House" folder; James Agee with Walker Evans, *Let Us Now Praise Famous Men* (Boston: Houghton Mifflin, 1941; paperback, 1980), 322.

35. Olin E. Hughes, "An Analysis of Farm Building Costs" (M.A. thesis, University of Missouri at Columbia, 1932), 25–27, 130–31.

36. John Egerton, *Speak Now against the Day: The Generation before the Civil Rights Movement in the South* (Chapel Hill: University of North Carolina Press, 1994), 205–6; Danbom, *Resisted Revolution*, 133–34.

37. Harvey Green, *The Uncertainty of Everyday Life, 1915–1945* (New York: Harper Collins, 1992), 61–65, 101–2; George J. Hildner, *One Hundred Years for God and Country: St. John's, the Church and the Community, 1839–1940* (Washington, Mo.: Washington Missourian, 1940), 66.

38. Quoted in Jane Adams, *The Transformation of Rural Life: Southern Illnois, 1890–1990* (Chapel Hill: University of North Carolina Press, 1994), 210; Edward Skillin, "Granger Homesteads," *Commonweal*, May 24, 1940, 95.

39. Thomas Carey, quoted in *Catholic Rural Life*, November 1925, 3; Edgar Lee Masters, *Spoon River Anthology* (New York: Collier; Macmillan, 1962), 254.

40. David M. Chalmers, *Hooded Americanism: The History of the Ku Klux Klan* (1965; repr. New York: Franklin Watt, 1981), 292; Carol Coburn, *Life at Four Corners: Religion, Gender, and Education in a German-Lutheran Community, 1958–1945* (Lawrence: University of Kansas Press, 1992), 63; Leonard J. Moore, *Citizen Klansman: The Ku Klux Klan in Indiana, 1921–1928* (Chapel Hill: University of North Carolina Press, 1991), 11; Christopher J. Kauffman, *Faith and Fraternalism: The History of the Knights of Columbus 1882–1982* (New York: Harper and Row, 1982), 1–9.

41. Quoted in J. E. Biehler, *One Hundred Years in Rock Creek Valley: A History of St. Joseph Parish at Flush, Kansas* (Topeka, Kans.: Central Press, 1954), 126; Catherine Albanese, "Exchanging Souls, Exchanging Selves: Contact, Combination, and American Religious History," in *Retelling U.S. Religious History*, ed. Thomas A. Tweed (Berkeley: University of California Press, 1996), 203.

42. *St. Martin's Parish, Caldwell, Kansas, Golden Jubilee: 1888–1938*, CCUA, Drawer 28, reel 19; Jeane Gilmore, *The Legacy: The History of the St. Joseph Catholic Church, Edina, Missouri* (Quincy, Ill.: Jost & Kiefer, 1974), 74–75.

43. Green, *Uncertainty of Everyday Life*, 190; Carmen Welch to Dorothy Day, undated, MUA, DD/CW, W-4, Box 1, Nazareth House folder; Ray Wortmann, "Coughlin in the Countryside: Father Charles Coughlin and the National Farmers Union," *U.S. Catholic Historian* 13 (1995): 97–120.

44. Edgar Schmiedeler, "Trailing the Trailer Chapels," *Homiletic and Pastoral Review* 42 (1942): 245; Schmiedeler, "Motor Missions, 1940," *Homiletic and Pastoral Review* 41 (1941): 399–400; Curtis W. Ellison, *Country Music Culture: From Hard Times to Heaven* (Jackson: University Press of Mississippi, 1995), 20; David Fillingim, *Redneck Liberation: Country Music as Theology* (Macon, Ga.: Mercer University Press, 2003).

45. Thomas and McShane, "Farmers Must Reform Methods of Farming," *Catholic Rural Life Bulletin*, November 1941, 100–102; Danbom, *Resisted Revolution*, 138–42; Warren Susman, *Culture as History: The Transformation of American Society in the Twentieth Century* (New York: Pantheon, 1984), 211–29.

46. Yzermans, *People I Love*, 84.

47. Andrew Greeley, *The Church and the Suburbs* (1959; repr. Red Bank, N.J.: Deus and Paulist Press, 1963), 58.

48. Cf. Stephen J. Gross, "The Grasshopper Shrine at Cold Spring, Minnesota: Religion and Market Capitalism among German-American Catholics," *Catholic Historical Review* 92 (April 2006): 215–43.

49. Examples of bishops' statements include "This Land is Home to Me," the 1975 statement by Appalachian bishops (http://www.catholicconferencewv.org/docs/ThisLandIsHome.pdf) and "The Columbia River Watershed: Caring for Creation and the Common Good," from Pacific Northwest bishops (2001; http://www.thewscc.org/uploads/3/4/9/4/34945816/crplp.pdf). For "green sisters," see Sarah McFarland Taylor, *Green Sisters: A Spiritual Ecology* (Cambridge, Mass.: Harvard University Press, 2007).

FIVE

"An Embassy to a Golf Course?": Conundrums on the Road to the United States' Diplomatic Representation to the Holy See, 1784–1984

Roy Domenico

When the fourth-century Roman emperors accorded Christianity a formal state role, they wrote the first page in a long story of complex relations between the papacy and Christian powers. In the seventeen hundred years that followed, meddlesome princes, opportunists, zealots, and manipulators, from Constantine to Pepin, from Philip II to Benito Mussolini, attempted to influence, bully, cajole, and champion the Holy See. The modern era, furthermore, added its own list of conundrums in the affairs between the papacy, or Holy See, and temporal powers—beginning with Protestantism in the sixteenth century and followed by secular ideologies in the eighteenth, nineteenth, and twentieth centuries. These issues periodically placed the pope and his church at odds with European states, and they colored dealings across the Atlantic, particularly diplomatic relations at the ministerial level with the United States. Quintessentially modern and Protestant America embraced what became known as liberal principles—secular, representative, and pluralist democracy anchored in civil rights and a free market or capitalist system. The Holy See contested those values, which nonetheless triumphed in the United States and Europe, while at the same time the papacy suffered the extinction of its temporal power. After the pope surrendered his last earthly provinces, the Papal States, to the new Kingdom of Italy in 1870, many wondered why he should receive diplomats at all. Should Washington accord an embassy to a state that did not exist? Then, with the creation in 1929 of the tiny Vatican City State, new quandaries surfaced—should the United States send a representative to a postage-stamp territory enveloped by the city of Rome?

Despite their differences, the Holy See welcomed formal diplomatic ties with the United States, particularly after the Italian Kingdom wiped the Papal States off the map in 1870, a time when links with any nation would help to maintain its international presence. On the other hand, after that date, American Protestant and secularist liberal prejudices worked against relations, requiring justifications to send a representative to Rome, reasons not normally needed for diplomatic exchanges elsewhere. Through its first century and a half, the United States' small but growing Catholic population and its small but growing role in European and world affairs meant that diplomatic ties with the Papal States remained largely inconsequential and, after 1867, virtually nonexistent. From 1867, America sent no minister or ambassador to the Holy See, a situation that persisted until 1984 when the two formally exchanged diplomatic representatives, a U.S. ambassador to Vatican City and a papal nuncio to Washington.

Protestant suspicions toward the Holy See, which worked against the exchange of diplomats, ran deep and surfaced shortly after the American Revolution in the highest corridors of power. John Adams, for instance, argued against any Roman presence in the United States and branded the pontiff "an ecclesiastical tyrant." In 1824 a confident James Madison wrote to then president James Monroe on America's role as an "antidote" against the doctrines and "vices" of what he saw as Europe's reactionary and implicitly pro-Catholic Holy Alliance. In an 1832 letter, Madison noted that the papal system constituted the "worst form of government." Nineteenth-century American culture, moreover, was replete with a robust nativist anti-Catholicism displayed in such sensational works as Maria Monk's 1836 *Awful Disclosures of the Hotel Dieu Nunnery.* These sentiments expressed themselves in nativist slogans such as "Rum, Romanism and Rebellion" and others that damned the pope as "the whore of Rome." The Holy See reciprocated these feelings and ideas in Catholic teaching that dismissed Protestants as heretics.[1]

The United States in some regard shared with France the guilt of materialist liberalism and capitalism, transgressions released in their revolutions. While the American republic's first steps and the French revolution did not unduly preoccupy the papacy, France's outrages of regicide, the Terror, and its military occupation of Rome in 1798 provoked reaction. The kidnapping of Pope Pius VI and his death in a French prison (1798–99), followed in 1809 by the abduction of his successor, Pius VII, sealed the issue. All subsequent pontiffs, at least through Pius IX, would be justly regarded as enemies of modernity and its ideologies. Gregory XVI's 1832 encyclical, *Mirari vos,* "on liberalism and religious differentism," for instance, lamented that "science (was) impudent, liberty, dissolute," and that the church had been "subjected to human reason." Gregory XVI complained that the liberal and nationalist calamities that plagued the age, "destruction of public order" and the "fall of principalities," were rooted in "heretical societies and sects in which all that is sacrilegious, infamous, and blasphemous has gathered as bilge water in a ship's hold, a congealed mass of all filth." Particularly relevant to pluralist and Protestant America was *Mirari vos'* condemnation of the "perverse opinion . . . that it is possible to obtain the eternal salvation of the soul by the profession of any kind of religion, as long as morality is maintained." Thirty-two years later, Pope Pius IX's 1864 encyclical, *Quanta cura,* with its famous "Syllabus of Errors," stands alone as perhaps the greatest reactionary manifesto of the nineteenth century. That list of eighty fallacies included the separation of church and state, secular education, civil marriage, freedom of religion, and the notion that "the Roman Pontiff can, and ought to, reconcile himself, and come to terms with progress, liberalism and modern civilization." The Syllabus's reference to many other less notorious documents served to illustrate the extensive list of Catholic condemnations of liberalism, socialism, nationalism, secular society, and other monstrosities unleashed by the Age of Reason and the revolutions that it spawned.[2]

Unlike France, however, the United States never invaded the Papal States; nor did it kidnap and kill the pope. The king that Americans rejected in 1776, furthermore, had been one of their fellow Protestants and not a Catholic like Louis XVI. Shortly after independence, therefore, in July 1783, the Holy See's nuncio in Paris communicated to Benjamin Franklin the pope's wish to detach the American Catholic Church from the vicar apostolic's control in London. On December 15 of the following year, Pius VI, in a friendly gesture, opened his ports of Civitavecchia and Ancona to American ships. This led on June 26, 1797, to the establishment of consular, but not fully diplomatic, relations in the commission of Giovanni Battista (or John) Sartori as the United States' first consul to the Papal States. A native of Rome, he served until 1823, although he moved to the United States, where he simultaneously acted as the Holy See's representative. In 1826 Washington received the Neapolitan count Ferdinando Lucchesi as consular representative of both the Holy See and the Kingdom of the Two Sicilies. At one point, some twenty-one papal consuls served in cities across the United States.[3]

Relations in this early period proceeded with little incident. In an age of sail, an ocean separated the two countries. Both had fairly small populations in 1790, about three million in the papal territories and just over four million in the United States, although the latter enjoyed an influx of immigrants that would outpace both the former and all of Italy. Affairs were limited to minor commercial dealings and occasional needs of travelers. "Trade between the United States and the Papal States," according to one historian, "was practically nonexistent, and the work of the pope's consul in New York consisted merely of issuing three or four passports a year."[4] Soon, however, ideology and politics tempered relations between the United States and the Holy See.

The wave of European revolutions in 1848–49 and the convulsions of Italy's unification, the *Risorgimento*, demanded more of Washington's attention and the desirability of an official presence in Rome above the consular level. In 1846, Giovanni Maria Mastai-Ferretti came to the throne of St. Peter as Pius IX at a time when Catholic intellectuals such as Vincenzo Gioberti pushed for a "guelph" option of papal leadership in a united and free Italy. It all depended on the new pope, and in the early stages of his very long reign, Pius appeared to sympathize with Italian nationalism and at least some of the liberal ideas that went along with it. Upon his accession, he released political prisoners, enacted a customs union with the neighboring Grand Duchy of Tuscany, and took the first steps toward an advisory assembly, or *Consulta*, moves that found great sympathy in the United States. He also let it be known to the U.S. consul, Nicholas Browne, that he would welcome full diplomatic ties with Washington. The spirit of Pius's measures earned the endorsement of the New York and Louisiana state legislatures. Former president Martin Van Buren applauded his patriotism, and Vice President George Dallas discerned "hope in the real sublimity of his genius." Reaction like this in the United States prompted President James Polk in December of 1847 to elevate America's representation in Rome to the ministerial level. Congress agreed and dispatched Jacob Martin, secretary of the U.S. legation in Paris, to Rome as *chargé d'affaires* in preparation for the move.[5]

Martin reached Rome in August 1848 but succumbed to a fever and died shortly after his first meeting with Pope Pius IX, an indication of the trouble that would soon plague the Holy See and its relations with the United States. In the ensuing months the revolution spread to Rome. Pius, however, retreated from his early enthusiasm for reform, and by autumn real misgivings emerged. On November 15 the chief minister of his government (and his former ambassador to France), Pellegrino Rossi, fell victim to an assassin's knife while he entered the chancellery palace, an atrocity that triggered the Roman insurrection. Nine days later the pontiff, "disguised as a simple priest," fled the city. A revolutionary triumvirate, soon guided by Giuseppe Mazzini, established a Roman Republic based on liberal principles and inspired in part by the American example, as were many of the other regimes that exploded across Italy at the time. Giuseppe Garibaldi, the hero of Italian independence, arrived the following March as commander of a citizens' militia.

With his battle cry of "Rome or Death!" (*Roma o morte!*), Garibaldi, a convinced democrat and Mason, became the face of the *Risorgimento*, and the liberal world accorded him a hero's status. A figure of Olympic anticlericalism, he blamed the church and its priests for much of Italy's woes. They were "traitors of the deepest die," "descendents of Torquemada," "ministers of falsehood," and members of the "black brood, pestilent scum of humanity . . . still reeking with the scent of human burnt offerings where tyranny still reigns."[6] Garibaldi's own novel of Roman intrigue, *Clelia*, or as it was known in English translations, *The Rule of the Monk*, never missed a chance to expose the evil of Catholic authority, from the "languid luxury" of the cardinals, "present(ing) every temptation to corruption and libertinism of the very worst kinds," to the pope, whose idea of Christian humility was to have emperors kiss his toe. In a chapter entitled, "Torture," Garibaldi lamented that "the world still tolerates these fiends in human form . . . God grant the people of Italy may before long have the will and the courage to break this hateful yoke from off their necks."[7] The Jesuit review *Civiltà Cattolica* snatched up the gauntlet and dismissed Garibaldi as a "comic hero" who at least possessed one attribute, the skilled use of the dagger. "This valiant lion," wrote the Jesuits, "this Achilles, this Hercules, this Mars, this Jove—the more you try to force him into the light of day, the more he retreats into the shadows; the more he melts before your very eyes." In the United States, the Jesuits found an echo in the Catholic *Pilot* of Boston, which attributed "robberies, cruelties and debauchery" to this "modern Attila" and decried his hatred for "Christ and His Church." The *Pilot*, however, could not sway Protestant Americans, nor even factions within the nation's growing Italian population. Along with the celebrated statue to Garibaldi erected in New York's Washington Square, Washington D.C.'s Italian community presented the U.S. Senate with a bust of the great man in 1887, five years after his death. The Senate accepted it "with the assurance of the admiration of the people of this land for his noble life and distinguished deeds."[8]

At the end of 1848, in the pitch of revolutionary fervor and until Jacob Martin could be replaced, Nicholas Browne took charge of the U.S. office in Rome with orders from Secretary of State James Buchanan to withhold recognition of the republic until it proved itself a viable political entity. Browne's letters and actions, however, reveal examples of liberal and Protestant America's anti-papist sentiment, as well as his own inclination toward insubordination. In his historical treatment of the events of 1848–49, Leo Francis Stock concluded that Browne "far over-reached himself" and "openly acted against the papal government." The consul clearly preferred the revolutionary regime. He marched through the Roman streets with its Constituent Assembly, and to its minister of foreign affairs, Prince Carlo Rusconi, he confided his "fullest belief" that Washington would grasp "the earliest opportunity to recognize (the new state)." To Buchanan, Browne argued the republic's case with no sympathy for the pontiff's "pseudo-religious sway." The revolution brought "great and beneficial innovations" to a people who had been denied the same liberties long enjoyed by Americans. He wrote that the pope considered the Romans mere "vassals only of the soil, created alone for the support and glorification of the Papal See."[9]

Despite Browne's enthusiasm, the Roman Republic crumbled before a French-led international army. None of Italy's revolutions succeeded, and the *Risorgimento* had to wait for another decade. In the Eternal City, the papal administration reestablished itself, and Pope Pius returned in 1850 from the nearby port of Gaeta, where the King of the Two Sicilies had sheltered him. The Papal States resumed its embattled existence for two more decades. The defeated revolutionaries fled; Mazzini found refuge in London, while Garibaldi experienced more difficulty finding a safe haven, although for a time he breathed the free air of Staten Island, New York. "Rome's fresh young life has bled in vain," penned the sympathetic American poet John Greenleaf Whittier, "the ravens scattered by the day come back with night again," while the victims of "the Nero of our time (lay mangled) in (his) stately Quirinal."[10]

U.S. recognition of the Roman Republic never came, and Lewis Cass arrived in the city to replace Jacob Martin. Lacking Browne's gusto, Cass, the son of a Michigan senator, assumed full ministerial rank in 1854, and he and his successors oversaw cordial if uneventful relations with the pope, who thanked him that Washington had held back on recognition. The legation, however, failed to dampen occasional but persistent bursts of American anti-popery, even on the part of U.S. government personnel. In 1867 Edwin Cushman, a consular official, was even reported to have taken up arms in support of Garibaldi's last, ill-fated attack on papal territory at Mentana. By that year, furthermore, all residual American hopes for Pius IX had clearly worn off. He had bluntly distinguished himself as the enemy of Italian unification and, as his "Syllabus" confirmed, of practically any sign of liberal progress.

For its part, when Cass became U.S. minister, the Holy See vaguely indicated a notion to reciprocate and send someone of ministerial rank to the United States. The visit to the United States by Archbishop Gaetano Bedini, the papal nuncio to Brazil, was seen as a kind of papal feeler toward that end. Bedini arrived in New York on June 30, 1853. While never clear, the cleric's visit was generally explained as a fact-finding and good-will visit to the United States and Canada. Arriving in New York City on June 30, 1853, Bedini's tour included the Great Lakes, the large eastern cities, New Orleans, and the Ohio Valley. At almost every stop, however, anti-Catholic nativists and anticlerical immigrants dogged him. One renegade Italian priest campaigned against him and alleged that, as papal governor of Bologna in 1849, he had collaborated with the Austrian occupation force in the execution of Ugo Bassi, the patriot-priest and friend of Garibaldi. Threatening handbills marred Bedini's journey, and in many places he was hanged or burned in effigy. The greatest danger came in Cincinnati, where a Christmas riot exploded, mainly among German immigrants bent on revenge against the "butcher of Bologna." By January 1854 the archbishop returned to Washington, where President Franklin Pierce hosted him with supper at the White House. By then, however, Congress joined much of the United States in questioning the real purpose of the nuncio's visit. The Senate even debated the question on January 23 and 24 and delivered a request for any State Department correspondence that could shed light on the issue. Despite the loss of some key material, it nonetheless became apparent that, whatever its purpose, Bedini's exploratory and good-will trip had ended in disaster; although the archbishop's report to the pontiff recommended the establishment of a nunciature, the Holy See's diplomatic representation in Washington remained a dead letter.[11]

In the 1860s the *Risorgimento* lurched toward completion and jeopardized what remained of the pope's domains. The still incomplete Kingdom of Italy absorbed the eastern Papal States in 1860, linking the peninsula's north and south, moved its capital from Turin to Florence in 1865, and took Austrian Venetia the following year, leaving Rome as the last prize. By 1867, with less and less reason to maintain a minister in the imperiled city, the U.S. Congress quietly dropped funding for the mission and sealed its fate, justifying its decision on incorrect information that Pope Pius had expelled the American Protestant church to beyond the Rome city walls. America's last minister, Rufus King, dismissed the accusation as completely groundless, but his protests fell on deaf ears in Washington. Some explained the end of the embassy as a bit of vengeance against Pius IX for his alleged friendliness toward the Confederacy during the Civil War. This was a U.S. misconception, concluded the historian David Alvarez, who wrote that, indeed, "by the spring of 1862 the Vatican perceived the preservation of the Union as not only probable, but as actually desirable." Some of the confusion stemmed from two diplomatic missions that the Confederacy sent to Rome, under A. Dudley Mann in 1863 and under Charleston's bishop Patrick Lynch in 1864.[12] After the war, however, Rome emphasized its good will by arresting John Surratt, who was wanted by U.S. authorities regarding his involvement in the assassination of President Abraham Lincoln. Surratt had made his way to Rome under a false name and joined the Papal Zouaves before a Canadian in the corps exposed him. Not bound by an extradition treaty, the Holy See nevertheless acted on its own as evidence of good faith and arrested Surratt. He escaped from the pope's prison, however, and fled to Egypt, where he was later captured. Rufus King pointed to such gestures and concluded that the United States had been unfair to the Holy See. In an April 1868 letter to Secretary of State William Seward, the minister complained that he had done all that he could "to correct the misapprehensions (concerning the American church) . . . but, apparently without the slightest effect." The government's brusque action, King thought, had insulted a pontiff who had displayed only kindness and generosity to him and to the U.S. government.[13]

The end of America's mission could not have inordinately depressed Pius because, by that time, weightier issues plagued him. On September 20, 1870, troops of Italy's King Vittorio Emanuele II breached Rome's ancient walls at the Porta Pia and captured the city from the pope, who chose a self-imposed exile as "the prisoner of the Vatican." "The despotism of a thousand years," recorded the poet Whittier, "fell at a touch in noiseless rottenness." Temporal papal business now functioned at the largesse of the Italian government, which was usually reluctant to do anything more to disturb it. The kingdom, however, drew the line at the maintenance of diplomatic relations between other nations and the "deposed" prince of the Papal States, an act that could delegitimize the touchy new nation. The pontiffs, therefore, were condemned to what the historian Robert Graham termed "a state of worldly humiliation," deprived of territory and the diplomatic status that went with it. After conquering the Papal States, the Italian Kingdom formally frowned on any continuation of diplomatic relations between the Holy See and foreign states. Recognizing, however, that such a policy might create as many problems as it solved, it pretended to ignore the issue, opting often to turn a blind eye. Thus, while the diplomatic corps of the Holy See suffered some notable defections like Belgium between 1880 and 1884 or France after 1905, Graham noted that the Holy See enjoyed remarkable success during those difficult years by actually increasing the number of permanent missions accredited to it from eighteen in 1890 to twenty-seven in 1929.[14]

The United States occupied a place on the list of nations with which the Holy See attempted to revive ties between the fall of Rome and the accords of 1929. At the same time, the United States maintained an embassy to the Italian Kingdom that had been formally established in March 1861. That year, Abraham Lincoln appointed the first minister, George Perkins Marsh, a Vermonter who achieved fame as an environmentalist. Marsh followed the new state's capitals, from Turin to Florence in 1865 and ultimately to Rome, where he served from 1871 until his death in 1882.[15] Undaunted, the Holy See searched for ties with Washington and extended feelers during an 1886 American visit by Monsignor Paolo Mori. A subsequent extended trip to the United States by Archbishop Francesco Satolli illustrated the wish of Pope Leo XIII, who succeeded Pius IX in 1878, to achieve some sort of presence. While a nuncio to the United States was still impractical, perhaps a papal representative to America's Catholic episcopate, as apostolic delegate, might resolve some of the dilemma. Apostolic delegates have no diplomatic standing; rather, according to church canon law they are entrusted to "watch carefully over the state of the churches (dioceses) in the country to which (they are) assigned and to give regular reports to the Holy See regarding their condition."[16]

Satolli came to America only through an official invitation to exhibit Vatican items at Chicago's Columbian Exposition of 1892. On January 14, 1893, however, while still in the United States, he received a telegram from Rome informing him of the creation of the apostolic delegation and of his appointment. In his new capacity, Satolli remained in the United States until October of 1896. He quickly discovered a sometimes-blurred line between his duties toward the church and involvement in the host country's politics, where he might appear to "lobby" for a certain position. In the 1890s, for instance, Satolli and his successor, Archbishop Sebastiano Martinelli, tried to use their office to mobilize the U.S. hierarchy against Italy's annexation of Rome.[17] Church business, however, clearly dominated the agenda, and Archbishop Satolli became embroiled in ecclesiastical politics and debates over "Americanism" on both sides of the ocean. In the United States, battling conservative and liberal clerics dragged him into their own squabbles, while in Rome Pope Leo XIII undercut liberal positions and condemned Americanism through his encyclical *Longinqua oceani* (1895) and his apostolic letter *Testem benevolentiae* (1899). As the Jesuit historian Gerald Fogarty wrote, these anti-liberal proclamations "breathed (a new spirit) into the American Church, the spirit of Roman authority and discipline, of loss of American independence and episcopal collegiality. With it also came the stifling of intellectual life in the new nation."[18]

The U.S. government had no interest in such debates, and for its part, Washington's negligible diplomatic interest in the Holy See briefly peaked only after the Spanish-American War, when it privately sought the pontiff's assistance regarding a property-rights dispute in the newly won Philippines. President William McKinley's administration worried that widespread resentment there over large expanses of church-held lands might fuel the anti-American insurrection. Through Archbishop John Ireland of St. Paul, Minnesota, Secretary of State Elihu Root contacted the papal secretary of state, Cardinal Mariano Rampolla del Tindaro, with the aim of relieving the owners of their estates. In 1902 Root sent the American governor of the Philippines, William Howard Taft, to Rome for negotiations. Rampolla accorded Taft full diplomatic honors in the hope that this might lead to U.S.–Holy See recognition—something in which the Americans still had no interest. On June 5, Taft met with Pope Leo XIII and found the nonagenarian "bubbling with humor (and) as lively as a cricket." The talks floundered over the expulsion from the Philippines of the Spanish clerical landholders, and Taft left without a settlement, although an agreement was later reached in which the United States bought the properties. While such relatively insignificant contacts served to illustrate the subdued relations between the United States and the Holy See at that time, as one historian concluded, the Taft episode "laid the basis for further understanding" between the United States and the Holy See.[19]

The 1929 Lateran Accords between Italy and the Holy See created a sovereign Vatican City State and revived the question of diplomatic ties with the United States.[20] The magnate and influential Catholic layman Joseph P. Kennedy discussed the possibility with President Franklin Roosevelt in November 1935, and in 1936 Cardinal Eugenio Pacelli, Pope Pius XI's secretary of state and the future Pius XII, broached the issue with the president during a celebrated tour of the United States. Boston's auxiliary bishop Francis Spellman acted as Pacelli's guide through most of the trip, an excursion marked by quite a bit of ecclesiastical politics and jockeying between Spellman and Amleto Cicognani, the apostolic delegate. The final trump came when Spellman organized Pacelli's visit to President Roosevelt at his Hyde Park estate, torpedoing Cicognani's plans to meet at the White House. In 1939 a grateful Pacelli, now Pope Pius XII, appointed Spellman as archbishop of New York and raised him to the cardinalate in 1946.[21]

Roosevelt's decision to send Kennedy, then ambassador to Britain, as his representative to Pacelli's coronation in March 1939 signaled movement in a new direction. The issue assumed added significance as Europe slid into war during the late spring and summer of that year, prompting New York congressman Emanuel Celler to urge recognition of the Holy See in a letter to President Roosevelt and Secretary of State Cordell Hull. Celler, a Jew, circulated a draft among his district's Catholic parishes and sent a copy to Monsignor Michael J. Ready, the general secretary of the National Catholic Welfare Conference (NCWC, the U.S. bishops' organization), who wondered if the letter "might do more harm than good." Nevertheless, Ready secured the help of the NCWC lawyer, William Montavon, to collaborate with Celler on a final copy. Sent on July 14, the congressman's letter lauded the pontiff's opposition to racism and "the savage and merciless inroads of Fascism, Nazism and Communism." Washington would be wise, it concluded, to "re-establish diplomatic relations with the Holy See." Two weeks later, on July 28, Cardinal Enrico Gasparri, the nephew of Pius XI's secretary of state, who had negotiated the Lateran Accords, arrived in New York as Spellman's guest. It was only a three-day visit before the cardinal left for a more extended tour of Canada, although the *New York Times* surmised that Gasparri would take advantage of his brief sojourn by "preparing the juridical status for the possible opening of diplomatic relations" between Washington and the Holy See.[22]

Secretary Hull corroborated the *Times* conjecture when he recorded in his memoirs that President Roosevelt and the State Department began to discuss diplomatic relations in the summer of 1939. Both Undersecretary Sumner Welles and William Philips, the U.S. ambassador to Italy, advanced the cause, although Philips insisted that the envoy be a Protestant. The diplomats argued that the Vatican could serve as an intelligence source regarding German, Italian, and Spanish developments, but President Roosevelt agreed to pursue the matter "solely on the refugee question."[23] Following the start of the European war, in December 1939 the president announced his decision to send Myron C. Taylor as his personal representative to the Holy See. The pressures of the conflict, said Roosevelt, justified Taylor's mission to Rome, a haven of peace in a war-ravaged continent that could help not only with the refugee situation, but provide valuable information and serve as a conduit for communication. An Episcopalian with experience in refugee issues as U.S. representative to the 1938 Evian Conference, Taylor had also chaired the United States Steel Corporation. In addition, he was an Italophile who enjoyed frequent visits to his Tuscan villa Schifanoia, which he later presented to the pontiff. The industrialist-turned-diplomat arrived in Rome in February of 1940.

Traditional anti-Catholic and anti-papist sentiment resurfaced. American Protestant groups responded immediately and with fury to the Taylor appointment, prompting a letter from Roosevelt to George A. Buttrick, the president of the Federal Council of Churches, which explained that Taylor was merely his "personal representative." This appointment, the president emphasized, "(did) not constitute the inauguration of formal relations with the Vatican."[24] Despite such assurances, Protestants continued to hound the Roosevelt White House and later the Truman White House over any hint of U.S. representation to the Holy See.[25]

Pearl Harbor and America's entry into the war invigorated a patriotism that muted most of the criticism to the Taylor mission and permitted a closer working relationship between the White House and the Holy See. It also clarified Washington's new openness in relations. The Vatican proved to be of some value to the United States as a listening post in wartime Europe, but other potential uses rarely bore fruit. Roosevelt had already worked with Pius XII, for instance, to persuade Mussolini to maintain neutrality in the war's early stages, an effort that failed when the *Duce* declared war on Britain and France in June 1940. Washington also sought to secure papal blessings in the struggle against the Axis powers, a wish that intensified after the Japanese attack on Pearl Harbor and one never satisfied. While Pius XI had criticized Italian Fascist methods and German Nazi racism in the 1930s, his successor refrained from hailing the Allied cause over the Axis agenda once the war began. That America's most powerful ally was the Soviet Union complicated the issue. Roosevelt pleaded with Pius XII to sanction U.S. aid to Moscow, and on this the pope compromised a bit, instructing his apostolic delegate in America to temper disparagement of Stalin's regime insofar as it would not be misunderstood as scorn for the embattled Russian people. But this was not enough, and the frustrated president threatened the pontiff that his reluctance to publicly endorse the Allied cause might weaken his moral authority. Such unfortunate counsel, along with Anglo-American insistence on unconditional Axis surrender and the decision to bomb Rome in 1943, did nothing to secure Pius XII's support. Both Allied and Axis agents, nonetheless, badgered the pope throughout the war to solicit his support and claim his endorsement for their causes to the point that he simply resigned himself to their activities and did not bother to deny them.[26] The Holy See, however, secured a back-handed victory of sorts when, following Pearl Harbor and Italy's declaration of war against the United States on December 11, 1941, Taylor's office had to relocate out of the city of Rome and onto Vatican grounds. This did not much affect Taylor, who was rarely in Rome, but it changed the status of his assistant and man on the spot, Harold Tittmann, who was accorded the formal diplomatic status of *chargé d'affaires*. Roosevelt acquiesced, although the move did not help relations, which only deteriorated a few weeks later when Pius XII accepted a diplomatic mission from Japan.[27]

At the war's end, ties between the Holy See and the United States drew closer, joined in a community of purpose, perhaps even a de facto alliance, as anti-Communists. After the defeat of the Axis, the Cold War took center stage as the great international drama and caused Pius XII to remark to Tittmann that the Holy See must "look to the United States." In January of 1946, the pope emphasized the new situation by elevating four Americans, including Spellman, to the College of Cardinals.[28] On its part, as the historian Dianne Kirby has written, the Harry S Truman administration considered religion during those early postwar years as an "integral part" of its "campaign to persuade the American people to abandon isolationism, embrace globalism and world leadership, and roll back communism."[29] The president consequently rejected State Department proposals to close the Vatican mission and chose instead to maintain relations. In May 1946 Truman asked a reluctant Taylor to remain at his post, no longer as personal envoy but as "personal representative of the President," a linguistic deviation that appeared to give Taylor more of an official status and, as the State Department predicted, triggered a fresh barrage of

Protestant criticism.[30] In its new fight against Bolshevik Moscow, the United States now enjoyed some clear measure of the papal approval that it had failed to secure in its war against Germany and Italy. It appeared that America had become the next in line as the sword of the Holy See. Suddenly images of Pope Stephen II and the Frankish King Pepin or Leo III and Charlemagne offered themselves in reflections of Pius XII and President Truman. America's attitude toward the Holy See hinted of Charlemagne's congratulatory letter to Pope Leo III on his coronation in 796: "Your task, holy father, is to raise your hands to God like Moses to ensure the victory of our arms."[31] Truman's renewal of the Taylor mission in 1946 and his July 1947 draft letter to Pius, which declared that real peace must rest on Christian principles, emboldened the pontiff, who reciprocated often with hands raised to God in the late 1940s and early 1950s.

If this was indeed an alliance, the historian Peter Kent concluded that it lasted for but a brief moment—peaking when the 1948 Italian elections brought decisive victory to the Christian Democrats over the Socialist and Communist front, a victory followed the next year by the Holy Office's decree *Responsa ad dubia de communismo*, which excluded collaboration between Catholics and Communists. Kent noted that the Holy See never wholeheartedly occupied America's corner and that Washington frequently disappointed the pope. On his part, for instance, Pius doubted the worth of the 1949 NATO alliance and needed the persuasion of Italian Christian Democratic leaders to accept their country's adherence to it. The *Civiltà Cattolica* and the Vatican daily *Osservatore Romano*, moreover, both flatly rejected any papal alignment in the Cold War. Toward that end, two emphatic articles written in June 1947 by the *Osservatore*'s conservative editor, Giuseppe Dalla Torre, brought a State Department protest, delivered to Italy's ambassador in Washington. The Vatican paper, however, retracted and stated that the pieces conveyed only Dalla Torre's opinions. Criticisms of U.S. policy, nevertheless, continued, and Pius XII often condemned the atomic game played by both America and the Soviet Union. In a different regard, the Holy See could prove more hawkish than the Americans. Where the United States sought to contain the Soviet Empire, the pontiff wanted to fight back and defeat it. It can be said that the Soviet conquest of Eastern Europe did not launch a Cold War with the Vatican but, rather, a hot one in which many members of the Catholic clergy and faithful were perfunctorily arrested, exiled, or liquidated. This emergency, however, brought "no help and little sympathy from policy-makers in Washington." One such case where America and the Holy See parted ways involved Yugoslavia. Charles Gallagher's examination of events there has shown how Washington, anxious to draw the regime of Marshal Tito (Josef Broz) from the Soviet orbit, did nothing regarding the arrest of Archbishop Aloysius Stepinac, who had been charged as a collaborator with the wartime Croat Nazi puppet state. Stepinac was condemned in 1946 and died under house arrest fifteen years later, a martyr destined for canonization.[32]

More difficulties hampered formal U.S. diplomatic recognition of the Holy See, which, in the months after the 1948 Italian electoral crisis, seemed less and less of a pressing issue.[33] The end came when Myron Taylor finally retired on January 18, 1950. Washington hastily recalled Taylor's last assistant, Franklin C. Gowan, and ended a formal U.S. presence at the Holy See. "The office is closed," Gowan told the press, "that is all we know."

As in 1867, America's Vatican representation ended abruptly, and, as it occurred at the start of the 1950 Holy Year, many observers discerned a note of particular callousness. The *New York Times* noted that Taylor's move came as "an unpleasant surprise" that "disturbed and even affronted" the Holy See, which, however, still hoped that Truman would send a replacement.[34] Undaunted, members of the hierarchy, led by Cardinal Spellman and the apostolic delegate, continued to lobby for diplomatic relations. The president stalled until October 20, 1951, when he dropped a bombshell by announcing that he would not send a personal representative but would instead establish a full Vatican embassy and nominate as ambassador General Mark Clark, the Fifth Army commander who had liberated Rome in June 1944. Truman's press release noted that the decision to reopen the U.S. embassy after over eighty years was "in the national interest . . . in coordinating the effort to combat the Communist menace." "Purposes of diplomacy and humanitarianism," he added, "(would) also be served by this appointment."[35]

Within two days the *New York Times*, which still hoped that the United States would eventually establish diplomatic relations, nevertheless condemned the Clark nomination as "inept" and predicted "terrible consequences."[36] Protestant reaction had reached the boiling point. The normally staid *Christian Century*, for example, had already launched an apoplectic attack on Truman's "Vatican embassy fraud" born of "chicanery and deceit" in 1946 when he announced the continuation of Taylor's mission. That act, felt the magazine, had deserved "swift and overwhelming rebuke from all intelligent and patriotic Americans, whether they are Protestants, Roman Catholics or neither. This does not seem to be a time for polite and conciliatory language."[37] Protestants, then, did not hesitate to mobilize against the Clark appointment. Ten thousand of them held a rally in St. Louis' Kiel Auditorium, and the National Association of Evangelicals designated October 28, 1951, Reformation Sunday, to organize a nationwide protest. Among the most outspoken was Paul Blanshard, an ordained minister who also ferociously carried the banner for secularist sentiment in America. Debating Arthur Schlesinger Jr. in the pages of the *Atlantic Monthly*, Blanshard appreciated America's wish to enlist the Vatican as an ally against Moscow but claimed that the establishment of an embassy toward that end "strikes me as wishful thinking." The president's move to send an ambassador to "the single, absolute dictator of . . . the semi-religious and semi-political empire of Catholic power" was for Blanshard "a political stunt designed to attract Catholic voters." "We do not need," he wrote, "an ambassador to a territory the size of a golf course."[38] The columnist and editor for the Catholic *Commonweal*, John Cogley, joined the fray, responding that while not all opposition was delivered "with the vulgarity of a Blanshard" and not all of it was simply anti-Catholicism, it sadly revealed "the shocking deterioration of Catholic, non-Catholic relations in this country."[39]

The mechanics of the Clark nomination, furthermore, dashed most hopes for an American embassy to the Holy See. A rock-ribbed Protestant from Missouri and a Mason, Truman had revealed his secret reservations in 1946 after he asked Taylor to remain at his Roman post. To a gathering of disgruntled ministers, he confessed, "I inherited this thing. I would not have done it this way."[40] Five years later the president displayed, at best, poor judgment when he nominated Clark just hours before the 82nd Congress recessed, forcing him to resubmit the proposal when the legislature convened the following January. Clark also caused some discomfort when he refused to surrender his military position to become ambassador, an act that required Congressional action to overcome. Perhaps most damning, however, was ill-feeling toward Clark from the chair of the Senate Foreign Relations Committee, Tom Connally of Texas. War veterans from his state delivered harsh criticism of Clark for his alleged "sacrifice" of their comrades in the 36th Infantry National Guard Division during the Italian campaign. Connally subsequently opposed Clark as unfit for the Vatican embassy post, and Truman withdrew the nomination on January 13, 1952. Shortly thereafter, the House of Representatives voted to deny any funding for a revived U.S. mission, ending hopes for formal relations between Washington and Rome.[41]

The end of the Taylor mission and the Clark debacle cast a pall over U.S.–Holy See relations for almost two decades. "The consequences of this political firestorm," concluded one study, "was that Presidents Eisenhower, Kennedy and Johnson refused to establish any ties with the Holy See."[42] In Rome, Archbishop Giovanni Battista Montini at the Secretariat of State berated Cardinal Spellman over the "vulgar, bitter and entirely unjustified attacks" from American "non-Catholics"; in January 1953, even the archbishop of New York admitted defeat during a meeting with Pope Pius XII.[43]

As long as atheistic Soviet power maintained its stranglehold on Catholic nations, however, and as long as Communist states persecuted the church and the faithful, some measure of identification with America's side in the Cold War was inevitable. To Myron Taylor, for instance, Pius XII's nuncio to Paris, Archbishop Angelo Roncalli (the future Pope John XXIII), hoped, albeit privately, that American arms would prevail during the Korean War. Indications of good will included Dwight Eisenhower's courtesy call on the Vatican and his meeting with Pope John on December 6, 1959. Highlighted by a twenty-five-minute talk, this marked the second time a sitting American head of state visited the Holy See.[44] Real cooperation, moreover, occurred when America aided in the efforts to assist Catholic refugees from North Vietnam in 1954.[45] The U.S. embassy in Budapest also famously provided political asylum for the primate of Hungary, Cardinal József Mindszenty, who fled the Communist regime after the collapse of the 1956 revolution. The cardinal received safe haven within its four walls for fifteen years until he was allowed to leave for the Vatican in 1971.[46]

On another occasion, Pope John used his good offices to help break the deadlock during the October 1962 Cuban missile crisis. The Cold War thaw had enabled Rome to act as arbiter between the two superpowers rather than to be dismissed by many as a moral prop for the Americans. By 1961 John had already made clear his willingness to talk with the Soviets, and in November of that year, through his ambassador to Italy, Premier Nikita Khruschev sent birthday greetings to the pontiff, the first formal communication between Moscow and the Holy See since the Bolshevik revolution. Two days after Khruschev's greetings, John secretly transmitted his own best wishes to Moscow. A year later, during the darkest days of the Cuban missile crisis, President John Kennedy contacted Norman Cousins for help with the Holy See. A writer and international activist who had already called for a papal role in conflict resolution, Cousins was attending a conference at Andover, Massachusetts, along with Soviet scientists and writers. Also present was the controversial

Belgian Dominican Felix Morlion, who had been close to Clare Boothe Luce, the U.S. ambassador to Italy in the 1950s, and who was suspected of links to the Central Intelligence Agency. On the urging of Cousins and perhaps Morlion, Pope John, at his Wednesday audience of October 23, praised statesmen of both sides "who strive to come together to avoid war and bring peace to humanity." He also begged the heads of state "not to remain insensitive to the cry of humanity, peace, peace." In an extraordinary turn, the Communist organ *Pravda* printed this message on page 1 of its October 26 issue. It has been argued that John's actions presented Khruschev with an honorable exit from the crisis, a sentiment that the premier seemed to confirm in a subsequent discussion with Cousins. "The pope's message," he told the American, "was the only gleam of hope." In December of 1962, finally, Cousins had the honor of presenting Christmas greetings to the pontiff from both Kennedy and Khruschev, and he engineered the choice of Pope John XXIII as *Time* magazine's "Man of the Year."[47] The president intended to visit John the following summer, but the pope died on June 3, 1963. Kennedy then met in July with his successor, Paul VI.

While papal actions during the Cuban missile crisis may have been sanctioned by the Americans, the outcome was further confirmation that the Holy See intended to distance itself from one side or the other on the international stage. In the 1960s, U.S. involvement in Vietnam further divided the Holy See and Washington. Paul VI's one-day October 4, 1964, visit to the United Nations in New York constituted a cry to end the conflict. A nadir in this regard was reached in December 1967 when President Lyndon Johnson visited the Vatican and received a harsh rebuke from Paul.[48] Washington soon concluded, however, that some form of permanent contact with the Holy See was still called for and resumed the practice of sending personal representatives. Starting in 1970, President Richard Nixon and later Gerald Ford sent the Massachusetts Republican Henry Cabot Lodge; Jimmy Carter chose David Walter, the first Catholic envoy, followed by the former New York mayor Robert F. Wagner Jr.; Ronald Reagan tapped his long-time friend from California, William Wilson.

The setting for formal diplomatic relations, however, had to wait until 1978, when Karol Wojtyla came to the throne of St. Peter as Pope John Paul II, and 1981, when Ronald Reagan entered the White House. By then cracks in the Soviet empire had appeared in Catholic Poland, where the Solidarity movement opposed the Communist dictatorship; and the struggle, now invigorated by fresh hope, brought Rome and Washington together. Already in 1976, on his first visit to the United States to attend the Philadelphia Eucharistic Conference, Cardinal Wojtyla spoke in veiled references to Poland's "deep hunger for freedom and justice." As pope, John Paul II chose to travel as no pontiff had ever done, with clear consequences for Poland's struggle for freedom. In 1979, his first papal trip to Poland revealed that, probably more than any other world leader, John Paul II had the ability to attract colossal throngs of people. Watching developments from California, Ronald Reagan noted "then and there" to his advisor, Richard Allen, that "the pope was the key figure in determining the fate of Poland."[49] By 1980 and 1981 fears of Soviet intervention in Poland and John Paul's stubborn support of liberation, particularly for the Solidarity movement, earned him Reagan's increased attention and admiration, while in Washington a clique led by Central Intelligence Agency director Bill Casey, Secretary of State Alexander Haig, Deputy Secretary of State William Clark, National Security Advisor Richard Allen, and General Vernon Walters formed and pressed for closer work with the Holy See, using John Paul's formidable intelligence network and the force of his personality as a symbol to Poland. Their actions led to such measures as the channeling of two billion dollars through the Holy See to assist Polish farmers. In June of 1982, Reagan and John Paul II met for the first time in Rome.[50]

The mechanics of diplomatic recognition began with a one-hour talk on August 3, 1982, between Reagan and the Vatican secretary of state, Cardinal Agostino Casaroli, at the Knights of Columbus centenary celebration at the Hartford Civic Arena in Connecticut. Some weeks later, Reagan told his Roman liaison Wilson, "I realize the importance of having diplomatic relations with the Vatican and I've got to find a couple of senators and a couple of congressmen to support this." In the House of Representatives, key backing came from Clement Zablocki, the chair of the Foreign Affairs Committee. A Wisconsin Democrat from the heavily Catholic and Polish south side of Milwaukee, Zablocki introduced a resolution on June 30, 1983, to repeal the 1867 ban on funding. In the Senate, the Indiana Republican member of the Foreign Relations Committee, Richard Lugar, a Methodist, headed the drive to "end the awkward charade" of nonrecognition and attached the Zablocki resolution to a State Department authorization bill.[51] Neither the House nor the Senate held hearings, and President Reagan remained aloof during the process, but his press secretary, Larry Speakes, later credited America's recognition as partly a result of the high esteem held for Pope John Paul. "We respect the great moral and political influence which he and the Vatican exercise throughout the world," he stated. "We admire the courageous stands he takes in defense of western values."[52]

Consequently, on January 10, 1984, President Reagan announced the resumption of full diplomatic relations, designating William Wilson as America's first twentieth-century ambassador to the Holy See. A source of big financial contributions to Reagan's political career beginning in the early 1960s, Wilson was a convert to Catholicism whose fortune came from the oil tool industry and California real estate. John Paul reciprocated America's action in elevating the rank of Archbishop Pio Laghi, his representative in Washington, from apostolic delegate to papal pro-nuncio.[53] Congressman Zablocki, however, died, literally at his desk, in November 1983, never witnessing the fruit of his efforts. John Paul later acknowledged Zablocki in 1991 by naming a wing of a Polish hospital in his honor.

Protestant hard-line objections emerged from the start, although with less vigor than on previous occasions. The National Council of Churches opposed the development, and the Reverend Jerry Falwell warned that the Reagan administration was "making a very serious mistake" in diplomatic recognition. Protestant critics were joined by civil liberties organizations, some Jewish groups, and the *New York Times*, which dismissed recognition as mere pandering to the Catholic vote. In the Senate, South Carolina Democrat Ernest Hollings spoke against recognition as a violation of the First Amendment, and Gerald Fogarty noted in a *New York Times* interview that most, perhaps 90 percent, of U.S. bishops opposed formal diplomatic relations. A Gallup poll, however, revealed that the hierarchy split with lay Catholics, who favored recognition 79 to 11 percent, as did their Protestant brothers and sisters, although by a narrower margin of 48 to 29 percent. Some fundamentalist church groups and Americans United for Separation of Church and State brought court injunctions to halt recognition, but to no avail. In May 1985 the U.S. District Court of Eastern Pennsylvania dismissed the challenge, as did the Third Court of Appeals in Philadelphia the following March. Finally, on October 20, 1986, the U.S. Supreme Court refused to hear the case.[54] The embassy was there to stay.

Historical detachment will require more time, although it is safe to say that formal U.S.–Holy See relations have survived despite bumpy relations that followed the fall of the Muscovite empire. Even in 1986, Pope John Paul II's decision to visit Communist Cuba raised some eyebrows in the Reagan administration and illustrated that the new diplomatic relations between the two states did not quite constitute an alliance.[55] Vatican criticisms of capitalism, such as John Paul's 1987 encyclical *Sollicitudio rei socialis*, or its dismay over U.S. interventions in the Middle East in 1991 and 2003, served to further illustrate this. Social and cultural divisions also disturbed relations. The Clinton White House, for example, clashed with the Holy See over abortion and family issues at the 1994 International Conference on Population and Development in Cairo and at the Fourth World Conference on Women at Beijing in September 1995; at the United Nations Food and Agricultural Conference at Rome in November 1996, Pope John Paul sided with the Third World bloc against the United States over a proposed right to food. Arguments have continued into the twenty-first century. The Barack Obama administration and many American Catholics on the political left found fault with positions taken by Pope Benedict XVI, until, it was rumored, the United States even pressured the pontiff to abdicate in 2013.[56] Relations between Pope Francis and the Donald Trump administration (and his presidential campaign) have sometimes been distinguished by bizarre exchanges. In the summer of 2017 the *Civiltà cattolica* published an article very critical of an unholy alliance between conservative U.S. Catholics and Evangelical Protestants in support of President Trump, unleashing a firestorm from the right.[57]

Some old fights over "papism" or between Catholics and secularists still appear in these flaps; but the U.S. embassy to the Holy See remains open and somewhat special. That the United States has chosen to send an ambassador to a nation the size of a golf course is not typical of its diplomacy; many larger nations have not merited such a diplomatic presence. Washington's mission to Andorra, for instance, is under the jurisdiction of its embassy in Spain. U.S. representation in Monaco is conducted through its offices in France, and the U.S. ambassador to Liechtenstein doubles with, and resides in, Switzerland. The United States, nonetheless, has rejected the option of conducting affairs via its embassy to the Italian Republic and continues instead to maintain separate formal relations with the Holy See. In 2015 the embassy raised some eyebrows when it appeared to have moved from its spot near the Mazzini monument at the base of Rome's Aventine hill into a new location—namely, the U.S. embassy to the Italian Republic across town. During a June 2017 appointment, however, I entered not through the main entrance in the Via Veneto, but through a different door around the corner in the Via Sallustiana. The State Department official who welcomed my students and me emphasized that, truly, we were in a separate building and that, indeed, we were visiting America's embassy to the Holy See.

NOTES

1. On Madison, see Massimo L. Salvadori, *L'Europa degli Americani dai padri fondatori a Roosevelt* (Rome-Bari: Laterza, 2005), 101. On more general American Protestant treatments, see Jenny Franchot, *Roads to Rome: The Antebellum Protestant Encounter with Catholicism* (Berkeley: University of California Press, 1994); On "Maria Monk" see, particularly, chap. 7, 135–61.

2. Claudia Carlin, ed., *The Papal Encyclicals, 1740–1878* (Ann Arbor, Mich.: Pierian, 1990), 234–41. Pope Gregory XVI began his reign in 1831 during a period of revolutionary activity that foreshadowed 1848. During the deliberations leading to his election, a "harmless" bomb exploded inside of the conclave, and the cardinals received word that, if the affair did not end soon, restless Romans threatened to establish a republic. More serious revolts in Bologna, Ancona, and other northern reaches of the Papal States broke out immediately after Gregory XVI's ascension to the throne, prompting him to ask for Austrian aid in their suppression; Owen Chadwick, *A History of the Popes 1830–1914* (Oxford: Clarendon, 1998), 4–6. *Mirari vos* can also be located at http://www.papalencyclicals.net/Greg16/g16mirar.htm, and the Syllabus of Errors at http://www.papalencyclicals.net/Pius09/p9syll.htm, both accessed May 29, 2012. Many of the modern pronouncements of the Holy See can be accessed through the Vatican website, www.vatican.va.

3. Massimo Franco, *Parallel Empires: The Vatican and the United States—Two Centuries of Alliance and Conflict*, trans. Roland Flamini (New York: Doubleday, 2008), 29; see also James F. Connelly, *The Visit of Archbishop Gaetano Bedini to the United States of America (June, 1853–February, 1854)* (Rome: Libreria editrice dell'Università Gregoriana, 1960), 77–78, f. 12.

4. David J. Alvarez, *Spies in the Vatican: Espionage and Intrigue from Napoleon to the Holocaust* (Lawrence: University of Kansas Press, 2002), 19.

5. Howard R. Marraro, *American Opinion on the Unification of Italy, 1846–1861* (New York: Columbia University Press, 1932), 5–16.

6. Christopher Hibbert, *Garibaldi and His Enemies: The Clash of Arms and Personalities in the Making of Italy* (Boston: Little Brown, 1966), 105.

7. Giuseppi Garibaldi, *The Rule of the Monk; or Rome in the Nineteenth Century* (London: Cassell, Petter and Galpin, 1870).

8. Peter D'Agostino noted that this admiration extended to the progressive Jane Addams. The front hall of her Hull House in Chicago boasted a bust of Garibaldi; D'Agostino, *Rome in America: Transnational Catholic Ideology from the Risorgimento to Fascism* (Chapel Hill: University of North Carolina Press, 2004), 40, 73. Canada also honored Garibaldi in naming a mountain and a provincial park for him. On the bust in the Capitol, see http://www.senate.gov/artandhistory/art/artifact/Sculpture_21_00007.htm; accessed May 30, 2012.

9. Leo Francis Stock, ed., *Consular Relations between the United States and the Papal States; Instructions and Dispatches* (Washington, D.C.: American Catholic Historical Association, 1945), xxix–xxx, 159–78; Robert A. Graham, *Vatican Diplomacy: A Study of Church and State on the International Plane* (Princeton, N.J.: Princeton University Press, 1959), 335. Regarding the impact of the Roman Revolution on the United States, see D'Agostino, *Rome in America*, 26–31. In her recent study, Paola Gemme convincingly cautioned that America's image among the Italian revolutionaries can be easily exaggerated; Gemme, *Domesticating Foreign Struggles: The Italian Risorgimento and Antebellum American Identity* (Athens: University of Georgia Press, 2005). On Browne's march through Rome, see also Gemme's "Imperial Designs of Political Philanthropy: A Study of Antebellum Accounts of Italian Liberalism," *American Studies International* 39 (February 2001): 20.

10. From the poem "To Pius IX," in John Greenleaf Whittier, *The Complete Poetical Works of John Greenleaf Whittier* (Boston: Houghton Mifflin, 1892), 370–71. A short introduction to the poem nonetheless emphasized that Whittier was "no enemy of Catholics." It was translated into Italian in Sara Antonelli, Daniele Fiorentino, and Giuseppe Monsagrati, *Gli Americani e la repubblica romana del 1849* (Rome: Gangemi, 2000), 275–77.

11. Connelly, *Visit of Archbishop Gaetano Bedini*, especially 98–99, 118–22, 131–34; see also Franco, *Parallel Empires*, 6–19; Gemme, *Domesticating Foreign Struggles*, 131–34; and Gerald Fogarty, S.J., *The Vatican and the American Hierarchy from 1870 to 1965* (Stuttgart: Anton Hiersemann, 1982), 115, 117. The Italian renegade was Alessandro Gavazzi, who published a letter detailing his accusations in the August 27, 1853, *New York Times* under the title, "Ugo Bassi and Bedini."

12. Alvarez, "The Papacy in the Diplomacy of the American Civil War," *Catholic Historical Review* 69 (April 1983): 241–44.

13. "It was not," wrote King, "a courteous exit nor a dignified ending of this chapter of American diplomacy"; Stock, ed., *United States Ministers to the Papal States: Instructions and Dispatches, 1848–1868* (Washington, D.C.: The Catholic University of America Press, 1933), Introduction and 435–36.

14. Graham, *Vatican Diplomacy*, 25, 181–214. Graham noted that the number dipped to fourteen just before the First World War. On American Catholic reactions to the events of September 20, see D'Agostino, *Rome in America*, 74–80. The Whittier passage can be located in a letter of January 4, 1871; Whittier, *The Letters of John Greenleaf Whittier*, ed. John B. Pickard (Cambridge, Mass.: Harvard University Press, 1975), 3:247–49. U.S. president Woodrow Wilson experienced the fiction for himself when he visited Rome on January 4, 1919. He called on King Vittorio Emanuele III in the morning and then was obligated to return to the U.S. embassy before crossing the Tiber to see Pope Benedict XV. The *New York Times* reported that the two discussed Armenia, Palestine, and "social issues." Perhaps to emphasize the trip's dual purpose, the president abandoned his automobile, which took him to the king's Quirinal Palace, and then employed a horse-drawn carriage for the route to the Vatican. The Roman interlude also included a visit to Emilio Gallori's equestrian statue of Garibaldi atop the Janiculum Hill, where Wilson doffed his hat to the general. To further deemphasize his visit to the pontiff, the president met with Rome's Protestant leaders; "Half-Hour Talk with Pope," *New York Times*, January 5, 1919.

15. George Perkins Marsh is buried in Rome's Protestant cemetery.

16. William J. Lallou, *The Fifty Years of the Apostolic Delegation, Washington, D.C., 1893–1943* (Paterson, N.J.: St. Anthony Guild, 1943), 9.

17. D'Agostino, *Rome in America*, 74–80.

18. On Satolli and the "Americanism" debate, see Fogarty, *The Vatican and the American Hierarchy from 1870 to 1965*, 115–94; regarding *Longinqua Oceani*, 137; and regarding *Testem Benevolentiae*, 177–85. See also Daniela Saresella, *Cattolicesimo italiano e sfida Americana* (Brescia: Morcelliana, 2001), 91–95.

19. John T. Farrell, "Background of the 1902 Taft Mission to Rome," *Catholic Historical Review* 36 (April 1950): 1–32; Alvarez, "Purely a Business Matter: The Taft Mission to the Vatican," *Diplomatic History* 16 (Summer 1992): 357–69; Alvarez, *Spies in the Vatican*, 61–69; Frank T. Reuter, *Catholic Influence on American Colonial Policies, 1898–1904* (Austin: University of Texas Press, 1967), 137–59; Graham, *Vatican Diplomacy*, 341–43; and Luigi Bruti Liberati, *La Santa Sede e le origini dell'impero Americano: La Guerra del 1898* (Milan: Edizioni Unicopli, 1984), 115–22. Taft's opinion of Pope Leo was recorded in Reuter, *Catholic Influence*, 141. Reuter's optimistic conclusion can be found on p. 147.

20. On the impact of the Lateran Accords in the United States, see D'Agostino, *Rome in America*, 199–223. During the First World War, the United States saw the need for some ties but relied on the new British embassy to the Holy See. Washington asked London to station a diplomat there "who was informed about American affairs, including the attitudes of American Catholics." Toward that end, the British transferred Robert Wilberforce from their consulate in New York City to the Vatican. The United States also partly relied on the services of a confidant of Baltimore's Cardinal James Gibbons, Father Cyril Fay, who was ostensibly in Rome on Red Cross business; Alvarez, *Spies in the Vatican*, 125.

21. On the Pacelli visit, see Fogarty, *Vatican and the American Hierarchy*, 246–48; Leon Hutton, "The Future Pope Comes to America: Cardinal Eugenio Pacelli's Visit to the United States," *U.S. Catholic Historian* 24 (Spring 2006): 109–30.

22. Copies of the Celler letter and various drafts can be seen at the American Catholic History Research Center of the Catholic University of America, Collection 10, Box 11, File 1. On Gasparri's trip, see "Cardinal Gasparri Here for a Visit," *New York Times*, July 29, 1939.

23. Cordell Hull, *The Memoirs of Cordell Hull* (New York: Macmillan, 1948), 713–16; Fogarty, *Vatican and the American Hierarchy*, 259–61.

24. Graham, *Vatican Diplomacy*, 327–28. President Roosevelt also sent a copy of the letter to the president of the Jewish Theological Seminary, Cyrus Adler.

25. Michael H. Carter, "Diplomacy's Detractors: American Protestant Reaction to FDR's 'Personal Representative' at the Vatican," in *FDR, the Vatican, and the Roman Catholic Church in America, 1933–1945*, ed. David B. Woolner and Richard G. Kurial (New York: Palgrave Macmillan, 2003), 178–208. Carter considered the Protestant response as part of the broader movement toward "ecumenical unity and political activism within the mainline denominations" and noted that "while anti-Catholic rhetoric was prominent throughout the debate . . . neither bigotry nor sincere fear of pernicious Catholicism are sufficient to explain the Protestant reaction."

26. John S. Conway, "Pope Pius XII and the Myron Taylor Mission: The Vatican and American Wartime Diplomacy," in Woolner and Kurial, *FDR, the Vatican, and the Roman Catholic Church*, 146–49; see also Conway's "Myron C. Taylor's Mission to the Vatican, 1940–1950," *Church History* 44 (March 1975): 85–99; Alvarez, *Spies in the Vatican*, chaps. 5 and 6; Fogarty, *Vatican and the American Hierarchy*, 259–71; and Fogarty, "United States and the Vatican, 1939–1984," in *Papal Diplomacy in the Modern Age*, ed. Peter C. Kent and John F. Pollard (Westport, Conn.: Praeger, 1994), 222–31. On the problems raised by the Soviet Union, see also Peter Kent, "Toward the Reconstitution of Christian Europe: The War Aims of the Papacy, 1938–1945," in Woolner and Kurial, *FDR, the Vatican, and the Roman Catholic Church*, 165; Frank J. Coppa, "Pope Pius XII and the Cold War: The Post-War Confrontation between Catholicism and Communism," in Wolner and Kurial, *FDR, the Vatican, and the Roman Catholic Church*, 50–52; and Graham, *Vatican Diplomacy*, 347. On the bombing of Rome, see Robert Trisco, "The Department of State and the Apostolic Delegation in Washington During World War II," in Woolner and Kurial, *FDR, the Vatican, and the Roman Catholic Church*, 226–31; and Elisa A. Carrillo, "Italy, the Holy See and the United States, 1939–1945," in Kent and Pollard, *Papal Diplomacy in the Modern Age*, 139–45.

27. Fogarty, *Vatican and the American Hierarchy*, 278–84.

28. Ibid., 310–11.

29. Dianne Kirby, "Harry Truman's Religious Legacy: The Holy Alliance, Containment and the Cold War," in *Religion and the Cold War*, ed. Dianne Kirby (Basingstoke, Hampshire: Palgrave Macmillan, 2003), 77–78. The Italian historian Ennio Di Nolfo also raised the question of "convergence or alliance" between postwar America and the Holy See. He concluded that "two parallel lines never connect, by definition, but they travel in the same direction"; Di Nolfo, "Convergence ou alliance?," in *Actes du colloque: Nations et Sainte-Siège au XXe Siècle* (Paris: Fayard, 2003), 251–63.

30. On State Department reservations, see George J. Gill, "The Truman Administration and Vatican Relations," *Catholic Historical Review* 73 (July 1987): 408–9.

31. J. M. Wallace-Hadrill, *The Frankish Church* (Oxford: Clarendon, 1998), 186. Alcuin probably wrote the letter.

32. Kent, *The Lonely Cold War of Pope Pius XII: The Roman Catholic Church and the Division of Europe, 1943–1950* (Montreal: McGill-Queen's University Press, 2004), 5, 191–93; Charles R. Gallagher, "The United States and the Vatican in Yugoslavia, 1945–1950," in Kirby, *Religion and the Cold War*; see also Dennis J. Dunn, "Stalinism and the Catholic Church during the Era of

World War II," *Catholic Historical Review* 59 (October 1973): 385–428. On Pius XII and NATO in the Italian context, see Carla Meneguzzi Rostagni, *"Il Vaticano e i rapporti Est-Ovest nel secondo dopoguerra (1945–1949),"* *Storia delle relazioni internazionali* 4 (1988): 1; and Guido Formigoni, *La Democrazia cristiana e l'alleanza occidentale* (Bologna: Il Mulino, 1996). Formigoni notes (163) that the Dalla Torre articles earned praise from none other than the head of the Italian Communist Party, Palmiro Togliatti.

33. George J. Gill also considered Italian events to be crucial. "It was the future of Italy . . . that seems to have prompted action on Taylor's status." Already in 1947 Washington had started to pull the Taylor mission away from the Holy See and toward the U.S. embassy to Italy by attaching the office of Taylor's assistant, then J. Graham Parsons, to the latter. Pius's undersecretary of state, Domenico Tardini, protested, and Parsons remained assigned to the Taylor office; Gill, "Truman Administration and Vatican Relations," 411–14.

34. "Vatican Hopes U.S. Names Full Envoy," *New York Times*, February 24, 1950. By March 1950 the White House received about three thousand letters daily that opposed continuation of the Taylor office. At about the same time, Taylor's former assistant, Gowan, told Cardinal Spellman that letters to the State Department were running 25,000 to 27 against renewal. When Truman renewed the Taylor mission, he replaced Tittmann with J. Graham Parsons, who was, in turn, replaced by Gowan in February 1947; Gill, "Truman Administration and Vatican Relations," 419, 421; Fogarty, *Vatican and the American Hierarchy*, 315–20; and Fogarty, "United States and the Vatican, 1939–1984," in Kent and Pollard, *Papal Diplomacy in the Modern Age*, 231–37. Peter Kent noted that, since Taylor was rarely in Rome toward the end of his mission, his loss was not particularly upsetting. Rather, the U.S. timing and its lack of interest in replacing Taylor seemed to particularly offend the Holy See; Kent, *Lonely Cold War of Pope Pius XII*, 251–54.

35. On the Clark nomination, see Fogarty, *Vatican and the American Hierarchy*, 328–32; F. William O'Brien, "General Clark's Nomination as Ambassador to the Vatican: American Reaction," *Catholic Historical Review* 44 (January 1959): 421–39; "Gen. Clark Named First Ambassador of U.S. to Vatican," *New York Times*, October 21, 1951.

36. "Editorial Comment on Truman's Plan to Send Envoy to Vatican," *New York Times*, October 23, 1951.

37. "Vatican Embassy Fraud," *Christian Century*, April 3, 1946, 422–24.

38. Arthur Schlesinger Jr., "Relations with the Vatican: Why Not?," and Paul Blanshard, "One-Sided Diplomacy," both in *Atlantic Monthly*, January 1952. Blanshard went to Rome in 1950 as the correspondent for the left-wing review, *The Nation*. On his campaign against U.S.–Holy See relations, see Fogarty, "United States and the Vatican, 1939–1984," in Kent and Pollard, *Papal Diplomacy in the Modern Age*, 364–67.

39. John Cogley, "Call It the Thing," *The Commonweal*, November 9, 1951. In 1953 the *Osservatore Romano* claimed that America, for a while in World War II, had indeed sent a man of formal diplomatic status to the Holy See in the person of Harold Tittmann. As *chargé d'affaires*, he had set a precedent that later was conveniently forgotten; Graham, *Vatican Diplomacy*, 331–32.

40. Carter, "Diplomacy's Detractors: American Protestant Reaction to FDR's 'Personal Representative' at the Vatican," in Woolner and Kurial, *FDR, the Vatican, and the Roman Catholic Church*, 189.

41. "Clark Withdraws as Vatican Choice; Another Planned," *New York Times*, January 14, 1952.

42. Andrew M. Essig and Jennifer Moore, "U.S.–Holy See Diplomacy: The Establishment of Formal Relations, 1984," *Catholic Historical Review* 95 (October 2009): 744.

43. Fogarty, *Vatican and the American Hierarchy*, 329; Fogarty, "United States and the Vatican, 1939–1984," in Kent and Pollard, *Papal Diplomacy in the Modern Age*, 234–36; Essig and Moore, "U.S.–Holy See Diplomacy: The Establishment of Formal Relations, 1984," 744n8. The archbishop had become so identified with the idea of an embassy to the Holy See that one Protestant

critic branded the whole effort one of "Spellmanism"; O'Brien, "General Clark's Nomination as Ambassador to the Vatican: American Reaction," 428.

44. "Talks with Pope John at Vatican," *New York Times* December 7, 1959. On the first visit, that of President Wilson, see note 14. In his study on religion and the U.S. presidents, Merlin Gustafson wrote that "the Eisenhower administration was noted for its religiosity." Although the president enjoyed warm relations with two Jesuits from Creighton University, men who had access to the White House, his focus was clearly on U.S. Protestants. He first entrusted religious affairs to two Episcopalians, Sherman Adams and James Hagerty; while in his second term, he appointed Frederick E. Fox, a Congregationalist minister, as liaison with religious groups; Gustafson, "The Religious Role of the President," *Midwest Journal of Political Science* 14 (November 1970): 710–17.

45. Roy Domenico, "America, the Holy See and the War in Vietnam," in Peter C. Kent and John F. Pollard, *Papal Diplomacy in the Modern Age*, 206–8. On Roncalli, see Ennio Di Nolfo, *Vaticano e Stati Uniti, 1939–1952* (Milan: Franco Angeli Editore, 1978), 654–55.

46. Chadwick, *The Christian Church in the Cold War* (London: Penguin, 1993), 67–72.

47. Giancarlo Zizola, *The Utopia of Pope John XXIII*, trans. Helen Barolini (Maryknoll, N.Y.: Orbis, 1978), 117–20, 141; Peter Hebblethwaite, *Pope John XXIII: Shepherd of the Modern World* (Garden City, N.Y.: Doubleday, 1987), 445–48. I would also like to thank Professor Thomas J. Carty of Springfield College for sharing with me some of his research on this subject contained in his unpublished paper "A Catholic President at the Vatican? John F. Kennedy's Visit to the Holy See in 1963." On the roles of Cousins and Morlion during the Cuban Missile Crisis, see Karim Schelkens, "Vatican Diplomacy after the Cuban Missile Crisis: New Light on the Release of Josyf Slipyi," *Catholic Historical Review* 97 (October 2011): 694–99. Regarding the intriguing figure of Felix Morlion, see Alvarez, *Spies in the Vatican*, 253–57.

48. Domenico, "America, the Holy See and the War in Vietnam," in Kent and Pollard, *Papal Diplomacy in the Modern Age*, 213–14; Hebblethwaite, *Paul VI: The First Modern Pope* (Mahwah, N.J.: Paulist Press, 1993), 510–13.

49. Essig and Moore, "U.S.–Holy See Diplomacy: The Establishment of Formal Relations, 1984," 745–46. Allen recorded that the scenes of John Paul II in Poland brought tears to Reagan's eyes.

50. George Weigel, *Witness to Hope: The Biography of Pope John Paul II* (New York: Harper Collins, 1999), 399–411, 441–42. Weigel concludes that while Reagan and John Paul II shared the same motives in opposing the Soviet empire in Poland, "there was no conspiracy." Nevertheless, Andrew Essig and Jennifer Moore, drawing on the work of Mark Riebling, note that while refueling in Alaska during a return trip from Asia, John Paul II met with William Wilson, who presented him with a letter from President Reagan urging the pontiff to "use" the representative "for sensitive matters you or your associates may wish to communicate with me"; Essig and Moore, "U.S.–Holy See Diplomacy: The Establishment of Formal Relations, 1984," 746–47. Gerald Fogarty discerned other elements that may have been in the mix of diplomatic recognition. President Reagan, he wrote, wanted the pontiff to rein in the "activist American bishops opposing the vast American nuclear-arms buildup"; Fogarty, "U.S.-Vatican 'Alliance' Has Precedents in Church History," *National Catholic Reporter*, February 28, 1992. Regarding the Catholic group in the White House, William Clark succeeded Richard Allen as national security advisor in January 1982.

51. Essig and Moore, "U.S.–Holy See Diplomacy: The Establishment of Formal Relations, 1984," 750–51; Vicki Ann Crumpton, "An Analysis of Southern Baptist Response to Diplomatic Relations between the United States and the Vatican" (Ph.D. diss., Southwestern Baptist Theological Seminary, 1988), 51–52. North Carolina senator Jesse Helms was listed as cosponsor with Lugar of the Senate in that he had introduced an earlier measure.

52. Fogarty, "The United States and the Vatican, 1939–1984," in Kent and Pollard, *Papal Diplomacy in the Modern Age*, 237–40. Zablocki once recalled his chagrin when, at the funeral of Poland's Cardinal Stefan Wyszyńsky, Wilson, as President Reagan's representative, was not allowed to sit with the diplomatic corps. See also Essig and Moore, "U.S.–Holy See Diplomacy: The Establishment of Formal Relations, 1984," 756.

53. Pio Laghi remained in Washington as pro-nuncio until 1990, when Agostino Cacciavillan succeeded him. The latter served from that year until 1998. The Holy See's website attributes the full nuncio title to him; http://www.vatican.va/news_services/press/documentazione/documents/cardinali_biografie/cardinali_bio_cacciavillan_a_en.html (accessed June 28, 2012).

54. Fogarty, "The United States and the Vatican, 1939–1984," in Kent and Pollard, *Papal Diplomacy in the Modern Age*, 236. Fogarty noted that even in 1970, when President Nixon appointed Lodge, Protestant response had become "pro forma." Crumpton, "Analysis of Southern Baptist Response," 51–53. Ambassador Wilson, however, soon found himself involved in a scandal regarding relations with Libya that led to his resignation and return to private business in 1986.

55. Marie Gayte, "The Vatican and the Reagan Administration: A Cold War Alliance?," *Catholic Historical Review* 97 (October 2011): 734–35. In June of 1987 the U.S. ambassador Frank Shakespeare reported that the Holy See considered the Global North-South split to be as important as the East-West one.

56. See for example, Massimo Faggioli, "Benedict's Resignation: Blame Obama," *Commonweal*, March 8, 2017.

57. "Confidant of Pope Francis Offers Scathing Critique of Trump's Religious Supporters," *Washington Post*, July 13, 2017; James Carroll, "Pope Francis Is the Anti-Trump," *New Yorker*, February 1, 2017. The original article in question was Antonio Spadaro and Marcelo Figueroa, "Fondamentalismo evangelico e integralismo cattolico: Un sorprendente ecumenismo," *Civiltà cattolica* Q.4010, v. III, July 15, 2017. It can be read in its English translation, "Evangelical Fundamentalism and Catholic Integralism: A Surprising Ecumenism," on the *Civiltà cattolica* website: http://www.laciviltacattolica.it/articolo/evangelical-fundamentalism-and-catholic-integralism-in-the-usa-a-surprising-ecumenism/.

PART TWO

Engaging the World

SIX

American and Catholic and Literature:
What Cultural History Helps Reveal

Una M. Cadegan

For as long as there have been American Catholics, they have been writing what we can call "American Catholic literature." For the cultural historian, the trick is that what we call literature is a slippery category—it has changed a great deal over time and keeps changing as we speak. That is, "literature" is a historically contingent category—not everything written comes to be regarded as "literature," and much of what is included in that category at one time might be left out at another. Understanding how and why the criteria for inclusion change helps us see where Catholic literary culture fits into the big picture. Two questions will help us to orient ourselves—What were Catholics writing and publishing? And how did what they wrote and published relate to what was going on in the publishing world and the literary academy? When we answer these questions thoughtfully, we will see that we can learn more not only about Catholic literature, but about American literature as well.

Most of the earliest sustained narratives written by Europeans in the decades following first contact with the continents of North and South America are "Catholic literature" in the sense that they were written by Catholics, often by priests, and are also usually explicit explorations of how Catholicism was faring in the New World. So, for example, the diaries of Christopher Columbus, or Bartolomeo de las Casas's (1484–1566) passionate condemnation of the treatment of indigenous peoples by the Spanish *conquistadores* in his *Defense of the Indians*, or the massive (18,000 pages, in one English translation) *Jesuit Relations*, documenting the seventeenth-century history of the Society of Jesus's work among the natives in New France, all clearly form part of the literary history of Roman Catholicism in the New World.

Two things may seem to be missing here that will help us understand the boundaries of the amorphous thing we are calling "American Catholic literature": first, the works described include no fiction—no novels or stories or poems or plays. Second, the list does not include anything written originally in English in the colonies of Massachusetts and Virginia, where "American" histories usually begin. These two apparent omissions illustrate some important things about the history of American Catholic literary culture. First, the category of "literature" was much more capacious—it held more things and more different kinds of things—before about 1920 than it was for about the next seventy-five years. And when, after about 1920, the category narrowed considerably, one of the kinds of things that disappeared was most writing by Catholics. Second, the English-language focus of most definitions of American literature elides the presence of most Catholics from American literary history until the early national period, when figures such as John Carroll (1725–1815), the first bishop of the United States, emerged onto the national scene.

We can gain greater clarity on what we mean by "literature" if we understand it in relationship to the idea of "print culture." This term refers to the whole cultural system by which all print materials are produced, disseminated, and assimilated. The study of print culture includes not just the reading and interpretation of a work of "literature," such as *Moby-Dick*, but also the circumstances of its printing, the history of its reception (who read it? did they like it? what did book reviewers say about it?), the examination of other works published at the same time and now forgotten—in short, the entirety of the human activities surrounding the production and use of print. It thus also includes not just famous works such as *Moby-Dick*, but advertisements, magazines, religious tracts, newspapers, and dime novels—all of the printed material produced in a given society at a given time.

What does the study of print culture tell us that looking at "literary culture" alone does not? It helps us see the "extra-literary" factors that shape the category of the literary. Who decides whether a certain work gets into print? Whether it gets heavily advertised? Whether it is reviewed in major newspapers and prestigious literary magazines? Who plays a role in keeping an author's work in print after he or she dies? Answers to these questions are not always easy to obtain, and even if we do obtain them, we do not then necessarily know everything we need to know about how "literature" gets made and defined. But we do see things that we otherwise would not see. A cultural historian wants to see as much as possible of the whole system of meaning within which a work is embedded. That system includes things that are not "literary" as most critics would define the term, but for cultural historians that is much of the point.

Historians of print culture date its origins, reasonably, to the mid-fifteenth-century invention of movable type. Crucial transformations in the way knowledge was conceived and transmitted unfolded over the course of the following centuries. When industrialization got well underway after the mid-1700s, it brought about a less entirely transformative but nonetheless massive change in the role of print in society. This change stemmed from the development of steam-powered printing presses and was furthered by the wide distribution of printed material made possible by the growth of the railroad in the middle of the nineteenth century. By the late nineteenth century, printed materials of all sorts were more widely available more cheaply than ever before in human history.

This transformation coincided in time with the period of greatest growth in the U.S. Catholic population, as immigrants, first from Ireland and Germany and then from the countries of southern and eastern Europe, poured in and transformed the social, political, and religious landscape of the United States from the 1820s through the 1910s. In important ways, then, U.S. Catholicism and U.S. print culture grew up together, and each left its imprint on the other. One of the earliest and most successful nineteenth-century printers and booksellers, Mathew Carey, was responsible for the first Catholic (Douay Version) Bible printed in the United States.[1] The waves of immigrants to the United States included members of long-time European printing and bookselling families who established branches of their original houses that in some cases grew larger than the ones at home. From their earliest years, the U.S. bishops who met in plenary councils to decide on matters of importance to the church had print and its necessity and potential benefits and dangers always in their sight.

If, then, over the course of the nineteenth century, print was transforming the United States as a whole, what is there to say about its effect on Catholicism, and about Catholics' use of it, specifically? Was the relationship different from that of other Americans? In many ways, of course, Catholics used and were affected by print culture in ways very similar to other Americans—they read novels, newspapers, pamphlets, and periodicals, just as their compatriots did. But Catholics as Catholics—that is, as self-conscious members of a group set apart in certain important ways from their compatriots—also appropriated print culture in ways particular to themselves. Three factors in this appropriation emerge as distinctive and distinctively important.

For Catholics, print was always in the service of other (and, they would say, higher) goals. This is most clearly evident in the centrality within Catholic print culture of scriptural, liturgical, and devotional works used in the official and unofficial, public and private worship of the church. Approved Catholic versions of the Bible, sacramentaries and lectionaries (containing the prayers and readings for use at Mass and the other sacraments), missals and prayer books for individual worship and devotion—all of these colored the content of Catholic print culture as well as generating business for the printers and booksellers who produced and sold them. The centrality of scriptural and liturgical texts does not set Catholics off uniquely, however, because the same would also be true of Protestants; the larger point here is that the history of print culture itself changes if religious publishing is included.

Catholic print culture was genuinely distinctive, however, in two ways. First is the interdependence between print and material objects. The interdependence was on one level economic—it was conventional wisdom among nineteenth-century printers that one could not make sufficient profit selling books. Where religious booksellers made money was in the sale of church goods. Within Catholic culture, though, the economic connection was not the sole or, perhaps, the most basic one. Books and religious objects went together in other, more meaningful ways as well. Devotions very often connected some material object—scapulars, the rosary, statues, and pictures—with prayers and readings designed for meditation and study. This connection between print and object is not solely implicit. For example, in his widely reprinted advice book for young women in domestic service, George Deshon insisted that even if a young woman could not read, she should "not be cast down on that account." "There is one beautiful book, at least, we can read; and that is the Crucifix," which contains "fountains of knowledge and true wisdom." In addition, the rosary is "another lovely book you have that you can read, though you never learned a letter of the alphabet."[2]

The second way in which Catholic print culture was distinctive is related to the first. Since print was always in the service of other goals, especially worship, it was subject to the structures of Catholic authority. The church had established rules governing print from the earliest years of the print revolution; these rules had remained almost unchanged from the end of the sixteenth century through the end of the nineteenth. The most famous result of these rules was the *Index Librorum Prohibitorum*, a list of books Catholics were forbidden to read without permission because they were in some significant way contrary to church doctrine. The Index existed all the way up until 1966 and affected the way Catholics thought about literature in various ways throughout that time.

Pope Leo XIII (r. 1878–1903) is probably best known for his encyclicals such as the 1891 *Rerum novarum*, which outlined the church's responsibility to address the conditions created by industrialization; these encyclicals now form the basis for the contemporary understanding of Catholic social teaching. Another significant way in which Leo XIII attempted to address the church's relationship to the modern era was by ordering a review and revision of canon law (the official internal law of the church) concerning the church's censorship regulations. It makes intuitive sense that the church would be intent on ensuring that versions of scripture and liturgical texts, as well as theological and catechetical works, were consistent with church doctrine. But the regulations regarding publication— and reading, as well—applied to all kinds of texts. There were, to be sure, specific criteria that applied to official books for worship and the teaching of doctrine. But canon law regarding print and reading took into account all the possible reading experiences of believers and put at its center the importance of safeguarding faith. In a culture that, especially after the first decade of the twentieth century, tended to emphasize not communal standards and doctrinal integrity, but individual autonomy and intellectual freedom, this stance was one of the things that set Catholics and Catholic literary culture most clearly apart from their compatriots and had considerable impact on how they participated in the more explicitly literary parts of American print culture.

Seeing Catholic print culture in light of the development of print in the industrial era is important for context. What, though, did the more specifically "literary" dimensions of Catholic culture look like as the Catholic community in the United States grew and changed in the course of the nineteenth century? U.S. Catholics consciously emulated the aspects of American literary culture that they saw as worthy in aesthetic and social terms, but deficient in terms of the Catholic view of the world. That is, they largely accepted and advocated what scholars have called the "genteel tradition," the view of the arts and culture as crucial to the life of an educated person and to the uplift or social mobility of the immigrant classes. This genteel tradition was the most influential strain of American literary culture in the years between the Civil War and the First World War. Catholics parted company with their fellow Americans, however, when genteel culture took on an explicitly Protestant slant. In response, Catholics created an alternative network of literary institutions that attempted to achieve the same goals but with an explicitly Catholic doctrinal and cultural flavor.

For example, Isaac Hecker (1819–88), founder of the Paulists, was a fervent believer in the power of print culture to spread the gospel and the responsibility of Catholics to take every advantage to be in its forefront. In response to the (Protestant) American Tract Society's wide nineteenth-century distribution of religious pamphlets, Hecker established the Catholic Publication Society, which by the measure of material printed and distributed was probably the largest publisher of its time. In addition, he could see the value of popular middle-class periodicals such as *Harper's* and the *Atlantic Monthly* in cultivating educated good taste among upwardly mobile Catholic Americans, but he worried, too, about the Protestant bias of these magazines. So he established the *Catholic World* as a deliberate Catholic counterpart. It published, as did *Harper's* and the *Atlantic Monthly*, essays, stories, poetry, book reviews, and other material aimed at educating and uplifting its audience, but it did so in light of Catholic doctrine and inclusive of Catholic history and culture.

Other Catholic writers, such as Mary Anne Sadlier, wrote the kind of domestic novels that were probably the single most popular genre in the nineteenth century, when women constituted by far the majority of published authors and of the reading public. Sadlier's heroines, however, were Catholic women, most often Irish servant girls who learned that the seductive material comforts of American culture were, in the long run, inherently unsatisfying, and that embracing the faith first instilled in them beside the peat fires of the thatched cottages they had left behind in Ireland was the way to true happiness in this life and eternal happiness in the next.

American Catholics also aimed at creating and fostering an elite literary culture that would combine the rich tradition of Catholic art with the energy of the U.S. experience to produce a new contribution to the world's great literature. This endeavor would take on increased energy in the twentieth century, but its foundations were clearly in place by the end of the nineteenth century. A number of Catholic writers and critics such as Agnes Repplier (1858–1950) and Maurice Francis Egan (1852–1924) regularly exhorted Catholics to develop more cultivated tastes and work toward real literary greatness.

So, on the threshold of the Great War Catholic literary culture was lively, somewhat bifurcated, but with what seems like a clear trajectory—the unlettered immigrant population would be introduced to the great tradition of Western art and thought, and their upward mobility would be not only economic but cultural. For most U.S. Catholics in the intellectual classes in the early twentieth century, Matthew Arnold's description of the culture of the educated person as "the best that has been thought and said" required a bit of Catholic translation, but they did not question the description's assumption that there were lower and higher forms of art and that the aim of the writer should be to appeal to what was higher and better and train the tastes of the lower classes away from the former and toward the latter. As with the more general, culturally Protestant strain of the genteel tradition, these assumptions would be seriously shaken by the era that followed the Great War.

American literature was invented in the 1920s. The story is not quite that simple, of course—otherwise, excellent scholars would have written many fewer books on the topic. But, if by "American literature" we mean a body of work read in schools and universities, studied and written about by scholars, and embodying some meaningful essence of American identity and experience, then it came into being not in the 1490s or the 1620s or the 1770s or the 1850s but in the 1920s. Before that, literature (in the sense of recent creative writing in English) was not ordinarily the subject of university study nor of scholarly attention. Scholars of literature studied the Greek and Roman classics and the writing of the Middle Ages and Renaissance. The great English writers of the eighteenth and nineteenth centuries, writers such as Laurence Sterne and Samuel Richardson and Jane Austen and George Eliot and Charles Dickens, read now primarily in classrooms—this was the stuff of leisure time, not of serious study and scholarship. If this was true of the major English writers, it was even more true of American writing, which was largely presumed to reflect the general shallowness, youth, and crassness of American culture as a whole. This is not to say that the writings we call "American literature" were all *written* in the 1920s. There had by that time been a flourishing and nationalistically self-conscious literary culture in America for well over a century. But "American literature" as an object of serious study and scholarship did not enjoy widespread intellectual legitimacy until at least the third decade of the twentieth century. When this idea of "Americanness" in literature emerged and became prominent (if not dominant), it had significant consequences for American Catholic literary life.

As early as the 1880s, critics were talking about a "renaissance" in American literature, centered especially on the 1850s. What helped make this idea the most influential and pervasive way of thinking about American literature for the next fifty years was F. O. Matthiessen's 1941 book *American Renaissance.* By the time Matthiessen's book was published, the term had been in widespread use for decades. It reflected a definition of "American literature" that deemphasized the wide variety of things Americans wrote and published and read and instead emphasized a definition that was primarily nationalist and formalist—that is, literature was "American" if it reflected important elements of American culture and identity, and it was "literature" if it met certain requirements of formal and stylistic quality as determined by literary critics rather than by a wide range of readers.[3] When Matthiessen and other critics in the 1920s looked back in time, they recovered from the nineteenth century a tradition that included what most people even today would agree is a hall of fame of American writing: Ralph Waldo Emerson, Henry David Thoreau, Walt Whitman, Nathaniel Hawthorne, Herman Melville, Mark Twain, Henry James. (In recent years, we have also consciously reincluded women writers active in the same era, especially Emily Dickinson, Harriet Beecher Stowe, and Margaret Fuller.) To understand why this list has particular implications for American Catholic literary culture, it is worth thinking for a moment about what the term "Renaissance" meant in American culture in the 1920s.

It is not too strongly put to say that "the Renaissance" was an idea defined largely *against* Catholicism and Catholic history. Almost the entire emphasis of "Renaissance" in the early twentieth century, in both professional history and wider cultural colloquial use, was on the period's distinction from the Middle Ages. The Middle Ages were church-centered; the Renaissance was secular. Medieval meant blind faith; Renaissance meant increasing personal and political autonomy. Medieval meant hierarchy and tyrannical monarchy; Renaissance meant the recovery of classical notions of democracy and the seeds of modern self-government. So to cast the retrieval of a grand tradition of American literature as a "renaissance" was to ally it with freedom from traditional religion and emphasize instead the creation of a new tradition of individual autonomy and freedom from history.

One of the things a reader would never guess from reading *American Renaissance* or much mid-twentieth-century literary criticism is how interested its authors were in Catholicism.[4] Margaret Fuller, Herman Melville, and Ralph Waldo Emerson were all in Rome during the 1848 revolutions in that city and across Europe. These revolutions, especially the Italian one, were passionate nationalist movements against the involvement of the church in the temporal—that is, political and economic—affairs of the nation. Because these movements were usually at least anticlerical and often also actively antireligious, writing about them inevitably meant choosing how to depict the insular and anti-modern Vatican of Pope Pius IX (r. 1846–78). Writers like Fuller and Emerson had complicated and ambivalent reactions to the Roman Catholicism they saw and experienced during their time in Europe, but this aspect of their work seldom emerged as part of their credentials in the American Renaissance. Yet, the influence and the fascination were there. Fuller's dispatches to the *New York Tribune* helped inspire Walt Whitman's "Resurgemus," one of the poems in the first version of *Leaves of Grass*.[5] Scholars of Mark Twain and Harriet Beecher Stowe go out of their way to explain (or explain away) Twain's fascination (infatuation, even) with Joan of Arc and Stowe's sojourn in Renaissance Italy with *Agnes of Sorrento*. Why these works are less well known to us than *The Adventures of Huckleberry Finn* or *Uncle Tom's Cabin* may seem obvious, but that very obviousness demonstrates the extent to which the American Renaissance helped to write Catholics largely out of American literary history.

So, the redefining and refining of the category of literature in nationalist and formalist terms that took place between the two world wars effectively elided Catholics from the overall narrative. When we realize this—that and how this particular definition of literature shifted over time—Catholics and Catholicism reappear. The most important reappearance is that of Orestes Brownson (1803–76). Brownson was by any reasonable measure one of the most prominent and influential of the New England circle of Transcendentalists when he became a convert to Roman Catholicism in 1844.[6] Brownson's conversion meant renouncing much of his success and influence. He continued to write for the rest of his life, however, turning his talents to defending Catholicism against its American detractors. Reconstructed in the early twentieth century, the "American" renaissance could not encompass a story that told the history of modernity in reverse—from untrammeled visionary transcendentalism to Romanist apologia. And so when the pantheon of nineteenth-century American writing was put together in the 1920s it left out one of the main players.

This rethinking of the history and tradition of American literature was an enormously important element of the American literary scene after the Great War, but it was far from the only thing that affected American Catholic literary culture. What, in the years following this war, happened to the lively Catholic literary culture that had seen itself as so much a part of the genteel tradition? There are several important answers to this question. First is what we might think of as an alternative renaissance—the Catholic literary revival. This resurgence of Catholicism as a theme and force in contemporary literary culture took place largely outside the boundaries of the United States. American Catholics interested in literature and literary culture pointed to Europe with respect and some envy, seeing their increased interest in Catholic literature and an increase in admirable work from a variety of countries. In England, John Henry Newman (1801–90) made a public and rational case for Catholicism at a time when membership in the Catholic Church was still incompatible with public advancement and upper-class British identity, and G. K. Chesterton (1874–1936) spoke to the next generation through an endlessly prolific production of essays, journalism, fiction, poetry, and erudite amateur history that celebrated the resources Catholicism could draw on to counter the gray conformity and mindless mechanization of modern life.

As with the earliest years of U.S. exploration and settlement, one of the things that set Catholics apart was their identification with writers in languages other than English. The Catholic literary revival invited U.S. Catholics to celebrate their kinship with writers not just in the United States or even in England, but in France, Norway, Italy, Germany, and Spain. Georges Bernanos's (1888–1948) 1936 *Diary of a Country Priest* and Sigrid Undset's (1882–1949) 1929 *Kristin Lavransdatter* explored quintessentially European themes at precisely the time "Americanness" in American literature was becoming more and more important. These works and many others demonstrated to Catholics that they had a role to play yet in artistic modernity, that the philosophical and political upheavals of the preceding century of revolution had not so completely cut them off from their literary heritage that the connection was irretrievable. U.S. Catholics saw the European revival as a spur to their own achievement. When was the burgeoning literary culture of the United States going to produce work of real greatness? This question increasingly preoccupied American Catholic literary culture in the twentieth century.

What great work would look like was a much less simple question in 1925 than it had been twenty years earlier. In the intervening decades, literary modernism had entered public consciousness and established permanent residence. Instead of earnestly looking for the next Longfellow or the American Wordsworth, by the early 1920s American literary culture as a whole was badly split in reaction to modernism's subversion of literary (and social) convention. For some, modernism was exhilarating and liberating, a definitive means of slipping off the shackles of the past and meeting the modern world on its own terms. The rejection of rhyme and meter in poetry and of conventional linear narrative in prose fiction mirrored for modernism's supporters the rejection of stifling Victorian convention. Literary and social convention seemed to have been equally discredited by the atrocities of the Great War—the system that had produced the war's unimaginable horrors had no warrant any longer for the wholesomeness of its culture and no claim on the future.

Catholics had a somewhat contested relationship with artistic modernism (as with modernity in general). Because stylistic experiments were so explicitly linked to philosophical presuppositions that challenged (often overtly) Catholic orthodoxy, Catholic critics and writers rejected the stylistic innovation along with the philosophical underpinnings. "Free verse," for example, seemed to some a willful refusal to see and appreciate the order God had given to the universe. The tumultuous personal lives of so many modernist artists seemed to many Catholics (and to others who could not quite believe the genteel tradition was on its way out) to confirm that art, religion, philosophy, and the foundations of society itself were linked in an intricate pattern and that undermining one led to the eventual unraveling of the whole.

This critique of modernism led to much derision, then and now, of Catholics' inability to discern and appreciate the direction in which art and history were moving. Even by the time of the outbreak of the Second World War, however, the picture had become a bit more complicated. James Joyce, who had more than any other writer defined for Catholic critics the fracture between Catholic tradition and modernist liberation, seemed less the apostate and more the astute diagnostician of the ills at the heart of the bourgeois capitalist nationalism that was once more dragging the world into war (though his unconventional personal life and thorough excoriation of Irish Catholicism's repressive excesses continued to exasperate Catholic critics). T. S. Eliot, whose 1922 "Waste Land" defined modernist despair more comprehensively than any other single work, had by the outbreak of the second war rejected his own rejections and embraced tradition and belief in a not unproblematic but inarguably innovative and undoubtedly modern idiom.

This convergence of modernist critique with at least some aspects of Catholicism's tradition and its contemporary stance resonates ironically with another important strain of Catholic literary culture. The place where literary support for bourgeois convention flourished was in popular literature, which left much of Catholic literary culture near despair—the people who were attempting stylistic innovation and aiming for aesthetic achievement were abandoning Catholicism's great tradition of consonance between moral and artistic vision, while those whose moral vision posed no obstacles were content with pleasing the masses instead of aiming for the stars.

The best example of the popular author whose artistic achievement, in the eyes of the high-culture critics, left something to be desired was Kathleen Thompson Norris (1880–1966). Not to be confused with the similarly named contemporary spiritual writer, this Kathleen Norris surely ranks with the bestselling writers of the twentieth century. She published her first full-length work, an autobiographical reflection entitled *Mother*, in 1911 (it was still in print and a popular Mother's Day gift in the early 1940s), and went on to publish over ninety other books, most of them novels featuring the romantic, career, and family dilemmas of women of all ages.

Neither the most ardent fan nor the most committed feminist could make a case for the excellence of Kathleen Norris's prose or the extent of her formal literary innovations (though Ann Douglas has noted that her style owes something to Henry James!).[7] Nor is it useful to the cultural historian of U.S. Catholic literature to dismiss her work as unworthy of notice because of its conventionality. Instead, as good historians of popular culture and good scholars of women's literary work have confirmed over and over again, work such as Norris's repays close examination precisely on account of its timeliness and ephemerality. It speaks to and of the concerns of people living in a particular historical moment and encapsulates many of the most immediate cultural issues in ways that more widely addressed writing does not. The conventionality of its style and plot can obscure the breathtaking scope of its ambitions—it takes hold without apology of the most powerful modern engines of culture and turns them to spreading its view of life, relationships, family, work, home, culture, economy, and religion. In its way, work like Norris's is considerably more "modern" than that of the modernists, for all its apparent support for the status quo.

The example of Kathleen Norris underscores one of the realities of Catholic literary culture in the early years of the twentieth century—it reflected the needs and complexities of a community divided by class and ethnicity but simultaneously tied together by faith and institution. One of the reasons that the identification of the American literary canon in the 1920s is so resonant with the history of American Catholicism is that it was virtually simultaneous with the drastic reduction of U.S. immigration through legislation passed by Congress temporarily in 1921 and made permanent in 1924. That legislation deliberately engineered a reactionary reorientation of immigration away from heavily Catholic (and Jewish) countries of origin and toward those more likely to be Protestant and English-speaking. The anti-Catholicism that informed this legislation was a significant cultural factor in the United States of the 1920s. Seen from one angle, the overwhelming tendency of the majority of the Catholics in the United States. was toward adapting and assimilating to modernity—surely the whole-hearted drive toward upward mobility and participation in American political life are evidence of the thorough absorption of American values by wide swaths of the U.S. Catholic community in the years after the Great War. At the same time, however, Catholics maintained a certain distance from the American mainstream—a distance arguably forced on them at least in part by anti-Catholicism, but also articulated and defended by Catholics themselves, who saw their own distance from the mainstream and were able to articulate a critique of certain American—and certain Catholic—tendencies even as they were seeking recognition and success within the society they were critiquing.

For much of the late nineteenth and early twentieth century, the story of American Catholic literature, like that of American Catholicism itself, was inextricable from the history of immigration and assimilation. The writers who chronicled that experience in fiction are more often identified as American than as Catholic, but any history of American Catholic literary culture would be incomplete without them. They raise very starkly the question of what the term "Catholic" includes or refers to when we talk about Catholic history or Catholic literature.

In the work of writers who were children of immigrants, such as German Theodore Dreiser (1871–1945) or Italian Pietro di Donato (1911–92), Catholicism appeared as part of the world that immigrants brought with them to the United States. In defining themselves against their immigrant parents as American, the first generation born in the United States often identified Catholicism with the Old World, with the heritage of foreignness and oppression that needed to be shed or escaped to take up the full promise of America. American art and popular culture seem most often to have framed this as a clear either/or choice, and not only for Catholics. For example, in the iconic 1927 motion picture *The Jazz Singer*, the young boy "Jakie Rabinowitz" cannot be both the faithful son of his Orthodox Jewish parents and a "jazz singer"; by becoming "Jack Robin" in dress, hairstyle, and demeanor, he exhibits on his return home his distance not only from the emotional embrace of his parents but from the religious belief and practice they exemplify.

The identification of economic success with the rejection of religious heritage was complicated for U.S. Catholics by the role played by socialism and other leftist political philosophies. Because socialism was figured within U.S. Catholicism as a godless enemy, first-generation Catholics who instead saw it as a means of seriously working for justice for the poor came in turn to believe that the church was an obstacle that prevented its members from staking a claim to economic justice and thus kept them mired in poverty. A number of the children of Catholic immigrants turned to socialism as an alternative that seemed more authentically to side with the needs of the poor, even if the poor could not see this themselves. It is true that during these same years Catholic social tradition was emerging as a resource for addressing the same issues from a Catholic perspective, but the stark rejection of socialism as any kind of ally was an important factor in alienating writers of this generation from the Catholicism of their immigrant forebears. It plays this role in many of their most powerful stories, such as Dreiser's *Sister Carrie*, di Donato's *Christ in Concrete*, and James T. Farrell's (1904–79) Studs Lonigan trilogy.

Economic issues were only one of many areas in which Catholicism seemed to be attached to the stagnant past and American culture to look energetically toward the future. This opposition became a theme threading through many of the major narratives of the American imagination in the middle of the twentieth century. F. Scott Fitzgerald (1896–1940) said he left behind for good the Catholicism in which he had been raised when he entered Princeton as an undergraduate, but many readers have seen in *The Great Gatsby*, for example, a deep ambivalence about his being caught between the past and the future, in which the promise of America is exposed as sour at its heart but nonetheless still irresistibly attractive. Willa Cather (1873–1947) demonstrates the same thing from a slightly different angle. She was hailed early in her career as a major American novelist when she wrote about the heroic American present (and near past) in works such as *O Pioneers!* and *My Antonia*. But praise for her work cooled considerably when she turned toward subjects in the deep (Catholic) past of the New World, such as the nineteenth-century Santa Fe of *Death Comes for the Archbishop* and the seventeenth-century Quebec of *Shadows on the Rock*. Cather herself was not a Catholic, and she wondered publicly a number of times why U.S. Catholics were not writing these stories themselves. In seeing these stories as part of the American landscape, neglected and poorly understood, she stood apart from many of her literary contemporaries.

Contrasting literature with popular culture is once again useful here. The fairly bleak depiction of U.S. Catholicism that became embedded in American literature contrasts dramatically with the image Catholicism took on in mid-century popular culture. Vaudeville's ethnic humor vented the tensions of urban life and the struggle for assimilation riotously and irreverently. The picture of urban poverty that emerged in early film was not of dire desperation but of heroic (if often simultaneously criminal) survival—think James Cagney. By the middle of the 1930s, Catholics were arguably the most influential group in the country in determining the content of American movies; that and the healthy appreciation on the part of studio owners of the percentage of urban audiences who were Catholic helped make depictions of Catholic life on screen considerably more positive than they often were in the pages of modernist novels.

Many U.S. Catholics involved in literary work—not just writers, but editors, teachers, librarians, and critics—were quite aware of the negative views of Catholicism and immigrant culture that were becoming canonical in American literature. They had a complicated set of reactions to these depictions. Some saw them as full of hate, the revenge taken by those who had broken with the church and had to justify that break to themselves. Others saw the power and the truth and the empathy in the attempts to identify with the suffering of the poor and genuinely lamented the authors' inability to bring the resources of faith and tradition to bear on this task. Others accepted and helped to maintain the stark boundary between the aesthetic intentions of a work of art and the question of fidelity to faith in judging whether a novel was successful.

Increasingly after the mid-1930s, and ever more rapidly after the Second World War, successive generations of literary Catholics attempted to take in the whole landscape—modernism, American Renaissance, immigrant life, popular culture—and to try to identify some ground on which contemporary, self-confidently Catholic literature could be recognized as both American and as high-quality literature. One of the most active and influential Catholic public presences was Daniel A. Lord, S.J. He was a tireless and astonishingly prolific writer, exhorting American Catholics, among many other things, to live up to their vast and deep literary heritage by aiming to produce work of high quality that could speak to the modern age. In addition, his love of movies led him to help write the 1930 Motion Picture Production Code and to establish the system of monitoring and approval by which it shaped U.S. motion pictures for much of the twentieth century.[8]

Another pervasive presence on the Catholic literary scene was Sr. Mariella Gable, O.S.B., a Benedictine sister who saw her life's work as fostering Catholic writers and Catholic literary culture. She did this sometimes in very personally tangible ways (working, for example, to get a job for writer Harry Sylvester at St. John's University so that he could support his growing family while working on his novels). She also collected the work of a wide variety of American authors in the 1940s and 1950s into several anthologies of short stories with titles such as *This Is Catholic Fiction* and *Great Modern Catholic Short Stories* (which included stories by little-known Catholic writers, but some also by some of the most famous U.S. authors, such as Hemingway's "The Gambler, the Nun and the Radio"). Sister Mariella experienced some exasperation during her lifetime and even some ridicule since, but she saw quite clearly the predicament of Catholic writers in the landscape in which they found themselves and took decisive and persistent action to try to address the situation.

More centrally situated to influence national attitudes was Harold C. Gardiner, S.J., literary editor of *America* from 1940 to 1962. He wrote a widely cited and apparently widely consulted book, *Norms for the Novel*, that helped bridge the gap between the moral perspective Catholic readers brought to literature and modernist subject matter, bringing a number of twentieth-century Catholic writers if not quite back into the fold, then at least reclaiming them as part of the history and experience of Catholicism's encounter with modernity. He also edited several extensive projects that considered U.S. literature and the Great Books curriculum from the perspective of Catholic teaching and aesthetic philosophy. It is easy in hindsight to mock the assumptions behind such projects, but given the chasm between the worlds he was trying to bridge, they might have been more savvy strategies than they seem in retrospect. He also weighed in quite prominently on one of the most contested of twentieth-century issues, the censorship of books, in a volume written for the Hanover House/Image Books "Catholic Viewpoint" series (other titles included church and state, education, marriage and family, overpopulation, and race relations).[9]

Lord, Gable, and Gardiner exemplified a growing literary self-consciousness on the part of U.S. Catholics. One could argue that they represent a stage before true self-confidence, in that the need to announce and keep announcing one's confidence is not the clearest sign of its strength. But it could also be argued that they helped prepare the ground in important ways for a number of Catholic writers who were not necessarily less self-conscious but were perhaps more subtle about it. The first three twentieth-century writers who were both unapologetically Catholic in theme and intention and clear unequivocal successes in mainstream high culture were Flannery O'Connor, Walker Percy, and J. F. Powers. Beginning in the late 1940s and continuing for the next half-century, they produced a body of stories and novels (and letters and essays) that—though very different from each other—shaped Catholic writing more than any other voices and definitively put to rest the worry that somehow Catholics were incapable of encountering American life with the same profundity and power as members of other groups.

O'Connor herself dismissed this concern at what was perhaps its crest in U.S. Catholic consciousness—in the years following John Tracy Ellis's "American Catholics and the Intellectual Life." In this 1955 analysis (first a paper given at the annual meeting of the Catholic Commission on Intellectual and Cultural Affairs, then expanded to book length), the most prominent historian of U.S. Catholicism launched a blistering critique of the state of American Catholic intellectual life.[10] While Ellis did not explicitly address artistic achievement, his concerns echoed those that had been resounding within Catholic literary circles for decades at this point. But Flannery O'Connor seemed to see those days as behind her: in a March 1963 letter to Sally and Robert Fitzgerald, she wrote, "I haven't seen it in print but somebody told me he thought [Robert] got the Bollingen Prize. I congratulate you. You should have got it if you didn't. I guess you saw that Powers got the National Book Award. I was much cheered at that. I got the O. Henry this year. Walker Percy got the N'tl Book Award last year. Katherine Anne [Porter] will probably get the Pulitzer Prize. I think you ought to judge the prize by the book but even so these hold up and all these people are Catlicks so this should be some kind of answer to the people who are saying we don't contribute to the arts."[11] O'Connor had some of the key details wrong here, but the appearance of increasing literary prominence for U.S. Catholics is borne out by the correct information as well as by her impression.[12]

O'Connor did not include in her list a writer who invented his own category, but whose Catholic roots and influences have been increasingly appreciated in recent years. Jack Kerouac's very grounding of the notion of "Beat" in the beatific vision—the direct encounter with the face of God—gives the game away, but the autobiographical resonances with the culture of French Catholic New England add additional depth and information to the centuries-deep encounter between Catholicism and New World culture.

There is probably something to be made here of the fact that these four successful and influential Catholic voices emerged from outside of New York City. O'Connor and Percy fell in step in some ways with the flowering of southern literature that characterized the middle part of the twentieth century. O'Connor tried to move to New York; it is interesting to consider what shape her work might have taken if her lupus had not forced her to remain at home in rural Georgia for most of her adult life. Powers spent his life in the Midwest (with regular sojourns in Ireland). Kerouac's origins on the fringes of New England were far in culture if not in distance from centers of power in publishing and cultural guardianship in New York and Boston. Perhaps Catholicism's route to mainstream literary influence in the United States lay along the path of regionalism, rather than by way of laying a direct claim to the center.

The achievement of mainstream literary success and visibility by Catholic writers was not limited to these four. Others less often identified primarily as Catholic—such as Robert Lowell, Allen Tate, Caroline Gordon, and Robert Fitzgerald—were very well known and successful as novelists, poets, critics, and translators. In addition, there was something like a flowering of Catholic memoir in these years. The first of the wave and perhaps the most influential was Thomas Merton's *The Seven-Storey Mountain*. This autobiography of a worldly and cosmopolitan young man who decided to become a Trappist monk captured the national imagination, a place Merton occupied for the next two decades, publishing a long list of books that combined autobiography, theological reflection, and witness to the churning complexities of the contemporary political scene. His early work shared the public's attention with at least two other stories of young men articulating widely divergent stances but sharing a serious and culturally contemporary Catholicism. William F. Buckley in 1951 helped define modern conservatism with his account of his undergraduate years in *God and Man at Yale: The Superstitions of Academic Freedom*. In 1956, with *Deliver Us from Evil*, medical missionary Tom Dooley published the first of a number of books on his work with Vietnamese refugees that helped make him a hero to a generation of Catholic young people. Memoirs by women provide equally good evidence of the wide range of Catholic experience in postwar America. Dorothy Day distilled more than a half-century of committed social activism and journalistic witness into *The Long Loneliness* in 1952. Novelist Mary McCarthy described her journey from six-year-old orphan to convent-school apostate to the center of New York literary life in her 1957 *Memories of a Catholic Girlhood*. Conservative and radical, active and contemplative, following paths into and out of the church and sometimes back again—these writers make clear the mater-of-fact relevance of Catholic experience to the postwar American landscape, the presence of a self-aware Catholic voice in public discourse. They critiqued the public discourse, and they critiqued the church, and they critiqued their fellow U.S. Catholics. They also indicated that the lines along which U.S. Catholicism would divide in the next two decades were already rather clear by the middle of the 1950s at the latest.

As with so much else about Catholic culture in the 1960s, the ecumenical council convened by Pope John XXIII in 1962 culminated in changes that had been long underway and propelled further changes. The upheaval—whether seen as bracing "aggiornamento" or frightening destabilization—had the effect of shifting literature and literary experience temporarily into the cultural background. Reality was where the drama was; fiction took a backseat for a while. Thousands of bishops in full regalia converging on Rome in front of the television lights dramatized the confrontation of Catholicism with modernity as no novel could. Within three years of the Council's close, the divisive reception of *Humanae vitae* would heighten this confrontation and deepen gulfs that in the 1950s seemed more bridgeable than they had in over half a century.

As a consequence, Catholic literary culture after the Council had, for a while, a pronounced partisan character—critique and defense of the church became a more significant focus than they had been a decade earlier. Garry Wills's 1972 memoir *Bare Ruined Choirs*, for example, shares with those by Merton and company the young person's exploration of Catholicism's place in the contemporary landscape, but Catholicism, instead of a stable element of the backdrop against which to dramatize one's own story, becomes a protagonist in the drama—variable, unstable, exciting but unpredictable.

In the generation since the Council, Catholic literary culture has become less self-conscious, but not necessarily less active or interesting. The lessened self-consciousness is evident in the decline of the institutional and organizational activity that surrounded Catholic writers for much of the century. On the most official level, the censorship structures that had been in place since the Reformation were dismantled (with the explicit caveat that Catholics should always be aware of the power reading has to influence ideas, and therefore the responsibility readers have to protect their faith); on an unofficial level, many of the efforts by Catholic writers and critics to encourage and promote U.S. Catholic literary work seemed to have faded away. They were, arguably, at least to some extent, victims of their own success, for, while American Catholic literary self-consciousness may have diminished, American Catholic literary activity surely has not.

While U.S. Catholicism was changing in response to the forces set in motion by Vatican II, U.S. literary culture was changing around the same time. The consensus that had emerged by the 1950s about what American literature was had by the end of the 1960s begun to fray irreparably. The confidence that one relatively short list of canonical literary texts could encapsulate the motley and variegated spectrum of American experience was one of the less traumatic casualties of the 1960s' questioning of authorities of all sorts. The collapse of overall consensus gave rise to a new flexibility and freedom for writers from a wide variety of perspectives to write newly "American" stories. Within this looser, more deliberately expansive framework, Catholics laid claim to at least as many components of U.S. literary culture as they had in the more parochial climate of the preconciliar era. The unremarkable nature of this claim is part of what makes it remarkable.

There have been in the years since the Council a large number of writers who are Catholic and who write (by some definition) about Catholics and Catholic culture. Mary

Gordon, Anna Quindlen, Julia Alvarez, and Alice McDermott have focused intently on women's experiences, critiquing exclusivist church policies while meticulously delineating the distinctiveness and intimacy with which women enter into the symbols and relationships at the heart of church traditions. Jon Hassler, Richard Rodriguez, Ron Hansen, and Alice McDermott have deepened and extended the regional embodiment of U.S. Catholicism, helping to flesh out its common Americanness in ways F. O. Matthiessen could not have comprehended. Andrew Greeley and James Carroll have used fiction and nonfiction in equal measure to develop a prophetic polemic in which liturgy and politics, history and tradition, collide and coalesce with the American and Catholic culture of the last forty years. It is difficult to imagine an array of novels and novelists that could be more satisfying to early and mid-twentieth-century proponents of the need for U.S. Catholics to do their part in expressing and documenting the American experience.

Catholic literary culture continues to have additional dimensions as well. Catholic literary critics explore and highlight the religious dimensions of contemporary writers such as Don DeLillo, Annie Dillard, John Irving, Anne Tyler, Anne Rice, and Marilynne Robinson. For better or for worse, there is still an active literary machinery in place—lay and clerical, formal and informal—with an interest in assessing key popular culture phenomena such as the Harry Potter books, the "Left Behind" series, and *The Da Vinci Code*—in light of their religious and literary significance for Catholics. And explicitly, institutionally Catholic publications such as the *Catechism of the Catholic Church* and myriad writings of popes John Paul II, Benedict XVI, and Francis become surprise (then reliable) bestsellers. The laments about the decline of Catholic literary culture have not entirely disappeared, and there may be somewhat less sense of a collective enterprise, an embattled church arrayed against an engulfing culture, but awareness of a distinctive, occasionally prophetic stance persists and animates the work of Catholic writers from every literary realm.

Conclusion

Writers and critics, readers, students, and teachers who have over the course of American history defined "the literary" narrowly have often missed the things written and published by Catholics. The criteria that led "American literature" to become a constricted category often gave "American" an implicit definition that made it difficult to encompass Catholic experiences and Catholic views of history and society. Using broader definitions of literature—which are, interestingly, both very old and rather new—makes clear that Catholics have been there all along, all over the spectrum, in every genre, at all levels of achievement—not outside of time, but deeply immersed in whatever time they find themselves; defined not just by relationship to their church, but by individual encounters with the church, with the transcendent reality the church embodies and mediates, with the time and place in which they live, and with their own personal history and circumstances.

The "literary" lens—the critical view that emphasizes a work's formal and aesthetic qualities as an independent object—is important and illuminating. Art can often mean something regardless of time and place. But the historian's lens—the view that connects a work of art to the dense set of circumstances in which it is created and received and preserved—helps us to see how often and how substantively and how fascinatingly the definition of the literary changes. And observing these changes closely helps us to see the American experience of Roman Catholicism more clearly.

NOTES

1. See Paul Gutjahr, *An American Bible: A History of the Good Book in the United States, 1777–1880* (Stanford, Calif.: Stanford University Press, 1999), 23–31.

2. Rev. George Deshon, *Guide for Catholic Young Women, Especially for Those Who Earn Their Own Living* (repr. 29th ed., 1897; New York: Arno Press, 1978), 78.

3. The categories of "nationalist" and "formalist" come from Eric Cheyfitz, "What Work Is There for Us to Do? American Literary Studies or American Cultural Studies?," *American Literature* 67, no. 4 (December 1995): 843–53.

4. A number of literary scholars from quite different perspectives have noticed just this slant in the trajectory of American literature in the middle of the twentieth century; see Nina Baym, "Melodramas of Beset Manhood: How Theories of American Fiction Exclude Women Authors," *American Quarterly* 33 (1981): 123–39; Jenny Franchot, *Roads to Rome: The Antebellum Protestant Encounter with Catholicism* (Berkeley: University of California Press, 1994); Paul Giles, *American Catholic Arts and Fictions: Culture, Ideology, Aesthetics* (New York: Cambridge University Press, 1992); Sharon O'Brien, "Becoming Noncanonical: The Case Against Willa Cather," in *Reading in America: Literature and Social History*, ed. Cathy N. Davidson (Baltimore, Md.: Johns Hopkins University Press, 1989): 240–58.

5. Michael Rogin, "Recolonizing America," review of *European Revolutions and the American Literary Renaissance*, by Larry J. Reynolds, *American Literary History* 2, no. 1 (1990): 144–49.

6. Patrick W. Carey, *Orestes A. Brownson: American Religious Weathervane* (Grand Rapids, Mich.: W. B. Eerdmans, 2004).

7. Ann Douglas, *Terrible Honesty: Mongrel Manhattan in the 1920s* (New York: Farrar, Straus and Giroux, 1995).

8. See the account of the significant extent of Catholic influence on this process in Frank Walsh's *Sin and Censorship: The Catholic Church and the Motion Picture Industry* (New Haven, Conn.: Yale University Press, 1996).

9. Harold C. Gardiner, S.J., ed., *Fifty Years of the American Novel: A Christian Appraisal* (New York: Scribner, 1951); *The Great Books: A Christian Appraisal; A Symposium on the First-Fourth Year's Program of the Great Books Foundation*, 4 vols. (New York: Devin-Adair, 1949–53); *Catholic Viewpoint on Censorship* (Garden City, N.Y.: Hanover House, 1958).

10. John Tracy Ellis, *American Catholics and the Intellectual Life* (Chicago: Heritage Foundation, 1956).

11. Flannery O'Connor, *The Habit of Being: Letters* (New York: Farrar, Straus and Giroux, 1979), 511.

12. Robert Fitzgerald received the Bollingen Poetry Translation Prize in 1961 for his translation of the *Odyssey* but did not receive the 1963 Bollingen Prize for Poetry. Katherine Anne Porter did not receive the Pulitzer Prize for *Ship of Fools* in 1963 but did receive it in 1966 for her *Collected Stories*. J. F. Powers won the National Book Award in 1963 for *Morte D'Urban*; Walker Percy had won the previous year for *The Moviegoer*. Six of O'Connor's stories were included in the annual O. Henry Award *Prize Stories* anthologies; three ("Greenleaf" [1957], "Everything that Rises Must Converge" [1963], and "Revelation" [1965]) became the first-prize stories.

SEVEN

Gospel Zeal: Missionary Citizens Overseas and Armchair Missionaries at Home; American Catholic Missions in China, 1900–1989

Robert E. Carbonneau, C.P.

In a 1911 letter to his fellow U.S. bishops, Cardinal James Gibbons of Baltimore (1834–1921) addressed the growing competition between Catholics and Protestants to convert China to Christianity. Gibbons stridently voiced his support for a new venture—that is, an American Foreign Missionary Seminary later known as Maryknoll. "The prestige of our country has become wide-spread; and Protestants, especially in the Far East, are profiting by it to the positive hindrance of Catholic missioners. I understand," Gibbons added, "even the educated classes in China, misled by the almost complete absence of American Catholic priests, believe that the Church of Rome has no standing in America."[1]

Motivated to convert the Chinese, establish the local church, and counter Protestant initiatives, gospel-driven zeal for China dominated the twentieth-century American Catholic missionary movement. Between 1900 and 1950, as many as thirty-five American Catholic religious congregations sent priests, brothers, sisters, or lay workers to China as part of a worldwide Catholic missionary movement.[2]

This Catholic China mission story combines themes from U.S. Catholic and Chinese history. This chapter explores that historical narrative by examining two interlocking cohorts operating throughout the first half of the twentieth century. One group is the American citizens serving as missionaries in China. In addition to their national passports, spiritual citizenship in conjunction with the Holy See proved to be of paramount influence in the evangelization process. Oftentimes contentious, this fostered encounters between bishops and diplomats, priests, sisters, and laity and the local transnational political actors in China. Essentially, this chapter highlights the lived tension of missionaries as they diligently balanced national and spiritual allegiances during the tumultuous decades of Chinese social and political change in the first half of the twentieth century.

The second group is the armchair missionaries. I suggest that these important benefactors on the American home front first came to identify with associated events when they attended the dramatic departure ceremonies for missionaries proceeding on to China. American Catholic journals, newspapers, and ecclesial resources published from the early 1900s to the mid-1950s provided regular news of the missionaries' efforts in the mission field. Frequently, mission education undertaken by returning missionaries proved a key element in reaching local audiences via personal appearances and promotional literature. Over time, these elements became increasingly linked to the Guomindang Nationalists' agenda under Chiang Kai-shek (1887–1975) while eschewing the Communist agenda of Mao Zedong (1893–1976) that redefined China in 1949 under the People's Republic of China.

This chapter concludes by providing a synopsis of how the Deng Xiaoping Era in China (1978–89) necessitated that seasoned missionaries who had returned home from China and their armchair missionary counterparts reposition their spiritual legacy. During this decade, multiple ecumenical symposia and Catholic-sponsored annual meetings proved to be important steps in creating a new paradigm: the Chinese Catholic Church and the reconciliation narrative.

Introduction

Empowered by the words of Jesus Christ found in sacred scripture, "Go forth and make disciples of all nations" (Mt 28:19), the fulfillment of this mandate to bring Christ to China proved most challenging to both American Catholic missionaries and their supporters back home. Initially, many priests, brothers, and sisters chosen for the China mission were volunteers who had answered calls issued by their religious superiors. These volunteers regarded missions to China as lifelong assignments. Not until the 1930s did furloughs become more common. Missionaries' departures were typically marked by a series of tearful farewells. For instance, front-page headlines in the Baltimore *Catholic Review* (June 7, 1924) lauded Passionist missionaries of the Passionist Congregation at St. Joseph's Monastery, Irvington, Maryland, when they left for China. The subheading read, "Touching Scene Witnessed at Departure Ceremonies of Passionist Missionaries. Kiss of Peace Moves Congregation to Tears. Young Levites Kneel and Give Pledge of Loyalty before Crucifix."[3]

Early twentieth-century Chinese culture was an unknown world to the American Catholic missionaries, educators, and people in the church pews. Readers of the 1908 *Catholic Encyclopedia* would have learned that China was a "dynastic Empire." An introduction to the transliteration system of that day would have forced such readers to plod through the text that covered the Catholic mission legacy of the eleventh-century Nestorian

Christians, which reached into the Modern Missions period of the first decade of 1900. In 1908, proselytizing efforts were completely under the auspices of European-based religious congregations. Overall, the 1908 encyclopedia offered an image of China that provided rudimentary respect for Chinese tradition even as it hinted that a struggle was in place to embrace new ideas, with technology serving as an inspiring foundation for Catholic missionaries. When the opportunity came to preach the gospel, missionaries would have a clear challenge; specifically, convert the Chinese and foster modernization.[4]

Before their departure to China, some missionaries did receive basic medical training, but virtually none were trained in the Chinese language. The Pacific crossing took a month or longer, and assignment to a rural mission meant enduring additional weeks of travel by riverboat and horseback, as paved roads were virtually nonexistent. Beginning in March 1919, the *American Ecclesiastical Review*, a monthly journal of pastoral theology for clergy, published letters written by the first four Maryknoll missionaries in China. The 1918 letter by Father Francis X. Ford (1892–1952) captured both the excitement and anxiety in the hearts of every missionary traveling to China:

> Whoever wrote[,] Ye ho, my lads, the wind blows free,
> A pleasant gale is on our lee,
> never crossed the Pacific.[5]

Such published letters allowed U.S. readers to "travel" with the missionaries as they encountered this "new" Asian culture. In 1924, for example, Passionist Father Anthony Maloney (1900–1982) described how he and his fellow priests began to learn the Chinese language in western Hunan, China. "Our teacher, pagan and an opium smoker, knew no English. He would point to a Chinese character and utter a sound which we tried to imitate; if there was a drawing on the page we might guess the meaning of the sound."[6]

Novice American Catholic missionaries to China operated schools, health clinics, and orphanages to attract potential converts to the village church for instruction. In the late 1920s, Maryknoll initiated two separate evangelization approaches in southern China. The first sent local Chinese village "catechists out to local village sites to instruct potential converts, catechumens, through direct evangelization." The second approach dispatched teams of priests to live with the Chinese and establish new parishes. Maryknoll sisters were commissioned to go in pairs into the countryside.[7]

A listing of religious congregations engaged in China in the *Official Catholic Directory* confirms the direct link that existed between the American domestic church and the foreign missions in the first half of the twentieth century.[8] Maryknoll's undertaking in Kwangtung (Guangdong) in the 1923 *Official Catholic Directory* was the first mention that Americans had taken responsibility for a China mission.[9] After the 1927 citation of the Vincentian effort in Kiangsi (Jiangxi), the directory added details on additional American religious orders ministering in other vicariates apostolic.[10] By the start of the Anti-Japanese War (1937–45), eleven American groups were listed with locations in China.[11] By the time Communists took over in 1949, the directory reveals a strong commitment to China involving five religious orders serving in multiple provinces while other religious congregations ran staffs in four locales.[12]

Missionary Citizenship Overseas

Catholic missionaries in China quickly learned that their passports were as important as their bibles, catechisms, or mass kits. Looking back in the historical mirror, we now see how these aspects led to a fluid understanding of gospel zeal and citizenship. In this case, passports clearly identified U.S. citizenship. However, like it or not, Catholic missionaries easily became both real and/or symbolic representatives of shifting U.S.-China diplomatic relations. In turn, protocol demanded that American diplomats in China exhibit diligent care for these American Catholic men, women, and laity who preached the gospel in China.[13]

Catholic missionaries going to China also possessed a kind of spiritual passport in that they also followed missionary directives issued by the Sacred Congregation for the Propagation of the Faith (SCPF), also known as Propaganda Fide: the mission office in Rome.[14] Once in China, U.S. missionaries often joined in ministry with their European missionary counterparts in various provinces of China. Concretely, this secondary notion of spiritual citizenship created a dilemma whereby in some cases, Catholic missionaries paid more attention to Propaganda Fide's directives than to those issued by U.S. diplomats in China. One might say that Catholic missionaries to China possessed dual citizenship; that is, they were asked to be loyal to the directives from their homeland and those sent from Rome, as all would help them promote the gospel.

Of course, missionaries' success or failure always depended on local circumstances. Political turmoil might be found as near as the next river bend, the next village, or even at a mission residence. The first letter home of Passionist Father Cuthbert O'Gara (1886–1968) in September 1924 from West Hunan ended with "a very harrowing scene" involving a boy with a sign around his neck announcing a public execution. "We hurried down to the river's bank to find a large crowd of the idle natives gathered about a prostrate figure. A handkerchief was spread over his face, the body was stark and rigid; the head had just been severed by the public execution." O'Gara proceeded to explain how the head was sewn with needle and thread onto a tree trunk to the interest of the spectators. "The children ran in and out as though it were a common occurrence. These people are going to take a lot of civilizing; it is not going to be the work of a day."[15]

American Catholics back home read an array of publications that espoused similar themes of violence, suffering, self-sacrifice, and the burdens of a "civilizing mission." Most notable were *The Field Afar* (1907–59), published by Maryknoll in New York; *The Far East* (1919–71), produced by the Missionary Society of St. Columban in Nebraska; and *The Shield* (1921–71), circulated by the Catholic Student Mission Crusade (CSMC) in Ohio. Since its beginnings in 1918 at Techny, Illinois, historian David J. Endres explains how the CSMC—a national group of seminarians and college and high school students—valued using prayer, study, and sacrifice to educate themselves and others about the missions and promote financial support.[16]

Readers of these periodicals generated widespread support for the China missions throughout Catholic America. Mission clubs were abundant, and their members participated in the effort to save Chinese "pagan babies," with numerous adults and children putting their spare coins into small collection containers called "mite boxes," named after the scripture story (Mk 12: 41–44) of the poor widow who gave generously from the little wealth she had. Others lighted prayer candles at church side altars and offered prayers for the missions. Some were lucky enough to attend a departure ceremony in person. Supporters of the China missions knew, for example, that Union City, New Jersey, was home to the Passionist cause; Techny, Illinois, was home to the Society of the Divine Word; Cincinnati, Ohio, was headquarters for the ministry undertaken by the Sisters of Notre Dame de Namur and the Franciscans Minor of St. John Baptist province; and Springfield, Illinois, was the staging area for the Hospital Sisters of the Third Order of St. Francis. Thus, it came to pass that the experiences of the missionary citizenship overseas began to influence the armchair missionaries who followed events from their homes. Interest in the historic day-to-day political, social, and spiritual realities of the China mission intensified, and missionaries often functioned in symbiotic relationships with those back home.

Also uniting the China missionaries in the field with supporters back home in the United States was the scripture passage, "Our citizenship is in heaven" (Phil 3:20). Armchair missionaries offered prayers and money. In turn, they received decades of mission education by reading missionary literature and sharing letters and personal contacts with furloughed missionaries. The imaginations of those with faith that made the missionaries long for home also allowed the armchair missionaries to feel as if they were eating rice with a Chinese missionary without ever leaving home. This fluid understanding of gospel zeal and missionary citizenship was evident through four distinct periods from 1900 to 1955—the latter being the year virtually all foreign missionaries were expelled from China by the Communists, who had come to power in 1949.

1900–1919: Fragile Foundation

Beginning in 1907, the publication *Catholic Missions*, released by the Society for the Propagation of the Faith in New York, educated readers about the importance of spreading the gospel to foreign lands. Merging in 1924 with the *Annals of the Propagation of the Faith*, it kept the same title but received new numbering. Well into the 1950s, issues of *Catholic Missions* solicited essays from U.S missionaries in the field. Their historical narratives brought China to life. Readers viewed these missionaries as modern-day apostles. *Catholic Missions* upheld the mystique that China was a sometimes backward, pagan society.

Often ignored or simplified was the complex role played by Christianity during dynastic change. Nestorian Christian missionaries, who believed that Jesus was two people—a man and the divine son of God—traveled to China from southeastern Europe, only to be banned by the Tang dynasty (618–907). Christianity in China was reestablished in the Yuan dynasty (1279–1321). The evangelization efforts of Matteo Ricci (1552–1610) and his fellow Jesuits in the last decades of the Ming dynasty (1644) are legendary. Christianity struggled through the Qing dynasty (1644–1911). In 1692, the Kangxi emperor's Edict of Toleration provided a regal nod toward Christianity. Conditions worsened, however, and the Holy See through Propaganda Fide responded harshly. In 1704, Pope Clement XI forbade Chinese Catholic participation in rituals that honored Confucius or family ancestors. In 1724, the Yongzheng emperor banned Christianity altogether, although it managed to survive in many rural areas. Only in 1939 did Propaganda Fide lift the ban on the Chinese Rites, thereby acknowledging that the rituals had only civil and social importance.

In the nineteenth century, increased opportunities for trade had Christians knocking on China's door again. The Opium War (1839–1842)—which broke out when China wanted the opium drug trade banned and the British refused—further damaged Christianity's reputation. Defeated by Britain, China was forced to submit to an 1842 treaty that opened five Chinese ports to foreign traders, diplomats, and Christian missionaries. Some European Catholic missionaries took advantage of the unequal treaties to profit from mission property bought in China. While Catholics and Protestants rejoiced in this newfound opportunity to evangelize, many Chinese labeled all foreigners as imperialists. Moreover, the Taiping Rebellion (1850–64) degraded Christianity's reputation. Leader Hong Xiuquan (1814–64) had read a missionary tract that left him convinced he was the younger brother of Jesus Christ. In 1851, Hong proclaimed the new Taiping dynasty. Years of reform and chaos followed until Chinese and Western troops defeated Hong in 1864. Later, longtime anti-Christian sentiment in northern China led to the 1870 Tianjin massacre of Catholic missionaries.[17]

In 1900, almost 100 European Catholic missionaries and over 30,000 Chinese Catholics—Protestants and Orthodox suffered as well—were killed during the Boxer Uprising. Traditionally, many have interpreted the Boxers as an antiforeign, anti-Christian movement. Historians of China have understood the Boxers as part of a larger sociopolitical rebellion targeting both Chinese and foreigners. In recent years, greater attention has been paid to the Catholic influence.[18] In 1900, the Boxers were defeated by an international rescue effort of foreign troops sent to China. These same foreign powers, through their diplomatic representatives, imposed the indemnity system throughout China. As a result, all foreign citizens, including Catholic missionaries, were given more legal protections than ever before. Although these foreigners rejoiced, many Chinese leaders of the time interpreted this as another layer of imperialism. More than ever, this made all foreigners, including Catholic missionaries, "political."[19] Remnants of this debate over the legacy of imperialism resurfaced in 2000, when St. Pope John Paul II (1920–2005) canonized the 120 Blessed Martyrs of China killed in the Boxer Uprising.[20]

China became a republic in 1912. Due to the efforts of late nineteenth- and early twentieth-century priests, sisters, and brothers from European-based religious congregations, Catholicism had a rural rather than urban foothold in most provinces. Although China's provinces sought greater independence and Confucian tradition was reexamined in light of Western influence and business during this period, warlords and bandits wreaked havoc, instability, violence, and death.

The more China struggled during this first part of the twentieth century, the more American Catholic armchair missionaries grew committed to assisting in the cause to convert the homeland of Confucius. Promoters for the Catholic China missions took advantage of the situation by encouraging armchair missionaries to reach into their pockets and donate money at church, pray for the missions, or go to mission club socials. Through the grace of God, there was every hope that the education about China would inspire new missionaries who wished to leave all behind for the conversion of China. To that end, American Catholic colleges became a place to champion this push for new recruits.

The Sanctum, a student monthly publication at Duquesne University in Pittsburgh, Pennsylvania, typified the campus effort to convert China. A 1915 essay, "One Way to Convert China," described how a Chinese man became Catholic while living in Missouri. He then returned to his home village in China to help an English Sister of Charity convert its inhabitants. Another story from that year described the visit to campus of Maryknoll superior Father James A. Walsh (1867–1936). His talk at the Duquesne college chapel "no doubt fired many" students "with the noble ambition of devoting their lives to the conversion of the infidels." Because Holy Ghost [Spiritan] Father E. J. Knaebel, director of the Holy Childhood in the United States, resided at Duquesne, he had the opportunity to address assembled students on April 12, 1916. The priest explained the importance of financially supporting the foreign missions because the war had cut off European sources of income. Following up on the Walsh visit, the *Sanctum* publicized the priestly ordinations of Maryknoll missionaries. In May 1919, Columban Father Matthew Dolan (1888–1957) spoke at Duquesne to promote the China venture of his missionary society. Those present were asked to subscribe to the *Far East* magazine for one dollar.[21]

The devastation of World War I (1914–18) resulted in many European Catholic foreign missionaries being called home. Few replacements were sent during or after the German defeat in November 1918. Before the ink was even dry on the April 1919 Paris Peace Conference treaty, diplomats gave Japan control of Shandong province. German citizens—including the German Catholic missionaries of the Society of the Divine Word—were pressured to leave the region. To prevent the missionaries' expulsion, on January 30, 1919, Divine Word bishop Augustin Henninghaus (1862–1939) in Shandong cabled Cardinal James Gibbons in Baltimore asking that he contact U.S. Department of State diplomats to intervene on behalf of his German missionaries. Although they were not American citizens, Gibbons made the case to the State Department.[22] With assistance from Archbishop George Mundelein (1872–1939) of Chicago, Gibbons successfully asserted that the German missionaries were spiritually linked with the armchair missionaries back in America, despite the fact they were from Germany. Mundelein explained that the Chicago suburb of Techny, Illinois, was the American base for the Society of the Divine Word and that some of its missionary recruits were likely destined for Shandong. Mundelein and Gibbons pointed out that American Catholic money had been offered in support of the Shandong effort. Mundelein also played his World War I patriotism card. Because Catholics had been "loyal to our Government in critical times," they had every reason to expect that their American government would support church interests. Finally, Mundelein explained that the uprooting of so many priests from every Catholic European nation as a result of World War I meant that U.S. Catholics were in the best position to come to the aid of mission areas that might require diverse assistance. On March 21, 1919, Gibbons learned that the U.S. government had agreed to support any remaining Shandong missionaries. In Peking on August 21, 1919, Bishop Henninghaus personally met with U.S. diplomat Paul Reinsch (1869–1923) to thank him for the diplomatic support, but when Henninghaus requested that the Shandong mission be put under the specific protection of the American legation, Reinsch balked. Missionaries holding a German passport could not be offered such protection by the U.S government in China.[23]

American armchair missionaries were able to follow the Henninghaus case as it developed. In March 1919, *Catholic Missions* published the Henninghaus cable, requesting that the magazine "do all [it] can to prevent the expulsion of our missionaries from China." The following month, *Catholic Missions* informed readers that its office had prompted Gibbons to contact the State Department, arguing that the Shandong mission "is at present almost solely supported by our contributions and may be rightly considered an American mission." The May issue reported that no Divine Word German missionaries were to be expelled. Subsequent issues of *Catholic Missions* proclaimed a missionary is "never" a "political agent," as "the only interests he has at heart are those of the Church and souls he has come to evangelize." Bishop Henninghaus personally summarized the collaborative process undertaken by the respective parties to assure uninterrupted preaching of the gospel in Shandong. This was both a clear expression of thanks to the magazine and a firsthand account of the layered status pertaining to missionaries in China at that time.[24]

1920–1934: Missionary Hope and Reorganization

The apostolic letter *Maximum illud* (1919) was in direct response to the missionary vacuum in China and the world. Shaped in part by the progressive ideas of a Belgian missionary to China, Father Vincent Lebbe (1877–1940), the document inspired a Catholic worldwide mission initiative with unprecedented leadership from American congregations.[25] Americans proved quite zealous—sometimes naively so—compared with seasoned Europeans in their quest to create the indigenous Chinese Catholic Church envisioned by *Maximum illud*. In 1922, Passionist Father Timothy McDermott (1897–1963) found himself in the midst of this fragile pastoral situation. The Columbans, he wrote, "are not well liked over here, nor is Maryknoll any too well liked according to most reports I have received. One reason is because they are just upstarts, according to the older Orders who resent their spirit of independence and sophistication."[26]

The 1920s was a turbulent decade in China. The May Fourth Movement, launched in 1919, promoted Chinese nationalism and independence. In 1921, the Chinese Communist Party was founded, giving life to Mao Zedong's revolutionary movement. In 1925, Nationalist leader Sun Yat-Sen died. Chiang Kai-shek succeeded him. The Nationalist-Communist First United Front (1924–27) was short-lived. Rather than create peace, Chiang's Northern Expedition (1926–28) was a military and political effort to create power. In the long run, it offered the nation a false sense of unity because Communist "Reds," bandits, and warlords continued to fight each other.

Catholic missionaries were caught up in the turmoil. Nationalist anti-imperialist and anti-Christian sentiments forced many missionaries to evacuate from the interior in 1927.

Some European missionaries were killed, and a number of European and American Catholic missionaries were held for ransom. Armchair missionaries followed the drama in the U.S. Catholic and secular press. In 1926, this led American William J. Cusack to write Department of State officials over concern for the safety of his daughter, Maryknoll Sister M. Mercedes Cusack (1893–1972). She proved to be safe in Hong Kong.[27] Despite all this chaos, some missionaries in the provinces were able to negotiate local disputes, care for wounded soldiers, or assist Chinese displaced by flood and famine.

In 1922, the Holy See appointed Archbishop Celso Costantini (1876–1958) as the apostolic delegate to China. He coordinated the efforts of the Catholic Church there until 1934, when he resigned due to ill health. In 1924, the First Plenary Council of Shanghai brought together European, American, and Chinese bishops and regional leaders (no women) to reorganize mission priorities. The 1926 promulgation by Pope Pius XI (1857–1939) of apostolic letter *Ab ipsis pontificatus primordiis* and the papal encyclical *Rerum ecclesiae* provided a wider context of missionary awareness for clergy and laity in China. Interest had also increased as a result of the 1925 Vatican Missionary Exhibition, the Missionary Union of the Clergy, the relationship of missions to St. Therese of Lisieux (1873–97), and the need for missionaries to study the sciences associated with the missionary effort. Pius XI reaffirmed the growth of a local Chinese Catholic Church by personally ordaining six Chinese bishops in the Sistine Chapel on October 28, 1926.[28]

In 1927, Costantini wrote the *Instructions Issued by the Apostolic Delegate to the Bishops Who Have to Act on Questions of Indemnity*. Concretely, Costantini was promoting awareness that missionaries possessed a spiritual allegiance. Coupled with their respective passports, the situation increasingly came to mean that all foreign Catholic religious men and women in the China missions were aware that they held a dual citizenship of sorts to spread the gospel. This was to have concrete applications in the mission field.

Representatives of the Holy See increasingly frustrated foreign diplomats in China, such as the United States, by not following historic extraterritorial law, which had allowed for payment of indemnity—monetary compensation—"upon the violent death of a missionary."[29] An example of this scenario came to pass in May 1929, when the Passionists decided not to seek indemnity after three of their missionary priests—Walter Coveyou (1894–1929), Godfrey Holbein (1899–1929), and Clement Seybold (1896–1929)—were murdered the previous month in western Hunan. These first American Catholic missionaries killed in China made front-page news.[30] The following poem, published in the May 1929 issue of *Michigan Catholic*, indicates just how deeply the armchair missionaries had become attached to the American Catholic missionary effort in China.[31]

American Passionist Martyrs

When China's soul is white with grace
And fair her face to see
When Cross of Christ has found a place
Where now no Cross there be:

When all the toil and sacrifice
Of mission pioneers.
Has conquered pagan dark device
And overcome their fears:
When calm and peaceful is the land
Of Asia old and wise.
Will sound the solemn anthem grand
The song of praise arise.
For three brave Passion Fathers who
In white robes watch on high.
The China that their labors knew
The land that saw them die!
That saw them die for Christ the King.
By bandit hand cut down:
Oh, ever will their praises ring
Who wear the martyr crown!
Coveyou, Seybold, Holbein.
Martyrs one and all.
For America's glory shine
Answering God's call.

In contrast, the 1927 *Instructions* meant that it was becoming more common for missionaries to ignore diplomatic directives from their home countries. At a 1931 meeting in Washington, Costantini heard the complaints in person from U.S. diplomat Stanley K. Hornbeck (1883–1966). As chief of the Division of Far Eastern Affairs, Hornbeck was frustrated by the inconsistency of American Vincentians—as American citizens—in following consular citizen safety directives in hostile Jiangxi province, controlled by Mao Zedong. In response, Costantini told Hornbeck about spiritual citizenship—that is, that all missionaries worked together regardless of their nationality. "If a missionary were killed, they regretted it, but they [the Holy See] considered that he had fallen in action, in the line of duty; he had become a martyr and they were not inclined to make a disturbance about it." The meeting ended with both sides respectfully holding to their positions without compromise.[32]

Despite all of the difficulties, the first three decades of the twentieth century showed an increase in the Chinese Catholic population. For example, the 1903–4 period boasted 842,000 Catholics in China. In 1929–30, the number was 3,498,015 Catholics in China, in addition to the large number of foreign missionaries ministering there. Throughout these same decades, foreign missionaries held most of the leadership positions in Catholic China, even as the indigenous voice of Chinese Catholic leadership became stronger. For example, the 1903–4 period showed that none of the 42 ecclesiastical regions of Catholic China were led by Chinese (534 Chinese priests, 1,110 foreign priests). In the 1923–24 period, 2 of the 69 ecclesiastical regions were led by Chinese (1,132 Chinese priests, 1,685 foreign priests, 272 Chinese brothers, 239 foreign brothers, 2,384 Chinese religious, 1,039 foreign religious). In the 1933–34 period, 21 of the 121 ecclesiastical regions were led by Chinese (1,660 Chinese priests, 2,443 foreign priests, 607 Chinese brothers, 541 foreign brothers, 3,319 Chinese religious, 1,831 foreign religious).[33]

US. Catholic armchair missionaries continued to support the China missions during the Great Depression of the 1930s as missionary organizations stepped up the cause of self-promotion. New publications were founded. For example, *Lotus Leaves* (1929–51) became the voice of the Sisters of Charity in Cincinnati, Ohio. Through the well-coordinated efforts of the CSMC's education unit, the missionaries' message reached almost every Catholic seminary, college, and diocese. News of the China mission was everywhere. In 1929, *The Gothic*, published at Sacred Heart Seminary in Detroit, Michigan, reported on the Catholic University in Peiping [Beijing]. In 1931, the journal highlighted the China mission efforts of Detroit native Benedictine Father Sylvester Healy (1891–1979). In a similar vein, the spring 1932 issue of *The Grackle*, a student journal published at Mount Saint Joseph College in Chestnut Hill, Philadelphia, Pennsylvania, reported on an illustrated lecture presented at the women's college by Vincentian Father and China mission veteran Francis J. Moehringer.[34]

1935–1949: Combined Allegiance

During this era, the dual aspects of missionary citizenship and the interests of armchair missionaries became increasingly blurred, as most American Catholic missionaries, Holy See representatives, U.S. diplomats, and American Christians viewed Chiang Kai-shek's Nationalist government as a symbol of anti-Communism. In a sense, gospel zeal and democratic values joined together through a variety of events that shaped the understanding of the China mission during the last half of the twentieth century.

China faced many challenges during the 1930s. In 1931, Japan invaded Manchuria. Chiang Kai-shek—to the delight of at least some Catholic and most Protestant missionaries—became a Methodist in 1932. Mao Zedong made his Long March to Yan'an in 1934. In 1936, Chiang's capture during the Xi'an Incident led to forced cooperation between the Nationalists and the Communists. The relationship was formalized as the Second United Front (1937–41) after the Japanese invaded China in 1937. The defeat of Japan in 1945 began the Nationalist-Communist civil war. By 1949, victory belonged to the Communists.

In 1934, the more cautious Archbishop Marius Zanin (1890–1958) replaced progressive apostolic delegate Costantini. By the time his tenure ended in 1946, Zanin had organized new dioceses and vicariates. Even though the number of Chinese bishops, priests, sisters, and laity holding positions of leadership in the Chinese Catholic Church remained limited, Zanin proved successful in creating a Catholic network for refugees displaced during the Anti-Japanese War (1937–45). In fact, the refugees and Catholic missionaries were alike in that both groups had fled the coastal province to find safety in the interior provinces. Back in the United States, priests, sisters, brothers, and lay people worked with their European counterparts to coordinate assistance for the displaced Chinese in need of food, medical supplies, and sacraments—often in that order. Due to this concentrated effort, Catholic missionaries proved to be more successful in gaining Chinese converts in the 1930s than they had been in the 1920s.

During the Anti-Japanese War, Catholic missionaries knew that their national passports were linked to the political fortunes of the countries to which they belonged. Given that the Anti-Japanese War started as a Japan-China conflict, during the late 1930s, most missionaries held passports that identified them as noncombatants. In theory, missionaries were safe. In reality, it did not stop the Japanese from bombing mission sites in Nationalist territory. To prevent this injustice, some American Catholic missions decided to accent their neutrality by placing the U.S. flag atop the mission compound roof. A U.S. Department of State report revealed that the bombings continued between 1937 and 1938, suggesting that Japan did not often respect this action taken by the missionaries. U.S. diplomatic protests of damage inflicted by bombs to the Japanese counterparts in Tokyo did little to rectify the situation. In many cases, U.S. Catholic missionaries did their best to continue serving the Chinese people during the Japanese occupation. For instance, in 1939, the Sisters of Providence from St. Mary of the Woods, Indiana, tried to maintain their neutrality while simultaneously following new Japanese educational regulations to keep their school open.[35]

The December 1941 Japanese attack on Pearl Harbor and Hong Kong created a new situation. Suddenly, most missionaries—except those from nations supporting Japan—held passports identifying them as enemy combatants. In turn, the Japanese sent numerous foreigners—including U.S. Catholic and Protestant missionaries—to internment camps in Weihsien, Shandong, and Shanghai. In 1942 and 1943, the Japanese allowed the refugee ship the SS *Gripsholm* to carry many of these same prisoners back home to safety.[36] This scenario symbolized an important point. In most cases, when faced with a crisis or disaster, Catholic and Protestant missionaries who regularly applied their zeal to compete for the conversion of the Chinese soul redirected that same zeal to sustain ecumenical cooperation.

Anyone holding a passport from the Irish Free State was fortunate, as Ireland was neutral. Moreover, because the Japanese applied a fluid interpretation of ancestor lineage, freedom was just around the corner for anyone who could prove they had Irish relatives. In 1941, this was the case of the Canadian-born leaders of the U.S. Passionists, Bishop Cuthbert O'Gara and Maryknoll Father Mark Tennien. They carried British and U.S. passports, respectively, but because they also had Irish ancestry, the Japanese acknowledged their neutral status. As a result, they escaped death and endured a short time of hardship before the Japanese allowed them to leave occupied Hong Kong.[37]

In 1937, the Holy See added another layer of diplomatic confusion for China when an increased European fear of Communism led Pope Pius XI to issue his encyclical *Divini redemptoris* against atheistic Communism. It did not take long for Catholics to see Chinese Communists in an evil light. By 1940, the Catholic population had reached 3,262,678 and spread across 138 regions. There were 2,091 Chinese priests and 3,064 priests from other countries. In 1943, Mr. Xie Shoukang presented his credentials to the pope as the first Chinese minister to the Holy See, the same year the United States finally ratified an end to long-standing laws on extraterritoriality. In 1946, Chinese bishop Tian Gengxian (1890–1967) was named the cardinal of Beijing. That year, the Holy See made two pro-Nationalist appointments that were unpopular with the Communists. Archbishop Antonio Riberi (1897–1967) replaced Zanin as apostolic internuncio. Riberi held the post on the mainland and later in Taiwan until 1959. However, Mr. John Wu Jingxiong (1899–1986) was named Nationalist representative to the Holy See. As a result, the Communists erroneously began to view all Catholic missionaries as part of a larger spiritual missionary army of the pope.

During the first half of the 1940s, Chongqing, Sichuan, became the Nationalist wartime capital. Representatives from the Chinese Communists, the United States, and Catholic and Protestant missionary organizations were involved in constant lobbying to influence Chinese government policy. During his time in Chongqing (from 1940 to 1944), American Franciscan Father Leo Ferrary (1894–1944) successfully collected funds to support refugees in China. Upon receipt of donations from the CSMC in the United States, Ferrary personally presented the funds to Chiang Kai-shek and General Ho Yin-ch'ing (He Yingqin, 1890–1987), minister of war in Chongqing. Publicity surrounding the event led to a photo showing Ferrary with Bishop Paul Yu-Pin (1901–78) of Nanjing and General Pai Chung-hsi (Bai Chongxi, 1893–1966), the assistant minister of war. As a result, missionaries' daily life in Chongqing reflected the dual Catholic understanding of missionary citizenship—support for their country and gospel.[38] Despite this public face, the Nationalist-sponsored *China Handbook* shows that the Nationalists maintained a restricted view of the Catholic missionaries. Between 1943 and 1947, the Chinese Ministry of Information published several Chinese editions of the book under the direction of editor in chief Hollington K. Tong (1887–1971). English editions—each over eight hundred pages, divided into twenty chapters—appeared in 1943 and 1947. Written in encyclopedic fashion, it resembles a tutorial lesson upholding the Nationalist agenda, offering data on government structure, military, and foreign affairs and a wide range of social and economic issues. Neither Catholicism nor Protestantism is listed among the five accepted Chinese religious expressions. However, the Nationalists acknowledged the contribution of Christianity. The 1943 edition included a list of all 134 Catholic bishops by location and nationality and a distribution list of Catholic institutions by province. The 1947 edition opted for summary over detail, as it updated the "Catholic mission's" effort in three pages. It emphasized how all missionaries and Catholic workers were "ordered by the Bishops of the Catholic Church to cooperate with the Chinese Government in the national emergency" as they conducted refugee and medical relief and child welfare and educational work. Subsequently, it concluded that the dispossessed "had a friend in the missionary of the Catholic Church."[39]

The inclusion of Bishop Paul Yu-Pin of Nanjing in "Chinese Who's Who" was important. Standing well over six feet tall, Yu-Pin was an impressive symbol of Catholic China–Nationalist relations. He had served as inspector of Catholic schools in China (1933–36) and was a member of the People's Political Council (since 1938), a leader in the Association of Religious Believers in China, and president of the Chinese Catholic Cultural Association. Founded in 1941, this association promoted Catholic culture in China in the wider context of European and U.S. Catholic culture through the publication of *Christian Life* and *Religion and Culture*.[40]

On September 16, 1944, U.S. vice president Henry A. Wallace gave the *China Correspondent* magazine as a gift to the Library of Congress in Washington, D.C. The journal originated in Chongqing when Catholic officials decided to change the French-language Catholic weekly *Le Correspondent Chinois* into an English-language Catholic monthly. Published from December 1943 to September 1944 under the direction of Father Leo Ferrary, Benedictine Father Thaddeus Yang (1905–82) and American Passionist Father Cormac Shanahan (1899–1987), the *China Correspondent* operated under Nationalist press restrictions. Yet, the publication also valued a relationship whereby U.S. planes carried each issue to Catholic soldiers stationed at military bases in China. The journal's aim was "to know China better," and wartime China was the backdrop. Many articles summarized Catholic religious thought or explained Chinese culture for the soldier in the field. Sometimes, Nationalist government officials wrote for the magazine.[41]

During the summer of 1944, before production disputes brought an end to the magazine in September 1944, *China Correspondent* editor Father Shanahan was given permission by the Nationalist government to represent Catholic magazines and travel with five other foreign reporters, including Harrison Forman, to personally visit Mao Zedong in Yan'an. Shanahan's diary of the trip was written on one of his old American passports, symbolically calling to mind his position as Catholic priest and citizen. It is easy to imagine him sitting in the Yan'an caves making daily notations. Shanahan eventually reported the story to armchair missionary Catholics back home via his *Sign Magazine* articles of 1946. They learned about the positive aspects of daily life at the Chinese Communist stronghold, but Shanahan also described the lack of religious freedom for Yan'an Catholics under Mao. He made it clear to U.S. Department of State officials and in later publications that Yan'an was no utopia.[42]

Chinese Communist officials during the Chongqing era were suspicious of American Catholic missionaries employed as contract military chaplains. Maryknoll Father Mark Tennien (1900–1983) worked in Chongqing while Passionist Father Marcellus White (1908–2002) worked with the Flying Tigers in Zhijiang, western Hunan. Later, during the Korean War (1950–53), Communist interrogators accused numerous captured U.S. Catholics of colluding with chaplains to help the Nationalists gain military information. The public nature of these conflicts enhanced American armchair missionaries' support for the China mission and the Chinese Nationalist cause. This position was staunchly backed by the U.S. government and the National Catholic Welfare Conference (NCWC), which fervently publicized the China mission effort in Catholic diocesan newspapers and the national and regional secular press.

Armchair missionaries grew deeply enamored of Bishop Paul Yu-Pin. His February 1939 visit to the United States as special envoy of the Chinese National Government Relief Commission led to the creation of the West Meets East Committee. Located at 115 Mott Street, New York, the committee distributed *The Truth About Communism in China*, a ten-cent pamphlet extolling the Nationalist effort. In 1945, Yu-Pin published a book of essays linking the basic principles of Chinese philosophy and culture with U.S. democratic values. The work included his 1945 talk before a U.S. House of Representatives Committee on Immigration.[43]

Bishop Yu-Pin went on to use his position as honorary chairman of the *China Monthly: The Truth about China* to lobby U.S. Catholics on behalf of the Chinese Catholic Church and Nationalist China. From 1939 to 1949, the journal's main office was in New York City. After 1945, offices were opened in Nanjing and Shanghai. As first rector of the Catholic University of Peking (1925–33) and later a faculty member at Duquesne University (1934–37) and the Catholic University of America (1937–39), Monsignor George Barry O'Toole (1886–1944) used his international connections to edit the *China Monthly* from 1939 until his death in 1944. Father Mark Tsai then took over and served as editor until 1949. The *China Monthly* demonstrates how well-organized interest groups sought to educate and politicize armchair missionaries to support the Nationalist regime. Articles were penned by Catholic officials, American politicians, and business and military leaders with interests in both America and China.

Finally, the 1944 movie *The Keys of the Kingdom* had a memorable effect. Starring Gregory Peck (1916–2003) as Father Francis Chisholm, the film brought the China mission into mainstream American culture with scenes depicting the rigors inherent in Catholic and Protestant missionary zeal.

1949–1956: Missionary Citizenship and Armchair Missionaries in the Communist Era

China changed dramatically in 1949 with the triumph of Mao Zedong's revolutionary forces. Promoting *Ai-guo* (love of country), Mao instituted harsh economic and political programs. Many Chinese people suffered during the national anti-corruption purge (1951–52) and participation in the Korean War (1950–53). Although the Communists praised religious freedom, they simultaneously increased persecution against Chinese Christians and foreign Christian missionaries. The Chinese Communists now viewed missionaries holding U.S. passports as spies abetting the American "police action" in Korea. Most of the Catholic missionaries were also suspected of colluding with the Holy See's special mission to gather a spiritual army of Chinese Catholics, organized around membership in the devotional organization known as the Legion of Mary. Founded in 1921 by Frank Duff, a Catholic layman from Ireland, Columban Father W. Aedan McGrath had introduced it to his Hubei parish in 1937.[44] All of the foreign missionaries faced a difficult choice; that is, leave China with the Nationalists or stay under the Communists. U.S. diplomats urged all U.S. citizens to leave the country, but just as in the 1930s, the Holy See asked all essential Catholic missionaries to remain at their posts. Most of the foreign missionaries were evacuated, but a small percentage of Catholic missionaries remained, including some Americans. Many were veterans well versed in Chinese culture and language and well loved by the community of Chinese Catholics. Within a short time, these missionaries and indigenous Chinese Catholics faced systematic persecution. Catholic life in China became a trial in every sense. During the 1950s, thousands of Chinese Catholic citizens faced imprisonment, torture, or death and thus had to make difficult decisions. Some believed that following the gospel meant they should boycott the Chinese Communist government and practice their Catholic faith in silence as part of an "underground" or unregistered church. Other Chinese Catholics chose to practice their Catholicism in public cooperation by registering and following the Communist regulations as part of an "open church."

Holy See–China relations continued to deteriorate. In 1952, armchair missionaries were shocked to learn that U.S. Maryknoll bishop Francis X. Ford had died as the result of his captivity in a Chinese prison. The Holy See's Internuncio Riberi was officially expelled from China. He subsequently relocated from Hong Kong to Taipei, Taiwan, where the Nationalists had established the government of the Republic of China in 1949. In 1954, Pope Pius XII (1876–1958) promulgated *Ad sinarum gentem*. The encyclical comforted faithful "underground" Chinese Catholics loyal to the pope inside and outside China who had chosen to defy the Communist government while criticizing loyal Chinese Catholics who had participated in the government-sponsored "Three Self Movement," which stipulated that Chinese Catholic (and Protestant) loyalty went hand in hand with loyalty to the state. In 1955, Catholics inside and outside China were frustrated by the news that Archbishop Gong Pinmei (1901–2001) of Shanghai, about 40 priests, and 1,000 Catholics had been accused of disloyalty to the government and maintaining open communication with imperialist interests outside China.[45]

Although the public was eager to obtain news of U.S. Catholic and Protestant missionaries, American armchair missionaries were exposed to constant reminders of China's culture of persecution. In 1953, Maryknoll Father Robert W. Greene (1911–2003) published a book about his time in a Chinese prison, as did Gretta Palmer (1907–53) in *God's Underground in Asia*. She told "the full story of the Red war against the Church in China, a story of organized terror and Christian heroism." Bishop Fulton J. Sheen (1895–1979), editor of *Worldmission* magazine published by the Society for the Propagation of the Faith, kept the China story alive among the American people. His 1953 article describing how "wet martyrs" shed their blood for the faith while "dry martyrs" suffered martyrdom without shedding blood painted a vivid picture of 1950s Catholic missionary life and persecutions in China and throughout the world. In 1956, seminarians at St. Mary's Seminary in Baltimore felt the sting of Chinese persecution in a personal way when the school journal reported that alumni Father John Nien, who had graduated in 1947 and had been ordained a priest of the Yuanling, Hunan, diocese in 1948, had been imprisoned by the Communists. Only years later did his death become known.[46]

During these Cold War troubles, armchair missionaries raised their voices to pray for Catholics suffering in China. When missionaries expelled from China returned home, they were hailed as Cold War heroes. In the decades to come, many of these armchair missionaries, with financial and promotional assistance from Alfred Kohlberg (1887–1960)—a right-wing former FBI agent turned entrepreneur—created a powerful anti-Communist "China lobby."

Catholic piety toward the Blessed Mother led many armchair missionaries to pray for the suffering Chinese by reciting the popular *Union of Prayers for the Persecuted Church in*

China. The prayer read, "Almighty and eternal God, Comforter of the afflicted, and Strength of the suffering, grant that our brothers of China who share our faith, may obtain through the intercession of the Blessed Virgin Mary and of our holy Martyrs, peace in Thy service, strength in time of trial, and the grace to glorify Thee, through Jesus Christ our Lord. Amen." The prayer was circulated via holy cards on which it was inscribed. A Pittsburgh high school student, Theresa Weyandt, received her holy card in 1956 at St. Mary's Church in downtown Pittsburgh as a member of the Missionary Confraternity of Christian Doctrine. In 1959, the same card was handed out to students at the Loyola College chapel in Baltimore.[47]

Popular anti-Communist tracts and pamphlets further amplified the vigilance of armchair missionaries. Paul K. T. Sih (1910–78) of Seton Hall University in South Orange, New Jersey, and Passionist bishop Cuthbert O'Gara, among others, detailed not only the perils faced by Christians in Red China, but also the ease with which Communist Chinese tactics might be used by those bent on infiltrating the United States. Later, the prison memoir of American Franciscan missionary Father Boniface Pfeilschifter (1900–1985) depicted the loss of China as a distinctly Catholic tragedy.[48]

Still, with an eye to the future, several scholars quietly tried to build on the past experience of missionary citizenship and armchair missionaries. For example, as early as 1951, Vincentian Father Julius M. Schick avoided conventional Cold War rhetoric by objectively addressing tensions in China that in the 1930s had pitted American Vincentians against U.S. diplomats. In addition, Passionist Father Thomas Berry (1914–2009) promoted a greater understanding of Chinese history and culture. Assigned to China in 1949, Berry was forced to evacuate that same year when the Communists assumed power. In a 1956 essay for *Worldmission,* Berry offered an urgent message to former missionaries and other interested parties. "Communists or no Communists, we must get on with [the] work" of Sinology.[49]

Generally, the armchair missionaries believed that increased public knowledge about these suffering missionaries put pressure on China to release them. In contrast, diplomats shied away from public protest during the Korean War years, when a U.S. passport meant little to the Chinese. As early as February 8, 1952, U.S. Secretary of State Dean Acheson (1893–1971) sent a two-page secret security memo to U.S. officials. It reminded them just how cautious a diplomat had to be when speaking about Americans in a Chinese prison. At the end of the memo, Acheson laid his cards on the table. "It has been the Department's view that acrimonious and denunciatory statements by the Department would in all likelihood be marked off by the Chinese Communists as political propaganda designed to exploit the situation of Americans in China."[50]

International diplomats often worked behind the scenes together to get missionaries released. Following the model of communication set up during World War II, they consulted with families, the provincial superiors of their respective American Catholic religious congregations, the offices of the NCWC, U.S. representatives in the Senate and House of Representatives, officials at the United Nations, and U.S. diplomats. In March 1954, at least thirteen U.S. Catholic missionaries still languished in Communist prisons. As the public pressed for their release, a cadre of diplomats around a negotiating table in Geneva, Switzerland, worked with the Office of Special Consular Services of the Department of State, the NCWC, and Secretary of State John Foster Dulles to secure their eventual release.[51]

Conclusion

Popular opinion was that the oppressive Cultural Revolution (1966–76) had resulted in a death blow for Chinese Catholic believers.[52] As surprising as the 1972 visit of President Richard M. Nixon to China and the establishment of diplomatic relations in 1979 were to Americans, few anticipated renewed contact between Chinese Catholics of the People's Republic of China and the U.S. mission-sending congregations that had been active in China until the 1950s or with the armchair missionaries who had supported them.

This unexpected rapprochement with the new China Catholic milieu (and ecumenical audiences) resulted in the 1980s giving life to experienced congregants and a new generation of participants seeking to build paradigm-based learning, dialogue, and friendship with religious believers in China.[53]

International inquiry of scholars seeking to establish an ecumenical common ground was paramount. For example, in Chicago on May 4–5, 1979, the Chicago Cluster of Theological Schools sponsored the Midwest Consultation on Christian Perspectives toward the New China. In 1981 in Montreal, Canada, this discourse gained credence when Chinese Catholic and Protestant leaders were participants in a historic meeting with 150 Christians to foster sharing and forge personal relationships.[54]

On the U.S. scene, annual meetings during the 1980s coordinated by Catholics in America Concerned About China (CAAC) proved equally important in paying respect to the accrued wisdom of missionary congregations and armchair missionaries with a vested interest in China. A selective sampling of CAAC participants and themes is instructive to appreciate emerging voices who were seeking to understand the interactive pulse of Chinese Catholicism.[55]

Gathering at Maryknoll, N.Y., for CAAC 1980 were forty representatives of religious congregations with past China interaction. Planners included Sister Ann Gormly, SND-deN, of the U.S. Catholic Mission Council, China Liaison Group, and Donald MacInnis, Maryknoll Mission Research, while Dr. Edmond Tang of Pro Munda Vitae spoke on "the Catholic Church in China Today."

Building upon the positive shared dynamics of the early CAAC gatherings, in 1984 and 1985, the CAAC Executive Committee developed agendas whereby the respective annual meetings successfully addressed more nuanced theological issues relevant to religion and society in a wide framework to include China.[56] Throughout the 1980s CAAC meetings assisted in providing a forum and confidence to a multitude of scholars and organizations in their quest to understand Catholic China.[57]

In sum, this chapter examines the 1900 to 1989 legacy of missionary citizens abroad, armchair missionaries at home, and a new China paradigm. Lessons of resiliency learned during these years proved essential in coping with the shock and immediate impact of

Tiananmen Square in 1989. Moreover, in subsequent years reflection on the diverse contours that make up this American missionary context facilitate the reconciliation narrative espoused in the last decades of the twentieth century[58] and during the twenty-first century by Pope Benedict XVI and Pope Francis.[59]

NOTES

Previously published by the Centre for Catholic Studies, CUHK, in the book *Foreign Missionaries and the Indigenization of the Chinese Catholic Church*, Chapter 3: "Gospel Zeal. Missionary Citizens Overseas and Armchair Missionaries at Home: American Catholic Missions in China, 1900–1956," pp. 35–67.

1. John Tracy Ellis, ed., *Documents of American Catholic History*, vol 2, *1866–1966* (Wilmington, Del.: Michael Glazier, 1987), 577.

2. This information is compiled from Wu Xiaoxin, ed., *Christianity in China*, 2nd ed. (Armonk, N.Y.: M. E. Sharpe, 2009), and R. G. Tiedemann, *Reference Guide to Christian Missionary Societies in China: From the Sixteenth to the Twentieth Century* (Armonk, N.Y.: M.E. Sharpe, 2009).

3. *Catholic Review*, June 7, 1924, 1.

4. Henri Corder, "China," *The Catholic Encyclopedia* (New York: Robert Appleton, 1908), 3:663–68.

5. "Two Letters from the Rev. Francis X. Ford, A.F.M., to the Maryknoll Communities. About 2000 miles S.W. of Frisco. Sept. 26, [19]18," *American Ecclesiastical Review* 60 (March 1919): 305–12. Quote on p. 305.

6. Reflections of Father Maloney, written July 26, 1973, in 505.04_023.003b, the Passionist China Collection [Hereafter the PCC]. From 2012 to 2015 the PCC was digitized at the Ricci Institute for Chinese-Western Cultural History at the University of San Francisco, San Francisco, California, and is now open for research by scholars. The Weinberg Memorial Library, Special Collections, University of Scranton, Scranton, Pennsylvania has the original and a digital copy. All number references in the PCC refer to the digital copy.

7. Jean-Paul Wiest, *Maryknoll In China* (Maryknoll, N.Y.: Orbis, 1997), 73–131. Maryknoll's progressive approach can be identified in Rev. Thomas F. Price, "The Present Condition of the Foreign Mission Field," *American Ecclesiastical Review* 56 (April 1917): 375–87.

8. The overall context for this relationship between domestic and foreign missions is in Angelyn Dries, O.S.F., *The Missionary Movement in American Catholic History* (Maryknoll, N.Y.: Orbis, 1998).

9. *The Official Catholic Directory* (New York: P. J. Kenedy & Sons, 1923), 751. Administrative offices of Maryknoll and the Columbans refer to China as well; 752–53.

10. *Official Catholic Directory* (1927), 695–96.

11. Maryknoll ministered in Kongmoon and Kaying, Kwangung province; Wuchow, Kwangsi province; and Fushun, Manchuria. The Chicago Franciscans were in Chowtsun, Shandong province. The Columbans were in Hanyang, Hupeh province. The Eastern Province Vincentians were in Kanchow, Kiangsi. The Holy Name Franciscans of New York were in Shasi, Hupeh. The Cincinnati Franciscans were in Wuchang, Hupeh. The Passionists were in Yuanling, Hunan province. The Western Province Vincentians were in Yukiang, Kiangsi. The Columbans were in Kien Chang, Kiangsi. The East Coast Dominicans of St. Joseph were in the Independent Mission of Kienningfu, Fukien province; *Official Catholic Directory* (1938), 665–74 [original spelling of Chinese regions has been retained].

12. Chinese locations of Divine Word Missionaries, Franciscans, Jesuits, Maryknoll, and Columbans in *Official Catholic Directory* (1950), 639–54, passim; Vincentians staffed two dioceses, while the Passionists and Dominicans each had one (657–58).

13. Greater study is needed on the process by which the National Catholic Welfare Conference (NCWC) and U.S. government agencies facilitated and coordinated information about all religious congregations engaged in missionary activity during the Depression Era through the 1950s. The U.S. Department of State officials worked closely with the staff of the National Catholic Welfare Council. Their archives are at the American Catholic History Research Center and University Archives at the Catholic University of America in Washington, D.C.

14. On August 15, 1967, the name of the congregation was changed to the Congregation for the Evangelization of Peoples.

15. Cuthbert O'Gara, to Stanislaus Grennan, C.P., in PCC, 505.04_027.007a to 007d.

16. David J. Endres, *American Crusade: Catholic Youth in the World Mission Movement from World War I through Vatican II* (Eugene, Ore.: Pickwick, 2010).

17. A basic summary of Protestant and Catholic efforts throughout Chinese dynastic change into the modern era is in Daniel H. Bays, *A New History of Christianity in China* (Malden, Mass.: Wiley-Blackwell, 2012).

18. These dimensions are seen in Paul A. Cohen, *History in Three Keys: The Boxers as Event, Experience and Myth* (New York: Columbia University Press, 1997); Henrietta Harrison, *The Missionary's Curse and Other Tales from a Chinese Catholic Village* (Berkeley: University of California Press, 2013), 92–115; and Anthony E. Clark, *Heaven in Conflict: Franciscans and the Boxer Uprising in Shanxi* (Seattle: University of Washington Press, 2015).

19. Ernest P. Young, *Ecclesiastical Colony: China's Catholic Church and the French Religious Protectorate* (New York: Oxford University Press, 2013).

20. Arnluf Camps, O.F.M., "The Chinese Martyrs among the 120 Martyrs of China, Canonized on the 1st of October 2000," in *Silent Force: Native Converts in the Catholic China Mission*, ed. Dr. Rachel Lu Yan and Dr. Philip Vanhaelemeersch, Leuven Chinese Studies 20 (Leuven: Ferdinand Verbiest Institute, 2009), 507–33.

21. *Sanctum* 23 (November 1915): 63; *Sanctum* 23 (January 1916): 138; *Sanctum* 23 (May 1916): 289; *Sanctum* 25 (February 1918): 165; *Sanctum* 26 (June 1919): 344. All in Duquesne University Archives, Duquesne University, Pittsburgh, Pennsylvania.

22. Gibbons cable: RG 59:393.116/164; American government support: RG 59:393.116/170; both in the National Archives of the United States, College Park, Maryland (hereafter: NARA).

23. Mundelein letter of support is RG 59:393.116/171; Henninghaus meeting Reinsch is RG 59:393.116/193; both in NARA.

24. Henninghaus had strong ties to the United States. The *Chicago Daily Tribune* (March 25, 1908) reported his arrival in New York for fund-raising and offered a summary of evangelization in "Missionary Notes and News," *Catholic Missions* [hereafter *CM*] (May 1918). The Shandong case is as follows: "We enter our most emphatic protest . . . of the greed of certain nations which do not hesitate to sacrifice prosperous Christian missions to extend their commercial supremacy"; Editorial: "An Alarming Situation," *CM* 13 (March 1919): 70; Editorial: "The South Shantung Mission," *CM* 13 (April 1919): 91; "Missionaries in Shandong undisturbed," editorial: "'Expelled From China' The South Shantung Mission," *CM* 13 (May 1919): 142; "A missionary who is faithful to his vocation must entirely forget the material interests of his mother land and never be its political agent; the only interests he has at heart are those of the Church and souls he has come to evangelize"; Editorial: "Plea of German Missionaries," *CM* 13 (June 1919): 166; Right Rev. A. Henninghaus, S.V.D., "The Other Side of the Story," *CM* 13 (August—June 1919): 178–79.

25. Greater insight on Father Lebbe is in Young, *Ecclesiastical Colony*.

26. McDermott to Grennan, February 22, 1922, in PCC 505.02_012.05.

27. Cusack correspondence, in RG 59:393; NARA 1163/61, 63, 64.

28. Paul Mariani, S.J., "The First Six Chinese Bishops of Modern Times: A Study in Church Indigenization," *Catholic Historical Review* 100 (Summer 2014): 486–513.

29. The 1930 English translation of the document is in the NCWC Papers, File: Church: Missions: China: State Department 1930, 136-C.

30. Robert E. Carbonneau, "Life, Death and Memory: Three Passionists in Hunan, China and the Shaping of an American Mission Perspective in the 1920s" (Ph.D. diss., Georgetown University, 1992).

31. Poem by Anthony F. Klinker, of Dubuque, Iowa, *Michigan Catholic*, May 16, 1929, 3.

32. *Foreign Relations of the United States* (FRUS), 1931, 3:965–69; quote on p. 965.

33. *Annuaire des Missions catholiques de Chine* (Shanghai: Bureau sinologique de Zi-ka-wei, 1935), 2 and 5.

34. *The Gothic*: Charles Freegard, "The Catholic University of Peiping" (December 15, 1929): 28; Francis Lynch and Stanley Bowers, "Father Healy and His Labors" (April 15, 1931): 7 and 33. The journal is at the Edmund Cardinal Szoka Library, Sacred Heart Major Seminary, Detroit: *The Grackle* 9 (1932–33): 18. The journal is at the Logue Library, Chestnut Hill College, Philadelphia.

35. Bombings in RG 59:393.1163/868; Sisters in RG 59:393.1163Am3/430. Both in the NARA. For context, see Sister Ann Colette, S.P., *Against All Odds: Sisters of Providence Mission to the Chinese, 1920–1990* (St. Mary-of-the-Woods, Ind.: Sisters of Providence, 1990), 119–37.

36. The two best studies on Weihsien are Langdon Gilkey, *Shantung Compound* (New York: Harper & Row, 1966), and Jonathan Henshaw, *Beyond Collaboration and Resistance: Accommodation and the Weihsien Internment Camp, China, 1943–1945* (M.A., University of Alberta, 2010). Six internment sites were also in Shanghai. A case study that includes internment is "Father Leonard Amrhein, C.P.: Missionary Zeal and Shared Experience of Suffering and Compassion with Chinese Catholics in Wartime and Late-Twentieth-Century China," in *China's Christianity*, ed. Anthony E. Clark (Boston: Brill, 2017), 175–98, www.bris.ac.uk/history/customs/ancestors /internees/zikaweicamp.pdf; on *Gripsholm*, see http://salship.se/mercy.php.

37. Ronald Norris, C.P., "The Church in Internment," *The Sign* 22 (November 1942): 224–28; Mark Tennien, *Chungking Listening Post* (New York: Creative Age, 1945), 10–21.

38. Information comes from a newspaper clipping entitled, "The Mission Crusade of the U.S.A. Gives a Pledge to China's People." There is also the photo, the content of which is mentioned in the previous text; circa 1940s, in PCC 800.30_050.011.

39. *China Handbook: 1937–1943* (New York: Macmillan, 1943), and *China Handbook: 1937–1945*, rev. and enlarged with 1946 supplement (New York: Macmillan, 1947), respectively; quote in 1947, p. 570.

40. *China Handbook: 1937–1945*, 592, 600–601, and 705.

41. David J. Endres, "The Legacy of Thaddeus Yang," *International Bulletin of Missionary Research* 34 (January 2010): 23–28. An original run of the *China Correspondent* can be found at the Library of Congress in Washington, D.C.; also available in digital copy of the PCC.

42. Cormac Shanahan, "Red China Today," *The Sign*, July 1945, 629–31, and "Holy Mass in the Heart of Red China," *The Sign* 25, November 1945, 42–43. Thoughts of Shanahan to the State Department are in *FRUS*, 1944, 479–82. Robert E. Carbonneau, "Journalist and Priest: The Participation of Father Cormac Shanahan, C.P., in the 1944 Press Party to Yan'an China, His Experience with Communist Leaders and Ministry to Yan'an Catholics," in *A Lifelong Dedication to the China Mission: Essays Presented in Honor of Father Jeroom Heyndrickx, CICM, on the Occasion of His 75th Birthday and 25th Anniversary of the F. Verbiest Institute K.U. Leuven*, Leuven Chinese Studies 17 (Leuven: Ferdinand Verbiest Foundation, K.U. Leuven, 2007), 29–52; PCC 502.01_001 is a digital copy of the Cormac Shanahan Diary.

43. Dr. Harry McNeil, *The Truth about Communism in China* (New York: West Meets East Committee. 1939). On May 19, 1943, Yu-Pin spoke on "Repeal of the Exclusion Act"; see Bishop Paul Yu-Pin, *Eyes East* (Paterson, N.J.: St. Anthony Guild Press, 1945), 31–34.

44. John Witek, "Legion of Mary," ed. R. G. Tiedemann, in *Handbook of Christianity in China*, vol. 2, *1800–Present* (Boston: Brill, 2010), 568–70.

45. Paul P. Mariani, *Church Militant: Bishop Kung and Catholic Resistance in Communist Shanghai* (Cambridge, Mass.: Harvard University Press, 2011).

46. Robert W. Greene, M.M., *Calvary in China* (New York: G. P. Putnam's Sons, 1953); Gretta Palmer, *God's Underground in Asia* (New York: Appleton Century-Crofts, 1953); Fulton J. Sheen, "Wet Martyrs and Dry Martyrs," *Worldmission* 4 (Fall 1953): 259–75; Special editorial announcement on Nien, in *The Voice* 31 (January 1954). The journal is located at the Knott Library, St. Mary's Seminary and University, Baltimore, Maryland.

47. Theresa Weyandt to author; "The Church Silent," editorial, *The Greyhound*, April 29, 1959, 2.

48. Paul K. T. Sih, *Decision for China: Communism or Christianity* (Chicago: Regnery, 1959); Norbert Schmalz, O.F.M., and Boniface Pfeilschifter, O.F.M., *Shen-Fu's Story: The Memoirs of Two Missionaries in the China of Yesteryear* (Chicago: Franciscan Herald, 1966); Most Rev. Cuthbert O'Gara, C.P., *The Surrender to Secularism* (St. Louis, Mo.: Cardinal Mindszenty Foundation, 1967). In 2015 *Surrender* was still in circulation, selling for $4.00. For more on O'Gara's anti-Communist voice, see Robert E. Carbonneau, C.P., "'It Can Happen Here': Bishop Cuthbert O'Gara, C.P., and the Gospel of Anticommunism in Cold War America," *Mission Studies* 15, no. 2 (1998): 2–30.

49. Julius M. Schick, C.M., "Diplomatic Correspondence Concerning the Chinese Missions of the American Vincentians 1929–1934" (Master's thesis, The Catholic University of America, 1951); Thomas Berry, C.P., "Our Need for Orientalists," *Worldmission* 7 (Fall 1956): 301–14; quote on 301.

50. NARA, RG 59: 293.1111/2-852.

51. NARA, RG 59: 293.1111/3-1854, and RG 59: 293.1111/3-2254, show this process.

52. My research showed a dearth of references to the Catholic Church in China in the *Catholic Periodical Index* from 1955 to 1970,

53. Sources and insight used in the conclusion of this chapter essay is based upon my attending these events and my personal archives.

54. "Western Christianity and the People's Republic of China: Exploring New Possibilities" was the Chicago theme. The organizer was Prof. James A. Scherer, Lutheran School of Theology at Chicago. Discussants included Dr. Ross Terrill, Harvard; Dr. Donald MacInnis, director of the Midwest China Resource Center; Dr. Arne B. Sovik, Lutheran World Federation; and Fr. Joseph Spae, C.I.C.M, Vatican secretariate for Non-Christians; 1981 Montreal proceedings are in *A New Beginning: An International Dialogue with the Chinese Church*, ed. Theresa Chu and Christopher Lind (Montreal: Canada China Programme of the Canadian Council of Churches, 1983).

55. Awaiting to be written is the history of the CAAC, which met annually between 1980 and 1988.

56. Board members in advance of the 1984 CAAC annual meeting pondered, "What is the role of CAAC? CAAC members want/need? They must feel that the CAAC meeting is worthwhile, or meets some needs." Thus, a specific question: "What is the role of CAAC? CAAC plays a needed role, as coordinator, educator, stimulator, challenger, provider of ideas and information." Planning for the CACC December 6–8, 1985, meeting at Maryknoll, N.Y., resulted in Robert J. Schreiter, C.PP.S., speaking on "A Theology of Christian Presence in a Secular Society." Attuned to China, it was published as "A Theology of Christian Presence," *Tripod*, no. 32 (1985): 34–48.

57. From 1980 to 1985, the following were among the numerous CAAC participants. Many attended multiple meetings. In the post-CACC era of the 1990s all continued to seek understanding of China church relations: Father Robert E. Carbonneau, C.P. (1980); Sister Janet Carroll, M.M. (1980); Father John Cioppa, M.M (1980) and Father Laurence Murphy, M.M (1980), then of

New York and Seton Hall University, respectively; Father Peter Barry, M.M. (1981) and Father John Tong (1981), both from Hong Kong; K. H. Ting, president of the China Christian Council (1981); Father Michael Chu, S.J., associate general counselor to Jesuit Superior General and special advisor on China (1982); Sister Goretti Lau, Hong Kong (1983); Dr. Richard Madsen, sociologist, the University of California, San Diego, (1984); Father Edward Malatesta, S.J., of the Ricci Institute of Chinese-Western Culture, University of San Francisco, (1984); Father Michel Marcil, S.J. of Canada, (1984); Dr. Franklin Woo, China Program of the National Council of the Churches of Christ in USA (1985); Father Jeroom Heyndrickx, C.I.C.M., Leuven, Belgium (1985); Dr. Jean-Paul Wiest, Maryknoll China Project (1985).

58. Robert E. Carbonneau, C.P., "The Chinese Catholic Church and the Quest for a Reconciliation Narrative," *Canon Law Society of America Proceedings* 59 (1997): 105–22.

59. Ongoing international efforts of the Holy See and other parties with the approximately 10 to 12 million Chinese Catholics in China in 2017 can best be followed by consulting the website of the Holy Spirit Study Centre, Hong Kong, www.hsstudyc.org.hk.

EIGHT

Northern Settlement Houses and Southern Welfare Centers: The Sisters of Our Lady of Christian Doctrine, 1910–1971

Margaret M. McGuinness

By the age of nineteen, Veronica McCarthy knew exactly how she wanted to spend the rest of her life: she wanted to be a "sister," and she wanted to work with the poor. Having very little knowledge about the differences among women's religious communities, she turned to her parish priest for guidance. He told her about a "fairly new" community, she remembered, whose members lived with and ministered to the poor of New York City's Lower East Side. Shortly after this conversation, Veronica found herself ringing the doorbell of Madonna House, a social settlement founded and staffed by the Sisters of Our Lady of Christian Doctrine.[1] The sisters were very welcoming, and Veronica, who was given the religious name of Sister Dorothea, had found what she was seeking.[2]

Sister Dorothea's story is not unique. Since the arrival of six French Ursulines in New Orleans in 1727 and continuing into the present day, thousands of women have answered God's call and devoted all or part of their lives to prayer and apostolic work within the framework of a religious community. Some, seeking a more contemplative life in cloistered communities, pray for the work of the church and the well-being of the world—a world they have chosen to leave. Others, without denying the importance of prayer in their lives and apostolate, have built, administered, and staffed schools, hospitals, orphanages, settlement houses, and other charitable institutions.

Women Religious in the United States

During the colonial era, British laws restricting the practice of Catholicism forced women who believed they had a vocation to join a religious community on the European continent. Ann Matthews (Mother Bernardina Teresa Xavier of St. Joseph), a Maryland native, left her homeland to enter the Discalced (shoeless) Carmelites, a community dedicated to the contemplative life. In 1790, three years after the ratification of the U.S. Constitution, Matthews was able to return home and, along with three other sisters from the Antwerp and Hoogstraeten Carmels, establish the first women's religious foundation in the new nation.

Although Baltimore archbishop John Carroll (1787–1815) warmly welcomed the Carmelites, they were not quite the group the first U.S. bishop (Carroll was named archbishop in 1808) needed as he began the arduous task of establishing and solidifying the Catholic Church in the United States. Carroll sought religious women who were engaged in active apostolates, especially those willing to educate girls and women or work with the poor. He would begin to realize his dream in 1799 when Alice Lalor, Maria McDermott, and Maria Sharpe, who would be formally professed as Visitation Sisters in 1816, arrived in Georgetown to live in community and begin a ministry devoted to the education of young Catholic women.

John Carroll's efforts to provide a strong religious foundation for American Catholics would be helped immeasurably in 1809 when Elizabeth Ann Bayley Seton, a convert to Catholicism, established the Sisters of Charity of St. Joseph. Although Seton modeled her community on the Daughters of Charity founded by saints Vincent de Paul and Louise de Marillac, she adapted the French order's rule to meet the needs of religious women living and working in a country where Catholics were the minority. Founded as a distinctly American order—with no ties to a European religious community—the Sisters of Charity opened the first free Catholic school for girls in the United States (St. Joseph Academy and Free School). In 1823, they became the first American women religious to staff a hospital when they began work at the Baltimore Infirmary.[3]

European women religious were among the thousands of immigrants arriving in America during the antebellum period. United States' bishops, who often found themselves surrounded by poor Catholics in need of both education and social services, begged European superiors to send some of their community's members to the United States. Many European religious communities took the entreaties of American bishops to heart and sent their sisters across the ocean to teach school, staff hospitals, visit the poor, and prepare children and adults to receive the sacraments. After hearing that Bishop Joseph Rosati of St. Louis had appealed for missionaries willing to work in his frontier diocese, for instance, Mother St. John Fontbonne, CSJ, agreed to dispatch six Sisters of St. Joseph to minister to local Catholics. She was even willing to honor Rosati's special request that two sisters be able and willing to teach deaf children. As a result, in 1836 the first Sisters of St. Joseph arrived in the St. Louis area from France.[4]

By the end of the nineteenth century, women religious were common sights in cities and towns with significant Catholic populations. Some communities journeyed to the

United States to work with a specific immigrant group and either kept their ties with their European foundation or severed their relationship and developed their own governance structure. At the same time, young American Catholic women called to serve God and the poor were entering religious communities throughout the United States. In addition, two congregations of African American women religious, the Oblate Sisters of Providence and the Sisters of the Holy Family, had been founded to minister to black Catholics. A third congregation, the Franciscan Handmaids of Mary, was established in 1916.

When Sister Dorothea began to realize that she indeed had a vocation (a calling from God) to the religious life, she had to determine which of the several hundred women's religious communities was the "right fit." Any young women in the process of choosing a religious community would first have to decide whether she was interested in an active or a contemplative apostolate. Contemplative communities remove themselves from the distractions of the world to give themselves to God through the medium of prayer. The life of a contemplative is very structured; there are set times for prayer, meals, recreation, and work. Members of active communities live the word of God through the particular ministry of their community, which may include teaching, nursing, social work, or domestic or foreign mission work. Each religious community is devoted to its own particular apostolate.

The Sisters of Our Lady of Christian Doctrine, the community to which Sister Dorothea was called in 1936, was, at the time, a relatively new religious order. Indigenous to the United States, the congregation was dedicated to meeting the material needs of Catholic immigrants while, at the same time, helping them remain faithful to their church. The sisters' primary means of reaching the people they were called to serve was through the establishment and staffing of settlement houses, institutions that allowed them to offer residents of a given neighborhood material assistance, social activities, and religious education classes.

London's Toynbee Hall, the first social settlement, was founded in 1884 by Canon Samuel Barnett. American progressive reformers quickly embraced the idea of settlements, and two years after the opening of Toynbee Hall, Stanton Coit established the Neighborhood Guild in New York City. In 1889, Jane Addams and Ellen Gates Starr founded Hull House in Chicago, the most well known of American social settlements. By the 1890s, Protestant, Jewish, and secular settlements were operating in most major U.S. cities. Catholic bishops were slow to endorse and encourage the founding of these institutions; several bishops claimed they were hotbeds of secularism and radicalism. The *New World*, Chicago's Catholic newspaper, for example, described settlements as "mere roosting-places for frowsy anarchists, fierce-eyed socialists, professed anti-clericals and a coterie of long-haired sociologists intent upon probing the moonshine with pale fingers."[5]

Recognizing the need to convince Catholic immigrants, particularly the Italians, that their church had not abandoned them, some bishops began to permit the establishment of Catholic social settlements in their dioceses by the end of the nineteenth century. In 1897, at the invitation of Cincinnati's Archbishop William Elder, Sisters Blandina and Justina Segale—who were biological sisters as well as members of the Sisters of Charity— were assigned the task of working with that city's Italian community. The sisters quickly determined that a settlement would best meet the needs of Cincinnati's immigrants and their children and founded the Santa Maria Institute, the first Catholic social settlement in the United States, in 1897.[6]

Marion Gurney (1868–1957), the foundress of the Sisters of Our Lady of Christian Doctrine, was appointed headworker at the newly established St. Rose's Settlement in New York City in 1898, shortly after she left the Episcopal Church and converted to Catholicism. Associated with the parish of St. Catherine of Siena on East 68th Street, the settlement's expected constituency was "that class of poor who have proven their infidelity to their Catholic birthright, remaining Catholics in name only."[7] In 1910, Gurney founded a religious community dedicated to providing material and spiritual sustenance to poverty-stricken Catholic immigrants. She and her sisters established Madonna House on New York City's Lower East Side in 1910, and in 1931 the community opened Ave Maria House in the Bronx. In 1940, the sisters were invited to adapt the community's urban apostolate to meet the needs of the working poor in rural South Carolina. Through the work of the "welfare center" (as it was called in the South), the sisters offered the same physical and spiritual sustenance to their southern neighbors that they provided to needy New Yorkers.

The Sisters of Christian Doctrine staffed religious education programs in many parishes throughout the mid-Atlantic and southeastern United States, but their two major institutions were Madonna House (New York) and the Horse Creek Valley Welfare Center (South Carolina). Unlike most other U.S. religious communities, the Sisters of Christian Doctrine never intended to emphasize teaching or nursing, but an examination of the congregation serves as a case study for those interested in the place of women religious in American Catholic life and reveals that the sisters served as the face of Catholicism for the people to whom they ministered.

The Beginning of a Religious Community

Marian Gurney was actively involved in the founding and work of several settlement houses, Protestant and Catholic, prior to founding a religious community. Along with other urban Catholic leaders of her era, lay and clerical, Gurney feared that Protestant settlements and social organizations were luring immigrant Catholics—particularly Italians—away from their ancestral church. According to the prevailing Catholic thought of this era, Protestant churches, sponsoring settlements that offered social activities, lessons in Americanization, and evangelization, were proving irresistible to their Catholic neighbors.[8]

Unlike many of her secular and Protestant counterparts, Gurney never claimed settlement houses were the definitive answer to the issues confronting immigrants streaming into U.S. cities during the late nineteenth and early twentieth centuries. Social services and Americanization classes were valuable, but more was needed; the souls of the poor also demanded attention. "'[T]he city of New York will be saved if it is,'" Gurney reflected, "'not by the distribution of clothing and groceries, nor yet by the study of Browning and the cultivation of fine arts, but by regeneration of individual human lives as one by one they are brought back to the Sacraments of the Catholic Church.'"[9]

Convinced God was calling her to religious life, Gurney was unable to find a community whose apostolate combined working with the poor through settlement houses with providing religious instruction and sacramental preparation to the local Catholic population. In 1908, after consulting with a number of people including her spiritual advisor, Francis McCarthy, S.J., Gurney and four other women began living in community to implement her vision. Two years later, they were formally recognized as the Institute of Our Lady of Christian Doctrine.

In 1910, the pastor of St. Joachim's, an Italian national parish located in the Cherry Hill section of New York City's Lower East Side, invited the new community to offer religious education classes to the parish children, most of whom were completely unfamiliar with the church's teachings. The sisters immediately discovered their job was not going to be easy. According to Gurney, now known as Mother Marianne,

> The Italian element which was very numerous was honest and hard-working but terribly pinched by poverty, and this poverty and simplicity was being shamelessly exploited by the non-Catholic missionaries who abounded. Although the religious census shows that only one-half to one per cent of the district are Protestants, the remainder being Hebrew or Roman Catholic, there are seven large Protestant Missions in the immediate neighborhood all filled with Catholic children and young people.[10]

Despite Protestant competition and parental indifference, the sisters struggled to interest the parish children in religious education, but nothing seemed to work. Mother Marianne quickly diagnosed the problem. "They were going to the people from afar," she opined. "They were not a part of the neighborhood life, in touch with all its humble joys and sorrows. Cherry Hill had no desire to be taught, but would it not respond to practical sympathy? Was not this method divinely chosen by Incarnate Love to win the hearts of men?"[11]

The new community submitted a memorandum to New York archbishop (later cardinal) John M. Farley (1902–18) detailing the conditions—spiritual and temporal—they had observed in Cherry Hill. After consulting with his advisors, Farley granted the women permission to establish a day nursery for the children of the neighborhood's working mothers. Although the sisters had never intended to include day care in their apostolate, as temporarily professed women whose rule was pending, they complied with Farley's "request." They agreed that the absence of a Catholic day nursery in the neighborhood left mothers with no alternative but to leave their children with non-Catholic childcare providers. Many of these agencies accepted young children on the condition "that the older children would attend classes of religious instruction and the parents would be present at the weekly gospel meeting."[12] With the archdiocese's help, the sisters rented a five-story house at 173 Cherry Street, on the border of St. James and St. Teresa's parishes. The neighborhood was primarily Italian, and the sisters claimed it was the poorest in the entire city. Most of the area's working mothers were employed as garment workers; they received 3.5 cents for "finishing" a coat (lining the coat and sleeves and sewing on the buttons). Many were the single parents of large families; most of their salaries were being used to pay rent.

On June 29, 1910, the first Mass was celebrated in the building's chapel. Sr. Pauline Orlando, one of the first members of the community, remembered that the weather that day was very hot and the sisters were very tired because they had stayed up until 2 a.m. making sure the house was ready for its first liturgy. During the next six weeks, a sister fluent in Italian visited neighborhood families and informed them of the soon-to-be operational nursery. The message must have been received, because on August 15 the sisters found themselves with thirty children—all crying for their mothers—representing many different nationalities, including Irish, Italian, Syrian, and Greek.[13]

Since the day nursery's mission was to serve as a substitute for the children's mothers while they worked, the sisters believed they were obligated to offer more than quality physical care. An article in *Mary's Mission*, the community's magazine, explained: "But a mother is not a mere nursemaid and the nursery, to be true to its high mission, must give the child more than mere physical care." A child's religious training must begin as early as possible.[14]

The number of children enrolled in the day nursery soon grew to fifty. Although the new community was delighted that their neighbors were taking advantage of their services, the sisters were having difficulty allocating space in which to conduct catechism classes. The building consisted of four floors, and the nursery occupied the entire second floor. The third and fourth floors served as living quarters for the sisters, and the first floor was devoted to a chapel and parlor. Even the ground floor was utilized as a kitchen and dining room. Religious education classes were conducted in the only available spaces: in the halls and on the stairs.

In response to the sisters' lack of space, the archdiocese purchased an adjoining building to accommodate the nursery's growing number of children. Once the nursery was transferred to "new" quarters, the sisters were able to dedicate some space for catechism classes intended to prepare children and adults to receive the sacraments. During their first year on Cherry Street, the sisters taught catechism to public school children three afternoons a week and spent weekday evenings instructing working boys and girls in the tenets of their faith. They accompanied children to Confession on Saturday afternoons and to Mass on Sunday mornings. The new community also taught religious education classes at San Rocco—a mission of St. Joachim's—and Our Lady Help of Christians, located on East 12th Street.

Protestant missionaries, according to the sisters, continually attempted to thwart their efforts, especially in the area around San Rocco's. They reported that "newly arrived immigrants are told that the [Protestant] mission is the true Catholic Church and the deception is aided by the frequent distribution of pictures of the Madonna and of the saints, while the children are carefully drilled in the usual anti-Catholic arguments and slanders against the clergy." The sisters countered these missionary efforts with tactics of their own and often stationed a sister nearby whose task was to stop everyone she saw on their way to the mission and inform them they had no business attending non-Catholic services.[15]

As long as the church supported their work, the sisters claimed, they would, "without doubt, be able to hold the great bulk of Catholic immigration and so help fulfill the dream of those who pray daily for the conversion of America."[16] Neighborhood mothers were invited to attend religious instruction classes on Sunday afternoons, and the sisters took pride in the fact that some women returned to the church's sacraments after many years away. Some had not received the Eucharist since their wedding day; others approached the Communion rail for the first time since they left their country of origin for the United States.

Mother Marianne firmly believed that the day nursery was not adequate to meet the many material needs of Cherry Hill's impoverished residents. She expressed her sentiments in a 1910 letter to Rt. Rev. M. J. Lavelle, vicar general of the New York archdiocese. Mother Marianne reminded Lavelle that her earlier report to Archbishop Farley recommended a "wider development of Catholic activity" in Cherry Hill. "To compete with the proselyting [*sic*] agencies," she wrote, "there should be classes for older children, evening classes for young working people, and systematic neighborhood visitation"; in other words, a social settlement. In closing, she assured Lavelle of her community's "hearty desire to do everything which is humanly possible for the salvation of these souls."[17]

Madonna House—A Northern Settlement House

Convincing John M. Farley that a community of women religious should be allowed to operate a social settlement was not an easy task. Many American bishops were either suspicious of the very idea of a settlement house or had not yet recognized the place of women religious in social service work. Mother Marianne was adamant, however, that a social settlement could and should be able to provide for the immigrants' material and spiritual needs, and she eventually prevailed. "We had come," Mother Marianne reflected in 1936, "not merely to found a social settlement, to advance the temporal interests of our neighbors, to share with them certain cultural advantages, nor even to demonstrate the brotherhood of man founded on the possession of common humanity. . . . We would have all to know that above and beyond them was a Christian zeal which seeks to share the treasures of the spirit, and a Christian solidarity based on membership in the Mystical Body of Christ."[18]

The statistics prepared by the Sisters of Christian Doctrine indicate that they indeed offered both material and spiritual support to their neighbors during the first two years of Madonna House's existence. During 1911 and 1912, in addition to recording baptisms (2 adults), First Communions (101 children), Confirmations (93), and marriages legalized (2), they also noted the number of children attending the day nursery (24,021), the number of meals served to children (41,238), meals served to the poor (704), baskets sent to families (357), and night shelter offered to adults and children (21).[19]

The sisters hoped the settlement's programs would solve the problem that had confronted them since they first agreed to provide religious education for the children of St. Joachim's: convincing young men and women (school-age) to attend catechism classes. Mother Marianne knew from past experience in social settlement work that young men in particular had to be enticed to leave the streets and enter the world of the settlement. The sisters began to form clubs and recreational groups for boys and young men, hoping that they would find "settlement gangs" more attractive than street gangs. The plan apparently worked, because chroniclers of Madonna House reported that the St. Aloysius

Sodality for young men actually evolved from the "Cherry Blossoms," a neighborhood gang whose members had asked to hold their meetings at Madonna House. The sisters, along with a layman, worked with the boys and counted it among their successes that many of the group's members enrolled in catechism classes. In addition, the Immaculata Club was designed to appeal to the schoolgirls of the neighborhood, and the "Lambs," a club for adolescent boys, was established.[20]

Within a few years of its founding, Madonna House was providing a full complement of activities similar to those found in non-Catholic social settlements. In addition to clubs for boys and girls, the settlement offered a sewing school, dressmaking classes, a kindergarten, millinery instruction, music classes (including ukulele lessons), and courses in public speaking and citizenship. By 1926, Boy and Girl Scout troops were sponsored by the settlement, along with mothers' clubs designed to offer support to English- and Italian-speaking mothers. The settlement even boasted a volunteer military unit known as the Columbus Volunteers in which young men were able to acquire the discipline necessary to serve in the United States' armed forces.

Neighborhood outreach was an essential component of the sisters' apostolate. By 1913, two sisters were serving as "parish visitors"; their task was to introduce themselves and their work to neighborhood families whose children were not attending Madonna House's religious and social programs. Although many neighbors welcomed the sisters' efforts, some did not. Sister Pauline Orlando recounted the story of two sisters who arrived at an apartment only to find that the husband of the couple was regularly attending the local Protestant mission. He was not happy to hear that Catholic sisters were visiting, and his wife told them, "Quick go out he have knife in his hands [*sic*]." Orlando concluded her story by saying, "They ran!"[21]

During the 1918 influenza epidemic, home visitations proved crucial as the sisters went throughout the neighborhood's tenements offering to nurse those too ill to care for themselves. Although nursing was not one of the ministries Mother Marianne envisioned in her plan for a religious community, their neighbors were among those afflicted by the epidemic, and anything that impacted the citizens of Cherry Street concerned the Sisters of Christian Doctrine. When hospitals and nurses proved unable to care for all the stricken, the sisters found themselves transformed into practical nurses "overnight." Sister Mary Rosaria Perri remembered, "The homes we went into were scenes of horror and sadness. The members who were already dead (and at times there would be two, three and more) could not be taken out for burial because of the great number dying in the district and undertakers were inadequate."[22] In addition to nursing the sick and arranging to bury the dead, the women tried to be a positive presence for the living. Despite the risk of infection, they refused to wear masks as they went in and out of tenements tending to the sick because they "terrified the children" and thus created a barrier to their work.[23]

Nursing the influenza victims was difficult; consoling the survivors took even more time. When those who had opposed the sisters' presence on the Lower East Side came to respect and admire the women and the way they lived and worked among the poor, however, the sisters realized their efforts had not been in vain. "No more would ripe tomatoes fall on passing Sisters from Jewish windows. No longer would small boys chalk insults on the convent steps, for all Cherry Street and its environs now knew that the Sisters of Madonna House were there for the good of all without respect to race or creed," wrote Mother Marianne.[24]

Soldiers passing through or stationed in New York City during World War I received both physical care and friendship from the sisters. Members of the community often visited wounded soldiers at the makeshift hospital that had been set up in a former department store, and they also tended to soldiers at a home they owned in Elberon, New Jersey. Recognizing that not all of their charges shared their religious beliefs, they did not initiate conversations about religion, but would answer questions when asked.[25]

Mother Marianne herself wrote letters to her "boys" serving overseas and kept them apprised of the news from home. In a letter dated August 14, 1919, she apologized that she had not been in New York to welcome the returning soldiers, but was busy in "Elberon, some fifty miles from New York . . . with three houses full of wounded boys on my hands." She assured them that she was looking forward to seeing them on Labor Day, and urged them to "wear all the ribbons, crosses and insignia" they had been awarded. She never failed to remind her military friends that those at home took pride in their accomplishments. "Did I tell you that John Cuccioli has received the French Cross of the Legion of Honor, the highest French Decoration?" she asked the group. She went on to assure them, "We are immensely proud of all of you and the splendid work you are doing over there."[26]

By 1920, the sisters and their Cherry Hill neighbors viewed each other as family. Even after they had followed the pattern of other U.S. religious communities and established a separate motherhouse and novitiate in rural Nyack, New York, to be "far from the madding crowd," the sisters in the city made sure that their country counterparts were kept abreast of neighborhood activities. In addition, there was constant interaction between the settlement house and the motherhouse. The Madonna House Annals for September of 1929, for instance, report that the sisters from the Lower East Side had been out to the motherhouse for a visit and "left behind them in the garb of a postulant, 'little Josephine' Saitta, who has been loved and tended at Madonna House, as a little daughter of the convent, as it were since she was [a few] years old." Happy as they were over Josephine's (later Sister Bernadette) vocation to their community, they rejoiced equally over the wedding of Josephine's "inseparable companion," Antoinette Manuzza, "who is engaged to a lad who has grown up in the organizations of the house, and known her since their boy and girl scout days."[27]

The wedding of Antoinette and John Gorman was the talk of the settlement for weeks. The sisters found themselves serving as Antoinette's surrogate mother and enthusiastically helped to prepare for the nuptial Mass and the reception that was to follow. The settlement's Girl Scout troops hosted a "kitchen shower" for the bride-to-be, and Sister Rosaria helped prepare the newlyweds' apartment for occupancy. Mother Marianne herself arrived from the motherhouse to attend to the final details, and she and six other sisters observed the ceremony from the relative privacy of the church choir loft. It had been many years, according to neighborhood legend, since a nuptial Mass had been celebrated in St. Teresa's church, and the sisters hoped that by "teaching the neighborhood how to get married" many more would follow.[28]

When Mr. and Mrs. Gorman returned from their honeymoon, Mother Marianne decided to visit the newlyweds to make sure their apartment contained all of the essentials necessary for setting up housekeeping. Her visit proved somewhat problematic, however; when the boys who participated in the activities of Madonna House learned of her plan, they insisted on inviting Mother Marianne to their homes as well. The annalist's notation explained the boys did not understand that "Antoinette being our own charge, the case was different, and although we do not visit unless in case of need, Reverend Mother had the charity to lend them her encouragement by a few moments visit at as many of their homes as she could reach before dark."[29]

Despite the evident success of Madonna House's programs, the sisters usually found themselves operating at a deficit. In 1920, Mother Marianne wrote to Catholic Charities' Rev. Bryan McEntegart, requesting that the organization pay a $600 milk bill. Although the archdiocese contributed $100 a month to Madonna House, she informed McEntegart, that money was put toward the rent; it did not cover any expenses associated with the settlement's work. The Sisters of Our Lady of Christian Doctrine supported themselves entirely through donations and by assigning sisters to the task of "collecting," a euphemism for begging. Each sister was expected to use her talents to improve the financial health of the community. Since Sister Amelie Merceret, one of the first women to join the community, had grown up around horses, she assumed the responsibility of taking the settlement's horse and wagon out every day to solicit food from area grocers.

In a 1929 letter to Vicar General Lavelle, Mother Marianne boasted that Madonna House was the "most completely organized Catholic community center in the Archdiocese." An average of seven hundred people passed through the settlement each day, and the system devised by the sisters allowed them to keep in touch with their neighbors "literally from the cradle to the grave." She worried, however, that a shortage of space prevented them from doing all they could, and as a result, some of the neighborhood's Catholic young people continued to frequent non-Catholic settlements. The sisters simply did not have the financial resources to do all they wished. "We cannot give our people the attractive meeting room, the showers and swimming pools, the domestic science and industrial class equipment, the basketball courts and auditorium provided in the [other] settlements," she told Lavelle; the sisters would have to receive some monetary assistance from the archdiocese if they were to continue their work. "We are, indeed, glad to be numbered among Christ's poor," she explained, "but there are necessary expenses which must ultimately be met and we have now reached the point when we must either have more material support or retrench our work and let our people drift back to the neighborhood houses from which we have withdrawn them."[30]

Most of the money received by the sisters was, in one way or another, given to their neighbors. An integral part of the Madonna House operation, for instance, was a bread line for the neighborhood's unemployed and poor. Not only were the sisters able to provide bodily nourishment, they also offered their guests the chance to think about the state of their souls. Sister Bernadette Saitta recollected that Madonna House "had what we called . . . a 'Bread Line' so that all the poor could come any time to take what they needed, beside [sic] that they could have a nice hot bowl of soup and bread on very cold days, and in this way, the Sisters could feed their souls with a spiritual talk and bring them back to the Church and sacraments."[31]

The Sisters of Christian Doctrine believed a combination of educational activities, social activities, and religious instruction would transform their neighbors into faithful Catholics and solid citizens. If statistics are any indication, Madonna House was an unequivocal success. The settlement's 1926 annual report demonstrates there was a good deal more to the religious program than catechism classes and sacramental preparation. The sisters boasted that 106 adults had returned to the sacraments that year (after an absence of between one and eighteen years); 84 businesswomen had attended a Day of Recollection; and 107 teachers had made a three-day retreat under their direction.

The 1926 report also documented the sisters' attempts to alleviate the physical sufferings experienced by many of their neighbors. Four hundred and eleven quarts of milk had been donated to families; other needy neighbors received a total of 5,500 pounds of coal; and the sisters provided 522 neighborhood families with either Thanksgiving or Christmas baskets. About 1,200 articles of clothing (new and used) were distributed, 91 people received shoes, and the Cherry Street sisters gave out 644 pairs of stockings. They also managed to help 18 people find work and obtained legal aid for another 89.

Recognizing that both children and adults enjoyed leisure activities, the sisters noted that they had tried their best to entertain the settlement's visitors. In addition to organizing 3 parades, they distributed about 1,250 Christmas presents and sponsored a neighborhood health contest complete with a baby parade and pageant that attracted 1,435 participants and spectators. In an attempt to teach their neighbors that reading could be fun as well as educational, the sisters loaned 2,209 library books to children and adults.[32]

Boy and Girl Scout troops played an important role in the life of Madonna House. Girl Scout troops, Mother Marianne believed, should be organized first because "they are easier to handle than the boys and their equipment is not so expensive." Scout meetings offered perfect venues for religious instruction, and in a 1924 letter she offered a possible two-hour meeting outline to demonstrate her idea. The first fifteen minutes should be spent on calisthenics, followed by thirty minutes of needlework. Fifteen minutes of singing came next, followed by one-half hour of "[r]eligious instruction and story telling." The final thirty minutes of the meeting could be spent playing games.[33]

Following the pattern established by settlement house workers in other U.S. cities, the Sisters of Christian Doctrine willingly lobbied city officials when decisions were being made that affected the Lower East Side. In 1923, the sisters learned that the city intended to lease a section of "unimproved" land to a private citizen who planned to build a garage on the property. Although the land might not have seemed important to the bureaucrats involved, the sisters knew that particular piece of land was the only spot in the "most congested and worse housed district in New York" where boys could play baseball or any other games that were "so necessary if they are to develop into healthy men."

The city's decision promoted Mother Marianne to write Mayor John F. Hylan on behalf of the neighborhood's boys. She informed the mayor that if this section of land were developed for business purposes, the only sources of recreation remaining were "the crap game, and the frequenting of the so called 'Pool Rooms.'" She reminded Hylan that the settlement's goal was to decrease the number of neighborhood juvenile delinquents rather than the opposite, and taking away the ball field would diminish the work of the sisters in this regard. In closing, she asked Hylan to think of the effect this would have on the boys "in memory of your own boyhood days."[34]

The poverty and unemployment that characterized the years of the Great Depression meant that Cherry Hill needed the Sisters of Christian Doctrine and their settlement house more than ever. During these years, the sisters often found themselves ministering to boys and men who left their homes in other parts of the country hoping to find work in New York City. In January of 1930, Sister Antonia Parilli approached a boy new to the settlement's bread line. A conversation with the young man revealed he had left New Hampshire for New York in the hope of finding a way to make a living. Sister Antonia convinced the boy to write his mother and was delighted to report that the young man received a telegram responding to his letter; he was to come home at once.[35]

By 1937, under the direction of Sister Mary Elizabeth Lammers, Madonna House's activities reflected the changing neighborhood and its needs. The annual report for that year claimed that a total of 2,185 people were "registered" at the settlement; 668 of these were adults. The sisters were now actively involved in relief work and in that year alone had provided 72,628 loaves of bread, 16,116 quarts of milk (reserved for families with babies), and 1,102 baskets of food to hungry neighbors. They were also sending coal, furniture, and clothing to needy families. The bread line was fully operational; 2,674 meals were served to adults in 1937. The sisters continued to visit the sick and arranged doctors' visits and medication for those unable to pay for treatment

Despite the extra demands placed upon them by the poor economy, the women did not neglect the work they were called to do: providing religious education and sacramental preparation to children and adults. In 1937, 31 children and 22 adults received either First Communion or Confirmation under the sisters' tutelage. In addition, they obtained First Communion outfits for 26 children. A ministry to Chinese immigrants who had recently moved into the area had been established, and they were currently providing religious education classes for 40 Chinese children. An average of 250 children were attending "Christian Doctrine School" on the weekend; 45 high school students were enrolled in weekly classes, and 130 children were preparing to receive either First Communion or Confirmation. The settlement also hosted a number of religious clubs and sodalities, including the Little Flower Club (girls ages eight to ten), the Infant Jesus Sodality (children up to age six), the Immaculata Club (working girls), and the Kings of Constantine and Little Crusaders (for Greek boys and girls).

During the Depression the neighborhood surrounding Madonna House was in need of the cultural and social activities sponsored by the settlement, and the fourteen resident sisters did not neglect this aspect of their work. They held weekly parent meetings for English-, Italian-, "Young English-," and Greek- (Byzantium-) speaking neighbors. Classes in pottery, woodcarving, sculpture, dance, and dramatics were offered; and the sisters continued to sponsor Brownie, Girl Scout, and Boy Scout troops. Those hoping to learn a skill leading to employment were invited to enroll in sewing, dressmaking, or leather craft classes. Like other settlement workers, the sisters' philosophy included the idea that the urban poor should spend some time in the country each year. In 1937, 112 children, 33 mothers, and 72 working girls were able to spend at least a week outside of New York City.[36]

The ministry of Madonna House continued during the years in which the United States was involved in World War II. Both residents and participants helped cultivate a victory garden, and everyone, of course, prayed for a speedy Allied victory. The issues facing the Lower East Side remained unchanged, and the sisters persisted in their struggle to improve the physical and spiritual lives of their neighbors. What will happen, they wondered, "if we win the war against a foreign foe, only to lose on the domestic front in the conflict with moral disorder?"[37] They continued to believe that by duplicating the values found in the home, the Catholic settlement house could offer a solution to the problems resulting from urbanization and industrialization. Settlements offered young people the chance to participate in art, music, drama, and craft classes; befriend other Catholics; and take part in the settlements' various social activities. Above all, however, one could always find a sympathetic ear at Madonna House because the sisters were "always at home to them, never too busy to receive a confidence, to help solve a problem, to share, with ready sympathy, life's joys and sorrows."[38]

Madonna House continued its mission to its neighbors during the postwar years. In 1946, First Communion and Confirmation classes were meeting three times a week with a total enrollment of 133 children, and 271 additional children were receiving religious instruction during the week. In addition, the settlement continued to provide activities designed to enrich the lives of their neighbors; 89 Boy Scouts and 94 Girl Scouts were involved in troops led by the sisters and lay workers. In 1950, the settlement was offering classes in drama, music, art, ballet, English, and military training. Six years later, the resident directress reported Madonna House was operating six and one-half days per week.[39]

A Southern Welfare Center

In 1940, Rev. George Smith formally invited the Sisters of Christian Doctrine to bring their ministry to rural South Carolina. When New York governor and presidential candidate Alfred E. Smith met the pastor of Our Lady of the Valley mission located in Gloverville, South Carolina, he told Father Smith of the work the sisters were doing on New York's Lower East Side. The mission, located in the Horse Creek Valley section of Aiken County between Aiken, South Carolina, and Augusta, Georgia, was poor and struggling, and Smith hoped that Mother Marianne would send sisters willing to transplant the work of Madonna House—an urban settlement—to the rural South. Convinced that the methods used by settlement workers would prove successful in rural areas, he assured Mother Marianne that he could raise money from wealthy northerners who spent their winters in the vicinity of Aiken and had already arranged for a "Miss Coleman" to support the sisters during their first year in the mission.[40] After Mother Marianne and Sister Elizabeth Lammers visited the area, she assented to Smith's proposition, and in February of 1940 Sisters Dolores Carty, Anne-Marie Bach, and Clare Dennis arrived in what the sisters fondly called "the Valley."[41]

Before the sisters arrived, Smith warned Mother Marianne that "the vast majority of 'poor whites' are non-Catholic. The problem of helping them is not particularly a Catholic problem—it is a social problem."[42] The sisters' initial work would not be to teach religion; they would focus instead on hygiene, cooking, and sewing. Despite their willingness to downplay the theological aspect of their work, they still had to contend with anti-Catholicism upon their arrival in South Carolina, often with comic results. According to the *Aiken Standard*, the local chapter of the Ku Klux Klan decided to demonstrate its dislike of the sisters on the very day of their arrival. "As [the sisters] were driving down the street [they] came upon the tail end of a parade, so they followed it. . . . They were very visible because they were dressed in black and white habits. Everyone on the street was laughing and pointing. They asked what all the commotion was about. Someone said, 'You're riding at the end of a Ku Klux Klan demonstration. They don't want you here.'"[43]

Anti-Catholic demonstrations were, in some respects, the least of the new arrivals' problems. Since there were only thirty-four resident Catholics in the city of Aiken at the time of their arrival, one of their first tasks was simply introducing themselves to their new neighbors, many of whom had never seen a Catholic sister. The area residents' lack of knowledge about Catholic women religious led to some humorous incidents. "As they entered one cabin, the lady of the house cried to her neighbor, 'Go get my kids out of school,' and then, turning to the Sisters said by way of explanation, 'They ain't never seen things like you-all before.'" When they called at another home, a member of the family said, "'Ladies, won't you take your hat off? I forgot to ask when you came in.'"[44]

It was obvious to the sisters that residents of the valley were not even sure how to speak with a Catholic, especially a Catholic sister. Shortly after arriving in their new home, they stopped someone to ask directions. The stranger willingly supplied the necessary information, and the sisters politely responded by saying, "Thank you," and "God bless you." The stranger, at a loss for how to respond, replied, "Yours truly."[45]

Mother Marianne and the sisters she sent to South Carolina believed that their work would not show results for at least a generation. They envisioned the building of a settlement house and chapel where they would help develop "cottage industries to build up the income of those who are incapable of hard manual work, cooking classes to remedy the inadequate nutrition, and above all the inspiration of religion, by which human nature, however degraded, may be lifted up and spiritualized."[46]

Recognizing the pressing material needs of the people they had come to serve, the sisters distributed food, clothing, and medicine while advising people to eat fresh greens to avoid pellagra. In February of 1941, Smith and the sisters were able to break ground for what would become the Horse Creek Valley Handicraft and Welfare Center. The facilities eventually included a main building to be used for recreational purposes, garage, carpenter shop, pool, and playground. There was also space for a kindergarten, library, craft room, clinic, and laundry.[47] The center's activities were designed to promote character building, vocational training, and health improvement.

The sisters who ministered in the valley loved their work, and they fell in love with the people. When others demonstrated prejudice based on the residents' socioeconomic status and/or lack of education, the sisters defended them in words and action. In 1942, for instance, the Red Cross was invited to offer a class in first aid at the welfare center. The instructor arrived and announced that the course could not be taught if the men insisted on wearing overalls. The sisters, however, "regarded overalls as badges of honorable labor and not only welcomed the men and women of the mills in their working clothes and invited them to make use of the shower rooms before class, but joined the class themselves."[48]

Valley residents eventually embraced the sisters as both neighbors and friends. By 1945, when two sisters returned to South Carolina after spending some time away, they reported that two men helped them with their luggage. "What a difference," they commented, "compared to the cold reception our Sisters received a few years ago."[49]

In addition to rural settlement work, the sisters continued to impress upon their southern neighbors, Catholics and non-Catholics, the message of the church. In a 1945 appeal, Sister Dorothea McCarthy described their ministry in language similar to the rhetoric being used to garner support for America's war effort. The sisters won their first battle when a few non-Catholics began to allow their children to attend programs in the "Catholic Building," Sister Dorothea explained. She continued her analogy by telling the audience that fighting began in earnest when the children started to attend cooking and handicraft classes at the welfare center because they began to learn "Catholic viewpoints and practices." Sister Dorothea asked for her listeners' help. "We have come to find recruits. Every Catholic is a member of Christ's Army. As a member, each must take an active part in His Campaigns. To-day you cannot take an active part, but you can help here at home in two ways; by prayer and alms deeds." She concluded by asking her audience to join them as they worked for "V-C day" (Victory for Christ).[50]

The sentiments expressed by Sister Dorothea were endorsed by Mother Marianne. The years she spent helping to prepare religious education teachers, along with her knowledge of the area (gleaned from personal visits and reports sent by sisters ministering in the valley), meant that the foundress understood the difficulty involved when trying to impress upon people the value of Christian doctrine, and she was fully aware the community faced an uphill battle.[51] In a letter to the sisters stationed in South Carolina, Mother Marianne reported she had told Smith no progress would be made in the valley until the presence of the Lord was felt there: "That is the lesson of the Incarnation—men's hearts are won by Our Lord's coming among them."[52]

Annual reports indicate that the Sisters of Christian Doctrine successfully transplanted the work of social settlements to rural South Carolina. From April 1943 to February 1944 the sisters provided area residents with 14 Thanksgiving baskets, 15 Christmas baskets, and 451 pieces of clothing, including 16 layettes. They initiated classes in sewing and cooking, started Boy and Girl Scout troops, and were conducting between 3 and 21 home visitations a day for an annual total of 1,894. They had less success providing for the spiritual needs of the valley's inhabitants, reporting only 2 baptisms and 4 First Communions during that same time period.[53]

By 1951, however, the sisters ministering in the valley could claim that the spiritual side of their work was beginning to bear fruit. They were conducting religious instruction classes for 30 adults and 58 children and boasted that 8 converts had been received into the church. The social and educational life of the center was also thriving. The women were leading 5 scout troops with 81 members, as well as conducting a kindergarten in which 45 children were enrolled.[54]

The End of Northern Settlements and Southern Welfare Centers

Between 1960 and 1971, the Sisters of Our Lady of Christian Doctrine ceased their work at New York City's Madonna House and the Horse Creek Valley Welfare Center. Their reasons for leaving these ministries were the result of both practical considerations and changes taking place in communities of U.S. women religious. In 1964, the number of American sisters peaked at 180,015; since that time the number of women involved in religious life has steadily declined. Like other U.S. religious communities, the Sisters of Christian Doctrine began to experience both declining numbers and an aging population during the 1960s and 1970s, forcing them to make hard decisions about where they could be most effective.

The initial difficulties with the operation of Madonna House, the sisters' first foundation, began in 1958 when an inspection of the property revealed "hazardous" living conditions that would cost between $300,000 and $600,000 to repair; the sisters determined that this sum was "prohibitive." The New York archdiocese, anxious for the congregation to continue ministering in the area, offered to help find a new location for the settlement. The original proposal called for the settlement to relocate to a new building that would have space for the Day Care program as well as housing facilities for the sisters.[55] This plan did not materialize, however, and the community reluctantly began phasing out the settlement's activities

On November 6, 1960, the Sisters of Christian Doctrine regretfully closed the Madonna House settlement. The decision was not made lightly, and, in the end, the sisters believed they had exhausted all other options. Social and educational activities they had once offered were now being handled by other agencies and organizations; and perhaps most important, the building was crumbling around them. It was no longer physically safe to offer childcare services and religious education classes in the Cherry Street buildings. Some of the settlement's activities were transferred to surrounding parishes, but the cultural programs (such as music classes) were discontinued. The Children's Building was closed on June 30, 1960, and the Youth Activities Division of Catholic Charities of the New York archdiocese assumed responsibility for the childcare services.[56] By November 1 of that year the sisters had relocated to a new residence on East 94th Street.

Leaving Madonna House was, for many of the sisters, the end of an era. "It was there that Reverend Mother Marianne and her first band of Sisters labored indefatigably among the immigrants," wrote annalist Sister Cecily Berretti. "It was there too that many of us younger Sisters in later years also labored zealously, happily leading souls to the Sacred Heart." The sisters recognized, however, that the role of social settlements had changed over the years. "Gradually, as The Music School and the Scout Troops were closed, it hardly felt to some of us as though living there were of much use for we could go to our missions from some other location."[57]

Although the Sisters of Christian Doctrine remained in Horse Creek Valley until 1971, they began to consider closing the welfare center at the same time its urban counterpart was being phased out. As early as June of 1959, Sister Ursula Coyne—who succeeded Mother Marianne as Mother General upon her death in 1957—expressed her concerns to Charleston bishop Paul Hallinan when she told him that despite the extensive programs administered by the sisters in the valley, they were not reaching many people. At the very least, the name of the Horse Creek Valley Welfare Center should be changed; such a title "connotes organized social service of a wide variety," and the fact that the sisters were not offering such services was misleading to some.

In later correspondence, Sister Ursula wondered if the time had come to dissolve the welfare center. It was expensive to operate, and the sisters faced considerable competition from other religious traditions. In addition, times had changed, as had the conditions the sisters found in the valley upon their arrival in 1940; in fact, the primary purpose of the welfare center had been achieved. The Sisters of Christian Doctrine, Sister Ursula explained, were now primarily expected to do catechetical work, and an active CCD program would serve the needs of several parishes and be less expensive to operate.[58] Hallinan vigorously disagreed with Sister Ursula and claimed the sisters were essential to the work of the church in rural South Carolina. She assured the bishop that the sisters would remain in the valley as long as their presence had a positive effect on the state of South Carolinian Catholicism.

In 1970, the sisters stationed in the valley reported that they were continuing to offer material help and religious education classes to their rural neighbors. Two sisters were currently leading Brownie and Girl Scout troops (which were open to non-Catholics), and they were trying to recruit lay people to work with the Cub and Boy Scouts. An integrated sewing class was being offered at the center, and the sisters were actively involved with several programs designed to help the area's residents solve local problems related to issues such as sewers, roads, and electricity. They occasionally still visited people in their homes, and often ministered to neighbors who had been hospitalized. In addition to supplying bread, food, and clothing to black and white families, they were helping people apply for and receive Food Stamps.

The valley sisters noted that 27 children in grades one through six and 15 students in grades seven through twelve were enrolled in religious education classes. These were obviously very small numbers, and the sisters also cited a need for a viable religious education program for adults. In addition, the maintenance costs of the center had become overwhelming and were consuming most of their salaries.[59]

These concerns prompted Sister Dorothea McCarthy, who succeeded Sister Ursula Coyne as the community's president, to inform Charleston bishop Ernest Unterkoefler that the Sisters of Christian Doctrine would no longer be able to staff the Horse Creek Valley Mission. Sister Dorothea cited several reasons for the decision, including: a lack of sisters to staff the center; "apparent lack of need for the Sisters as evidenced by the very poor attendance at religious instruction"; less need for the kindergarten; and the difficulty she had convincing sisters to volunteer to minister in the valley.[60] Despite Unterkoefler's entreaties, the decision was firm, and the sisters made plans to leave the mission by May of 1971.

The decisions to close Madonna House and withdraw sisters from the welfare center meant that by the 1970s the Sisters of Christian Doctrine were focusing almost exclusively on catechetics. The sisters and their settlements, however, are remembered fondly by former residents of the "old neighborhoods." Now scattered throughout the country, those who grew up on the Lower East Side and in Horse Creek Valley have vivid memories of participating in the activities sponsored by the sisters as well as attending religious education classes. Many, such as Isabelle J. Gambino, credit the sisters with teaching her valuable lessons about life in addition to their other work. In a 1985 letter to Sister Angela Palermo, Gambino praised them for teaching her a great lesson: "It is more Blessed to give than receive."[61]

In the twenty-first century, a number of U.S. religious communities have been forced to confront similar realities to those faced by the Sisters of Christian Doctrine when they elected to close their northern settlement house and, eleven years later, withdraw from their southern welfare center. Despite steadily declining numbers, however, women religious not only continue to administer and staff schools, colleges, and hospitals, they also work directly with the poor, lobby for social justice, and provide pastoral support in parishes. Religious communities have had to pick and choose which institutions will remain under their care based on institutional viability and the availability of financial and personnel resources, but the story of the Sisters of Our Lady of Christian Doctrine serves as a reminder that despite changes in numbers and streamlined apostolates, women religious continue to play a pivotal role in the life and work of the U.S. Catholic Church.

NOTES

1. For a full history of the Sisters of Our Lady of Christian Doctrine, see Margaret M. McGuinness, *Neighbors and Missionaries* (New York: Fordham University Press, 2011). Much of the material in this essay is found in greater detail in this book.

2. Interview with Sr. Dorothea McCarthy, Archives, Sisters of Our Lady of Christian Doctrine Papers (hereafter RCD), Archives Archdiocese of New York (hereafter AANY), March 21, 2004.

3. See James J. Hennessey, S.J., *American Catholics: A History of the Roman Catholic Community in the United States* (New York: Oxford University Press, 1981) and McGuinness, *Called to Serve: A History of Nuns in America* (New York: New York University Press, 2013) for further discussion of the Discalced Carmelites, Visitation Sisters, and Sisters of Charity.

4. For the complete story of the arrival of the CSJs in the United States, see Carol Coburn and Martha Smith, *Spirited Lives: How Nuns Shaped Catholic Culture and American Life, 1836–1920* (Chapel Hill: University of North Carolina Press, 1999).

5. Quoted in Rudolph J. Vecoli, "Prelates and Peasants: Italian Immigrants and the Catholic Church," in *The Other Catholics*, ed. Keith R. Dyrud, Michael Novak, and Rudolph J. Vecoli (New York: Arno Press, 1978), 226n35.

6. See Anna C. Minogue, *The Story of the Santa Maria Institute* (Cincinnati: Santa Maria Institute, 1922).

7. Clement W. Thuente, O.P., "Charity in New York," *St. Vincent de Paul Quarterly* 40 (May 1910): 164.

8. See Theodore Abel, *Protestant Home Missions to Catholic Immigrants* (New York: Institute of Social and Religious Research, 1933), 103–4.

9. Quoted in Thuente, "America's Pioneer Catholic Settlement House," *Rosary Magazine*, October 1923, 3.

10. Mother Marianne, dictated by *The Sisters of Our Lady of Christian Doctrine*, ca. 1912, 16, RCD, AANY. As of this writing, the RCD papers are being processed so some of the ways in which I have cited material may not be helpful to those interested in some of these primary sources.

11. Ibid., 19.

12. Ibid., 25.

13. Sr. Pauline Orlando, RCD, "Open [*sic*] of Madonna House, 173 Cherry St., New York, June 29, 1910," n.d., typescript, RCD Papers, AANY.

14. "The Spiritual Influence of the Day Nursery," *Mary's Mission*, January 1932, 6.

15. Orlando, "Open [*sic*] of Madonna House."

16. "The Madonna Day Nursery," 1910–11, RCD Papers, AANY.

17. Marian Gurney, to Rt. Rev. M. J. Lavelle, (1910), RCD Papers, AANY.

18. Mother Marianne of Jesus, RCD, "Looking Backward: Silver Jubilee Reminiscences," *Mary's Mission*, September 1936, 2.

19. Mother Marianne, *Sisters of Our Lady of Christian Doctrine*, 28–29.

20. History of Madonna House, Typescript (1960), RCD Papers, AANY.

21. Orlando, "Open [*sic*] of Madonna House."

22. Sr. M. Rosaria, "Sisters' Writings about Rev. Mother," file, RCD Papers, AANY.

23. Mother Marianne of Jesus, RCD, "Looking Backward: Silver Jubilee Reminiscences," *Mary's Mission*, February 1938, 2.

24. Ibid., 3.

25. Mother Marianne of Jesus, RCD, "Looking Backward: Silver Jubilee Reminiscences," *Mary's Mission*, May 1938, 2–3.

26. Sr. Marianne of Jesus to "My dear Boys," October 29, 1918, "Madonna House Columbus Vol.," file, RCD Papers, AANY.

27. "Annals Madonna House, Institute of Our Lady of Christian Doctrine," September 12, 1929 (hereafter as AMH), RCD Papers, AANY.

28. "AMH," November 5, 1929.

29. "AMH," November 13, 1929.

30. Mother Marianne of Jesus to Rt. Rev. M. J. Lavelle, December 6, 1920, "St. Joachim" file, RCD Papers, AANY.

31. Sr. Bernadette Saitta, RCD, to Mother Elizabeth, March 10, 1957, "Sisters Writings About Rev. Mother Attestations" file, RCD Papers, AANY.

32. "Statistical Report, 1926," "Madonna House 1925–" file, RCD Papers, AANY.

33. Mother Marianne to Jane Curran, March 27, 1924, "Madonna House 1925–" file, RCD Papers, AANY.

34. Mother Marianne to Honorable John F. Hylan, June 13, 1923, "Ladyfield Peekskill N.Y." file, RCD Papers, AANY.

35. "AMH," January 10, 1930.

36. "Catholic Settlement 1937," "Madonna House 1925–" file, RCD Papers, AANY.

37. "Juvenile Delinquency," *Mary's Mission*, January 1943, 3.

38. "Some Remedies for Juvenile Delinquency," *Mary's Mission*, March 1943, 9.

39. See "Settlement Questionnaire, 1946," "Settlement Questionnaire, 1947," "The Greater New York Fund—1950 Yearly Report of Participating Agencies on Operations and Standards," and "Settlement House Annual Report for Catholic Charities—1956," "Catholic Charities 1925–" file, RCD Papers, AANY.

40. Msgr. George Smith to Mother Marianne, January 19, 1940, "Horse Creek Valley Mission 1940–1971" file, RCD Papers, AANY.

41. "Our Lady of the Valley Catholic Church Fiftieth Anniversary 1946–1996," clipping in a scrapbook entitled "Mary's Mission and Our former *Maryknoll Seminarians* at the Valley, now *Maryknoll Priests*," RCD Papers, AANY.

42. George Smith to Mother Marianne, December 14, 1939, "Horse Creek Valley Mission 1940–1971" file, RCD Papers, AANY.

43. Nina J. Nidiffer, "Catholic Church Has 50-Year Anniversary," *Aiken Standard*, May 19, 1991, 3–4.

44. "Article for N.C.C.S.," undated, "Horse Creek Valley South Carolina" file, RCD Papers, AANY.

45. "A Devil Is Loose in the Valley," *Mary's Mission*, April 1940, 11.

46. Mother Marianne, "Looking Forward," *Mary's Mission*, November 1939, 10–11.

47. "Article for N.C.C.S.," n.d.

48. "Field Notes," *Mary's Mission*, September 1942, 12.

49. "Horse Creek Valley Mission," *Annals*, September 18, 1945, RCD Papers, AANY.

50. "Address by Sr. M. Dorothea to Schools in So. Carolina—1945," "Horse Creek Valley South Carolina" file, RCD Papers, AANY.

51. Gurney was involved in the founding of the New York Normal Training School for Catechists while working at St. Rose's Settlement.

52. Mother Marianne to "My Dear Children," February 12, 1945, "Correspondence from Mother Marianne 1941–54" file, RCD Papers, AANY.

53. "Horse Creek Valley Mission, Warrenville, S.C. Report: April 1943–February 1944," "Horse Creek Valley South Carolina," file, RCD Papers, AANY.

54. "Horse Creek Valley Mission, Langley, S.C. Jan. 1–Dec. 31, 1951," "Horse Creek Valley South Carolina" file, RCD Papers, AANY.

55. Sister Ursula Coyne, RCD to Dear Sisters, September 24, 1958, "1957–1963 Mother Ursula Cong. Correspondence" file, RCD Papers, AANY.

56. Sister Ursula Coyne, RCD, "Reports of the Mother General," Sister Ursula Coyne Papers, RCD Papers, AANY.

57. "AMH," November 1, 1960.

58. Sister Mary Ursula Coyne, RCD, to Most Rev. Paul J. Hallinan, "Memorandum Concerning Horse Creek Valley Welfare Center, Our Lady of the Valley Parish," June 1959, "Horse Creek Valley Mission" file, RCD Papers, AANY. See also her letters to Hallinan dated February 27, 1961, and May 15, 1961, RCD Papers, AANY.

59. "Our Lady of the Valley Convent, Langley, S.C., House Profile 1970," "Horse Creek Valley South Carolina" file, RCD Papers, AANY.

60. Sister Dorothea McCarthy, RCD, to Most Reverend Ernest L. Unterkoefler, July 6, 1970, "Horse Creek Valley South Carolina" file, RCD Papers, AANY.

61. Isabelle J. Gambino to Sr. Angela Palermo, RCD, May 16, 1985, "Apostolate" file, RCD Papers, AANY.

NINE

Pulp Catholicism: Catholics in American Popular Film

Anthony Burke Smith

Catholics in the United States have been deeply involved in the film industry since its beginnings, shaping both their own image and that of the nation itself. To understand the role of Catholics in film is, in fact, to engage the history of American cinema. From film pioneer D. W. Griffith's fascination with immigrant Catholics to Mel Gibson's early twenty-first- century retrieval of Baroque Catholicism in *The Passion of the Christ*, Catholicism and the movies have enjoyed a long, intimate, and contentious relationship. The mutual attraction between Catholics and film testifies to the unlikely but enduring home that movies provided Catholics in America.

Hollywood allowed Catholic outsiders to devise new roles for themselves as American insiders, simultaneously performing their religion and crafting stories that spoke to mass audiences. It also provided a space for Catholic filmmakers and moviegoers to revise their understanding of themselves and their society by critiquing older representations and projecting new ones. In the process, American films absorbed and refracted a range of Catholic sensibilities and imaginations. The result has been a cinema richly sedimented with Catholic images, perspectives, and preoccupations. Movies, the popular enterprise of the modern age, also proved to be a deeply Catholic one.

The intertwined history of Catholics and the movies is suggested by the simultaneous development of the Catholic subculture and the studio system of the nation's film industry after World War I. As the major studios such as MGM and Warner Bros. were establishing their industrial model of mass production during the 1920s, a parallel system of cultural integration and coordination characterized Catholic life. Parishes, schools, and popular devotions provided a way of life as powerful as anything devised by a movie mogul for his contract players. Only five years separated the creation of the American Catholic bishops' national lobbying organization, the National Catholic Welfare Conference in 1919, and MGM in 1924.[1] Very soon after their modern formations, the movie studios and the church worked out an agreement that benefited each other in the form of the industry's self-regulation of moral content in movies. And while the studio system began to unravel a decade before the Catholic subculture came apart in the 1960s, in the 1970s such products of that subculture as Martin Scorsese and Robert Altman became leading rebel auteurs of Hollywood.

This larger cultural history of Catholics in the movies has until recently been largely overlooked.[2] Instead, film study tends to equate Catholicism with cultural reaction. Central to such interpretations is the Legion of Decency, the popular and influential pressure group formed by the Catholic bishops in the early 1930s that waged a campaign of moral reform.[3] Beyond the Legion, Catholics in Hollywood movies rarely register more than brief mention. Censorship, conservatism, piety, and sentimentality are the terms that have traditionally framed scholarly discussions of Catholics in movies.

The putatively conservative role of Catholicism in film history had the bishops and their censors play the leading role within critical film scholarship. Yet a peek behind the academic veils that separate religion from modern culture studies reveals a varied, richly complex, and diverse presence of Catholics of many kinds, challenging, watching, and creating American movies. A partial list of Catholic directors comprises a sizeable portion of significant American filmmaking: John Ford, Frank Capra, Leo McCarey, Alfred Hitchcock, Fritz Lang, John Farrow, Martin Scorsese, Francis Ford Coppola, Robert Altman, Brian De Palma, Nancy Sacova, Kevin Smith, Abel Ferrara, and Mel Gibson.[4]

Catholic actors and actresses who helped craft images of Catholics as well as popular America itself include Bing Crosby, James Cagney, Irene Dunne, Pat O'Brien, Maureen O'Sullivan, Loretta Young, Walter Connolly, Andy Devine, and Grace Kelly. In addition, Catholicism courses through numerous genres of American movies both as subject and as implicit source of influence, popping up in all kinds of unexpected places. Not only did Catholicism enjoy its own cycle of very successful movies at mid-century, oriented around all-American priests and nuns, it materialized in romantic comedies, gangster films, war films, film noir, social realism, Westerns, historical epics, and horror movies. Yet our concern is not so much whether Hollywood's Catholicism reflected actual Catholic experience so much as the construction of Catholicism in America through the movies and the ways in which cinematic Catholicism helped shape understandings of U.S. society.[5]

The persistent Catholicity manifested in film was grounded in the distinctive character of the immigrant church, with its vast ethnoreligious subculture close to the heart of the urbanizing, industrial forces transforming American society. While many late nineteenth-century Anglo-Americans found the religious practices of Catholics hopelessly "foreign," the new ways of seeing offered by movies found this old-world religion an alluring attraction. Catholics made for prominent film subjects early in the movie business. As film historian Lee Lourdeaux argued, pioneering filmmaker D. W. Griffith sensed the power of ethnic Catholicism: his 1909 films *Pippa Passes* and *A Baby's Shoes* evinced a fascination with immigrant Catholic culture. However, Griffith utilized Catholicism to sustain his own Anglo-Protestant vision of the United States. In particular, Catholicism was figured in terms of celibate priests and virginal women who sanctioned a Victorian middle-class social order. Griffith conveyed at best a stilted feel for ethnic Catholicism. Nativist anxieties about the expanding presence of Catholic immigrants in national life further limited Griffith's approach to urban-immigrant Catholicism, which was represented in attenuated form in his films.[6]

Catholic responses to the new medium varied in the early decades of cinema. Urban Catholics constituted a large portion of the immigrant and ethnic working classes that flocked to nickelodeons in America's cities. Some parish priests even facilitated Catholic moviegoing. Father Francis Finn of Cincinnati endorsed films, sensing their democratic appeal, and installed a "moving picture machine" in St. Xavier's parish school hall. He believed the

> moving picture is a good thing for the average man and woman. All classes of people have begun transferring their patronage from the vaudeville shows to the five-cent theater, and as there is less vulgarity and suggestiveness in a month of moving picture shows than in one ordinary vaudeville performance, the change is undoubtedly for the better.[7]

Yet movies also provoked deep anxieties among Catholic leaders. Much of Catholic discourse on the burgeoning film industry echoed concerns of other moralist critics from that era.[8] The threat posed by moving pictures to the moral health of children was a persistent theme. The *Catholic Fortnightly Review* complained that a "considerable proportion of them [films] are of a demoralizing character. The low price of admission allures boys and girls of tender years to these places, some of which are nurseries of vice."[9] The *Ecclesiastical Review* fretted over the "allurement of immoral shows" where children "seek their pleasure in places where their virtue becomes sullied or lost."[10]

Not surprisingly, many Catholics advocated censorship of motion pictures, contributing their own voices to a movement for regulation spearheaded by Protestants.[11] The popular weekly *Ave Maria* asserted "censorship should be systematic and exercised frequently."[12] The Jesuit *America* magazine cited the state of Pennsylvania's new film censorship law in 1911 as an "excellent piece of legislation" and wrote that "there can be no question of the restraint of any liberty of individuals in the suppression of the stories of crime and horror exhibited to children at some of the cheap shows in our cities."[13] The following year the *Catholic Fortnightly Review* supported the Woman's Municipal League of New York's call for a censorship ordinance in the city, insisting, "To keep the shows clean, eternal vigilance on the part of local authorities will be necessary."[14]

Calls to regulate films joined hopes that Catholics would create their own cinema. Reverend F. Schulte of Remsen, Iowa, wrote in 1911 that "here is a field for some benevolent and enterprising Catholics to do a great deal of good. Why cannot a few of our moneyed co-religious combine into a manufacturing company for making films that can be shown without offense to virtue?"[15] Similarly, *America* asserted, "The extension of the Catholic picture show is eminently desirable, in itself and as an antidote, but is greatly hampered by a scarcity of suitable films. Yet the history of the Catholic Church, its heroes, martyrs, missionaries, discoverers, its architecture and paintings and sculpture, and the Bible itself present inexhaustible material. There is a fortune awaiting the Catholic genius who will construct from it adequate scenarios."[16]

One organization, the Catholic Art Association, did, in fact, produce films with Catholic subjects and themes. This group made at least six movies in the late teens and early 1920s, such as *The Victim* (1920), a drama involving a Catholic priest falsely accused of murder and based on the book *A Victim to the Seal of Confession*, by the Rev. Joseph Spillman; *The Burning Question* (1921), featuring fictionalized members of the Knights of Columbus; and *The Eternal Light* (1919), a dramatization of the life of Christ that was barred from exhibition by the Boston police because of its violent depictions of the Passion.[17] Many of these films were made by the same group of individuals, including the director Joseph Levering, scenarioists O. E. Goebel and Conde B. Pallen, and actress Inez Marcel, suggesting that the Catholic Art Association acted as something of a tight production unit. Goebel was at one time head of the St. Louis Motion Picture Company; he shared roots in the heavily German-Catholic Gateway City with Conde Pallen.[18]

Pallen was the most prominent Catholic within this fledgling movie production unit. Born in 1858, a graduate of Georgetown University, he earned a Ph.D. in philosophy from St. Louis University, where he later held a chair in philosophy. Pope Leo XIII granted him the *Pro Ecclesia et Pontiface* medal, and Pius XI made him a Knight of St. Gregory. An active writer of literary commentary, novels, and poetry and editor of the St. Louis *Church Progress*, Pallen also coedited the *Catholic Encyclopedia* with, among others, the noted Catholic psychologist and philosopher Rev. Edward Pace and Catholic University of America rector Thomas J. Shahan between 1904 and 1920. A political conservative, Pallen became chairman of the National Civic Federation's Department of Subversive Movements in the 1920s. His *New York Times* obituary reported that his opposition to the noted progressive Catholic social reformer Monsignor John A. Ryan "took up much space in the public press."[19]

While many Catholic leaders advocated local and state censorship of films as the most effective means of reforming the motion picture industry, Pallen proposed a national censor to supplant "blue law" censors and "a Puritanism ignorant of morality" that he saw characterizing local censorship efforts. "In the zeal for reform," he wrote in *America* in 1921, "prudery is apt to usurp the throne of common sense." Pallen proposed instead censor boards "composed of people of such high character and intelligence as to ensure sane and balanced decisions" that he believed could only be realized at the national level under federal supervision.[20]

One of the films produced by the Catholic Art Association, *The Transgressor* (1918), is a particularly interesting example of early cinematic representation of American Catholics. It is simultaneously a labor story, a depiction of the ethnic working class, a critique of anti-Catholicism, and an early cinematic rendering of Catholic Marian devotionalism.[21] The film revolves around Andrew Carnegie–like steel magnate Charles Carson, who rules with a despotic hand over his steel mills, oblivious to the sufferings of his Irish and French workers. When a female steel mill worker, Claire Daudet, exhausted from overwork, accidentally falls down an elevator shaft because there is no safety guard, Carson responds to his son Charles, "They are only employees and must learn to be more careful." He is also an anti-Catholic bigot. When his elder daughter, Edith, informs him that she is engaged to a respectable doctor named Delaney, he proclaims, "Why that man is a Roman Catholic. I will never permit my daughter to marry a Catholic!" The worldly, powerful Carson, as source of economic exploitation and social prejudice, is the transgressor of the film's title. As Father Conway, the Catholic pastor of the ethnic workers in Carson's steel mill, tells the capitalist, "You are blinded by your avarice. Do you think you can transgress the laws of God and Man and not be brought to justice?"

Ethnic Catholic workers are the primary victims of Carson's tyranny. Among them are Claire Daudet and her mother, living devout, materially sparse lives in a simple but clean home. There are also the Reillys, who are portrayed as poorer than the Daudets. Lumber is piled on their residential street, suggesting the hard-scrabble character of their neighborhood. Reilly works in Carson's mill and is the head of a family that includes little Nora, who is a friend of Claire. The numerous scenes of the laborers toiling in Carson's steel mill, assembling for a labor meeting and eventually striking, all dramatically demonstrate the film's attention to working-class life, albeit a laboring world composed largely of men who are susceptible to the radical calls of revolutionaries like Petroski, the labor agitator who convinces the workers to strike against Carson.

Between oppressive and heartless capitalism and gullible workers stands the Catholic devotionalism of the ethnic working-class women. The domestic scenes that take place within the Daudet and Reilly homes are replete with traditional Catholic imagery including the crucifixion, Jesus in the garden, the Virgin Mary, and female saints. Carson's younger daughter Mary is drawn to the Marian devotions that Claire and Nora practice. Initially ignorant of Catholic spirituality, Mary comes eventually to sleep in her palatial mansion with a statuette of Mary in her hand and prays to the Virgin Mary, asking her, "If papa is a tyrant, please help him."

Mary is led into this redemptive world of Catholicism through Claire and Nora. One day, while Claire and Nora are out in front of their houses, they see Mary, with whom they have become friends. Claire invites them all back to her home. When Nora first learns that this wealthy girl could be so ignorant of Catholic reality, she asks her, "Your name is Mary and you don't know who the Blessed Virgin Mary is?" Nora then introduces Mary to the Catholic faith through an account of Bernadette of Lourdes. Offering an early film treatment of Catholic devotionalism, *The Transgressor* depicts Bernadette's encounter with the Virgin Mary in the rocky hills of the French countryside and her later vocation as a nun. The film signals the transition from the story of Bernadette back to Claire's home through an iris-in shot in the shape of a cross. The camera then lingers on Claire and Nora in prayer, underscoring for the film spectator the spiritual significance of the Lourdes story the girls have shared with Mary.

Later, Nora is run over by Carson's car. The workers, already brought to a fevered pitch by Petroski's radicalism, are ready to revolt. Nora's father confronts Carson outside the factory gates and is about to attack him when Father Conway intervenes. The priest calms not only Reilly but the other workers as well. The film then takes a melodramatic turn involving the flight of Petroski, which culminates in his driving off a cliff to his death, a fire in the Daudet home, and the rescue of little Mary from the burning home by the respectable Doctor Delaney. In the final scene, Carson, realizing the sacrifice the Catholic Delaney has made to rescue Mary, gestures to Edith that he accepts her engagement. Carson also extends his friendship to Father Conway. Finally, Carson agrees to support his son Charles's efforts to improve the safety of the steel mill. In one final sign of union, Charles walks over to Claire and puts his arm around her, suggesting a more intimate relationship. Thus, Catholic and Protestant, workers and industrialists, ethnic and Anglo-American are united. But in this film, the renewal of social harmony occurs on Catholic grounds. The young Mary's religious conversion to Catholicism is but the most dramatic in a series of conversions from Anglo-Protestant to Catholic the film imagines as central to social well-being. If, as Tom Gunning has argued, the emergence of narrative film within early cinema by the mid-1910s was predicated on its development into a moral discourse, *The Transgressor* suggests an attempt to give this cinematic discourse a Catholic accent.[22]

While *The Transgressor* and the other films of the Catholic Art Association may not have made a dramatic impact upon early motion pictures, they indicate an alternative source of Catholic imagery from that of Griffith and the Hollywood studios. They are also evidence of early Catholic efforts to utilize the new medium of film to represent themselves within the terms of ethnicity, class, and urban industrial life. From the earliest years of the twentieth century Catholics were among the immigrant working populations that made movies a new national medium. Yet within a regulatory social space of the 1910s and 1920s, shaped not only by movie censorship but immigration restriction and the prohibition of alcohol, Catholic involvement during the first three decades of U.S. film was circumscribed by the demands of assimilation defined in highly Anglo-American terms. It was largely on the fringes of movies that Catholics were to be found during an era when cultural guardians looked at both cinema and ethnic religious outsiders as threats to true Americanism. It therefore should not be surprising that early efforts to create films from Catholic perspectives, such as the Catholic Art Association, gained little traction among the early twentieth-century public and have all but vanished from the records of film history.

As Hollywood repeatedly failed in the eyes of moral critics to reform film production practices and as the Catholic population grew increasingly self-confident during the 1920s, some Catholics believed the time had come for a more deliberate effort to reform what they considered the immorality of the movies.[23] The failure of Protestant groups to unite on a course of action in regard to the film industry emboldened Catholics to take the lead. Simultaneously, renewed calls for federal regulation of the movies in the early 1930s led movie producers to seek new allies in the debate over morality and Hollywood. Will Hays, the head of the film industry trade group the Motion Picture Producers and Distributors of America, looked to Catholics for help in addressing the vexing issue of movie reform. Crucial in this regard was a group of Catholics who took seriously the need for Catholic action in the movies.

This cohort included the Jesuit Daniel Lord, who had consulted on Cecil B. DeMille's epic life of Jesus, *The King of Kings* (1927); Martin Quigley, publisher of the *Exhibitor's Herald*, a leading trade journal in the film industry; Father Wilfred Parsons, S.J., editor of

America, the Jesuit weekly magazine; and Cardinal George Mundelein of Chicago, who had the ear of major bankers to the film industry. In 1930 Lord and Quigley wrote a new production code that provided filmmakers with moral guidelines on how to treat a variety of controversial subjects, including crime, sex, marriage, religion, and the law. These Catholic reformers reasoned that if filmmakers adhered to clear standards for making morally acceptable movies, there would be no need to censor films after they were completed and distributed to the public. With the strong urging of Hays, the major studios approved the code written by the two Catholics.

Yet the voluntary agreement reached between the studios and the Catholic reformers quickly broke down. The early 1930s saw the studios' fortunes plummet as movie audiences shrank due to the economic crisis of the Depression. Filmmakers turned to what seemed the only reliable subjects to get people back into theaters—sex and violence. Catholics were outraged. But not until 1933 were the Catholic bishops ready to take action. They created a Legion of Decency, organized by each individual bishop in his diocese, designed to prevent Catholics from viewing morally offensive movies. The film studios feared that a united Catholic boycott would threaten a large portion of their market, particularly since many Catholics lived in the major northern and midwestern cities, where the studios owned their most lucrative theaters. The heads of the major film production companies therefore sought a deal with the church. The result was the creation of the Production Code Administration (PCA), headed by the Catholic Joseph Breen, whose responsibility was to certify that every film released by the studios conformed to the Lord Quigley–written production code that they had signed onto in 1930.

For their part, the bishops and the Legion of Decency created a ratings system, classifying films as A-I, "morally unobjectionable for the general public," A-II, morally unobjectionable for adults, B, "morally objectionable in part," and C, condemned as immoral.[24] Throughout the United States, Catholics pledged an oath to abide by the Legion and its ratings system. Catholic newspapers published the Legion's evaluations of movies. Hollywood trade papers kept careful note of the Legion's pronouncements. While this agreement was, to a degree, a capitulation to Catholic power, the studios found much to their liking in this new arrangement. They were more than happy to find an alternative to federal regulation that the industry feared in the early 1930s. Movie producers also believed this system would resolve the time-consuming and quite costly process of placating the numerous state and local censorship boards that had continued to plague their movies throughout the 1920s.

This system of censorship involving the PCA, the Legion of Decency and its rating system, and the major studios would hold sway over American films for over two decades. Yet, as Francis G. Couvares suggests, the power of Catholic reformers in Hollywood should not be construed "as a simple tale of artistic freedom struggling against repressive moralism."[25] Rather, Catholic action and changes in the ways the studios policed themselves in the 1930s represent a larger struggle in early twentieth-century America over cultural authority.[26] Enjoying strong organizational coherence and leadership, Catholics were able to succeed where the older Anglo-Protestant reformers had failed and thus stepped into a void within an already established regulatory context of movies that had shaped films into a moral discourse. Catholics did not create the censorship of films, but, because of their extensive urban subcultures throughout the United States at mid-century, they were able to shift the terms of that regulatory context in ways that allowed them new authority as cultural guardians of the nation's films.

Equally important for understanding why Catholics become so central to movies at mid-century was the larger shift in sensibilities within films beginning in the early 1930s. As historian Lary May has shown, the Depression inaugurated not only a political revolution of the New Deal, but also a cultural revolution as ethnic and religious outsiders moved from the margins of American culture to the center.[27] In the process they transformed the character of American identity. Movies were a central vehicle of this cultural development in America during the 1930s. As an organization that represented ethnic Catholics, the Legion was one manifestation of the shifting cultural landscape of mid-century as new voices increasingly asserted themselves via popular culture.

Yet Catholic actors and filmmakers themselves were also key agents of cultural change. As they crafted new personas, stories, and images suitable for a more complex and religiously diverse population, Catholics helped imbue classical Hollywood films with the cultural textures and social concerns of ethnic struggle and were instrumental in forging a more inclusive kind of popular Americanism. As Hollywood turned its gaze to ethnic urban life, Catholicism became a crucial ingredient in the transformation of American cultural identity. The neighborhood priest, the prison chaplain, the nun at the orphanage, the Catholic church looming on the city street all became signs of a new national landscape populated by ethnic, working Americans. No longer a manifestation of decay, corruption, and old-world foreignness, Catholics now functioned as an expression of a robust, pluralist America itself.[28]

In fostering a new pluralist public sphere, the movies of the 1930s and 1940s opened a cultural space for Catholic actors and actresses to participate in the construction of new American identities. This cohort of Catholic performers included the Gonzaga University–educated Bing Crosby, the former students of Milwaukee's Marquette Academy Pat O'Brien and Spencer Tracy, the Kentucky Catholic Irene Dunne, and New Yorker James Cagney.[29] Lesser stars included Walter Connolly, a graduate of Xavier College in Cincinnati and a frequent character actor in the films of Frank Capra and Andy Devine who studied for the priesthood before becoming an actor and whose most memorable role may be Buck the stagecoach driver in John Ford's *Stagecoach*.[30] Collectively these Catholic performers embodied a new ethnoreligious dynamic that transformed Hollywood in the 1930s and 1940s. Ethnic Catholics were not simply reflected on screen; these "new Americans" were reshaping the very look and images of the movies.

Even within the numerous constraints of Hollywood convention and moral censorship, a varied and exciting portrait of ethnic American Catholicism emerged. If Pat O'Brien embodied the tough but decent neighborhood priest, James Cagney perfected, through the course of such films as *Angels with Dirty Faces*, *The Roaring Twenties*, and *The Fighting 69th*, the persona of the lapsed Catholic. He gave expression not simply to the "city boys" of America but to the specifically urban Catholic who could neither accept his faith nor fully escape the church.[31] Indeed, Cagney's career was tied to his ability to translate his own

Irish Catholic working-class background into a new kind of aggressive, street-smart movie hero that resonated with ethnic moviegoers.

Cagney was born in 1899 and grew up on the Upper East Side of Manhattan, attending Mass and volunteering as an altar boy at the family parish, St. Francis De Sales.[32] His social life was shaped by his neighborhood milieu, learning to fight street kids and frequent parish dances. In 1918, however, Cagney left the church after a parish priest failed to provide a funeral prayer service for his father.[33] This combustible mix of Catholic formation and resentment imbued Cagney's screen rebels with their palpable dynamism. In 1931 he burst upon the cinema in his role as the decidedly secular Irish gangster, Tom Powers in *The Public Enemy*. Yet Catholicism is the absent presence in this film populated with working-class cops, civil servants, pious, doting mothers, and people with names like Ryan and Doyle. The later film *Angels with Dirty Faces* (1938), in which Cagney played the gangster Rocky Sullivan who returns to his urban neighborhood and eventually helps the local priest, played by Pat O'Brien, reform street kids, made explicit the Catholic presence on the ethnic urban landscape that had been implied in the earlier gangster film. Commenting on the set of the urban streets Warner Bros. had created for the picture, Cagney stated, "I thought I was back in Yorkville in 1910. . . . I was right back at home."[34]

Angels with Dirty Faces helped launch a decade-long cycle of highly successful "Catholic" films that gave dramatic expression to the interpenetration of Catholicism and American motion pictures. From *Boys Town* to *The Fighting 69th* (1940), *Knute Rockne, All American* (1940), *The Song of Bernadette* (1943), *Going My Way* (1944), *The Keys of the Kingdom* (1944), *God Is My Co-Pilot* (1945), *The Bells of St. Mary's* (1945), *The Miracle of the Bells* (1948), and *Fighting Fr. Dunne* (1948), Catholicism defined the religious film of the late New Deal–World War II era.[35] Collectively these movies constituted a turning point in the history of U.S. Catholicism. These films, far more than "Americanist" bishops such as John Ireland or public intellectuals such as John Courtney Murray, gave American audiences a new image of Catholics as part of a shared national project of pluralism. Masculine but virtuous priests, endearing and caring nuns, ethnic neighborhoods where decency vied with and ultimately triumphed over criminality were all pieces of the Catholic portrait that movies arranged into a compelling picture at mid-century.

Going My Way, perhaps more than any other film, epitomized this Catholic moment in U.S. cultural history.[36] Winner of seven Academy Awards, including Best Picture, Best Director for Leo McCarey, and Best Actor for Bing Crosby's role as Father "Chuck" O'Malley, *Going My Way* broke numerous box-office records on its release. Its success spawned a sequel, *The Bells of St. Mary's* (1945), which enjoyed even greater commercial success than the first Father O'Malley movie. *Going My Way*'s success is not hard to fathom. Only those averse to the alchemic possibilities of popular culture could fail to recognize Crosby's portrayal of the adept young cleric as a remarkable instance of cultural border-crossing.

A man in both Roman collar and straw boater, Crosby/O'Malley is a multicultural hybrid, addressing both all Americans generally and Catholics in particular at a moment of deep transition in the nation's modern history. An alternative to stereotypes of Catholics as un-American, *Going My Way* locates Catholics at the very core of a popular, pluralist nation. It simultaneously gathers other Hollywood depictions of the priest such as *Angels with Dirty Faces* and *Boys Town* and moves beyond them, creating an image of Catholicism that both reflects an ethnic, urban subcultural reality and reworks it through a dreamscape of Catholic longings and aspirations.

Going My Way and the other films of the Catholic cycle therefore manifested an expanded sense of American community that movies in the 1930s and 1940s helped forge. As historian Charles Morris noted, these films confirmed "Catholics were becoming Everyman."[37] Yet even more remarkable was how the Catholic priest had come to signify a broader transformation of just who everyman *was* by the 1940s. Indeed, Catholicism in movies at mid-century traced the contours of a new national landscape as religious outsiders functioned as consummate insiders traversing high/low cultural divides, ethnic diversity, and the line between public and private. These films helped construct a new kind of public sphere characterized by ethnic and religious pluralism, urban experiences, and mass culture.

Clearly, the influence of the Legion of Decency played a role in the emergence of these films. But these movies took on a life of their own, as evidenced by their enormous popularity and box-office success among American moviegoers. Catholic movies, in fact, contributed to a new sense of "the public" not only through the stories of religious outsiders now firmly planted at the center of the modern nation, but in their ability to create urban social events that gathered a pluralist public arena. For instance, the 1938 world premiere of *Boys Town* was held in Omaha, Nebraska, the home of the original home for wayward youth founded by Catholic priest Father Edward J. Flanagan. On September 7, 1938, thirty thousand people gathered outside the Omaha Theater to celebrate the film. The movie's stars, including Spencer Tracy, who played Father Flanagan, and Mickey Rooney, spoke to the crowd as did the real Father Flanagan. In addition, Omaha's Bishop James Ryan and the head of the local B'nai B'rith offered brief remarks to moviegoers.[38]

Catholic influence in movies was not limited to the onscreen representation of religion. The Catholic moment in movies also featured a large number of filmmakers whose works manifested Catholic sensibilities. Director John Ford, son of Irish immigrants who settled in Portland, Maine, practiced a poetics of ethnic Catholic acculturation by exploring national myths such as the Western from the perspectives of cultural outsiders.[39] *Fort Apache* (1948), for instance, is a story of a cavalry unit on the western frontier after the Civil War. Yet this movie of a hierarchical community populated by Irish grunts existing on the boundaries of civilization while cultural elites look down upon their efforts reads like a barely concealed exercise in displaced Irish Catholic psychology.[40]

Ford represents the tip of a Catholic filmmaking iceberg. Frank Capra's Italian Catholic populist vision of the country, Leo McCarey's sophisticated comedies, which adroitly sublimated a Catholic anxiety about social climbing, and Alfred Hitchcock's complex explorations of the visual gaze that reworked a traditional Catholic moral concern for the "custody of the eyes" all demonstrate how Catholic imaginations and perspective enriched American cinema at mid-century.[41] Each filmmaker created movies that articulated Catholicism differently, suggesting a range of Catholic sensibilities inscribed within movies. Leo McCarey, born into a southern California middle-class family, made romantic comedies that in genre, tone, and style were worlds apart from Ford's Westerns. For McCarey, high society provided a screen to project a comic assault on cultural respectability. The immigrant Capra charted the possibilities and dangers of success, infusing a Catholic communitarianism into his idealization of the American dream.[42] Collectively these directors indicate the extensive participation of Catholic filmmakers in crafting American cinema as the medium of popular imagination. Further, they suggest the role that Catholic difference played in mediating the cultural transformations of America from an Anglo-Protestant–identified nation to a modern, pluralist, mass culture.

Catholics both on-screen and off, therefore, were ubiquitous in movies at mid-century. But cultural tensions also characterized this era of Catholic ascendancy in movies. Films that privileged Catholics both managed and masked serious ethnoreligious conflicts in the United States. If Bing Crosby's cool Father O'Malley always seemed ready with the reassuring response, beneath that confidence surged darker impulses, for movies also functioned as an arena where Catholic anxieties about modernity unfolded. The Catholic Joe Breen of the PCA was a raging anti-Semite who received no admonishment from Catholic officials for his tirades against Jews.[43] Catholic discourse on movies during the 1930s and 1940s was replete with condemnations of the "materialist" godless Hollywood that functioned as barely veiled attacks on Jewish movie producers. Furthermore, many Catholics were constantly on the lookout for Communist infiltration of movies. A hard-edged stance therefore accompanied movie-made Catholicism, undercutting some of the more uplifting tendencies the films expressed.

The very presence of Catholics in films generated cultural anxieties as well. Some Protestants worried about a Catholic takeover of the movies and interpreted the popular Catholic films as evidence of an unnatural Hollywood favoritism toward Catholics. Liberal journals such as the *Nation* believed Catholic influence threatened the possibilities of cultural democracy in American.[44]

Assimilation, therefore, is too simple an explanation for the widespread Catholicism found in movies from the 1930s to the 1950s. Instead, Catholic involvement in the movies manifested significant changes reshaping American cultural identity. Movies became an important arena in remaking the national community along more pluralist lines that could accommodate ethnic, religious outsiders. This entailed both a pervasive role of Catholics in American popular imagination and serious cultural tensions.

While converts like Thomas Merton and Clare Booth Luce gave American Catholicism a new intellectual respectability in the late 1940s, film noir directors took the image of Catholics into the fetid streets of criminals, murderers, and cops. Henry Hathaway's *Kiss of Death* (1947) and *Call Northside 777* (1948) charted an ambiguous vision of social possibilities through urban Catholic neighborhoods. Perhaps most brilliant of all, Robert Siodmak's great film noir set among Italian Catholics, *Cry of the City* (1948), starring Victor Mature and Richard Conte, which climaxes in a dimly lit Catholic church on the Lower East Side, plays like an embryonic version of Martin Scorsese's *Mean Streets*. Indeed, the genre of film noir, so beloved of many film critics, sustained a fascination with the Catholic vernacular. The shadowy, gritty crime films imagined a different kind of Catholic from that of *Going My Way* and *Boys Town*, one in which ethnic Catholicism provided a visual and social terrain to project post–World War II anxieties about democracy in America. The result was an expanding presence of Catholic imagery in popular imagination.

After World War II, the conventions of the Catholic priest and nun that had been created during the late 1930s and 1940s continued. By the late 1950s, the genre of Catholic films had grown quite tired, as evidenced by Frank Tashlin's *Say One for Me* (1959). Even the title indicates its specifically Catholic address. Playing yet another Manhattan priest, Father Conroy, who ministers to show biz folk, Bing Crosby looks like he is going through paces he devised fifteen years before. Debbie Reynolds, who plays an aspiring dancer the priest seeks to safeguard from unsavory influences, provides the film's ingredient of youth that Crosby himself had offered in the mid-1940s.

Efforts were made in the 1950s to infuse this genre of Catholic religious films with new energy: attention was paid particularly to Catholic nuns as evidenced by John Huston's *Heaven Knows, Mr. Allison* (1957) and Fred Zimmerman's *The Nun's Story* (1959). *Heaven Knows Mr. Allison*, which starred Deborah Kerr as a nun marooned on an island with a marine, Corporal Allison, played by Robert Mitchum, used the nun's commitment to her vocation as a parallel to a soldier's duty to his mission.[45] Yet by severing the nun from her religious community and any sense of social rootedness, the film reflected the erasure of ethnicity and urban memory that characterized much of 1950s culture.

Exceptions to the 1950s articulation of religion in bland, deracinated terms were provided by the neorealist idiom of New York filmmaking from the period.[46] *On the Waterfront* (1954) and *Marty* (1955) offered powerful depictions of working-class Catholic ethnics. Each film was highly acclaimed and won the Academy Award for Best Picture. As one of the most important films of the second half of the twentieth century, *On the Waterfront* explores the plight of working-class Catholics on the New Jersey docks as they struggle against a corrupt union boss. Best known for Marlon Brando's performance as the young Terry Malloy, the film has often been considered a reflection of director Elia Kazan's own experience testifying before the House Un-American Activities Committee.[47] Yet as James T. Fisher has shown, *On the Waterfront* is deeply rooted in the story of an actual Jesuit labor priest, John "Pete" Corridan, who worked the New Jersey–New York waterfront championing Catholic social justice for dockworkers.[48] Karl Malden's role as Father Pete Barry, who encourages Terry to testify against the waterfront racketeer Johnny Friendly, is a fictionalized account of Corridan's own activism among Catholic workers.

Marty, which won the Best Picture Award the following year, was another tale of ethnic working-class Catholics. Ernest Borgnine played a thirty-two-year-old Italian American butcher who longed to escape his bachelorhood and find a woman to marry. Taunted by neighbors and family for his lack of a wife, Marty seems destined to live out his Saturday nights with his buddies, aimless and bored, until he meets another ugly duckling, Clare. At first excited about having finally found a woman who likes him, Marty has second thoughts as he realizes this might mean giving up his ties to his mother and friends. Ultimately Marty chooses the prospects of domestic life with Clare over his ethnic family and male camaraderie. As historian Judith E. Smith has argued, *Marty* reflects the new valorization of private life that characterized much of the 1950s.[49] However, the screenwriter Paddy Chayefsky's depoliticization of the ethnic neighborhood simultaneously highlighted the urban neighborhood as a sphere shaped by a Catholic sense of time and place. The references to Sunday Mass and church that pepper Marty's conversations with Clare, his brother-in-law, and his friends mark the religious parameters of his world. No wonder that Catholic reviewers liked the film. *Extension* noted the "strong Catholic undertones" of *Marty*. *Commonweal* wrote that the movie "has caught beautifully the sights and sounds of a big city—and most of all it has caught the vernacular of the people who live in a big city."[50]

Noted for their realism, *Marty* and *On the Waterfront* were not so much a dramatic break with the earlier Catholic films as signs of the continuing role of Catholicism in contributing to the social terms of urban ethnic life on screen. These films suggested that an alternative memory of America—one that retained a sensitivity to the importance of particular, rooted identities—existed beneath the happy façade of 1950s suburban consensus that informed the era.

In the 1960s Catholicism attracted the epic treatment that had characterized the biblical spectacles popular in the postwar decade. These films eschewed the complex portraits of Catholicism that films such as *On the Waterfront* pursued. Social realism and ethnic culture were largely abandoned in favor of popes, cardinals, and the Vatican. Films such as *The Shoes of the Fisherman* (1968) and *A Man for All Seasons* (1966) reflected the new attention the world was paying to Rome as the site of the historical events transforming Roman Catholicism during the Second Vatican Council from 1962 to 1965. The spectacle of Rome rather than the intimate spaces of ethnic city streets that Father O'Malley and Father Barry walked became a preferred image of Catholicism in the movies.

Then, in the late 1960s and 1970s, the auteurs hit Hollywood, bringing in their wake a new wave of Catholic sensibilities.[51] The major studios' willingness to gamble on a young generation of film directors and their personal visions of movies opened another chapter in the history of Catholics in American cinema. Though many of these filmmakers were not Catholic, three of the most creative, Martin Scorsese, Francis Ford Coppola, and Robert Altman, brought Catholic cultural memories to a new era of movies. The films of Scorsese, Coppola, and Altman offered a critical revision of themes featured in films from the "Catholic moment" era of the 1930s and 1940s. These younger Catholics drew upon, often implicitly, their formative Catholic backgrounds and education to craft powerful and challenging new images of America. Taken together, their movies represent additional evidence of how films have been central to the Catholic articulation of the nation now expressed by these filmmakers' own contentious relationship with both their religion and their society.

Unique among recent filmmakers, Martin Scorsese, director of such movies as *Taxi Driver* and *Goodfellas*, has been most explicit about his Catholicism.[52] He has stated, "I'm a lapsed Catholic. But I am a Catholic—there's no way out of it."[53] From his exploration of ethnic Catholicism in *Mean Streets* to his controversial depiction of the life of Jesus, *The Last Temptation of Christ*, to his rendering of the tribal wars between nativists and Irish Catholics in Civil War–era Manhattan, *The Gangs of New York*, Scorsese's movies have continually explored the social, theological, and even historical dimensions of Catholicism.

Scorsese emerged out of the ethnic Catholic subculture of postwar America, growing up in New York City's Little Italy and educated at Catholic schools, including brief study at a minor seminary when he considered becoming a priest.[54] His youth reads like a real-life version of the Italian American street kid Tony Scaponi of *Going My Way*, whom Father O'Malley befriended. In his early years, Scorsese came under the influence of a dynamic priest who introduced him to classical music, took him to movies, and helped steer him from the criminal influences in his neighborhood. Encouraging him to appreciate an alternative world of art and culture to the rough-and-tumble world of Little Italy, the priest became a model for the young Scorsese.[55] He would eventually attend New York University to study filmmaking after failing to get into the Jesuit Fordham University due to poor grades.[56] Catholicism and a deep sensitivity to the cultural codes that structure communal life are inexorably entwined in the films of Scorsese.

Where the Catholic films of the studio era of the 1930s and 1940s highlighted the church's vitality as a sign of a reinvigorated American society, Scorsese's *Mean Streets* (1973) explores the personal and moral struggles of a Catholic in the contemporary world. The protagonist, Charlie, played by Harvey Keitel, is modeled on Scorsese's own anxious conflict with his Catholic faith. Charlie's hero is St. Francis, but he chafes against the ritual demands of the church. He seeks to live his Catholicism beyond the boundaries of Mass and confession in the streets of his daily existence. *Mean Streets* offers perhaps the most sustained exploration of Catholicism in Scorsese's body of work, though as numerous critics have noted, a Catholic sacramental sensibility informs the treatments of the physical, tangible, and corporeal in virtually all of Scorsese's films.[57]

The blood that flows freely in a Scorsese film suggests his Catholic training in the sacramental meanings of the Passion. *Raging Bull*'s (1980) Jake LaMotta works out his own punishments through the only thing he understands—his physical body.[58] It is just through such physical realities that Scorsese's characters play out their sins and search for redemption. Likewise, Scorsese's almost anthropological attention to social codes, rules, and hierarchies, whether manifested in the East Coast mob of *Goodfellas* (1990) or the high-society world of turn-of-the-century Manhattan in *The Age of Innocence* (1993), reflects a Catholic sensitivity to the importance of communal forms and practices.

Scorsese epitomized the refashioning of Catholicism through the movies during the 1970s. Two other directors of that era, Francis Ford Coppola and Robert Altman, joined Scorsese in drawing upon their Catholic experiences to craft movies that highlighted the contradictory, often oppressive character of Catholicism.[59] Coppola's mixing of brutal violence and Catholic ritual in his *Godfather* films (1972 and 1974) and Altman's ridiculing of Catholic priestly authority in *M*A*S*H* (1970) evidenced how a new generation of filmmakers depicted a Catholicism far less wholesome than earlier Hollywood films. Their work relished subverting the older movie imagery of Catholics, reflecting an iconoclastic impulse born from intimate acquaintance with Catholicism itself. But even as the films of Scorsese, Coppola, and Altman utilized Catholicism as a rich source for critique, their movies evoked traces of a latent Catholic communal sensibility. All three directors gave primacy to the complexities of community and the interrelationships that structure large groups, whether it be Little Italy, the Mafia, or Nashville.[60]

If *The Godfather* and *Mean Streets* indicated how movies offered a postwar generation of creative Catholics opportunities to examine their Catholicism critically, they also signaled in a wider revision in the Catholic representation in Hollywood cinema. Films in the last third of the century, such as *True Confessions* (1981) and *The Verdict* (1982), imagined a corrupt and hypocritical church of compromised priests and hierarchs. Though not the only image of Catholics presented in late twentieth-century movies, such depictions reflected an increasing alienation among filmmakers and audiences toward established social institutions. The very visibility of the Catholic Church, which once allowed it a privileged place in the visual culture of film, now made it an easily recognizable and useful symbol of oppressive authority. These films marked the cultural distance movies had traveled from the era of *Going My Way* and Father O'Malley.

By the 1980s the pleasure of looking at Catholics had greatly diminished for American film audiences. The image of Catholics could no longer suture a compelling vision of the nation as it had done at mid-century. Similarly, assimilation meant that many Catholics no longer felt the need to explain themselves and their distinctive traditions to their fellow citizens.[61] The end of the twentieth century, in fact, witnessed the fragmentation of the Catholic signifier in American culture. The political character of such widely acclaimed films during this era as *The Mission* (1986) and *Dead Man Walking* (1995) underscored this changed status of cinematic Catholicism as a fractured image. Catholicism in these films was now harnessed to the depiction of controversial issues—such as Western militarism in South America and capital punishment in the United States. Further, U.S. Catholics in the 1980s and 1990s were directly involved on both sides of these deeply contested social issues. Catholic social action was far from dead in the late twentieth century, but whatever ability it had to unify American Catholics was in ruins.

That Catholic subculture that had played such an important role in the cultural history of American film during the mid-century was now long gone. Instead, Catholics were divided among themselves and pulled in numerous directions. Many Catholics seemed intent on fiercely debating the consequences of assimilation. Tensions between the proper relationship between U.S. Catholics and Vatican authority also characterized the era. Further, an ascendant younger generation knew nothing but a post-subcultural Catholicism.[62] This generation of Catholic filmgoers thus had little to shape their visual gazes to identify Catholic concerns on the screen.

The film industry too had changed: during the 1980s movie studios became parts of multimedia corporate behemoths that pursued strategies of synergy to maximize profits from films. This change had enormous impact on the status and reception of movies in the nation. Increasingly they became less unique cultural expressions and instead "products," merely the first and ultimately not the most important node in a whole chain of consumer opportunities that stretched from the movie house through cable, video rentals and purchases, DVDs, traditional television, and theme park rides. Further, the new technologies of cable, video, and DVD allowed the home to become a primary site for movie viewing. These developments within the film industry refigured the cultural space of American movies, making it harder for films with traditional religious subjects to find large audiences. Indeed, it is hard to imagine a Father O'Malley ride at Paramount King's Island.[63]

The result of these changes in Hollywood, Catholicism, and the nation itself was that the treatment of Catholicism in American films moved in several directions simultaneously. Each direction, however, constituted, with rare exception, a small ripple in the film culture of late twentieth-century America. Ironically, it is only in the 1980s and 1990s, *after* the collapse of the Catholic subculture, that Catholic films became "ghettoized" into niche markets that engaged small audiences

Films that addressed the role of religion in social-justice issues signaled one trajectory. Examples include *The Mission* (1986), *Romero* (1989), *Dead Man Walking* (1995), and *Priest* (1994). *The Mission* (1986), the winner of the Cannes Film Festival Palm D'Or award, is a particularly interesting film for the numerous Catholic associations that extended beyond the movie's story of Jesuits in seventeenth-century Paraguay. Written by Robert Bolt, who also wrote the screenplay based on his own play, *A Man for All Seasons*, which enjoyed critical success in the mid-1960s, *The Mission* took as its backdrop liberation theology, debates over Rome's increasing authority over the worldwide church, and American military involvement in El Salvador and Nicaragua. The director, Roland Jaffe, had just made his powerful film treating the Cambodian genocide, *The Killing Fields*. The radical Jesuit Daniel Berrigan's presence in the film suggested that this movie had more on its mind than simply entertainment.[64]

The film's leading role was played by Robert De Niro, widely known for his involvement in Scorsese's portraits of Italian Catholic criminal worlds of New York. Jeremy Irons, fresh from his performance as a convert to Catholicism in the British television production of Evelyn Waugh's *Brideshead Revisited*, also starred. The film thus swam amid a sea of popular cultural associations to Catholicism; in treating the conquest of indigenous peoples in the Americas it also resonated with concerns about American military involvement in Central America that shaped U.S. political culture in the 1980s. *The Mission* demonstrated how Catholicism could be utilized to offer narratives that questioned reigning ideological impulses within the country during the 1980s. The movie, however, failed to attract a mass audience: critical theology was not able to gather these diverse signifiers into an attractive representation.

While such films as *Dead Man Walking* and *The Mission* evidenced a willingness to treat Catholicism in terms of controversial, politicized subject matter, they also sustained elements of earlier film depictions of social Catholicism, carrying forward older associations between Catholicism and social morality. For all its realism, for example, *Dead Man Walking* drew upon the prison chaplain motif that populated films in the 1930s. Susan Sarandon's nun character had more in common with Pat O'Brien's priests from the Warner Bros. crime films than some may have wished to acknowledge.

Other popular films, including *Sister Act* (1992) and *Keeping the Faith* (2000), evoked traditional portrayals of Catholic religious clothed in updated material. *Sister Act*, one of the big hits of 1992, starred Whoopi Goldberg as a nightclub singer who had been placed by a witness protection program in an urban convent passing as a nun to avoid detection by her gangster boyfriend. At first chafing at the restrictions of convent life, Goldberg's character soon takes over as director of the nuns' choir and turns it into a crowd-pleasing attraction. With the money the choir raises, as well as the new confidence she inspires in the sisters, Dolores saves the convent from closing. The story and theme drew heavily from 1944's *Going My Way* in its fusion of popular music and urban Catholicism. Some critics at the time, pointing to the clichéd depiction of nuns, savaged the film.[65] Few commentators, however, bothered to notice how *Sister Act* brought together two groups—Catholics and African Americans—deeply influential in twentieth-century popular culture. The time-worn story and characterizations highlighted the centrality of mass culture itself in the formation of identities in modern America. In fact, the film gave Goldberg, a comic master of playing with racial conventions, an opportunity to extend her explorations of passing as a cultural phenomenon through her role of a nightclub singer masking as a Catholic nun. The film struck a chord with audiences, becoming one of the biggest hits of 1992, and spawned a sequel that also landed in the top twenty in 1993.

Freed from the burden of older Hollywood conventions and the demands of the older ethnic "ghetto," the sign of Catholicism in many late twentieth-century movies sank under the weight of its newfound freedom. *Priest, Entertaining Angels* (1998), *Black Robe* (1991), and *The Mission* all sought to inject social relevance, politics, and/or history into the representation of Catholicism, yet struggled to find audiences. Such films attempted to move beyond the tradition of ethnic Catholic urbanism in Hollywood films that stretched back to the 1930s but without much success.

Kevin Smith, director of *Clerks* (1994) and *Dogma* (1999), began to craft just such a path by infusing Catholic concerns into a new context of disaffected college-age suburbanites. *Clerks* focuses on Dante, a twenty-two-year-old slacker, who finds working in a convenience store to be his own personal hell. *Dogma* is an irreverent rendering of Catholic preoccupations about the sacramental, heaven, and hell set in contemporary New Jersey and saturated with comically blasphemous, profane, yet often moving dialogue between individuals who might be said to have grown up, in the words of a song by the Clash, "all lost in the supermarket."

Kevin Smith began his career as an independent filmmaker in that precarious creative territory where the most interesting manifestations of Catholicism in movies were often located in the final decades of the century. Here emerged fascinating films that operated within Catholic movie conventions to creatively explore new dimensions of Catholic experience. Nancy Savoca's *Household Saints* (1993) and the movies of Abel Ferrara are examples of this new Catholic cinema.

Savoca's film examines the familiar terrain of New York Italian Catholicism but organizes its narrative around three generations of Italian Catholic women. This represents a new development and highlights the gendered character of Catholicism in the movies. If movies have often functioned to stage and contain anxieties about gender and masculinity, then the pervasive presence of Catholic priests and nuns in movies and the overwhelmingly male character of Catholic filmmakers suggest that Catholicism has served an important role in articulating gender and its contradictions in popular movies.[66] The tradition that has been explored in this chapter, in fact, can be considered a decidedly male Catholic gaze at Catholicism and America. By focusing on immigrant, mid-century, and postwar baby boomer Catholic women, Savoca gave expression to the domestic and devotional experiences neglected in the masculine versions of ethnic Catholic life that Hollywood movies have made normative.

Abel Ferrara, well known in independent film circles, combines raw violence with thoughtful considerations of faith through his distinctive rendering of gangster and crime movies. Born in the Bronx and a product of Catholic schooling, Ferrara teamed up with schoolboy friend Nicholas St. John to make a series of films in the late 1980s and 1990s, including *The Addiction* (1995) and *The Funeral* (1996), that addressed significant theological issues.[67] Ferrara has been quite explicit about the seriousness with which he takes moral and spiritual issues in his filmmaking. He admits that he shares the intense struggles over faith and redemption that define many of his characters:

> It's not my films. It's my life. A film is not a ninety-minute thing. A film is everything that I am. We keep coming back to the point of, "Who are we? Where do we come from? What's our future?" We do plenty of dealing with the now. But I don't know how you can fucking live and not question where you're from. When you're brought up in a Catholic school, they tell you, "Don't ask those questions, they'll make you crazy."[68]

It is in his films that Ferrara explores the questions his Catholic upbringing cultivated but then prevented him from addressing, further evidence of how the movies have functioned as a displaced religious arena for Catholics.

Bad Lieutenant (1992) is perhaps Ferrara's most noted film, pushing an exploration of sin and forgiveness to extreme limits. Harvey Keitel plays the "bad lieutenant," a self-destructive New York City cop who snorts lines of coke on photographs of his daughter's First Communion and lives a life of degradation. Charged with investigating the brutal rape of a nun, the lieutenant descends into a nightmarish world of personal drug and sexual abuse. The movie graphically depicts the lieutenant's many vices, dramatizing the cop's self-absorption. Yet when he confronts the nun praying at her church, astounded that she has forgiven her rapists, the lieutenant collapses in the nave and has a vision of the crucified Christ. Simultaneously outraged at the absence of God in his life and confessing his weakness, the lieutenant repents before Christ. In his own act of forgiveness, the cop finds the two rapists and puts them on a bus out of New York. In the final scene, the lieutenant is killed by a drive-by shooter. The film ends ambiguously but with a suggestion that the cop had achieved some kind of redemption through his repentance and sacrifice.

The violence and sexual explicitness of Ferrara's films may have prevented them from gaining mainstream audiences. But their preoccupation with issues of faith in a violent, distorted world made them distinctive. Further, they suggest that pushed to the margins of recent movies, thoughtful new filmmakers such as Ferrara continue to find Catholicism a rich subject for serious exploration.

Given the lack of popular appeal for movies about Catholics in the late twentieth century, one could have reasonably wondered if Catholicism's ability to influence movies had run its course. Then Mel Gibson made a movie that got everyone talking about Catholicism again.[69] Gibson, known for his action adventure films, made what at first seemed to be an esoteric movie about Jesus's final hours spoken in the ancient languages of Aramaic and

Latin. By the time of its release, *The Passion of the Christ* (2004) had become a part of the nation's culture wars of the early twenty-first-century as the movie's extreme violence and depiction of Jewish religious leaders provoked fierce debate. Surprisingly to many, the movie also scored a huge commercial success.[70]

While commentators and scholars sought to place the film in various historical contexts, including the history of Catholic anti-Semitism, movie depictions of Jesus, and Catholic devotionalism, less attention was paid to how Gibson's movie became the latest manifestation of the long tradition this chapter has explored—namely, the Catholic use of movies to negotiate American society. Gibson's own style of Traditionalist Catholicism rejects many of the modern reforms inaugurated by the Second Vatican Council.[71] *The Passion of the Christ* is the cinematic equivalent of the traditional Catholic devotion of the Stations of the Cross that was popular in the older Catholic subculture of the early and mid-twentieth centuries. By crafting his story of Jesus in terms of this devotion, Gibson ignored advances in Catholic-Jewish dialogue regarding depictions of the Passion. He also signaled his disregard for Hollywood's conventional pious portraits of Jesus. Movies proved once again to be an effective vehicle for inserting Catholic sensibilities into popular culture.

If Gibson therefore treads, intentionally or not, within a long-standing cultural tradition of Catholic engagement with the movies, he also charts new territory. In the past, Catholic filmmakers were adept at practicing a multilayered language and making movies in which Catholic concerns were embedded in stories that spoke to a wide range of audiences. Catholic filmmakers have therefore often been consummate crossover artists, simultaneously Catholic and players within a modern secular culture. Martin Scorsese and Abel Ferrara are recent examples of Catholics whose films gained critical attention beyond their coreligious. Secular critics have often embraced their movies without concern for the Catholic nuances of their work.

Yet Gibson and his film represented a different kind of crossover. Gibson made *The Passion* as an intentionally religious film, courting not so much other Catholics, but evangelical churches. This deliberate effort to bring Traditionalist Catholicism and evangelical Protestantism together made Gibson unique among Catholic filmmakers.

Over the course of one hundred years, Catholics have helped create American movies. The density and polyvocality of Catholicism in U.S. movies engages a panorama of American society. Ethnicity, class, urban life, family, gender, crime, the law, the body, theology, and mass culture itself are but some of the subjects that Catholicism in the movies have absorbed and articulated.

But if a dialogic process characterized Catholicism and film whereby Catholics helped create the movies while Hollywood constructed Catholicism for mass audiences, this complex history also possessed significant limitations. The predominance of urban Catholicism in movies has made it difficult to literally see other social realities of the U.S. Catholic experience. For all Kevin Smith's efforts, Catholicism in the suburbs, for instance, remains in the cinematic shadows cast by the gritty and colorful ethnic Catholic neighborhood. Other subjects, including the Catholics of recent immigration, more regional variants of Catholicism, and women's experiences also need richer, more creative treatment. Perhaps the second century of cinema will incorporate these and other dimensions of Catholic life into the movies.[72]

Three trajectories of the twentieth century coalesced to foster the widespread Catholic presence in films. First, the rise and development of the specifically U.S. film industry, organized around major studios that operated on mass-production lines, created the material conditions for Catholics in the movies. It was this very particular studio arrangement with its corporate organization, vertical integration, genre typologies, and cultivation of star personalities that produced the classical Hollywood film in which Catholic filmmakers and actors worked.[73]

Second, the emergence of a substantial Catholic subculture in America provided the social and religious basis for Catholic encounters with movies. Many of the Catholics who worked and succeeded in film were shaped by the formative influence of this particular ethnic-inflected Catholicism that prevailed in the United States during the twentieth century. In addition, millions of Catholic moviegoers over the decades were parishioners as well as film spectators. The result, sometimes explicitly, often indirectly, was an ongoing Catholicization of the movies through distinctly Catholic memories, characters, and imaginations on screen.

Finally, the role of movies in remaking the modern United States drew Catholics into wider conversations about the character and direction of American society. From the crisis of Anglo-American authority to the forging of a pluralist nation to the culture wars of the late twentieth century, movies provided a forum to debate the terms of national belonging. As a medium particularly attuned to the desires and experiences of the masses, movies moved Catholics to the center of popular understandings of America.

Movies therefore broaden and complicate the study of Catholics in the United States. They offer additional contexts and sources to explore the wide-ranging but elusive presence of Catholicism in American culture. As important as the parish, the school, bishops, and papal encyclicals may be to understanding U.S. Catholicism, the movie house, the fan magazine, and the images that flickered on-screen embodied equally important influences shaping Catholics in America. They reveal that as significant as the subculture was to Catholic life, it did not exhaust Catholic experience in the twentieth century. Indeed, film represents a cultural form where the centrality of Catholics to the history of modern America has been substantial and long-lasting. Far from representing a minor element in the development of cinema, Catholics helped give movies their look, appeal, and influence. Movies with Catholic themes reveal the importance that religious identities and communities continued to have in a century long considered increasingly secular. Recognizing the Catholic imprint upon popular film opens both the history of Catholics and American culture to new complexities and resonances.

NOTES

1. On the creation of the National Catholic Welfare Conference, originally named the National Catholic War Council, in 1919, see Douglas Slawson, "National Catholic Welfare Conference," in *The Encyclopedia of American Catholic History*, ed. Michael Glazier and Thomas J. Shelley (Collegeville, Minn.: Liturgical Press, 1997). On the creation of MGM in 1924, see

Richard Koszarski, *An Evening's Entertainment: The Age of the Silent Feature Picture, 1915–1928* (New York: Charles Scribner's Sons, 1990), 80–83.

2. Recent works that have begun the reevaluation of Catholics in American film include Anthony Burke Smith, *The Look of Catholics: Portrayals in Popular Culture from the Great Depression to the Cold War* (Lawrence: University Press of Kansas, 2010); James T. Fisher, *On the Irish Waterfront: The Crusader, the Movie, and the Soul of the Port of New York* (Ithaca, N.Y.: Cornell University Press, 2009); Colleen McDannell, ed., *Catholics in the Movies* (New York: Oxford University Press, 2008). Other studies include Lee Lourdeaux, *Italian and Irish Filmmakers in America: Ford, Capra, Coppola and Scorsese* (Philadelphia: Temple University Press, 1990); Paul Giles, *American Catholic Arts and Fiction: Culture, Ideology, Aesthetics* (New York: Cambridge University Press, 1992); Richard A. Blake, *AfterImage: The Indelible Catholic Imagination of Six American Filmmakers* (Chicago: Loyola University Press, 2000); Charles Morris, *American Catholics: The Saints and Sinners Who Built America's Most Powerful Church* (New York: Vintage, 1997), 196–200. An early effort to consider Catholicism as a lens through which to consider filmmakers is Leo Braudy, "The Sacraments of Genre: Coppola, DePalma, Scorsese," *Film Quarterly* 30 (Summer 1986): 17–28. Les Keyser and Barbara Keyser, *Hollywood and the Catholic Church: The Image of Roman Catholicism in American Movies* (Chicago: Loyola University Press, 1984) is one of the few older works that gave extensive attention to the portrait of Catholics in movies.

3. On the Legion of Decency, see Gregory D. Black, *Hollywood Censored: Morality Codes, Catholics and the Movies* (New York: Cambridge University Press, 1994); Frank Walsh, *Sin and Censorship: The Catholic Church and the Motion Picture Industry* (New Haven, Conn.: Yale University Press, 1996); Leonard J. Leff and Jerold L. Simmons, *The Dame in the Kimono: Hollywood Censorship and the Production Code*, 2nd ed. (Lexington: University of Kentucky Press, 2001); Francis G. Couvares, "Hollywood, Main Street, and the Church: Trying to Censor the Movies before the Production Code," in *Movie Censorship and American Culture*, ed. Francis G. Couvares (Washington, D.C.: Smithsonian Institution Press, 1996), 129–58.

4. For an awareness of the numerous Catholic filmmakers in American cinema, see also McDannell, *Catholics in the Movies*, 20.

5. On assessing movies in regard to their accuracy of Catholic experience, see Keyser and Keyser, *Hollywood and the Catholic Church*.

6. Lourdeaux, *Italian and Irish Filmmakers in America*, 26–42.

7. "Dramatic Notes," *America*, March 26, 1910, 652.

8. See Terry Lindvall, *The Silents of God: Selected Issues and Documents in American Film and Religion, 1908–1925* (Lanham, Md.: Scarecrow, 2001).

9. "Flotsam and Jetsam," *Catholic Fortnightly Review* 17, no. 13 (1910): 409.

10. Quoted in *Catholic Fortnightly Review* 19, no. 5 (1912): 154.

11. On the "regulatory space" that emerged in the 1910s as a central context for cinema in twentieth-century America, see Lee Grieveson, "Fighting Films: Race, Morality and the Governing of Cinema, 1912–1915," in *The Silent Cinema Reader*, ed. Lee Grieveson and Peter Kramer (New York: Routledge, 2004), 169–86.

12. Quoted in *Catholic Fortnightly Review* 19, no. 4 (1912): 120.

13. "To Censure Moving Picture Films," *America*, July 8, 1911, 306.

14. *Catholic Fortnightly Review* 19, no. 9 (1912): 283.

15. F. Schulte, "Moving Picture Shows," *Catholic Fortnightly Review* 18, no. 23 (1911): 702.

16. "Abuses and Uses of Motion Pictures," *America*, August 16, 1913, 448.

17. The descriptions of these films draw upon the entries for each film in the online American Film Institute Catalog. Additional source for the barring of *The Eternal Light* is Conde B. Pallen, "Motion Pictures and Censorship," *America*, March 12, 1921, 497.

18. On Goebel, see the entry "Goebel, Otto E.," in Eugene Michael Vazzana, *Silent Film Necrology* (Jefferson, N.C.: McFarland, 2001), 201. On Pallen, see the entry "Pallen,

Dr. Conde B.," in *Silent Film Necrology*, 408, and "Conde B. Pallen, Noted Editor, Dies," *New York Times*, May 27, 1929, 25.

19. See "Conde B. Pallen, Noted Editor, Dies"; C. Joseph Nuesse, *The Catholic University of America: A Centennial History* (Washington, D.C.: The Catholic University of America Press, 1990), 151; Aaron I. Abell, *American Catholic Thought on Social Questions* (New York: Bobbs-Merrill, 1968), 204–13.

20. Conde B. Pallen, "Motion Pictures and Censorship," *America*, March 21, 1921, 497.

21. My analysis of *The Transgressor* is based upon repeated viewings of a copy of the film held by the UCLA Film Archives. This copy consists of eight reels. While some scenes may be missing from this safety print, which is in otherwise good condition, enough of the film remains to allow a strong sense of the narrative.

22. Tom Gunning, "From the Opium Den to the Theatre of Morality: Moral Discourse and the Film Process in Early American Cinema," in Grieveson and Kramer, *Silent Cinema Reader*, 146.

23. My discussion of Catholic efforts to reform movies and the Legion of Decency draws heavily upon Frank Walsh's careful history *Sin and Censorship*, particularly pages 46–162. Francis Couvares also provides an excellent account of how and why Catholics assumed a major role in the reform of movies in the 1930s in his "Hollywood, Main Street, and the Church."

24. Quoted in Walsh, *Sin and Censorship*, 135.

25. Couvares, "Hollywood, Main Street, and the Church," 152.

26. See ibid., 129–58. Jonathan Munby also argues for interpreting the Catholic role in film censorship in terms of a struggle over cultural authority in early twentieth-century America, in his *Public Enemies, Public Heroes: Screening the Gangster from Little Caesar to Touch of Evil* (Chicago: University of Chicago Press, 1999).

27. Lary May, *The Big Tomorrow: Hollywood and the Politics of the American Way* (Chicago: University of Chicago Press, 2000); see also Munby, *Public Enemies, Public Heroes*.

28. I discuss this cultural history in more detail in my *Look of Catholics*.

29. On Crosby, see Gary Giddins, *Bing Crosby: A Pocketful of Dreams; The Early Years, 1903–1940* (Boston: Little Brown, 2001). On Pat O'Brien and Spencer Tracy, see their respective entries in the online *American National Biography*. On Dunne, see Wes D. Gehring, *Irene Dunne: First Lady of Hollywood* (Lanham, Md.: Scarecrow, 2003). On James Cagney, see John McCabe, *Cagney* (New York: Alfred A. Knopf, 1997).

30. On Devine, see Leonard Maltin, ed., *Leonard Maltin's Movie Encyclopedia* (New York: Dutton, 1994), 227. On Connolly, see Ephraim Katz, *The Film Encyclopedia*, 3rd ed. (New York: HarperPerennial, 1998), 284.

31. On the construction of the "city boys" in popular film of the 1930s and 1940s, see Robert Sklar, *City Boys: Cagney, Bogart, Garfield* (Princeton, N.J.: Princeton University Press, 1992).

32. McCabe, *Cagney*, 18.

33. Ibid., 34, 35–36.

34. Ibid., 162.

35. Morris also highlights these movies as evidence of the growing Catholic presence in America during the twentieth century in his *American Catholics*, 196–200.

36. See Anthony Burke Smith, "Entertaining Catholics: Bing Crosby, Religion and Cultural Pluralism in 1940s America," *American Catholic Studies* 114 (Winter 2003): 1–19.

37. Morris, *American Catholics*, 200.

38. "*Boys Town* Premiere," 1938 Clippings File of *Omaha World-Herald*, Historical Society of Douglas County, Nebraska.

39. On Ford, see Anthony Burke Smith, "Sinners, Judges, and Cavalrymen: John Ford and Popular American Catholicism," in *American Catholic Traditions: Resources for Renewal*, ed. Sandra Yocum Mize and William L. Portier (New York: Orbis, 1997), 115–29. See also Blake, *AfterImage*,

129–76; Giles, *American Catholic Arts and Fiction*, 296–308; Lourdeaux, *Italian and Irish Filmmakers in America*, 88–128. Biographies of Ford include Tag Gallagher, *John Ford: The Man and His Films* (Berkeley: University of California Press, 1986); Scott Eyman, *Print the Legend: The Life and Times of John Ford* (New York: Simon and Schuster, 1999).

40. Paul Giles has also suggested interpreting the frontier in Ford's films as a "psychological state of mind" manifesting an "ambivalent" insider/outsider identity of Ford as an Irish American Catholic; see Giles, *American Catholic Arts and Fiction*, 304.

41. On Capra, see Lourdeaux, *Italian and Irish Filmmakers in America*, 130–62; Blake, *AfterImage*, 87–127. On Hitchcock, see ibid., 49–86; Giles, *American Catholic Arts and Fiction*, 324–35. Surprisingly, there is little written on McCarey. Besides Silver, which simplifies McCarey's Catholicism, see Jerome M. McKeever, "The McCarey Touch: The Life and Films of Leo McCarey" (Ph.D. diss., Case Western Reserve University, 2000). McCarey still awaits a published biography.

42. Lourdeaux, *Italian and Irish Filmmakers in America*, 130–62; Blake, *AfterImage*, 87–127.

43. See Walsh, *Sin and Censorship*, 84.

44. See "Vatican Over Hollywood," *Nation*, July 11, 1936, 33; Winchell Taylor, "Secret Movie Censors," *Nation*, July 9, 1938, 38–40; Elizabeth Yeaman, "The Catholic Movie Censorship," *New Republic*, October 5, 1938, 233–35.

45. See Lesley Brill, *John Huston's Filmmaking* (New York: Cambridge University Press, 1997), 125–42.

46. On the "American new realism" in late 1950s American movies, see Peter Lev, *History of the American Cinema*, vol. 7, *Transforming the Screen, 1950–1959* (New York: Charles Scribner's Sons, 2003), 241–44.

47. See May, *Big Tomorrow*, 205.

48. Fisher, "John M. Corridan, S.J. and the Battle for the Soul of the Waterfront, 1948–1954," *U.S. Catholic Historian* 16 (Fall 1998): 71–87, and Fisher, *On the Irish Waterfront*.

49. Judith E. Smith, *Visions of Belonging: Family Stories, Popular Culture, and Postwar Democracy, 1940–1960* (New York: Columbia University Press, 2004), 255–80.

50. *Extension*, June 1955, 51; "Boy Meets Girl, 1955," *Commonweal*, April 22, 1955, 77; see also J. E. Smith, *Visions of Belonging*, 277–78.

51. The notion of the film director as an auteur is a contested concept in film studies. For both a useful introduction and a stimulating reinterpretation of auteurism, see James Naremore, "Authorship," in *A Companion to Film Theory*, ed. Toby Miller and Robert Stam (Malden, Mass.: Blackwell, 2004), 9–24.

52. On Scorsese, see Blake, *AfterImage*, 25–47; Giles, *American Catholic Arts and Fiction*, 335–50; Lourdeaux, *Italian and Irish Filmmakers in America*, 217–66.

53. Quoted in Blake, *AfterImage*, 25.

54. Lourdeaux, *Italian and Irish Filmmakers in America*, 220–24; Blake, *AfterImage*, 25–27.

55. Ian Christie and David Thompson, eds., *Scorsese on Scorsese* (London: Faber and Faber, 2003), 12; see also Lourdeaux, *Italian and Irish Filmmakers in America*, 221–22.

56. Blake, *AfterImage*, 26.

57. Ibid., 25–48; Lourdeaux, *Italian and Irish Filmmakers in America*, 218–62; Giles, *American Catholic Arts and Fiction*, 335–50; Braudy, "Sacraments of Genre," 17–28.

58. Giles, *American Catholic Arts and Fiction*, 341.

59. On Coppola, see Blake, *AfterImage*, 177–215; Lourdeaux, *Italian and Irish Filmmakers in America*, 171–215. On Altman, see Patrick McGilligan, *Robert Altman: Jumping off the Cliff* (New York: St. Martin's, 1989), 35–38, 244; Giles, *American Catholic Arts and Fiction*, 308–23.

60. On Scorsese and Coppola, see Blake, *AfterImage*, 25–47, 177–215; Giles, *American Catholic Arts and Fiction*, 335–50; and Lourdeaux, *Italian and Irish Filmmakers in America*, 171–262. On Altman, see Giles, *American Catholic Arts and Fiction*, 308–23.

61. On the idea of the engagement of religious minorities with mainstream America as a cultural project of explanation, I draw upon Lila Corwin Berman's study of Reform rabbis' efforts to gain the respect of non-Jewish Americans in the mid-twentieth century; Berman, "Mission to America: The Reform Movement's Missionary Experiments, 1919–1960," *Religion and American Culture* 13 (2003): 205–39.

62. For an argument that makes the collapse of the Catholic subculture rather than Vatican II the central feature of twentieth-century American Catholicism, see William L. Portier, "Here Comes the Evangelical Catholics," *Communio* 31 (Spring 2004): 35–66.

63. On changes within the movie industry during the 1980s, see Stephen Prince, *History of American Cinema*, vol. 10, *A New Pot of God: Hollywood Under the Electronic Rainbow, 1980–1989* (New York: Charles Scribner's Sons, 2000).

64. Judith Miller, "'The Mission' Carries a Message From Past to Present," *New York Times*, October 26, 1986, section 2, page 19.

65. Richard Corliss, "And Then She Was a Nun," *Time*, June 1, 1992, 81; Janet Maslin, "Whoopi Goldberg on the Run, Disguised as Nun," *New York Times*, May 29, 1992, section C, page 10.

66. For a study of the construction of masculinity in Westerns, see Lee Clark Mitchell, *Westerns: Making the Man in Fiction and Film* (Chicago: University of Chicago Press, 1996).

67. On St. John, see J. A. Hanson, "Spiritual Subversion: The Films of Nicholas St. John," *Image* 20 (Summer 1998): 108–14.

68. Gavin Smith, "Dealing with the Now," in *American Independent Cinema: A Sight and Sound Reader*, ed. Jim Hillier (London: British Film Institute, 2001), 186.

69. See Christopher Noxon, "Is the Pope Catholic . . . Enough?," *New York Times Magazine*, March 9, 2003; Peter J. Boyer, "The Jesus War," *New Yorker*, September 15, 2003, 58–71; Frank Rich, "The Pope's Thumbs Up for Gibson's 'Passion,'" *New York Times*, January 18, 2004.

70. Recent books of the film and the controversies it created include Kathleen E. Corley and Robert L. Webb, eds., *Jesus and Mel Gibson's The Passion of the Christ: The Film, the Gospels and the Claims of History* (New York: Continuum, 2004); Jorge J. E. Gracia, ed., *Mel Gibson's Passion and Philosophy: The Cross, the Questions, the Controversy* (Chicago: Open Court, 2004); S. Brent Plate, ed., *Re-Viewing The Passion: Mel Gibson's Film and Its Critics* (New York: Palgrave, 2004).

71. See Boyer, "Jesus War."

72. For a discussion of *Santitos*, a recent example of film treatment of Mexican Catholicism, see Darryl V. Caterine, "Border Saints: Santitos" (1999), in McDannell, *Catholics in the Movies*, 277–96.

73. See David Bordwell, Janet Staiger, and Kristin Thompson, *The Classical Hollywood Cinema: Film Style and Mode of Production to 1960* (New York: Columbia University Press, 1985).

PART THREE

Prophetic Catholicism

American Catholic Social Thought in the Twentieth Century

Christopher Shannon

What is "social thought"? Modern secular intellectuals came to understand the "social" first in terms of economics: the social is the sum total of contractual exchanges made between free, autonomous individuals. Over the course of the twentieth century, this narrowly economic vision gave way to a more capacious understanding of the social proceeding from the anthropological conception of culture as a whole "way of life": the social is a deep pattern of values that shapes and structures organic communal life prior to relations of consent and contract. What is Catholic social thought? It is both more and simply other than its secular equivalent. The European Catholic intellectual tradition never accepted the primacy of contractual economic relation posited by the Enlightenment tradition running from Hobbes through Rousseau. Catholics confronted modernity equipped with an organic vision that secular moderns would only begin to approximate with their turn to culture in the early twentieth century; the challenge for Catholics would be to incorporate the realities of modern capitalist economics into a social theory that would remain true to fundamental Catholic moral and spiritual principles.

How to do this? Throughout the twentieth century, liturgy provided a firewall, so to speak, separating engagement from assimilation. How one understood the relation between the natural and the supernatural profoundly shaped how one understood political action and social justice; to the degree that Catholic intellectuals placed liturgy and the supernatural at the heart of their understanding of the social, Catholic social thought remained distinctly Catholic. In America, this dialectic of engagement and assimilation has played itself out in three main stages: a liturgical period, covering most of the first half of the twentieth century; a liberal/assimilationist period, stretching from the 1950s through the early 1980s, in which mainstream intellectuals came to subordinate liturgy and orthodox theology to secular norms of social justice; and finally, a renewed liturgical social vision that, since the 1980s, has sought to synthesize the best of the earlier two periods.

Historians conventionally date the birth of modern Catholic social thought with the publication of Leo XIII's encyclical *Rerum novarum*. Leo's landmark encyclical inaugurated the church's official engagement with the challenges industrial capitalism posed to a Catholic understanding of social order, but this understanding was itself the fruit of some nineteen hundred years of reflection and teaching on the relationship between faith and life. The biblical account of the early church presented in the Acts of the Apostles shows the new faith to be an all-encompassing communal commitment. St. Luke writes that "all who believed were together and had all things in common; and they sold their possessions and goods and distributed them to all, as any had need."[1] In the letters of St. Paul, this vision of the common life of the early Christians took on deeper theological significance through the metaphor of the church as the body of Christ: "For as in one body we have many members, and all the members do not have the same function, so we, though many, are one body in Christ, and individually members of another."[2] Taken together, these visions of the early church bequeathed a tradition of understanding social life as an organic unity modeled on the unity of organisms found in nature—most importantly, the human body. Even as the passage from Acts suggests a kind of egalitarian distributive ethic, so Paul's writings on the church as the body of Christ emphasized hierarchical ordering along with functional differentiation.

The Christianization of the Roman Empire in the fourth and fifth centuries added a political and juridical element to this understanding of the social nature of the church. Seeking to carve out an independent public role for itself within the empire, the church developed the theory of the "two swords." This theory received its classic early formulation in Pope Gelasius I's letter to the emperor Anastasius in 494, in which Gelasius insisted that while the church and the emperor were co-rulers of Christendom, the church possessed ultimate authority due to the primacy of the spiritual to the temporal. The church maintained this view of the ordering of spiritual and temporal authority throughout the Middle Ages, yet organic metaphors would persist through the imaginative rendering of medieval Christendom as a social body. The twelfth-century writer John of Salisbury acknowledged the temporal prince to be the head of this body, but insisted that the church, as the soul of the body, had "rulership over the whole thereof."[3] The juridical claims of the church, in particular of the papacy, proved a source of constant tension in Western Christendom up through the period of the Reformation. The so-called wars of religion of the sixteenth and seventeenth centuries were as much battles over conflicting ideas of political sovereignty as over conflicting understandings of theological truth.[4]

The Peace of Westphalia, which brought an end to these wars in 1648, seemed to settle this matter in favor of the princes. Protestant rulers secured their right to be free from the Roman Church; Catholic rulers affirmed their allegiance to Rome but set the terms for that allegiance by severely curtailing the independent authority of the church within their kingdoms. The additional shock of the French Revolution and the subsequent rise of liberal parliamentary regimes in nineteenth-century Europe threatened to reduce the legal status of the church to at best that of a private, voluntary association. Throughout the eighteenth and nineteenth centuries, popes continued to insist on the legitimacy of the church's earlier, pre-Westphalia claims to public authority. More broadly, papal encyclicals of this period affirmed what the historian Michael J. Schuck called "a 'territorial' communitarian ethic." Against the Enlightenment social-contract tradition that conceived of society as an assemblage of autonomous, rights-bearing individuals, the popes insisted on an understanding of self and society in which people derived identity and purpose from nonvoluntary obligations rooted in local attachments to family, friends, parishes, and villages.[5]

This short history of a long tradition is essential to navigating the twists and turns of twentieth-century Catholic social thought in the United States. The communitarianism of the broader Catholic social tradition informed Leo XIII's support for labor associations in *Rerum novarum*, yet it also informed his condemnation of "Americanism" in the apostolic letter *Testem benevolentiae* (1899). Americanism is a complicated issue, but the term basically refers to a movement to adapt the church in the United States to indigenous theological traditions of the primacy of individual conscience and political traditions of democracy and republican government.[6] Leo saw in both capitalism and Americanism an unrestrained individualism that respected no authority outside of the individual will.

Leo's successor, Pius X, also appears to be a sign of contradiction from the perspective of mainstream American liberalism. In his 1907 encyclical *Pascendi dominici gregis*, Pius issued a blanket condemnation of "modernism"—understood as the attempt to integrate modern, scientific, historical-critical methods into Catholic biblical scholarship and theology in general. Yet even as Pius closed down one area of theological exploration, he dedicated much of his papacy to enriching the spiritual life of the laity through a renewal of the liturgy. Distressed by the extravagance of operatic styles of singing that had crept into the liturgy during the nineteenth century, Pius encouraged the revival of Gregorian chant as a simpler singing style that the laity would be capable of learning so as to more fully participate in the liturgy. Pius also wished to draw the laity more into the liturgy of the Mass by encouraging the frequent reception of Communion with the decree *Sacra tridentina synodus* (1905). In extending to the laity a practice once thought the privilege of the clergy, Pius was no crypto-democrat. Critical modern reason and virtuoso operatic singing both struck Pius as expressions of modern individualism. The alternative to such fragmentation was integration through the liturgy. Catholic thinkers of the first half of the twentieth century shared Leo's and Pius's commitment to an ideal of integration, but often differed dramatically in the relative weight they gave to economics and liturgy as principles of integration; more contentiously, those who stressed economics often did so by embracing the language of at least one form of modern critical reason, social science.

The career of Monsignor John A. Ryan provides the best guide to the trajectory of social-scientific economic thought among Catholics in the United States. Ryan was ideally situated, in both place and time, to appreciate the radical critique of capitalism offered by *Rerum novarum* and translate its Catholic principles into an American idiom. Born May 25, 1869, in Vermillion, Minnesota, Ryan grew up that rarest of entities: an Irish

Catholic midwestern farm boy. The son of Irish immigrants, he grew up in a household that received Patrick Ford's *Irish World and Industrial Liberator*, a New York–based newspaper that provided the immigrant community in America with news of developments in the old country and preached a radical politics that equated capitalism with usury. News of the eviction of Irish tenant farmers at the hands of evil English landlords, along with Ford's critique of big business, resonated with the growing radicalism of midwestern American farmers who saw their way of life threatened by the development of an industrial economy. Ryan's father was a member of the populist National Farmer's Alliance, and John himself came under the rhetorical spell of the alliance's most charismatic orator, Ignatius Donnelly.[7]

Ryan's Minnesota upbringing also provided a more moderate model of Catholic engagement with America: the example of John Ireland, archbishop of St. Paul. A staunch Republican, real estate speculator, and close friend of railroad tycoon James J. Hill, Ireland was in certain respects a midwestern populist's worst nightmare. He was, however, in his own way, a progressive. As one of the leaders of the "Americanist" wing of the Catholic Church, Ireland was open to the possibilities offered by modern democracy and committed to ensuring that the Catholic Church would exercise a positive influence on American society as a whole. Educated as a youth by the Christian Brothers, Ryan early on sensed a vocation to the priesthood. In 1893, after five years of classical study, Ryan committed himself to his vocation and began the six-year program of clerical study at St. Paul Seminary. The timing of Ryan's enrollment would prove auspicious. That same year, Archbishop Ireland responded to Leo XIII's call to action in *Rerum novarum* by adding courses in economics and sociology to the seminary training of his priests. Soon, Ryan would blend Ireland's quintessentially American faith in social progress with the social critique found in Leo's encyclical to take U.S. Catholic economic thought in a direction well to the left of anything Ireland would have imagined.

A cursory reading of *Rerum novarum* could easily leave one wondering just what direction Leo himself wished faithful Catholics to take. As with subsequent social encyclicals, it is long on high ideals and short on practical programs. At the most basic level, *Rerum novarum* takes a clear stand against what in the 1890s seemed to be the two main social/political options facing the modern industrial West: individualistic, free-market capitalism and collectivist state socialism. Leo attacked both systems as practically and/or theoretically atheistic in their commitment to an amoral scientific understanding of social life. He insisted that the "social question"—that is, the fate of the working class under industrial capitalism—was fundamentally a moral and religious question; furthermore, he looked to the natural-law philosophy of Thomas Aquinas as the only intellectual tradition with the necessary resources for securing a just resolution to the conflict between labor and capital. In appealing to Thomas, Leo affirmed the church's traditional understanding of society as a hierarchical order, based on submission to rulers who ultimately derive their authority from God. At the same time, Leo steered the church in a decidedly modern direction by endorsing (nonsocialistic) labor unions as the legitimate representatives of the working class and affirming the duty of the state to intervene in economic matters to promote economic justice for the poor.[8]

Exposure to *Rerum novarum* turned Ryan away from his agrarian populist roots to a more direct engagement with the labor problem under industrial capitalism. As he moved on from seminary to pursue graduate study in moral theology at the Catholic University of America (CUA), Ryan managed to keep the social question at the center of his studies. Firmly rooted in Leo's understanding of medieval Thomism, Ryan nonetheless came to see the social question in comparatively modern terms as primarily the problem of achieving a more equitable distribution of the world's material resources—a goal he would later call "distributive justice." In 1905, he completed his doctoral dissertation on the "living wage," arguing that for a social order to be considered just, it must guarantee each worker a wage capable of supporting his family in modest comfort, regardless of what market competition might enable an employer to get away with paying. The following year, with the assistance of Richard T. Ely, a leading progressive economist, Ryan saw his dissertation published by the Macmillan Company as *A Living Wage: Its Ethical and Economic Aspects*. The reviews were plentiful, but mixed. Despite Ryan's Thomism, many Catholic moralists refused to accept the moral necessity of a living wage; because of his Thomism, mainstream secular economists dismissed his work as unscientific. Critics inside and outside the church were quick to tar Ryan with the damning brush of "socialist."[9]

Ely's endorsement pointed to the ultimate fate of Ryan's ideas. Hardly representative of his discipline, Ely was nonetheless at the intellectual center of that strain of Progressive Era reform that fought for a greater role for the state in the regulation of the economy. With the eventual triumph of this brand of reform in the New Deal, Ely and Ryan would both appear, in retrospect, as prophets of the new order. Ryan's intellectual alliance with a prominent non-Catholic also proved prophetic with respect to the ecumenical trajectory of Catholic social reform. In 1907, Ryan's willingness to work with Protestant and secular Progressives aroused in Catholics as much suspicion as his economic theories. Ryan looked to Jane Addams's Hull House as a model of forward-thinking social activism and bemoaned the lack of Catholic equivalents; many Catholic charity workers at the time thought the very idea of professional social work was nothing short of mercenary.[10] Still, while desiring to maintain separate institutions, socially concerned Catholic leaders were slowly following the lead of non-Catholic reformers in moving from charity toward new models of scientific social work. By 1910, Father William Kerby, a sociologist from CUA, presided over the first meeting of the National Conference of Catholic Charities (NCCC).

For Ryan, sociology provided an entering wedge into the whole gamut of Progressive reform. At the most basic level, it meant a shift from poor relief to the investigation and reform of the root structural causes of poverty. As early as 1909, Ryan mapped out an agenda for social reform virtually indistinguishable from the cutting edge of secular and Protestant Progressivism. In an article published in the *Catholic World* that year, Ryan called for a sweeping series of labor-reform measures, including a guaranteed minimum wage, an eight-hour day, unemployment and disability insurance, and legal protection for the right to organize unions. Beyond labor relations proper, Ryan advocated the public ownership of utilities, mines, and forests; public control of monopolies either through regulation or anti-trust legislation; and a progressive income tax.[11]

To the left of mainstream Catholic opinion, Ryan's position as professor of moral theology at CUA placed him at the center of the institutional developments that would shape Catholic social policy for the next fifty years. War is the health of bureaucracy, and the outbreak of World War I accelerated the trend toward bureaucratic centralization of Catholic institutional life initiated by the founding of the NCCC in 1910. In 1917, the American bishops created the National Catholic War Council (NCWC) primarily as an organization to provide for the material and spiritual needs of Catholic soldiers—not the least need being protection from similar Protestant efforts sponsored by the National Council of Churches. Located in Washington, D.C., the Catholic University became the natural home for this organization.

Catholics were as impressed as secular Progressives by the potential for positive social action offered by the bureaucratic centralization. After the war, the bishops established the renamed National Catholic Welfare Council (later Conference) as a permanent institution to gather and disseminate information relating to all aspects of Catholic life in the United States. Tapped to head up the council's Department of Social Action, Ryan used his position to continue to advocate for the reform agenda he had outlined in his 1909 *Catholic World* article. In 1919, through Ryan's influence, this agenda became, somewhat improbably, the official position of the U.S. Catholic bishops. In the face of a postwar recession and widespread fears of a Communist takeover of the United States, the National Catholic Welfare Council released a Ryan-drafted pastoral letter titled the "Program of Social Reconstruction." The letter explicitly endorsed the whole Progressive agenda, from protective labor legislation to the government regulation of monopolies. The novelist and socialist activist Upton Sinclair declared it a "Catholic miracle."[12]

In terms of practical impact, the "Program" was a bit of a false start. Then, as now, Catholics could be selective in what they chose to accept as authoritative teaching. Many Catholic business leaders dismissed the document as socialistic. At the same time, bitterness over the war and the eventual return of prosperity somewhat dampened the Progressive reform impulse in the nation's intellectual life. Ryan and other reform-minded Catholic intellectuals found themselves additionally challenged by a revival of anti-Catholic nativism, a development culminating in the national hate campaign directed against Al Smith, the Irish Catholic Democratic candidate for the presidency in 1928.

Ironically, Smith's loss ultimately proved a political gain for Catholics. Spared the blame for the ensuing Depression, Democrats came roaring back in 1932 with Franklin Delano Roosevelt. Personally quite contemptuous of Catholics, Roosevelt at least seemed to stand for much of the reform agenda progressive Catholics such as Ryan had advocated for decades. This reform agenda had recently received a papal reaffirmation in Pius XI's *Quadragesimo anno*, a document Roosevelt was politically savvy enough to cite in several key campaign speeches. Initially unenthusiastic about Roosevelt (his campaign speeches offered no clear sense of how he planned to address the economic crisis), Ryan eventually came on board, serving on several New Deal labor committees. Ryan was in no way personally close to Roosevelt (they met no more than four times during Roosevelt's twelve years in office), and his influence on actual New Deal policies is debatable. His biographer has judged that he "was more the New Deal's ambassador to Catholics than a Catholic legate to the New Deal." Still, he defended Roosevelt against the attacks of the popular radio priest Father Charles Coughlin in 1936, thus earning from Coughlin the nickname "Right-Reverend New Dealer." His delivery of the benediction at Roosevelt's Second Inaugural in 1937, moreover, helped to forge a symbolic link between the New Deal and Catholic social teaching, a link reinforced by overwhelming Catholic support for Roosevelt at the polls.[13]

This seemingly united Catholic front in support of the New Deal has obscured real divisions among Catholic intellectuals of the time with respect to the interpretation of Catholic social teaching. *Rerum novarum* endorsed both labor unions and an activist state as instruments for achieving a just social order but left unclear the precise nature of unions and the permissible extent of state intervention in the economy. As a general guide to judgment in matters of social organization, *Quadragesimo anno* offered subsidiarity, the principle that "no higher level association, like the State, should undertake a task that a lower level one, like a union or the family, could do as well."[14] Subsidiarity could of course cut either way—toward statism or localism—depending on how you judge a task well done. Ryan had from the start been partial to the state as an instrument of reform; prior to the 1930s, he had engaged in bitter battles with Catholics who viewed protective legislation regulating child labor as an unwarranted intrusion of the state into family life. Similarly, Ryan consistently supported the right of labor to organize, yet the trade and industrial unions of the 1930s were a far cry from the medieval guilds that provided the models for the "occupational groups" lauded by the papal social encyclicals. Ryan defended some notion of joint labor-management control of the means of production yet raised no serious opposition to the New Deal drift toward the ideal of a broker state, in which the national government would serve as a mediator between labor and capital, conceived of as distinct, if not necessarily hostile, interest groups.

The most consistently thoughtful alternative to the mainstream Catholic view developing under Ryan came from a German American layman, Frederick P. Kenkel. Inspired by the papal social encyclicals, Kenkel also drew on a specifically German tradition of Catholic social thought rooted in the life and work of Wilhelm von Ketteler, bishop of Mainz and one of the leading European Catholic critics of capitalism in the decades preceding *Rerum novarum*. In the first decades of the twentieth century, Kenkel opposed mainstream Progressivism in the name of a German Catholic alternative known as "Solidarism." Against piecemeal reform and bureaucratic regulation, Solidarism promoted a vision of economics rooted in small-scale communities of independent producers bound together in a harmonious social hierarchy of occupational groups. Kenkel feared that Progressive reform, including Ryan's Catholic version of it, accepted the division of society into antagonistic classes and simply sought to ameliorate the worst excesses of social conflict. Kenkel would settle for nothing short of the restoration of some sort of hierarchical organic society as had existed in the Middle Ages.[15] This uncompromising idealism put Kenkel at odds with the modern, egalitarian, bureaucratic welfare state developing under the New Deal.

Kenkel possessed something of the zeal of a convert. Baptized a Catholic, he grew up in a religiously indifferent household, and by the time of his young adulthood he considered himself a "New Pagan."[16] His family's financial circumstances allowed him to travel in Europe, where he indulged in a fully Romantic engagement with European culture. He married a German woman in a Lutheran ceremony, but her early death provoked a profound spiritual conversion. His continued attachment to European culture now took a more distinctly medieval direction. Long before his exposure to the social encyclicals, Kenkel had learned from German Romanticism to see the Middle Ages as a time of ideal spiritual and social order in which faith, art, and life were integrated into a harmonious whole. Some historians have dismissed Kenkel as a utopian dreamer, yet even skeptics concede the practical institutional achievements of his work with the Catholic Central Verein (CCV).[17] Founded in 1855, the CCV was a national union of local German American mutual aid societies. From its headquarters in St. Louis, the CCV served as a kind of national clearing house for coordinating local activities relating to social welfare, understood primarily in terms of charitable activities and life insurance. Drawn to the institution by its combination of ethnic culture and social concerns, Kenkel assumed the directorship of the Verein's Central Bureau in 1909. In the spirit of the Progressive Era, Kenkel used his position of leadership to move the organization beyond traditional charity to structural social reform. Still, unlike the scientific reform ideals of secular Progressives, Kenkel understood "structure" in terms of the medieval organicism extolled by German Romanticism and Leo's *Rerum novarum*. During the first ten years or so of Kenkel's directorship, the CCV experienced tremendous growth. Catholic social reform provided a new source of German identity in the wake of the decline of German language and culture among second- and third-generation German Americans. As director of the Central Bureau, Kenkel began publication of the *Central Blatt and Social Justice* to disseminate his corporatist ideas. Kenkel tempered his medieval organicism somewhat to accommodate the American situation, supporting fairly mainstream reform programs such as the recognition of labor unions and protective labor legislation.[18] Still, throughout the four decades in which he directed the Verein, Kenkel would serve as a consistent voice of opposition to state centralization. Even prior to the New Deal, Kenkel invoked the principle of subsidiarity to oppose legislation he felt would authorize "the Federal government . . . [to] engage in activities which, in their very nature, should be left to individuals, private organizations, municipalities, counties, and states."[19] Unlike mainstream American conservatism, Kenkel's opposition to centralized government power carried with it no endorsement of free-market economics. The state and the market were both impersonal "mechanical" institutions that threatened the integrity of "organic" local communities. Sadly, the New Deal consensus that triumphed in the 1930s largely wiped out this tradition of localism in mainstream Catholic thought.

As Kenkel's star fell in the years following World War I, there appeared other, deeper sources of dissent from the top-down, statist vision of social reform promoted by Ryan and the NCWC. For leaders of the emerging Liturgical Movement, Ryan's social vision suffered not merely from a somewhat loose interpretation of economic subsidiarity, but from a near-total neglect of the spiritual dimension of social life.[20] Historians usually date the emergence of the Liturgical Movement proper from 1926 with the founding of the journal *Orate Fratres* by Virgil Michel, a Benedictine monk of St. John's Abbey in

Collegeville, Minnesota. Michel shared much in temperament and ideals with Kenkel. He too had a life-changing experience after traveling in Europe and sought to transplant the organic, unified culture he found in rural Germany to the United States.[21] Committed like Kenkel to social reconstruction in line with *Rerum novarum*, Michel insisted that such reconstruction was impossible without the kind of liturgical renewal called for by Pius X.

The precise nature of the relation between the liturgical and the social was, of course, always somewhat unclear. The liturgy is, literally, "the work of the people," and Pius X clearly understood it as itself a social action, not merely an ornament to some more basic, material activity. Pius believed that the social and communal nature of liturgy had suffered in the modern world. Adopting a defensive posture in response to the institutional challenge of the Reformation, the church had for too long emphasized the external hierarchy at the expense of the understanding of the church as the mystical body of Christ; in defending the true presence of Christ in the Eucharist, the church had lost sight of the Eucharist as a communal sacrifice.[22] Reverence for the Eucharist had, unwittingly, discouraged Catholics from reception of the special sacramental grace that set them apart from Protestants.

Even in the United States, where Mass attendance was high, the central liturgy of the church hardly seemed to be the work of the people. As one liturgical reformer commented:

> To watch the average Catholic congregation at a morning Mass is often disedifying. . . .
> One is reading some private devotions in a prayer book. Another, is saying the Rosary.
> Another, perhaps, is making the Stations.
>   Possibly some, turning their backs on the altar, are kneeling before the shrine of some saint.[23]

Pius objected to what he saw as a kind of spiritual individualism and called for a communal ethic of "[a]ctive participation in the most holy mysteries and in the public and solemn prayer of the Church."[24] In addition to the frequent reception of Communion, he also insisted on the necessity of congregational singing at High Mass and promoted the revival of Gregorian chant.

In the pages of *Orate Fratres*, Michel took up the challenge of Pius X and provided a forum for reformers to exchange ideas on how to involve the laity more directly in the liturgy. Michel and his followers promoted early experiments in the use of dual language (Latin/vernacular) missals, the *Missa recitata* or dialogue mass, the popularization of the Divine Office, and of course, the revival of Gregorian chant. A friendly but serious critic of John Ryan, Michel insisted, "Not paper programs, not high sounding unfulfilled resolutions once renewed the world . . . but new and living men born out of the depths of Christianity."[25] Without directly opposing the liturgical movement, Ryan simply confessed his inability to see what Gregorian chant had to do with the fight to secure a living wage for workers. Yet for Michel, liturgy itself was the primary social action of Catholics, and any meaningful material reform would have to flow from a prior liturgical renewal. The liturgy was less a tool for social reform than a vessel of social order that would inspire analogous orderings in other areas of social life.[26]

This idea of analogies of order linked the Liturgical Movement to the broader program of Catholic Action promoted during the pontificate of Pius XI. Building on the work of his papal predecessors, Pius XI encouraged Catholic lay people to organize themselves in distinct apostolates organized according to specific social milieu—that is, workers minister to fellow workers, students to fellow students. Lay initiative and leadership were central to these organizations, but each was to have a clerical advisor to ensure its social work retained a proper and orthodox spiritual dimension.[27] As Michel believed the liturgy to be central to the spirituality of all Catholics, he forged links to various Catholic Action groups, most especially the National Catholic Rural Life Conference (NCRLC). Though founded by a priest, Father Edwin V. O'Hara, it met the Catholic Action goal of addressing Catholics in a particular milieu—a milieu that fit nicely with the rural, agrarian ideals Michel drew from his understanding of medieval Catholic culture. Michel's medievalism proved too anti-modern for O'Hara and the other leaders of the NCRLC. Though open to Michel's liturgical reforms, the NCRLC thought his social ideals impractical and, more tellingly, un-American.[28] Ironically, Michel found his true kindred spirits in a Catholic Action movement that began in an urban, industrial setting, the Catholic Worker (CW).

Though its legacy is ambiguous and contested, the Catholic Worker remains the gold standard for Catholic radicalism in the United States. Founded in 1933 by Dorothy Day and Peter Maurin, it stood at the far opposite pole from John Ryan's New Deal, statist Catholicism. Like Kenkel, Day and Maurin rejected centralized state action in favor of local community; like Michel, they insisted that the material problems of modern civilization were ultimately spiritual problems that needed to be addressed through liturgical renewal. Day and Maurin met in December of 1932. Day had spent much of her adult life working as a secular journalist and activist in service of a variety of left-wing labor causes. Following her conversion to Catholicism in 1927, she had been searching for some way to combine her new faith with her old commitment to social justice. Maurin was a French émigré vagabond, well-versed in the social teachings of the church but searching for some way to put them into practice. By early 1933, the two had agreed upon a three-pronged strategy to reconstruct the social order along Christian lines: first, they would publish a newspaper, the *Catholic Worker*, to disseminate their ideas; second, they would establish "houses of hospitality" to practice the corporal works of mercy among the urban poor; third, they would set up farms that could become the basis for a renewed Catholic agrarian order.[29]

Against the growing impersonal order of state and corporation, the Catholic Worker promoted the idea of personalism that Maurin had learned from his reading of the French philosopher Emmanuel Mounier. Though reflecting elements of modern existentialism and phenomenology, personalism served Day and Maurin as a modern idiom through which to revive a Franciscan ethic of holy poverty. For Day and Maurin, the true Christian was called not simply to serve the poor, but to be poor. Maurin distinguished holy poverty from destitution less by material wealth than spiritual circumstances. Acknowledging that many urban workers lacked basic material subsistence, he saw the social and spiritual rootlessness of modern urban life as the greatest injustice. Drawing on his own peasant childhood in the south of France, Maurin insisted that the model of rural life developed in premodern, Catholic Europe was the only antidote to modern rootlessness.[30]

Day did not always see eye to eye with Maurin on rural life, but their shared commitment to holy poverty put them at odds with other Catholic groups seeking to address the plight of the modern worker. One such group, the Association of Catholic Trade Unionists (ACTU), actually grew out of discussions among Catholic laymen meeting around the kitchen table at the Catholic Worker house in New York City. Unlike the Catholic Worker, the ACTU drew exclusively on actual union members for its membership and leadership.[31] The ACTU understood its particular charism in terms of training Catholic labor activists who would then assume leadership positions in their particular unions. Catholic labor leaders would then work to purge unions of the influence of Communists and organized crime as they strove to direct unions toward building up an authentically Christian social order. Though very much a grassroots organization, the ACTU's social vision shared more with the top-down vision of a John Ryan than with the anti-modern localism of the Catholic Worker. As articulated by founding member John C. Cort, the ACTU's labor goals were not readily distinguishable from that of the non-Catholic (and non-Communist) labor organizations: decent wages and working conditions, job security, the right to strike, and collective bargaining.[32] This rough consensus on goals united the ACTU with the clerical labor education institutions by the Jesuits.

Top-down statists such as John Ryan and grassroots labor leaders such as John Cort continued to speak a distinctively Catholic language derived from the social encyclicals throughout the 1930s. Still, some within the mainstream of Catholic activism began to share the Catholic Worker's suspicion that involvement in practical politics was compromising a distinctive Catholic social vision. The most significant critic of the mainstream Catholic reform agenda came from Paul Hanly Furfey. A professor of sociology at CUA during the 1930s, Furfey rejected Ryan's NCWC brand of activism for the more radical models offered by groups such as the Catholic Worker. For Furfey, just as "the sources of revelation form our textbook of Catholic social theory," so the lives of the saints "form our textbook of Catholic social action."[33] An academic insider, Furfey could speak with some authority on the limitations of the dominant scientific approaches to social problem solving. Conceding that the social sciences offered certain investigative techniques that facilitated some necessary fact gathering, he nonetheless insisted that facts were at best second premises in a theological syllogism that begins and ends with revealed truth.

Furfey saw more deeply and radically than earlier Catholic critics of professional social work just how the new scientific models of social problem solving inhibited the production of heroic saints. In his 1936 manifesto *Fire on the Earth*, Furfey critiqued the limitations of secular reform through a kind of anti-litany of the saints: we denounce racial injustice but have no St. Peter Claver; we call out for economic justice but have no St. Francis of Assisi; we organize Boy Scout troops but have no St. John Bosco; we have Catholic social workers but no Blessed Angela of Foligno. On this last point, Furfey offers an explicitly liturgical critique of modern textbook social science: "Our social workers learn their methods from Mary Richmond; but Blessed Pierre Eymard learned his from the Blessed

Sacrament." Scientific social work may accomplish some real natural good, but it will never accomplish real Catholic social action.[34]

Furfey located the distinguishing marks of authentic Catholic Action in two dimensions: "personalist" motivation and the model of the cross. He defined personalist action as "external action which is performed by a person as a member of the Mystical Body rather than as a member of the state." Here Furfey directly attacked the drift toward secularism that he saw in the thought of John Ryan and the Catholic social-work profession. Motivation was more important than results. The natural goods of social work lack the spirit of charity if pursued for reasons other than the building up of the mystical body of Christ; Furfey condemned them as St. Paul condemned those good works performed without the spirit of love. Though often associated with a kind of Catholic romanticism, Furfey explicitly rejected the ethics of authenticity commonly associated with romantic politics: people act most authentically not when they are true to themselves, but when they direct their action outward toward participation in a distinctly Catholic social whole, the mystical body of Christ.[35]

Like Michel, Furfey insisted that the liturgy is the primary social action of the Catholic. Perhaps more so than Michel, however, Furfey offered some intimation as to how liturgy connects with life. Lest the middle-class professional appropriate mystical body imagery to provide a theological gloss on modern social work, Furfey offered the following model of how Catholic social action "works":

> Think of what this means! A priest in Burma is overwhelmed by the difficulties of his position, but he suddenly finds his burden lifted because a peasant girl in Belgium has made a good Communion. A despairing man in Paris is saved from suicide because a woman in Brazil gives some money to a beggar. Something like this—if we were permitted to see it—would be the activity of the Mystical Body of Christ.[36]

Such action does not, of course, lend itself to program planning, outcomes assessment, and the whole bureaucratic toolbox of what passes for social action in the modern world. This was precisely the reason Furfey embraced it as an authentically Catholic model of social action.

Deliberatively provocative, Furfey affirmed this "supernatural sociology" not as a romantic reaction against modern reason, but as part of a broader affirmation of the model offered by Jesus, the folly of the cross. Furfey rejected realism, or what he called "prudence," because Jesus rejected it. Jesus's lack of prudence led to his death on Calvary, but that in turn led to his resurrection and the birth of the church, whose continued existence two thousand years after the crucifixion testifies to the triumph of the cross. Confronting the catastrophic material suffering of the Great Depression, Furfey still insisted that Catholics are called not simply to help the poor but to be poor, to share in the poverty and humiliation of the poor: "Such must be the keynote of Catholic social action. We must steel ourselves for suffering. We must joyfully embrace the cross."[37] As a guide to Catholic Action, Furfey pointed to the saints who imitated the suffering of Christ:

> They teach us the eloquence of suffering. They teach us that hard methods are more likely to get results simply because their difficulty is itself eloquent. This does not mean

that propaganda always fails when it is painless, but it does mean that in the long run, we must suffer to succeed.[38]

Furfey conceded that this model of sainthood may not be for all. Poverty and suffering voluntarily undertaken may bring great grace; imposed from without, they may be occasions for sin. Still, Catholics must look to the saints rather than to secular modes of social activism. Catholic social action is primarily a matter not of solving problems, but of bearing witness. Success in bearing witness, in turn, depends on the grace of God rather than the approval of the world.

Furfey's hard sayings were at once traditional and radical. At one level, they reflected a peculiarly Catholic struggle to realize the premodern social and theological ideals of medieval Catholicism within a modern social setting largely the product of an explicit rejection of those ideals. At another level, Furfey's critique reflected a broader questioning of the assumptions of the modern world on the part of the secular heirs to the Enlightenment. The Great Depression called into question not only the virtues of free-market capitalism, but also the whole economic worldview that understood human beings primarily as rational utility maximizers motivated by material self-interest. Secular intellectuals began to argue (or at least, to hope) that the root of social unity lay not in the smooth functioning of economic exchange relations, but in a deeper set of shared values—a culture, a whole way of life. Inspired by the work of anthropologists such as Margaret Mead and Ruth Benedict, intellectuals looked to "primitive," non-Western cultures for alternative models of social organization.

Mead and Benedict rejected the notion of a generic "primitive" and stressed the unique nature of each culture they studied. Still, they argued that non-Western societies seemed to share a common trait of subordinating economic life to other, noneconomic values; in each of these societies, some deeper set of values provided the foundation or unifying "pattern" for the people's culture. Adapting this mode of analysis to modern America, anthropologically minded intellectuals located the deep pattern of American culture in the values of individual liberty and political democracy, timeless values that transcended the historically contingent environment of free-market economics in which they happened to develop during the nineteenth century.[39] As Furfey called Catholics to the folly of the cross, so secular intellectuals sought to transform democracy from a set of political institutions to something like a transcendent faith.

Secular intellectuals were as divided as Catholics over the relation between economics and culture. If a figure such as John Ryan simply could not see the relation between liturgy and social action, then many secular intellectuals thought the turn to culture a positive distraction from the real issues of the day. Significantly, a key group of secular intellectuals, led by the philosopher Sidney Hook, saw the turn to culture as a symptom of a kind of creeping Catholicism in American intellectual life.[40] To be fair, the appeal to culture was indeed in many ways a search for a substitute Catholicism—a social ideal that could evoke the organic unity associated with the Catholic Middle Ages without sacrificing the individual freedom understood as the great achievement of the modern world. With the outbreak of World War II, the appeal to culture, and increasingly to myth and symbol, struck Hook alternatively as fostering either a retreat from the real problems facing America or a kind of homegrown totalitarianism through the propagandistic manipulation of cultural symbols and values.

Far from bringing these issues to a head, the war ultimately swept them under the carpet. Military victory obscured a multitude of intellectual divisions, and postwar prosperity rendered the culture vs. economics debates of the 1930s moot. Hook's brand of intellectual anti-Catholicism survived into the early postwar period, but Catholics by and large emerged from World War II with a sense of themselves as solidly in the American mainstream, indeed as major players in a new national "consensus" that embraced religious diversity as never before in U.S. history.[41] The triumph of the New Deal welfare state lent something like canonical status to John Ryan as the authoritative interpreter of the papal social encyclicals. Catholics debated the relative merits of top-down vs. bottom-up labor activism, and some held the emerging corporate order to the medieval guild model evoked by the papal encyclicals.[42] Prosperity and the Cold War demand for unity made this debate moot. By the material standards of the Great Depression, postwar America was a worker's paradise.

Postwar Catholics retained the language of the prewar tradition, but the meaning of the old terms underwent a significant shift. "Social justice," once a broad term evoking Aristotelian and Thomistic notions of the proper order of society, now pointed almost exclusively to a narrower notion of distributive justice, understood as the more-or-less egalitarian distribution of wealth, power, and opportunity.[43] By virtue of their location in the industrial centers of the Northeast and Midwest, Catholics shared somewhat disproportionally in postwar prosperity. Commitment to distributive justice thus often led Catholic activists to consider the plight of non-Catholic populations, most especially African Americans.[44] Participation in the civil rights movement reinforced the ecumenical sense of a common American identity that transcended "narrow" denominational or confessional traditions.[45] In light of this common identity and a shared commitment to distributive justice, most of what was unique to Catholic social thought now appeared as an obstacle to the "common good." Poverty and suffering, once a means to sanctity, now came to be seen as problems to be solved along with any number of other social injustices.[46] Still largely aligned with the Democratic Party, Catholics followed the trajectory of reform from F.D.R.'s New Deal to Lyndon Johnson's Great Society, with increasingly less of anything distinctively Catholic to bring to their activism.

By the late 1960s, liberal reform gave way to radical revolt in the New Left, Black Power, and antiwar movements. Catholic radicals found inspiration in the Catholic Worker, but as with their liberal counterparts, they were very selective in their appropriation of the Catholic past, discarding most of the liturgical and devotional elements of Catholic social thought. In his 1972 work *The Renewal of American Catholicism*, historian and activist David O'Brien rendered this assessment of the Catholic Worker tradition:

> By today's standards they were theologically conservative, for they found in the liturgy a
> basis for community and a model of society, the Mystical Body of Christ. Today's
> Catholics have been greatly influenced by the Catholic Worker's insistence on personal

responsibility, but they are less able to regard the liturgy as central to their social and political concerns, even if many find it crucial to their religious life.[47]

Short of endorsing atheistic Marxism, the economic agenda of post–Vatican II liberal and radical Catholics remained within the bounds of orthodoxy. Still, the tendency of progressive Catholics to link their social concerns to a rejection of old devotional and liturgical forms made even conventional attacks on poverty seem, by association, almost heretical. The near-universal rejection by liberal Catholics of the church's reaffirmation of its traditional ban on artificial birth control in *Humanae vitae* lent further weight to the conservative tendency to associate the social justice agenda with heresy. That the emerging Catholic conservative intellectual movement rallied less around a defense of *Humanae vitae* than an endorsement of free-market economics shows how far both liberals and conservatives had fallen from the distinctly Catholic vision of the early twentieth century.[48]

Much of Catholic life in the postwar period appears as a revolt against Catholic intellectual and social traditions. Distinctly Catholic terminology suggested attachment to the world of the Catholic ghetto that assimilated Catholic activists were happy to leave behind.[49] Such assimilation anxiety undermined efforts to deal with the most pressing "social" challenge facing the church in the postwar United States: the pastoral care of the growing Latino population. Latino Catholicism in the postwar United States became a battle ground for the two visions of Catholic social thought that we have examined so far. From this battle we also see the emergence of a new synthesis capable of rejuvenating the best of these two earlier visions.

At first glance, new immigration from Puerto Rico and Mexico would seem to have provided an opportunity for building on older traditions of Catholic Action to forge a distinctly Catholic response to the struggle for racial justice. Puerto Ricans and Mexicans were, unlike African Americans, predominantly Catholic; despite certain language barriers, Catholic activists at least had a common faith to bridge what was perceived to be a racial divide. Still, the question remained, which Catholicism? The traditional folk Catholicism immigrants brought with them from their native countries, the standardized, pan-ethnic devotions of the "traditional" American parish, or some new forms being concocted by liturgical reformers now less concerned with reviving Gregorian chant than proving their independence from the ghetto Catholicism of their parents? The most unlikely answer came from the most unlikely of places: a revival of folk religion under the careful watch of that arch-Americanizer, Cardinal Francis Spellman.

Cheap flights and U.S. citizenship flooded Spellman's New York archdiocese with Puerto Rican immigrants in the early 1950s. Heir to an Irish American tradition of relegating new immigrants to basement masses, Spellman hardly saw the Puerto Rican migration as an opportunity for the church to make a statement about racial justice; nevertheless, he sincerely feared the loss of Puerto Rican Catholics to the secularism, materialism, and cultural Protestantism that threatened all Catholics in the United States. In seeking to reach out to Puerto Rican Catholics, Spellman found his most successful missionary in the figure of Father Ivan Illich. A brilliant, cosmopolitan intellectual of noble Austrian descent, Illich arrived in New York in 1952 ostensibly to pursue further historical studies at

Princeton University; in actuality, he came to America largely to flee a promising though undesirable career in the Holy See's diplomatic corps. Assigned to Incarnation parish, a historically Irish American parish in the Washington Heights section of Manhattan, Illich found himself at the heart of the Great Migration of Puerto Ricans to New York. Because of his ability to master Spanish, a feat that eluded his largely working-class Irish colleagues, Illich quickly assumed control of Spellman's outreach to Spanish-speaking Catholics.[50]

Attracted to the challenge, Illich may have perhaps succumbed to an enduring intellectual weakness for exoticizing the culture of the "other." Still, he was clearly no more a conventional progressive than was Spellman. Illich was a traditionalist in the mode of Paul Hanly Furfey—not by direct influence, but by virtue of a common Catholic intellectual patrimony. He recognized the real material needs facing Puerto Rican immigrants, yet like Furfey realized that Catholic witness demands that one not simply help the poor, but be poor. To break down the physical distance at Incarnation between the Euro-American parish staff and the Puerto Rican congregation, Illich rented an apartment in a tenement and turned it into *El Cuartito de Maria* (the Little House of Mary). As a service project, *El Cuartito* provided free childcare for the women of the tenement. Illich nonetheless saw the primary purpose of the apartment as simply establishing a neighborly presence for the church in the Puerto Rican community.

Illich's greatest achievement was undoubtedly the establishment of the Fiesta de San Juan. Having traveled to Puerto Rico to soak up the folk Catholicism of the countryside, Illich returned to New York inspired to recreate the folk community in the city. In 1955, he organized a *Fiesta de San Juan* to serve as a day for Puerto Rican Catholics to celebrate their religious and cultural heritage. Naming the event after the patron saint of Puerto Rico, Illich conceived of the celebration on the model of traditional *fiestas patronales*, which freely mixed religious processions and a solemn High Mass with picnicking, card playing, music, dance, and theatre. If the Irish could have St. Patrick's Day on March 17, Illich reasoned, the Puerto Ricans should have St. John's Day on June 24. Spellman could hardly argue with that logic, so he agreed to allow the use of the great quadrangle at Fordham University for the event—with himself as the guest of honor, of course. Illich took charge of promotional efforts, placing ads in Spanish-language newspapers and eliciting support from slick Madison Avenue executives. On June 23, the eve of the feast, the police estimated they would need officers to control a crowd of about 5,000; the next day, 35,000 people descended on Fordham for a celebration of ethnic cultural identity unprecedented in postwar America.

Illich's success proved his undoing. Pushed upstairs, in a sense, to direct a missionary training program at the Catholic University of Puerto Rico, Illich found himself increasingly at odds with church leaders on the proper goals of missionary work. Despite his success in New York and the continued support of the very powerful Cardinal Spellman, Illich found little enthusiasm for his folk-revival strategy of missionary work. The hierarchy in the United States and Latin America was instead committed to some type of modernization—that is, remaking Latin America in the image of the United States—as the only "realistic" response to the pastoral challenges faced by widespread poverty and a severe shortage of priests. Illich drifted around Latin America until he found a sympathetic clerical patron in Sergio Mendez Arceo, bishop of Cuernavaca, Mexico. Under Arceo's protection, Illich founded the Center for Intercultural Documentation (CIDOC), an all-purpose intellectual meeting ground that he fondly referred to as his "center of de-Yankeefication." From his base at CIDOC, Illich would go on in the 1960s and 1970s to produce the most profound critique of the culture and economics of Western capitalism to emerge from that general intellectual ferment known as the "counter culture." Illich never sought laicization, but his continuing run-ins with church authorities and his unwillingness to subordinate the gospel to a political program led him to withdraw from active service in the priesthood. His refusal to speak publicly as a Catholic priest obscured the Catholic origins and substance of his thought and deprived American Catholics of the most compelling model of radical traditionalism available in the late twentieth century.

Back in New York, Illich's successors in the Spanish-speaking apostolate were stumbling toward a new form of Yankeefication under the rubric of "social justice." Whereas Illich understood the *Fiesta de San Juan* as an intrinsically political act by virtue of its ability to embody and display traditional Puerto Rican communal values, progressive-minded U.S. priests (mis)understood the festival as a potential tool for political consciousness raising. The promiscuous mingling of the sacred and the secular, the essence of the spirit of carnival, soon came under attack. Monsignor Robert Fox, who assumed the position of director of the Office of Spanish-American Catholic Action in 1963, sought to "free" the festival from its medieval "parochialism." Attempting to reach out to the broader Latino population, he changed the name of the event from the *Fiesta de San Juan* to the *Fiesta de la Comunidad Hispaña*. In the name of opening the church to the world, the next year he accepted federal government funds from the War on Poverty programs, thus barring religious figures from leadership positions in the festival. Finally, Fox shifted the focus of the celebration from class harmony to class resentment, using the festival as an occasion to call attention to the economic subordination of Latinos in America.

Fox was completely in tune with the best liberal-progressive thinking of the day—and completely out of touch with the Puerto Ricans under his pastoral care. Puerto Rican Catholics resented being subsumed under the multinational category of "Latino" and shifted their loyalties toward the secular, nationalistic Puerto Rican Day Parade held on the first weekend of June. Fox's social-justice agenda could never quite shake the assumption of the need for racial uplift, and his new-model festival seemed too dour an affair to attract non-Puerto Rican Latinos, who expected something called a festival to be, well, festive. Fox's tenure in the Puerto Rican apostolate appears in retrospect a classic melodrama of middle-class alienation, with an intellectual trying to connect to a vision of "the people" that merely reflected the idealized self-image of the intellectual.[51]

Fox's work with Puerto Ricans did have one redeeming moment worthy of Illich's original vision. In 1967, a riot broke out in Spanish Harlem following a police shooting of an unarmed Puerto Rican man. As night fell, Mayor John Lindsay pleaded with people to stay off the streets. Reasoning that such a course of action would only leave the streets open to the most violent in the community, Fox instead organized a night-time peace procession in which he led Puerto Rican Catholics in the recitation of the rosary. The presence of the rosary procession was enough to keep the peace through the night and restore order to the community. The lesson, of course, is that Fox finally succeeded in inspiring action for social justice only after appealing to an indigenous Puerto Rican—and Catholic—tradition not explicitly related to modern conceptions of "social justice." Fox's rosary procession did not put an end to police shootings of poor minorities, but then again, neither have more conventional or "practical" programs of social protest. By the standard of effectiveness, few programs of protest can claim more than a mixed record. Regardless of their ability to affect tangible social change, the rosary and the *Fiesta de San Juan* connect people to a mythic story capable of unifying them in the face of life's failures and disappointments.

For progressive, non-Latino Catholics, the lesson of the Harlem rosary fell on deaf ears. Still, Latinos of the late 1960s raised up for themselves an authentically Catholic social activist capable of combining concrete social activism with an orthodox Catholic liturgical sensibility: Cesar Chavez. A Mexican American working as a migrant farm laborer in California, Chavez was for his time what Catholic labor organizers of the 1930s had been for industrial unionism. Chavez was schooled both in the social encyclicals and in *Cursillo*, a mid-century Catholic Action program geared toward developing a more interior spiritual life. He combined these Catholic traditions with the principle of nonviolent resistance drawn from Gandhi and Martin Luther King Jr. to fight the exploitation of migrant workers. Chavez organized the workers into a union, the United Farm Workers, and led a successful five-year strike (1965–69) for fair labor contracts with California's grape growers.[52] Progressive Euro-American Catholics rallied to Chavez's heroic witness, yet as with their treatment of the legacy of Dorothy Day, they tended to subordinate the theologically orthodox dimensions of Chavez's activism to his social-justice concerns.[53]

At the opening of the twenty-first century, Catholic social thought appears to be coming full circle. Liberal and conservative Catholics still fight the battles of the 1960s, yet there have in recent years been signs of an emerging consensus perhaps best captured by the label "radical orthodoxy."[54] The intellectuals comprising this movement share a conventionally radical disdain for the social and political norms of middle-class American life with a very unconventional insistence that the only real alternative to this life lies in a fruitful engagement with the Catholic tradition on its own terms. In the work of Robert Brimlow, the much-derided "ghetto" once again becomes an ideal of community; in the work of a William Cavanaugh, the Eucharist itself becomes a political act.[55] Among Latino Catholics, theologians such as Roberto Goizueta look to traditional rituals such as the *Via crucis* as embodying an alternative vision of community against the dominant Western individualism imposed on Latinos in the name of social uplift.[56] In different ways, these scholars seek to break the grip of a progressive narrative that dismisses appeals to tradition as nostalgia for a past that never existed. They share a common intellectual experience of having been through the mill of progressivism and found it wanting. As mainstream U.S. Catholics fight to hold on to the middle-class comforts they achieved in the postwar years and Latinos struggle to secure their piece of the American dream, it remains to be seen if this radical orthodoxy will find an audience beyond the increasingly academic world of Catholic intellectual life.

NOTES

1. Acts 2:44–45 (RSV).

2. Rom 12:4–5 (RSV).

3. Quoted in James Bruce Ross and Mary Martin McLaughlin, *The Portable Medieval Reader* (New York: Viking Penguin, 1949), 47.

4. On this point, see William T. Cavanaugh, *The Myth of Religious Violence: Secular Ideology and the Roots of Modern Conflict* (New York: Oxford University Press, 2009).

5. Michael J. Schuck, *That They Be One: The Social Teaching of the Papal Encyclicals, 1740–1989* (Washington, D.C.: Georgetown University Press, 1991), 31, 32.

6. For a full-length account of this controversy, see Thomas T. McAvoy, C.S.C., *The Great Crisis in American Catholic History, 1895–1900* (Chicago: Henry Regnery, 1957).

7. Francis L. Broderick, *Right Reverend New Dealer: John A. Ryan* (New York: MacMillan, 1963), 3–8.

8. This summary owes much to Joseph M. McShane, *"Sufficiently Radical": Catholicism, Progressivism and the Bishops' Program of 1919* (Washington, D.C.: The Catholic University of America Press, 1986), 30–36.

9. Broderick, *Right Reverend New Dealer*, 37, 40–47.

10. Ibid., 57, 65.

11. Ibid., 57–58.

12. Charles Morris, *American Catholics: The Saints and Sinners Who Built America's Most Powerful Church* (New York: Vintage, 1998), 151.

13. Broderick, *Right Reverend New Dealer*, 208, 211, 227, 230.

14. Morris, *American Catholics*, 150.

15. Philip Gleason, *The Conservative Reformers: German-American Catholics and the Social Order* (Notre Dame, Ind.: University of Notre Dame Press, 1968), 131–35.

16. Ibid., 91.

17. For this mixed assessment, see ibid., 143.

18. Ibid., 128–29.

19. Quoted in Kevin E. Schmiesing, *Within the Market Strife: American Catholic Economic Thought from "Rerum Novarum" to Vatican II* (Lanham, Md.: Lexington, 2004), 92.

20. Keith F. Pecklers, *The Unread Vision: The Liturgical Movement in the United States of America: 1926–1955* (Collegeville, Minn.: Liturgical Press, 1998), 87–90.

21. Ibid., 20.

22. Godfrey Diekmann, O.S.B., "The Primary Apostolate," in *The American Apostolate: American Catholics in the Twentieth Century*, ed. Leo R. Ward (Westminster: Newman Press, 1952), 29–31.

23. Paul Hanly Furfey, *Fire on the Earth* (New York: Macmillan, 1936), 57. I would like to acknowledge a special debt to Gene McCarraher, who first introduced me to the work of Furfey. For the best short treatment of Furfey's intellectual career, see Eugene B. McCarraher, "The Church Irrelevant: Paul Hanly Furfey and the Fortunes of American Catholic Radicalism," *Religion and American Culture* 7, no. 2 (Summer 1997): 163–94.

24. Quoted in Diekmann, "Primary Apostolate," 31.

25. Quoted in David J. O'Brien, *American Catholics and Social Reform: The New Deal Years* (New York: Oxford University Press, 1968), 191.

26. For the distinction between "tool" and "vessel" as two distinct spiritual orientations, see Max Weber, *The Protestant Ethic and the Spirit of Capitalism* (Mineola: Dover, 2003), 113–14.

27. On this brand of Catholic Action, see Jim Cunningham, "Specialized Catholic Action," in Ward, *American Apostolate*, 47–65.

28. See Craig Prentiss, *Debating God's Economy: Social Justice in America on the Eve of Vatican II* (University Park: Pennsylvania State University Press, 2008), esp. chapter 2, "Sanctifying Life on the Land."

29. O'Brien, *American Catholics and Social Reform*, 196.

30. For the social philosophy of the Catholic Worker, see Francis J. Sicius, *Peter Maurin: Apostle to the World* (Maryknoll, N.Y.: Orbis, 2004).

31. Prentiss, *Debating God's Economy*, 102.

32. Ibid., 103.

33. Furfey, *Fire on the Earth*, 9.

34. Ibid., 10–15.

35. Ibid., 36, 92.

36. Ibid., 48.

37. Ibid., 78.

38. Ibid., 110.

39. See, in general, Christopher Shannon, *Conspicuous Criticism: Tradition, the Individual and Culture in American Social Thought, from Veblen to Mills* (Baltimore: Johns Hopkins University Press, 1996).

40. For Hook's attack on Catholicism, see Sidney Hook, "The New Failure of Nerve," *Partisan Review* 10 (January–February 1943): 17, 19, 20. For the best detailed historical account of this controversy, see John T. McGreevy, "Thinking on One's Own: Catholicism in the American Intellectual Imagination, 1928–1960," *Journal of American History* 84 (June 1997): 97–131.

41. On this, see McGreevy, *Catholicism and American Freedom: A History* (New York: W. W. Norton, 2003), especially Chapter 6, "American Freedom and Catholic Power," 166–88.

42. See Prentiss, *Debating God's Economy*, Chapter 6, "Industrial Councils," 199–235.

43. For a nice vignette on changing notions of social justice, see the account of Father Andrew McDonagh's attempts to advance this new notion of distributive justice at a Chicago parish in Alan Ehrenhalt, *The Lost City: The Forgotten Virtues of Community in America* (New York: Basic, 1995), 120, 122.

44. The definitive study of how the civil rights movement transformed the Catholic understanding of social justice remains McGreevy, *Parish Boundaries: The Catholic Encounter with Race in the Twentieth-Century Urban North* (Chicago: University of Chicago, 1996).

45. The classic primary text on this political ecumenism is Will Herberg, *Protestant, Catholic, Jew: An Essay in American Religious Sociology* (Garden City, N.Y.: Doubleday, 1960).

46. On this point, I draw on the argument advanced in Joseph P. Chinnici, O.F.M., "From Sectarian Suffering to Compassionate Solidarity: Joseph Cardinal Bernardin and the American Catholic Language of Suffering," unpublished paper delivered at the Cushwa Center for the Study of American Catholicism, University of Notre Dame, March 9, 2000.

47. O'Brien, *The Renewal of American Catholicism* (New York: Paulist Press, 1972), 20.

48. On the emergence of conservative, free-market Catholicism, see Prentiss, *Debating God's Economy*, Chapter 4, "Sanctifying American Capitalism." For a better sense of the range of Catholic conservatism in the postwar period, see Patrick Allitt, *Catholic Intellectuals and Conservative Politics in America, 1950–1985* (Ithaca, N.Y.: Cornell University Press, 1993). The church's official response to President Obama's recent HHS mandate requiring Catholic institutions to provide medical insurance for the purchase of birth control is revealing. For all of the supposed traditionalism of the current generation of bishops, the leaders of the church in America have framed the issue almost entirely as one of religious freedom for Catholics rather than an opportunity to evangelize Catholics and non-Catholics on the truth of the church's teaching on birth control. One can only surmise that "conservative" American bishops believe that the American principle of religious liberty is a more effective rallying cry than the church's teaching on birth control.

49. For a nice account of the fate of the Catholic ghetto written at the time of its demise, see Gleason, *Conservative Reformers*, 2, 216–20.

50. My account of Illich and his successor, Robert Fox, draws primarily on the following sources: Francine du Plessix Gray, *Divine Disobedience: Profiles in Catholic Radicalism* (New York: Knopf, 1970); Ana María Díaz-Stevens, *Oxcart Catholicism on Fifth Avenue: The Impact of the Puerto Rican Migration upon the Archdiocese of New York* (Notre Dame, Ind.: University of Notre Dame Press, 1993); Jaime R. Vidal, "Puerto Rican Catholics," in *Puerto Rican and Cuban Catholics in the U.S., 1900–1965,* ed. Jay P. Dolan and Jaime R. Vidal (Notre Dame, Ind.: University of Notre Dame Press, 1994); and Joseph P. Fitzpatrick, S.J., "Ivan Illich as We Knew Him in the 1950s," in *The Challenges of Ivan Illich: A Collective Reflection,* ed. Lee Hoinacki and Carl Mitcham (Albany: State University of New York Press, 2002), 1–7.

51. See Díaz-Stevens, *Oxcart Catholicism,* 151–75: for example, her contention that "the essential service to preserve the faith among Puerto Ricans was subordinated to vocational soul-searching for adults recently freed from the cloister" (159), and "The mirth and frivolity of the crowds of people who annually came to picnic at the fiesta was seen as inimical to the higher purpose Fox had set" (162).

52. The literature on Chavez is growing. For a good short introduction, see Richard W. Etulain, ed., *César Chávez: A Brief Biography with Documents* (Boston: Bedford and St. Martin's, 2002). For an excellent treatment of Chavez's Catholicism, see Stephen R. Lloyd-Moffett, "The Mysticism and Social Action of César Chávez," in *Latino Religious and Civic Activism in the United States,* ed. Gaston Espinosa, Virgilio Elizondo, and Jesse Miranda (New York: Oxford University Press, 2005).

53. See again Lloyd-Moffett, "Mysticism and Social Action," for a critique of the various efforts to downplay the role of orthodox Catholicism in Chavez's activism.

54. For an introduction to this movement, see James K. A. Smith, *Introducing Radical Orthodoxy: Mapping a Post-Secular Theology* (Grand Rapids, Mich.: Baker Academic, 2004). This is not a distinctly Catholic movement; the Christian theologians who identify themselves with this school of thought more often than not wind up being Protestants who wish to speak the language of tradition and orthodoxy without making the leap to Rome. The unofficial leader of the movement, the Anglican John Milbank, is the best example of this tendency. Milbank's *Theology and Social Theory* (Oxford: Blackwell, 1993) offers an insightful critique of modern social theory as a disguised, and thus perverse, theological discourse, yet owes far more than it appears willing to acknowledge to the recovery of "tradition" in the work of the Catholic philosopher Alasdair MacIntyre. On MacIntyre, see his *After Virtue: A Study in Moral Theory* (Notre Dame, Ind.: University of Notre Dame Press, 1981), and *Three Rival Versions of Moral Enquiry: Encyclopedia, Genealogy, and Tradition* (Notre Dame, Ind.: University of Notre Dame Press, 1990). I am concerned less with the movement as an academic phenomenon than with the general opening up to tradition as a basis for a true Catholic cultural and intellectual life that will incidentally, but not primarily, run counter to most of the cultural and intellectual norms of modern American life.

55. Robert W. Brimlow, "Solomon's Porch: The Church as Sectarian Ghetto," in *The Church as Counterculture,* ed. Michael L. Budde and Robert W. Brimlow (Albany: State University of New York Press, 2000), 105–25; Cavanaugh, *Theopolitical Imagination: Discovering the Liturgy as a Political Act in an Age of Global Consumerism* (New York: T & T Clark, 2002).

56. See in general Roberto S. Goizueta, *Caminemos con Jesús: Toward a Hispanic/Latino Theology of Accompaniment* (Maryknoll, N.Y.: Orbis, 1995).

ELEVEN

Catholics, Communism, and African Americans

Cecilia A. Moore

Dr. Thomas Wyatt Turner arrived in St. Louis the Sunday after Christmas 1925. He was on his way to a meeting of the Botanical Society of America. "As any good Catholic ought to do," he looked for a church.[1] Finding St. Ann's in time for the 9:00 A.M. Mass, Turner took a seat in the middle aisle on the right side, as was his custom. Not long after settling in the pew, "a corpulent happy-faced youngster" who was ushering asked Turner to take a seat at the back of the church on the far-right side. His request struck Turner as odd. He recalled, "I was already quite cold, so a proffered banishment to a distant corner of that large church did not appeal to my thermal sense at all."[2] Turner asked the usher why he wanted him to move, and the youth explained that the pastor had designated the rear as the place for blacks at St. Ann's. Demonstrating his offense, Turner retorted, "Why even colored people go to a Catholic church, and further if I were looking for associations with colored people they would not be those of his selection." He also informed the youth that he did not take orders about how to be Catholic from any man but only from "Jesus Christ." Finally, he dismissed the usher, saying, "You have done your bidding, so please get you hence that I may assist at Mass."[3] And with that, Turner remained in the pew of his choice.

Turner's experience at St. Ann's was not a singular experience for him, for other black Catholics in St. Louis, or for black Catholics in almost any other city or town in the United States in the 1920s.[4] This experience was but one manifestation of a strict Catholic color bar that prevailed in many Catholic churches, schools, hospitals, colleges, universities, and social organizations throughout the country. Hence, the young usher's request that Dr. Turner move to the "colored" section was not at all an uncommon experience or practice. Most black Catholics did not exercise the temerity Turner did. They sat in the areas they knew were "reserved" for them and did not refuse to move when asked, but their obedience did not signify their happiness or satisfaction with their treatment in the church or in the larger society. No, the request was not uncommon, but Turner's response certainly was.

The practice of racial segregation and discrimination this incident illustrates did not reflect a particularly Catholic form of racism but is illustrative of American racism and Catholic *capitulation* to it. From the end of Reconstruction in 1877 until the beginning of the modern civil rights movement in the 1950s, state legislatures throughout the country—especially in the South—stripped African Americans of civil rights. The 1896 Supreme Court ruling in the case of *Plessy v. Ferguson* upheld the right of states to enact racial segregation laws. This ruling had a chilling effect on all aspects of black life, including education, employment, and housing. Segregation laws also helped to buttress the tacit acceptance of mob violence against African Americans enshrined in the practice of lynching that took the lives of thousands of black men and women. In addition to these laws, enduring social customs and practices circumscribed the freedom of blacks in American society. The discrimination, deprivations, and danger that African Americans faced in this period prompted historian Rayford Logan to characterize the period from the late nineteenth to the early twentieth centuries as "the nadir" of African American history and experience.

While the United States regarded its black citizens as a "problem" to be solved and laws and customs that limited and confined blacks as the answer, African Americans responded by fighting for their freedom and civil and political rights. In the period between the end of Reconstruction and the beginning of the civil rights movement, African American leaders led countless campaigns for racial justice and looked for allies outside of their immediate community. By the 1930s, two mutually antagonistic potential allies emerged: the Catholic Church and the Communist Party. This essay examines the role of Catholics and Communists in the struggle for racial justice; the response of African American and particularly African American Catholics; the fruits of these collaborations; and the heretofore unexamined relationship among three groups who, working at times together and at times against each other, helped to prepare the way for the full-blown civil rights movement of the 1950s and 1960s.

Starting with their experience of racism in their own church, in the 1920s and 1930s black Catholics sought to redress the color line in the Catholic Church in the United States through the Federated Colored Catholics, a lay Catholic organization that Dr. Turner founded in 1924 and led through the early 1950s. The Federated Colored Catholics grew out of the Committee for the Advancement of Colored Catholics that originated in the late 1910s. The primary goal of the FCC was to unite black Catholics throughout the United States to work for racial justice in the church and in society.[5] The church's teachings on the equal dignity of all men and women before God drove the FCC's mission; its members believed it was the vocation of black Catholics to lead the campaign for racial reform in the church. One of their initial though unsuccessful efforts in advocacy targeted the Catholic University of America, whose policy of racial segregation was especially scandalous given the university's governance by some of the nation's leading bishops.[6] The FCC invested its energies into fostering a national Catholic conversation on racism in the church, to developing strategies to end racist practices and policies, and, finally, to the work of dismantling the Catholic color line. They believed that if they could achieve justice for African Americans in the church, then surely they could do the same in the wider society.

Turner and the black Catholics he represented believed that everything about Catholicism from its history, geography, theology, and ancient traditions destined it to be the institution most true to the ideal of universal brotherhood. But, in the American context it fell woefully short of its promise, and, in falling short, it squandered the good will most African Americans otherwise would accord it. Catholic refusals, particularly those of priests, to collaborate as equals with African American Catholics on racial problems were also destructive and alienating. As Turner explained the effects of this institutional racism:

> In many places parish priests are "marking time," blind to the needs and necessities of the colored group. They are not living in close enough touch with the real problems confronting Negro life to render effective aid. They have not been able, in a majority of cases, to work in harmony with the intelligent people of their churches, and thus get the benefit of their advice, they commit the basic error of thinking that they are wholly sufficient in communities to speak for colored people and that colored leaders are superfluous and troublesome.[7]

Turner saw this failure of engagement as the primary cause of Catholic failings to aid the cause of black freedom, especially when compared with the willingness of non-Catholic advocates to listen and collaborate. Turner observed that "the dominant non-Catholic forces working for the betterment of the colored people are getting much better results, because they have learned long ago that real, permanent progress, spiritual or temporal, is assured only when a racial group is helped to fall in line behind its own leaders."[8] Catholics were failing, Turner concluded, because they were helping blacks from "the side lines," but did not "help him either as layman or priest to participate in his own uplift."[9] Catholics would continue to fail in their efforts to do justice so long as they continued to work on behalf of blacks instead of with blacks. And, as they continued to fail, blacks suffered more and more and cast about for allies in their quest for justice in America.

Other African American leaders were equally attentive to the incongruity between Catholic theology and doctrine on equality and universal brotherhood and the racial practices operant in most Catholic parishes in the United States. Dr. Kelly Miller, an English professor at Howard University, noted that the church's "historic policy embraces all men without regard to race or color":

> The historical Church senses its strategic opportunity, but stands appalled at the magnitude of the difficulty. The Catholic Church is willing to go the limit short of social equality. This it lacks the courage to dare in the face of the Protestant majority whose creed cannot cross the color line. . . . When in Rome, do as the Protestants do. The Catholic Church lacks the courage to violate that ancient motto and shrinks from the bold attempt to capture the Negro race.[10]

Miller correctly identified the compromise American Catholics made with the culture. They would not challenge the nation's dominant racist practices even though they could not square them with Catholic theology, doctrine, or history, choosing instead to further the cause of the church's advancement within the United States. The unnamed Catholic author of the "Red Menace," an article on Communism and blacks in *Interracial Review*, the leading Catholic journal on interracial concerns, succinctly restated Miller's thesis by asserting, "Catholics lack the courage to go all the way with Christ."[11] While the author had kudos for Catholic organizations that were teaching Catholic doctrine to non-Catholics, he charged that Catholics continued to fail to live the doctrine of universal brotherhood, particularly when it came to African Americans. Blacks wanted to see evidence of the Catholic doctrine of universal brotherhood in the ways that white Catholics acted toward them. The author regarded the situation as particularly dangerous because Communists were making inroads into African American communities. The author warned that "Communism gives no internal evidence with a book, but it is giving plenty of evidence in a practical interest in America's 'tenth man.'"[12]

American Catholic theology on the "race question" developed tentatively in the decades following the "Great Migration" of African Americans from the rural South to the urban Midwest and Northeast during the first third of the twentieth century (a process reaccelerated by the onset of the Second World War). This migration brought large groups of white Catholics and African Americans into daily if wary contact with each other at work, in neighborhoods, at school, and in church.[13] Catholics knew that American law and culture for the most part disenfranchised and devalued blacks, especially in the South, but they looked to their religion for answers about how they should treat and regard African Americans in an era of unprecedented proximity. Over a period of about twenty-five years, theologians employed history, sociology, and economics to develop a theological response to the "race question" for the faithful. Hallmarks of prevailing American Catholic theological and ethical approaches to race stressed the essential equality of all created in God's image; drew distinctions between natural and civil rights; championed a living wage and adequate educational opportunities for blacks; and defined Christian love and justice to emphasize the importance of outward acts of charity to African Americans.[14]

These mainline Catholic theologians privileged the ethic of self-love or self-regard when it came to interactions with African Americans but prescribed the virtue of prudence as the answer to the race question in its social and political contexts, counseling that in time things would change for the better for blacks in America. Until the change came, white Catholics owed blacks a minimum of Christian justice and charity. Fundamentally, this minimum demanded working for or at least not standing in the way of opportunities for African Americans to advance economically and educationally—a low standard that did not include "social equality" for African Americans with white Americans. Anything that required one to regard another person as one would a peer, a member of one's social set or social status, an associate, a mate, a sibling or other kinsman, or a friend constituted "social equality." As far as many Catholics were concerned, church seating arrangements fell into the category of social equality. In justice, a place had to be reserved for black parishioners and visitors. To fail to provide seating was unjust and sinful. However, it was considered neither unjust nor sinful to require blacks to sit in segregated and marginal areas in the church.[15] So the young usher who meant to apply the seating rule to Dr. Turner and the priest who set the rule in place were actually conforming to the reigning Catholic social ethic.

This mainline Catholic approach to the "race problem" was not without its critics. Monsignor Paul Hanly Furfey, a sociology professor at the Catholic University of America, represented the radical Catholic position on the "race problem." Furfey believed the gospels were the best and only source from which to build a theology of racial justice because they directly challenged Christians with Jesus's teachings. From these teachings, Furfey advanced in the 1930s and 1940s an alternative that he called the theology of "interracial love."

Furfey was most critical of mainline American Catholic theologians of racial justice who used the virtue of prudence as a justification for racial prejudice and claimed it was simply a way for Catholics to excuse themselves for not confronting evil in the world. He dismissed theologians' counsel of "prudence" in racial justice as "tommyrot" lacking a shred of theological justification. Furfey wrote, "To lift up our voices against race prejudice people say would be to create a sensation and cause opposition, and prudence is a virtue which forbids extremes."[16] But, he continued,

> the application of prudence to the present subject is obvious. By subtle casuistry it may be possible to justify some of our discriminations against the Negro. Some of our hackneyed excuses *may* be valid. For this or that act, we *may* escape hell. But with all our ingenious and devious reasoning we are playing fast and loose with the dignity of God whom we can offend by offending the Negro. The prudent man will not dare to run such risks. He will prefer the safer and secure path of interracial love.[17]

"Interracial love" was the only love in the world that could truly honor Jesus's teaching. Furfey described "interracial love" as an intense and fearless love. It was not colorblind; it recognized difference as the presence of God in the person. "Interracial love" was the only kind of love fit for the mystical body of Christ; interracial love accepted blacks as fully human not only in God's plan of creation but also in the world: a mere concern that blacks receive a just wage or enjoyed access to adequate schools failed to meet the standard of Christian love.[18] Christian love also demanded respect and affection. Furfey vociferously criticized Catholics who urged prudence in American race relations lest they upset the American social order or embarrass the church. The church could never be embarrassed to follow Jesus's commandment to love as Jesus loved.[19]

Furfey distinguished himself among white Catholics writing on race in this period by consulting with African American Catholics about issues of racial prejudice in the United States. Dr. Louis T. Achille, a native of Martinique and a Howard University professor, was a black Catholic who significantly influenced Furfey's thought and activism. From blacks, Furfey learned about their experiences of racial prejudice, how prejudice affected them, the role Christianity played in race prejudice, and the ways in which whites and blacks engaged in race prejudice. Furfey's direct engagement with African Americans sharpened his critique of the mainline Catholic approach to race prejudice and especially that approach's dependence on the virtue of prudence. It also deepened Furfey's convictions regarding the necessity of interracial love. This radical theology of interracial love did not enjoy the broad support and application that the mainline theology and ethics on race did. Furfey's greatest influence was witnessed at Friendship House, an interracial apostolate in Harlem founded in 1938 by the Russian émigré Baroness Catherine De Hueck. Yet if Catholics expected to compete with Communists for the allegiance of black Americans, they needed to adopt a radical theological stance akin to that of Paul Hanly Furfey.

Conscious of the indignities and injustices blacks experienced, American and European Communists spent time, effort, and money in the 1920s, '30s, and '40s to build alliances with African Americans because they believed African American support and participation were essential in their quest to build just and classless societies throughout the world. In its formal foundation in 1919, the Communist Party United States of America (CPUSA) identified black Americans as being in "'economic bondage and oppression,'" while Soviet Communists regarded the struggle of African Americans as setting the global paradigm. Soviet Communists thought that if they could secure the commitment of African Americans to the Communist Party, then they would be able to reach blacks throughout the colonial and postcolonial world.[20]

Historians continue to debate the effectiveness and significance of Communist overtures to African Americans during the Depression and its aftermath, from the numbers of African Americans that actually became Communists to the degree of racism American and Soviet Communists harbored in their relationships with African Americans. But, a consensus apparently formed. The primary point of agreement is that most African Americans who engaged with Communism were not duped into the relationship but did so for their own reasons. African American Communists exercised a certain degree of independence from the Comintern and the CPUSA and were regarded as Communist leaders in their own rights in their own communities. Robin D. G. Kelley's groundbreaking work *Hammer and Hoe: Alabama Communists during the Great Depression* is the leading scholarly exemplar of this theme.[21]

The historical records preserved in the United States and in Russia show that in fact Communists played an integral role in working for social-justice reforms that improved the lives of African Americans. Communist activism on behalf of civil rights for African Americans gained them the respect and admiration of many African Americans, if not members of the party. According to Mark Solomon, a historian of African American Communism, "to win the Negro, the Party had to yoke class to race and correlate its objectives 'with their [black] ideology and their immediate wants and sufferings.'"[22] Solomon argued that Communists worked to put "the human factor" into their work with blacks and focused on initiatives that placed equality and human dignity at the forefront. In helping African Americans to make gains in labor and political rights, they hoped to "place the blame for black suffering at the feet of the capitalists."[23]

Communism also had strong appeal for many black intellectuals, artists, and writers whose ideas and works received scant recognition outside of the African American community. Communists in the United States and Europe were appreciative of the gifts black artists offered. Dorothy West, Langston Hughes, W. E. B. DuBois, Claude McKay, and Paul Robeson were among the black intellectuals who made the "magical pilgrimage" to Moscow in the 1920s, '30s, and '40s.[24] According to George Streator, an African American anti-Communist, Communists reached out as well to a broader spectrum of African Americans. "Where previously few Negroes ever ventured as far away as Russia, now, small-town school teachers somehow got trips to Moscow," Streator explained. "Washington elite saw their children married in the shadow of the Kremlin. Young ministers who had never been able to venture from home sailed en route to Moscow, and came back, as a face-saver, via Jerusalem. Moscow was the Mecca of the black bourgeoisie and Communism was its passport."[25]

Communists offered comradeship to blacks. As comrades, they wanted black Americans to believe they shared the same desires and destinies of workers all around the world. They wanted African Americans to see themselves as engaged in a class struggle that they could win if they would join with workers throughout the world under the mantle of Communism. United they could dismantle capitalist structures that injured all workers. Publicly Communists did not shirk from regarding African Americans as their social equals; to do otherwise would belie their fundamental philosophy. Communists wanted to be seen as walking beside African Americans in a march toward freedom and justice. They offered their organization and platforms to African Americans to gain a hearing in the United States and in the rest of the world. Communists also offered material, legal, and moral support to the most disadvantaged African Americans, particularly those in the urban areas and the deep South. One of the most striking examples of this kind of support was the CPUSA's involvement in the defense of the Scottsboro Nine in 1931. In March 1931, nine African American male youths were arrested and charged with the rape of two white women. Less than two weeks later they were tried and convicted in Scottsboro, Alabama. The U.S. Supreme Court ordered a retrial, and the CPUSA stepped in to help by hiring Samuel Liebowitz to defend the "Scottsboro Boys." Their trials gained national attention. Many civil rights groups, such as the National Association for the Advancement of Colored People, and religious leaders and groups, Catholics among them, spoke out against the injustices leveled against these black youth, but none were credited with advocacy as staunch as that of the Communists.

Catholics were loath to ally themselves with causes where Communists enjoyed an influence of any kind. The Catholic Church condemned Communism as early as 1846, a position reaffirmed by Pope Pius IX in his 1864 *Syllabus of Errors*, which declared Communism contrary to the natural law. Pius IX ominously warned that Communism would destroy the rights of the person and ultimately dismantle civilization. In 1878 in *Quod Apostolici Muneris*, Pope Leo XIII called Communism "the fatal plague which insinuates itself into the very marrow of human society only to bring about its ruin." And in his encyclicals on differing topics such as *Miserentissimus redemptor*, on reparation to the Sacred Heart of Jesus (1928), *Quadragesimo anno*, on the fortieth anniversary of *Rerum novarum* (1931), *Caritate Christi compulsi*, on devotion to the Sacred Heart of Jesus in response to worldwide economic depression (1932), *Acerba animi*, on the persecution of the church in

Mexico (1932), and *Dilectissimo nobis,* on the oppression of the church in Spain (1933), Pope Pius XI reiterated the church's condemnation of Communism and protested acts of violence by Communists against Catholics in Russia, Mexico, and Spain.

On March 19, 1937, the Feast of St. Joseph, the patron saint of workers, Pius XI issued the encyclical *Divini redemptoris* (On Atheistic Communism).[26] This was the Catholic Church's true declaration of war against Communism, calling Catholics around the world to the service of militant Catholic Action against the "satanic scourge."[27] Pius XI urged the Catholic hierarchy, priests, religious, and laity to band together to unmask Communism for what it was, "a false messianic idea" that used claims of justice, equality, and fraternity to appeal to the working poor and miserable throughout the world. He acknowledged that Communism did not manufacture the real economic and political suffering that so many people endured because of "the unequal distribution of goods in this world."[28] He also acknowledged that Christians had played a role in creating this injustice. But Communism could never be the answer to justice because it was atheistic and did not recognize the God-given rights of the person.

Pius XI believed Communism was an all-encompassing plague with outposts spreading everywhere, tremendous financial resources, huge organizations, and trained workers throughout the world. Communists made expert use of the print media, radio, and theatre and could be found making their appeals in schools and universities. The pope was particularly concerned about the Communist appeal to "the younger intelligentsia who are still too immature to recognize the intrinsic errors of the system" and racial minorities who suffered the most in all parts of the world.[29] This was the way that Communism worked itself into the fabric of so many cultures and into all classes.[30]

Affirming the dignity of the worker, Pius XI pleaded for Catholics everywhere to strive to detach from earthly things and to embrace the practices of charity and justice. These were the surest defenses against Communism and the greatest tools in reconstructing society in Christ. He asserted, "The more the workingmen and the poor realize what the spirit of love animated by the virtue of Christ is doing for them, the more readily will they abandon the false persuasion that Christianity has lost its efficacy and that the Church stands on the side of the exploiters of their labor."[31] The pope urged Catholics to suffer for the poor and disadvantaged as Christ suffered and sacrificed and to "forget self for love of neighbor." He also warned there could be no true charity unless it took justice "into constant account."[32] Giving alms instead of providing jobs was not justice. Giving small donations to charities did not exempt a person from what justice demanded. He bemoaned the fact that Catholics in many countries were acting in ways that hurt working people and helped turn the working class away from Christianity.

Social justice demanded that workers must be paid well enough to provide "proper sustenance for themselves and for their families," the pontiff asserted. He advocated public and private insurance for old age, periods of unemployment, and illness; he also championed "an intensive program of social education adapted to the varying degrees of intellectual culture."[33] The foundation of this social education would be the social teachings of the Catholic Church. Pius XI saw a significant role for Catholic print media to devise "attractive ways" to foster a better understanding and application of Catholic social teaching and to warn of the "insidious deceits with which Communists endeavor, all too successfully, to attract even men of good faith."[34]

The pope was particularly concerned about the Communist promotion of class identity that led to class warfare and that had caused "rivers of blood to flow" in Europe. He also was greatly troubled by Communist infiltration of a variety of social institutions, including some with Catholic affiliations. "Communism is intrinsically wrong," he declared, "and no one who would save Christian civilization may collaborate with it in any undertaking whatsoever."[35] The pontiff called upon Catholics to take up the work of Catholic Action in response to the threat, enlisting this new social apostolate to "fight the battles of the Lord." Catholic Action was the work the Catholic laity did to assist the hierarchy in proclaiming and practicing the message of the Gospel of Jesus in the world. Catholic Action was formally defined as "the participation of the laity in the work of the hierarchy." As conceptualized, bishops directed Catholic Action. The sacramental graces all Catholics received in baptism and Confirmation conferred the gifts and responsibilities to evangelize. The fundamental goal of Catholic Action was to "bring souls to God" and to establish a society based on Christian principles. From the 1930s until well into the 1960s, most lay Catholic movements and projects in the United States fell under the rubric of "Catholic Action."

To combat Communism, Pius XI called for the creation of study circles, conferences, lecture courses, and other activities that would educate people about Christian solutions to the problems Communism purported to solve. "The militant leaders of Catholic Action," he asserted, "thus properly prepared and armed, will be the first and immediate apostles of their fellow workmen."[36] These militant Catholics would work with their priests to carry "the torch of truth" and to relieve people suffering from spiritual and material privations. Together they would work to break down the anticlericalism and religious indifference that Communists used to their advantage and would "collaborate, under the direction of especially qualified priests, in that work of spiritual aid to the laboring classes on which We set so much store, because it is the means best calculated to save these, Our beloved children, from the snares of Communism."[37]

For the next twenty years or more, Catholics, particularly young adults, enlisted in the Catholic army against Communism in the United States, with a major focus on African American communities. Using Pius XI's plan of attack, they created study groups, adopted resolutions, worked to reform their attitudes regarding African Americans, wrote articles, delivered lectures, became catechists and social activists in black communities, and founded organizations to promote justice and to reach out to African Americans in friendship. This campaign against Communist influence in black communities required Catholics to embrace the new papal ideology on the one hand and take up the work started earlier in the century by black Catholics to break down the Catholic color bar on the other—to balance their challenge to mainline Catholic theology and ethics on race relations with the militant agenda of Catholic social thought.

Events suggested that on the American scene young Catholics were less concerned with papal mandates than making authentic witness against injustice. Women attending a

March 1933 meeting of the Catholic Action Forum of Manhattanville College adopted the pledge:

> *Whereas: I am enjoying the privilege of a Catholic education, I recognize that I have certain duties and obligations toward my fellow man, among which I must consider my conduct and attitude toward the American Negro.*[38]

Led by the "Banner Students," the Catholic Action group at this prominent women's college in suburban Westchester County, New York, students "engaged in warm discussion of Catholic teaching on race relations" and debated the twelve resolutions the Banner Students had composed with the help of George K. Hunton, a prominent Catholic interracialist and editor of the *Interracial Review*.[39] At an all-campus assembly, after an exposition on the question of racial discrimination in the United States and the "Christian response" by two students, a question-and-answer session, and the reading of the Resolutions, Manhattanville students unanimously voted to accept the Resolutions as their own.[40]

Students making this pledge accepted eight resolutions designed to convert their thinking and engagement with African Americans. Chief among their resolutions was a pledge to "maintain that the Negro as a human being and as a citizen is entitled to the rights of life, liberty, and the pursuit of happiness and to the essential opportunities of life and the full measure of justice."[41] In their meetings and encounters with African Americans, Manhattanville students promised to be "courteous and kind," to refrain from calling blacks by nicknames, and to "say a kind word to him on every occasion," remembering the "heavy yoke" of injustice and discrimination that American blacks labored under daily. Manhattanville women believed that the Catholic Church and the Catholic program of social justice was the "Greatest Hope of the Colored Race" and that African Americans shared with them membership in the mystical body of Christ. Finally, Manhattanville's students pledged their financial support to "the heroic missionaries laboring among the Negro group" and dedicated their work in Catholic Action to "the betterment of his conditions, spiritually and materially."[42]

According to George Hunton, the Manhattanville students and their resolutions had a profound influence on the Catholic community's thinking on racial justice. Hunton was present for the adoption of the Manhattanville Resolutions; in his autobiography he recalled telling the young women, "'What you have done here today is a matter of interest not only to yourselves, or even to students and faculties of other Catholic colleges. It is a matter of national interest and concern.'"[43] As editor of *Interracial Review*, Hunton published the Manhattanville Resolutions, and news of what these young Catholic women were committing to do to work for racial justice spread quickly. Hunton noted that even *L'Osservatore Romano*, the Vatican's semi-official newspaper, published the Manhattanville Resolutions in full; they were also published in Catholic newspapers in Asia and Africa.[44] The Manhattanville Resolutions were then printed in a pamphlet that was distributed to Catholics editors and teachers. And eventually, "they were taken up, endorsed, elaborated, and commented on by all manner of bodies."[45] Ultimately, the Manhattanville Resolutions inspired the creation of "All Men Are Equal: A Brief for the Black Man," a document that reached 162 Catholic colleges in the United States. "All Men Are Equal" challenged Catholic faculty and students to become involved in working for justice for African Americans.

The Manhattanville Resolutions were influential beyond the academy. On May 4, 1934, the Brooklyn Catholic Social Action group adopted a set of resolutions that were almost identical to the Manhattanville pledge. The Brooklyn group was comprised of "over two hundred Catholic men and women from the various parishes in the diocese." They determined after "having analyzed the various kinds of prejudice in American [*sic*]" that the Negro was "the greatest sufferer from bigotry and injustices." Therefore, they would focus their attention on blacks because they were in the most danger from Communism, which "constantly strives to foster class hatred, misunderstanding and conflict between all groups and is the most persistent foe to peace, understanding and the brotherhood of man."[46]

Two years later, on March 19, 1935, Manhattanville students gathered for an interracial forum to hear addresses from nationally recognized interracial justice leaders alongside student peers who were emerging as young Catholic interracialists. In the presence of Father John LaFarg, S.J., and George K. Hunton of the National Catholic Interracial Justice Committee, Manhattanville sophomore Betty Farley spoke on the ethics of interracial justice, arguing that most white Catholics held attitudes toward African Americans that were inconsistent with Christian principles.[47] Senior Mary Ursula Morris presented her classmates with specific examples of discrimination blacks faced in religious, social, economic, and political contexts. Morris coupled the elimination of racial barriers with the struggle against Communism, later noting that "the relation between Communism and the interracial question immediately inspired the interest of students."[48]

At the end of the interracial forum, the students readopted the "Manhattanville Resolutions" and pledged to make the college a place where principles of interracial justice reigned. The students requested that the college begin to admit African American women and continue to support the work of Manhattanville students for racial justice. Just two years after adopting the resolutions, student leaders declared that "the interracial question is now one of great interest to all Manhattanville students and the forum obtained much new sympathy and support for these who are working so hard for a recognition of Negro rights."[49]

Three years later, Manhattanville students, faculty, and administrators tested the courage of their convictions on their own campus when Manhattanville became one of the first Catholic colleges to admit African American students. Manhattanville's president, Mother Grace Cowardin Dammann, R.S.C.J., announced to the students and alumnae that in the fall of 1938 they would welcome the first black Manhattanville student to the freshman class. Mother Dammann asserted, "She is coming for an education that will equip her for the work of uplifting her own racial group. She needs an education for leadership. Would it be just to refuse her?"[50]

This development greatly pleased African American Catholics who had advocated for their inclusion in Catholic higher education for quite some time. They also believed that Catholic education had a strong role to play in protecting blacks from Communism. George W. B. Conrad, vice president of Cincinnati's Federated Colored Catholics, contended that most education for blacks, delivered principally by public segregated schools and Protestant private schools for blacks, focused on their material development but neglected their spiritual education.[51] Conrad claimed, "Protestantism has not brought to him the 'returns in religious and material life which he anticipated.'"[52] While public education and Protestant education failed, Communists were waiting in the wings with promises that by accepting Communist beliefs "the Negro may come into his own."[53] Conrad believed Communists concealed a "plan of destructiveness" that appealed to the emotions of blacks. He insisted, "It fosters and promotes racial antipathy and is harmful to the furtherance of interracial good will and better understanding."[54] But, he asserted, "Catholic training (including college and university) will solve many, if not all, of the Negroes' problems."[55]

In the 1940s, many Catholic colleges and universities followed Manhattanville's lead as the American church looked to young people to provide the surest offensive against Communism, especially within the African American community. The Intercollegiate Interracial Council of Catholic Colleges, which included colleges and universities in the Philadelphia metropolitan area, offered religion courses on Sunday mornings in over sixty Catechetical Centers established in black neighborhoods throughout Philadelphia. Young women and men went to these neighborhoods to show that the Catholic Church was concerned for both the souls and daily concerns of black Americans in hopes they might become members of the Catholic Church. Writing for *Interracial Review*, Father Aloysius Donadieu, a recently ordained priest of the Archdiocese of Philadelphia and a member of the Negro Apostolate in Philadelphia, proclaimed young Catholics to be the surest guard the Catholic Church had in protecting African Americans from Communism. He remarked:

> Such a movement as this is the seed of inspiring hope not only that the Negro will be enlightened about things Catholic but also that the tremendous influence that Communism can exert on the Negro may be combated. A wonderful work! It shows the immense interest youth has taken in the interracial problem and the good he can accomplish. It is the work that each of us should do.[56]

Donadieu believed that Catholic youth were the best missionaries to blacks because they were the most willing and able to take up "the cudgels of interracialism to fight for the Negro."[57] Interracialism was "attractive" to youth, and it generated their enthusiasm. It appealed to the "adventurous spirit" of youth and was "new," "startling," and "something exciting." Donadieu predicted that by fighting for justice Catholic youth would become the heroes of African Americans: "A challenge to a willing spirit—a challenge which causes pride and gallantry to swell up in him and bring him to the defense of the mistreated and underrated Negro."[58] Young people were "less contaminated" than their ancestors and elders with racial prejudice. Because of this, youth were more willing to "associate" with blacks, to learn about the problems blacks faced, and to do what they could do to help blacks solve these problems. Though he admitted that not all Catholic youth were so open to blacks and dedicated to racial justice, Father Donadieu did believe that there were enough youth willing to do this work and to make a difference. This small group combined zeal, sincerity, and determination. He also believed, as the Manhattanville Resolutions suggested, that precisely because these young women and men had the benefits of Catholic higher education, they were more "easily won over to the cause of the Negro" and understood and could correctly use Catholic principles to achieve justice. Of this kind of student Donadieu wrote:

> He realizes that certain actions toward the Negro are morally inconsistent with Catholic teaching. He has learned that full import of the truth that all men are equal—equal in their dignity, for all are created equal in the image and likeness of God; equal also because their bodies are temples of the Holy Ghost—temples that are not to be defiled or desecrated; and what is most important, equal in their destiny, for all men are destined by God for eternal glory in heaven.[59]

Catholic doctrine, discipline, and sacraments provided all Catholic youth needed to build a case and foundation for friendship with African Americans and an alternative to the comradeship Communists offered.

In 1931, Baroness Catherine De Hueck opened the first Friendship House in Toronto, Canada, at the behest of Archbishop Neil McNeil.[60] Designed as a Catholic bulwark against Communism where the poor and unemployed could "pass away the long, dreary, empty hours which hung heavily on their hands,"[61] Friendship House was also "an experiment in Catholic Action." When Archbishop McNeil asked De Hueck to survey the extent of Communism and Communist propaganda in Toronto and New York, she set about infiltrating a variety of Communist organizations to find out just what the Communists were up to and the secrets of their appeal.[62] In her undercover investigations, De Hueck discovered that Communism was making its greatest inroads with youth between the ages of eighteen and thirty. Although their parents could scarcely imagine why or how children imbued with British and American values could be attracted to Communism, De Hueck clearly understood that Communism was much more than a political or economic philosophy; it was also a religion whose appeal was nearly irresistible to young men and women coming of age in the Depression in a culture characterized by despair. She reported that these young men and women knew only "appalling injustices," "tragic misery," "millions in poverty in the midst of plenty," "war madness," "and "greed and selfishness run rampant." "It is the Religion of Irreligion with its gods," the baroness explained, "Marx and Lenin; its gospel; its apostles; its proselytizers; its martyrs. How is all of this possible you will say; when obviously they are lacking in the foundation of truth?"[63]

The Communist banquet offered youth an attractive array of food for the body, mind, and spirit, including: recreation facilities for workers and their families, labor organizations, and libraries in "shabby shops in slum areas." The libraries were filled with books, pamphlets, magazines, newspapers, and tracts published in a multitude of languages available for free or for very little cost. Communists seemed ever-ready to engage and to challenge youth in conversation about things that mattered to them; the party also provided night schools, arranged debate clubs, and sponsored lectures for the intellectual development of youth. As an example of the vast and expanding Communist network, De Hueck claimed that Harlem alone had twenty-nine Communist Centers, some publicly known as Communist and others operating underground.

Communists had transformed public protest against social injustices into a well-organized art form that won the attention and support of the poor and marginalized "among people of all creeds and nationalities." Communists provided the services of doctors, lawyers, and dentists for people who could not afford such help otherwise. They addressed material, social, and intellectual needs of people that governments and religious institutions seemed to have forgotten, especially African Americans. The awareness and concern that Communists expressed for the poor, for workers, and for African Americans was returned in the form of appreciation and respect from the poor, the workers, and blacks to Communists.

Catherine De Hueck's experiences observing Communism and its appeal to young people convinced her that Catholics could lose no more time in providing an alternative to Communism. It was imperative for Catholics to honestly look at the injustices in Canadian and American societies, to acknowledge how they contributed to and supported these injustices, and to resolve to reform themselves so that they could win the hearts, minds, and souls of the poor, the worker, and the black for the church. "For Catholics must not forget that before a hungry, naked, miserable world will listen to their voice," she pleaded, "they must alleviate its material misery while at the same time they are pointing out the way to the complete renovation of the social order based on Christian principles."[64]

The first Friendship House opened in a rented room in Toronto, which the baroness stocked with Catholic newspapers, magazines, and books: "a little Catholic library."[65] The archbishop agreed to pay the rent for Friendship House, but for everything else De Hueck relied on begging and prayers. Stores, manufacturers, and friends of Friendship House provided furniture and food. De Hueck used donated paint to spruce up the place and "transform these three neglected rooms into a clean cozy place."[66] Friendship House's aesthetic appeal was important to her because she believed poverty was no reason for anyone to live in filth or to be deprived of beauty. No one ever left Friendship House without receiving some kind of gift. It might be a garment, a rosary, a prayer book, or a religious medal. De Hueck explained that these gifts were necessary so that "a shivering body might be clothed and a tired questioning soul set at rest with the grace of God."[67]

After hearing of Friendship House's success in Canada, Father Michael S. Mulvoy, C.S.Sp., pastor of St. Mark the Evangelist Church, invited the baroness to open a Friendship House in Harlem. Mulvoy was a community activist who enjoyed the respect of African Americans in Harlem because of his forthright commitment to racial justice, particularly in housing and employment, and his fearless advocacy for the rights for blacks; he was known locally as "'the blackest white man in Harlem.'"[68] He saw the gains Communists were making in Harlem and believed Friendship House could be a worthy Catholic champion for blacks in the community. With a guarantee of rent from Father George Barry Ford, pastor of Corpus Christi Church on W. 121st Street between Broadway and Amsterdam Avenue and moderator of the Newman Clubs of Greater New York, Catherine De Hueck arrived in Harlem in 1938 with three dollars, two suitcases of books, and a portable typewriter to establish a Friendship House.[69]

De Hueck did not receive a warm welcome. She perplexed Harlemites and roused their suspicion. Why would a white woman choose to live in the roughest part of Harlem and devote herself to working with blacks? Catholic journalist Edward Doherty, who would marry her in 1943, described the incongruity between the average Harlem resident's experience of white women generally in Harlem and that of De Hueck. Most "white women didn't come to Harlem for any good."[70] Doherty said people thought she was crazy, dumb, or had a racket going. Most of her white friends similarly thought something was wrong with De Hueck and discounted what she was doing in Harlem, thinking, "Catherine was crazy, or perhaps just giving rein to a whim that would pass. Just Harlem-happy, maybe like some men get slap-happy; but she'd get over it."[71] After blacks and whites saw that the baroness was staying and was serious about establishing a Catholic presence and alternative to Communism in Harlem, she began to gain the respect and assistance of many who had mistrusted her. Neighbors offered household items, furniture, and food to her and admonished her not to give what they had given her away, though her generosity was essential to the mission to build friendship between Catholics and African Americans.

Within the first year of coming to Harlem, De Hueck turned a ten-by-fourteen room into the Blessed Martin de Porres Friendship House of Harlem, complete with a Catholic Youth Organization that was wildly popular with Harlem teens and fueled rapid expansion to a small storefront CYO clubhouse on 135th Street. This venue also featured a library, games, and a piano.[72] The library was stocked with religious, economic, sociological, and interracial literature; its walls were adorned with pictures of Pope Pius XI and notable African Americans. Racks of Catholic periodicals invited guests to "Take One." The focal point of the library, however, was the shrine to Blessed (now St.) Martin de Porres. "Arranged in the manner of a European wayside shrine, Blessed Martin attracts the attention of all passers-by as he looks out over Harlem, giving an invitation to his colored brothers to come and share with him the teachings and glories of the Catholic Church."[73] So that Blessed Martin would be visible at all hours, the baroness kept a vigil light for the intentions of Friendship House by the statue at all times. From the 1930s through the 1960s, Blessed Martin de Porres served as the patron of the cause of Catholic interracialism.[74]

As the son of a Panamanian free woman of color, Anna Velasquez, and Juan de Porres, a Spanish knight in Lima, Peru in 1569, Blessed Martin embodied interracialism. As a young man he was trained as a barber-surgeon, and at age fifteen he became a Third Order Dominican and eventually a professed lay brother. His dark skin and African features and his status as an illegitimate son made the priesthood off-limits to him. Still he dedicated his life to works of charity and justice and was known throughout the city of Lima among the Spanish, Indians, free blacks, and enslaved blacks as a miracle worker and servant of the poor. Martin de Porres had charge of the Dominican's infirmary, where he cared for his sick Dominican brothers. He also went out into the city of Lima to care for the sick wherever they were. He helped found an orphanage and a foundling hospital and cared for all manner of animals. Martin de Porres's iconography always depicts him with a broom to emphasize his lowliness and life of service; he is also usually portrayed with a bowl of milk at his feet and a dog, a cat, and a mouse feeding from the same dish. These three "natural enemies" represent the races present in Lima, the Europeans, the indigenous Indians, and the Africans, all of whom received Martin's care and regard. He was the saint who brought all races together in peace, harmony, and brotherhood, making Martin de Porres the perfect saint to represent Friendship House's mission.

Friendship House provided material goods and services to Harlemites ravaged by the Depression and systemic poverty and racism of longer duration, without regard for race, religion, or political affiliation. The house depended on volunteers for all of its resources and programs. Most volunteers were young white and black Catholics, though the house was open to all people. Newman Club members and Manhattanville students were especially faithful Friendship House volunteers. Among the most successful endeavors of Friendship House was the story hour offered each week by Ellen Tarry, an African American Catholic children's book author and Friendship House volunteer. Most of all, Friendship House offered itself as a spiritual outpost to any person in need of a place to pray and to receive the benefits of prayer.

The baroness was good at garnering attention, both with her striking and stately physical presence and her luminous personal charisma, which helped attract middle- and upper-middle-class young men and women to Harlem to live on watery soup, wear donated clothing and shoes, and transgress the racial boundaries the culture sought to enforce. One Friendship House volunteer, Ann Harrigan, described her attraction to the work of Friendship House in this way:

> The ambience was unforgettable: walls lined with books, flickering lights muted by smoke. . . . White people, black people—talking, laughing, friendly, sipping coffee. How simple the solution all seemed then: the sooner we of different races, learned to work together, to pray together, to eat, to study, to laugh together, the sooner we'd be on the way to interracial justice. Little did we know then the complexities of the sin of segregation.[75]

As much as Friendship House sought to transform the social, economic, political, and religious culture of Harlem, it sought to transform the young men and women who volunteered there into aware, active, and critical Catholics unwilling to yield when it came to the missions of racial justice and the defeat of Communism in the United States. In order to do this, the baroness developed a rule of life for volunteers similar to that of a religious community. Of Friendship House, Edward Doherty said, "It isn't a monastery, nor is it a convent. But it's something between the two, and something of both of them. That's why I call it a conastery. My conastery."[76]

De Hueck, who was affectionately called "the B" by volunteers, served as the abbess "of shining holiness." Black and white female volunteers lived together in an apartment they called "Madonna Flat." They shared in common all that they received, from clothing to books to day-old bread and bruised vegetables. She sent volunteers out into the neighborhood to do works of mercy and charity. Young women went to tenements to feed the hungry, to take care of the sick, and to comfort the afflicted. She encouraged volunteers to see Christ in those they served and to see themselves as members of the mystical body of Christ.

Among the many beneficiaries of Friendship House's service was famed Jamaican poet Claude McKay. Probably best known for his searing 1919 protest poem about the horrors of lynching, "If We Must Die," McKay was among the most important artists of the Harlem Renaissance and a controversial figure in African American arts and letters. In the 1920s he made the "magical pilgrimage" to Moscow and spent a couple of years there writing, speaking, and promoting the cause of Communism and advocating it as a vital ally for oppressed black people throughout the world. By the middle of that decade, however, McKay renounced Marxism and charged that Communists never intended to treat blacks as their equals. McKay believed that Communists had cruelly exploited him; he spent the rest of his life as an ardent anti-Communist and promoter of black self-reliance.

McKay entered into communion with the Catholic Church in 1944 and was baptized by Auxiliary Bishop Bernard J. Sheil in Chicago. His relationship with Friendship House, and in particular with Friendship House volunteers Ellen Tarry and Mary Jerdo Keating, was instrumental in his conversion. According to McKay, his friend and fellow writer Tarry asked, "'Claude, why don't you become a Catholic? It is the only religion for a man like you who has traveled all over and seen everything.'" When McKay replied that he was an agnostic, Tarry challenged him: "'It is easier for an intellectual not to believe than to believe.'"[77] McKay later acknowledged that Tarry's question caused him to do some "thinking hard." He reevaluated his conviction that Christianity had "destroyed the glory of pagan life." McKay's reeducation in Christianity taught him that this claim was not true, that there had been African popes and saints, that Catholicism embraced the notion of the dignity of all persons, and that there were thousands of African Catholics.[78] During this investigation, McKay said, "I was flooded by the True Light. I discovered a little of that mystical world of the spirit that eludes the dictators, the agnostics, the pure materialists. I saw too, the Roman Catholic Church in a light different, indeed, from the many in which I had previously visioned it."[79] This experience opened the way for McKay to accept Catholicism, but his experience receiving the care and protection of Catholics helped to finally convince him.

On many occasions Ellen Tarry and Mary Jerdo Keating came to McKay's aid and nursed him back to health. In 1943, Keating offered her cottage in Connecticut to McKay for his convalescence. She also introduced him to Bishop Sheil, who hired McKay as his advisor on Russian and Negro affairs.[80] McKay welcomed this new career, as it provided him with the opportunity to join forces with the Catholic Church in combating the encroachment of Communism in the African American community. According to McKay biographer Wayne Cooper, McKay's first year in Chicago working for Sheil was his happiest.[81] He lectured on black culture in Chicago and throughout the Midwest, made friends and participated in the Chicago Friendship House, and regularly briefed Sheil on Russian Communism, race relations, and world affairs and summarized articles on such topics for him.[82] But ill health prevented Claude McKay from maintaining this hectic pace. By the time of his 1948 death McKay had grown wholly dependent on his Catholic friends. They fed him, nursed him, visited him, and helped to bury him. Being there for McKay in his need was at the heart of the mission of Friendship House.

As ardently as Friendship House volunteers practiced the corporal works of mercy, they pursued justice; indeed, Friendship House members insisted there could be no Catholic social justice without racial justice. De Hueck declared that if racial justice did not prevail, "the only alternative for the Church in the United States is the Catacombs."[83] A series of "Social Forums" prominently treating issues of racism and Communism became a staple of Friendship House. She adapted the "Social Forums" idea from a Canadian priest who sponsored discussion groups that took up current events and problems. Discussion participants received topical readings on a problem to prepare for these "Social Forums"; they would gather to discuss the problem and to apply Catholic social teaching to it. In Harlem these gatherings were the source of enormous appeal to volunteers. As Ellen Tarry wrote of her initial experience of Friendship House:

> I went to the Monday night meeting. It would be truer to say the meeting met me as I climbed the steps. Boys and girls were standing on the stairway, leaning against the banisters, sitting wherever they could. . . . The grey-haired woman was passing out tea and cakes, and others were talking about the Negro and his problem. I sat on the floor next to an attractive Creole-looking girl, who I soon learned was from New Orleans. Across the room was one brown-skinned boy. Though the others were talking about my people I could tell that few of them had known or associated with Negroes. I could catch phrases like "the Fatherhood of God, and the Brotherhood of man," or "the Negro and the Mystical Body" which indicated much more depth than I had attributed to these youngsters. Then the Baroness talked about "Christ in the Negro" and along with all others in the room I came under the spell of Catherine De Hueck. I had entered the room a Doubting Thomas and left as an ardent disciple. I was convinced that Friendship House needed me and many other Negroes if it was to be the Catholic Center the Baroness said was needed to combat the forces of Godless Communism in Harlem.[84]

Ellen Tarry not only became a faithful volunteer at the Friendship House in Harlem, she and Ann Harrigan, a white Friendship House volunteer, were chosen to establish a Friendship House in Chicago. Tarry took her role as a black Catholic spokesperson seriously. It was important to her that her Catholic audience understood she spoke as a Catholic and as a black woman. Tarry's experiences gave her perspectives on African American life that the baroness and other white Friendship House volunteers could never have and often had difficulty understanding. It was not easy for Tarry to offer these perspectives, but it was crucial that she share them and for them to be received if Catholics truly hoped to provide a real alternative to Communism.

Probably the most important statement Ellen Tarry made on the relationship of African Americans to Communism was an article she published in *Commonweal* in 1940. In this acclaimed essay, "Native Daughter," Tarry challenged Catholics for their sharp critique of Richard Wright's groundbreaking protest novel *Native Son*. "In Catholic circles," she wrote, "many have lamented the fact that the Negro writer who has arisen as the spokesman for his race should be a communist."[85] Tarry may have shocked the theological sensibilities of her fellow Catholics when she suggested that not all Communists were atheists. According to Tarry, who was a friend and colleague of Richard Wright, Wright considered himself "a God-fearing communist." In Tarry's experience this was eminently possible because "we [African Americans] learned about *Him* long before the communists *discovered* us."[86] Belief or nonbelief in God had very little to do with why Communism held an appeal for African Americans. While Tarry, a quite devout Catholic convert, embraced the principles of Friendship House and its work against Communism, she also knew the social, economic, and political circumstances that made Wright and so many other blacks willing to give it a fair chance. Communists seemed willing to give blacks a fair chance; they accepted blacks, remarked Tarry, "as men and women, despite our black skins."[87] In this acceptance Communists seemed to understand better the idea that God was not a respecter of persons, which was the central teaching about the nature of God that had attracted Ellen Tarry to Catholicism in the first place.

In "Native Daughter," Tarry did not set out to extol the virtues of Communism, but she did wish to awaken Catholics, especially Catholics who were working for interracial justice, and to combat Communism among African Americans. While they were right to reject Communism, she wanted them to see that they ought to be very careful in condemning those who saw its value and found hope in it. Catholics had something to learn from Wright. Tarry asked her fellow Catholics, "Did you ever stop to think that Catholics may be among those who are responsible for some of the conditions that have led Richard Wright and scores of others into the ranks of the reds?"[88] Finally, she pled for Christian America to "shed its coat of hypocrisy and to admit its sin."[89] To Tarry these were hard truths that Catholics had to come to terms with to accomplish their mission. In this case, Tarry "preached to the choir" because she knew it was possible for even those most engaged with the work of interracial justice to persist in negative attitudes regarding blacks and hypocrisy that undermined the good they tried to achieve.

Ellen Tarry was devoted to Friendship House, and she worked to bring more African Americans into association with it. But there were always many more white volunteers at Friendship House than black volunteers, even though Friendship House was located in a black community. According to Tarry, many Harlemites never felt complete confidence in Friendship House or the baroness because they did not understand the reasons for the house's existence. "Knowing why she had come to Harlem, the 'B' saw no need to explain her reason for being among us. Rather, she depended upon her good works to speak for her. However, as Friendship House and all it represented was built around her, the organization was often viewed with suspicion which the 'B's' presence had aroused in our midst."[90] At times the baroness experienced working with blacks as being like "walking on eggshells," but during her time in Harlem she came to an understanding of why many blacks had such a hard time trusting whites.[91] Tarry observed that the baroness came to understand the privileges she enjoyed because she was white while living in Harlem and used these privileges whenever she could to "open doors, purses, mouths, or ears, which are closed to a Negro, but open for a white person."[92]

Though Tarry thought Friendship House was making progress as a Catholic witness against Communism in Harlem, she believed its greatest achievements fell outside its stated mission. Friendship House was a clearinghouse for information on all sorts of matters as they related to African Americans; it was a place where blacks and whites met to talk about problems, church teachings, faith, and interests they shared in common, a sanctuary where "defeated men and women" knew they would receive help, and it was "a haven where some few of them found their way back to God."[93]

In some ways, Catholic anti-Communism as it related to African Americans brought Catholics into closer association and identification with Communists. Anyone who supported the full enfranchisement of black Americans or spoke out for justice for blacks ran the risk of being labeled a Communist. Catholics, the most ardent American anti-Communists, did not escape from being so labeled themselves when they ardently crusaded on behalf of interracial justice, a cause that found Catholics deliberately employing many of the methods used by Communists. Like Communists, they established connections in black neighborhoods, provided educational opportunities for black youth, assisted poor blacks with material assistance and medical services, used friendly media outlets to plead the case for justice for African Americans, engaged with black intellectuals, and transgressed cultural boundaries to meet blacks as social equals. These efforts brought Catholics failure when they allowed their history, theology, and prejudices to get in the way. But as often as they failed, these Catholics succeeded in showing true good will and sincere commitment to justice, Christian love, and equality. Communists desired blacks as their comrades in creating a new social order, while Catholics desired blacks as their friends in their quest to "go all the way with Christ." Communists and Catholics alike did not always convert African Americans to their way of thinking or believing, but they opened the way for conversation and collaboration and prepared foundations for building new relationships rooted in equality.

Throughout the 1930s, '40s, and early '50s, Catholic endeavors in African American communities against Communism flourished. During these decades, Catholics paid more attention to African American concerns and engaged with African American religious, civic, cultural, and political leaders more than they ever had or have since. George Schuyler, A. Philip Randolph, George Streator, Ellen Tarry, Claude McKay, Theophilus Lewis, Thomas Wyatt Turner, and Arthur G. Falls were among the black intellectuals, writers, and leaders whose thoughts on Communism, religion, racism, politics, and culture Catholic journals like the *Interracial Review*, *Commonweal*, *Catholic World*, and *America* sought and published.[94] Catholic schools, colleges, and universities began to open their doors to black students, and some Catholic dioceses formally desegregated, like the Archdiocese of St. Louis in 1946 and the Diocese of Raleigh, North Carolina, in 1953. Catholic seminaries began to train black men for the priesthood, and previously all-white religious communities began to accept the religious vocations of black women and men.

The numbers of African Americans who entered into the Catholic Church surged during this period as well. This Catholic engagement with African Americans was in large part spurred on by their anti-Communism and their fears of Communist infiltration of African American communities, and it primed Catholics for participation in the civil rights movement. And most importantly, it began to erode the Catholic color line that African American Catholics like Dr. Thomas Wyatt Turner and the Federated Colored Catholics had worked to dismantle since the early twentieth century.

NOTES

1. Thomas Wyatt Turner, "Experiences of a Colored Catholic," *Fortnightly Review*, April 1, 1926, 143.

2. Ibid.

3. Ibid., 143–44.

4. Well into the 1950s, African American Catholics were still dealing with the color bar in St. Louis, despite the fact that Archbishop Joseph E. Ritter formally desegregated Catholic institutions in 1946. In a letter to Dr. W. E. B. DuBois, Mrs. Monica Morrison, a black Catholic from St. Louis, complained of racism in Catholic hospitals, schools, and churches. She described how the color bar prevented her son from serving as an altar boy at their parish, and how this devastated him and discouraged him from pursuing his vocation to the priesthood; Mrs. Monica Morrison to W. E. B. DuBois, September 11, 1950, in *Selections: Correspondence of W. E. B. DuBois, 1944–1963*, ed. Herbert Aptheker (Amherst: University of Massachusetts Press, 1973), 290–92.

5. Cyprian Davis, *The History of Black Catholics in the United States* (New York: Crossroads, 1990), 220.

6. Marilyn Nickels, *Black Catholic Protest and the Federated Colored Catholics, 1917–1933: Three Perspectives on Racial Justice* (New York: Garland, 1988). Nickels details this particular initiative and provides a comprehensive account of the work of the Federated Colored Catholics and a biography of Dr. Thomas Wyatt Turner.

7. Turner, "Experiences of a Colored Catholic," 145.

8. Ibid., 145.

9. Ibid.

10. "The Red Menace," *Interracial Review* (November 1933): 203.

11. Ibid.

12. Ibid. Catholics and others used the euphemism "tenth man" often when referring to African Americans because statistically at that time they made up about 10 percent of the U.S. population. In 1937, a Josephite priest, Father Edward F. Murphy, published a novel on the Catholic apostolate to African Americans called *The Tenth Man* (Philadelphia: Dolphin, 1937).

13. John McGreevy, *Parish Boundaries: The Catholic Encounter with Race in the Twentieth-Century Urban North* (Chicago and London: University of Chicago Press, 1996).

14. Francis J. Gilligan, *The Morality of the Color Line* (Washington, D.C.: The Catholic University of America Press, 1928); John T. Gillard, S.S.J., *Colored Catholics in the United States* (Baltimore: Josephite, 1941); John LaFarge, S.J., *The Race Questions and the Negro: A Study of the Catholic Doctrine on Interracial Justice* (New York: Longmans, Green, 1943); and John A. Ryan "The Place of the Negro in American Society," address delivered at Howard University, March 2, 1943. The first three books were standard texts to which Catholics referred. Fathers Gilligan, Gillard, and LaFarge were all considered leaders in racial justice and experts on the "race problem." The hallmarks of Catholic thinking on racial justice between 1925 and 1945 appear in various ways in their writings, as well as those of lesser-known Catholics writing on race and justice.

15. The Catholic color bar also prevented black Catholics from sending their children to Catholic schools that they financially supported and from receiving treatment at Catholic hospitals. It denied the sacrament of holy orders to black men on the grounds that they could not possess the intellectual capacities or moral characters necessary to serve as good priests in the American church; see Stephen J. Ochs, *Desegregating the Altar: The Josephites and the Struggle for Black Priests, 1871–1960* (Baton Rouge: Louisiana State University Press, 1990), for extensive treatment on this subject.

16. Paul Hanly Furfey, "How Not to Go to Hell, and One Might Add: One Way of Not Going to Hell," *The Sign*, January 1937, 345.

17. Ibid.

18. Furfey, *The Mystery of Iniquity* (Milwaukee: Bruce, 1944), 149.

19. Furfey, "How Not to Go to Hell, 345.

20. Kate A. Baldwin, *Beyond the Color Line and the Iron Curtain: Reading Encounters between Black and White, 1922–1963* (Durham and London: Duke University Press, 2002), 35–37.

21. Robin D. G. Kelley, *Hammer and Hoe: Alabama Communists During the Great Depression* (Chapel Hill: University of North Carolina Press, 1990).

22. Mark Solomon, *The Cry Was Unity: Communists and African Americans, 1917–1936* (Chapel Hill: University of North Carolina Press, 1998), 19.

23. Ibid.

24. Ibid., 15. Baldwin says that "magical pilgrimages" went on throughout the 1920s, 1930s, and 1940s, but dropped off significantly by the 1950s when black interest in Communism dropped to an all-time low.

25. George Streator, "The Black Man Turns Away from Communist Appeal: 13,000,000 Negro Americans Wait for Saner Leader," *America*, October 7, 1939, 609.

26. Pius XI, *Divini redemptoris: On Atheistic Communism with Discussion Outline by Reverend Gerald C. Treacy* (New York: Paulist Press, 1937), 5.

27. Ibid.

28. Ibid., 6.

29. Ibid., 9.

30. Pius XI taught that civil society was an instrument of God. God-given rights were the right to life, to bodily integrity, to necessary means to existence, the right to move toward one's God-given destiny, the right to associate, and the right to own and to use property.

31. Ibid., 21.

32. Ibid., 22.

33. Ibid., 25.

34. Ibid.

35. Ibid., 26.

36. Ibid., 29.

37. Ibid.

38. "Resolutions Adopted by the Students of the College of the Sacred Heart, Manhattanville, New York City," *Interracial Review*, July 1933, 126.

39. George K. Hunton, *All of Which I Saw, Part of Which I Was* (Garden City, N.Y.: Doubleday, 1967), 94.

40. Ibid.

41. "Resolutions Adopted by the Students of the College of the Sacred Heart, Manhattanville, New York."

42. Ibid.

43. Hunton, *All of Which I Saw, Part of Which I Was*, 94.

44. Ibid., 95.

45. Ibid.

46. Ibid.

47. Mary Ursula Morris, "Youth and Interracial Justice," *Interracial Review*, April 1935, 58.

48. Ibid., 59.

49. Ibid.

50. Mother Grace Cowardin Dammann, R.S.C.J., Announcement of Integration of the College of the Sacred Heart, May 1938; http://www.mville.edu/News/News mayo3 diverse.

51. George W. B. Conrad, "The Negro and Communism," *The Chronicle*, July 1932, 139.

52. Ibid.

53. Ibid.

54. Ibid.

55. Ibid.

56. Aloysius Donadieu, "A Challenge to Catholic Youth," *Interracial Review*, June 1941, 89.

57. Ibid., 88.

58. Ibid., 89.

59. Ibid.

60. Catherine De Hueck was a Russian noblewoman and lost much of her family at the hands of the Bolsheviks during the Russian Revolution.

61. Baroness Catherine De Hueck, *The Story of Friendship House* (New York: privately printed), 2.

62. Ibid.

63. Ibid., 2–3.

64. Ibid., 2.

65. Ibid., 8.

66. Ibid.

67. Ibid., 14.

68. Ellen Tarry, *The Third Door: The Autobiography of an American Negro Woman* (New York: Guild, 1966), 158.

69. J. G. Shaw, S.J. "The Baroness in Harlem," *Catholic World*, January 1940, 476.

70. Edward Doherty, "Harlem's Holy House," Fund-raising literature, undated; Paul Hanly Furfey Papers, Archives, The Catholic University of America.

71. Ibid.

72. Shaw, "Baroness in Harlem," 477.

73. Ibid.

74. Martin de Porres was beatified by Pope Gregory XVI in 1836. In 1962, Pope John XXIII canonized de Porres.

75. Ann Harrigan Makletzoff quoted from her unpublished memoir in Albert Schorsch III, "Uncommon Women and Others: Memoirs and Lessons from Radical Catholics at Friendship House," *U.S. Catholic Historian* 9, no. 4 (Fall (1990): 373.

76. Ibid.

77. Claude McKay, "On Becoming a Roman Catholic," in *Epistle: A Quarterly Bulletin* 11, no. 2 (Spring 1945); reprinted in *Stamped with the Image of God: African Americans as God's Image in Black*, ed. Cyprian Davis and Jamie T. Phelps (New York: Orbis, 2003), 107.

78. Doherty, "Poet's Progress," *Extension*, September 1946, 46.

79. McKay, "On Becoming a Roman Catholic."

80. Wayne Cooper, *Claude McKay: Rebel Sojourner in the Harlem Renaissance; A Biography* (Baton Rouge and London: Louisiana State University Press, 1987), 359.

81. Ibid., 362.

82. Ibid., 363.

83. Ibid., 15.

84. Tarry, *Third Door*, 165.

85. Tarry, "Native Daughter," *Commonweal*, April 1940, 524; see also Cecilia A. Moore, "'My Spirit Soared': Ellen Tarry's Conversion to Catholicism," *Sacred Rock: Journal of the Institute for Black Catholic Studies* 2 (Summer 1999): 19–24.

86. Ibid.

87. Ibid.

88. Ibid.

89. Ibid.

90. Tarry, *Third Door*, 147.

91. Ibid.

92. Ibid., 168.

93. Ibid.

94. George Schuyler was a black conservative and ardent foe of Communism. He was also the father of Phillipa Duke Schuyler, an internationally famous child piano composer and prodigy. Phillipa and her mother converted to Catholicism, though George never did. Ellen Tarry, Theophilus Lewis, and Claude McKay were all converts to Catholicism. In the 1920s, Claude McKay was a Communist and was a guest of the Soviet Communists in Moscow. Not long after his visit to Moscow, McKay repudiated Communism and became an ardent anti-Communist. He converted to Catholicism in 1944.

TWELVE

Praying in the Public Square: Catholic Piety Meets Civil Rights, War, and Abortion

James P. McCartin

As thousands of truant school children poured into Milwaukee's streets to march for racial equality in October 1965, one figure among them stood out not only for his age and enthusiasm, but also for his clerical collar. Asked why he was there among children twenty or more years his junior, James Groppi, a white priest and prominent activist who gained a national reputation by organizing over 100 civil rights marches in his native city, simply declared, "I didn't think I had a choice"[1] In fact, Groppi was one of a dozen priests and two dozen religious sisters who that day became conspicuous symbols of a growing Catholic commitment to the forces of political change. A vocal minority of Catholic laity, both in Milwaukee and elsewhere, likewise joined such priests and sisters in embracing activism, and those who did so tended to affirm, like Groppi, that their faith compelled them to do so. In the process, these Catholics embodied Groppi's claim that "marching is not only a protest, it is a prayer."[2] Hailed by supporters and denounced by opponents, these Catholic activists garnered national attention, sparked controversy, and exercised profound influence within and beyond the U.S. Catholic community as they brought their prayers into the public square.

Religion and public activism converged in the late twentieth century as Americans devoted themselves to a whole range of initiatives designed to procure social and political change. The rising influence of Protestant Evangelicals in the decades after 1945, a development that would eventually help secure Republican dominance in post-1980 U.S. politics, has attracted historians' generous attention.[3] But Catholics, too, played a vital and transformative role in the engagement between religion and public life in this era. Particularly through their participation in the African American civil rights movement, the anti–Vietnam War movement, and the movement to oppose legalized abortion, Catholic activists went a long way in assuring religion's continued prominence in the U.S. public square, and in the process, they fostered a changing understanding of the meaning of religious devotion. Indeed, attending to the public prayers of Catholic activists amid the pitched national battles of the late twentieth century can help us to gain a more textured understanding of the recent history of religion and public life in the United States, revealing how Catholics were ultimately decisive actors in this history.

Though historians have too often underemphasized the religious impetus behind the struggle for African American civil rights, activists frequently saw themselves as participants in a religious movement. Civil rights demonstrations frequently began in churches and employed the scriptural language of justice and judgment to encourage marchers to persevere despite resistance, violence, and imprisonment. Leaders like Martin Luther King Jr. insisted that the notion of rights itself was endowed with profound religious significance and not subject to undue limitation by human regulation.[4] Writing from Rome amid increasing civil rights demonstrations in 1963, Pope John XXIII likewise did his part to foment and justify activism on behalf of God-given rights: "If civil authorities legislate for, or allow, anything that is contrary to [the moral] order and therefore contrary to the will of God, neither the laws made nor the authorizations granted can be binding on the consciences of its citizens, *since we must obey God rather than men.*"[5] Citing their religious conviction, Catholic civil rights supporters thus joined a growing community of religiously inspired Protestants, Jews, and Muslims in the fight for equality before the law.[6]

Though Catholic support in general expanded throughout the 1960s, many working-class white ethnic Catholics in the urban North rejected religious arguments for civil rights. For them, the large-scale migration of southern blacks into northern cities in the decades after World War I was an unwelcome invasion that threatened to dissolve tight-knit white ethnic communities with nineteenth-century roots. In white majority neighborhoods, African Americans were often seen as competitors for scarce jobs. Viewing the advancement of African Americans as a symptom of their own social and economic instability, many white Catholics therefore found it easy to brush off calls for racial equality.[7]

But particularly among African American and many white, northern, suburban Catholics, civil rights found enduring support—support that would have significant reverberations because it helped, over a series of decades, to redefine what it meant to be a "good Catholic." Though only a small percentage embraced civil rights activism, they represented both a gathering consensus around racial equality and an increasing willingness among Catholics to support social and political change as a religious priority. These activists also promoted the notion that engagement in public life could be a means of advancing personal "holiness"—a development that helped bestow new spiritual legitimacy on popular activism. Subsequently, support for "social justice" and an elevated sense of personal "vocation" to improve the world would become a highly valued measure of religious commitment within the U.S. Catholic community.[8] Yet as it emerged in tension with a more traditional measure of piety—which had long been determined by dutiful performance of religious rituals, especially regular Mass attendance—the expectation of public activism would become a critically divisive theme in postwar U.S. Catholicism.

Growing support for civil rights during the 1960s rested in substantial part on Catholic leaders' challenges to racism in the preceding decades. Already in the 1930s, Jesuit John LaFarge, an editor at *America* magazine, launched a sustained attack on the evils of racism, especially as practiced by Catholics. In the wake of World War II, bishops in St. Louis, the District of Columbia, New Orleans, and Raleigh ordered the integration of diocesan organizations and schools—decisions that prompted angry standoffs with recalcitrant parishioners. In a 1958 document that the NAACP labeled "one of the strongest statements yet issued in the USA in support of racial integration," the National Catholic Welfare Conference, an organization sponsored and led by U.S. Catholic bishops, asserted that "the heart of the race question is moral and religious." "Can enforced segregation be reconciled with the Christian view of our fellow man?" the bishops asked. No, they answered, since "all men are equal in the sight of God . . . [and this] confers on all men human dignity and human rights."[9] All the while, a growing number of Catholic parishes, schools, and colleges became local organizational sites for a slowly expanding support for racial justice.[10] Though concern for potential Communist influences ensured that postwar church authorities shunned any hint of radicalism in pursuit of racial equality, they nevertheless demonstrated commitment to challenging racist attitudes and encouraging white Catholics to advance black civil rights.[11]

Developments in mid-century theology and devotional life likewise contextualized and shaped how a growing number of Catholics understood racial attitudes in relation to their religious commitments. In particular, a postwar focus on the integration of Christian practice into all the activities of everyday life provided a spiritual foundation for Catholic activism. Influential European-born intellectuals like Emmanuel Mounier and Jacques Maritain stressed that true holiness consisted not simply in the performance of traditional rituals, but instead in living an actively Christian life within the context of the secular world. Echoing such writers, Gerald Ellard, an American Jesuit and popular spiritual writer, asserted that all the baptized were called to embody *the life of Christ living within us.* For Ellard, as for other postwar spiritual writers, private prayer and public celebration of the sacraments were ideally the context in which each individual nurtured a closer relationship with Jesus, thus enabling him "to dominate our lives, to have full sway over our thoughts, aspirations, and activities."[12] Thus, the depth of an individual's religious commitment was ultimately measured by his or her actions in the "temporal order" rather than according to ritual observance.

At the same time, the faithful became immersed in the theology of the mystical body of Christ, a dominant theme among U.S. Catholics between the 1930s and 1960s. Drawing on the work of European theologians and boosted by a 1943 encyclical on the mystical body by Pope Pius XII, U.S. spiritual writers and preachers encouraged their audiences to see themselves as part of Christ's living body in the contemporary world. Each individual was a living agent of Christ's saving power—wherever he or she lived, whatever his or her status in life. Just as each part of a body has its ordained purpose and function, so too did each living Christian have a specific vocation and purpose to serve God within the secular world. One typical writer on the topic challenged readers to consider the meaning of their political and social activities: "Incorporated into the Mystical Body of Christ, filled with His Life, taking part in His Action . . . what should be our impact, our effect on the world?"[13] Like the drive to integrate Christian practice and everyday life, mystical-body theology encouraged individuals to make the world more just—more as God intended. According to Bernard Sheil, a Chicago auxiliary bishop who spearheaded efforts at interracial collaboration, the implication of mystical-body theology for racial attitudes was irrefutable: "Jim Crowism in the Mystical Body of Christ is a disgraceful anomaly."[14]

To give practical force to these ideals, lay-led "Catholic Action" organizations—clubs or fellowships that drew upon pastoral models developed in Europe in the 1920s— proliferated between 1945 and 1960. National groups like the Young Christian Workers, Young Christian Students, and Christian Family Movement, organizations that together claimed well over 100,000 U.S. members organized into local "cells," each made up of perhaps ten or twenty members, promoted the ideal that Catholics were called to transform the world through public action. Racial equality was often foremost in the minds of those who joined Catholic Action groups, along with a concern for economic justice and an interest in peaceful resolution of global conflict. Though their membership peaked in the late 1950s, these organizations helped prepare the way for Vatican II reforms and spawned many 1960s Catholic civil rights activists.[15]

Together, these developments broadened the concepts of religious devotion and personal holiness to include actions undertaken both in the private sphere and in the public, thereby affirming the religious significance of the postwar movement for racial justice. In devotional magazines and diocesan newspapers, commentators continually highlighted the fundamental connection between the life of true holiness and the life of love for one's neighbor, no matter of what race. One writer concluded in 1956:

> The race problem is a sacramental problem because it has to do with the Eucharist. . . . When those Catholics who indulge in racial prejudice receive Communion they do not really mean what they do. They do not really mean to be united to all members of Christ's Body, white or colored. For them the Eucharist is not the Bread of unity and love. It is a sacramental lie. . . . The truth of our love and the truth of our Communion will lead us to a solution of the racial problem this side of time and will determine our eternal destiny the other side of time.[16]

"We trumpet the blasphemous triumph of Satan," the distinguished liturgical scholar and Benedictine priest Godfrey Diekmann declared, "if we eat the Bread and drink the cup, and refuse to accept the Negro as our daily table guest."[17]

Trappist monk Thomas Merton, who had gained fame with his 1948 memoir *The Seven Storey Mountain*, likewise applied religious principles to the problem of racial inequality and called lay Catholics to embrace the spirit of social and political change. "Our social actions must conform to our deepest religious principles," he argued in 1966. "Beliefs and politics can no longer be kept isolated from each other." Ultimately, he concluded, "every man is to be regarded as Christ, and treated as Christ."[18] Within this context, he invited lay people to consider the implications of their position on civil rights for their personal aspirations to live a Christian life in the contemporary world.

By the time the Second Vatican Council opened in Rome in the fall of 1962, the civil rights movement had gained a national momentum that found resonance in the Council's later pronouncements on social justice and human rights. In the 1964 "Pastoral Constitution on the Church in the Modern World," for example, Council fathers affirmed the position that had gained ground for well over a decade: holiness and public action were intimately related, and Catholics were called upon to accomplish "the work of Christ Himself" by advancing the "brotherhood of all men." Highlighting the inviolable character of human rights, church leaders at Vatican II made clear their own position: "With regards to the fundamental rights of the person, every type of discrimination, whether social or cultural, whether based on sex, race, color, social condition, language, or religion, is to be overcome as contrary to God's intent." Asserting a "Universal Call to Holiness" shared by all the baptized, church leaders enjoined the faithful to confront inequitable social and political relations through the transformative power of Christian action. "All the faithful of Christ of whatever rank or status are called to the fullness of the Christian life," the Council proclaimed. Lay people were thus called to "devot[e] themselves to the glory of God and the service of their neighbor," becoming "a shining witness and model of holiness" before the world.[19]

Prominent leaders like Milwaukee's James Groppi proudly appealed to Vatican II in the service of racial equality. A national media figure by his mid-thirties, Groppi became for many younger priests across the nation a prototypical model for a new "Vatican II style" of ministry. His own archbishop complimented Groppi for "doing things maybe others of us don't have the courage to do," and Martin Luther King Jr. hailed the priest's capacity to push beyond "sentimental and timid supplications for justice."[20] Yet because prominent figures like Groppi also represented a distinctly assertive manifestation of the religious imperative for change, they also provoked the critical reaction among some of their fellow Catholics. At times employing severe rhetoric, Groppi claimed to have "felt no sorrow" amid the Milwaukee riots of 1967, implying that white Milwaukeeans got what they deserved. "I don't believe in violence," he insisted, "but we had done everything possible to relieve the conditions under which [impoverished African Americans] lived."[21]

Beyond individual leaders, groups like the Christian Family Movement (CFM) focused intently on the issue of racial justice by the mid-1960s. Drawing on earlier developments in theology and spirituality, as well as on the teachings of Vatican II, CFM engaged in a campaign to enlist its 80,000 lay members in the cause of civil rights. As small groups of married couples, CFM cells regularly met to engage common readings and discussion exercises, each designed to deepen their mastery of a social problem and inspire them to infuse their local communities with social justice. Like those of other Catholic Action organizations, members followed three basic steps in confronting social problems: observe, judge, and act. First, members observed the multiple aspects of the specific issue at hand, such as racism, poverty, or warfare. Then, within the context of group prayer, study, and discussion, they judged its economic, sociological, and political basis while determining what concrete actions might augment the problem. Finally, CFM members together committed themselves to undertake the desired actions and thereby assume their Christian responsibility to transform the world.

As secular activism accelerated, the pursuit of racial equality through actions of religious commitment consumed CFM groups across the nation—prompting one member to assert that "the Negro question seems to creep into virtually every meeting." Members encouraged one another to reconsider the meaning of Christian "devotion" in the midst of contemporary struggles, and throughout 1964 and 1965, local cells across the nation confronted impediments to African American equality. Aiming "to effect *change* within ourselves and on the world around us," as the organization's nationally distributed study guide put it, members undertook a range of actions to improve race relations and win civil rights for African Americans. Chicago-area groups hosted interracial parties and community lectures on civil rights and escorted African American Catholics to Sunday Mass in neighborhoods where whites threatened violence. In Oakland and New York, they put their energies behind fair-housing campaigns. Elsewhere, members marched, boycotted, initiated interracial dialogues, and helped establish inner-city youth programs. One crowning achievement for CFM was the participation of several dozen members in the Selma March in the spring of 1965, an event that proved critical in securing popular support for the Voting Rights Act that became law that year. From all regions of the nation, members traveled to Selma to help ensure a visible Catholic presence there.[22]

Though it spread Catholic commitment to civil rights, the integration of faith and activism also yielded division within CFM, underscoring the significance of the broader religious transformation that was underway. While detractors within and outside the organization argued that it had become more a political movement than a religious one, supporters maintained that the organization merely embodied a style of religious expression and commitment suited to contemporary demands. Amid such division, some local CFM groups scaled back on public activism and returned their attention to more traditional and private devotions like the rosary. But others sustained the activist momentum and, by the late 1960s, moved beyond civil rights to confront the challenges of urban poverty and the war in Vietnam. Regardless, a persistent tension over the proper place of activism within CFM sparked a general decline in membership, and the organization faded into obscurity by the following decade.[23]

Yet despite such divisions, the measure of religious commitment changed significantly during the post–World War II era. An individual's ritual observance was arguably the single standard by which to gauge religious devotion in the 1940s, but by the 1960s commitment to social justice and to the welfare of others emerged as an alternative measure. Over time, the boundary between piety and activism became fluid as church leaders and lay organizations, aided by the historical convergence of the civil rights movement and Vatican II, together affirmed the notion that Christian devotion could be measured through engagement in public life. Civil rights thus became an entryway for idealistic Catholics who accepted the call to public engagement as a religious imperative.

Support for civil rights thus highlighted and elevated Catholics' place within the postwar public square and put them on the winning side of history. Engagement in the struggle for rights and equality would therefore highlight Catholics' commitment to the celebrated American ideals of freedom and equality. But by the late 1960s and early 1970s, debates over war and abortion frequently placed Catholic activism in a decidedly different light.

Burning napalm has a noxious odor—quite distinct from the sweet-smelling incense burned during Catholic liturgies to symbolize prayers rising up to God. But at the hands of a cadre of activist Catholics in May 1968, napalm stood in for incense at one dramatic ritual performed in a parking lot outside the Selective Service Office in Catonsville, Maryland. For years, American military aircraft unleashed enormous payloads of napalm on the jungles of Vietnam, destroying villages and burning the skin of Vietnamese peasants who were doused in the process. This day, however, it was deployed in an act of prayer and protest against American military actions in Southeast Asia.

As seven men and two women made the sign of the cross and prayed aloud for a cessation of violence in Vietnam, the smoke from the burning heap of several hundred draft files, freshly stolen from the draft board and smothered in homemade napalm, drifted over their heads into the sky. In a written statement, the "Catonsville Nine," as they would be called, declared their opposition to the war was "in utter fidelity to our Faith," and they pledged to devote "whatever strength of mind, body and grace that God will give us" to the cause of ending it. Soon, the police arrived, as expected, and hauled the nine activists off to jail. Each subsequently pleaded innocent at trial, asserting that their religiously formed consciences compelled them to violate the law by destroying federal property.[24]

The Catonsville Nine's combination of religious ritual and public protest both indicated continuity with earlier civil rights activists and highlighted the advancement to a new stage of Catholic activism in the late 1960s. Earlier protesters enshrined activism as a legitimate expression of religious devotion by affirming the American values of freedom, equality, and individual rights. But Catholic antiwar activists made their mark by offering a profound critique of U.S. nationalism. In doing so, they challenged Catholics' hard-won reputation as loyal Americans—a reputation solidified only in the recent past amid the Catholics' World War II patriotism and Cold War anti-Communism. Consequently, in the eyes of many fellow citizens—including many Catholics—religious war resisters appeared far more radical than the religious civil rights activists who emerged earlier in the decade.

As they brought the work begun by civil rights activists to a new stage that was more challenging to many Americans' patriotism, Catholic antiwar protesters established boundaries on the convergence of piety and public protest. Ultimately, their demonstrations highlighted the limits of popular Catholic enthusiasm for public activism.

As antiwar demonstrations began to proliferate in the mid-1960s, they supplied an important context for the merger of Catholic conviction and political dissent. Whether provocative or benign, antiwar protests staged by Catholic activists received generous publicity in the national media, assuring broad public awareness of the connection between Catholicism and growing opposition to the Vietnam War. A few weeks after Pope

Paul VI's 1965 appeal for peace at New York's United Nations headquarters, Roger La-Porte, a twenty-two-year-old former Trappist monk, entered the U.N. Plaza and poured gasoline over his body, immolating himself in protest. "I am against war, all war," he told paramedics before his death. "I did this as a religious action."[25] On the Pentagon concourse in November 1969, roughly 170 activists trespassed onto federal property to gather for a Mass protesting U.S. involvement in the war, only to be arrested.[26] During the summer of 1973, several groups of Catholic protesters were detained for staging "pray-ins" in the White House: gaining entrance as tourists, they knelt down, prayed for peace, and refused to vacate until forcibly removed.[27] In various locations throughout the late 1960s and early 1970s, Catholic war resisters joined others in publicly burning their government-issued draft cards, sometimes going on to serve prison terms for what they deemed a religious act.[28]

As such religious acts of political dissent mounted, they triggered an intergenerational struggle that James Carroll, a prominent priest and antiwar activist in the late 1960s and early 1970s, would later dub an internal "holy war" over the proper place of the Catholic faith in the U.S. public square. At the center of this struggle was the question of whether American Catholics should be willing to affirm their nationalism in uncritical fashion or should boldly challenge the United States' anti-Communist campaign in Vietnam.[29] Between different generational camps, charges of the zealotry and dangerous fanaticism of the young were matched by accusations of the older generation's complaisance with evil. Catholic activists typically came of age in the 1950s and 1960s—making it easy for their critics to characterize them as "young radicals" and associate them with the anti-American strain of the secular New Left. For their part, many older Catholics interpreted a critical attitude toward the war as scandalous disloyalty and a rejection of hard-won reputation of Catholic patriotism. Strident affirmations of patriotic support by authorities like New York's Cardinal Francis Spellman—"My country, may it always be right," he said in late 1965. "Right or wrong, my country"—met with popular approval among those who had already been adults by the outbreak of World War II.[30]

Making matters more complex, those who publicly opposed the war also fielded criticism from war opponents of a more moderate disposition, a group that notably represented roughly a quarter of the total U.S. Catholic population.[31] Political moderates who rejected U.S. policy on Vietnam, for example, sometimes worried that activists were ultimately counterproductive in their public protests. As one Catholic editorialist asserted, the Catonsville draft board raid, for example, tended to "raise other questions which obscure the point the [activists] are trying to make: questions related to respect for the law and for other individuals, questions of public order and of propriety and taste."[32] Even prominent peace advocates like Thomas Merton and Dorothy Day, founder of the pacifist Catholic Worker movement, questioned the means of protest chosen by activists. To them, destruction of government property seemed excessive, even potentially immoral. While Merton worried that such acts conveyed hopelessness and cynicism, Day feared that they skirted too closely to physical aggression and might devolve into a "whole turning toward violence in the Catholic Left."[33]

Yet for many of the most dedicated war opponents, their religious commitment far exceeded their commitment to nationalism and could not be curbed by chiding from fellow war opponents. Especially as military intervention escalated after 1967, Catholic protesters, painfully aware that their protests did not foment significant policy change, self-consciously rejected concerns about offending sensibilities and committed themselves to actions of "prophetic witness." Drawing on the tradition of the Hebrew prophets, the project of prophetic witness implied two things: first, exposing the nation's most glaring moral problems; and second, urging renunciation, atonement, and change at the national level.[34] The federal government and military, along with those who actively supported these organized instruments of war and violence, thus became targets of relentless criticism by Catholic activists. Draft-board raids and the destruction of government-issued draft cards, as well as willingly serving prison terms for such offenses, dramatized and underscored the dire necessity of reform—and over time, these developments helped form popular attitudes toward the wider antiwar movement and Catholic activism alike.

The most prominent Catholic advocates of prophetic witness against the war were the two brothers who orchestrated the Catonsville protest of 1968, Jesuit priest Daniel Berrigan and Philip Berrigan, a Josephite priest. Together, the Berrigans demanded a rejection of the systemic violence wrought by the U.S. military, drawing hundreds—if not thousands—of the faithful into public activism. In the three years after the Catonsville protest, Catholic antiwar activists staged or joined scores of similar draft raids. Just as Groppi became a nationally recognized Catholic face within the civil rights movement, the Berrigans were recognizably linked with the antiwar cause. Even from federal prison, where they landed after the Catonsville event, the brothers urged ongoing activism through their correspondence. Writing in 1972, historian David J. O'Brien highlighted what drove the Berrigans' relentlessness:

> In the past ten years Daniel and Philip Berrigan have experienced little if any change in their central beliefs about their faith or in the basic direction of their lives. What has changed is their view of America, the gradual transformation of the almost naive faith in the goodness of America and the ability of its people to live up to its ideals to a shocked awareness of the scandalous failure of the nation to resolve its moral, and its economic, contradictions.[35]

Supporters and detractors alike reacted to the same characteristic in the Berrigans: their ability to articulate a piercing critique of U.S. policies while standing on the foundation of their deep religious faith. Simultaneously, the brothers represented the best and the worst of Catholics' engagement in the postwar public square. Some saw in them the logical progression of the public activism prompted by mystical-body theology and Catholic Action and earlier borne out in the civil rights movement and the teachings of Vatican II. But these brothers distinguished themselves by their dim appraisal of U.S. military actions—a fact that drew either affirmation or rage from observers. Critics like FBI chief J. Edgar Hoover branded them terrorists, while several prominent American church leaders publicly disapproved of the Berrigans' activism. But as one supporter maintained, their radicalism was "best understood as priestly activity." "They are attempting to regain an ancient heritage of power: to become practitioners of the healing of souls," he argued. "They have sensed the demons at loose in the spiritual depths of modern man and society— the onslaught of absurdity and death. And they have undertaken to recapture the original priestly task and calling—the struggle of exorcism and liberation."[36] For them, as for other prophetic witnesses of their time, exorcism and liberation meant loosening the bonds of nationalism that led to wrongful support for a corrupted political system and an immoral war.

Other practitioners of prophetic witness followed the Berrigans in defending their actions by appealing to their Catholic faith. In 1970, Francis Kroncke, a young layman who destroyed draft files in Minneapolis, asserted that his protest was "a sacramental act" that was a "proper, reasoned and measured response to the immorality of the [Vietnam War] and to the moral imperatives and guidelines of the Second Vatican Council." His intention, Kroncke said, was to "begin the removal of the evil present in America, and allow God's sanctifying and reconciling presence to be felt and discerned." The seven other activists who joined him, he concluded, were

> people who believe that the meaning of their Catholic sacramental system extended through and beyond intra-personal acts into social acts. . . . They believe that sacramental actions, for example, the Eucharist which effects the religious solidarity of what is called theologically, the "Body of Christ," carried over concretely into and through the State's socio-political body.[37]

Along with the Berrigans, Kroncke clearly echoed the earlier strains of mystical-body theology and Catholic Action that helped inspire Catholic civil rights activism.

Beyond the challenge to nationalism, two other characteristics further limited popular sympathy with those who undertook acts of prophetic witness: first, the abstractness of their claims; and second, their moral stridency. These activists, often individuals with advanced education and theoretical sophistication, relied upon what was ultimately a technical language to explain the convergence of holiness and public dissent—a language that often failed to resonate with many ordinary observers, including many of their fellow Catholics. Declarations that linked "sacramental actions" to the "State's socio-political body" turned many into skeptics of prophetic witness and made activists' moral claims easier to dismiss. Earlier in the decade, civil rights demonstrations could more concretely link personal holiness with the issue of race: postwar social and cultural circumstances brought interracial contact to new heights, creating personal experiences that more easily connected to theological assertions. But antiwar activists seemed comparatively strained and abstract in linking piety to politics. Broad characterizations of the government as morally bankrupt and the implication that ordinary citizens were accomplices in its systemic immorality could come off as arrogant. In their unflinching moral critique, activists' outrage often lacked connection to the outlook of many ordinary citizens. Consequently, activists became susceptible to charges of extremism and detachment.

Finally, in the late 1960s prophetic witness combined with an emerging set of contradictory reactions to recent changes in Catholic piety that made public protest a profoundly divisive force among U.S. Catholics. Conflict grew both from differing views about the activist orientation sparked by civil rights protesters and from the liturgical reforms of Vatican II. Such conflict generated a backlash against Catholic progressives and radicals who employed piety to advance social or political reform. By the mid-1960s, Vatican II–era liturgical reforms allowed for rituals to be tailored to express particular circumstances and interests. Many African American and Latino Catholics, for example, took this opportunity to make their public worship reflect their cultural distinctiveness and dramatize their work for "social justice."[38] Catholic feminists likewise adapted traditional rituals, forging them into protests against patterns of social and ecclesiastical patriarchy.[39] By 1967, most of the faithful had reached their conclusions about the reform of worship spurred by Vatican II. While the majority attested to welcoming changes such as the use of the vernacular language and sustained lay participation in Catholic liturgy, a vocal minority denounced changes as undignified, even heretical revisions that allowed political interests to dominate over reverence for God. Such divergent attitudes hardened into distinct camps. "Traditionalist" critics organized to lobby for a return to the limited liturgical options of the pre–Vatican II era, and they decried experimentation as a divisive misuse of liturgy perpetrated by "new-breed innovators" and "liturgical beatniks."[40] Such critics tended to regard recent changes as the "politicization of piety," while advocates understood them as the "sanctification of politics." Either way, the combination of piety and politics instigated a debate over Catholic piety that continued to divide the faithful into the next century.

In the context of the antiwar movement, piety channeled and intensified existing political and cultural tensions, fostering polarization within both the Catholic community and the broad American populace.[41] This polarization had three major implications. First, due to its often antinationalistic character, many dismissed prophetic witness and even turned their disapproval against more demure forms of Catholic activism. Second, polarization over innovations in piety after Vatican II sparked internal conflict among Catholics that would endure into the next century. Third, in the more immediate future, the polarization generated by antiwar protests would forecast the contours of public activism within the emerging pro-life movement.

Every seven seconds on January 26, 1972, Manhattan's Church of the Epiphany tolled its bell in solemn protest. Visitors across the street entering an open house at a Planned Parenthood clinic where abortions were performed each morning also encountered Epiphany parishioners holding signs proclaiming the "right to life" of the unborn. While city officials and curious New Yorkers toured the new medical facility, several female parishioners spent the afternoon inside the church praying for an end to abortion. "Perhaps it's good that this place is across the street from a church," argued one. "Maybe some woman will look at the church as she is about to enter the door here and have another thought and do what is right."[42] Through similar demonstrations in New York and in a dozen other states during the late 1960s and early 1970s, Catholic abortion opponents projected their religiously inspired opposition to new state laws that offered legalized accessed to abortion, proclaiming their own political stance regarding the "right to life."

Such demonstrations underscored two things about the early antiabortion movement: first, its modest, grassroots organizational character; and second, Catholics' crucial public opposition as access to abortion entered a period of increasing legalization. In its early years, the antiabortion movement coalesced at the local and state levels as committed Catholics advocated recognition of fetal rights. The goal of these activists was either to maintain and affirm old state antiabortion statutes or provoke the reversal of new, more permissive state laws. As legal access to abortion expanded in states beginning in 1967, public activism attracted many Catholics who stood on the sidelines of other 1960s protests. In the process, parish halls and parochial school cafeterias became vital centers for local "right to life" initiatives that would utilize a wide array of tactics, including public protests, petitions, letter-writing campaigns, legislative lobbying, and lawsuits. Many who had never previously understood themselves as activists—middle-aged Catholic women, for example—often represented the majority of participants in local organizations, demonstrating that the call to religious activism would not be confined to the young activists or male leaders that dominated the civil rights and antiwar movements.[43] Like the civil rights movement, the early antiabortion movement demonstrates how religion bolstered the mounting call for political rights in the 1960s.

Yet the character of antiabortion activism changed significantly in the decade after the U.S. Supreme Court's January 1973 rulings in *Roe v. Wade* and *Doe v. Bolton*, which secured wide access to abortion across the fifty states. Organizationally, opposition to abortion became a national and ecumenical initiative, and in the process, participants in the newly energized movement adopted more strident modes of activism. Modest sidewalk protests attended entirely by Catholic participants gave way to Catholic participation in vast, interdenominational marches in Washington, D.C. By the late 1970s, acts of nonviolent civil disobedience and the arrest of rosary-bearing protesters became commonplace scenes outside abortion clinics. By the early 1980s, antiabortion Catholics also staged regular "rescues" in which participants physically blocked access to what they termed "abortuaries" or "abortion mills." Amid such drama, activists would also serve as "sidewalk counselors," pleading with clients to forgo abortions, and some even moved beyond the sidewalks, infiltrating clinics to sabotage costly medical equipment.[44] Though many Catholic activists would denounce the use of violence by protesters, a contingent of leaders within the broader movement advocated destructive acts that caused no harm to human life.[45] In the process, the combination of national coordination and the use of more dramatic tactics represented transformation in the movement after *Roe*.

Among the new post-*Roe* recruits was Joan Andrews, a laywoman whose relentless leadership would inspire hundreds to welcome arrest and imprisonment. "In 1973, when *Roe vs. Wade* was decided, I was shocked. I felt that I had returned to Nazi Germany. I had always figured we had lived in a civilized world," she later said, "but now that had changed."[46] Over the next decade, Andrews built a network of likeminded activists and coordinated some of the nation's most highly visible and tenacious antiabortion protests. During the 1980s, Andrews led fellow Catholics in collaborating with Evangelical leader Randall Terry in his well-publicized "Operation Rescue" campaigns. "We got 15 days [in jail] for our first rescue, 30 for the second, 45 for the third, 60 for the fourth, 75 for the fifth. . . . We were not backing down, and [judges] realized that the long sentences were not going to do any good."[47] Condemning the political system that fostered state-protected "death camps,"

Andrews concluded that "Jesus would not cooperate with authorities in the midst of mass murder."[48] Such views led her to a five-year prison sentence in 1986 after being convicted of burglary, criminal mischief, and resisting arrest at a Florida protest. Still undeterred in the late 1990s, she denounced what she called the "Un-Supreme Court" and declared that

> Catholic doctrine is clear and must be universally accepted. It is infallible truth. . . . The
> Catholic Church teaches with the force of infallible doctrine that abortion is a heinous
> sin, the act of killing an innocent child. . . . As this holocaust of the Culture of Death has
> shown time and again, this whole struggle goes far beyond unjust laws and a government
> gone bad; it is a war between good and evil.[49]

Like frustrated antiwar activists of the late 1960s, many Catholic antiabortion advocates followed Andrews in embracing both radical protest methods and extreme rhetoric during *Roe*'s long aftermath.

In the face of ongoing disappointment throughout the 1970s, activists altered the focus of their work from ensuring the rights of the unborn to procuring cultural reform, a transition that helped foster the most radical manifestations of Catholic antiabortion activism. In the process, activists increasingly distinguished themselves from the politically and theologically liberal Catholics who joined earlier movements in favor of civil rights and against the Vietnam War. Having congealed in the late 1960s around the political project advancing the "right to life," throughout the 1970s the movement increasingly focused on promoting "pro-life" sensibilities, raising public awareness that life itself is "sacred." In working to reform cultural attitudes about the value of human life beginning at conception, Catholic activists often appropriated an anti-liberal perspective that shaped their movement into the 1980s and 1990s. As they voiced angry critiques of the "liberalization" and "secularization" of U.S. culture, the earlier political goal of securing legal rights became increasingly diffuse. In the process, Catholic antiabortion activism came to evoke a religious crusade rather than a social or political movement. Though U.S. Catholic bishops maintained that respect for human rights was the centerpiece of their lobbying efforts, at the hands of mostly lay Catholic activists and their Protestant counterparts, against abortion access, the focus of the movement shifted from politics to culture.

It was hardly inevitable that lay activists like Joan Andrews would adopt such a radical orientation. During the 1960s and early 1970s, outspoken Catholic opponents of abortion articulated arguments that echoed the African American civil rights movement, voicing their position in terms of a liberal appeal for the rights of the unborn.[50] Consequently, the movement for the fetal "right to life" became one among many contemporary movements to expand legal rights, including the rights of women, handicapped persons, prisoners, and of a host of other minority groups.[51] The respected Jesuit moral theologian Richard A. McCormick argued this way in 1965: "Every man possesses the right to life from God. . . . There must be no man, no human authority, no science, no indication (whether medical, eugenic, social, economic, or moral) that can justify deliberate and direct destruction of innocent human life."[52] A string of statements from U.S. Catholic bishops likewise applied the rhetoric of individual rights to the abortion question, and even Vatican officials at the Congregation for the Doctrine of the Faith voiced its position in the language of legal rights: "The first right of the human person is his right to life. . . . Hence it must be protected above all others."[53]

So, why did post-1973 Catholic antiabortion activism become increasingly anti-liberal and shift its focus away from political "right to life" and toward the effort to promote a "culture of life"? First and foremost, the alignment of political forces against the antiabortion movement encouraged this shift. In the years after *Roe*, the National Organization for Women (NOW), founded in 1966, had long since popularized the language of individual rights to affirm women's right to choose an abortion. Swayed by the growing influence of the women's movement, Democratic politicians at both state and national levels increasingly adopted NOW's "right to choose" perspective, and in the process, the Democratic Party moved from encompassing real diversity of opinion on abortion in 1970 to adopting the 1984 official party platform, which included a statement affirming that access to abortion was a "fundamental human right."[54] In the face of such developments, abortion opponents failed in their efforts to promote a constitutional amendment and restrictive federal legislation that could reverse or substantially augment the post-*Roe* status quo. Activists were thus burdened by persistent political disappointment after 1973. Overcome by powerful political advocacy among liberals, those who had advocated the political recognition of the "right to life" were left to voice contempt for the liberal political establishment as they shifted their focus toward promoting a culture of respect for the sanctity of human life beginning at conception.[55]

Further, the tenor of Catholic activism changed due both to growing hostility toward the church's post–Vatican II "liberalization" and to Catholic activists' increased collaboration with conservative Evangelical and Fundamentalist Christians. Rejecting changes within the church associated with the 1960s, Catholic activists in growing numbers self-consciously embraced "traditional" teachings of the church. In the process, the rhetoric and protest antiabortion Catholics helped to spark would later be deemed "culture wars," bitterly dividing conservatives and liberals into distinct, adversarial camps in American life.[56]

Among Catholic antiabortion activists, the public dissent of the faithful from official church teaching on human reproduction and abortion helped foster their own more emphatic assent to authoritative church teachings. After the release of Pope Paul VI's 1968 encyclical, *Humanae vitae*, over half of U.S. Catholics rejected the pope's assertion that use of artificial birth control was immoral—and lay opposition to church sexual teachings only increased thereafter.[57] In the face of these developments, the urgency of affirming the traditionalist perspective on sex and reproduction became still more apparent. Added to the pervasive dissent on birth control, public opinion polls suggested that opposition to abortion was weakening among Catholics throughout the 1970s. Some 40 percent of U.S. Catholics affirmed the *Roe* decision in 1973, up from 36 percent who approved of the "right to choose" the previous year. Numbers among younger Catholics were still more revealing, with one poll indicating that 89 percent of Catholics under thirty supported abortion access in the case of rape and 74 percent supported access "if there is a strong chance of a serious defect in the baby."[58] Among women seeking abortions, data was similarly bleak from antiabortion activists' perspective, as polls showed that Catholic women were only marginally less likely to seek an abortion compared with non-Catholics.[59] For Catholics in the antiabortion movement, such revelations made cultural reform essential: to sustain and expand opposition to abortion, it became a priority to convince Americans of both the "sanctity" of human life beginning at conception and the immorality of the pro-choice position. In the process, the focus on cultural reform widened the chasm between the two camps within the church: as one activist argued, "It is almost as if the pro-abortionists and pro-lifers live in different universes. There are whole chunks of our world which seem missing from theirs."[60]

Further, immediately after *Roe*, conservative Evangelicals and Fundamentalists joined Catholics in opposing abortion rights, publicly demonstrating in substantial numbers for the first time. In the post-*Roe* decade, Catholic and Protestant activists became agents in a common struggle, driven by the same religious imperative to stop abortion. Consequently, a movement once almost entirely Catholic became heavily ecumenical (though still decidedly Christian), and Catholics, Evangelicals, and Fundamentalists shaped the character of one another's advocacy. By the early 1980s, Evangelicals and Fundamentalists, for example, adopted the arguments employed by Catholics regarding the sanctity of all human life. In turn, Catholics became adept with the language of cultural degradation and the apocalyptic rhetoric that Evangelical and Fundamentalist Christians utilized in their critiques both of post-*Roe* abortion policy and post-1960s American life more generally.[61]

Under such collaboration, activists nourished a synthesis that critics called "Catholic Fundamentalism" or "Revivalist Catholicism."[62] Mirroring the moral assuredness of post-1960s Evangelicalism and Fundamentalism, prominent figures like Joan Andrews, Benedictine priest Paul Marx (who founded an organization called "Human Life International" in 1981), and layman Joseph Scheidler (leader of various Catholic antiabortion groups, including the Pro-Life Action League, founded in 1980), along with traditionalist periodicals like *Fidelity* and *Crisis*, led Catholic activists to become a distinct and sometimes isolated community within the larger American Catholic setting. As they privileged cultural arguments about the sinful and immoral character of abortion over political arguments for protecting fetal rights, Catholic activists affirmed their traditionalist identity and confirmed their isolation from secular political discourse. Already by the late 1970s, towering crucifixes and representations of the Virgin Mary often eclipsed handmade signs asserting the rights of the unborn at abortion clinic protests. Characterized by an uncompromising focus on the church's moral teaching authority and a propensity for "traditional" devotions, the movement had the effect, as one commentator had earlier predicted, of "turning off many Catholics who are themselves not ideological pro-abortionists. They step to the sidelines, where they are spared the embarrassment of association with zealots."[63]

Straining to refocus antiabortion activities around the political affirmation of rights, U.S. Catholic bishops in the 1980s continually suggested that opposition to abortion should not be so tightly bound to traditionalist Catholicism. Instead, bishops stressed the alternative framework of the church's social teachings and its affirmation of universal human rights. "The abortion question is not purely an issue of Catholic doctrine," one bishop explained in 1984. "It is a basic issue of human rights, the right of the unborn child to exist. . . . The issue cannot be presented simply as one religious community seeking to impose its doctrinal beliefs on the body politic. . . . Antiabortion legislation is essential because it deals with the fundamental human right, the right to life itself."[64] In the same vein, Cardinal Joseph Bernardin of Chicago argued for a "consistent ethic of life" that affirmed human rights from conception until natural death: opposition to abortion, he argued, should be connected to opposition to the death penalty and to euthanasia as the defense of the inviolable human right to life. By thus framing the issue, he maintained, the antiabortion position could return to an earlier emphasis on affirming human rights and promoting the "common good" through political reform.[65] Further, in advancing an alternative framework, the whole administrative body of U.S. Catholic bishops, in the form of a pastoral letter on war and peace, treated abortion in the context of the threat of nuclear annihilation in the 1980s:

> We must ask how long a nation willing to extend a constitutional guarantee to the "right" to kill defenseless human beings by abortion is likely to refrain from adopting strategic warfare policies deliberately designed to kill millions of defenseless human beings, if adopting them should come to seem "expedient." . . . We plead with all who would work to end the scourge of war to begin by defending life at its most defenseless, the life of the unborn.[66]

Emphasizing the broad political context, bishops affirmed the centrality of the "right to life" position and the need to advocate for rights protection in a range of areas.

Yet into the 1990s, many of the most committed activists maintained the cultural framework they had adopted after the 1973 *Roe* decision. In doing so, they helped to foment and sustain the late twentieth-century "culture wars," even as they achieved limited success either in changing popular attitudes toward abortion or in altering the *Roe* decision. On the whole, both Catholic and non-Catholic Americans continued to support widespread access to abortion; and though the 1989 case of *Webster v. Reproductive Health Services* and the 1992 decision in *Planned Parenthood v. Casey* both opened the door to curbs on abortion, the *Roe* decision maintained the force of law.

Comparison with the African American civil rights movement highlights an important aspect of the history of antiabortion activism, while similarities with the antiwar movement underscore antiabortion activists' limitations. In the civil rights movement of the 1960s, the rhetoric of sin and divine judgment bolstered the argument for African American rights. But within the abortion debate, the focus on divine judgment ultimately diminished the political effectiveness of the antiabortion movement. In one case, public displays of religious faith and the use of religious rhetoric energized political change. In the other, praying in the public square blurred the focus on political change and moved activists in the direction of cultural reform. Like the antiwar movement, the antiabortion movement underscored the difficulty of appealing to religion in the public square: faith could just as easily become a wedge of division as a mediator of solidarity and political reform.

The encounter between religion and activism after 1960 shaped how Catholics understood the meaning of religious devotion and holiness in the context of the secular world.

It also made them central actors in some of the most controversial and significant episodes in late twentieth-century U.S. life. Nearly twenty years into the twenty-first century, the meeting of faith and public action continues to foster substantial division in U.S. society.

NOTES

1. "Priests and Nuns Back Milwaukee School Boycott," *New York Times*, October 19, 1965, 27. On Groppi's civil rights leadership, see Patrick D. Jones, *The Selma of the North: Civil Rights Insurgency in Milwaukee* (Cambridge, Mass.: Harvard University Press, 2009).

2. Groppi, quoted in John T. McGreevy, *Parish Boundaries: The Catholic Encounter with Race in the Twentieth-Century Urban North* (Chicago: University of Chicago Press, 1996), 202.

3. Joel A. Carpenter, *Revive Us Again: The Reawakening of American Fundamentalism* (New York: Oxford University Press, 1997); Darren Dochuk, *From Bible Belt to Sun Belt: Plain Folk Religion, Grassroots Politics, and the Rise of Evangelical Conservatism* (New York: W. W. Norton, 2010); Lisa McGirr, *Suburban Warrior: The Origins of the New Right* (Princeton, N.J.: Princeton University Press, 2002); Matthew Avery Sutton, *American Apocalypse: A History of Modern Evangelicalism* (Cambridge, Mass.: Harvard University Press, 2014); Daniel K. Williams, *God's Own Party: The Making of the Christian Right* (New York: Oxford University Press, 2010); and Bruce Schulman and Julian E. Zelizer, eds., *Rightward Bound: Making America Conservative in the 1970s* (Cambridge, Mass.: Harvard University Press, 2008).

4. David Chappell, *A Stone of Hope: Prophetic Religion and the Death of Jim Crow* (Chapel Hill: University of North Carolina Press, 2004).

5. John XXIII, "Peace on Earth," in *Catholic Social Thought: The Documentary Heritage*, ed. David J. O'Brien and Thomas A. Shannon (Maryknoll, N.Y.: Orbis, 1992), 139; emphasis in original.

6. Recent relevant works include: R. Bentley Anderson, *Black, White, and Catholic: New Orleans Interracialism, 1947–1956* (Nashville, Tenn.: Vanderbilt University Press, 2005); Danny Duncan Collum, *Black and Catholic in the Jim Crow South: The Stuff That Makes Community* (Mahwah, N.J.: Paulist Press, 2006); Jones, *Selma of the North*; Amy L. Koehlinger, *The New Nuns: Racial Justice and Religious Reform in the 1960s* (Cambridge, Mass.: Harvard University Press, 2007); and Justin Poché, "Religion, Race, and Rights in Catholic Louisiana, 1938–1970" (Ph.D. diss., University of Notre Dame, 2007).

7. McGreevy, *Parish Boundaries*, 79–110.

8. Claire Wolfteich, *American Catholics through the Twentieth Century: Spirituality, Lay Experience and Public Life* (New York: Crossroad, 2001).

9. For the text of the National Catholic Welfare Conference document "Discrimination and the Christian Conscience," see *Documents of American Catholic History*, vol. 2, *1866–1966*, ed. John Tracy Ellis (Wilmington, Del.: Michael Glazier, 1987), 646–52. For the NAACP's endorsement, see *The Crisis*, January 1959, 15.

10. Timothy B. Neary, *Crossing Parish Boundaries: Race, Sports, and Catholic Youth in Chicago, 1914–1954* (Chicago: University of Chicago Press, 2016); Martin Zielinski, "'Doing the Truth': The Catholic Interracial Council of New York, 1945–1965" (Ph.D. diss., Catholic University of America, 1989); and Helen Ciernak, "Catholic College Students in the San Francisco Bay Area and the Civil Rights Movement," *U.S. Catholic Historian* 24 (Spring 2006): 131–41.

11. The National Catholic Welfare Conference's 1958 statement included this warning against political radicalism in the pursuit of racial justice: "We hope and earnestly pray that responsible and sober-minded Americans of all religious faiths, in all areas of our land, will seize the mantle of leadership from the agitator and the racist. It is vital that we act now and act decisively. All must act quietly, courageously, and prayerfully before it is too late"; Ellis, *Documents of American Catholic History*, 2:651–52.

12. Gerald Ellard, S.J., *Christian Life and Worship* (Milwaukee: Bruce, 1956), 398, 403.

13. Mary Ward Perkins, ed., *The Sacramental Way* (New York: Sheed & Ward, 1948), 309.

14. Bernard Sheil, quoted in McGreevy, *Parish Boundaries*, 44.

15. Jeffrey M. Burns, *Disturbing the Peace: A History of the Christian Family Movement, 1949–1974* (South Bend, Ind.: University of Notre Dame Press, 1999); Steven Avella, *This Confident Church: Catholic Leadership and Life in Chicago, 1940–1965* (Notre Dame, Ind.: University of Notre Dame Press, 1992); Mary Irene Zotti, *A Time of Awakening: The Young Christian Worker Story in the United States, 1938–1970* (Chicago: Loyola University Press, 1991); and Dennis M. Robb, "Specialized Catholic Action in the United States, 1936–1949: Ideology, Leadership, Organization" (Ph.D. diss., University of Minnesota, 1972).

16. Kilian McDonnell, O.S.B., "Racism and the Eucharist," *The Sign*, May 1956, 59.

17. Godfrey Diekmann, quoted in McGreevy, *Parish Boundaries*, 206.

18. Thomas Merton, *Conjectures of a Guilty Bystander* (Garden City, N.Y.: Doubleday, 1966), 81–82, 219.

19. "Pastoral Constitution of the Church in the Modern World," in *Documents of Vatican II*, ed. Walter Abbott, S.J. (New York: Guild, 1966), 201, 227–28; "Decree on the Apostolate of the Laity," in ibid., 498; and "Dogmatic Constitution of the Church," in ibid., 66–67.

20. Archbishop William E. Cousins and Martin Luther King Jr., quoted in McGreevy, *Parish Boundaries*, 200, 202.

21. "1967 Rioting in Milwaukee Made Groppi Want to Sing," *New York Times*, March 29, 1969, 15.

22. Burns, *Disturbing the Peace*, 126, 129; Andrew Moore, *The South's Tolerable Alien: Roman Catholics in Alabama and Georgia, 1945–1970* (Baton Rouge: Louisiana State University Press, 2007), 105–11.

23. See Burns, *Disturbing the Peace*.

24. Patrick E. McGrath, "Napalm in Baltimore," *Ave Maria*, June 8, 1968, 16; and Shawn Francis Peters, *The Catonsville Nine: A Story of Faith and Resistance in the Vietnam Era* (New York: Oxford University Press, 2012).

25. "Man, 22, Immolates Himself in Antiwar Protest at U.N.," *New York Times*, November 10, 1965, 1, 5; and "Pope Paul's Visit to New York and Peace Appeal at U.N.," *New York Times*, October 11, 1965, 59.

26. "Testimony on Mass at Pentagon Given by Senator's Wife," *New York Times*, June 17, 1970, 28.

27. "Four Nuns Arrested in White House," *New York Times*, July 7, 1970; "Six Arrested in White House, during War Protest Prayers," *New York Times*, July 11, 1973, 25; "Four Arrested at Pray-In at White House," *New York Times*, July 14, 1970, A1; and "Fourteen More Protesters Arrested at White House," *New York Times*, August 11, 1973, 7.

28. Marian Mollin, *Radical Pacifism in Modern America: Egalitarianism and Protest* (Philadelphia: University of Pennsylvania Press, 2006); Michael S. Foley, *Confronting the War Machine: Draft Resistance during the Vietnam War* (Chapel Hill: University of North Carolina Press, 2003).

29. James Carroll, *An American Requiem: God, My Father, and the War That Came between Us* (Boston: Houghton Mifflin, 1996), 157.

30. "Spellman Arrives for Four-Day Visit with Vietnam G.I.'s," *New York Times*, December 24, 1965, 6.

31. Jay P. Dolan, *The American Catholic Experience: A History from Colonial Times to the Present* (New York: Doubleday, 1985), 426.

32. "The Spoken Word, the Written Word . . . and Napalm?" *Ave Maria*, June 8, 1968, 4–5.

33. Penelope Adams Moon, "'Peace on Earth—Peace in Vietnam': The Catholic Peace Fellowship and Antiwar Witness, 1964–1976," *Journal of Social History* 36 (Summer 2003): 1046; and Anne Klejment, "War Resistance and Property Destruction: The Catonsville Nine Draft

Raid and Catholic Worker Pacifism," in *Revolution of the Heart: Essays on the Catholic Worker*, ed. Patrick G. Coy (Philadelphia: New Society, 1988), 292.

34. On "prophetic witness" in the post-1945 era, see Leilah Danielson, "'It Is a Day of Judgment': The Peacemakers, Religion, and Radicalism in Cold War America," *Religion and American Culture* 18 (Summer 2008): 215–48.

35. O'Brien, *The Renewal of American Catholicism* (New York: Oxford University Press, 1972), 199–200.

36. John C. Raines, "The Followers of Life," *Holy Cross Quarterly* 4 (Jan. 1971): 69.

37. Francis X. Kroncke, "Resistance as Sacrament," *Cross Currents* 21 (Fall 1971): 373–75.

38. Timothy Matovina, *Latino Catholics: Transformation in America's Largest Church* (Princeton, N.J.: Princeton University Press, 2011), 162–89; James P. McCartin, *Prayers of the Faithful: The Shifting Spiritual Life of American Catholics* (Cambridge, Mass.: Harvard University Press, 2010), 148–57; and Mary McGann, Eva Lumas, and Ronald Harbor, *Let It Shine!: The Emergence of African American Catholic Worship* (New York: Fordham University Press, 2008).

39. Mary Henold, *Catholic and Feminist: The Surprising History of the American Catholic Feminist Movement* (Chapel Hill: University of North Carolina Press, 2008).

40. "St. Patrick's Cathedral Picketed by Traditionalist Catholic Unit," *New York Times*, March 3, 1968, 28.

41. See James Hitchcock, *The Decline and Fall of Radical Catholicism* (New York: Image, 1972); and George Kelly, *The Battle for the American Church* (Garden City, N.Y.: Doubleday, 1979).

42. "Abortion Clinic Formally Opens as Nearby Church tolls Protest," *New York Times*, January 27, 1972, 30.

43. Williams, *Defenders of the Unborn: The Pro-Life Movement before Roe v. Wade* (New York: Oxford University Press, 2016); Kristin Luker, *Abortion and the Politics of Motherhood* (Berkeley: University of California Press, 1985); and Allison Vander Broek, "Rallying the Right-to-Lifers: Grassroots Religion and Politics in the Building of the Broad-based Right-to-Life Movement, 1960–1984," (Ph.D. dissertation, Boston College, 2017).

44. Joseph M. Scheidler, *Closed: 99 Ways to Stop Abortion* (San Francisco: Ignatius, 1985). Such tactics were prefigured in the pre-*Roe* years by a Catholic organization called the "Sons of Thunder," organized by conservative activist Brent Bozell; see Patrick Allitt, *Catholic Intellectuals and Conservative Politics, 1950–85* (Ithaca, N.Y.: Cornell University Press, 1993), 148–56.

45. Jeffrey Kaplan, "America's Last Prophetic Witness: The Literature of the Rescue Movement," *Terrorism and Political Violence* 5 (Autumn 1993): 58–77.

46. Joan Andrews, *I Will Never Forget You* (San Francisco: Ignatius, 1989), 27.

47. Ibid., 87–89.

48. Ibid., 191.

49. "Statement of Conscience in the Court of Common Pleas of Allegheny County, Pennsylvania [Dec. 22, 1997]," *Commonwealth of Pennsylvania vs. Joan Andrews*, http://www.catholicculture.org/docs/doc_view.cfm?recnum=248, accessed August 30, 2005.

50. McCartin, *Prayers of the Faithful*, 157–65.

51. John D. Skrentny, *The Minority Rights Revolution* (Cambridge, Mass.: Harvard University Press, 2004).

52. Richard A. McCormick, S.J., *The Wrong of Abortion* (New York: America Press, 1965), 3.

53. Congregation for the Doctrine of the Faith, "Declaration on Procured Abortion," *Origins*, December 12, 1974, 388.

54. "Democratic Platform of 1984," quoted in *Abortion: A Documentary and Reference Guide*, ed. Melody Rose (Westport, Conn.: Greenwood, 2008), 128.

55. See N. E. H. Hull, Williamjames Hoffer, and Peter Charles Hoffer, eds., *The Abortion Rights Controversy in America: A Reader* (Chapel Hill: University of North Caroline Press, 2004), 85–121.

56. For the classic definition of "culture war," see James Davidson Hunter, *Culture Wars: The Struggle to Control the Family, Education, Art, and Politics in America* (New York: Basic, 1992).

57. Leslie Woodcock Tentler, *Catholics and Contraception: An American History* (Ithaca, N.Y.: Cornell University Press, 2004), 264–79.

58. John Deedy, "Catholics, Abortion, and the Supreme Court," *Theology Today*, October 1973, 279–86; "Catholics Agree with Protestants that Abortion and Contraception Should be Widely Available," *Family Planning Perspectives*, (January 1980), 53.

59. Jeff A. Borders and Phillips Cutright, "U.S. Determinants of Legal Abortion Rates," *Family Planning Perspectives* (July 1979): 227–33; and Susan B. Hanson, "State Implementation of Supreme Court Decisions: Abortion Rates since *Roe v. Wade*," *Journal of Politics* 42 (May 1980): 372–95.

60. Dave Andrusko, ed., *To Rescue the Future: The Pro-Life Movement in the 1980s* (Toronto: Life Cycle, 1983), 147.

61. Ted G. Jelen, "Changes in the Attitudinal Correlations of Opposition to Abortion, 1977–1985," *Journal for the Scientific Study of Religion* 27 (1988): 211–28; and McCartin, *Prayers of the Faithful*, 157–65.

62. Patrick M. Arnold, "The Rise of Catholic Fundamentalism," *America*, April 11, 1987, 297–302, and Michael W. Cuneo, *Catholics against the Church: Antiabortion Protest in Toronto, 1969–1985* (Toronto: University of Toronto Press, 1989), 185–213.

63. Deedy, "Catholics, Abortion, and the Supreme Court," 283; see also Philip S. Kaufman, O.S.B., "Abortion—Catholic Pluralism and the Potential for Dialogue," *Cross Currents* 37 (Spring 1987): 76–86.

64. Bishop Howard J. Hubbard, "A Response to Gov. Cuomo," *Origins*, October 25, 1984, 304.

65. Cardinal Joseph Bernardin, "Consistent Ethic of Life," *Origins*, December 29, 1983, 492–93.

66. U.S. Catholic Bishops, "The Challenge of Peace: God's Promise and Our Response" (1983), in O'Brien and Shannon, *Catholic Social Thought*, 554.

THIRTEEN

The Resurrection Project of Mexican Catholic Chicago: Spiritual Activism and Liberating Praxis

Karen Mary Davalos

This essay traces the formation and activism of the Resurrection Project/*El Proyecto Resurrección*, a community development organization that predominantly builds and secures housing for Latino residents, and locates the organization within the historical context of *mexicano* Catholicism in Chicago.[1] Focusing on the organization's first fifteen years, 1990–2005, and inaugural efforts in Pilsen (in that period, the most densely populated *mexicano* community of Chicago), it uses historical archives, oral history interviews, and ethnographic material to view the programs for housing, community development, and leadership as a strategy to create a life of dignity, as revelation, and as an expression of "the faith of the people."[2] This research investigates a liberating faith-based embodiment of Catholicism among Mexican Chicago. Moreover, it argues that the framework of "spiritual activism" helps to illuminate the organization's two campaigns—the building of housing and the formation of a communal consciousness—as profound integration of lived experience, faith and culture.[3]

The Resurrection Project/*El Proyecto Resurrección* is a neighborhood development corporation whose mission has much in common with Chicana/o social movements, faith-based community organizing, and Catholic activism in the United States.[4] Orlando Espín's observations about Latina/o faith as located in human experience, as well as the rejection of any attempt to disconnect faith from the lived realities of Latina/os, is appropriate for this case study of Mexican Catholic Chicago.[5] Building on his observation, this article traces the experience of oppression, specifically the unequal structures of society that produce poverty, inadequate education, political powerlessness, and unstable and substandard housing in Chicago's Mexican neighborhood of Pilsen. As an organization whose mission is to "build relationships and challenge people to act on their faith and values to create healthy communities through organizing, education and community development," the Resurrection Project/ *El Proyecto Resurrección* (TRP) illustrates the penetrating connection between daily life, faith, and culture through the creation of "decent, safe, affordable and high-quality housing" for low-income and working-class families who realize, embody, and engage their place in Chicago.[6]

The building of homes and healthy communities is historically, affectively, and culturally rooted in places and relationships across the Americas, and the consideration of lived realities requires attention to a transnational sensibility. The primary reality for this setting is the relationship between the United States and Mexico, which is marked by invasion, conquest, annexation, exploitation, and oppression. This intertwined historical relationship makes it impossible, or at least untenable, to view migratory experiences in the United States as if they were separate from centuries of U.S. hegemonic control in the Americas. This is a structurally contingent point to which I turn later, but here I register my argument that the historical and socioeconomic conditions through which Mexicans migrated to the Midwest, their social location as disposable laborers or second-class and gendered citizens, their removal or segregation from specific neighborhoods in Chicago, as well as memories of exclusion from the Catholic Church comprise the transnational sensibilities that shape and inform the work of TRP.[7] The value for community development, a term that TRP defines as housing and empowerment, or "tangible and intangible assets," is articulated in Chicago by Mexicans, but it emerges from that long historical relationship between the United States and Mexico.[8] At the same time, an account of migrants is not a story of an unanchored community living in the netherworld of fragmented identities.[9] Instead, the transnational sensibilities of TRP drop cultural anchors in the United States and Mexico and blend the cultures found within both of these nations. Their transnational attachments, a sense of belonging to two nations, further informs the programs of TRP. The residents of Pilsen are physically distant from Mexico, but it is both their distance from Mexico and their relational and affective ties to Mexico that invigorate their desire to build, renovate, and own a home in Chicago and thereby challenge notions of citizenship, belonging, and the nation-state.

During the organization's first fifteen years, its programs focused on belonging measured in intangible and tangible ways. The campaigns included the following: (1) community organizing and empowerment through the congregations' block clubs, which are street-level advocacy groups that are related to and sometimes coterminus with *las comunidades de base* (grassroots Christian communities); (2) homeownership services that help residents attain and sustain homeownership through counseling and educational and housing programs; (3) asset management that develops and renovates rental property for low- to moderate-income households; and (4) economic development that assists construction-related small businesses through a cooperative. These programs, especially the creation of "decent, safe, affordable and high-quality housing" and the consciousness that leads to the call for such housing, are a form of "spiritual activism" or "liberating praxis" designed to transform the unjust conditions of Pilsen.[10]

"Spiritual activism," a term coined by Chicana lesbian feminist philosopher Gloria Anzaldúa, is a critical process of renewal, a radical assessment of oppression, and "a liberatory and holistic spirituality in tandem with social justice work, usually drawing from alternative spiritualities rather than mainstream religions."[11] It is a process that shares several characteristics with "the principle of liberating praxis." Latina feminist theologian Maria Pilar Aquino writes, "Latina/o theology is internally articulated by the principle of liberating praxis. Under this light, U.S. Latina/o theological reflection understands itself as a praxis of accompaniment *with*, *within*, and *from* the Latina/o communities in the latter's struggle for a new reality free of violence, dehumanization and exclusion."[12] While Aquino emphasizes an internal reflection or discourse and Anzaldúa implies external action that emerges from the assessment of one's reality, both posit that a radical consciousness manifests—as Aquino notes—"with, within, and from" the Latina/o communities' "struggle for a new reality free of violence, dehumanization and exclusion."

While the origins and orientation of TRP are fundamentally Catholic and do not draw from "alternative spiritualities," the organization challenges the patriarchy and hierarchy of the Catholic Church. Women and men parishioners are central to its call to action, leadership, and perception of lived realities. Pilsen residents identify the violence done to them and the forces of dehumanization and exclusion, and this knowledge begins their development and application of critical consciousness and faith. An examination of TRP explicitly supports a joining of Chicana feminist scholarship with U.S. Latina/o theology in an analysis of the creation of housing for working-poor and working-class *mexicanos* and *mexicanas* in Chicago as an expression of Mexican Catholic faith in action.[13]

Therefore, I interpret the work of TRP—the building of 140 new single and multiunit houses, at a total of 200 new housing options; the renovation of 12 buildings to create 156 affordable rental units; the development of 2 childcare centers that serve 400 children; the training of 86 Mexican and other Latino contractors to begin, develop, or expand their own construction businesses; the closure of over 300 loans, including home, conventional, refinance, and home improvement loans; the creation of a bilingual second-stage housing program for homeless single mothers; and the generation of more than $65 million in community investment—as a form of spiritual activism and liberating praxis as it accompanies and transforms the lives of Mexicans in Chicago.[14]

Structural Contingencies

To illustrate the context for the spiritual activism and liberating praxis of TRP, I turn to a brief historical portrait of *mexicano* Catholicism in Chicago since the early 1910s and through the 1990s, the decade in which TRP was founded. Included within this historical analysis is a description of the significant moments at which Mexican parishioners exerted their spiritual activism within and against the Catholic Church. This account of Mexican Catholic history, therefore, does not follow the historiography of American Catholicism of Chicago in its description of clergy, ministry, and devotional practices *inside* the church.[15] Moving outside of the church allows for the voices and experiences of men and women parishioners to be heard and to register their actions as devotion, their reflections as revelation, and their actions as a "struggle for a new reality."

Limited inclusion, outright exclusion, and dispersal as well as resistance and cultural affirmation characterize the historical presence of Mexicans in Chicago. The ebbs and flows of systematic racism and institutional neglect, as well as Mexican claims to space and identity, have shaped the goals of TRP. It is not surprising that "decent, safe, affordable, and high-quality housing" became the central campaign as the Catholic leadership and clients defined shelter as a basic human right, fundamental to other social-justice issues.

Unlike Mexican presence in the American Southwest, which predates the formation of the United States, Mexican Catholic Chicago began in the early twentieth century and is directly tied to industrialization, labor struggle, and urban development as well as patriarchal norms. For example, Mexican workers, usually single men, were a commodity that suited capitalist strategies for labor control and were recruited to Chicago as strikebreakers. The American Beet Sugar Company used a different gender strategy and recruited entire Mexican households because they felt that women would promote stability within a temporary labor force.[16] These households, which included women and men, were directed to urban areas when the harvest ended, and this in turn produced the initial sanctioned route for women migrants to Chicago.[17] Similar to the dominant pressures such as racism, sexism, and classism that Mexican-heritage populations experienced in the Southwest, Mexican migrants faced ongoing exclusion and invisibility in multiple social arenas: education, housing, employment, and politics. In addition, Mexican migrants coming to Chicago in the early decades of the twentieth century were primarily Catholic but did not find churches and social institutions they could call their own. Congregations may have received Spanish-speaking pastors, but pastoral care was not culturally directed at Mexicans,[18] and this disconnect played a key factor throughout the century in the emergence of lay people as spiritual leaders and cultural advocates.

During the first few decades of the twentieth century, Mexican Catholic lay leadership developed under the pressures of assimilation in Chicago. Between 1916 and 1929, the Archdiocese of Chicago founded forty-two parishes; only nine were national parishes and of these, two were for Mexicans: Our Lady of Guadalupe Parish established in 1923 and St. Francis of Assisi Church, officially converted in 1927 from an Italian into a Mexican parish.[19] Even as the assimilationist agenda permeated the Archdiocese of Chicago at this time, Mexican parishioners maintained their own faith practices and cultural heritage. Several important examples are worth mentioning. By the late 1920s, the congregation of St. Francis of Assisi Parish had a vibrant Guadalupana organization. It sponsored a carnival and an elaborate altar, participated in the dedication ceremony for Our Lady of Guadalupe Church when the facility was finally built in 1928 on Chicago's south side, and organized a celebration for the feast day of the patroness of Mexico, which by the 1930s became a twelve-day event that included a reenactment of the apparition and the miracle.[20] Elsewhere in the city, working-class Mexican Catholics undertook a campaign to purchase a storefront chapel in their Back of the Yards neighborhood. Beginning in the early 1930s, over 100 Mexican Catholic families independently inaugurated an effort to secure a place for worship after years of renting one location, refurbishing it, and then losing the lease. In 1941, the Mexican Catholic spiritual activists of the Back of the Yards converted an old butcher shop into a chapel to serve over two thousand people. After applying a fresh coat of paint and a decorative motif, the laity adorned Our Lady of Guadalupe Chapel on South Ashland, a major artery of the Yard's community, with flowers and images of Guadalupe, the Sacred Heart of Jesus, and the Madonna.[21] The desire to establish a sense of belonging, their own place of worship, their own forms of popular Catholicism, and their own images of the divine was a precursor to the spiritual activism and liberating praxis initiated by TRP in the 1990s.

After steadily increasing in the first few decades of the twentieth century, Mexicans in Chicago formed the fourth-largest Mexican-origin community in the United States by 1930.[22] However, racism played a major factor in the disavowal of Mexican and Mexican American political representation and inclusion in Chicago. The Great Depression proved useful to nativists who called for repatriation campaigns, which disproportionately targeted midwestern communities. Mexican neighborhoods were nearly devastated in the 1930s, and the setback cannot be underestimated as the dynamism and social capital of Mexican Catholic Chicago evaporated. Households were divided, congregations dwindled, and families were forced to uproot, even though they had invested in the city and the nation as Catholics, citizens, workers, students, and parents.

While labor control drove migration to Chicago in the 1910s and 1920s and racist scapegoat policies forced the deportation of Mexicans in the 1930s, market interests in the United States during World War II eventually helped to restore Mexican neighborhoods. The Bracero Program, a bilateral agreement between Mexico and the United States (1943–64), in which the former nation was to provide temporary labor to U.S. capitalists at both rural and urban worksites, was a major factor in the repopulation of Mexican Catholic Chicago. For example, more than 15,000 workers were contracted to work on the Chicago railroads between 1943 and 1945, or 11 percent of the total imported laborers for U.S. railroads.[23] Yet it structured their inclusion as low-wage and disposable laborers, which in turn limited their housing options.

Chicago urban policy after the war reinforced Mexicans residents' disadvantaged socioeconomic position. Chicago planners designed the devastation of the industrial sector through an aggressive urban policy that prioritized downtown investment, and the relocation of manufacturing companies produced high unemployment rates among Mexican and African American communities. By concentrating private development in the downtown area and shifting the economy from heavy industry and railway transportation to finance, management, and service, Chicago created a two-tier municipal structure that neglected industrial districts, the areas where most Mexicans lived, to favor business and commercial development.[24] Included within Chicago's urban policy, which privileged downtown financing, was the building of a new public university, the University of Illinois, Chicago, on the Near West Side (the community area directly north of Pilsen), which at the time was predominately populated by Eastern Europeans and a sizable Mexican community. The Near West Side was, as it is, home to St. Francis of Assisi Parish and thus, as I have described previously, the site of significant *mexicano* leadership and popular Catholicism. Approximately 14,000 housing units were destroyed by the time the university opened in 1965.[25] The displaced residents of the Near West Side dramatically changed the landscape of Pilsen, including the religious terrain. Several Pilsen parishes rapidly transitioned into Mexican Catholic congregations: St. Pius V Church celebrated the first Spanish-language Mass in 1963, and masses at St. Vitus and St. Procopius parishes soon followed. Unofficial estimates by historian Louise Año Nuevo Kerr indicate that of the 9,000 *mexicanos* forced to leave the area, nearly half of those residents moved to Pilsen. By 1970, 26,000 *mexicanos* comprised 55 percent of Pilsen's total population.[26]

The physical removal of Mexican residents was duplicated and supported by national policy in the late 1960s and early 1970s. Apprehensions by the Immigration and Naturalization Services (INS) "increased roughly 800 percent of its 1965 level by 1971 [and] . . . Mexican nationals accounted for 85 percent of the 8,728 INS apprehensions during the 1971 fiscal year."[27]

The INS used intensive workplace raids and neighborhood roundups, including apprehensions of parishioners as they left Mass, particularly after the Spanish-language service at St. Vitus Parish.[28] In response, St. Vitus's parishioners enacted protest demonstrations in 1974 and 1976, denouncing the racial profiling of the Mexican community.[29] But the creation of a community relations committee in Chicago did not stop racial profiling and assumptions of illegality, and St. Vitus and the wider community of Pilsen continued to struggle for local empowerment.

A brief detour about St. Vitus Parish is important as it eventually became the facility for TRP: the founding executive director had been a member of the parish before it was closed by the archdiocese in 1990. During the 1970s and 1980s, St. Vitus Church was a major force in mobilizing and uniting the neighborhood around social issues and popular Catholicism, and their activism helped to establish and maintain lay leadership among Mexican Catholic Chicago. Pastor James Colleran was a worker-priest who welcomed community organizers, undocumented families, and union activists into the parish facilities.[30] The parishioners initiated and organized worker strikes; boycotts against stores with poor labor practices; demonstrations against municipal neglect; a campaign against the Chicago Transit Authority for employment inequity; and confrontations with the INS during attempted illegal detentions of *mexicanos*.[31]

In addition, the congregation of St. Vitus organized the first *Vía Crucis* (Way of the Cross enacted on Good Friday) in 1977 after an apartment building fire took the lives of several children. The community felt that firefighters' inability to communicate in Spanish contributed to the tragedy.[32] For the congregation of St. Vitus, the *Vía Crucis* was one of many actions of solidarity and calls for social justice. Within a few years, the *Vía Crucis* became an event organized by Mexican laity and helped to unify the Catholic parishes in Pilsen who formed the Pilsen Cluster. For the organizers of the Way of the Cross, many of whom later became leaders and founders of TRP, the *Vía Crucis* was envisioned as a rite to "take back the neighborhood," as the procession would reveal God's salvation in the streets of Pilsen. They deliberately located the Stations of the Cross at businesses known for unfair labor practices, the site of a recent homicide, a corner used by drug dealers, and in front of rental properties owned by absentee landlords. The closing of St. Vitus Parish in 1990 created only a temporary setback for the neighborhood because interparish solidarity based on social justice, resistance to the abuses of power, and a claim for local autonomy were sufficient to maintain momentum, some of which was channeled into the formation of TRP, the subject to which I now turn.

Spiritual Activism and Liberating Praxis

The Resurrection Project is a faith-based community federation of Catholic parishes, largely comprised of the Pilsen Cluster, and it has grown to include other parish members in Little Village and the Back of the Yards.[33] This research focuses on the organization's first fifteen years and its inaugural work in Pilsen, because the core of the organization's activism and leadership has remained in Pilsen.[34] Indeed, some criticism of the organization points to the overwhelming resources located in Pilsen compared to Little Village and the Back of the Yards.[35] Nevertheless, a systematic exploration of the organization's formation and earliest initiatives illuminates the foundational role of spiritual activism and liberating praxis, a profound integration of lived experience, faith, and culture.

TRP was established in 1990 with an initial investment of $30,000 from six founding parishes in Pilsen. The membership parishes of the Pilsen Cluster had been structurally linked since the 1980s through the coordination of sacraments, religious education, and ministry, as well as community-wide events, such as the *Vía Crucis*. Their systematic integration and collaboration generated a robust dialogue across otherwise autonomous parishes. In 1988, six of the nine Catholic parishes in Pilsen began organizing residents. With the help of the Industrial Areas Foundation organizer Mike Loftin, lay and clerical leadership from the parishes of Holy Trinity, Providence of God, St. Adalbert, St. Pius V, St. Procopius, and St. Vitus formed the Catholic Community of Pilsen (CCP). Reverend Charles W. Dahm of St. Pius V Church had been instrumental in developing the theological, critical, and activist orientations in Pilsen and later by extension in TRP, and he urged the CCP to consider community-based strategies to create social change.[36] Through group meetings and formal organizing efforts, the CCP learned that Pilsen residents were most concerned about municipal neglect, poor education, housing, and crime. Continuing over a decade of advocacy and activism in Pilsen, the CCP began to create a base of leaders through training classes on empowerment, *comunidades de base*, and the participation of lay members, not just leaders. For example, in 1990, CCP worked during the Lenten season with the congregations' sixty *comunidades de base* and encouraged the small Christian neighborhood groups to reflect on their experiences with gang violence and Catholic teaching about compassion and justice.[37] The CCP also asked the groups to discuss possible solutions to drug-trafficking and its related violence. After four weeks of meetings in residents' homes, over four hundred people assembled at the St. Pius V auditorium to meet officials from the city's police, housing, and building departments and the state's attorney general. Three committees formed, each to address and solve a particular issue: regular and increased trash pickup, communication with police, and a comprehensive housing strategy to meet the needs of the residents. Concerned with overcoming oppression, as it is defined by residents, and grounded in faith, the housing committee rapidly captured the imagination of the community.[38]

Why Housing?

While the organization was developing and still designated as the CCP, displacement of low-income families and substandard housing threatened community formation and the growing political power of Mexican Chicago. Similarly, Mexican residents experienced on-going vulnerability that resulted from the ways in which they had been racialized and considered illegal regardless of their documentation and status. Families hoping to stay in Pilsen had limited opportunities. During the decades in which Pilsen's Mexican population swelled, nearly 2,000 units were destroyed. In addition, Pilsen has some of the oldest housing stock in the city, with 78 percent of all units built before 1939. Only 23 percent of these homes were owner-occupied in the 1980s. The area was plagued by violence and municipal neglect, including a lack of police programs and presence. Moreover, despite their demographic majority in Pilsen, Latinos owned less than half of all owner-occupied units in the 1980s.[39] The majority of housing options were, and continue to be, small apartment buildings. Rent studies indicate that Latinos tend to pay higher rents than non-Latinos, and this trend increases for areas with higher concentrations of Latinos, suggesting that realtors and landlords participate in race-based speculation and indicating that Pilsen rents are disproportionate.[40] Housing became a foundational goal for achieving social justice and answering Jesus's call as the residents articulated cultural and spiritual values for attachment to place: a desire to claim physical rootedness as a way of knowing where one belongs, how one is connected to the larger world, and how existence is understood.

The housing committee transformed into the Pilsen Resurrection Development Corporation, which merged in 1994 with the CCP, forming the Resurrection Project.[41] Member institutions provide the faith-based development corporation with financial support, facilities, and advocacy. By 2005, the institutional membership included fourteen parishes in Pilsen, Little Village, and the Back of the Yards, although the ties to the Back of the Yards have waned over the years.[42] The congregations of St. Pius V and St. Procopius are at the forefront of leadership, and St. Francis of Assisi (a parish outside the boundaries of Pilsen, but historically significant to many residents on the Southwest side) provides informal guidance and support. TRP is an example of Mexican Catholicism in which clerics and laity "use their social experiences as the starting point for theological discourse" and social action.[43]

Similar to other faith-based organizations and federations, TRP practices many of the mobilization tactics developed by "the dean of community organizing in the United States, Saul Alinsky," who founded the Industrial Areas Foundation.[44] However, periodic and systematic modifications to Alinsky's organizing methods—an emphasis on one-to-one meetings, evaluation of meetings, challenging and holding people accountable—have resulted in church-based organizing that acknowledges, strengthens, and makes use of social relationships, cultural knowledge, and Catholic values. As Woods and Wilson independently note, faith-based organizing is frequently described as less aggressive than Alinsky's organizing methods, and to this, employees would add, it is also accountable to the Divine, not union leadership or political officials.[45] By employing Catholic values of accountability and transparency to a higher source and by using prayer, reflection, and relationships, TRP participates in a unique form of democracy and empowerment.

For example, as is common among other faith-based institutions, TRP employs Catholic rituals and reflections at meetings, events, and actions to reinforce and build on the faith of its clients and to register the divine source of its work. Biblical stories and testimony are part of public programs, newsletters, and the website, and these frequently attest to the revelation of God in daily experience, such as the purchase of a home or the lease of an affordable and decent rental unit. For the first round of sales of TRP homes, Cardinal Joseph Bernadin symbolically baptized the organization at a ceremony inside Providence of God Parish and blessed the participants who entered a lottery to purchase a house, "the first new housing plan in Pilsen in nearly five decades."[46] Anointment is also made in public spaces, sanctifying the everyday and material realities of Pilsen. Lay leadership often organizes summertime street masses that begin with a procession and blessing of homes. The houses built by TRP are often singled out for anointment, especially during *las posadas*, in which the reenactment of Mary and Joseph's quest for lodging has symbolic meaning for new homeowners. Some parishes combine *las posadas* celebrations with activism for affordable housing, calling for "*Vivienda Digna para Todos*" (Dignified Housing for All) as they journey from home to home.

Yet even the most basic of Alinsky's techniques—the one-to-one meetings—is reformulated as a goal, not a means to an end. One-to-one meetings are a strategy for "building healthy communities," as relationships are essential to TRP's vision of communal well-being, organized action, collective empowerment, and critical consciousness. The dialogue forms a relationship, but it also embodies the process whereby Pilsen residents become "'masters of their thinking' and aware of their 'significance as human beings.'"[47] From the collective experience and sharing of stories emerge new ways of placing oneself in the world and exercising one's vision of salvation on Earth.

Equally relevant to faith-based organizing, TRP relies upon the networking strategies of women who coordinate actions, share resources, develop networks, and offer support on a daily basis, particularly the domestic chores of childcare, cooking, cleaning, and maintaining family ties. This feminine source of knowledge and action supports a value for women as leaders and agents of social change. TRP creates a Latina/o liberating praxis and spiritual activism that unites the mundane and the sacred through a theological premise that envisions the revelation of God on Earth through the transformation of the social order, including reevaluations of patriarchy.

Rebirth and Renewal

The official name of the organization, the Resurrection Project/ *El Proyecto Resurrección*, signifies the linguistic social realities of Mexicans in Chicago. The founders wanted a cognate title that monolingual Spanish and English speakers could recognize in either language. The Resurrection Project/ *El Proyecto Resurrección* values the various combinations of Spanish and English and does not privilege one language over the other. This sensibility, one that affirms multiple cultural experiences, is part of a transnational life enriched by cultural foundations in the United States and Mexico.

In addition, the spiritual significance of the name foregrounds the larger theological vision of the organization. Although early critics of the organization emphasize the precondition of resurrection—death—and claim the name is offensive because it implies that Pilsen, or more generally the Mexican community in Chicago, was lifeless, the leadership, active participants, and clients emphasize renewal, rejuvenation, and rebirth. For them, the word "resurrection/*resurrección*" inspires hope for social transformation, new possibilities, and a sense of responsibility and ownership. The title articulates the politics of potentiality—that something more can come from a dispossessed transnational community living in the shadows of municipal and economic power. Cecilia Paz, founding board member, parishioner, and former staff of St. Procopius Church, makes an allegorical reference to a stream that replenishes the body or the community. She states, "You are drawing from it like a spring of fresh water that you need to replenish [yourself] . . . a spring of life that we [the leadership of TRP] were using to get us going to where we accomplished [something] for our community."[48] For Paz, the name serves as a symbol for revitalization that is simultaneously spiritual, in that people connect to other-worldly phenomena, and material, in terms of accomplishments—be it housing, childcare, or cleaner streets. The potentiality for salvation echoes one of Maria Pilar Aquino's preconditions for U.S. Latina/o theology; *el empapamiento*, an ability to "saturate ourselves," "imbue ourselves," or "permeate ourselves" with hope, to believe that life will improve or that change will occur.[49]

Raúl Raymundo, the founding executive director of TRP, also makes a connection between Christian celestial and worldly salvation. He elaborates:

> We wanted a name that means "new life," and new life means creating a healthy community with good housing, solid family relationships, strong economic growth, job and educational opportunities and positive attitudes. These things surface when we work to build the Kingdom of God on Earth. Jesus' resurrection is all about new life, and as a primarily Catholic community, we believe in His life and message.[50]

Articulating one orientation of a liberating praxis, Raymundo clarifies how the work of TRP is a strategy to establish salvation through the elimination of poor housing and substandard schooling and by creating economic opportunities for Mexicans. TRP literally *builds* God's kingdom on Earth. It draws on a gospel of liberation through a praxis that eliminates the sins of exploitation, violence, and dehumanization.

As a community development corporation focused on housing, TRP's spiritual activism and liberating praxis take physical form. Renovation of industrial buildings allows the organization to reclaim and transform blight into rental units and to remove derelict properties that support crime hot spots from the community. In the design of housing, TRP makes use of cultural values. In one instance, TRP challenged a city policy that subsidized single-family homes because the policy did not serve a cultural norm among Mexicans who live as extended families, or *familia*. The city policy could not accommodate a preference for *familia*, and TRP aimed to build affordable multiunit homes. In the mid-1990s, TRP was able to successfully lobby the city's housing department to include multiunit housing in its development program, New Homes for Chicago. This allowed TRP to build and subsidize three-level units with ground-floor apartments, often rented to grandparents, single parents, or relatives of the family that occupied the two-level house above the garden apartment. However, both family and nonfamily renters provided homeowners with significant economic advantages. In some cases, family renters cosigned loans or jointly shared the property. The three-level units became bestsellers for TRP, and these living arrangements reinforced kin networks that extend beyond the nuclear family while aligning female and age-based labor in the maintenance of family relationships. In short, TRP crafted a city policy that suited *la familia* and gender expectations to provide culturally informed living arrangements.

A specific example of physical transformation, which also illustrates how TRP depends upon the leadership and organizing skills of women, comes from the work of Alicia Rocha, block club leader and advocate for affordable, safe, and decent housing. In 1996, Rocha successfully mobilized for the city-financed demolition of two abandoned grain silos across the street from her home. She could not imagine a decent and secure life in which massive concrete silos threatened the safety of her neighborhood. But the vision of human dignity did not end with the demolition; Rocha organized her community to mobilize city officials to convert the empty lot into housing options for low- and moderate-income households. To build support, Rocha scheduled an annual street Mass to educate and empower residents, and she met with the local alderman to obtain a commitment to the block club's vision for the empty lot. Rocha explains that her organizing gives her faith and that her faith inspires action: *Toda mi actividad me ha dado fe*. Offered as *testimonio* to the public through TRP annual reports and newsletters, Rocha's words express the lived reality of TRP leaders, and the ways in which action and faith are intertwined. TRP plans to build affordable condominiums on the site.[51]

Housing and Salvation

The Resurrection Project builds decent, safe, affordable, high-quality apartments for low-income residents because it dignifies human life and understands relationships among its neighbors as the revelation of God's promise. In this way, TRP has expanded the common understanding of brick-and-mortar development to include intangible human development. As Raymundo illustrates in his description of the organization's name, the mission of TRP is a combination of secular and spiritual purposes that formulate a liberating praxis. The mission—"build relationships and challenge people to act on their faith and values to create healthy communities through organizing, education and community development"—is a call to action and a process of radical consciousness.[52] The mission requires residents to "reflect on [their] action in light of faith" and, through this reflection, to recognize the ways in which their realities can be transformed by their faith in action.[53]

It is from this awareness that intangible assets develop. Thus, even as TRP aims to change the lives of *mexicanos* by providing support services, housing, and training for workers, it has also invested in a radical oppositional stance and way of seeing the world and one's place in it. Investing in intangible assets requires a proactive education agenda, a major but flexible campaign that consistently changed over the organization's first fifteen years.

At the inception of the new millennium, TRP organized a public life campaign, *Un Buen Cristiano Lucha Por Su Pueblo* (A Good Christian Works for the People/Community), but it also continued to support the initial methods of developing intangible assets, the block clubs, and *las comunidades de base*. The central point is that between 1990 and 2005, TRP continued to seek new strategies for creating and preparing local leaders for full participation in the civic life of Mexican neighborhoods and the larger metropolitan area and to help it understand that education of Pilsen residents is foundational to spiritual renewal and revelation.

Staff members also connect spiritual salvation or a higher calling with their everyday labor. In general, professionally trained staff members, who also insist on the acknowledgment of their cultural credentials, speak about their work as a calling; they are devoted to eliminating social inequity among Latinos. For instance, Edgar Hernandez makes a personal connection to each client he meets and imagines them "as someone that I know, I can relate to because it could be my uncle, it could be my father, it could my mother, it could be my sisters or my brother that may come here and look for some services."[54] This relational vision of clients is distinct from the expectations he found in "corporate America," for which he trained in college, but soon thereafter recognized that he disliked the profit-driven motive. Hernández explains: "Most of us are here [working at TRP] because this is a passion and this is definitely something that you have a vested interest in." Staff members such as Alvaro Obregón and Salvador Cervantes acknowledge that TRP campaigns emerge from experiential knowledge of the residents, and staff invoke the experiential knowledge with sacred and earthly value. Furthermore, leadership and clients of TRP frequently invoke the Holy Spirit when they talk about the achievements and programs of the organization. Founding board member and staff at Holy Trinity Church Esperanza Godínez describes the early work of TRP as a "miracle" because, although the original leadership had experience with social services and activism, none had built homes, negotiated with developers, or investigated purchasing tax-delinquent and other properties. With a laugh in her voice, she claims that the early successes of TRP were the result of divine intervention.[55] Guacalda Reyes, a Latina staff member of TRP states, "We have to try to make heaven here . . . otherwise, I don't think there is a reason for us to be here."[56]

Conclusion

Legal and de facto disempowerment has not provided the opportunity for consistent, meaningful, or equitable civic participation of Mexicans in Chicago. Because the residents' perspectives and experiences are central to the mission and action of the organization, TRP offers a critical reformulation of historical and everyday erasures, exclusions, and denials as well as new methods and ideas for belonging. The Resurrection Project approaches salvation through the elimination of poverty and oppression by bringing the sacred into daily life and defining homeownership services, including the construction of new homes, the renovation of abandoned buildings for rental housing, and financial education as a path to emancipation and spiritual rejuvenation. Respect for impoverished and racially marginalized people, as well as women, also calls into question the dominant expectations and myths of assimilation, meritocracy, individualism, and neoliberalism. Home ownership might appear to reinforce an American expectation of settlement and assimilation, but the lived realities of Mexican Catholic Chicago complicate an interpretation that would satisfy master narratives of accommodation and accomplishment. TRP residents invoke their cultural heritage, generally Mexican but also other Latin American identities, when they account for or describe feelings of belonging. Indeed, TRP housing designs, floor plans, and color schemes of architectural elements are consistently depicted as relevant among Latino households: the yellow of mangos and the green of the *selva*. The brightly hued door and window frames index "Mexicanness" to the Pilsen community in the same way that multiunit homes confirm their *familia* households. Simultaneously, Mexican residents claim attachment to their homeland and Chicago when they anoint their homes in Mexican Catholic rituals, such as *las posadas*, or reclaim their community and demand a better life through the *Via Crucis*. A transnational sensibility is strong enough to register among Chicago-born Mexican American youth of St. Pius Parish who, for example, saw their family history in the oral histories they gathered at the El Paso–Juárez border in summer 2004. Although their parents had migrated decades earlier to the Midwest as children or young adults, the youth associated testimonies of suffering, exhaustion, and dehydration with Jesus's final hours and with the contemporary experiences they documented at the border. In the same way that the youth of St. Pius Parish fashion a transnational sensibility by linking their family history to Jesus and contemporary border crossers, TRP fashions a sense of belonging that reaches across national borders.

More importantly, the spiritual activism of TRP among Mexican migrants challenges neoliberalism and its dependency on individualism and patriarchy. When I asked *mexicana* elders who were celebrating the fortieth anniversary of Father Dahm's ordination about their work with the block clubs and why it was important to them, they spoke about creating and maintaining networks among women. Street masses and other public events were sometimes thinly veiled but officially endorsed practices for "leaving the house" and sharing information and resources. Catholic events, particularly those outside the church, allowed women to come together without a threat of violence or reprimand for leaving the home. Moreover, the women used these public events to share private stories and embody the liberating praxis so fundamental to the organization's mission. They found in the block clubs a space to affirm their feminine solidarity, critique of patriarchy, and sense of *compartir*.

The English translation of *compartir* (to share or sharing) does not fully capture the meaning the women described to me. They explained how they share with others who have less material goods or emotional support and how they share resources even when their own families are in need. For example, if a woman experienced domestic violence, then her closest friends and neighbors would help her seek shelter or solutions; or if a woman needed employment, then the group could refer her to employers. A knowledge of and value for *compartir* creates an alternative value system, indeed a radical notion of self-in-community, collective justice, and social equity.

Other clients of TRP embody *compartiendo* when they offer to assist their neighbors. Raúl Hernández, former president of the board, states that residents who live in TRP rental properties frequently approach him after Mass and praise the housing, the organization, and its services. Each testimony is followed by the offer to "help in any way." He is amazed that single mothers with little free time, working-poor, and disabled residents have offered to "give something back" to their community. These contributions emerge from a spiritually informed communal obligation or Catholic sense of accountability to a social body beyond one's household. They profess an "ethic of accompaniment" and offer to be with each other as they witness strife, violence, or struggle.[57] In this way, TRP's spiritual activism and liberating praxis do not mimic the master narrative of meritocracy and individualism, but draw instead upon salvation, rebirth, and a moral obligation to others while challenging and questioning the structures that limit possibilities for low-income, Mexican households and women. The Resurrection Project is a method of radical transformation of material, spiritual, and spatial conditions.

As a case study of Mexican Catholic Chicago, the Resurrection Project is linked to a variety of faith practices, such as the *Via Crucis, la quinceañera* (a rite of passage for girls), *las posadas, las comunidades de base*, the celebration of a Mass in the streets of the community, or the feast-day celebration for Our Lady of Guadalupe, Patroness of the Americas.[58] Moreover, I aim to identify TRP as *one* of the faith practices of Mexican Catholic Chicago and a form of "popular religion" because of its relational and communal processes that characterize the organization's mission to engage the sacred.[59] From my perspective, the study of "the faith of the people" allows for the possibility of many types of actions to be read as "popular religion," not simply those rituals and activities affiliated with devotional practice, church-based celebrations, and events that are marked in obvious ways as faithful or spiritual. The daily experience of creating a home as an expression of belonging, as witness to the Divine, and as the embodiment of salvation are mundane, but nevertheless vital articulations of *mexicano* faith that springs from everyday realities. As with other forms of popular religion, the work of TRP is deeply revelatory, and clients, staff, and leaders view their work as bringing to light God's Kingdom and making a sacred landscape in Pilsen. Even those who have very little material wealth offer to accompany their neighbors through the wounds and pressures of life in Chicago, and they understand *compartiendo* as part of God's promise and calling. The spiritual activism and liberating praxis of TRP illuminate a moment of transformation, albeit fragile, but nevertheless affectively and effectively meaningful in people's everyday and spiritual lives. It is these moments of transformation that challenge notions of citizenship, belonging, and the nation-state because none depends on a singular homeland, cultural identity, or sense of self.

Epilogue

With new housing built or renovated by TRP, Pilsen has received more attention from real estate speculators. During the final phases of my research, particularly the summers of 2003 and 2004 and Holy Week of 2005, I observed "For Sale" and "For Rent" signs throughout Pilsen, and parish leaders and TRP staff noted that the telephone numbers on these signs indicate suburban area codes. The landlords, real estate contractors, and property owners live elsewhere. Ironically, the physical transformation of Pilsen housing and community development generated additional signs of economic instability and exploitation. Reinforcing this pattern of displacement, the eastern part of Pilsen has seen an increase in European American residents since the redevelopment of Pilsen's northern neighbor, the University of Illinois, Chicago, which is now pushed up against the viaduct that separates the two areas. Empowerment and belonging are fragile conditions for which TRP must consistently renew and replenish through spiritual activism and liberating praxis in its effort to build healthy communities and housing.

While fragile footholds on belonging and empowerment can strain the spiritual, political, and economic resources of Pilsen, the neighborhood is generative for Mexicans born in Chicago, particularly those who are college educated. That is, the sense of place is strong enough to support a "return migration" among second- and third-generation Mexican professionals in the new millennium. While current ports of entry are suburban Mexican enclaves outside of Chicago, Pilsen is the community in which professional Mexican American youth want to live. Although it is an emergent phenomenon, the "return migration" of young professionals offers another challenge to the model of the European immigrant in which successive generations move from the urban core to the suburbs. It also exposes the myth of assimilation, as these youth are not interested in abandoning their heritage but reaffirming it and seeking spaces in which their cultural capital translates into social action, spiritual vitality, and political power. Suburban municipalities and some parishes are not responding to the needs of Mexican Catholics.[60] Young Latino professionals identify Pilsen as a place that provides for their cultural and spiritual nourishment, health, and the bilingual and bicultural education of their children. Although it is unclear if the return migration of young professionals supports or undermines gentrification, it is clear that the Resurrection Project has helped to establish a transnational sensibility, confront daily struggles, and affectively as well as physically create dignity and basic necessities for Mexican Catholic Chicago. The spiritual activism and liberating praxis offer insights for the ways in which the Resurrection Project strengthens the heart of Mexican Catholic Chicago.

Please note: Financial support allowed this project to come to fruition. The research was initiated and was partially funded in 1991–92 by the Cushwa Center for American Catholicism at the University of Notre Dame; Carlos Tortolero, executive director of the National Museum of Mexican Art (formerly the Mexican Fine Arts Center Museum), allowed my family and me to stay at the museum's apartment in Pilsen in 2004 and allowed me the use of a computer while I concluded the research over two summers; two grants from Loyola Marymount University supported this research at critical stages; and a NEH Summer Stipend Award in 2003 enabled me to conduct interviews with the Resurrection

Project staff and other community leaders. Any views, findings, conclusions, or recommendation expressed in this essay do not necessarily reflect those of the National Endowment for the Humanities. Spiritual and research assistance came from members and staff of the Resurrection Project. Michael J. Zuccaro, library assistant at Loyola Marymount University, provided technical and media assistance. Glennon and María Olivia helped me prepare the tapes for transcription and translation. As small children, they accompanied me on several trips. Finally, I wish to acknowledge the intellectual communities of MALCS and ACTUS, as well as my students at Loyola Marymount University, who nourished this work. Chuck Dahm deserves special thanks, as he served as interlocutor, colleague, participant, and pastoral advisor. I dedicate this work to the people in Pilsen who opened their hearts to me, giving this *pocha* hours of their time and energy when they could have been organizing, resting, or solving problems.

NOTES

Previously published as "The Resurrection Project of Mexican Catholic Chicago: Spiritual Activism and Liberating Praxis," *Dialogo* 16, no. 1 (Spring 2013), pp. 5–19.

1. All labels are polysemous, but ethical obligations and understanding required from over two decades of research in Chicago cause me to interchangeably use the terms *"mexicano"* and "Mexican," because they are common in Chicago's Mexican-origin neighborhoods. The terms do not designate a specific citizenship status, place of birth, or political consciousness. See also Nicholas De Genova, "Race, Space and the Reinvention of Latin America in Mexican Chicago," *Latin American Perspectives* 25, no. 5 (1998): 97–116, and Dionicio Nodín Valdés, *Barrios Norteños: St. Paul and Midwestern Mexican Communities in the Twentieth Century* (Austin: University of Texas Press, 2000).

2. Orlando Espín, *Faith of the People: Theological Reflections on Popular Catholicism* (Maryknoll, N.Y.: Orbis, 1997). While the focus on the organization's first fifteen years may appear arbitrary, it corresponds to the historicizing scheme used by the organization. Annual Reports (2005, 2006, and 2010) and various publications at the fifteenth-anniversary celebration divide the organization's development into two periods: 1990–2005 and 2006–10. My funded research corresponds with the first period, and I conducted fieldwork in 1990–92 and every subsequent summer until 2005. See the Resurrection Project, Annual Reports (2005, 2006, and 2010), retrieved from http://www.resurrectionproject.org/About-Us/TRP-Reports-Publications/index.html.

3. Gloria E. Anzaldúa, *Interviews/Entrevistas: Gloria E. Anzaldúa*, ed. Ana Keating (New York: Routledge Press, 2000). I acknowledge Irene Lara for pointing out to me the connection between the Resurrection Project and Anzaldúa's notion of spiritual activism.

4. Carlos Muñoz Jr., *Youth, Identity, Power: The Chicano Movement* (London: Verso, 1989); Heidi J. Swarts, *Organizing Urban America: Secular and Faith-Based Progressive Movements* (Minneapolis: University of Minnesota Press, 2008); Catherine E. Wilson, *The Politics of Latino Faith: Religion, Identity, and Urban Community* (New York: New York University Press, 2008); Richard L. Wood, *Faith in Action: Religion, Race, and Democratic Organizing in America* (Chicago: University of Chicago Press, 2002); Interfaith Funders, *1999 Annual Report* (Jericho, N.Y.: Interfaith Funders, 2000). Critics will likely find this work too celebratory, as most of my scholarship strategizes to delineate the struggles against oppression and those moments in which the messy dynamics of hegemony are defeated. The Resurrection Project is simply one case study of Mexican Catholic Chicago during a specific time period, 1990–2005, and this work is not meant to exemplify the experience of all contemporary Mexican Catholics in Chicago or the entire record of the organization.

5. Espín, *Faith of the People*.

6. Resurrection Project, http://www.resurrectionproject.org/index.html.

7. The premise of structural contingency is found in the work of Latino theologians such as Virgilio Elizondo (*Galilean Journey: The Mexican-American Promise* [Maryknoll, N.Y.: Orbis, 1983], 50), who describes Mexican Americans as "twice conquered, twice colonized and twice oppressed," and scholars of Chicana/o history such as Rodolfo F. Acuña (*Occupied America: A History of Chicanos*, 3rd ed. [New York: Harper & Row, 1988]), who describes an "occupied America."

8. Interview with Raúl Raymundo, conducted by Karen Mary Davalos, June 27, 2003, Chicago.

9. Timothy M. Matovina and Gary Riebe-Estrella, eds., *Horizons of the Sacred: Mexican Traditions in U.S. Catholicism* (Ithaca, N.Y.: Cornell University Press, 2002).

10. Anzaldúa, *Interviews/Entrevistas*; Maria Pilar Aquino, "The Theological Method in U.S. Latino/a Theology: Toward an Intercultural Theology for the Third Millennium," in *From the Heart of Our People: Latino/a Explorations in Catholic Systematic Theology*, ed. Orlando Espín and Miguel H. Diáz (Maryknoll, N.Y.: Orbis, 1999), 6–48. See also Janise D. Hurtig, "Hispanic Immigrant Churches and the Construction of Ethnicity," in *Public Religion and Urban Transformation: Faith in the City*, ed. Lowell W. Livezey (New York: New York University Press, 2000), 37; and Wilson, *Politics of Latino Faith*, 180, for an interpretation of TRP as a liberating praxis.

11. Theresa Delgadillo, *Spiritual Mestizaje: Religion, Gender, Race and Nation in Contemporary Chicana Narrative* (Durham and London: Duke University Press, 2011), 18.

12. Aquino, "Theological Method," 32; italics in original.

13. Although a liberating praxis among U.S. Latinos might resonate with Latin American liberation theology, the comparative analysis is beyond the scope of this work. At various times during my research, 1990–2005, the leadership of TRP has used and rejected the term "liberation theology," a contradictory position we should expect from Catholics aware of the revolutionary vision of Latin American liberation theologians and the reformist strategies among U.S. Latinos. In addition, the Roman Catholic Church waged an attack against liberation theologians so that any reversal of positions among TRP leadership must be understood in this light. For example, former pastor of St. Pius V Parish Charles Dahm has rejected a characterization of his ministry or that of the Resurrection Project as liberationist, but scholars such as Janise Hurtig and Nile Harper argue that the U.S. form of liberation theology undergirds the primary mission and identity of St. Pius V and TRP. Wilson, in *Politics of Latino Faith*, offers another perspective, and her interviews with Dahm document a claim to liberation theology.

14. Since 2005, TRP has continued to build and renovate additional housing options in Pilsen, Little Village, the Back of the Yards, and in Chicago suburbs. These figures represent accomplishments to date in December 2003.

15. Cf. Peter R. D'Agostino, "Catholic Planning for a Multicultural Metropolis, 1982–1996," in Livezey, *Public Religion and Urban Transformation*, 269–94; Charles Shanabruch, *Chicago's Catholics: The Evolution of an American Identity* (Notre Dame, Ind., and London: University of Notre Dame Press, 1981); Edward R. Kantowicz, *Corporation Sole: Cardinal Mundelein and Chicago Catholicism* (Notre Dame, Ind., and London: University of Notre Dame Press, 1983); Steven M. Avella, *This Confident Church: Catholic Leadership and Life in Chicago, 1940–1965* (Notre Dame, Ind., and London: University of Notre Dame Press, 1992); Charles W. Dahm, *Power and Authority in the Catholic Church: Cardinal Cody in Chicago* (Notre Dame, Ind.: University of Notre Dame Press, 1981).

16. Valdés, *Barrios Norteños*, 53.

17. Gabriela F. Arredondo, "Navigating Ethno-Racial Currents: Mexicans in Chicago, 1919–1939," *Journal of Urban History* 30, no. 3 (2004): 402.

18. David A. Badillo, *Spiritual Strangers: Mexican-Americans and Catholicism in the Urban Midwest, 1910–1965*, Latin American Studies (Chicago: University of Illinois at Chicago, 1991), 63–64.

19. Jay P. Dolan, *The American Catholic Experience* (Garden City, N.Y.: Image, 1987), 254.

20. For archival information about Our Lady of Guadalupe Parish, see Claretian Missionary Archives, Eastern Province, Oak Park, Ill.: Our Lady of Guadalupe folder. Also see New World Archives, Parishes Collection, Our Lady of Guadalupe Parish folder. Chicago Archdiocese Publications, Chicago, Ill.

21. For archival material about the chapel, see New World Archives, Parishes Collection, Holy Cross/Immaculate Heart of Mary Parish folder, clippings "Mexican Chapel and Center Opens on S. Ashland Ave.," September 7, 1945, and "New Chapel Opens with Mission," November 16, 1945.

22. This demographic fact has been hidden by paradigms in Chicana/o Studies that presume the Southwest is the normative object of study and experience. Even as Chicago's rank in the nation for one of the largest populations of Mexicans and Mexican Americans jumped to second place by the twenty-first century, Chicana/o Studies has yet to reformulate its assumptions; see Davalos, Eric R. Avila, Rafael Pérez-Torres, and Chela Sandoval, "Roundtable on the State of Chicana/o Studies," *Aztlán: A Journal of Chicano Studies* 27, no. 2 (2002): 143–54.

23. Louise Año Nuevo Kerr, "Mexican Chicago: Chicano Assimilation Aborted, 1939–52," in *The Ethnic Frontier: Essays in the History of Group Survival in Chicago and the Midwest*, ed. Melvin G. Holli and Peter d'Alroy Jones (Grand Rapids, Mich.: William B. Eerdmans, 1977), 300.

24. Gregory D. Squires, Larry Bennett, Kathleen McCourt, and Philip Nyden, *Chicago: Race, Class, and the Response to Urban Decline* (Philadelphia: Temple University Press, 1987).

25. *Local Community Fact Book: Chicago Metropolitan Area Based on the 1970 and 1980 Censuses* (Chicago: Chicago Review Press, 1984), 76 and 79.

26. Kerr, "Chicano Settlements in Chicago: A Brief History," *Journal of Ethnic Studies* 2, no. 1 (1976): 29.

27. De Genova and Ana Yolanda Ramos-Zayas, *Latino Crossings: Mexicans, Puerto Ricans and the Politics of Race and Citizenship* (New York and London: Routledge, 2003), 37.

28. Chicago, Ill., Archdiocese of Chicago's Cardinal Joseph Bernardin Archives and Records Center (hereafter, AAC); St. Vitus Administrative Files, 1977–91 (Box BB, 10044.07) and Parish Bulletins Files (Box HH, 10715.04).

29. Robert H. Stark, "Religious Ritual and Class Formation: The Story of Pilsen, St. Vitus Parish, and the 1977 Vía Crucis" (Ph.D. diss., unpublished, University of Chicago, 1981), 175–78.

30. In a Catholic context, the worker-priest movement was an experiment in France during the 1940s during which priests took factory jobs to reach out to workers that were alienated from the church. James Colleran worked "first at loading docks in the fruit market" and later at the gas station near St. Vitus Parish; see Stark, "Religious Ritual and Class Formation," 180.

31. Historical information about St. Vitus Parish is from Chicago, Ill., AAC, St. Vitus Administrative Files, 1977–91 (Box BB, 10044.07) and Parish Bulletins Files (Box HH, 10715.04).

32. Stark, "Religious Ritual and Class Formation," 196–97.

33. For the definition of faith-based organizing federation, see Wood, *Faith in Action*, 68.

34. Additional research on the organization's twenty-year history might reveal how its inaugural efforts extend to residents of Little Village and the Back of the Yards as well as the suburbs. It was not until 1998 that TRP opened Casa Tabasco, its first affordable-rental building in Little Village, with eight units. The critical mass of TRP residents and thus the presence of a critical consciousness remains, in Pilsen, although the first residence for single mothers, Casa Sor Juana, opened in Little Village, not Pilsen, in 2000. In addition, major new developments were scheduled for the Back of the Yards in 2011.

35. Wilson, *Politics of Latino Faith*, 187.

36. Dahm, a priest of the Dominican Order who served in South America and who cofounded the Eight Day Center for Justice in Chicago, is an experienced advocate for the poor. His ministry emphasizes human dignity and the struggle for justice, rejecting material inequality and denouncing discrimination against women and social outcasts. He has been very vocal against domestic violence and has organized separate workshops for victims and perpetrators. Since his arrival in 1986, and particularly since the closing of St. Vitus, Fr. Dahm has influenced TRP spiritual activism. His retirement as pastor of St. Pius V Parish in 2004 allowed him to devote considerable time to TRP as well as campaigns against domestic violence and immigration reform.

37. According to Catherine Wilson, TRP strategized to replace *comunidades de base* with Social Ministry Action and Reflection Teams (SMART) at every member parish because the Christian base communities were not as robust in the new millennium. See Wilson, *Politics of Latino Faith*, 181.

38. Dahm, with Nile Harper, "St. Pius V Roman Catholic Church and the Pilsen Area Resurrection Project," in *Urban Churches, Vital Signs: Beyond Charity Toward Justice*, ed. Nile Harper (Grand Rapids, Mich.: William E. Eerdmans, 1999), 168–81.

39. Squires, Bennett, McCourt, and Nyden, *Chicago*, 99; *Local Community Fact Book*.

40. John J. Betancur, "The Settlement Experience of Latinos in Chicago: Segregation, Speculation and the Ecology Model," *Social Forces* 74, no. 4 (1996): 1299–1325.

41. It is important to register that housing was an issue across Mexican Catholic Chicago, even in the most geographically isolated Mexican community, South Chicago, located at the Illinois and Indiana border. In 1980, Our Lady of Guadalupe Parish of South Chicago founded Claretian Associates Neighborhood Development (CANDO). This neighborhood-housing program provided "attractive, moderately priced homes" for low-income residents and built four new homes; purchased seven vacant lots for additional homes; began work with the city's Urban Affairs Office to secure additional sites; and formed block clubs to support homeowner maintenance and education; see Claretian Missionary Archives, Eastern Province, Oak Park, Illinois: Our Lady of Guadalupe Parish folder and "History of the Parishes," 694.

42. Catherine Wilson reports that "from 1998 until 2001, Holy Cross/IHM Parish [of the Back of the Yards] was a member institution of TRP" but formally separated in 2001 because of TRP's lack of attention to the Back of the Yards; Wilson, *Politics of Latino Faith*, 187. My fieldwork in the summers of 2003 and 2004 suggests that the relationships with Back of the Yards parishes continued in the twenty-first century with and without membership status.

43. Gilbert R. Cadena and Lara Medina, "Liberation Theology and Social Change: Chicanas and Chicanos in the Catholic Church," in *Chicanas and Chicanos in Contemporary Society*, ed. Rorberto M. De Anda (Boston: Allyn and Bacon, 1996), 103.

44. Wood, *Faith in Action*, 6.

45. Ibid.; Wilson, *Politics of Latino Faith*.

46. Jim Langford, "Ray Raymundo," in *Happy Are They: Living the Beatitudes in America* (Liguori, Mo.: Triumph, 1997), 155.

47. Jacques Maritain, quoted in Wilson, *Politics of Latino Faith*, 180.

48. Interview of Cecilia Paz, conducted by Karen Mary Davalos, June 24, 2003, Chicago, Ill.

49. Aquino, "Latina Feminist Theology: Central Features," in *A Reader in Latina Feminist Theology: Religion and Justice*, ed. Maria Pilar Aquino, Daisy L. Machado, and Jeanette Rodríguez (Austin: University of Texas Press, 2002), 149.

50. Langford, "Ray Raymundo," 150.

51. Interview of Alicia Rocha, conducted by Karen Mary Davalos, July 14, 2003, Chicago, Ill.

52. The Resurrection Project, http://www.reurrectionproject.org/index.html. See also interview of Raúl Raymundo, conducted by Karen Mary Davalos, June 27, 2003, Chicago, Ill.

53. Cadena and Medina, "Liberation Theology and Social Change," 103.

54. Interview of Edgar Hernandez, conducted by Karen Mary Davalos, July 18, 2003, Chicago, Ill.

55. "The Resurrection Project: Building Relationships, Creating a Healthy Community" [video] (Chicago: Chicago Video Project, Producer, 2000).

56. Interview of Guacalda Reyes, conducted by Karen Mary Davalos, July 16, 2003, Chicago, Ill.

57. Roberto S. Goizueta, *Caminemos con Jesus: Toward a Hispanic/Latino Theology of Accompaniment* (Maryknoll, N.Y.: Orbis, 1995).

58. See Davalos, *La Quinceañera*: Making Gender and Ethnic Identities," *Frontiers: A Journal of Women Studies* 16, nos. 2/3 (1996): 101–27, and Davalos, "'The Real Way of Praying': The Via Crucis, *Mexicano* Sacred Space and the Architecture of Dominatio," in Matovina and Riebe-Estrella, *Horizons of the Sacred*, for a discussion of *la quinceañera* and *Via Crucis* in Chicago, respectively. The clerical backlash against *la quinceañera* that surfaced in the 1970s and 1980s was not sufficient to undermine Mexican Catholic popular religion in Pilsen.

59. Virgilio Elizondo, "Popular Religion as Support of Identity: A Pastoral-Psychological Case Study Based on the Mexican-American Experience in the USA," in *Popular Religion*, ed. Norbert Greinacher and Norbert Mette (Edinburgh: T & T Clark, 1986).

60. For the case in which Cicero, a western suburb of Chicago, attempted to deny St. Anthony Parish enactment of the Way of the Cross, see Matovina, *Latino Catholicism: Transformation in America's Largest Church* (Princeton and Oxford: Princeton University Press 2012), 169.

FOURTEEN

The Church and American Catholics

Chester Gillis

American Catholics have witnessed remarkable changes in the church since Vatican II (1962–65). Their attitudes toward the church and their relationship with it have also changed. While still very important in the lives of many Catholics, the church no longer commands all dimensions of Catholic's lives the way it did in the 1950s. It now competes with everything, including careers, technology, leisure activities, and popular culture, for the attention and commitment of Catholics. A smaller percentage of Catholics attends Mass weekly, with fewer priests, and with sisters and brothers disappearing. African and Asian priests now stand at American altars in a reversal of mission work. Many disagree with church teachings and moral positions yet still identify as Catholic. Churches are being closed in the Northeast and Midwest, but dioceses are growing in the Sunbelt. Permanent deacons and lay people keep parishes running. Catholics value the ritual and dogmas of the church, but do not want them to intrude on their lifestyle. The church continues to be a robust part of American life and a voice for continuity, but it cannot help but change if it wants to continue to flourish. This chapter chronicles that change.

Periodically, the Roman Catholic Church convenes councils of its hierarchy to determine doctrines and set a direction for the future. The most recent of these councils, the Second Vatican Council, took place in Rome from 1962 to 1965. In one of the documents promulgated by the Council, the "Dogmatic Constitution on the Church" (*Lumen gentium*), the bishops defined the church as "the People of God." Another Vatican II document, the "Pastoral Constitution on the Church in the Modern World" (*Gaudium et spes*), explored the church's relationship with culture. The two phrases "People of God" and "Church in the Modern World" captured much of the essence of Vatican II's direction. For unlike most previous councils, this assembly of bishops and cardinals, under the direction of the pope, addressed the pastoral, not the dogmatic, dimension of the church. In so doing, Vatican II urged Catholics to assume responsibility for their commitment to the church made in baptism and referred to the church as "the people of God," a description quite different from Robert Bellarmine's (1542–1621) "perfect society," which had been used for centuries.[1] Bellarmine, a Jesuit theologian, cardinal, doctor of the church, and saint, described the church as a "perfect society," implying that it stood independent of and superior to civil society. His "perfect society" view in scholastic language explained the church as an institution. The perfection of the church did not mean that it was without defect, but that it was an organic unity whose externals were subject to change, but whose essence was consistent throughout history.

The shift from "perfect society" to "people of God" may not seem significant to contemporary Catholics, but it constituted a dramatic change in focus from a hierarchical institution in which priests and bishops were the church to a notion of church as a community of the baptized—laity and clergy together working under the reign of God within the world.

In 1958 Cardinal Angelo Roncalli, the archbishop of Venice and a former church diplomat in Turkey and France, was elected pope and chose the name "John XXIII." Both church observers and the cardinals who elected him expected that he would largely be a caretaker pope. After all, at the age of seventy-seven, his electors expected a relatively short pontificate. He was also a compromise candidate selected by cardinals who were divided about choosing a younger candidate who would be either decidedly conservative or liberal. Most observers, and likely cardinal electors, as well, thought that John XXIII would be a capable administrator and caring pastor, but few thought he would emerge as the visionary he proved to be. Within months of his election on January 25, 1959, the new pope announced his intention to convene an Ecumenical Council. The announcement surprised the Roman Curia, the body of officials who administer the Holy See, and some among them opposed the idea. They did not believe that the church either needed to or should embrace the modern world. Indeed, they thought that the church should oppose modernity and hold steadfastly to its traditions. Some members of the Roman Curia wanted to control the agenda, but John XXIII planned the Council so that it would involve bishops from every corner of the globe and be open to a variety of perspectives.

Even though Vatican II occurred a generation ago, it continues to shape the church. A recent indication of its continued importance came within days of Benedict XVI's election as pope in 2005, when he reassured Vatican officials and the faithful that he would continue to carry out the reforms initiated by Vatican II. In his first homily after being elected, addressed to the cardinals who elected him pope, he stated:

> Thus, as I prepare myself for the service that is proper to the Successor of Peter, I also
> wish to confirm my determination to continue to put the Second Vatican Council into
> practice, following in the footsteps of my predecessors and in faithful continuity with the
> 2,000-year tradition of the Church. This very year marks the 40th anniversary of the

conclusion of the Council (8 December 1965). As the years have passed, the Conciliar Documents have lost none of their timeliness; indeed, their teachings are proving particularly relevant to the new situation of the Church and the current globalized society.[2]

The church embraces the twenty-first century as a people and an institution shaped by Vatican II and its aftermath. But that formation is as yet incomplete, and the church continues to interpret, implement, and aspire to fulfill the vision of the Council documents. Doing so faithfully and effectively, without dividing the world's Catholics, has posed a challenge since the close of the Council in 1965. Thus far, the church in the United States, as well as worldwide, has managed the transition required by this landmark Council, which urged the church to return to its roots in the gospel and tradition and to interact creatively with the contemporary world. It has not done so, however, without internal disagreements or dueling ideologies. Reflecting on the effects of the Council, the American Jesuit theologian and cardinal Avery Dulles (1918–2008) commented:

> Vatican II has become, for many Catholics, a center of controversy. Some voices from the extreme right and the extreme left frankly reject the council. Reactionaries of the traditionalist variety censure it for having yielded to Protestant and modernist tendencies. Radicals of the far left, conversely, complain that the council, while making some progress, failed to do away with the church's absolutistic claims and its antiquated class structures. The vast majority of Catholics, expressing satisfaction with the results of the council, are still divided because they interpret it in contrary ways.[3]

Perhaps the church would have adapted to the modern world even if Pope John XXIII had not convened the Council, forced to do so by the inertia of contemporary culture in which it was enmeshed. In the United States, the social upheaval of the 1960s may have spilled over into the church whether or not there was a historic Council in Rome. In the U.S. Catholic community, the period immediately following Vatican II brimmed with hope and promise but was forced to grapple with some serious difficulties as well. Chronologically, it coincided with the tumult that characterized the 1960s in the United States. The sexual revolution, the Vietnam conflict, rock music, recreational drugs, a more permissive media, distrust of government and authority, widespread access to higher education, the rise of a consumer culture, the Cold War, increased personal freedom, and more all contributed to a unique era in American history. The church's opening up to the world meant that a tide of change would sweep through the church as it did society and culture.

Maybe the post–Vatican II generation's attitude toward the church is affected more by the general decline in trust of institutions after the Vietnam War, Watergate, the civil rights struggle, increased divorce, corporate scandals, gay rights, and feminism's fight against patriarchy, among other social movements, than it is by church actions and policies. The institutional church has contributed to its own marginalization in the lives of some American Catholics by refusing to deal openly and directly with myriad problems and issues ranging from sexual abuse by clergy to women's call for equality.

Whether the Council accidentally coincided with this social transformation or was an integral part of it cannot be definitively known. In the second decade of the twenty-first century, the Roman Catholic Church in the United States faces a host of challenges and opportunities. How it responds to them will affect its future, but it will not make or break this enduring institution, which has survived many trying times in its history.

The Church, Public Policy, and Politics

As noted elsewhere in this volume, throughout its history, the Roman Catholic Church in America has faced bitter anti-Catholicism. Although there remain vestiges of this era in the post–Vatican II period,[4] anti-Catholicism has largely abated since the election of John F. Kennedy in 1960. Evidence of this can be found on the U.S. Supreme Court, where in the early years of the twenty-first century an unprecedented majority of its members—Roberts, Scalia, Sotomayer, Thomas, Kennedy, and Alito—were Catholic. With Catholics no longer considered outsiders, the institutional church has been proactive in trying to influence American culture and public policy. In particular, the U.S. bishops have mounted several efforts to suggest an agenda for all Americans to consider. In *Living the Gospel of Life: A Challenge to American Catholics*, the American bishops wrote, "'Citizenship' in the work of the Gospel is also a sure guarantee of responsible citizenship in American civic affairs."[5]

The attempt to influence public policy was carefully structured. For example, in the 1980s the American bishops addressed a number of sensitive public policy issues. In doing so, they appealed to both the ecclesial community and the civil community, using arguments constructed from the scriptures and from natural law. By grounding their documents in the Bible, they appealed to revelation that underpins all Christian theology. By employing a natural-law argument they were being consistent with Catholic theology that has relied on natural-law reasoning since at least the time of Thomas Aquinas. Using natural law, they attempted to influence public opinion and government policy by explicitly employing a philosophical argument that did not require that the public and public officials share the faith disposition of the bishops. The resultant pastoral letters, *The Challenge of Peace: God's Promise and Our Response* (1983), and *Economic Justice for All: Catholic Social Teaching and the U.S. Economy* (1986), were not only bold in content, but also the product of an extraordinarily consultative process, something new for the American bishops and for American Catholics. These pastorals addressed all Americans, not simply Catholics. As Rev. Theodore M. Hesburgh, C.S.C., a prominent educator and former president of the University of Notre Dame, remarked, "The bishops do not cease to be citizens by becoming bishops."[6] They have a responsibility to raise moral issues in the public forum.

The impetus for these pastoral letters came from Vatican II and particularly from *Gaudium et spes*, the Pastoral Constitution on the Church in the Modern World, which encouraged the bishops to read the "signs of the times" and to respond to them in ways consistent with the gospel. In the area of war and peace, the bishops' reading of these signs in the 1980s indicated the need for a quest for peace, emphasized the unique destructive powers of nuclear weapons, and underlined the necessity of curbing the escalating arms race. The peace pastoral attempted to analyze the moral issues involved in nuclear warfare and to suggest ways to peace. The church has traditionally defended a just-war theory that allows for warfare under certain conditions, but nuclear war, the pastoral argued, no longer fit under this rubric, since nuclear weaponry cannot compare with conventional weapons. Nuclear weapons are capable of destroying entire countries in a matter of minutes, and they readily violate all principles of proportionality. It is virtually impossible to confine their destructive effect to exclusively military targets. Thus "a limited nuclear war" seems an oxymoron. War, in any form, is no longer morally viable in the modern world, according to the bishops. Citing one of Pope John Paul II's homilies, the document asserts:

> Today, the scale and the horror of modern warfare—whether nuclear or not—makes it totally unacceptable as a means of settling differences between nations. War should belong to the tragic past, to history; it should find no place on humanity's agenda for the future.[7]

To some lay people this sounded like a utopian dream. To others it was the only stance possible in an unstable world in which the weaker nations were likely to suffer at the hands of the powerful. The document was careful to distinguish those who are Christian (and Catholic) from those who "do not share the same vision of faith," although it was ultimately intended for everyone regardless of religious commitment. For Catholics, it was an internal authoritative voice; for other Christians, it was a plea for peace based on Christian scripture; for non-Christian America, it was an appeal to rationality and sanity in a time when all sense of reason could evaporate in the heat of nuclear conflict.

The committee charged with writing the draft of "The Challenge of Peace" included five bishops headed by Archbishop Joseph Bernardin of Cincinnati, who became archbishop of Chicago in 1982 and a cardinal in 1984, shortly after the bishops' approval of the document. Among the committee members was Bishop John O'Connor (later archbishop of New York and a cardinal), who held the rank of admiral in the U.S. Navy, and Auxiliary Bishop of Detroit Thomas Gumbleton, a pacifist. Prior to this document, most church statements were the exclusive product of bishops and perhaps theologians. The committee overseeing this pastoral invited comment from a wide range of constituents who reacted to the drafts, including scientists, government officials, members of the military, politicians, and ordinary Catholics and non-Catholics. The discussions were open and frank. People within and without the church debated the content. Such collaboration was unprecedented. The entire process took thirty months and required the scrutiny of hundreds of potential amendments. When the final draft, titled *The Challenge of Peace: God's Promise and Our Response*, was put before the assembled bishops on May 3, 1983, in Chicago, the document passed, 238 to 9.

The road to passage was not always a smooth one. Some Catholics who were more hawkish disagreed vehemently with the document's position that first-strike nuclear war cannot be justified under any conditions. In general, conservatives inside and outside the church disagreed with the bishops. For example, William F. Buckley Jr. (1925–2008), a conservative Catholic commentator and writer, decried the pastoral's message, fearing, in part, that it meant abandoning the fight against Communism.[8] Those with a more liberal bent agreed with the document, and those within the church were heartened by the support for the document in circles outside the church. Both sides were surprised and encouraged by the consultative process in which the pastoral letter was conceived.

Despite the widespread consultation in the creation of the pastoral and the accompanying publicity it received, many Catholics either ignored the letter or were unwilling to invest themselves in a quest for peace, partly because in the 1980s, as U.S. church historian David O'Brien pointed out, "Episcopal and papal authority is weaker, the church has become more voluntary, and few Catholics are familiar with church teaching on social justice and world peace, even fewer with the natural-law tradition on which so many of these teachings are based."[9]

The second major pastoral letter by the U.S. bishops in the 1980s, under the leadership of Archbishop Rembert Weakland, OSB, of Milwaukee, dealt with the moral questions underlying the American economy. The topic appeared to some as beyond not only the competency, but the authority of the bishops. After all, bishops are meant to be shepherds and administrators, not economists. The *Los Angeles Times* reported "that the letter will make the anti-nuclear statement seem like a 'Sunday-school picnic' by comparison."[10] But the bishops thought that it was time to address economic structures that favored the wealthy, spent more on weapons than welfare, fostered a permanent underclass, and distributed economic advantage unevenly. The pastoral "call[ed] for the establishment of a floor of material well-being on which all can stand" and "call[ed] into question extreme inequalities of income and consumption when so many lack basic necessities."[11]

Economic Justice for All dealt with a wide range of economic issues, principal among them being employment, poverty, food and agriculture, and the U.S. role in a global economy.[12] The pastoral, published at a time of high unemployment and its accompanying hardships, stated that individuals have a right to work and that every effort should be made to provide jobs in both government and the private sector. While the pastoral acknowledges that some of the reasons for unemployment, such as population growth and women increasingly entering the workforce, were beyond the control of the government or private industry, it was critical of policies such as moving manufacturing plants overseas because of lower labor costs, increased defense spending on high-tech weaponry, and lack of job training programs for the unskilled or under-skilled worker. The bishops deplored the fact that one in seven Americans lives below the poverty line in one of the wealthiest countries on earth. This was particularly reprehensible, since many of these are children. They also called for an overhaul of the welfare system, not to diminish the assistance given, but to improve it. Theologically, the pastoral favored a preferential option for the poor, a tenet that is biblically grounded, found in Vatican II documents, and stressed in many contemporary liberation theologies.

As creative as this pastoral was in addressing all Americans on such issues, it reflected the thinking and teaching of key church leaders as articulated as recently as 1981 by Pope John Paul II. In his encyclical *Laborem exercens* (On Human Work), the pope defended work for every individual as a God-given right, along with the right of workers to form legitimate unions. John Paul II said, "[U]nemployment, which in all cases is an evil, when it reaches a certain level, can become a real social disaster." Previously, Pope Leo XIII (1810–1903) defended the rights of workers to a living wage, the right to organize and bargain collectively, and the right of the church to teach on social issues in his 1891 encyclical *Rerum novarum* (On the Rights and Duties of Capital and Labor), and Pope Pius XI (1857–1939) confirmed these thoughts in his Depression-era 1931 encyclical *Quadragesimo anno* (Commemorating the Fortieth Anniversary of Leo *XIII's Rerum novarum*), claiming that "the opportunity to work be provided for those who are willing and able to work." Pope John XXIII, in his 1963 encyclical *Pacem in terris* (Peace on Earth), stated, "[I]t is clear that human beings have the natural right to free initiative in the economic field and the right to work"; and Pope Paul VI (1897–1978) also urged a new economic order in his 1967 encyclical *Populorum progressio* (Development of Peoples). In addition to these encyclicals, the Vatican II document *Gaudium et spes* (The Church in the Modern World) stated that "it is the duty of society . . . to help its citizens find opportunities for adequate employment." For decades, the church had decried the deleterious effects of increasing industrialization. "Economic Justice for All" addressed the problems associated with the deindustrialization of the United States as it farmed out manufacturing to the Pacific rim and developing countries and became a service economy.

So, the bishops built on an established tradition. They had spoken on similar topics in the past (unemployment in 1930, the social order in 1940, and the economy as recently as 1970), but this was the first time that the bishops, as a body, addressed American society as a whole on this topic and received a spirited public reaction. This prophetic action, in the sense of biblical prophets who brought God's message to the attention of a sometimes reluctant people, reflected the fact that Catholics in the United States and their episcopal leaders no longer thought it incumbent on them to support American public policy at all costs. The U.S. Catholic community was no longer an exclusively immigrant and ethnic church seeking confirmation of its patriotism. It had toed the mark long enough to gain respectability and had risen above the suspicion that it was beholden to a foreign power in Rome. These pastorals symbolically represented the U.S. bishops' recovery of some degree of episcopal collegiality that they had not exercised since the late nineteenth century.

The pastoral on the economy was directed at the American people, Catholic and non-Catholic alike, but it addressed issues of economic justice that affected people all over the world. The economy must serve all of the people, including the poor. The objectives were noble as noted in the pastoral: "Society has a moral obligation to take the necessary steps to ensure that no one among us is hungry, homeless, unemployed, or otherwise denied what is necessary to live with dignity." Some critics of the economic pastoral challenged the church to live by its own words. Joseph A. Pichler, president and chief operating officer of Dillon Companies, Inc., wrote the following:

> The Church must witness its commitment to self-determination and voluntarism through its own actions as employer, educator, and minister. Church-related institutions must be a sign to all of managerial behavior that respects the dignity of work and of workers. This entails multiple obligations to: avoid all forms of discrimination based upon race, sex, and other arbitrary dimensions; provide employees with full information regarding their performance and status; recognize the right to collective bargaining; limit restraint placed upon employees to those which are necessary for the effective performance of duties; hear and accommodate the personal needs of employees insofar as they are

consistent with the task at hand; and avoid actions that would foreclose the freedom of others to seek self-improvement.[13]

Economists took exception not to the objectives of the pastoral, but to the methods it proposed to achieve those objectives. Some argued that the bishops were naive or misdirected in their proposals to achieve admirable objectives. For example, the Nobel laureate economist Milton Friedman argued that the means proposed in the pastoral would result in effects diametrically opposed to those the bishops desired.[14] Adhering to the tenets of the pastoral would create more unemployment and weaken the economy. The bishops wanted to invest the government with greater authority over economic matters; Friedman saw little hope that the government could correct what it was largely responsible for creating. He wanted to empower the free-market private sector, not the government. Walter Block, senior economist at the Fraser Institute and director of its Centre for the Study of Economics and Religion, was troubled by the bishops' "lack of comprehension of the free marketplace."[15] Carl Christ, an economist at Johns Hopkins University, commented, "Admirable though the aims of the pastoral letter are, they are sometimes [perhaps deliberately] stated in imprecise terms and hence give little quantitative guidance."[16] Clearly, some among the professional ranks of economists thought that the bishops ventured beyond their area of expertise in writing such a document.

It may have been true that the bishops were beyond their competency as far as economic theory was concerned, but they had not exceeded their moral authority. The gospel is clear in its call for justice and its mandate to care for the poor. In lobbying the American people in such a direct and public manner, the bishops were fulfilling their role as prophetic voices. The details of the letter may be subject to legitimate debate and criticism, but the rationale for such a document is unquestionable in Catholic theology.

The U.S. bishops carved out a particular platform when they spoke about nuclear weapons and the economy. At the time, the Roman Curia made no secret of its displeasure with what it termed the American (and Western) "culture of death." Chief among the church's concerns is its opposition to abortion. On this issue, the American bishops supported the positions of the Holy See. The institutional church, via the hierarchy and the offices of the U.S. Catholic Conference, has attempted to influence public policy, and the church has joined its protest with the protests of evangelical Christians in an alliance that some call "unholy." In addition, individual bishops and priests have made it the focal point of their ministry. The American bishops issued a *Pastoral Plan for Pro-Life Activities* in 1975 to coordinate Catholic efforts to counter *Roe v. Wade*, to teach the value of life, and to assist women with unplanned pregnancies to have their babies. Thirteen years later, in 1998, they issued a document entitled, *Living the Gospel of Life: A Challenge to American Catholics*, that reiterated their opposition specifically to abortion and euthanasia. Recognizing that Catholics were not heeding the church's teaching, the document reminded Catholics of the church's consistent teaching with the words, "As Americans, as Catholics and as pastors of our people, we write therefore today *to call our fellow citizens back to our country's founding principles*, and most especially *to renew our national respect for the rights of those who are unborn, weak, disabled and terminally ill*."

In September 2003, the bishops issued a document, *Faithful Citizenship: A Catholic Call to Political Responsibility*, that articulated principles for Catholics to follow when choosing elected officials. Part of the statement reads:

> As we approach the elections of 2004, we renew our call for a new kind of politics—focused on moral principles not on the latest polls, on the needs of the poor and vulnerable not the contributions of the rich and powerful, and on the pursuit of the common good not the demands of special interests.
>
> Faithful citizenship calls Catholics to see civic and political responsibilities through the eyes of faith and to bring our moral convictions to public life. People of good will and sound faith can disagree about specific applications of Catholic principles. However, Catholics in public life have a particular responsibility to bring together consistently their faith, moral principles, and public responsibilities.

During the presidential election of 2004, some members of the church hierarchy injected themselves into the political process. Senator John Kerry, the Catholic Democratic candidate for president, came under severe criticism for his support for pro-choice legislation. Like some other politicians before him, for example, Mario Cuomo, governor of New York from 1983 to 1994, and 1984 vice presidential candidate Geraldine Ferraro, Kerry personally opposed abortion as a Catholic, but believed, as an elected official, that he had an obligation to uphold the law of the land. Hoping to dissuade Catholics from voting for him, some bishops openly condemned Kerry.

One example of such action drew both praise and condemnation. On May 1, 2004, in anticipation of the November national elections, Bishop Michael Sheridan of the Diocese of Colorado Springs wrote a pastoral letter to his diocese *On the Duties of Catholic Politicians and Voters*. The letter stated:

> When Catholics are elected to public office or when Catholics go to the polls to vote, they take their consciences with them. . . . Anyone who professes the Catholic faith with his lips while at the same time publicly supporting legislation or candidates that defy God's law makes a mockery of that faith and belies his identity as a Catholic.
>
> There must be no confusion in these matters. Any Catholic politicians who advocate for abortion, for illicit stem cell research or for any form of euthanasia *ipso facto* place themselves outside full communion with the Church and so jeopardize their salvation. Any Catholics who vote for candidates who stand for abortion, illicit stem cell research or euthanasia suffer the same fateful consequences. It is for this reason that these Catholics, whether candidates for office or those who would vote for them, may not receive Holy Communion until they have recanted their positions and been reconciled with God and the Church in the Sacrament of Penance.[17]

Some bishops agreed with him, but the majority decided not to instruct Catholics how to vote or to deny Communion to politicians. In response to such initiatives by individual bishops, the United States Conference of Catholic Bishops appointed a task force chaired by Cardinal Theodore McCarrick of Washington, D.C., to study the matter. The committee, after consultation with officials of the Holy See, produced an interim report in June 2004. The document encouraged all Catholics to examine their conscience before receiving the Eucharist. With regard to politicians and bishops, in a document accompanying the report, Monsignor William F. Fay, general secretary of the USCCB, wrote:

> Given the wide range of circumstances involved in arriving at a prudential judgment on a matter of this seriousness, we recognize that such decisions rest with the individual bishop in accord with the established canonical and pastoral principles. Bishops can legitimately make different judgments on the most prudent course of pastoral action. Nevertheless, we all share an unequivocal commitment to protect human life and dignity and to preach the Gospel in difficult times.[18]

Thus, the document did not interfere with the right of individual bishops to govern their dioceses. At the same time, not wanting the Eucharist to be an instrument of politics, the document recognized that "the polarizing tendencies of election-year politics can lead to circumstances in which Catholic teaching and sacramental practice can be misused for political ends." The bishops walked a tightrope that balanced the church's moral position against the separation of church and state.

In 2008 the bishops issued a similar document, *Forming Consciences for Faithful Citizenship*, that stated that abortion is an "intrinsic evil" that "must always be rejected and opposed" but softens this directive, stating that "there may be times when a Catholic who rejects a candidate's unacceptable position may decide to vote for that candidate for other morally grave reasons."

Respecting but Not Always Following the Church

In the post–Vatican II era, American Catholics continued to profess love of their church, but they adhered to its teachings selectively. Despite all of the efforts by the church to make its views clear and binding, for a variety of reasons, American Catholics continue to think and act independently. Much has to do with American society and culture, to which Catholics contribute and by which they are affected. Americans are democratic; Catholicism is not. Americans often follow—or even set—trends. Seldom has the church been accused of being trendy. Americans live in a pluralistic society that values tolerance for many views and practices, whereas many perceive that the church holds moral and dogmatic positions that do not abide tolerance in its beliefs or practices. Americans live in an affluent, developed, and materialistic country. The church promulgates the gospel mandate to identify with the poor. Americans prize their independence. The church "takes care of" her children. Often, Americans are asked to compete and win at work. The church asks them to form a community of forgiveness and compassion. Americans demand reasonable answers to difficult questions from their political leaders. The church asks them to accept some things on faith alone or on the sole basis of the authority vested in the church.

Informed observers of the church, such as the sociologist Father Andrew Greeley, have concluded that American Catholics began distancing themselves from church teachings in reaction to Paul VI's 1968 encyclical *Humanae vitae*, prohibiting, under pain of sin,

Catholics from practicing artificial birth control. Catholics might like or dislike liturgical changes, the reintroduction of the permanent diaconate, or contemporary musical instruments instead of the classical organ, and they might or might not be aware of the nuances of theological disputes, but none of these struck at the core of family and economic life the way banning artificial birth control did. It did not help when American Catholics and others worldwide learned that Paul VI had issued his encyclical against the advice of a commission established originally by Pope John XXIII to study the issue. Not permitting Catholics to limit the size of their families by the use of readily available and safe artificial birth control in an economy that required ever-increasing resources to feed, clothe, and educate a child loosened the ties that bind for the vast majority of the faithful. They refused to be faithful on this issue. Instead, they ignored the teaching against artificial birth control yet continued to practice the faith. Many went through heart-wrenching pangs of conscience, not wanting to disobey their church, but at the same time they were not willing to have more children whom they could not afford to raise with sufficient opportunities to succeed in the world. Some tried the church-approved natural family-planning method but found it cumbersome and sometimes unreliable. Some still favor this method, but they represent a small minority of American Catholics.

Whether or not the reaffirmation of the traditional teaching on birth control was the watershed event that signaled profound disagreement with their church, since that time many American Catholics—on a number of issues a majority—have elected to think and act contrary to numerous church teachings. Thus, they procure abortions at about the same rate as other Americans; they believe that divorced and remarried Catholics should be permitted to receive the Eucharist without going through the legal complexities of what many perceive to be the intrusive process of annulment; they favor ordaining women as priests; they are tolerant of same-sex relationships; and they favor capital punishment for the worst criminals. In other words, they remain Catholic, but they do not practice their Catholicism on Rome's terms.

Vatican II and Changing Attitudes

In 1987 a group of sociologists of religion began conducting surveys of American Catholics using the Gallup Organization to gather data every six years.[19] In 2011, the most recent version of the survey, the demographics have changed. In 1987, 31 percent of American Catholics were pre–Vatican II (born 1940 or earlier), 47 percent Vatican II (1941–60), and 22 percent post–Vatican II (1961–78). In 2011, pre–Vatican II were 10 percent, Vatican II 33 percent, post–Vatican II 34 percent, and millennial (1979 and later) 23 percent.

This is just a small sample of the survey, but it proves instructive about the future of the church. Put simply, younger Catholics relate differently to the church than do older Catholics, and as a whole Catholics today do not agree with, or likely follow, church teachings as faithfully as Catholics of a generation ago. Thus, they make judgments based on personal experience and interpretation as much as by taking into consideration the hierarchy's teaching, even when that teaching is consistent and clear, as in the case of

Table 14-1.   2011 Survey Results on Changing Attitudes of American Catholics

	PRE–VATICAN II	VATICAN II	POST–VATICAN II	GEN X AND MILLENNIALS
	Before 1940	1941–60	1961–86	After 1987
Attend Weekly Mass	56 percent	32 percent	28 percent	24 percent

Adapted from W. D'Antonio, M. Dillon, and M. Gautier, *American Catholics in Transition* (Lanham, Md.: Rowman & Littlefield, 2013).

Table 14-2.   2011 Survey on Catholics and American Politics

	PRE–VATICAN II	VATICAN II	POST–VATICAN II	GEN X AND MILLENNIALS
	Before 1940	1941–60	1961–86	After 1987
Party Affiliation				
Republican	38 percent	40 percent	40 percent	45 percent
Democrat	62 percent	57 percent	57 percent	55 percent

Adapted from W. D'Antonio, M. Dillon, and M. Gautier, *American Catholics in Transition* (Lanham, Md.: Rowman & Littlefield, 2013).

Table 14-3.   2011 Survey on Beliefs of American Catholics

When asked "Can you be a good Catholic **without . . .**"

	YES, YOU CAN
1. Believing Jesus physically rose from the dead	30 percent
2. Donating time or money to the poor	59 percent
3. Believing the bread and wine become the body and blood of Jesus during Mass	37 percent
4. Attending weekly Mass	78 percent
5. Donating time or money to help the parish	74 percent

Adapted from W. D'Antonio, M. Dillon, and M. Gautier, *American Catholics in Transition* (Lanham, Md.: Rowman & Littlefield, 2013).

abortion. It is not that they do not know what the church teaches; it is that they disagree with the teaching and likely therefore do not follow it. They also go to church less regularly than the previous generation. In 1958, on the eve of Vatican II, 75 percent of Catholics attended Mass weekly. Today, the percentage of Catholics who attend Mass weekly hovers around 33 percent, and some sociologists say that once-a-month church attendance has replaced weekly attendance for many active Catholics.[20] One cannot ignore this statistic. Today there are approximately 70 million Catholics in America, about one-third of whom go to church weekly. In 1958 there were 45 million Catholics, 75 percent

Table 14-4.   2011 Survey on Moral Issues

When asked of all Catholics polled, "Should individuals or church leaders have the final say on moral issues," the responses were:

	CHURCH LEADERS	INDIVIDUALS	BOTH LEADERS & INDIVIDUALS
1. Remarry without annulment	21 percent	44 percent	33 percent
2. Practice birth control	10 percent	66 percent	23 percent
3. Free choice on abortion	18 percent	52 percent	29 percent
4. Homosexual activity	16 percent	56 percent	27 percent
5. Sex outside of marriage	15 percent	55 percent	29 percent

Adapted from W. D'Antonio, M. Dillon, and M. Gautier, *American Catholics in Transition* (Lanham, Md.: Rowman & Littlefield, 2013).

(33 million) of whom attended Mass weekly. It is no wonder that parishes are merging or closing. This phenomenon no doubt is due in part to changing demographics in which city neighborhoods originally populated by Irish, German, French, Polish, and Italian Catholics were replaced with a religiously mixed population as Catholics moved to the suburbs where new parishes have been and, in some places, still are being established. But beyond shifting demographics, the changing habits of Catholics account for decreased participation in weekly church attendance. They simply do not go in the numbers (raw or percentages) that they used to. In part, they do not follow the church because they do not hear the church's voice. But additional factors account for changed attitudes and habits. Even when they do hear the church, they ignore the message, in particular as it relates to moral issues, and especially sexual issues. They have decided that personal experience and conscience override ecclesial authority.

Can these attitudes be traced directly to Vatican II?—only partly. Vatican II encouraged the laity to think critically and to take responsibility for their choices and for their church. Having done so for a generation, many Catholics now find themselves opposing or ignoring some church teaching, especially those regarding moral choices that directly affect their lives—for example, birth control or abortion. While the church exerts less influence in these areas, culture exerts more influence, and that reveals the other side of the equation. It is not only that contemporary Catholics are ignoring church teachings; they are also assuming cultural patterns. They are Americans and Catholics, and sometimes being American trumps being Catholic, so they follow cultural and social trends even if they are in opposition to church teachings.

Vatican II did not change the church as radically as some have believed. It did, as intended, change some practices and dispositions (for example, the liturgy in the vernacular and greater openness to other religions); it did not, however, again intentionally, change dogmatic or moral positions (for example, the necessity of Christ for salvation or its position against birth control). What has changed is culture and Catholics—and that is the difference. The culture and American Catholics in the 1950s differed dramatically from today's culture and Catholics. Consider some examples. First, in the 1950s homosexuality in America was a taboo topic. Gays and lesbians were virtually invisible. Very few homosexuals were public about their orientation. Rock Hudson, a major heartthrob of young American women, was quietly gay. Today, television shows like *Modern Family*, movies like *Call Me by Your Name*, rock stars like Elton John, and political figures like former Congressman Barney Frank of Massachusetts and Senator Tammy Baldwin of Wisconsin demonstrate that gays are both public about their orientation and successful in our society. In June 2015 the U.S. Supreme Court declared same-sex marriage legal in all states, a position that the American bishops fought against. The post–Vatican II church continues to condemn homosexual activity, but many contemporary Catholics are less inclined to condemn such activity or lifestyles; this is particularly true for younger generations. Second, in the 1950s, Catholic families often numbered five or more children. In part, more children made it easier for a family to encourage one or two children to embrace the celibate priesthood, sisterhood, or brotherhood. Today, a large Catholic family has three children, and many have fewer. Parents are less likely to encourage a celibate lifestyle when the family name may be in jeopardy. And in the 1950s the priesthood was a prized profession: respected, admired, even feared. Today, especially after the clergy sexual-abuse crisis, but also for other reasons such as multiple career options for well-educated third-, fourth-, and fifth-generation Catholics, the priesthood has lost some of its appeal.

Revisiting Vatican II

The momentum of Vatican II was purposely curbed by Pope John Paul II and by Joseph Cardinal Ratzinger as head of the Congregation for the Doctrine of the Faith and later as Pope Benedict XVI. Two specific examples will support my claim. One is practical, the other theological. First, in the years following Vatican II, national bishops' conferences began to issue statements that reflected the situation and concerns of their particular region of the world. Representatives of these conferences traveled to Rome to meet with the pope on a regular schedule. Early in John Paul II's pontificate, these meetings took the form of a dialogue between the pope and regional bishops. The pope listened to the local churches. Later in his pontificate, bishops gathered in the papal audience hall, were lectured to by the pope, and left—no dialogue. Sensing that national bishops' conferences were influencing church policies, the apostolic letter *Apostolos suos*, written under the direction of Cardinal Ratzinger and approved by John Paul II in 1998, states:

> The Second Vatican Council, in the Decree *Christus Dominus*, not only expressed the
> hope that the venerable institution of Particular Councils would be revitalized, but also
> dealt explicitly with Episcopal Conferences, acknowledging the fact that they had been
> established in many countries and laying down particular norms regarding them. Indeed,
> the Council recognized the usefulness and the potential of these structures, and judged
> that "it would be in the highest degree helpful if in all parts of the world the Bishops of

each country or region would meet regularly, so that by sharing their wisdom and experience and exchanging views they may jointly formulate a program for the common good of the Church."

. . . . In dealing with new questions and in acting so that the message of Christ enlightens and guides people's consciences in resolving new problems arising from changes in society, the Bishops assembled in the Episcopal Conference and jointly exercising their teaching office are well aware of the limits of their pronouncements. While being official and authentic and in communion with the Apostolic See, these pronouncements do not have the characteristics of a universal magisterium. For this reason the Bishops are to be careful to avoid interfering with the doctrinal work of the Bishops of other territories, bearing in mind the wider, even world-wide, resonance which the means of social communication give to the events of a particular region.

Early in his pontificate, in October 2005, Benedict XVI presided over a synod on the topic of the Eucharist that was attended by an international group of approximately 250 bishops. During the synod, bishops raised the possibility of changing the celibacy require-ment for priests and the necessity for Catholics in second marriages to have church-approved annulments of their first marriage to be eligible to receive the Eucharist. The synod acknowledged that "the lack of priests to celebrate the Sunday Eucharist worries us a great deal" but, instead of altering the discipline of celibacy, called for the church "to pray and more actively promote vocations." Regarding divorced Catholics, the bishops said that they "know the sadness of those who do not have access to sacramental communion because of their family situation," but reaffirmed the ban on them receiving the Eucharist.

Another example illustrates how the openness of the church to other Christian com-munities and other religions, articulated in Vatican II's *Declaration on the Relations of the Church to Non-Christian Religions* (*Nostra aetate*), was narrowed and redefined in the Dec-laration of the Congregation for the Doctrine of Faith, *Dominus Jesus*, issued in 2000. For example, regarding the Protestant churches, the declaration states, "The ecclesial com-munities which have not preserved the valid Episcopate and the genuine and integral sub-stance of the Eucharistic mystery, are not Churches in the proper sense; however, those who are baptized in these communities are, by Baptism, incorporated in Christ and thus are in a certain communion, albeit imperfect, with the Church." The effects of these re-trenchments were overshadowed by the crisis the church faced when a pattern of sexual abuse came to light.

The Saddest Chapter in the Church's History

The clergy sexual-abuse crisis and the cover-up, widely participated in by bishops, com-prises an important chapter in the church's post–Vatican II history. No one knows for cer-tain exactly when sexual abuse by priests began, but everyone knows that it came to light in the 1980s and 1990s. The abuse had been going on for decades, and the cover-up by bishops equally as long. As a result of this scandal, the Roman Catholic Church in the United States suffered the most painful, disturbing, and publicly embarrassing chapter in its history. Among the most notorious cases were those of John Geoghan and Paul Shanley in Boston; Rudy Kos in Dallas; James Porter in Fall River, Massachusetts; and Gilbert Gauthier in Lafayette, Louisiana. However, the abuse touched virtually every diocese in the United States to some degree. Many of the cases exhibited similar characteristics: an abuser who was himself abused by a priest, multiple victims over many years, negligent supervision, unsuccessful therapy, legal wrangling, the press's role in exposing the case, prison sentences, dismissal from active ministry or from the priesthood itself, and lawsuits against dioceses with sometimes devastating financial consequences. While no two cases are identical, most exemplify the complexity, the idiocy, and the tragedy of clerical sexual abuse and the institutional church's mishandling of cases.[21]

Unchecked power of the clergy also contributed to the sexual-abuse crisis. Because parishioners traditionally revered the role of priest, too many victims were intimidated as well as abused; this prevented them from coming forward. To make matters worse, instead of acting in a pastorally sensitive manner, some bishops relied mostly upon lawyers for advice when dealing with victims, which further exacerbated their pain and disenfranchisement. So clergy *and* bishops abused their power by acting in authoritarian ways. In an attempt to protect themselves and the institution, Rome and the bishops tried to neutralize the sexual-abuse crisis through a series of mechanisms that deflected admission of and responsibility for their malfeasance.

Many observers believed that John Paul II, by this time visibly affected by Parkinson's disease, did not react quickly enough to the crisis in the American church. The slow reaction from Rome may have been a result of the pope's illness, but it also may have been caused by underestimating the widespread nature of the abuse as well as the belief that the scandal was created by a hostile press or that self-absorbed Americans had exaggerated conditions in their church. Whatever the reasons for not acting swiftly, the growing cry from Boston Catholics and others for the resignation of Cardinal Bernard Law, archbishop of Boston, a close confidant of the pope, brought the crisis to papal attention. Cardinal Law met with the pope and offered his resignation, but the pope declined to accept it, preferring that Law remain in office so that he could address and correct the problems in his archdiocese. Boston Catholics and a number of the priests from the Archdiocese of Boston, however, completely lost confidence in Cardinal Law to the degree that it became difficult for him to appear in public without protests. Finally, he and the pope recognized that his leadership was no longer viable, prompting the pope to accept Law's resignation on December 13, 2002. In July 2003, his successor, Archbishop Sean O'Malley, a Capuchin with a record for cleaning up abuse scandals in the dioceses of Fall River, Massachusetts, and Palm Beach, Florida, became archbishop of Boston. He met with abuse victims, sold diocesan property, and settled outstanding lawsuits. But the damage had been done, and the Archdiocese of Boston suffered financially and morally as the abuse crisis took its toll, eroding the morale of priests and the trust of the laity. In part, as a consequence of the settlements, Archbishop O'Malley was forced to announce the closing of eighty parishes, the news of which led to angry protests by parishioners that included sit-ins in churches to prevent the closings and further hard feelings and alienation. Some parishes pressed all the way to the Holy See's highest court, the Apostolic Singatura, where parishioners lost their appeal.[22] Even after the financially devastating initial round of settlements with 554 victims, the diocese faced another 100 cases still in contention.

Boston may have been the center of media attention, but it was hardly the only place to be devastated by the abuse. Fifteen dioceses, the earliest Portland, Oregon, in July 2004 and the most recent Great Falls–Billings, March 2017, and three religious orders—Oregon Province of the Jesuits, February 2009; Christian Brothers, April 2011; and Crozier Fathers and Brothers, June 2017—filed for bankruptcy. Almost every diocese in the nation faced charges of sexual abuse by priests and paid hundreds of millions of dollars in claims. Bishop Tod Brown of the Diocese of Orange, California, made the largest payout, 120 million dollars, believing that victims deserved an apology from the church that had wronged them and just compensation without a protracted legal battle that served neither the victims nor the church well. Cardinal Roger Mahony of Los Angeles, facing over 500 allegations, employed numerous legal maneuvers to protect the church's privileged internal communications. In December 2006, the archdiocese agreed to settle 45 cases at a cost of 60 million dollars. In a statement issued at the time, Mahony admitted that settlement of the remaining cases "will not be without pain and may require the archdiocese to re-evaluate some ministries, services and nonessential properties."[23]

The U.S. bishops, under the leadership of the United States Conference of Catholic Bishops' president Wilton Gregory, were forced to do a great deal of soul-searching, damage control, and apologizing. They devoted their annual meetings in Washington in November 2002 and in Dallas in June 2003 to the crisis, creating detailed policies for dioceses to follow. At the Dallas meeting they invited key laypersons, R. Scott Appleby from the University of Notre Dame and Margaret O'Brien Steinfels of *Commonweal*, to address them about the laity's reaction to the scandal. The bishops established a distinguished panel to oversee the church's compliance with sexual-abuse polices. Bishop Gregory appointed former Oklahoma governor Frank Keating to head the oversight commission. Keating angered many bishops when he openly criticized them for covering up their negligence. The backlash among bishops to Keating's style of leadership led to his stepping down.

The bishops commissioned John Jay College of Criminal Justice to conduct a study.[24] At their semiannual meeting in June 2002, they approved a *Charter for the Protection of Children and Young People*. The John Jay report was an extensive study of the problem that shed light on a dark corner of the church. The report and media investigations across the country shocked even the most devout Catholics and opened the church to criticism, ridicule, and lawsuits, most of which the church brought upon itself by turning a blind eye to the immoral and illegal behavior of some of its clergy.

The sexual-abuse crisis was not confined to the United States. From Latin America to Europe, Australia, and elsewhere, the church has been dealing with sexual-abuse consequences to this day. In June 2017, Cardinal Pell of Australia was summoned from his service to the Vatican to answer personal sexual-abuse charges in an Australian court, the highest-ranking prelate to be formally charged in the scandal.

The consequences of the abuse scandal defy summarizing. It will take years, if not decades, for the church to recover. Horrified, the laity lost trust in the church as an institution, in individual priests and the priesthood, and in the bishops, whom they blamed for lack of oversight and action. Priests lost the respect of their people, had to endure harsh, and in some cases, unfair, criticism, and suffered a sharp decline in morale. Bishops became the targets of anger from laity and priests, the wider public, and the press. Tragically, the situation resembled Shakespeare's Romeo and Juliet, in which "all are punished."

Today's Challenges and Promise

In addition to dealing with the complications from the sexual-abuse scandal, today's U.S. Catholic Church faces a number of pressing issues. The foremost among these is the shortage of priests. In 1965, 549 parishes did not have a resident priest pastor; by 2016, that number had swelled to 3,499. The Eucharist is at the heart of Catholic spirituality. The celebration of the Eucharist requires that a priest preside. In many parishes across the nation, priests simply are not available to preside at Sunday liturgy. While the shortage is more critical in some geographical areas than others, every diocese is pressed to provide a sufficient number of priests to accommodate the needs of the faithful. The shortage has many implications and few solutions. Most important, some Catholics are being deprived of the Eucharist on a daily basis, though they usually have Sunday Eucharist. Beyond that obvious fact, however, lies a range of ancillary complications. Many of the priests who are serving find themselves stretched in too many directions and are often exhausted from the multiple demands they face. Many dioceses have begun to import priests from foreign nations, but this resolution is fraught with its own difficulties. Foreign priests, even the most well-intentioned and sincere of them, are, in the end, foreign. This often means that they encounter challenges with the language and culture of American Catholicism. The situation is quite different from that of the first half of the twentieth century when immigrant communities brought their own clergy with them. These priests, while new to America, were part of the immigrant communities that they served. They knew well the people, and the people knew them and shared with them a common native language and culture, as well as a common struggle to accommodate to American culture. Many of the priests who are imported to American altars today come from cultures that differ significantly from the parishes in which they serve. One does not become an American overnight, and the adjustment period can prove trying for both the priest and the parish.[25] While the church is a universal body, which means that priests should be able to serve anywhere in the world, cultural differences matter and must be addressed for international priests to function effectively. While importing priests has become a necessary measure in many dioceses, this solution to the priest shortage simply postpones an indigenous resolution to the problem. One benefit of Vatican II that offsets the effects of the clergy shortage is greater involvement of the laity, in particular women, in pastoral ministry.

Another component to the priest shortage involves the age of the clergy. The average age of priests in America has been rising steadily for the past twenty years, and currently, in the early years of the twenty-first century, is sixty-three years old. The average age was thirty-five in 1970. A sixty-year-old priest can serve as vibrantly and as well as a thirty-year-old priest, but he will not do so for long. Adding to the average age of active priests is the fact that the majority of newly ordained priests are now in their thirties, when a generation ago, they were in their twenties. And there simply are not enough of them. In 1965 there were 8,325 graduate-level seminarians, compared to 3,520 in 2016. In 1965 there were 994 ordinations to the priesthood, compared to 548 in 2016. Many newly ordained priests have discovered their vocation as a second career; they come to the pulpit and the parish with multiple credentials and significant life experience. In most cases, this benefits the people whom they serve. But it cannot ameliorate the fact that they will serve for fewer years in active ministry because they are being ordained later in life. Many dioceses and religious orders have extended the service of active priests by raising the retirement age to seventy or seventy-five. This helps to a degree, but it does not address the underlying issues that created or contributed to the shortage. Many priests do not mind working until age seventy-five, but some would like to do so voluntarily and not be forced to stay on beyond their most energetic years. The aging of the clergy is even more apparent in the selection of bishops, the vast majority of whom are elevated to their positions in their fifties or sixties; the average age of bishops is about sixty-five years old.

In 1965, when American Catholics numbered 45 million, 58,632 priests served. In 2016, when American Catholics numbered 70 million, 37,192 priests served.[26] The numbers are more dramatic for religious sisters, whose ranks have declined from 179,954 in 1965 to 47,170 in 2016, and whose average age is over seventy years. Similarly, religious brothers have declined from 12,271 in 1965 to 4,119 in 2016. These numbers do not tell the entire story because in 1965, a higher percentage of Catholics, nearly 70 percent, attended Mass weekly than attend in the twenty-first century, with estimates ranging from 24 percent to 33 percent.[27] This final statistic may be the most ominous of all, indicating that the majority of American Catholics simply sit on the sidelines of the church.

Much changed with the election of Pope Francis in March 2013. Francis has focused on the pastoral dimension of the church and appears less concerned with laws and regulations than with the circumstances of the people's lives. He has appointed bishops with the same pastoral approach and has given less attention to conservative voices in the church. He removed Cardinal Raymond Burke, a prominent conservative American voice at the Vatican during Pope Benedict XVI's reign, from his Vatican position, has resisted promoting conservative bishops to the rank of cardinal, has empowered national bishops' conferences to make decisions that affect their region of the world, has refused to condemn gay Catholics, and has focused on the poor and disenfranchised. His 2015 visit to the United States included a speech to a joint session of Congress, a first for a pope. Beloved by the media, his reforms are not popular with all in Rome or America, but he is undeterred by criticism.

Despite these daunting challenges, the church in the United States continues to be vibrant. While a considerably smaller percentage of Catholics attend Mass weekly, those who do generally find parish life engaging. Many parishes, particularly in the suburbs, have full churches on Sundays, extensive religious education programs, competent staffs comprised of clergy and lay persons working cooperatively, and outreach to a wide range of groups from the most engaged to the marginalized. Most priests are happy with their vocation, and while many American Catholics selectively follow church teachings, they continue to identify themselves as Catholic. Most value the sacramental life and spirituality found within the church. The days of blind obedience to church rules may be past, but there is also a benefit to better-educated, more critically aware Catholics in America. The laity is willing to assume responsibility for their individual practice of the faith and for the church. This may occasion sharper conflicts, but it also means less passivity and greater willingness to be the church.

NOTES

1. Robert Bellarmine (1542–1621); see John Courtney Murray, S.J., "St. Robert Bellarmine on the Indirect Power," *Theological Studies* 9 (December 1948): 491–535.

2. "First Message of His Holiness Benedict XVI at the End of the Eucharistic Concelebration with the Members of the College of Cardinals in the Sistine Chapel," *The Holy See*, http://www.vatican.va/holy_father/benedict_xvi/messages/pont-messages/2005/documents/hf_ben-xvi_mes_20050420_missa-pro-ecclesia_en.html, accessed Oct. 15, 2005.

3. Avery Dulles, *The Reshaping of Catholicism: Current Challenges in the Theology of the Church* (San Francisco: Harper & Row, 1988), 19.

4. See Philip Jenkins, *The New Anti-Catholicism: The Last Acceptable Prejudice* (New York: Oxford University Press, 2006); Mark Massa, *Anti-Catholicism: The Last Acceptable Prejudice* (New York: Crossroad, 2003); and Robert Lockwood, ed., *Anti-Catholicism in American Culture* (Huntington, Ind.: Our Sunday Visitor, 2000).

5. "Living the Gospel of Life: A Challenge to American Catholics," United States Conference of Catholic Bishops, 1998, http://www.usccb.org/prolife/gospel.htm, accessed January 2006.

6. Philip J. Murnion, ed., *Catholics and Nuclear War: A Commentary on "The Challenge of Peace"; The U. S. Catholic Bishops' Pastoral Letter on War and Peace* (New York: Crossroad, 1983), vii.

7. Ibid., para. 219.

8. William F. Buckley Jr., "Dubois Memorial Lecture," in *Right Reason* (Garden City, N.Y.: Doubleday, 1985), 111–20.

9. David J. O'Brien, "American Catholics and American Society," in Murnion, *Catholics and Nuclear War*, 26.

10. Quoted in John W. Houck and Oliver F. Williams, eds., *Catholic Social Teaching and the U.S. Economy: Working Papers for a Bishops' Pastoral* (Washington, D.C.: University Press of America, 1984), 4.

11. *Tenth Anniversary Edition of Economic Justice for All: Pastoral Letter on Catholic Social Teaching and the U.S. Economy* (Washington, D.C.: United States Catholic Conference, 1997), 43.

12. See Douglas Rasmussen and James Sterba, *The Catholic Bishops and the Economy: A Debate* (New Brunswick: Transaction, 1987); Walter Block, *The U.S. Bishops and Their Critics: An Economic and Ethical Perspective* (Vancouver: Fraser Institute, 1986); and Houck and Williams, *Catholic Social Teaching and the U. S. Economy*.

13. Joseph A. Pichler, "Capitalism and Employment: A Policy Perspective," in Houck and Williams, *Catholic Social Teaching and the U. S. Economy*, 67. For a study of the church's relationship to unions within its own organizations, including schools and hospitals, and with those of other church employees, see Patrick J. Sullivan, *U.S. Catholic Institutions and Labor Unions, 1960–1980* (Lanham, Md.: University Press of America, 1985).

14. Milton Friedman, "Good Ends, Bad Means," in *The Catholic Challenge to the American Economy*, ed. Thomas M. Gannon (New York: Macmillan, 1987), 99–106.

15. Block, *U.S. Bishops and Their Critics*, 11.

16. Carl Christ, "Unemployment and Macroeconomics," in Gannon, *Catholic Challenge to the American Economy*, 117.

17. Pastoral Letters, Catholic Diocese of Colorado Springs; to see the document, search Google with the URL http://www.diocs.org/CPC/Corner/pastoralletters_view.cfm?year =2004&month=May; accessed June 4, 2006.

18. "Catholics in Political Life," *United States Conference of Catholic Bishops*, http://www.usccb .org/issues-and-action/faithful-citizenship/church-teaching/catholics-in-political-life.cfm, accessed July 2, 2006.

19. In September 2006, the *National Catholic Reporter* provided results of the most recent survey. William D'Antonio, James D. Davidson, Dean R. Hoge, and Mary Gautier have an expanded study and analysis of these data in *Catholic Laity: Their Faith and Their Church* (New York: Rowman & Littlefield, 2007).

20. According to statistics compiled by the Center for Applied Research in the Apostolate located at Georgetown University.

21. Particularly damning but cogently and precisely expressed are the findings from the following that the bishops' conference itself published: *The Nature and Scope of Sexual Abuse of Minors by Catholic Priests and Deacons in the United States, 1950–2002* (Washington, D.C.: USCCB, 2002), and *A Report on the Crisis in the Catholic Church in the United States* (Washington, D.C.: USCCB, 2004).

22. O'Malley announced plans to close or merge more than 80 of the archdiocese's 357 parishes. Sixty-two eventually closed, leaving the archdiocese with 303 parishes.

23. Statement issued on December 1, 2006, and available on the archdiocese's website at http://www.la-archdiocese.org/news/story.php?newsid=821.

24. The formal title of the report was *The Nature and Scope of the Problem of Sexual Abuse of Minors by Catholic Priests and Deacons in the United States*; http://www.usccb.org/issues-and-action /child-and-youth-protection/upload/The-Nature-and-Scope-of-Sexual-Abuse-of-Minors-by -Catholic-Priests-and-Deacons-in-the-United-States-1950–2002.pdf.

25. The National Federation of Priests' Councils addressed this challenge in 2000 when it commissioned a thorough study of international priests serving in American parishes. The results of the study have been published as *International Priests in America* (Collegeville, Minn.: Liturgical Press, 2006), written by noted sociologist Dean R. Hoge and Aniedi Okure, former coordinator of Ethnic Ministers at the U.S. Catholic Conference. The authors present an even-handed assessment of the pros and cons of having international priests in U.S. parishes. While they concede that the practice cannot solve the problem of the priest shortage, they have several valuable suggestions for improving the lives of these international priests and enhancing their effectiveness in the American setting.

26. Statistics from the Center for Applied Research in the Apostolate at Georgetown University, http://cara.georgetown.edu.

27. This number has remained steady since 2000; see the Center for Applied Research in the Apostolate study "Self-Reported Mass Attendance of U.S. Catholics Unchanged Last Five Years," at http://cara.georgetown.edu.

Jeffrey M. Burns

This volume represents a coming-of-age for U.S. Catholic historiography. Many of the authors in this collection began their careers in the 1980s and 1990s, trained at non-Catholic universities, and have published significant monographs. The breadth and depth of their work reflect the depth and breadth of current U.S. Catholic studies. The studies in this volume are regionally diverse, covering the West, Southwest, South, Midwest, Northeast, and East; they examine rural, urban, and suburban life. The old focus on the East, Northeast, and Midwest, on immigrant working-class culture, is still present, but these studies move beyond that paradigm. These essays are multiracial, multicultural, interdisciplinary, and transnational and employ different methodologies and approaches that not only capture the richness and diversity of the U.S. Catholic past but reflect the richness and diversity of the current state of U.S. Catholic history.

The study of U.S. Catholic history has developed over the past century and a half and has generally mirrored the historic position in which the church found itself. The pioneer historians—John Gilmary Shea, Peter Guilday, and John Tracy Ellis—established the professional discipline of U.S. Catholic history, created the baseline for the U.S. Catholic narrative, and promoted the U.S. church as the institution and its people assimilated into American culture. They wrote in an era when Catholics perceived themselves as a besieged minority. Their approach focused on the institutional, episcopal, and intellectual; it was limited but necessary work. In a sense, it represented a church that was still in its building stage, a defensive minority attempting to define and claim its place in U.S. society. For the most part U.S. Catholic historians looked inward toward matters of importance to

Catholics but of little concern to those outside the church. The Catholic story was largely ignored by mainstream U.S. historians, as it was thought to be, and treated as, peripheral.

By the 1950s, the church had become increasingly assimilated, boasted a growing middle class, and had gained a public and physical presence in the U.S. cultural, political, civic, and religious landscape. In addition, Catholics were becoming increasingly assertive. One of their own was even elected president in 1960. Five years prior to that, John Tracy Ellis published a famous essay—"American Catholics and the Intellectual Life"—that provoked a vibrant internal debate dubbed the "Catholic intellectual crisis," which asked why the U.S. church had not yet produced a more substantial intellectual tradition. This reflected a newfound confidence, but also brought to light a serious problem. Catholics wanted to be taken seriously, but it would still be another decade before the Catholic story broached the mainstream narrative.

The 1960s opened up new vistas in church and society. The civil rights movements directed attention to the common person, to those who had been invisible and on the periphery. This discovery coincided with the Second Vatican Council's (1962–65) designation of the church as the People of God and its reassertion of the priesthood of all the faithful. Both movements dovetailed with the new social history that attempted to present history from the perspective of the least or "from the bottom up." Barton J. Bernstein's important *Towards a New Past: Dissenting Essays in American History* is an example of a work that explored these new possibilities.[1] Catholic historians soon followed. Philip Gleason's *The Conservative Reformers: German-American Catholics and the Social Order* (1968) and Jay P. Dolan's *The Immigrant Church: New York's Irish and German Catholics, 1815–1865* (1975) set the standard for the new Catholic social history.[2] Others followed their lead. Catholicism was now comfortably situated in mainstream U.S. culture—some felt a little too comfortably. Was there anything distinctive about the Catholic community? Did it have anything distinctive to say? Were U.S. Catholic historians saying anything worth listening to? Catholicism slowly drew the attention of mainstream historians, though it continued to be peripheral.

The authors in our volume represent the next stage in U.S. Catholic historiography. They represent serious scholarship that is better integrated into the U.S. story. These authors have benefited not only from the efforts of their predecessors but also from the more developed infrastructure of U.S. Catholic Studies.

Most significant was the establishment of the Cushwa Center for the Study of American Catholicism at the University of Notre Dame in the late 1970s. The Cushwa Center has advanced the field through its newsletter, seminars, lectures, conferences, travel grants, and book series. Equally important, Cushwa has provided a congenial meeting place where scholars can share their research, test new ideas, and build personal relationships and networks. Well before the Internet, the center connected a diverse and regionally disparate group of scholars and created a sense of community among them.

Other developments also boosted the growing community. The staid *Catholic Historical Review* continued to publish significant scholarship, though it was not limited to U.S. Catholic history. The field was enriched and expanded by two peripheral publications retooled to assist and promote the growing field—the *U.S. Catholic Historian* and *American*

Catholic Studies. Both publications have broadened the field and made research more accessible. Secular presses such as Cornell University Press, the University of North Carolina Press, and New York University Press no longer eschew Catholic topics and have published a number of U.S. Catholic monographs. The field was moving from the periphery to the mainstream of U.S. historiography.

Today's U.S. Catholic historians find themselves in an interesting position—they are no longer part of a struggling, defensive minority community, but are still on the periphery. The Catholic Church now matters, sometimes. In the twenty-first century, historians will have to unpack the incredible complexity of a church that is both post-immigrant and still essentially immigrant; a church that consists of all social classes and political parties; and a church that continually struggles to apply and integrate its social message in the face of an increasingly disjointed yet global world. Catholics are more than ever beset by the same struggles other Americans face. One historian has dubbed the era "the age of fracture,"[3] and the fracture that plagues U.S. society has also infected life within the U.S. church. Catholics have been active participants in the culture wars and in the polarization of U.S. social and political culture.

Immigration remains central. The immigrants from the nineteenth and early twentieth centuries are almost fully integrated, but the U.S. landscape has been dramatically changed by the influx of new immigrants since 1965. The majority of these new immigrants come from what has been designated the Global South—Latin America, Asia, and Africa. These newcomers have radically transformed the makeup and complexion of the church. Complicating matters, this influx occurred as the church's institutions and programs declined following Vatican II, as so many of the essays in this volume document. The integrated Catholic culture of the 1950s collapsed; Catholic schools declined; men and women left the priesthood and sisterhood in record numbers; seminaries and novitiates became wasteland; and apostolic movements lost their energy. In the midst of all this, the church was hit by one of the worst scandals in its history—the pedophilia crisis: the sexual abuse of children by the clergy and the ensuing mishandling of the crisis by the church hierarchy and bureaucracies, which only deepened the crisis. The church's newfound stature and stability were undercut by powerful currents that left it in a state of constant turmoil.

This complex reality has allowed our contributors to take a fresh and challenging look at U.S. and U.S. Catholic history. The entire volume builds on the good work of previous generations but offers a fresh interpretation of the relation of U.S. Catholicism to U.S. culture and of U.S. Catholic history to the larger U.S. narrative. Our authors have challenged or overturned many of the standard interpretations of Catholics and U.S. culture, notably:

> The traditional narrative of the Catholic minority being buffeted by intense
> anti-Catholicism and anti-immigrant bias is countered by the notion that the
> U.S. attitude toward immigrants is best described as "ambivalent"; while
> discrimination was no doubt a reality, Catholic immigrants successfully
> assimilated and succeeded in the United States (Allitt). Moreover, Catholicism

had a strange attraction for many non-Catholics, including such noted U.S. authors as Nathaniel Hawthorne (Cadegan).

Though the traditional narrative usually starts in Maryland, a fresh perspective can be gained by turning the story on its head and beginning in Spanish America (Matovina).

The notion that Catholics docilely followed their leaders in obedience and that the church was strictly authoritarian and hierarchical is countered by a vibrant tradition of dissent (Burns).

The normative urban experience has overshadowed an equally exciting and important rural Catholic component (Marlett).

Women religious did more than teach and serve as nurses and worked beyond parochial boundaries (McGuinness).

Catholic influence on movies went far beyond the Legion of Decency, and, through the movies, Catholics were central to the development of U.S. popular culture (Smith).

Catholics developed their own literary culture that, though ignored by the academic canon, made a significant contribution to U.S. and U.S. Catholic culture (Cadegan).

The U.S. Catholic Church was not just a local and national institution, but an international one (Domenico), and by the early 1900s U.S. Catholics began to look beyond the local to the global by supporting foreign missions, if only as "armchair missionaries" (Carbonneau).

The Communist Party challenged Catholics, who had absorbed some of the worst features of U.S. racism, to adopt and develop a more humane racial policy (Moore).

Contrary to Will Herberg's assertions, U.S. Catholics never fully assimilated, but kept a particular point of view, particularly in terms of what constitutes the good society, and the typical liberal-conservative split did not adequately capture the complexity of U.S. Catholic social thought (Shannon).

There was a consistency in Catholic protests from the left and right. Tactics pioneered during the antiwar movements were employed by the Right-to-Life movement shortly thereafter (McCartin).

The lived experience of new Catholic immigrants remains rooted in the familial and communal, much as it was in the nineteenth century, despite the radical individualism of modern U.S. society (Davalos).

As the authors of this volume demonstrate, Catholic historians offer a distinctive view of history in three significant ways. First, the Catholic view tends to be communitarian, privileging the family and community over the individual, while still advocating for the rights of the individual. Second, Catholics take an international perspective because they are tied to an international authority located in Rome, an authority that can influence their daily activities. As a result, Catholics were early attuned to and ready for the growing globalization of the modern world. Finally, Catholic social teaching informs the Catholic perspective. Solidarity, dignity of the human person, the dignity of work, and care for creation inform the selection of research materials and subject matter that Catholic historians engage.

The Future

The richness and diversity of these essays suggest the complexity future historians will have to confront. Catholic historians will continue to examine the internal workings of the church, but they will offer more complex perspectives not limited to the episcopal and institutional. U.S. Catholic historians must look at the church's interrelationship with mainstream U.S. culture, its impact on the church, and the church's impact on it, and they must address the concerns of mainstream U.S. historians. We have seen that U.S. culture has not always influenced the church in a positive way: church members have imbibed U.S. racism, adopted some of the worst trappings of U.S. market forces, and been trapped by a pervasive individualism. The church's attempt to create a more just and peaceful society has met with limited success. The historian will also have to pay attention to the church's international or transnational character. What happens in the Vatican has a direct impact on the United States, and what happens in the United States concerns the world church. The church's international structure will play an ever-more-important role in an increasingly global world culture.

The authors in this collection have set the table for future historians of U.S. Catholicism. Historians will undoubtedly spend a good deal of time unpacking the pedophilia crisis that ripped the church apart in the 1990s and 2000s. But this crisis was emblematic of much greater challenges, including authority within church and society, sexuality and gender, and the role of the laity. The mishandling of the crisis created a crisis of authority as lay groups called for greater accountability and transparency within the church and a reconsideration of Catholic authority.

The issue of authority has been a central issue for church and society since at least the 1960s. That dramatic decade undermined the basis of most authority, but the challenge was particularly felt in the Catholic Church. As the authors of this volume suggest, in the years following Vatican II the church saw much of its flourishing institutional life decline. Arguments erupted over the cause: some blamed the Second Vatican Council itself; others claimed liberals had "hijacked" the Council; while still others blamed the deliberate speed with which Council reforms were introduced, or worse, were blocked or ignored entirely. Pope Paul VI's encyclical *Humanae vitae* proved a flash point for dissent, as many Catholics found themselves questioning, perhaps for the first time, a papal directive in an open and public manner, and faith in papal authority was seriously undermined. All these factors created, whatever their source, a crisis of authority that remains to be studied, explained, and resolved.

By the 1980s, a new model of authority was being explored. That era saw the extraordinary collegial work of the National Conference of Catholic Bishops culminate in two important pastoral letters, *The Challenge of Peace* (1983) and *Economic Justice for All* (1986).

These pastoral letters used a broadly collaborative process that consulted lay experts, theologians, and other authorities in an unprecedented fashion. The successful pastorals represented the high point of what conservative critic George Weigel derisively called the "Bernardin Machine,"[4] consisting of Cardinal Joseph Bernardin of Chicago, Archbishop John Quinn of San Francisco, Archbishop Rembert Weakland of Milwaukee, and other liberal prelates. The process set off alarm bells in the Vatican, and popes John Paul II and Benedict XVI reined in the too-independent U.S. episcopacy, short-circuiting the pastoral approach and aggressively refashioning the episcopacy. By 2011, Weigel could declare the "end of the Bernardin era." But then a funny thing happened—Pope Francis became pope in 2013 and the Bernardin era was resuscitated. There is much here for future historians to unpack.

Of particular note in these developments is the increasing importance of the U.S. church to the Vatican. The U.S. church has always been a bit baffling to Vatican officials and various popes; from the election of the first bishop, John Carroll, through the trustee controversies of the nineteenth century, through the condemnation of the heresy of Americanism, the Vatican has struggled to understand the U.S. situation. Never was their concern as great as in the 1990s. The United States was not only the dominant world superpower, but its cultural power was seemingly all-pervasive. What happened in the United States was seen to be a precursor of what would soon occur in the rest of the world. The appointment of bishops was of special concern, but nowhere was Vatican fear more evident than in its concern about women religious in the United States. Two separate "investigations" of American nuns and sisters, in 1984 and again in 2010, tried to understand the changing sisterhood. Future historians will need to explore the impact of Vatican intervention in the U.S. church, but will also have to explore the impact of the U.S. church and U.S. culture on the Vatican.

A subset of this area of study will be the need to examine more closely the rise of conservatives and neoconservatives within U.S. society and the U.S. church. Conservative Catholic critics such William F. Buckley and Russell Kirk provided the intellectual backdrop of the triumph of the conservative movement in the United States as indicated by the election of Ronald Reagan in 1980. Gaining greater visibility were Catholic neoconservatives, or "neocons," as they were called, most notably Father John Neuhaus, George Weigel, and Michael Novak, who challenged the bishops' pastorals and led the charge in the culture wars. The main concern of Catholics in these culture wars was the liberalization of abortion laws following *Roe v. Wade* in 1973. Abortion became *the* issue, but it was eventually joined by other "nonnegotiables," including same-sex marriage, euthanasia, and stem-cell research. By the 1990s the culture wars were in full swing, and Catholics found themselves on both sides of the conflict. Historians will find most interesting the coalition forged between Catholic conservatives (and bishops) and the once hated and feared Catholic-bashing evangelicals. By creating common cause with evangelicals, Catholics would soon be tarred with the same brush that tarred their former enemies: they were seen as anti-intellectual, two millennia of the Catholic intellectual tradition seemingly abandoned or at least forgotten. The most curious moment may have been the presidential campaign of Catholic candidate John Kerry in 2004, where Kerry's Catholicism was attacked not by anti-Catholics but by Catholics, who could not abide Kerry's style of Catholicism—that is, his refusal to support the pro-life position that abortion must be made illegal. No middle ground was acceptable. Several bishops entered the fray forbidding Catholic politicians from receiving the Eucharist if they did not sufficiently oppose abortion. How will historians treat this era? Will the history be as divisive as the era?

Sexuality and gender will provide another rich source for future historians to mine. The hypersexualized nature of modern society has led to the increasing importance of these issues. Chastity, celibacy, family, vocation: what do they mean in the modern world? The impact of Paul VI's refusal to change the church's teaching on birth control has already received much attention,[5] but will undoubtedly come under further scrutiny, especially since the birth control debate was revived recently as a result of the federal mandate that Catholic institutions supply birth control to employees as part of their health insurance. The legal challenge to the mandate by the Little Sisters of the Poor would go all the way to the Supreme Court.

Of equal interest will be the church's relationship to the newly visible Lesbian, Gay, Bisexual, Transgender, and Questioning community (LGBTQ+). Same-sex marriage proved the focal point for discussion, but the larger of issue of how, or if, the church could welcome the LBGTQ community is still playing out. Other issues such as married clergy will be explored, as will the defection of many Catholic women to seek ordination in non-Catholic traditions.

Gender will also be of interest. Central to this discussion will be the ordination of women. Despite Pope John Paul II's attempt to suppress debate, the issue has raged in the United States since the 1970s. What effect will the Vatican's study of the possibility of ordaining women to the diaconate have? How does the church understand the role of women, and how has it continued to develop over time? Where will Catholic women place themselves? What is the future for women religious?

Traditional concerns of U.S. Catholic historians will also have to be addressed, most notably the effect of the new immigration. Projections suggest the church in the United States will have a Latino majority within a decade. What difference will this changing demographic make on the church and on the way the U.S. Catholic story is told? What effect will it have on Catholic spirituality and public presence? Another important group will be the new Filipino arrivals whose ubiquitous presence in parish life, especially on the West Coast, is slowly transforming the local church. How will their story be incorporated? Race will continue to be a major concern as the vast majority of the new immigrants are people of color and as black Catholics seek redress from past grievances and strive to create a church that is "truly black, and truly Catholic." Native Americans continue to question the role of missions in the destruction of their culture; the canonization of Junipero Serra, the apostle of California, in 2015 has become a rallying point for native dissent. The persistence of ethnicity will also need to be addressed as older immigrant groups struggle to maintain their heritage by attempting to maintain their traditional national parishes.

Historians will continue to grapple with the ongoing struggle to adapt Catholic Social Teaching to the U.S. experience, although U.S. Catholic historians will now be writing as insiders. Since the 1960s, Catholics—both right and left—have become increasingly critical of U.S. culture. The critiques have come from vastly different perspectives, from the U.S. bishops of the 1980s to the U.S. bishops of the first decade of the twenty-first century, from the social liberalism of the Nuns on the Bus to the social conservatism of Speaker of the House Paul Ryan. Abortion, euthanasia, the death penalty, and other social issues continue to concern Catholics, but so do issues of just peace and just war, income distribution, fair taxation, and a host of other issues. Popular culture will continue to be explored, though the lack of a clearly defined Catholic identity will make the films of nominal Catholics such as Martin Scorcese and Kevin Smith subjects of investigation and debate.

U.S. Catholic historians have arrived, but their arrival seems to have created more challenges than it has resolved. The larger questions remain: How do U.S. Catholic historians tell the U.S. Catholic story? What perspective do they take? What sources do they use? How do they relate the Catholic story to the U.S. narrative? How do they engage non-Catholic historians to make sure Catholic historians remain on the cutting edge of U.S. historiography, but still effectively speak to the U.S. Catholic community? The authors of this volume have offered a fresh and challenging interpretation of U.S. Catholic history. Though undoubtedly the future will provide its own challenges, these authors have provided a good bedrock on which to build.

NOTES

1. Barton J. Bernstein, *Towards a New Past: Dissenting Essays in American History* (New York: Pantheon, 1968).

2. Philip Gleason, *The Conservative Reformers: German-American Catholics and the Social Order* (Notre Dame, Ind.: University of Notre Dame Press, 1968); Jay P. Dolan, *The Immigrant Church: New York's Irish and German Catholics, 1815–1865* (Baltimore: John Hopkins University Press, 1975).

3. Daniel T. Rodgers, *Age of Fracture* (Cambridge, Mass.: Harvard University Press, 2011).

4. George Weigel, "The End of the Bernadin Era: The Rise, Dominance, and Decline of a Culturally Accommodating Catholicism," *First Things*, February 2011.

5. See especially Leslie Tentler, *Catholicism and Contraception: An American History* (Ithaca, N.Y.: Cornell University Press, 2009).

PATRICK ALLITT is the Cahoon Family Professor of American History at Emory University. He is the author of seven books, including *Catholic Converts: British and American Intellectuals Turn to Rome* and *Catholic Intellectuals and Conservative Politics in America.*

JEFFREY M. BURNS is Director of the Francis G. Harpst Center for Catholic Thought and Culture at the University of San Diego and Director of the Academy of American Franciscan History. He is the author of *Disturbing the Peace: A History of the Christian Family Movement, 1949–1974* and, with Joseph White and Ellen Skerrett, *Keeping Faith: European and Asian Catholic Immigrants.*

UNA M. CADEGAN is Professor of History at the University of Dayton. She is the author of *All Good Books Are Catholic Books: Print Culture, Censorship, and Modernity in Twentieth-Century America* and co-editor with James L. Heft, S.M., of *"In the* Lógos *of Love": Promise and Predicament in Catholic Intellectual Life.*

ROBERT E. CARBONNEAU, C.P., is a priest and historian for the Passionist Congregation (eastern U.S.) and Affiliated Research Fellow at the Ricci Institute for Chinese-Western Culture, University of San Francisco. Research, study, and publications have concentrated on the Passionist history in twentieth-century Hunan, China, the United States, and throughout the world. From 2014 to 2017 he served as Executive Director of the U.S. Catholic China Bureau, Berkeley, California.

KAREN MARY DAVALOS is a Professor in the Chicano and Latino Studies Department at the University of Minnesota, Twin Cities, where she launched the major initiative "Mexican American Art since 1848." Her research and teaching interests include Chicana feminist thought and praxis, spirituality, visual and cultural studies, and the archive.

ROY DOMENICO is a Professor of History at the University of Scranton. He has published on Italian Catholic politics in the postwar era as well as on U.S.-Vatican relations. He is currently the Executive Secretary of the Society for Italian Historical Studies.

JAMES T. FISHER is Professor Emeritus of American Studies and Theology at Fordham University, where he has taught since 2002. He previously taught American Studies at Rutgers and Yale and held the Danforth Chair in Humanities at Saint Louis University and the Will and Ariel Durant Visiting Chair at Saint Peter's University. He is the author of four books, including *On the Irish Waterfront: The Crusader, the Movie, and the Soul of the Port of New York*.

CHESTER GILLIS is Professor of Theology at Georgetown University. His book *Roman Catholicism in America* was selected as the book of the month by the Catholic Book Club.

JEFFREY MARLETT teaches religious studies and serves as interim dean of Arts and Humanities at the College of Saint Rose in Albany, New York. He is the author of *Saving the Heartland: Catholic Missionaries in Rural America*.

TIMOTHY MATOVINA is Professor and Chair of the Theology Department at the University of Notre Dame. His most recent book is *Latino Catholicism: Transformation in America's Largest Church*. His book *Theologies of Guadalupe: From the Era of Conquest to Pope Francis* is forthcoming.

JAMES P. MCCARTIN is Associate Professor of the History of Christianity in the Department of Theology at Fordham University. He is the author of *Prayers of the Faithful: The Shifting Spiritual Life of American Catholics* and is currently at work on a book project on U.S. Catholicism and sex in the nineteenth and twentieth centuries.

MARGARET M. McGuinness is Professor of Religion at La Salle University. With James T. Fisher, she co-edited *The Catholic Studies Reader* and is the author of *Neighbors and Missionaries: A History of the Sisters of Our Lady of Christian Doctrine* and of *Called to Serve: A History of Nuns in America*. She is the winner of the Catholic Press Association's award for general excellence and the Distinguished Book Award at the tenth triennial Conference on the History of Women Religious in 2016.

CECILIA A. MOORE is Associate Professor in the Department of Religious Studies at the University of Dayton. She is also an adjunct professor for Xavier University of Louisiana's Institute for Black Catholic Studies. Her work focuses on African American Catholic history.

CHRISTOPHER SHANNON is Associate Professor and Chair of the History Department at Christendom College. He is the author of several works, most recently *The Past as*

Pilgrimage: Narrative, Tradition and the Renewal of Catholic History (co-authored with Christopher Blum).

ANTHONY BURKE SMITH is Associate Professor of Religious Studies at the University of Dayton. He is the author of *The Look of Catholics: Portrayals in Popular Culture from the Great Depression to the Cold Wa*r.

James T. Fisher and Margaret M. McGuinness (eds.), *The Catholic Studies Reader*

Jeremy Bonner, Christopher D. Denny, and Mary Beth Fraser Connolly (eds.), *Empowering the People of God: Catholic Action before and after Vatican II*

Christine Firer Hinze and J. Patrick Hornbeck II (eds.), *More than a Monologue: Sexual Diversity and the Catholic Church. Volume I: Voices of Our Times*

J. Patrick Hornbeck II and Michael A. Norko (eds.), *More than a Monologue: Sexual Diversity and the Catholic Church. Volume II: Inquiry, Thought, and Expression*

Jack Lee Downey, *The Bread of the Strong:* Lacouturisme *and the Folly of the Cross, 1910–1985*

Michael McGregor, *Pure Act: The Uncommon Life of Robert Lax*

Mary Dunn, *The Cruelest of All Mothers: Marie de l'Incarnation, Motherhood, and Christian Tradition*

Dorothy Day and the Catholic Worker: The Miracle of Our Continuance. Photographs by Vivian Cherry, Text by Dorothy Day, Edited with an Introduction and Additional Text by Kate Hennessy

Nicholas K. Rademacher, *Paul Hanly Furfey: Priest, Scientist, Social Reformer*

Margaret M. McGuinness and James T. Fisher (eds.), *Roman Catholicism in the United States: A Thematic History*